Recirculating Songs
Revitalising the singing practices of Indigenous Australia

SONG COMPOSED FOR THIS VOLUME BY M. K. TURNER, 2017

Edited by
Jim Wafer and Myfany Turpin

SYDNEY UNIVERSITY PRESS

 This book includes QR codes. Download free QR scanning software to your smart phone, take a snapshot of the QR code and you will be able to hear the music and/or see it performed.

Reprint edition published by Sydney University Press 2025.
Print edition first published 2017 by Hunter Press.
Ebook edition first published 2017 by Asia-Pacific College of Asia and Linguistics, The Australian National University. Web: https://hdl.handle.net/1885/132161

This collection © 2017 Jim Wafer and Myfany Turpin
Individual chapters © 2017 by the respective authors
Cover photograph *ulpare-ulpare* (Arrernte) 'Perennial Yellowtop' (Senecio magnificus) © Lisa Stefanoff
Cover song by M. K. Turner. Transcriptions (text and music) by Myfany Turpin.
Book design: Christine Bruderlin

Reproduction and Communication for other purposes
Except as permitted under the Australian Copyright Act 1968, no part of this edition may be reproduced, stored in a retrieval system, or communicated in any form or by any means without prior written permission. All requests for reproduction or communication should be made to Sydney University Press at the address below:

Sydney University Press
Fisher Library F03
Gadigal Country
University of Sydney NSW 2006
Australia
sup.info@sydney.edu.au
sydneyuniversitypress.com

 A catalogue record for this book is available from the National Library of Australia.

ISBN 9781761540257 paperback
ISBN 9781922185402 ebook

We acknowledge the traditional owners of the lands on which Sydney University Press is located, the Gadigal people of the Eora Nation, and we pay our respects to the knowledge embedded forever within the Aboriginal Custodianship of Country.

Culturally sensitive content
Parts of this book may include material that is culturally sensitive in some Aboriginal communities and might not normally be used in public contexts. This material includes words, descriptions, names, sounds, images, videos and audio recordings. In particular, in some Aboriginal and Torres Strait Islander communities, seeing images of deceased persons or hearing them in recordings may cause sadness or distress, or offend against strongly held cultural prohibitions. Readers are asked to ensure that any disclosure of the material contained in this volume is consistent with the views and sensitivities of relevant Aboriginal and Torres Strait Islander people and communities.

Contents

List of figures iv
List of maps iv
List of tables v
List of musical examples v
List of audio examples vi
List of video examples vii
Acknowledgements viii
Notes on contributors ix
Abbreviations xiii

Introduction: everything got a song • *Jim Wafer* 1
1 *Maaya waab* (play with sound): song language and spoken language in the south-west of Western Australia • *Clint Bracknell* 43
2 *Thabi* returns: the use of digital resources to recirculate and revitalise *Thabi* songs in the west Pilbara • *Sally Treloyn and Andrew Morumburri Dowding* 56
3 *Ngadiji*: for women and men also. A song and dance continuing to be performed by the Yanyuwa of the Gulf area of the Northern Territory • *Margaret Sharpe* 68
4 Finding Arrernte songs • *Myfany Turpin* 88
5 Lone Singers: the others have all gone • *Luise Hercus and Grace Koch* 102
6 Songs performed by Willie Rookwood at Woorabinda in 1965 • *Mary Laughren, Myfany Turpin and Gemma Turner* 119
7 A survey of traditional south-eastern Australian Indigenous music • *Barry McDonald* 140
8 Applying multilingual knowledge to decipher an historical song of change • *Raymond Kelly and Jean Harkins* 172
9 Ghost-writing for Wulatji: incubation and 're-dreaming' as song revitalisation practices • *Jim Wafer* 187
10 Finding *laka* for *burdal*: song revitalisation at Mornington Island over the past 40 years • *Cassy Nancarrow and Peter Cleary* 245
11 Maintaining song traditions and languages together at Warruwi (western Arnhem Land) • *Reuben Brown, David Manmurulu, Jenny Manmurulu, Isabel O'Keeffe and Ruth Singer* 257
12 Songs that keep ancestral languages alive: a Marrku songset from western Arnhem Land • *Reuben Brown and Nicholas Evans* 275
13 Singing with the ancestors: musical conversations with archived ethnographic recordings • *Genevieve Campbell* 289
14 Children, knowledge, Country: child and youth-based approaches to revitalising musical traditions in the Kimberley • *Andrea Emberly, Sally Treloyn and Rona Googninda Charles* 305
15 Revitalising Meriam Mir through sacred song • *Helen Fairweather and Philip Matthias with Toby Whaleboat* 318
16 Recovering musical data from colonial era transcriptions of Indigenous songs: some practical considerations • *Graeme Skinner* 336
17 A checklist of colonial era musical transcriptions of Australian Indigenous songs • *Graeme Skinner and Jim Wafer* 360
Index 405

LIST OF FIGURES

Figure 3.1: *Ngadiji* performance layout 79
Figure 4.1: The Laughton family. 95
Figure 5.1: George McDermott on the veranda of Bourke Hospital in 1970 104
Figure 5.2: Arthur 'Igor' Reid and his wife, Margaret, with her sister's
grandchild, at Dareton in 1972. 108
Figure 5.3: Butoba tape recorder, model MT5 110
Figure 6.1: Willie Rookwood, aged 48 122
Figure 6.2: CD cover of Willie Rookwood's songs from the Flint recordings. 132
Figure 9.1: Sunset over Mount Yango, vernal equinox, 2017. 225
Figure 11.1: *Inyjalarrku* dance actions, performed by Jenny Manmurulu at Marrinymarriny . . 266
Figure 11.2: Rupert Manmurulu and David Manmurulu dancing the giant dance 267
Figure 11.3: Jenny Manmurulu demonstrating the *amurl* dance action 268
Figure 11.4: David Manmurulu and his sons (including Rupert on didjeridu)
and grandsons perform and record *Inyjalarrku* at Warruwi 271
Figure 12.1: Johnny Namayiwa and Henry Guwiyul singing *Milyarryarr* 282
Figure 12.2: Toby Cooper executes a spectacular leap while dancing to uneven
clapstick pattern in MR04, Stone Country Festival, Gunbalanya 2011. 286
Figure 13.1: Clementine Puruntatameri† with Leonie Tipiloura and Stephanie
Tipuamantimeri† listening to the old recordings, 2010. 294
Figure 13.2: Recording, Bathurst Island 2015. 295
Figure 13.3: Sydney musicians in the recording studio, January 2016 300
Figure 13.4: Eustace Tipiloura, Nelsina Portaminni and Karen Tipiloura
in the recording studio, Sydney, October 2015. 300
Figure 14.1: The importance of Junba (word collage created by youth
participants, 28–30 September 2015) 312
Figure 14.2: Drawings by Laurenzia Divilli illustrating Junba dancing
ground and healthy Country, September 28–30, 2015. 313
Figure 14.3: Drawing by Clintisha Bangmorra, September 29, 2015. 313
Figure 14.4: Drawings of Junba dancing by Selwyn Wungundin, September 29, 2015 313
Figure 14.5: Laurenzia Divilli leading the song writing session, September 29, 2015 315
Figure 15.1: Toby Whaleboat 326
Figure 15.2: Toby Whaleboat, with members of the Torres Strait Islander
community, the University of Newcastle chamber choir 'Echology', and
members of the Torres Strait Islander Sacred Music Network, with
Canon Rod MacDonald, St James Cathedral, Townsville, 2015 329

LIST OF MAPS

Map 0.1: Hypothetical musical regions of Indigenous Australia. 10
Map 0.2: Musical regions and language regions of Indigenous Australia. 12
Map 0.3: Study sites represented in the present work 14
Map 1.1: The Nyungar language region 44
Map 3.1: Portion of the Northern Territory, showing Borroloola and the surrounding area. . . . 70
Map 6.1: The Upper Warrego–Maranoa region of Queensland. 121
Map 10.1: Geographical location of Mornington Island 246
Map 11.1: A reconstruction of pre-contact language-land associations in western
Arnhem Land, Northern Territory. 258

LIST OF TABLES

Table 0.1: Overview of chapters and their geographical sequence, correlated with musical and linguistic regions. ...13
Table 0.2: Proposed schema for Aboriginal song classification (examples from Bardi) ...16
Table 1.1: Comparison of sung phrase with spoken equivalent. ...45
Table 1.2: Nyungar song text sources for this study. ...46
Table 1.3: A list of Nyungar suffixes found in song, illustrating some of their functions ...49
Table 1.4: Five Nyungar song texts and comparable spoken text. ...49–50
Table 1.5: Poetic alterations in song texts A, B, C, D and E. ...50
Table 3.1: Correlation of texts, beats and dance movements in *Ngadiji* performance ...84–85
Table 3.2: Key to the videoed illustrations ...85–86
Table 4.1: The Ada Sylvia Laughton collection of Arrernte women's songs. ...99–100
Table 5.1: Kuyani *Malkara* song, basic sections ...106
Table 6.1: Text-melody setting 'Red kangaroo' (song 3). ...126
Table 6.2: Text-melody setting in 'Two men fighting' (song 4) ...129
Table 6.3: Verse structure of 'Farewell' (song 1) ...130
Table 6.4: Text-melody setting in 'Farewell' (song 1) ...130
Table 6.5: Details of recordings analysed in this chapter ...132
Table 9.1: Reconstitution of 'Nung-Ngnun' ('Song'), based on Dunlop's 'Native poetry' (1848a) ...198–199
Table 9.2: Reports of the musical dream in Indigenous Australia, by date ...212–213
Table 9.3: Reports of the musical dream outside Australia, by region, then date ...213–214
Table 9.4: Vocabulary items from E. H. Dunlop's glossaries ...216–217
Table 9.5: Sketch genealogy of E. H. Dunlop's descendants and affines ...218
Table 11.1: *Manyardi/kun-borrk* and *manikay* recorded at Warruwi from 1940s to 2013 ...259–260
Table 11.2: Idiomatic expressions that involve the word *wirrngak* 'breath, life force'. ...264
Table 12.1: Distinct rhythmic modes featured in Milyarryarr songs performed by Johnny Namayiwa and Henry Guwiyul. ...281–282
Table 12.2: Events involving the performance of Milyarryarr, recorded by musicologists and linguists in western Arnhem Land. ...283
Table 13.1: List of ethnographic field recordings used in Ngiya Awungarra CD, showing song-type and subject, performers (living and deceased), AIATSIS catalogue references and dates of recording. ...296–297
Table 16.1: Textual comparison of three versions of 'Popela'. ...345

LIST OF MUSICAL EXAMPLES

Musical example 3.1: The three-descent melodic contour and its clapped beat ...73
Musical example 3.2: The four-descent melodic contour and its rattled and clapped beat ...74
Musical example 3.3: Sample transcription of sung Text 1 ('Yirrinju') ...75
Musical example 5.1: Laurie Moffat's song, sung by Laurie Moffat at Lake Tyers in 1963 ...112
Musical example 5.2: Kuyani *Malkara* song, sung by Stuart Patterson and Percy Patterson near Copley (SA) in 1966. ...113
Musical example 5.3: Tim and Mick's song (Seven Sisters verse 5, 'Karilya'), sung by Tim Strangways and Mick McLean at Port Augusta in 1968. ...114
Musical example 5.4: *Urumbula*, sung by Mick McLean, Yumpi Jack and Archie Allen, at Finke (NT) in 1974. ...115

Musical example 5.5: Igor Reid's song, sung by Igor Reid at Dareton (NSW), 1972. 116
Musical example 5.6: Owlet nightjar, *Yerrateth-kurrk*, sung by Stan Day at Echuca in 1965 117
Musical example 6.1: *Dyindidyindi* – the Willy-wagtail song 133–134
Musical example 6.2: *Bawurra* – the Red Kangaroo song 134–135
Musical example 6.3: *Unimila* – Two men fighting song 136–137
Musical example 6.4: Farewell song 137–138
Musical example 11.1: Musical transcription of line D (50) of Inyjalarrku
    song IL18 and associated dance actions 265
Musical example 12.1: transcription of verse of Milyarryarr song MR07
    (0:00–01:28 of Audio example 1) 279–280
Musical example 12.2: Transcription of Milyarryarr song MR13 284–285
Musical example 16.1: Yam II ['Yamaz Sibarud'], musical transcription
    by Charles Myers (1912) 338
Musical example 16.2: Tjitjingalla Corroboree song, as transcribed by Percy Grainger, 1909. . . . 339
Musical example 16.3: Transcription of first of two 'corrobboree songs'
    (published version) by Percy Grainger; in Spencer and Gillen (1912) 339
Musical example 16.4: Musical transcription of first recorded version
    of Fanny Cochrane Smith's song 'Popela' 342
Musical example 16.5: Edited transcription of the melody and words only,
    from the two manuscript copies of 'Song of the Aborigines of Van
    Diemen's Land arranged by Mrs Logan' 344
Musical example 16.6: 'Song of the Aborigines of Van Diemans Land [sic]
    arranged by Mrs. Logan' 348
Musical example 16.7: Edouard Garnier, 'Observations musicales sur les chants
    de Narcisse Pelletier' (1876) 351

LIST OF AUDIO EXAMPLES

Audio example 5.1: Laurie Moffat's song 105
Audio example 5.2: Kuyani *Malkara* song 106
Audio example 5.3: Tim and Mick's song 107
Audio example 5.4: *Urumbula* 107
Audio example 5.5: Igor Reid's song 108
Audio example 5.6: Owlet nightjar, *Yerrateth-kurrk* 109
Audio example 8.1: *Tiny man* sung by Raymond Kelly 177
Audio example 11.1: Inyjalarrku song IL18 265
Audio example 12.1: Verse of Milyarryarr song MR07 280
Audio example 12.2: Milyarryarr song MR13 285
Audio example 13.1: *Amparruwu*, 'Snake' 298
Audio example 13.2: 'Going to Canberra' 301
Audio example 15.1: Language hymn: Eastern Islands hymn no. 199 *Peirdi
    esoao meriba Ad*, composer unknown, performed by St Stephen's Torres
    Strait Islands Ministry Choir, Townsville, North Queensland 322
Audio example 15.2: *Kores: Debe lamar e zogo*, composed by Weser Whaleboat,
    performed by Toby Whaleboat and Elise Whaleboat 328
Audio example 15.3: *Kores: Omar, omar, omar*, composed by Jimmy [?] Wailu; all
    vocal parts (unaccompanied) performed and recorded by Toby Whaleboat 330

Audio example 15.4: *Kores: Debe ki wabim gaire le*, composed by Harry Whaleboat, performed by Gai Bero, Wya Sailor, May Simbolo, Merwez Whaleboat, Toby Whaleboat, Lelay Wailu and Victor Wailu 331
Audio example 16.1: 'Yamaz Sibarud, sung by Maino of Yam', recorded by Sidney Ray, Torres Strait, 1898 338
Audio example 16.2: 'Tjitjingalla Corroboree song', recorded by Spencer and Gillen at Stevenson's Creek, 1901 339
Audio example 16.3: Fanny Cochrane Smith singing 'Popela', recorded by Horace Watson, Hobart, 5 August 1899 341

LIST OF VIDEO EXAMPLES

Video example 3.1: '*Ngadiji*. It's for women and men too.' Videoed at Wandangula by Megan Morais, 30 August 1994 70
Video example 16.1: Ethel Munn and friends from south-east Queensland singing the 'Maranoa lullaby', 2014 349

Acknowledgements

The editors thank each of the contributors for their splendid collaboration. Our gratitude goes as well to the general editor (Bethwyn Evans) and board of Asia-Pacific Linguistics for their support and encouragement throughout the project, in particular to our designated 'shepherd', David Nash.

The book had its origins in a workshop held at the Australian National University (ANU), as part of the 14th annual Aboriginal Languages Workshop (ALW), on 6 March 2015. In the planning stage, the workshop had as its title 'Revitalising ancestral song traditions in south-eastern Australia', but the call for papers elicited responses from a number of people working outside the south-east, so the focus was broadened to cover the whole of the continent. The workshop was facilitated by Jim Wafer, who acknowledges gratefully the support received from the organisers of ALW, in particular Jane Simpson and the Centre for Excellence in the Dynamics of Language at ANU. Special credit to David Nash for technical assistance; to session chairs Jane Simpson and Harold Koch; and to the participants in the final panel discussion: Clint Bracknell (chair), Linda Barwick, Sharon Edgar-Jones, Nardi Simpson and Michael Walsh.

Six of the nine papers presented at that event (those by Bracknell; Brown and Evans; Hercus and Koch; Laughren and Turpin; Wafer; Whaleboat and Matthias) provided the basis for chapters in the present book. Discussions on that and subsequent occasions led Wafer and Turpin to approach Asia-Pacific Linguistics about the possibility of co-editing a volume based on the workshop, with additional contributions from interested parties. Potential contributors were contacted in the months following ALW, and a general call for papers was sent out in June 2015. This resulted in offers of additional papers, to give a total of 17 chapters in the work you have before you. Negotiations for a print version of the book began in March of 2017, and we are grateful to Hunter Press for taking on such a large, complex and challenging job.

Although our peer reviewers must remain unnamed, we acknowledge our deep indebtedness to them for their thorough reading of the chapters and helpful feedback to the authors.

We recognise also that this book depends for its very existence on the many Indigenous songmen and songwomen, past and present, whose compositions and performances it presents and interprets. We offer our heartfelt gratitude to them for their contributions, and we hope this book will be able to support their indispensable role in keeping the ancestral song traditions in circulation.

We thank as well the following people for their contributions:

Cover song: Margaret Kemarre Turner
Cover photo: Lisa Stefanoff
Cover design: Christine Bruderlin
Design for print version: Christine Bruderlin
Proofreading: Mark MacLean
Maps for the introduction: Brenda Thornley

Notes on contributors

Clint Bracknell teaches popular music studies and ethnomusicology at the Sydney Conservatorium of Music, University of Sydney. He researches Aboriginal Australian song and languages while simultaneously working on music composition, production and performance projects. His cultural elders from the south coast of Western Australia refer to their clan as Wirlomin Noongar.

Reuben Brown is an ARC research associate on the Discovery Project 'Hearing histories of the western Pilbara', based at the Wilin Centre for Indigenous Arts and Cultural Development, Faculty of the Victorian College of the Arts and Melbourne Conservatorium of Music, University of Melbourne. For his PhD thesis, Reuben collaborated with ceremony leaders from Gunbalanya and Warruwi to document and sustain *kun-borrk/manyardi*. His current research interests include investigating public ceremony of western Arnhem Land and the Pilbara as a site of intercultural exchange, and the role of digital environments in facilitating intergenerational transmission of language, song, and dance.

Genevieve Campbell is an Honorary Affiliate, Sydney Conservatorium of Music, University of Sydney. Having played horn in everything from Opera Australia to Australian Idol and instigating (in 2007) the Tiwi/jazz collaboration *Ngarukuruwala – we sing*, Genevieve now juggles horn with her commitment to Tiwi song preservation.

Rona Googninda Charles (Ngarinyin and Nyikina) is a cultural consultant and researcher based in the west Kimberley. Charles has been engaged as a consultant by researchers working in a range of disciplines, including archeology, ethnomusicology, and land conservation and management, and has played a key role in native title negotiations and management for several groups. Collaborating on ARC-funded projects with Treloyn since 2009, Charles co-leads The Junba Project, has presented at conferences and seminars in Cairns, Melbourne, Perth, Sydney, Ottawa and Toronto, and has co-written several papers and chapters on Junba and research collaboration.

Peter Cleary toured nationally and internationally with Lardil dancers from 1977 to 2004. Since then he has worked with arts funding bodies and as a coordinator of the Gulf Dance Festival. He continues to engage with cultural projects throughout Far North Queensland and is currently writing up the bigger story of Mornington Island dance history.

Andrew Morumburri Dowding is a Ngarluma man whose family is from the Roebourne area of Western Australia. His traditional lands lie 80 kilometres south of Whim Creek at Thalayindi. Andrew is a PhD candidate at the University of Melbourne and holds a Bachelor of Arts (Anthropology and History) from the University of Sydney. Dowding has over 10 years' experience working in the Indigenous cultural sector, as an anthropologist and researcher, and has served on the boards of multiple Indigenous organisations. He has a special interest in community-facilitated mapping projects that digitally capture Aboriginal knowledge for future generations, and his PhD focuses on mapping *Thabi* songs.

Andrea Emberly is an ethnomusicologist and assistant professor in the Children, Childhood & Youth program at York University, Canada. Her work focuses on the study of children's musical cultures and the relationship between childhood, wellbeing, and musical arts practices. At present she is focused on three major research projects in collaboration with communities in several countries: sustaining endangered initiation schools for girls in Vhavenda communities in South Africa (SSHRC Insight Development); using repatriation of archival materials as a means to maintain musical traditions and generate curriculum for young people in five countries (Australia, Canada, South Africa, Uganda, USA) (SSHRC Partnership Development); and the relationships between language, music and education in remote Aboriginal communities in the Kimberley region of Western Australia (ARC Linkage).

Nicholas Evans is an ARC Laureate Fellow at the Australian National University and directs the ARC Centre of Excellence for the Dynamics of Language. His central research focus is the diversity of human language and what this can tell us about the nature of language, culture, deep history, and the possibilities of the human mind. He is especially interested in the languages of northern Australia and southern New Guinea, and has carried out extensive fieldwork in these areas over three and a half decades.

Helen Fairweather (formerly, Reeves Lawrence), an ethnomusicologist with an interdisciplinary background, has previously undertaken research into the sacred music of eastern Torres Strait. She is a Conjoint Fellow, School of Creative Arts, the University of Newcastle (NSW), and a member of its Torres Strait Islander Sacred Music Network.

Jean Harkins is a lecturer in linguistics at the University of Newcastle (NSW) and a member of the university's PURAI Global Indigenous and Diaspora Research Studies Centre and the Endangered Languages Documentation, Theory and Application group. She specialises in intercultural communication and semantics, with a focus on Indigenous Australian languages and second language acquisition. She has published on emotions in cross-linguistic perspective and NSW contact languages.

Luise Hercus, formerly Reader in Sanskrit at the Australian National University, has been recording Aboriginal languages and songs since 1962 and is the author of grammars and dictionaries and some editions of texts.

Raymond Kelly is a member of the Thangatti and Anaiwan people from the Armidale region of New South Wales. After moving to Newcastle with his family, Ray took on leading roles with the Awabakal people and is a leading member in the community. Ray is a published playwright and in 2015 graduated with a Doctor of Philosophy (Aboriginal Studies). His thesis, 'Dreaming the Keepara: New South Wales Indigenous cultural perspectives, 1808–2007', investigates the Aboriginal intellectual heritage of the mid-north coast of NSW through a combination of family history, oral tradition and audio recorded songs, stories, interviews, discussions, and linguistic material. The research has uncovered an unsuspected wealth of cultural knowledge, cultural memory, and language heritage that has been kept alive and passed down within Aboriginal families and communities, despite the disruptions and dislocations endured over the past seven generations. Ray is currently a research academic with the PURAI Global Indigenous and Diaspora Research Studies Centre at the University of Newcastle (NSW).

Grace Koch is a Visiting Research Fellow at AIATSIS and a Visiting Senior Research Fellow at the National Centre for Indigenous Studies, ANU. She has published nationally and internationally on ethics of managing Indigenous collections, analyses of Indigenous music and audio archiving.

Mary Laughren is an Honorary Senior Research Fellow in the School of Languages and Cultures at the University of Queensland, where she taught linguistics from 1993 to 2009. Since 1975 she has documented the Warlpiri language and has supported the implementation of bilingual education programs in Warlpiri-speaking communities. In collaboration with musicologists Turpin and Barwick she is currently working with senior Warlpiri women in the documentation of traditional Warlpiri songs. Since 2000 her research focus has also included the Waanyi language.

David Winungudj Manmurulu is from the Mawng-speaking Yalama clan, part of the Ngurtikin clan aggregate who own mainland coastal estates opposite South Goulburn Island. He is the senior songman and custodian of the Inyjalarrku 'mermaid' songset and has been in high demand as a ceremony leader across western Arnhem Land. He is also on the steering committee of the National Recording Project for Indigenous Performance in Australia and has presented and performed at numerous seminars and conferences across Australia.

Jenny Manmurulu is from the Kunwinjku-speaking Mayirrwulidj clan. She is a senior Indigenous teacher and cultural adviser at Warruwi Community School, where she has helped to develop Indigenous culture and language programs for students. Jenny is the lead female dancer for the Inyjalarrku songset, and teaches the dances to women and girls at Warruwi. She is one of the directors of the Yagbani Aboriginal Corporation and has presented and performed at numerous seminars and conferences across Australia.

Philip Matthias is the Deputy Head of School (Research & Research Training), School of Creative Arts, the University of Newcastle (NSW), and Chief Investigator for the current research project 'Torres Strait Islander Sacred Music: protection, cultivation, revitalisation'. He is also the Artistic Director of Echology, the University of Newcastle's chamber choir.

Barry McDonald has spent most of his life on the New England Tablelands, a stretch punctuated by 15 years living and working in desert areas of Australia, particularly around Alice Springs. In 2001 he completed a doctoral dissertation, from which his chapter in this volume is drawn, after which he concentrated more on teaching than research. He has also facilitated the publication of books by Arrernte authors, including M. K. Turner's *Iwenhe Tyerrtye* (2010).

Cassy Nancarrow works as a teacher and linguist supporting language revitalisation and education in Far North Queensland, and is an adjunct lecturer with James Cook University. She has had a close association with Lardil songmen for 20 years and continues to engage in various language- and song-related projects at Mornington Island.

Isabel O'Keeffe is a research associate at the University of Sydney working on an Endangered Languages Documentation Programme project empowering young people in the Warruwi and Maningrida communities to document the endangered Kunbarlang language. She has researched the relationship between multilingualism and *manyardi/kun-borrk* songs in western Arnhem Land over the last 10 years and this was the subject of her recently completed PhD.

Margaret Sharpe, adjunct senior lecturer in linguistics (University of New England), and life member of ALS, has published analyses and dictionaries of Yugambeh-Bundjalung (NSW-QLD) and Alawa (NT). She worked on Yanyuwa music, and helped in analysis of Ngalia data (WA), and in editing for the Wangkatja dictionary (WA). In 2017 she was awarded recognition of her work as a *Gayalgam Yugambehgaya* 'champion fighter for the Yugambeh language', and continues to help both the Yugambeh and the Bundjalung in passing on their language.

Ruth Singer (University of Melbourne) is a linguist who has researched language use at Warruwi, Goulburn Island, western Arnhem Land for 15 years. She is currently taking a linguistic anthropological approach to multilingualism at Warruwi, and is particularly interested in practices and ideologies that support the maintenance of so many small languages.

Graeme Skinner is an Australian music historian, and an honorary associate in musicology at Sydney Conservatorium of Music, University of Sydney. He is author of the biography *Peter Sculthorpe: the making of an Australian composer* (UNSW Press ebook 2015). Since 2014 he has built and curated the research website Australharmony (*http://sydney.edu.au/paradisec/australharmony*), an open access academic resource for the musical history of the colonial and early Federation eras, both settler and Indigenous. He also curates a complementary virtual archive of colonial music resources and user tags inside Trove. With co-author Michael Noone, he is currently completing a catalogue of the plainsong and polyphonic choir books of Toledo Cathedral, Spain.

Sally Treloyn is an Australian Research Council Future Fellow and senior lecturer in ethnomusicology and intercultural research in the Faculty of Victorian College of the Arts and Melbourne Conservatorium of Music at the University of Melbourne. Treloyn's specialism is dance-song traditions of the Kimberley, where she has worked since 1999, and more recently the Pilbara. Treloyn's research focuses on repatriation and dissemination of recordings to address music endangerment, resilience, and sustainability.

Gemma Turner is an independent singer, songwriter, singing coach, voice researcher and writer with 30 years' experience, specialising in voice production across languages and musical styles. Her performance experience fed into a voice science research PhD at Sydney University and journal publications on the effect of body movement on singing voice intensity and quality. She was recently a facilitator of research into singing effects on post-natal depression and currently is a contributor to an Aboriginal language revitalisation project in the Northern Territory involving song.

Myfany Turpin is a linguist and ethnomusicologist at the University of Sydney. She specialises in languages and music of central Australia, has published on song and ethnobiology and has also compiled a dictionary of Kaytetye. She currently holds an ARC Future Fellowship to investigate the relationship between words and music in Aboriginal song-poetry.

Jim Wafer is a conjoint senior lecturer in anthropology at the University of Newcastle (NSW), and has worked with Aboriginal languages since 1976. He is currently collaborating with Wonnarua and Gathang people on language and song revitalisation, under the auspices of Muurrbay Aboriginal Language and Culture Co-operative.

Toby Whaleboat is the Senior Land Service Officer (Aboriginal Communities) for the Hunter Local Land Services in Newcastle, NSW, where he is a member of the eastern Torres Strait Islander community. He is a knowledge-holder, a singer-songwriter and, as an affiliate of the School of Creative Arts at the University of Newcastle, is a driving force in the Torres Strait Islander Sacred Music Network.

Abbreviations

A. General abbreviations and acronyms

AIAS	Australian Institute of Aboriginal Studies (earlier name of AIATSIS)
AIATSIS	Australian Institute of Aboriginal and Torres Strait Island Studies
AIDT	Aboriginal/Islander Dance Theatre
ANU	Australian National University
ANZAAS	Australian and New Zealand Association for the Advancement of Science
ARC	Australian Research Council
ASO	Australian Screen Online
BMI	Bathurst and Melville Islands (region)
BMN	Benesh Movement Notation
CA	Central Arid (region)
CAAMA	Central Australian Aboriginal Media Association
CLC	Central Land Council
CSIRO	Commonwealth Scientific and Industrial Research Organisation
DCITA	Department of Communications, Information Technology and the Arts
DECRA	Discovery Early Career Research Award
diss.	dissertation
DoBeS	Dokumentation bedrohter Sprachen (Documentation of Endangered Languages), Max Planck Institute for Psycholinguistics
E&CA	Eastern & Central Arrernte
ECA	East Central Arid (region)
ELAR	Endangered Languages Archive
ELCat	Catalogue of Endangered Languages
FATSIL	Federation of Aboriginal and Torres Strait Islander Languages
FEL	Foundation for Endangered Languages
HRLM	Hunter River-Lake Macquarie language
IAD	Institute for Aboriginal Development (Alice Springs)
IASPM	International Association for the Study of Popular Music
IPA	International Phonetic Alphabet
KLRC	Kimberley Language Resource Centre
LMS	London Missionary Society
MK	Margaret Kemarre Turner
ML	Mitchell Library (State Library of NSW)
MS	manuscript
MSA	Musicological Society of Australia
n.d.	no date
n.p.	no page number(s)
NAC	Ngarluma Aboriginal Corporation
NAIDOC	National Aboriginal and Islander Day Observance Committee
NE	North-east (region)
NFSA	National Film and Sound Archive
NLA	National Library of Australia
NNTT	National Native Title Tribunal
NPN	Non-Pama-Nyungan
NSW	New South Wales
NT	Northern Territory
NW	North-west (region)
NWCA	North-west Central Arid (region)
PARADISEC	Pacific and Regional Archive for Digital Sources in Endangered Cultures
PBC	Prescribed Body Corporate
PN	Pama-Nyungan [language family]
QILAC	Queensland Indigenous Languages Advisory Committee
QLD	Queensland
QSS	Queensland Speech Survey

RMIT	Royal Melbourne Institute of Technology
RNTBC	Registered Native Title Body Corporate
SA	South Australia
SRNSW	State Records NSW
SWALSC	South West Aboriginal Land and Sea Council.
TAS	Tasmania
trans.	translator(s)
transc.	transcriber(s)
TSI	Torres Strait Islands
UMI	University Microfilms International
UNE	University of New England
unpag.	unpaginated
V.D. Land	Van Diemen's Land (i.e. Tasmania)
VCV	vowel-consonant-vowel
VIC	Victoria
WA	Western Australia
WALSP	Western Arnhem Land Song Project
YCA	Cape York Central Arid (region)

B. Grammatical abbreviations used in the glosses

1	First person	IMPF	Imperfective
1PL	First person plural	in	Inclusive pronominal category
1SG	First person singular	INST	Instrumental
2	Second person	KIN	Kin term suffix
3	Third person	KRDP	Kreduplication suffix: encodes iterative or durative tenseaspectmood
3DU	Third person dual		
3PL	Third person plural	LL	Land gender
3PL.NOM	Third person plural nominative	LOC	Locative
ABL	Ablative case	MA	Masculine gender
ABS	Abstract (i.e. discourse demonstrative)	MT	Metrical element
ASS	Associative	NEG	Negative preverbal particle or prefix
COM	Comitative	NEG	Negative
CONJ	Conjunction	NP	Nonpast tenseaspectmood suffix
CONT	Continuous	OBL	Oblique pronoun
CT	Continuous	P	Proximal
D	Distant	pl	Nonsingular number (restricted mainly to humans)
DAT	Dative case		
DC	Daughter's child	PL	Plural
DEM	Demonstrative	PP	Past punctual tenseaspectmood suffix
DVB	Deverbaliser	PROG	Progressive
ED	Edible gender	PRS	Present tense
EMPH2	Emphatic postverbal particle	PST	Past
ERG	Ergative case	PURP	Purposive
FE	Feminine gender	REC	Reciprocal
GEN	NonMasculine gender (i.e. any gender but Masculine)	REF	Reflexive
		SEMB	Semblative suffix
GEN	Genitive case	sg	Singular number (restricted mainly to humans)
I1	Irrealis 1 tenseaspectmood suffix		
I2	Irrealis 2 tenseaspectmood suffix	VOC	Vocable

Introduction: everything got a song

Jim Wafer
University of Newcastle

> Everything got a song, no matter how little... plant, bird, animal, country, people, everything.
> – Eileen McDinny, in John Bradley with Yanyuwa families, **Singing saltwater country**

> The bodied voices of others will always escape full domestication in our writing.
> – Gary Tomlinson, **The singing of the New World**

Singing and its revitalisation in Indigenous Australia: the context

In 1985, Catherine Ellis formulated the succinct observation that song is the 'central repository of Aboriginal knowledge' (Ellis 1985:83) – a point that has since been confirmed by numerous others.[1] In light of this, it might be expected that there would be a body of literature on strategies for the maintenance and transmission of this crucial component of the Australian Indigenous cultural heritage. Yet the writing is sparse, and the present volume is the first to address itself specifically to the issue of Aboriginal song revitalisation. There are no doubt many reasons for this neglect, the most obvious being the comparatively trivial (in the sense of 'non-essential') role played by music in the broader Australian culture. There is little relevant education, even for those working in allied fields, such as Aboriginal studies, musicology, anthropology and linguistics. Only a small number of Australian tertiary institutions teach courses in ethnomusicology, and an even smaller number of these include ancestral Indigenous singing practices[2] in the curriculum.

---

1 For example, Clunies Ross 1987:1; Wild 1987:101–106; Barwick 2000; Stubington 2007:4; Turpin 2011:20–21; Turpin and Laughren 2013:406; Green 2014:60. Earlier writers making a similar point include Strehlow 1971; Payne 1978; Ellis 1984:142.

2 We focus on *song* revitalisation in the present volume because the ancestral music of Indigenous Australia is predominantly vocal – even if Jones's view (1965:368) that it includes no exclusively instrumental music is overstated. Bradley and Mackinlay's account (2000:30) of Yanyuwa ceremonies where there are no songs but 'all the sound [is] produced by percussion' is just one counter-example. On our use of the term 'ancestral', see below.

The concept of music revitalisation is also relatively new. One of its earliest appearances was in Victoria Levine's 'Musical revitalization among the Choctaw' (1993). In Australia, the concept, under various guises, such as 'applied ethnomusicology' (Harrison, Mackinlay and Pettan 2010; Pettan and Titon 2015, Harrison 2016) or 'music sustainability' (Grant 2011; see also Grant 2010, 2014), began to emerge in the first decade of the new millennium, and achieved a substantial presence with the publication, in 2013, of a special issue of *Musicology Australia*, edited by Dan Bendrups, Katelyn Barney and Catherine Grant, and devoted to 'Sustainability and ethnomusicology in Australasia'. Australia was also the home-base for an international research project called 'Sustainable futures for music cultures: towards an ecology of musical diversity', the results of which were published in 2016 (Schippers and Grant 2016).

Levine derived the term 'revitalization' from Anthony Wallace's 1956 article on 'revitalization movements'. This phrase has often been used in contexts that emphasise its messianic and nativistic overtones (Harkin 2004[3]), which is perhaps one of the reasons that 'revitalisation' has not found widespread favour with musicologists. Internationally, a more popular term is 'music revival', as indicated by the recent publication of an Oxford handbook (Bithell and Hill 2014) that uses this phrase in its title. But this expression, too, is suggestive of revivalist movements, and in any case, as the contents of the volume indicate, is used mainly to refer to the revival of the 'folk music' of majority cultures.[4]

Catherine Grant (in press, p. 4 of pre-publication version) has observed that, in Australia, 'the alternative rhetoric of sustainability has increasingly surfaced in the ethnomusicological space'. She sums up the implications of the current terminological disarray so well that her overview is worth quoting at length.

> The field of scholarly investigation dealing with the current and future health of music traditions and global musical diversity has not yet even definitively settled on a name for itself. This brings considerable attendant challenges for research and activism, including practicalities such as securing funding and resources for applied work, and gaining recognition and momentum both within and outside of academia for related efforts. For this reason, it is arguably hampering academic contributions to international efforts to keep music genres strong. In contrast, linguists can at least be confident of a shared understanding (even if not acceptance) of the meanings of language maintenance and revitalization, and have carefully articulated (and thoroughly critiqued) definitions of terms and concepts such as revival, renewal, reclamation and restoration, even if meanings vary between researchers, countries, and contexts.
>
> A sustained interdisciplinary conversation around the meanings and implications of these (and other) terms may significantly advance ethnomusicological consensus and understanding of key issues in music vitality and viability, particularly at this point in its trajectory. If linguists and ethnomusicologists were to develop over time a shared terminology with which to explore the commonalities and differences of their work, this could consolidate, expedite, and enrich ethnomusicological understandings of music sustainability, and make significant headway with applied initiatives in the area. Conversely, within the recent and ongoing ethnomusicological explorations of these issues (such as that mentioned previously around sustainability and stewardship), linguists may encounter new ways of thinking that may expand and deepen language revitalization theory and practice.

---

3 For perspectives on the Australian context, see also Beckett (2012).
4 While studies of Australian Indigenous music are sometimes included in works devoted to Australian folklore (e.g. Neuenfeldt and Kepa 2011; see also Greenway 1961:445–446), 'Australian folk music' is generally taken to refer to 'bush songs', which by and large have their stylistic origins in the British Isles and Ireland. On the slow development of Australian folklore studies as they pertain to Aboriginal oral texts, see Greenway (1961), Tonkinson (1976), Clunies Ross (1986). More recent contributions come from Waterman (1987), Klapproth (2004) and Clarke (2007).

The title of Grant's article is 'A case for greater interdisciplinary collaboration in language and music revitalization', and it is due to appear in *The Routledge handbook of language revitalization* (edited by Hinton, Huss and Roche, in press). This is probably a fair indication of the increasing acceptance of the term 'revitalisation' in relation to music.

Among linguists, the alternative terms and concepts that Grant mentions (revival, maintenance, renewal, retention, reclamation, restoration, sustainability and so on) are sometimes defined in ways that makes them applicable to particular types or stages of language loss (see, for example, Tsunoda 2005:9–15; Amery and Gale 2008, Disbray 2015:5). Nonetheless, the expression 'language revitalisation' is increasingly being adopted as the general term to cover all these types, both internationally (Hinton and Hale 2001:5, Hinton 2011, Coronel-Molina and McCarty 2016, Cowell 2016) and in Australia (Hobson et al. 2010).

Language revitalisation has a fairly long history in Australia (though not necessarily under this name), and has been on the national agenda at least since 1950. Brian Devlin (2017:12) notes that 'although it is customary to say that bilingual education in the Northern Territory (NT), Australia, began in December 1972 as a result of a Federal government initiative, it is apparent that the foundations of this policy change were formally laid in 1950'. He also observes that 'relevant pioneering efforts' had been made by missionaries in earlier years (Devlin 2017:11). In more recent times, Aboriginal and Torres Strait Islander languages were included in the National Policy on Languages that was adopted by the federal government in 1987 (Lo Bianco 1990) and were specifically targeted for assistance in the National Indigenous Languages Policy announced in 2009.[5] This has resulted in various kinds of support for Australian languages, including the establishment of Indigenous language centres in many parts of the country, the inclusion of Indigenous languages in state-level education policies, and funding for individual language revitalisation projects.

By comparison, Indigenous music revitalisation is a relatively new concept in Australia. Although its origins go back further, its formalisation as a national objective can be dated to 2002, when the National Recording Project for Indigenous Performance in Australia was conceived, at the inaugural Symposium on Indigenous Music and Dance, at Gunyaŋara in Arnhem Land (Marett and Barwick 2003, Corn 2013:269). The title and stated aims of this project make clear that its primary focus is the recording, documentation and archiving of Indigenous performance traditions. These are, of course, entirely laudable goals, and the Project pursues them for the sake of making the resulting resources available for cultural revitalisation purposes (Corn 2013:279).

Still, performance is only one aspect of music (and, for that matter, dance), and the processes involved in making a permanent record of it are only one aspect of its revitalisation. This means that Indigenous music revitalisation needs to be recognised as a broader field that:

- pays attention also to those aspects of music (and dance) that are not on immediate display, such as composition and transmission
- extends the concept beyond contemporary performance to the research and re-creation of musical traditions of the past
- can be put into effect in those regions of Australia where the performance traditions have suffered heavy attrition (which includes most of the south of the country).

---

5 See House of Representatives Standing Committee on Aboriginal and Torres Strait Islander Affairs (2012), ch. 3, 'Indigenous languages policy' (pp. 45–77).

Rethinking 'traditional' versus 'modern'

Our field of interest in the present volume is constituted by the kinds of songs that have been called 'traditional' (Magowan 1994, 2007) or 'ancestral' (Clunies Ross 1999:93[6]), as distinct from those that are variously called 'popular' (Magowan 1994), 'contemporary' (Oien 2000, Dunbar-Hall and Gibson 2004:16), 'new style' (Breen and Brunton 1989:118), 'modern' (Ellis n.d: n.p.), 'recent' (Ottosson 2015:118), and so on.[7] This kind of distinction has been criticised as 'futile, and possibly damaging', on the grounds that it implies a dichotomy between 'music deriving from the pre-colonial past and that of the present' (Dunbar-Hall and Gibson 2004:16; see also Marett and Barwick 2003:144). Nonetheless, it is clear that a conceptual division of this kind actually reflects Aboriginal categories in many regions of Australia.[8]

Åsa Ottosson (2015:118) points out that there are parts of the country, such as Central Australia, where Indigenous musicians 'keep more recent and ancestral musical forms and knowledge separate'. For people of the desert regions, she argues, 'these two expressive genres [recent and ancestral forms] have also come to address different dimensions of people's lives, and aim at different realms for their intended social effects' (Ottosson 2015:116). She contrasts this with the Top End of the Northern Territory. There, musicians 'mix ancestral song styles into popular song, may add ancestral songs on separate tracks on their albums, and often integrate detailed ancestral narratives into rock, country, pop and reggae lyrics' (Ottosson 2015:50).

This is another case where Catherine Grant's point about the need for greater clarity and consistency in our terminology is applicable. Let me offer just a few preliminary observations. It should be noted that, even in the Top End, there are 'ancestral songs' that would never be mixed with 'popular' or 'modern' styles. These are the 'sacred' (and often secret) songs that are regarded as having always existed. In principle, at least, and in spite of the phenomenon of 're-dreaming' (McConnel 1935:66, Nancarrow and Cleary, this volume, Chapter 10), these songs do not have a human authorship but are handed down from generation to generation, or from songperson to songperson.

The distinction between 'traditional' and 'modern' is therefore really only relevant to musical innovations, since the 'pre-existent' songs cannot, by definition, be anything other than 'traditional'. But the converse does not apply: not all 'traditional' music is of this sacred 'pre-existent' type. There are other factors which, singly or together, may cause a song to be perceived as 'traditional'. A short list would include:

- being found in a dream
- making use of 'old' musical forms
- having lyrics that index 'traditional' beliefs and practices.

Alice Moyle (1980:717) notes that in the Kimberley there is a sharp conceptual division between songs 'found in dream' and those 'made with the brain' (such as 'cowboy songs'). Whether or not a song has been 'found in dream' is undoubtedly a major factor in Aboriginal musical classification in many parts of Australia. Songs that fall outside this category are often called 'fun' songs (Breen and Brunton 1989:10; Turner 2010:69).

---

6   The usage here is probably indebted to Donaldson (1995), who applied it to language.
7   For coverage of 'popular' Indigenous music, we refer the reader to the fine studies in this field that have appeared in recent times, such as Breen and Brunton (1989), Dunbar-Hall and Gibson (2004), Magowan and Neuenfeldt (2005) and Ottosson (2015).
8   This is no doubt also true for many of the world's Indigenous peoples. Chickasaw writer Linda Hogan (2013:19) puts the matter quite bluntly: 'For tribal peoples, our relationships and kinship with the alive world is simply called *tradition*. We are either traditionally minded or we are still in the process of decolonizing ourselves'.

Nonetheless, that songs of oneiric[9] origin ('dream songs') are not *necessarily* regarded as 'traditional' is clear from the following observation by Catherine Ellis (n.d.: n.p.): 'in addition to those traditional performers in desert areas who maintain their old song forms, there are others who dream modern songs that can be considered Dreamtime songs that include reference to modern living'. In other words, the term 'traditional' is being used here to refer to a set of musical and textual characteristics ('old song forms') rather than to compositional technique. Ellis de-emphasises the traditional nature of 'finding song in dream' in order to focus on a different aspect of the distinction between 'traditional' and 'modern' music-making.

Separating out these factors allows us to posit a continuum between 'traditional' and 'modern' Aboriginal musics. At one end of the continuum we locate the pre-existent songs that are not susceptible to innovation; at the other end we place songs that are 'made with the brain' and expressed in musical and poetic languages that have no connection with traditional beliefs and practices. But there is also a large intermediate area, where the factors listed above may be combined in different ways, and the musical and textual structures may integrate traditional and modern features in varying proportions.

As mentioned already, our focus in this book is largely on the song types located towards the 'traditional' end of the spectrum, on the grounds that these musical forms face greater threats to their sustainability than the 'modern' ones, and are therefore in greater need of revitalisation. This proposition needs to be seen in the context of what might be termed the 'doomed cosmology' theory.[10] If non-Indigenous thinking about Aboriginal people was dominated, in the late 19th and early 20th centuries, by the 'doomed race' theory, in more recent times this has been replaced by the equally colonial notion that, even if Aboriginal people have, against all odds, managed to survive, at least their cosmology is doomed to extinction, as they come to terms with the consequences of colonial history.

In spite of the insidious (because usually implicit) and widespread nature of this ideology in contemporary Australia, Aboriginal land-based cosmologies have survived down to the present day in many places, and in the best-case scenarios, they are supported by an unbroken tradition of singing practices. No doubt these practices have changed over time, and in some cases they may include 'modern' elements. But the interesting and productive question is not so much whether the relevant components of a song are 'traditional' or 'modern', but rather whether any particular song, or song-type, plays a part, or is capable of playing a part, in the sustaining (and revitalisation) of cosmologies that relate Aboriginal people to place.[11]

The use of the term 'ancestral' as an alternative to 'traditional' raises other important questions. If we ask what kinds of music can be considered 'ancestral', we also need to ascertain who or what can be considered an ancestor, and whether the basis of 'ancestrality' changes over time. The relevance to musical evolution becomes clear when we consider that Central Australian musical forms could become more mixed once the contemporary generation of desert musicians – that is, those who play popular music – become ancestors themselves.

---

9 From Greek ὄνειρος (óneiros), 'dream'.
10 I owe this notion, if not the precise formulation, to an unpublished paper by Petronella Vaarzon-Morel (2016b), entitled '"For a cultural future": re-figuring the Coniston Massacre' and presented in the 'Cosmologies unbound' panel at the annual conference of the Australian Anthropological Society, 12–15 December 2016, University of Sydney.
11 For an excellent overview of the politics of tradition in contemporary Indigenous Australia, see Onnudottir, Possamai and Turner (2013:16–21). There are also helpful insights into this issue as it applies to music in Magowan (1994:135, n.2). See Eyerman and Jamison (1998:26–47) for a broader discussion of the notion of 'tradition' in the social sciences, and its specific applicability to music.

Australian Indigenous music and ethnomusicology: historical background

If we understand ethnomusicology as 'musical ethnography' – that is, the study of a particular musical practice (or set of practices) through participant observation (see e.g. R. Moyle 2001) – then it shares with other branches of ethnography a synchronic focus. In essence, the ethnographic approach is centred on the description and analysis of a socio-cultural form at a particular point in time.

In Australia, this factor combines with the shallow time-depth of written records to explain the scarcity of studies in the field of historical ethnomusicology. A recently published textbook (McCollum and Hebert 2014) that aims to provide reliable foundations for this emerging sub-discipline[12] mentions Australia only in passing. Nonetheless, if there has been little opportunity for the development of historical ethnomusicology in this country, there has been some attention paid to ethnomusicological history[13]; that is, the history of our own region's ethnomusicology.

Probably the earliest relevant publication is Trevor Jones's article of 1974, on 'ethnomusicological studies in Australia'. This title places the emphasis on ethnomusicology as a discipline rather than on its subject matter, and reflects the terminological catchall role it has played in the study and revitalisation of Indigenous music in Australia. The article also includes what is perhaps the first attempt at a bibliographic sketch of the literature on Aboriginal music. Subsequent bibliographic and audiographic contributions include Stubington (1985), Koch (1987), Koch (1992) and Barwick and Marett (1996). More recent updates have been incorporated into works that are not specifically bibliographic, such as Stubington (2007:290–304). I note also the relevance of the 'ethnochoreological' literature on Aboriginal dance, as surveyed by Wild (1986), Williams (1991) and Farnell and Wong Santos (2014).

Other publications (such as Ellis 1979b, Moyle 1984, Barwick and Marett 1995, Marett 2005:6–14, Stubington 2007:3–10) have provided overviews of the development of a field of 'professional musicology within Aboriginal Studies' (Clunies Ross 1987:3)[14], and the present volume could be regarded as an update on what Clunies Ross calls 'the state of the art'. The major difference, as already noted, is that the current work is oriented specifically to the revitalisation of singing, rather than, or in addition to, the documentation and analysis of songs and their contexts.

The term 'ethnomusicology' has been comprehensive enough in the past to be applicable to the activities of the various categories of scholars who work with Australian Indigenous musical

---

12 The term 'historical ethnomusicology' was probably first used by Ann Buckley (1998). But this new field could just as well have been called 'ethnohistorical musicology' or 'musical ethnohistory'. Other perspectives on the terminology are provided by Gary Tomlinson, who has made a number of pioneering contributions (including Tomlinson 1993, 2007, 2015) that attempt to 'read' behind and beyond the written records. He has played in important role in the creation of what he calls a 'space for a music that does not survive in its living, sounding tradition, or on record or CD, or written in a performable notation' (2007:4). In a more recent publication (2015:13) he coins a term that he applies to recent developments in archaeology, namely 'cognitive archaeology'. The field he himself is pioneering could perhaps most accurately be called a 'cognitive archaeology of singing'. In this context, it is worth mentioning also the relevance of the emerging field of archaeoacoustics (Scarre and Lawson 2006, Eneix 2014).

13 The concept 'history of ethnomusicology' is also of relatively recent date. The contributors to Nettl and Bohlman (1991) provide an overview of earlier sources (but make no mention of Australia).

14 There have been other attempts at naming this field as a subject area of intellectual history, more recent ones including Marett's 'traditions of scholarship in the study of Aboriginal music' (2005:6–9) and Stubington's 'ethnomusicology and Aboriginal music' (2007:4–9). No one has yet suggested 'Australianist ethnomusicology' (which at least has the advantage of succinctness), though the use of 'Australianist' in this sense is common in linguistics, where it applies to research into Australian Indigenous languages (or, more technically, into languages belonging to the Australian phylum). Moreover, there is a widely accepted precedent in the term 'Africanist ethnomusicology' (see e.g. Agawu 2014:xix and *passim*).

traditions – typically musicologists, anthropologists, linguists and folklorists.[15] Their fields are highly specialised, which means that work on Indigenous music in Australia has often been a matter of interdisciplinary collaboration, as 'the most productive way of approaching the study of Aboriginal songs in the full range of contexts essential to them' (Clunies Ross 1987:1–2).

If this was true at the time these words were written, how much more do they apply today, when we are witnessing the rapid proliferation of composite fields clustered under such ample banners as 'sound studies' (Sterne 2012, Pinch and Bijsterveld 2012) and 'music in the social and behavioural sciences' (Thompson 2014[16]). At the same time, the subject matter of ethnomusicological studies has been ramifying relentlessly through the development of new genres and subgenres. The cross-fertilisation of popular music[17] and 'world music' has resulted in a widespread regional diversification of global forms such as heavy metal, punk, hip hop, techno or 'the rave', and the remix or 'mash-up', all of which have developed their own specialised discourses and publications.

In Australia, the Aboriginal popular music scene, once heavily identified with country music (Walker 2000), now manifests a diversity in which most of the major global genres are represented, to varying degrees. Nonetheless, across this range there has been a developing trend to use words or lyrics from Aboriginal languages.

The music of Black transnationalism began to have an impact in the 1970s and 80s through the medium of reggae (Dunbar-Hall and Gibson 2004:47; Stratton 2015:396), and this influence has continued down to the present, although today it is more likely to take the form of hip hop (Mitchell 2006, White 2009[18]). But other genres with less specific racial associations have also made a significant impression in Aboriginal Australia, particularly heavy metal (Mansfield 2014[19]). Punk, techno and the remix are not quite so well represented, but there are some noteworthy examples of Aboriginal musicians whose work has links to these styles. Sydney band Dispossessed, for example, has strong punk affiliations.[20] As for techno: the late Yolngu com-

---

15 I use the term 'folklorists' in a broad sense to include all those who study oral traditions. As Clunies Ross (1986:236) has pointed out, 'there have never been professional folklorists (in the North American sense of the term) at work in Australia', and it is only since the middle of last century that the overlap between musicology, linguistics and literary studies has begun to develop as a discourse in this country (Clunies Ross 1986:237). See Samuels (2015) for a theoretical perspective, and Barwick (2012) for practical applications.

16 Thompson's encyclopaedic work on this theme covers the following topic areas: aesthetics and emotion; business and technology; communities and society; culture and environment; elements of musical examination; evolutionary psychology; media and communication; musicianship and expertise; neuroscience; perception, memory, cognition; politics, economics, law; therapy, health, wellbeing. Many of these topic areas are already developing as hybrid specialisations with their own technical literature. The new field of medical ethnomusicology (Koen, Lloyd, Barz and Brummel-Smith 2008) is a good example, drawing as it does on the more established disciplines of medical anthropology, ethnomusicology and music therapy.

17 For stylistic reasons, references for the remainder of this paragraph are listed here. Popular music: Bennett (2001), Borthwick and Moy (2004), Bennett and Waksman (2015); world music: Toner and Wild (2004), Taylor (2012); diversification of global musical forms: Hayward (1998), Langlois (2011); heavy metal: Wallach, Berger and Greene (2011); punk: Haenfler (2015), Dunn (2016); hip-hop: Terkourafi (2010); techno or 'the rave': St John (2009); the remix or 'mash-up': Sinnreich (2010), Navas, Gallagher and burrough (2014).

18 See also http://www.thecitizen.org.au/features/hip-hop-and-rap-giving-voice-young-indigenous-protest
    https://blogs.adelaide.edu.au/researchtuesdays/2015/06/01/hip-hop-saved-my-life/
    https://allaussiehiphop.com/2014/06/10/cairns-murri-crew-built-to-last/
    https://allaussiehiphop.com/2012/01/31/jimblah-capitol-city/ [all accessed 7 January 2017].

19 Mansfield (2014:239) notes that 'the extensive equipment required for producing heavy metal music has prevented any metal bands from forming in Wadeye [the site of his fieldwork]'. Nonetheless, Aboriginal metal bands have emerged in other communities, such as Santa Teresa, in Central Australia. See http://www.alicespringsnews.com.au/2015/10/20/set-to-head-from-isolation-to-world-fame/ See also
    https://www.vice.com/en_au/article/aboriginal-headbanging;
    https://www.vice.com/en_au/article/heavy-metal-gangs-of-wadeye-1-of-2; [all accessed 7 January 2017].

20 See   https://noisey.vice.com/en_au/article/dispossessed-are-the-most-uncompromising-unapologetic-and-import-

poser-performer Gurrumul (Geoffrey Yunupingu) had been working on an electronic music album called 'TRIBE2tribe' before his death, and is quoted as saying that he 'loves the sound of highly produced house, dance and club' music.[21] And the remix has a following in Melbourne, which is home to at least two Aboriginal remix artists, DJs Sadge (Dylan Clarke) and Sovereign Trax (Hannah Donnelly), both of whom are represented on Mixcloud.[22] Mention also needs to be made of the important Indigenous contributions to Australian art music, such as the work of composer-performers Deborah Cheetham, William Barton and the late David Page.

This diversification of Indigenous music in Australia is not, however, the only factor that has obliged ethnomusicologists to extend the scope of their collaborative endeavours. The pioneering revitalisation work of the last couple of decades has often entailed cooperation with experts from a variety of fields other than those typically associated with ethnomusicology. For example, the annual Symposium on Indigenous Music and Dance has, since 2003, brought ethnomusicologists, Indigenous law-holders and cultural practitioners together with a range of other specialists, including archivists, librarians, lawyers and historians (Corn 2013:275) – all of whom have a significant role to play in the revitalisation process.

'Ethnomusicology', then, may no longer be broad enough to cover all the developing specialisations that are relevant to our theme. What is required (to quote Catherine Grant again) is a 'sustained interdisciplinary conversation around the meanings and implications of [the relevant] . . . terms' with a view to 'develop[ing] over time a shared terminology with which to explore the commonalities and differences of [our] work' (Grant in press:4). Let me, then, offer a (very preliminary) sketch of the terminological vectors and their implications.

Over the last half century, the notion of 'music' has been undergoing a significant reappraisal, both internationally and in Australia. Of the various factors that have contributed to this cultural shift, the work of Canadian composer and environmentalist Murray Schafer stands out as especially noteworthy. Schafer invented the term 'soundscape' in the 1960s (see Schafer 1968, 1977) to apply to the relationship between humans and their acoustic environment, and it has since been used in the Australian context in a diverse range of publications, such as Richards (2007) and Bandt (2014).

'Sound world' is a related term, of which I have been unable to pinpoint the origin. But another pioneer in the field of 'sound studies', Stephen Feld (e.g. 2001, 2003), has used the phrase in a way that implies a certain contrast with the notion of 'soundscape'. The emphasis in the use of 'soundscape' is on the sounds of everyday life, including those of the natural environment. The concept of the 'sound world', on the other hand, relates rather to the social and cultural processes involved in the human creation and interpretation of sound. This is a more ethnographic orientation to the sonic environment, and is reflected in publications that appear under the rubric of 'sound and ethnography' (Feld, Fox, Porcello and Samuels 2004, Samuels, Meintjes, Ochoa and Porcello 2010, Centre for Imaginative Ethnography 2016).

One of the effects of this international reassessment has been a proliferation of studies that link music and the environment, with branches such as soundscape ecology (Farina 2013), ecomusicology (Rehding 2011, Seeger 2015) and zoömusicology (Martinelli 2009; Taylor 2013; Taylor n.d.). A helpful overview of the literature is provided by two scholars based in Australia, Hollis Taylor and Andrew Hurley (2015). They mention the Australian manifestations of this

---

ant-band-in-australia; https://www.sbs.com.au/nitv/article/2016/07/05/lyrical-activism-indigenous-metal-band-dispossessed [both accessed 7 January 2017].
21 http://www.northernstar.com.au/news/gurrumul-to-release-electronic-music-album/2905080/ [accessed 7 January 2017].
22 See https://www.edm.me/artist/dylan-clarke; https://beta.mixcloud.com/discover/dj-sadge/; http://mpavilion.org/collaborator/sovereign-trax/; https://beta.mixcloud.com/discover/sovereigntrax/ [accessed 7 January 2017].

movement only in passing, but a broader perspective on issues of local interest can be found in the special issue of *Soundscape: The Journal of Acoustic Ecology* (Knox and Magen 2009) devoted to 'the investigation of changing soundscapes in the Australasian region'.[23] Australians have made a number of significant contributions to this discourse, such as those in the volume *Hearing places*, edited by Ros Bandt, Michelle Duffy and Dolly McKinnon (2007), and it has had a major influence on Australian sound art (Kouvaras 2013:54–56 and chapters 3, 5 and 8). This 'humanistic' aspect of sound studies is complemented by a more technologically-oriented side, as reflected in fields such as sound engineering and acoustics (Greene and Porcello 2005), mobile music technologies (Gopinath and Stanyek 2014), field technology (Lane and Carlyle 2013), and so on.

The long-term implications of this comparatively recent explosion of discourses with potential relevance to Australianist ethnomusicology remain to be seen. Many of the studies include at least passing references to Australian Indigenous music, and in a number of cases this topic is elaborated in contributions to works that take a broader, often international, perspective. There are few clear trends of immediate relevance to our theme, but one that stands out as promising for the future of both song revitalisation and reconciliation in Australia is what we might call 'collaborative music-making as sound art'. The ethnomusicologist participates as a fellow musician in a community's musical projects (cf. Russell and Ingram 2013), with the aim of jointly creating new musical forms that have a basis in local tradition.[24] An example of the practice can be found in Genevieve Campbell's Chapter 13 in the present volume.

This is a fairly recent development in what has been called 'applied' ethnomusicology. A number of other 'applied' fields have been elaborating their own discourses around Indigenous Australian music (and its revitalisation) for some time, and no doubt their significance for the durability of Aboriginal and Torres Strait musical traditions will continue to grow. These include, for example,[25] music pedagogy, archiving and heritage conservation, information technology and intellectual property law.

The present volume is, then, necessarily part of the same interdisciplinary tradition that Clunies Ross referred to in 1987, but it includes contributions that reflect the current broader scope of our field of endeavour. The new century has seen the rate of change and innovation in this field accelerate, as reflected in the publication of an article by Kirkwood and Miller (2014) on the effects and possible uses of the 'new technologies' in the musical education of Indigenous children. Indigenous authors are increasingly contributing to the discussion, for example in the recent volume called *Collaborative ethnomusicology* (Barney ed. 2014; see also Chadwick and Rrurrambu 2004).

There has been at least one major exception to the broad policy neglect of Indigenous music prior to the establishment of the National Recording Project for Indigenous Performance, and it can be seen in the work of Catherine Ellis and the Centre for Aboriginal Studies in Music

---

23 This includes a report (Magen 2009) on the activities of the Australian Forum for Acoustic Ecology, which was formed in 1998 (*http://www.acousticecology.com.au/* [accessed 30 August 2017]).
24 This synthesis of ethnomusicology and musical practice could be compared with the overlapping of anthropology and artistic practice (Schneider and Wright 2010, 2013). Jenny Deger (2013) provides an Australian perspective, based on collaboration with Yolngu of Arnhem Land.
25 Music pedagogy: Ellis (1979a), Ellis (1979b), Kartomi (1988), Dunbar-Hall (1991), Neuenfeldt (1998), Mackinlay and Dunbar-Hall (2003), Swijghuisen Reigersberg (2010), Bartleet (2011), Dunbar-Hall and Mackinlay (2011), Bradley (2012), Kral and Schwab (2012); archiving and heritage conservation: Seeger and Chaudhuri (2004), Falk and Ingram (2011), Corn (2013), Treloyn and Emberly (2013), Gillespie and Lilley (2015); information technology: Ormond-Parker, Corn, Obata and O'Sullivan (2013); intellectual property law: Christensen (1996), Feld (1996a), Johnson (1996), Mills (1996), Battiste and Henderson (2000), Christen (2005), Seeger (2005), Janke and Quiggin (2006), Quiggin and Janke (2007), Toner (2008), Anderson (2009), Janke (2009), Glaskin (2010), Feld (2011), Coombe (2011), Glaskin (2011).

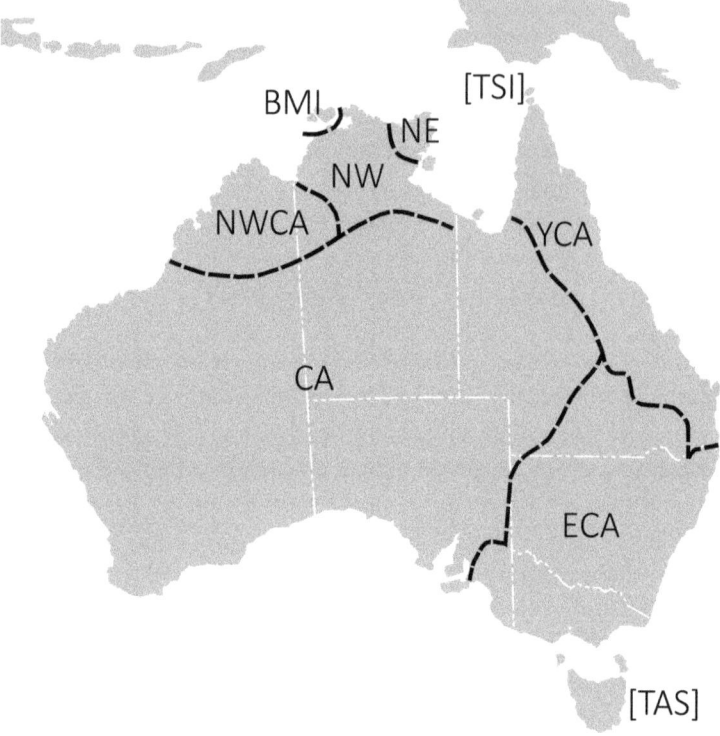

Map 0.1: Hypothetical musical regions of Indigenous Australia. Broken black lines indicate musical regions as proposed by Moyle (1966, map 3); broken white lines indicate state and territory boundaries. (Re-drawn by Brenda Thornley.)

(CASM), which Ellis was instrumental in establishing in 1975 at the University of Adelaide. Much of the song revitalisation work that has taken place in Australia has been influenced, directly or indirectly, by the initiatives at CASM (see Ellis 1979a, Ellis 1979b, Breen and Brunton 1989, Tunstill 1995 and Mackinlay and Dunbar-Hall 2003). These influences remain to be traced in detail, since there have been, as yet, no attempts at a history of Indigenous song revitalisation in Australia, and there is no directory of programs and projects, whether they be formal or informal, ongoing or sporadic (for example, occurring in the context of festivals or 'language and culture' camps).

The organisation of the chapters

We have organised the chapters geographically rather than thematically, at least partly because of the crucial link between Indigenous singing practices and *place*. From an Indigenous perspective, the source and origin of many songs is the land itself (see e.g. Turner 2010:194). The particular ordering we have used is intended to keep contiguous regions together and at the same time to make as transparent as possible the way the chapters (and regions they relate to) can be mapped onto the 'musical regions' proposed by Alice Moyle (1966:xv–xvii and map 3; see also Moyle 1967:35–43).

Moyle's work is now almost half a century old, and there have been no equally ambitious attempts in the interim to map Indigenous musical cultures in Australia, although more recent studies have filled in some of the gaps in the data, as Moyle had advocated.[26] This introduction is not the place to undertake a definitive contemporary survey, although the chapters that follow will yield much relevant information, to supplement the almost five decades of research that have taken place since Moyle's early work. The notion of 'musical regions' is not straightforward, so we draw attention also to Barry McDonald's Chapter 7 in the present volume, which interrogates a number of ramifications of the concept.

Map 0.1 (above) is based, then, on Moyle's map 3 of 1966. The codes Moyle uses (as adopted in Maps 0.1, 0.2 and 0.3, and in column 2 of Table 0.1, below) are as follows:

ECA = East Central Arid
CA = Central Arid
NWCA = North-west Central Arid
NW = North-west
BMI = Bathurst and Melville Islands
NE = North-east
YCA = Cape York Central Arid

Moyle attempted to map her regions onto an earlier map of 'Tribal areas' developed by Arthur Capell (see Moyle 1966:vii), which are omitted here. These were based on Capell's linguistic work (1963), which has since been superseded by better supported classifications of Australian languages. Note that neither Capell nor Moyle included the Torres Strait Islands in their surveys.[27] We have added to the map a coding ('[TSI]') for this region, in square brackets (to indicate that it did not originate with Moyle). Moyle did hypothesise one further region, namely Tasmania, but did not allocate a code to it. (We have coded it as '[TAS]' on our map.)

Eastern Arnhem Land ('NE') is not represented in the present volume. In compensation, some of the chapters included here cover regions for which Moyle was unable to list 'vocal features' (as she did for BMI, NW, NE and CA, 1966:xvi–xvii), presumably for lack of data or analyses or both. Specifically, the chapters we have grouped under the 'South-east' (Moyle's 'ECA') and the 'North-west/Kimberley' ('NWCA') may be relevant to any attempt to fill these gaps. In addition, Chapter 16 (Skinner), while not expressly focused on any particular locality, provides some valuable insights into the music of Tasmania ('TAS'), Cape York ('YCA'), and the Torres Strait Islands ('TSI'). The last of these regions also receives individual attention in our Chapter 15 (Fairweather, Mathias and Whaleboat).

In our second map (below) we have superimposed a sketch of Australian Indigenous language groupings on Moyle's musical regions. These patterns of linguistic classification are based on recent work on the Pama-Nyungan ('PN') languages by Bowern and Atkinson (2012), and on the non-Pama-Nyungan ('NPN') languages by Evans and his collaborators (2003). 'Pama-Nyungan' is geographically the largest language family of the continent, covering the whole of the mainland below a line that runs roughly from the west coast, south of the Kimberley, to the eastern end of the Gulf of Carpentaria. There are two Pama-Nyungan enclaves north of

---

26 Moyle's work (1966, 1967) was a preliminary study that called for further research to fill in details for those areas of Australia where the music had not been investigated. There are more recent overviews in *The Macquarie atlas of Indigenous Australia* (Arthur and Morphy 2005), which includes a chapter (11) on 'performing arts, sport and games'. This incorporates a section on music and dance (Barwick et al. 2005:126–133) that is illustrated with several useful maps covering stylistic features (such as instrumentation), but the authors have not attempted to define musical regions.
27 In this regard, it is worth noting that the Australia's Indigenous peoples identify as two distinct populations, 'Aboriginal' and 'Torres Strait Islander', on the basis of differences in language, land tenure, subsistence techniques and so on. Thus, the term 'Indigenous Australians' is often used as a shorthand way of saying 'Aboriginal and Torres Strait Islander Australians'. Capell and Moyle focused their studies specifically on Aboriginal Australians, rather than Indigenous Australians more broadly understood.

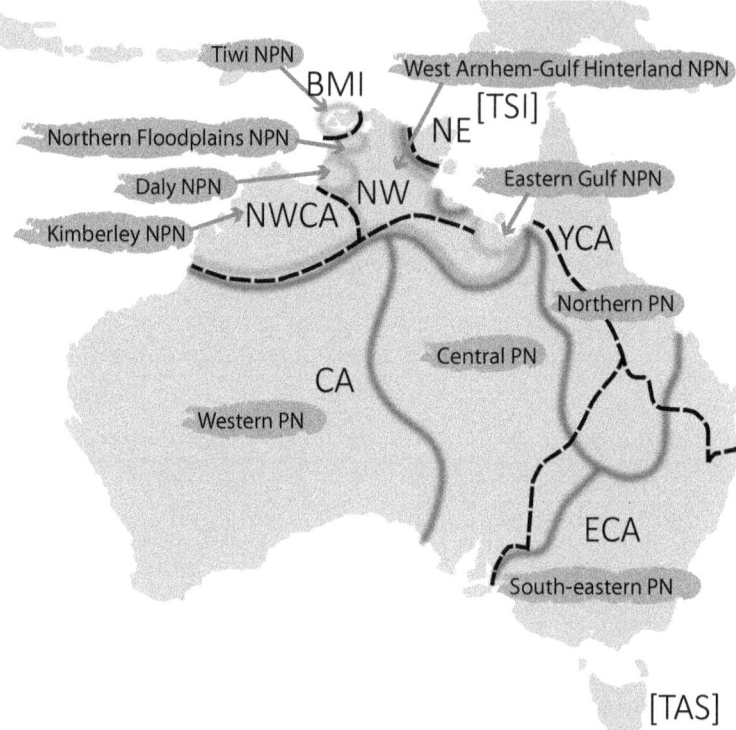

Map 0.2: Musical regions and language regions of Indigenous Australia. Dark grey lines indicate internal divisions of the Pama-Nyungan language family, light grey lines regional groupings of non-Pama-Nyungan. Where dark grey and light grey lines run parallel, there is a boundary between PN and NPN. These divisions are superimposed on Moyle's proposed boundaries of musical regions (see Map 0.1, above), indicated by broken black lines. (Cartography by Brenda Thornley.)

this line. These are constituted by the Yolngu languages of north-eastern Arnhem Land, and Yanyuwa, a language of the south-western Gulf of Carpentaria.[28]

Our division of the PN languages into four groups reflects the results of the phylogenetic analysis of Pama-Nyungan carried out by Bowern and Atkinson (2012:837–838), and we have adopted their nomenclature for these internal groupings: 'Western', 'Central', 'Northern' and 'South-eastern'. The non-Pama-Nyungan languages present a much more complex picture, with a large number of language families related in ways that researchers such as Evans (2003:4) acknowledge will take some time yet to understand fully. The mosaic-like nature of the phylogenetic relationships between the 20 or so NPN language families does not lend itself to simplification on a small map, so we have not attempted to represent these relationships here. Rather, we have grouped the NPN languages into six regions that are principally geographical. We use the regional designations 'Kimberley', 'Daly', 'Northern Floodplains', 'Tiwi', 'West Arnhem-Gulf Hinterland' and 'Eastern Gulf'. Readers who need specific phylogenetic detail are referred to Evans (2003), in particular to map 1 in that volume (2003:2).

In Table 0.1 (below), we present an overview of how the chapters in the present volume accord with the musical and linguistic groupings in Maps 0.1 and 0.2. Note that Chapters 16

---

28 Yanyuwa has been (re-)classified as PN (Blake 1988:76, Evans 2003:12), and is included in Bowern and Atkinson's re-analysis of Pama-Nyungan groupings (2012 supplementary materials:10) as a member of Western PN (to which the Yolngu languages also belong).

and 17 are not included in this table, because their geographical focus is not limited to any particular region but takes in the whole of Australia.

Table 0.1: Overview of chapters and their geographical sequence, correlated with musical and linguistic regions

REGION	MOYLE	BROAD LINGUISTIC CLASSIFICATION	LANGUAGE GROUPS~FAMILIES	LANGUAGE/LOCALITY	CHAPTER
THE SOUTH-WEST & PILBARA	CA	Western PN	Nyungic	*Nyungar*/ south-west of WA	1 Bracknell
			Ngayarta	*Ngarluma* & others/ western Pilbara WA	2 Treloyn & Dowding
WESTERN GULF	NW	Western PN	Yanyuwa	*Yanyuwa*/ Borroloola NT	3 Sharpe
CENTRAL ARID REGION	CA	Central PN	Arandic	*Arrernte*/ Alice Springs NT	4 Turpin
			Karnic	*Wangkangurru* & others/ Lake Eyre Basin SA & elsewhere	5 Hercus & Koch
CENTRAL QUEENSLAND	CA	Northern PN	Maric	*Gunggari*/ Woorabinda, central QLD	6 Laughren, Turpin & Turner
THE SOUTH-EAST	ECA	South-eastern PN	Various south-eastern groups	Various languages/ NSW, VIC, southern QLD	7 McDonald
			Yuin-Kuric	*Thangatti*/ Armidale NSW	8 Kelly & Harkins
			Yuin-Kuric	*HRLM*/ Hunter Valley NSW	9 Wafer
EASTERN GULF	NW	NPN (Eastern Gulf region)	Tangkic Family	*Lardil*/ Mornington Island QLD	10 Nancarrow & Cleary
WESTERN ARNHEM LAND & GULF HINTERLAND	NW	NPN (West Arnhem-Gulf Hinterland region)	Iwaidjan Family	*Mawng*/ Warruwi, Goulburn Island NT	11 Brown, O'Keeffe, Manmurulu, Manmurulu & Singer
			Marrku (family level isolate)	*Marrku*/ Croker Island NT	12 Brown & Evans
BATHURST & MELVILLE ISLANDS	BMI	NPN (Tiwi region)	Tiwi (family level isolate)	*Tiwi*/ Bathurst and Melville Islands, NT	13 Campbell
THE NORTH-WEST/ KIMBERLEY	NWCA	NPN (Kimberley region)	Worrorran Family	*Ngarinyin* & others/ Mowanjum & western Kimberley WA	14 Emberly, Treloyn & Charles
TORRES STRAIT	[TSI]	Papuan	Eastern Trans-Fly Family	*Meriam Mir*/ Murray Island QLD & other locations in QLD & NSW	15 Fairweather, Matthias & Whaleboat

In this table the chapters are listed in numerical sequence (far right column), and aligned with the relevant geographical region (column 1), the Moyle 'musical region' code (column 2), a

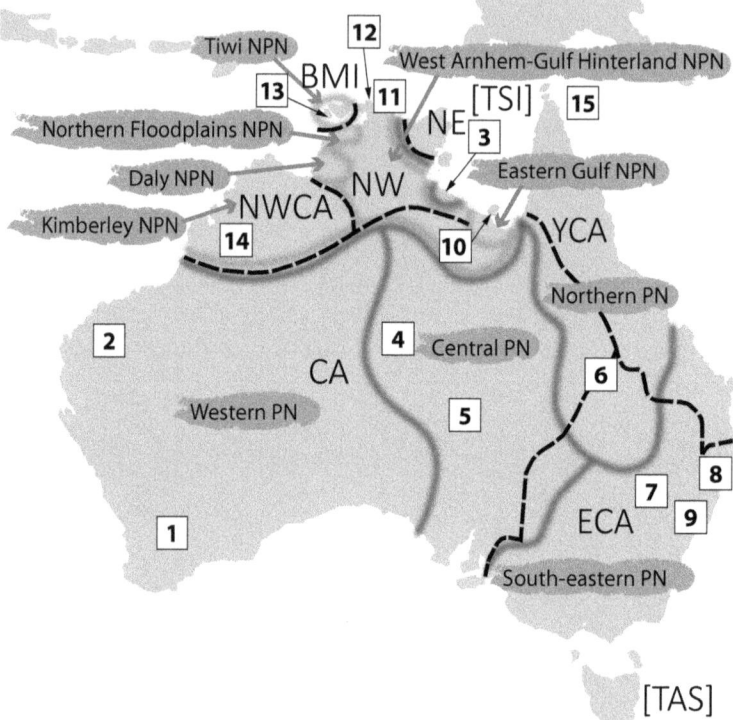

Map 0.3: Study sites represented in the present work. The numbers in boxes refer to the chapters in this book and have been overlaid on musical regions (broken black lines, see Map 0.1) and language groupings (dark grey and light grey lines, see Map 0.2.) (Cartography by Brenda Thornley.)

broad linguistic classification, as illustrated on Map 0.2 (column 3), the specific language group or family[29] (column 4) and the language name (italicised) and locality (after slash) (column 5).

In the allocation of regional names to our chapter groupings, we have subdivided two of Moyle's regions. Her 'CA' we have separated into the 'South-west and Pilbara', the 'Central Arid Region' and 'Central Queensland', while 'NW' has become 'Western Arnhem Land-Gulf Hinterland', 'Western Gulf' and 'Eastern Gulf'. These subdivisions were necessary to take into account certain disjunctive relationships between musical regions (as hypothesised by Moyle) and language groupings, which we will come to shortly.

The relevant correspondences are summarised in Map 0.3, above, which shows the approximate locations of the various accounts of Indigenous Australian singing practices to be found in the chapters of this volume.

This arrangement of the chapters allows certain relationships to be established at a glance. It is noteworthy that the geographical division between PN and NPN[30] corresponds reasonably well to Moyle's distinction between musical regions of the CA (Central Arid) type and

---

29 We have generally classified the PN languages by the group names given in Bowern and Atkinson (2012:837–838), and the NPN languages by the family names given in Evans (2003:2, map 1). For the classification of Meriam Mir, we have relied on Hunter, Bowern and Round (2011:109 and *passim*), who spell the language name as 'Meryam Mir'.

30 Both PN and NPN languages belong to the Australian Phylum. This does not apply to the East Torres Strait language of Chapter 15, which is generally considered to be a Papuan language of the Trans-Fly family (Evans 2005:255–256, Hunter, Bowern and Round 2011:109). We have not included chapters 16 and 17 in the table, since these are general chapters that deal with Indigenous singing from the whole continent.

the NW (North-west) type. (There is an apparent overlap in the case of NWCA, where NPN languages are spoken but there is an implied blending of NW and CA musical features.) This provides, perhaps, some justification for Jones's (1980:161) division of Aboriginal Australia into two musical blocs, roughly north and south of the Tropic of Capricorn (corresponding approximately to a division between Moyle's NE, NW, NWCA, BMI and (most of) YCA, constituting the north, and the rest of Australia – basically CA and ECA – making up the south).

But our arrangement also brings out some of the disjunctions that occur when overlaying language classifications and maps of other Indigenous cultural features. Language groups are not necessarily co-extensive with the groupings attributed to other social practices, such as music. This has been shown in detail in the work of AustKin on the relationship between languages and social category names ('skin names') in Aboriginal Australia.[31] The distribution of Aboriginal sign languages (Kendon 1988) is another case in point.[32]

To give some examples from Table 0.1 above: the arrangement of the table makes clear the anomalous position of Yanyuwa. This is a PN language, but located in Moyle's NW region.[33] (The great majority of the other PN languages are associated with the 'CA' regions – CA, ECA and YCA.[34]) We note also the ambiguous position of the Maric languages of south-central Queensland. Moyle did not investigate music from this region, but on her map it is divided up between CA, ECA and YCA. The chapter by Laughren, Turpin and Turner in the present volume (Chapter 6) suggests that the songs from this region that are the subject of their study have a number of features in common with the music of the CA region, but other features are distinctive. Further research may reveal what they share (or not) with ECA and YCA. Moyle's YCA is itself divergent, at least in terms of Jones's broad dichotomy of musical styles. In spite of this region's location largely north of the Tropic (which runs through Rockhampton), the languages of Cape York belong to the Pama-Nyungan family, and Moyle evidently regarded the region's musical features as having more in common with 'Central Arid' than with any of her northern groupings (e.g. Moyle 1966:xvii).

Stubbs (1974:109), in his map of prehistoric art styles in Australia, divides the continent into six regions that are to a large extent co-extensive with Moyle's. The differences are mainly matters of internal differentiation[35]. It is too early to know whether this overlap of hypothesised musical and artistic regions is actually indicative of something like 'culture areas', or whether the divisions on which these regions are based are just (as Barry McDonald puts it in his contribution to the present volume) a matter of convenience. Quite a lot more research will be needed before it is possible to investigate the relative distribution of musical (or art) styles in any phylogenetic depth – and this applies not just to Australia, but is almost universally true. As

---

31 For example, the distribution of subsections is restricted to an area of northern and central Australia that includes many (but not all) non-Pama-Nyungan languages and a (comparatively) small block of Pama-Nyungan languages. See http://www.austkin.net/ [accessed 31 March 2015] and McConvell, Kelly and Lacrampe (in press: ch. 2). For background on Austkin, see McConvell & Dousset (2012).

32 Kendon (1988:399) has shown, for example, that Warlpiri and Anmatyerre speakers share a much higher proportion of hand-signs than spoken vocabulary, so he classifies their sign languages as members of the same grouping, which he calls 'North Central Desert'. The spoken languages belong to quite distinct language groupings (Ngarga~Yapa and Arandic, respectively).

33 Moyle has created a separate region, 'NE', for the other PN enclave, the Yolngu languages, but it is not represented in the contributions to the present volume.

34 Myfany Turpin (pers. com.) has suggested that in fact Yanyuwa music probably does share features of the CA region, such as the use of short texts set to a longer repeating melodic contour.

35 First, Stubbs divides Moyle's Central Arid region (CA) into three parts (his region 1 incorporating the south-western section of South Australia and the south-east of Western Australia, his region 2 Central Australia, and his region 6 the south-west and Pilbara regions of Western Australia); second, his region 3 combines four of Moyle's regions (North-east, North-west, North-west Central Arid and Bathurst and Melville Islands) into one.

Le Bomin, Lecointre and Heyer (2016:1) put the matter, in their ground-breaking application of phylogenetic methods to the question of music transmission[36]:

> Numerous studies using computational methods derived from evolutionary biology have been successfully applied to varied subset of linguistic data. One of the major drawbacks regarding musical studies is the lack of suitable coded musical data that can be analysed using such evolutionary tools.

Implicit in this brief statement are a number of challenges for the current generation of ethnomusicologists, including those working in Australia.

Alice Moyle focused on formal features[37] in her proposal for Australian 'musical regions', but other factors are also relevant, in particular the emic classification of 'genres of singing'. The attention given to this issue is fairly limited, and this has led Michael Walsh (2007:133) to pose the question 'What is the ideal classification/categorisation of [Aboriginal] song?' The topic is too substantial to address in any detail here, but deserves some preliminary remarks.

Song types vary from group to group, and their categorisation is likely to depend less on strictly musical factors than on the social context in which a song is conceived and performed. Moreover, the particularity of local conventions for differentiating between song types is often a factor in the maintenance of a group's distinctive local identity. Nonetheless, the Bardi genres identified by Glaskin (2010:254–256) suggest a classificatory schema that is probably applicable across much of Aboriginal Australia. There are three main criteria of differentiation: first, whether a particular song type is 'oneiric' (that is, it originates in a dream) or 'made in the head'; second, whether the song type is 'pre-existent' or 'newly emerged'; third, whether it is considered 'public' or 'restricted'.

Among Bardi, the application of these principles would result in the following classification of genres:

Table 0.2: Proposed schema for Aboriginal song classification (examples from Bardi)

	ONEIRIC		MADE IN THE HEAD
	RESTRICTED	PUBLIC	PUBLIC
PRE-EXISTENT	ululung	anggwuy	
NEWLY EMERGED		ilma	ludiny

Ululung songs are those associated with 'a gender-restricted, male only initiatory stage'; *anggwuy* songs are part of 'an "open" or public stage of initiation'; *ilma* are 'public corroborees received in dreams' by living individuals, often from identifiable deceased persons; and *ludiny* are 'secular songs sung without accompanying dance or material representations' (Glaskin 2010:254–255). Note that all of these are 'traditional' genres, distinguished by Bardi from 'contemporary song

---

36 They show that, 'contrary to what is currently believed, vertical transmission plays a key role in shaping musical diversity' (Le Bomin, Lecointre and Heyer 2016:1). This is undoubtedly relevant to the Australian context, where linguistic borrowing (horizontal transmission) has also been shown to occur at a much lower rate than once supposed: 'loan levels ... as a whole have been overstated' (Bowern and Atkinson 2012:822). It is worth noting also that, in Australia, vertical transmission is generally lineal – that is, traceable through either a matriline (female descent) or a patriline (male descent). For other interesting applications of phylogenetics to music, see Liebman, Ornoy and Chor (2012) and Grauer (2011). For an overview of other approaches to 'computational analysis of a large corpus of music-related textual, sound, or image files', see McCollum and Hebert (2014:57–66).

37 Specifically: melody type (tonal and rhythmic characteristics); instrumental accompaniment; and relationship between song text and melody. A broader set of formal features has been analysed in detail by Jones (1965:351–374), who also makes some preliminary observations about regional differences.

genres [which] include Christian songs sung in Bardi, and rock and roll or country music' (Glaskin 2010:254).

There are two empty cells in the table. The one that is greyed out is logically impossible, since pre-existent songs, by definition, cannot be 'made in the head'. The other empty cell (restricted songs of the newly emerged type), however, is at least theoretically possible, and some of the Bardi genres mentioned by Glaskin but not described in detail, such as *wujuj* ('love songs') or *gurungara* ('songs used in sorcery'), might conceivably belong there.

Glaskin's particular interest is in the ambiguities of 'ownership' in the case of *ilma*:

> The different contexts in which these rituals are performed is also marked by a distinction in how 'ownership' of songs in the dreamt genres is considered: with songs associated with initiation rituals (even those that are dreamt and subsequently incorporated into the repertoire) being the collective responsibility of senior Law men (those who have achieved the highest ritual status), and *ilma* being the responsibility of the person who dreams them. When that person passes away, the question of the *ilma*'s ownership can, though, become complex . . . (Glaskin 2010:255; see also Glaskin 2011).

There are other kinds of ambiguity too. For example, the possibility of 're-dreaming' the pre-existent songs blurs, to some extent, their separateness from 'newly emerged' songs. Equivocal cases of this kind make it clear that my taxonomy is an ideal abstraction, not necessarily a guide to the way genres would be distinguished in any particular language. Moreover, this schema applies to just one possible set of factors relevant to the emic classification of singing practices – namely, those that pertain to a song's perceived origin and to (one aspect of) the social context of its performance.

Localised Aboriginal song genres have been described in a number of ethnomusicological publications, but there have been few attempts to consider them comparatively. Stephen Wild (1984) has made an important start in this direction, but as he notes, 'elaboration of [a] model to account for differences among musics of various Aboriginal cultures would require detailed comparison of those musics and cultures (1984:200).' Wild limited himself to a regional sketch that compared two Central Australian musical cultures (Warlpiri and Pintupi) with one from eastern Arnhem Land (Yolngu), and his model merits developing further.

The extant literature suggests that the other factors most commonly relevant to the naming of any particular musical practice include its function, the social groupings relevant to its production, and the formal aspects of its performance. For example, songs can classified according to the different functions of, say, putting children to sleep, or guaranteeing the success of a hunt, or guiding the spirit of a deceased person to its destination. Alternatively, they are often distinguished according to the nature of the relationship between classes of social actors – for example, men and women, opposite moieties, different clans or age grades or stages of initiation. In other cases it will be the formal elements of a performance that provide the basis for categorising song types – whether the performance includes dancing and/or the creation of visual symbols; what kind of instrumental accompaniment is used; and what musical, linguistic or choreological techniques are employed.

There is considerable potential for overlap between these classificatory principles, which is compounded by two additional factors: a particular song or song type may be used in different contexts, and a particular musical structure may be used with different song-texts. Further, any of these types, whether classified according to functional, social or formal characteristics, is liable to be designated in terms that are metaphorical or mythological. What this means is that an understanding of an Indigenous culture's song types requires some very fine distinctions to be made.[38]

The matter of Indigenous musical aesthetics pertains more to a song's reception than to its classification; but here, again, fine discriminations are necessary. There is an incipient literature on the topic,[39] and a good overview in Stubington (2007:115–120). It is worth noting, however, that this literature focuses largely on performance aesthetics rather than on Indigenous discourse around the 'texts' – that is, the words or musical structures in themselves, independent of their performance.

Many types of Aboriginal song are 'interauthorial'.[40] For example, a song received in a dream, wholly or partly, is rehearsed as soon as possible with the dreamer's immediate associates, who act as a kind of editorial committee, collaborating with dreamer to make the song performable. The language of this 'pre-performance discourse' no doubt includes criteria for the evaluation of the linguistic and musical texts, but these criteria have rarely been explicitly addressed in the literature.

The matter is complicated by the fact that a song's cultural appropriateness is likely to be judged largely in terms of social relationships or mythical narratives rather than the text's structural features. Nonetheless, it is probably safe to assume that what Stubington (2007:120) says of Aboriginal performance aesthetics is also true of the aesthetics of composition: 'the material for discrimination is there and Aboriginal musicians do discriminate.'

Thematic synopsis of the chapters

The chapters in this volume take a variety of perspectives on song revitalisation, and the strategies they describe or propose involve a wide range of contexts. Nonetheless, in this diversity there are some common themes. For the purposes of this brief summary, I treat each chapter as having particular relevance to one of the four essential processes into which Indigenous musical culture can be analytically divided, namely: composition, adaptation, performance and transmission. Needless to say, these are so closely interwoven that most of our authors touch on at least several of them. Still, the particular emphases that emerge from the individual chapters suggest the kind of topical arrangement that follows.

I begin with the relatively disregarded topic of **COMPOSITION**. John Sloboda (1985:103), referring to the field of music psychology, has observed that 'composition is the least studied and least well understood of all musical processes, and . . . there is no substantial literature to review' (see also Impett 2009). This is no doubt also true in the field of ethnomusicology. In his introduction to a special issue of *The World of Music* devoted to the music of Indigenous North America, Richard Keeling (1992:3) observes that Native American composition processes 'are so different in concept and method that they challenge our assumptions about the nature of music itself'. He proceeds to sketch out these processes, and sums them up as 'three separate but related ideas concerning the relationship between the singer and the song' (Keeling 1992:9):

> (1) Spontaneous origin. The idea that a song comes to a person all at once, in a relatively complete form, through a dream or vision;

---

38 Anderson (1995:13–17) provides a good example.
39 See, for example, R. Moyle (1979:71), Clunies Ross (1986:258–260, 1989), Grau (2000, 2004), Neuenfeldt and Costigan (2004), Barwick (2005), Corn and Gumbula (2007), Turpin (2007), Walsh (2007:133). The topic of aesthetics is more frequently discussed in relation to Aboriginal visual and plastic arts; see, for example, Morphy (1989) and, for a comparative perspective, the contributors to Coote and Shelton (1992) and Pinney and Thomas (2001).
40 I have borrowed this concept from Michael Frishkopf, who defines the interauthor as 'a social network of textual producers' (2003:85).

(2) Separate existence. The belief that a song has a separate existence or has always existed, possibly deriving from a sacred period before humans existed; and

(3) Representation or mimesis. The concept that the song can serve as a medium which captures the spiritual essence of a vision or important personal experience.

While it seems likely that Aboriginal people have analogous notions about the nature of music and its creation, the matter has rarely been explicitly addressed.

Composition in Indigenous Australia can be considered from two distinct but complementary perspectives. One approach analyses the externally observable techniques of musical, verbal and movement art on the basis of live performances or recordings or written texts. The other approach concerns itself with the cultural modelling of the processes involved in the conceiving and actualising of a song. These 'subjective' operations take place largely outside the purview of researchers and are often difficult for a song's originators to explain – particularly to an outsider. They may also have very little to do with the usual Western concept of 'composition'. Anthony Seeger (2005:81–82) writes, of the origin of a particular song among the Suya of Mato Grosso, Brazil: 'There is no one in this process of song creation that resembles the European notion of a composer ... If the song can be traced to anything, it is to the savannah deer spirit'. The situation in Indigenous Australia is similar, and this has led some writers to avoid the terms 'composition' and 'composer'. Marett (2000), for example, uses 'song-creation' rather than 'composition', and Nancarrow and Cleary (this volume, Chapter 10) use 'dreamer' and 'receiver' (of song) in preference to 'composer'.

There have been a number of fine analyses of the observable technical skills involved in an Indigenous 'composer's' work, but the processes involved in 'receiving' a song are generally mentioned only in passing, if at all, and, with a few notable exceptions (such as Dussart 2000:145–176; Marett 2000; Stubington 2007:98–120)[41], have not often been the subject of focused research. This points to a broader lack of attention to the nature of the soundscapes that Indigenous Australians inhabit; that is, to the role of sound, and, more specifically, vocalisation, in their understanding of the world.

The work of Gary Tomlinson[42] provides some excellent illustrations, from different cultures and historical periods, of the difficulties encountered by 'modern Westerners' in appreciating that their own sound world is specific and unique, just one of many, and that the role of language and song in other cultures needs to be understood in terms of the broader role of sound itself. A thorough application of such an approach to the aural distinctiveness of Indigenous Australian cultures is clearly beyond the scope of these preliminary remarks. Nonetheless, for present purposes, the Aboriginal sound world could perhaps most succinctly be characterised as an 'audible map', in which every sound, of whatever origin, is a kind of vocal inscription waiting to be interpreted.[43] Of particular importance are the sounds received in dreams and visions – that is, sounds that are not audible to an observer. These are the sounds that become songs once the dreamer brings them into waking reality and performs them.

---

41 See also Walsh (2007:333 and 140 n.2) for a listing of others who have written on the topic of Aboriginal song acquisition.

42 In particular Tomlinson (2007) – but see also the works of 1993 and 2015.

43 To give an example: Gumbaynggirr Elder Tony Perkins was told 'never to throw a pipi shell, as the high-pitched whistle that resulted could generate harmful consequences' (quoted in McDonald, this volume. See also Somerville and Perkins 2010:28). This kind of taboo on random auditory inscription is paralleled by similar constraints on marking the visible landscape. Galarrwuy Yunupingu was told by his father 'that if I made a mark, or dig, with no reason at all, I've been hurting the bones of the traditional people of that land. We must only dig and make marks on the ground when we perform or gather food' (quoted in Vaarzon-Morel 2016a:208).

This perspective is taken up in **Wafer**'s contribution (Chapter 9), which elaborates a rationale for revitalising Aboriginal singing practices by means of the traditional but endangered technique of composition through dreams. The author argues that, in spite of the widespread ideology of passivity in the composition process, which emphasises the role of spirits as the originators of song, there is good evidence that at least some Aboriginal cultures have techniques for what could be called 'song incubation'. These processes enable the songperson to be actively involved in the 'reception' of a song. The chapter is broadly concerned with the question of how local sound worlds can be 're-animated' through reconnecting songs with place, and it illustrates these points through the analysis of a particular song-text from the Hunter Valley that appears to be of oneiric origin.

But this account of traditional composition methods presents just one side of the two-way process of song revitalisation. On the other side are the techniques based on music literacy, as used in Australia's mainstream education system. The notion of 'two-way schooling' was formulated by Stephen Harris in 1990 and has since provided the basis for ongoing discussions around bicultural education, in which Indigenous participants have come to play a leading role. Outcomes of this discourse include the Ganma Curriculum, as developed by Yolngu of Eastern Arnhem Land, and the Milpirri Festival, which had its origins among Warlpiri of Central Australia. Wanta Steve Jampijinpa Patrick (2015:123) sketches out the connections in a recent article, where he says, 'Our inspiration for *Milpirri* comes from the way that *ganma* – a place where two rivers meet – is used by the Yolŋu of eastern Arnhem Land as a model for their intercultural and educational interactions with other peoples and cultures.'

The 'two-way' concept (though not necessarily under that name) has been applied to music pedagogy since the founding of CASM[44] in 1972 (Ellis 1979a). No doubt it continues to be implemented there and in some Indigenous schools, and possibly in other places, such as Boonderu Music Academy (in Roebourne, WA) and Winanjjikari Music Centre (in Tennant Creek). But the published accounts of such projects are scarce. There is no lack of data about rates of alphabetic literacy across the length and breadth of Indigenous Australia,[45] but the topic of music literacy in the education of Aboriginal students is rarely mentioned, and then only in passing (e.g. Tait et al. 2010:146, 149, 153). I have been unable to find any detailed studies or statistics, which suggests there are a number of research gaps in this area that are waiting to be filled.

Nonetheless, there are indications that rates of Indigenous music literacy are likely to increase. I base this assertion on several factors. One is that Aboriginal singers and instrumentalists from remote communities have become regular participants in dialogues with musicians whose work is informed by the literacy-based musical conventions that originated in Europe. Genevieve Campbell's Chapter 13 in the present volume illustrates a case where this is happening on a local level. No doubt there are other such interactions happening around the country, though most of them remain undocumented. An example on a national scale is provided by the 'Encounters' symposium hosted by Queensland Conservatorium in 2005, which brought together Indigenous and non-Indigenous composers and performers from around Australia for 'a week-long exploration of 200 years of interaction in Australian music between Indigenous and European cultures' (Catt and Lancaster 2005:8; see also Wolfe, Plush and Schippers, 2005).

Another factor is that music-based education methods are increasingly being recognised for their ability to improve outcomes in language learning and literacy for Aboriginal children (e.g.

---

44 The Centre for Aboriginal Studies in Music (University of Adelaide) – see above.
45 See, for example,
    https://www.creativespirits.info/aboriginalculture/education/aboriginal-literacy-rates#axzz4i8zCGyJq [accessed 30 August 2017].

Cotton 2011). And, finally, the overall importance of music in Indigenous societies seems likely to ensure that community members will make use of all available resources, including music literacy, to sustain their musical cultures.

So, although the present volume is focused on traditional singing practices, this emphasis does not preclude a 'two-way' approach that recognises the actual or potential usefulness of non-traditional means (such as music literacy and digital technology) in the revitalisation of these practices. If we look ahead to a time when two-way music education has become more widely established, it will be important for aspiring professional musicians, budding music teachers and potential composers in Indigenous communities to be able to develop their skills in description and analysis through the study of their own music. It is in the light of these considerations that I include here, under the rubric of 'composition', two chapters that use the methods of music literacy to analyse the technical skills involved in the creation of particular songs and song types.

The chapter by **Brown and Evans** (Chapter 12) deals with a songset from western Arnhem Land that uses a number of different languages, including untranslatable spirit dialects. In the case of some of the songs, their contemporary performance constitutes the only current active usage of the relevant languages. The authors concern themselves not just with the kind of analysis necessary to interpret the meaning of the songs and establish the nature of the linguistic material. They also outline the factors that create the 'aural identity' of the songset. Their account focuses on 'rhythmic mode'; that is, the way the tempo and rhythmic pattern of the clapstick beat is coordinated with the vocal and didjeridu rhythms. They recognise that dreamed songs are susceptible to innovation, and their account provides important insights into both the formal aspects of the novel elements and the rationale that underlies them.

The chapter by **Laughren, Turpin and Turner** (Chapter 6) adopts a similar approach to a group of traditional songs that were performed by William Rookwood in 1965 and recorded by Elwyn Flint. The songs come from a region (central Queensland) for which the musical information is otherwise very limited. The authors' analysis of the formal features of these songs enables a comparison with the characteristic attributes of Central Australian music, which has a much larger corpus and has been more extensively studied. On this basis, the authors are able to provide insights into what the two regions share musically and how they differ. This kind of approach, with its detailed examination of the structure of text, rhythm and melody, and the relationships between them, is important not only for the revitalisation of songs that are no longer performed, but also for understanding regional features.

McDonald's Chapter 7 is broadly devoted to surveying the literature on Aboriginal music in south-eastern Australia, but I discuss it at this point, within the broad topic area of 'composition', because it includes a section on 'song creation' that gives a rare comparative perspective on the processes involved. McDonald cites a distinction between receiving (and inducing) songs through dreams[46] and composing them in the 'ordinary way', although even the 'ordinary' practices possibly involve certain habitual, semi-ritualised, techniques for inducing a song (such as lying on one's back on the land, to 'make contact with the power' of the country). McDonald also touches on such aspects of the matter as 'group composition', as well as the intersection of these traditional methods of receiving song with the metaphysics of Christianity. The chapter, being a survey, has a much broader focus than just song creation, and covers also such matters as musical instruments, dance forms, song types, and musical education, as deduced from the surviving records of Indigenous music in the south-east. It also provides a useful discussion

---

46   Receiving songs in dreams is also mentioned in the chapters by Sharpe (3), Wafer (9), Nancarrow and Cleary (10) and Brown and Evans (12).

of the practical and theoretical problems involved in dividing Australia's Indigenous musical cultures into regions.

There is an aspect of composition that I have separated out for special attention as a topic area, and I treat it under the rubric of **ADAPTATION**.[47] This concept bears on variations in the cultural appropriateness of innovations in the development of new repertoire. How do Indigenous people negotiate the gap between the social expectations that would have surrounded song creation in the past and those that are operative in the in the early 21st century? As mentioned, our focus on 'traditional' song styles in the present volume means that we have not attempted to include 'modern' Indigenous music *per se*. Nonetheless, several of our contributors deal with the ways Indigenous Australians are using traditional song material in the creation of novel cultural forms, and how these hybrid genres can contribute to song revitalisation by adapting ancestral practices. This approach necessarily entails taking into account not just the 'source' songs themselves, whether they survive in active memory or in some archival form, but also their role in the sound world that produced them. This is what Gary Tomlinson (2015:63–99, 269–278 and *passim*) calls 'the taskscape'; that is, the 'work' the songs were intended to accomplish in their original cultural context.

Campbell's Chapter 13 provides a good example of the openness to experimentation and synthesis that characterises the Top End of the Northern Territory (as noted by Ottosson 2015:50). On Bathurst and Melville Islands, a large collection of ancestral song items dating back to 1912 has been used as the basis for a revitalisation project that brings together Tiwi and non-Tiwi musicians to create 'duets' with the recorded voices of deceased Tiwi songpersons. This enables the musicians to explore notions of improvisation and performance intuition that fit well with traditional Tiwi uses of singing. As the author notes, 'extemporisation within cultural, linguistic and musical frameworks is fundamental to Tiwi song practice, with perhaps its most defining feature being the composition of text specific to a song's performance and audience context'. In the case of this project, the genre (a jazz-based hybrid) and the context (the recording studio) are new, but both maintain significant continuity with traditional practices.

The interaction of ancestral and more recent musical forms is again the focus in Chapter 8. This contribution by **Kelly and Harkins** provides an exemplary account of musical adaptation on the east coast. The authors focus on a song recorded at Bellbrook (northern New South Wales) in the 1960s, which has hitherto resisted interpretation, and they succeed in showing that the text is a complex interplay of words and phrases from an ancestral language (Thangatti~Dhanggati), New South Wales Pidgin and Aboriginal English. Their exegesis is made possible by Kelly's local cultural background knowledge, which enables the 'work' of the song to be established and something of its sound world to be reconstructed. The song is in fact a 'multilingual welcome addressed by a senior man to members of a younger, multicultural generation who are soon to be put through the first stages of formal traditional education'. The analysis shows the creative response of a traditionally educated Elder[48] to a new context, where he needed to invite young men whose main language was English into a traditionally constituted educational space.

The chapter on Murray Island songs, by **Fairweather**, **Matthias** and **Whaleboat** (Chapter 15), provides an account of the music of a region (the Torres Strait Islands) not included in Moyle's 1966 mapping of Indigenous musical cultures, and it is the only such contribution to

---

47 See Sanders (2006:17–25) for a helpful overview of the theoretical literature, and Glaskin (2010, 2011) for an Australian case study.
48 In conformity with the Lowitja Institute's style guide (2015:6), I capitalise the noun 'Elder', when it is used as a noun to refer to a senior Aboriginal person.

the present volume. It is distinctive for a number of other reasons as well. First, it deals with a song corpus that is 'ancestral' in a different way from most of the other repertoires dealt with in this book. The songs are Christian hymns in Meriam Mir (the endangered language of the Island) and Torres Strait Creole. They were brought to the islands by missionaries in the 1870s, but they are 'ancestral' in that generations of ancestors of contemporary Islanders have sung them, and adapted them to their own needs in the process. Second, it exemplifies a case where non-ancestral religious texts have been incorporated into the ancestral repertoire. The songs, in fact, constitute a new cultural form that has become ancestral.

Skinner's Chapter 16 pertains to adaptation in two senses. It is based principally on the surviving corpus of colonial era transcriptions[49] of Indigenous songs, which are themselves adaptations of Indigenous music made by non-Indigenous people. Skinner considers their potential as a resource for song revitalisation, which implies a further step in the process of adaptation. There are fewer than 150 surviving notations of Aboriginal music from this period, and they have been widely impugned as unreliable, and also as tainted by the colonial attitudes of the time. But Skinner believes that this unique evidence simply cannot be ignored, and proceeds to demonstrate an approach that enables usable musical data to be extracted from it. His case is partly based on a comparison of the various early written sources for the Tasmanian song 'Popela' with the wax cylinder recordings made of the same song in 1899 and 1903. He is able to show that there are hitherto unsuspected consistencies across the various versions, and that these enable a 'restoration' with enough reliability to serve the purposes of song revitalisation. This approach, based on taking into consideration a range of evidence from different fields, is widely applicable to the sources from the colonial era, even in those cases (the great majority) where there are no sound recordings.

The 19th century musical data are organised schematically in the bibliographic chapter that **Skinner** has contributed, in collaboration with **Wafer** (Chapter 17). This chapter includes entries for all known notations of Indigenous music (113 in all) that originated in the 19th century. As well, it incorporates analysis and commentaries that provide basic contextual information about the transcriptions, to assist in establishing their historical, geographical and linguistic background.

My discussion of the topic area of **PERFORMANCE** opens with the contribution by **Turpin**, whose Chapter 4 illustrates many of the creative processes Indigenous people engage in for the sake of producing a contemporary song–dance series with ancestral roots. The Arrernte women's camp described in the article, which took place in 2015, was a deliberate effort to maintain and revitalise performance traditions, with the assistance of legacy recordings. The camp provided the opportunity for making new recordings, but also led to the discovery of additional song material recorded in an earlier period. The many facets of the event that are dealt with in Turpin's account include such crucial elements as: issues of ownership of recorded material; production and management of documentation; and the procedures involved in the organisation of 'culture camps'. This chapter provides insights into an innovative contemporary approach to creating opportunities for performance revitalisation.[50]

Chapter 10, by **Nancarrow** and **Cleary**, deals with a related approach, namely, the cultural festival. The chapter shows how festivals are integrated at Mornington Island with a number of allied activities, including culture camps, school classes and recruitment for the local

---

49 Skinner also takes into account the (far fewer) wax cylinder recordings from the same period.
50 It is worth noting as well that the camp made possible the kind of large community discussions that provide the catalyst for innovation. Myfany Turpin (pers. com.) considers it likely that the idea of deliberately creating new songs (as illustrated by M. K. Turner's song on the cover of this volume) was a result of these discussions.

performance troupe, which has toured nationally and internationally over many years. The discussion of 'authenticity' is of particular interest. This issue became a matter of deliberation for the performance troupe as a result of taking traditional songs and dances on tour and performing them publicly.

This bears on what Tomlinson (2007:51) refers to as the '*supraperformative* level, where we can glimpse not so much the specific manner in which a song was presented as what work its performance was expected to achieve'. What is crucial here is the nature of the criteria applied to the song's realisation, which underlie not just the means it uses to convey the 'aesthetic' tone appropriate to its social context, but also the desired social goals.

Apart from arguing for a broadening of the notion of 'authenticity', the authors also cover the issues of ownership of song material and the management of related documentation. But they make the important point that these organisational aspects of song revitalisation should not obscure the crucial element: 'an individual's commitment to a face-to-face teaching relationship with an elder songman'.

Sharpe's contribution on the Ngadiji ceremony, in Chapter 3, describes a context, in and around Borroloola (NT), where the opportunities for performance revitalisation occur mainly in the course of public events, such as the procession during NAIDOC week[51], and at festivals organised in other places. Sharpe notes that, even as 'more contemporary styles are competing for audience, performers and mental space', Ngadiji continues to be performed. She provides historical background on the ceremony, which could bear on its ongoing popularity. It has the formal characteristics of a women's ceremony from Central Australia, but its mythological theme justifies the participation of men and boys. Sharpe also analyses the melodic contours, the song language and the movement types and provides a substantial videoed example.

The contribution by **Hercus** and **Koch** (Chapter 5) considers performances that are at present lying dormant in recordings and have not yet been the subject of revitalisation activities. More specifically, it deals with songs recorded from solo singers, those who were the last, or among the last, to remember songs from various parts of central and south-eastern Australia, including a long series of history songs from the Lake Eyre district. The article focuses on a comparison with material recorded in its original collective context, which may, in some cases, still reflect current performance practices. This discussion raises a number of practical and theoretical issues relating to archived performances of this type. There is no doubt also a call to revitalisation here, in that 'the Lone Singers on many occasions said that they were sorry for the verses because in the future there would be no one left to sing them and to remember them'.

The call to revitalisation has been answered in different ways in different parts of Australia, and the chapters I group next, under the topic of **TRANMISSION**, illustrate the variety of approaches. I begin my review of this topic with a chapter by an Indigenous scholar from the south-west of Western Australia who is working to revitalise his own people's song traditions, **Bracknell**'s Chapter 1. The author makes the point that, because learning a song is easier than attaining fluency in a language, it is a very direct means of bringing an endangered language back into use, and this has benefits in terms both of pedagogy and of Indigenous empowerment. He uses as the illustrative example his own work with the Nyungar language revitalisation project, and focuses on several key issues, including differences between spoken language and song language, and also the matter of 'authenticity' that we have seen addressed in other chapters. He also formulates a perspective on his own work that is relevant to all of us working towards song revitalisation. It is so succinct that it is worth reproducing here. He observes that

---

51 NAIDOC Week is a national celebration of Aboriginal and Torres Strait Islander history, culture and achievements, held annually in the first full week of July. See *http://www.naidoc.org.au/* [accessed 30 August 2017].

his 'interpretation of meaning in Nyungar song texts can by no means be considered authoritative, but may be better conceptualised as entering into dialogue with the archive, the endangered language and the song tradition'.

Chapter 11, by **Brown**, **O'Keeffe**, **Manmurulu**, **Manmurulu** and **Singer**, concerns itself with western Arnhem Land, specifically with the community of Warruwi, 'where multiple small languages are still being spoken and song and dance traditions performed and passed on to children'. One of this chapter's major insights is that language revitalisation necessarily entails consideration of the relevant community's values with regard to language. Through a collaborative project that involved Indigenous musicians and educators as well as musicologists and linguists, the authors have been able to show that it is the creation and maintenance of linguistic and musical diversity that is valued by the community, rather than just the transmission of individual languages or song traditions. The paper also focuses on the extension of common meanings in the idiomatic (and often metaphorical) terminology of song and dance practices.

The chapter by **Treloyn** and **Dowding** (Chapter 2) takes an ethnographic approach to a contemporary song revitalisation project that uses high-tech methods to get archival material back into circulation. It details the social processes and digital technologies involved in the transmission of a genre of public solo songs that is called *Thabi* in several languages of the Pilbara (WA). These songs thrived in the period from the 1930s to the 1960s but are now endangered. Over recent years younger members of the community, including Dowding, have been active in revitalising the Thabi tradition, partly through preserving Elders' knowledge and instigating performances, and partly through repatriating legacy recordings and making them serviceable for song revitalisation purposes. In this case, the availability of the new technologies has coincided with the emergence of a generation, in Roebourne and associated communities of the north-west, who realised the urgency of maintaining and continuing performance practices that were at serious risk of being lost. They have seized the opportunities afforded by connectivity via the internet and mobile phones to bring the songs back into active use. This account is likely to become increasingly relevant to other Indigenous communities as digital technologies become more widespread.

The contribution by **Emberley**, **Treloyn** and **Charles** (Chapter 14) focuses on the active role of children and young people in motivating generational transmission of the *Junba* dance repertoire and of the songs that are essential to it. In their preparations for the annual cultural festival at Mowanjum, in the Kimberley (WA), the rising generation has taken a keen interest in researching and practising Junba dances that have fallen from the contemporary canon. They make use of archival photographs as well as video and audio recordings to prompt their Elders to recall and perform the songs that accompany the dances. The discussion situates the revitalisation of Junba in the context of pedagogical concerns about 'disconnections in the educational worlds of children' – in this case, a disjuncture between home communities (and Country) and the classroom. This is a problem that confronts many Indigenous communities throughout Australia, and the chapter provides a helpful overview of the theoretical and practical considerations involved in attempts to solve it.

Conclusion: of sonic spiritscapes and the Gatling gun

'Country' has always been the focus of Aboriginal and Torres Strait Islander political activism, and in the last half century this has resulted in the legal recognition of Indigenous prior occupation of Australia and the return of large areas of land through federal and state legislative processes (Tanner 2008). Connection to place has also been at the heart of a parallel cultural resurgence, as reflected in the proliferation of Indigenous cultural centres, language centres, music centres, keeping places, museums and festivals, and the programs and projects they support (Simpson 2007:163–169).

At the same time, Indigenous people from around the world have been organising themselves as a coherent international force, and their calls for greater control of their own affairs, extending to claims for political sovereignty, are substantially based on their historical and existential relationship to particular areas of land (Dirlik 2011). Music has played a role in Indigenous strategies for bringing about these changes, at both an international level (Walker 2009) and here in Australia (Dunbar-Hall and Gibson 2008).

These developments have taken place concurrently with what has been called 'the spatial turn'[52] in the world of scholarship, which entails a new 'academic valuing of the local and the oral' (Griffiths 1996:219). Around Australia, scholars, both Indigenous and non-Indigenous, have been able to offer support for the reclamation of Aboriginal and Torres Strait Islander links to Country[53], through place-based research in such fields as anthropology, history, genealogy, toponymy, language, music and so on. In the case of musicology, the spatial turn reflects also the emergence of what has been called 'ecomusicology'; that is, 'the study of music, culture, sound and nature in a period of environmental crisis' (Titon 2009:135; see also Pedelty 2011).[54]

The various disciplinary approaches to the relationship between music and place can be roughly divided into those that focus on the impact of sound on the human inhabitants of a place and those that treat sound as actually *constitutive* of place. Approaches of the first type often have a psychological or political orientation: the former in the case of studies that treat music as 'commemoration or evocation of place' (Taylor and Hurley 2015:2), or as a factor in local and individual identity (Stokes 1994); the latter when music (or sound more broadly) is treated as 'a medium for the negotiation of power' (Nooshin 2009:3); that is, as a force capable of being mobilised for an assault on place (Goodman 2010) or in defence of it (Eyerman and Jamison 1998, Pedelty 2016).

The other approach, which treats sound as constitutive of place, can be traced back to Murray Schafer's development of the concept of the 'soundscape' in the 1960s and 70s. Soundscapes are components of the physical structure of places, akin to the geological and biological constituents but less visible. Schafer developed the general hypothesis that 'people in some way echo their soundscape in language and music' (Feld 2003:225) – a notion that has been explored and refined in subsequent ethnographic studies, in particular by Steven Feld:

> Soundscapes, no less than landscapes, are not just physical exteriors, spatially surrounding or apart from human activity. Soundscapes are perceived and interpreted by human actors who attend to them as a way of making their place in and through the world. Soundscapes are invested with significance by those whose bodies and lives resonate with them in social time and space. Like landscapes, they are as much psychical as physical phenomena, as much cultural constructs as material ones . . . (Feld 2003:226).

Feld has illustrated the point in a number of accounts (e.g. 1982, 1996b, 2003) based on his fieldwork with a Bosavi group in Papua New Guinea. For these people, music is constitutive of place in an epistemological sense: it is what makes place humanly knowable. It is in reference

---

52 Defined by Warf and Arias (2008:1) as the 'reinsertion of space into the social sciences and humanities'.
53 When the noun 'country' is used in its distinctively Aboriginal sense, I capitalise it, in conformity with a convention that is becoming increasingly common among Aboriginal people themselves. For an example of this usage, and the reasons behind it, see *http://www.visitmungo.com.au/aboriginal-country* [accessed 9 May 2017].
54 Recent developments in human geography (e.g. Hudson 2006) have also played a part in musicology's 'spatial turn'. Jo Guldi has explored the implications of the spatial turn in a number of other disciplines, including anthropology (Guldi n.d.).

to this understanding of the relationship between people and places that Feld (1996b, 2003) invented the term 'acoustemology' (knowledge of the world through sonic means). From an acoustemological perspective, the relationship between humans and sound in Indigenous Australia probably has much in common with what Feld has observed in the case of the Bosavi.[55]

But there is one major difference. For many, perhaps most Aboriginal groups for which we have information, song is not just sound: it is also a kind of living substance that manifests the spiritual essence of a place and of the humans (and other beings) associated with that place. It joins people and place not just through an abstract commonality, such as expressed by the term 'identity', but also through a material 'consubstantiality'.[56] This is the implication of the quote from Eileen McDinny that I have used as an epigraph: 'Everything got a song, no matter how little . . . plant, bird, animal, country, people, everything' (in Bradley with Yanyuwa families 2010:1). Wanta Steve Jampijinpa Patrick (2015:120) has made a similar point: 'Country is expressing itself all the time'.

There are three aspects to this understanding of the world that are worth emphasising: first, Country is animate and intelligent; second, humans are, collectively, part of it, and, individually, extensions of it; and, third, sound (particularly the sound of the human voice) plays a central role in relationships with it. Aboriginal people communicate with Country as with a living being (Harrison and Rose 2010:257), and this happens both silently, in thought and dream, and audibly, in speech and song. John Bradley's commentary (2001:297) on Yanyuwa land management provides an excellent illustration of the role of the audible factors in these people's relationship to Country:

> According to the Western viewpoint, management is a one-way process where people do things to country, to look after it and make it productive. But for indigenous people such as the Yanyuwa negotiation is a two-way interaction between people and country. Yanyuwa often simply refer to concepts associated with negotiation as either *Yanyuwangala* or the Yanyuwa way of being; or doing things of *narnu-yuwa*, or Law. It is rare that the processes of negotiation are explicitly stated as such. Rather, the Yanyuwa would describe all the things I am incorporating into the word 'negotiation' by some of the following expressions: *wukanyinjawu ki-awarawu* 'speaking to country', *manhantharra awara* 'holding or embracing the land', *anykarrinjarra ki-awarawu* 'listening to country', *marakamantharra awara* 'making country safe', *yabirrinjarra awara* 'making the country good', and *wandayarra a-yabala ki-awarawu* 'singing the sacred songs belonging to the country'. It should also be noted here that *awara*, which I am translating here as 'country', can mean sea as well as land.

One of the reasons commonly given by Indigenous people for undertaking language revitalisation projects is that 'language is important to talk to country and ancestors' (Walsh 2014:331[57]). If

---

55 The explicit encoding of place in musical (as distinct from verbal) language in Aboriginal Australia has been suggested by Catherine Ellis (1985:103–104) and is implied also by Helen Payne's notion of 'aural identification markings' (1978:9; see also Payne 1993:11). The general principle has been summed up by Ellis and Barwick (1987:42) thus: 'we regard it as entirely possible that the formal structures of central Australian musical syntax may function with specific semantic intent'. This probably applies to other Indigenous musical cultures as well, though more research will be required to provide a firm foundation for this somewhat tentative (but highly plausible) hypothesis.

56 By contrast, most other contemporary soundworlds are characterised by 'schizophonia' and 'separability'. Murray Schafer, who invented the term 'schizophonia' in the 1960s, defined it as 'the split between an original sound and its electroacoustic reproduction' (Schafer 1977:273). In the interim it has undergone a number of conceptual refinements; see, for example, Feld (2011:41). The 'separability principle' is a concept we owe to Lydia Goehr (1992:157). It is the outcome of the historical trajectory that enabled music to be assimilated to the West's museum-based notions of an 'art form', 'estranging the work of art from its original external function so that its artness would now be found within itself' (Goehr 1992:173).

57 The other reasons in Walsh's short list are (paraphrasing slightly): reconciliation, right to redress, language as vehicle for culture, language as embodiment of knowledge systems that have been built up over thousands of years (Walsh 2014:331).

this is true of spoken language, then it is fair to assume that it would apply to song, and to song revitalisation projects, as well.[58] It implies also that these projects are being undertaken not just for the sake of the music itself, but rather as a means of renewing and re-activating relationships with Country. In effect, song revitalisation is a reclamation of sonic spiritscapes.

Denis Byrne, from whom I borrow the term 'spiritscape', has adopted it (Byrne 2010:55[59]) as a means of resisting reductionist approaches to the conservation of 'sacred natural sites',[60] which tend 'to be directed at conserving biodiversity for the sake of biodiversity rather than for its local religious value' (Byrne 2013:158). But the term's strategic utility is not limited to issues of conservation. It also provides linguistic support for resisting the rationalist-instrumentalist language of post-colonialism more broadly. Byrne has drawn out the political implications in his remarks on the rationale behind the 'anti-superstition' campaigns in Asia:

> It is not difficult to see how the landscapes of popular religion in Asia, populated as they are by numerous sites of the divine, each one of which might be considered to be a node of supernatural power, inevitably imposes limitations on the modern state's ambition to dominate space (Byrne 2013:162; see also Byrne 2012).

Byrne (2010:55) defines 'spiritscape', as 'a spiritual topography ... which coexists with the physical topography of [the] local landscape'. In Australia, as we have seen, the Indigenous spiritscape's 'material' manifestation is not limited to the visible landscape and but incorporates as well a significant sonic dimension.

A strategy that has been widely adopted in Australia for the reclamation of various aspects of Indigenous culture is 'counter-mapping'.[61] There is an outstanding example in the project undertaken by the Yanyuwa community in the south-west of the Gulf of Carpentaria, with the assistance of John Bradley, 'to map the sacred knowledge ... into atlas form so that future generations of Yanyuwa people may learn, in part at least, some of the knowledge their old people and ancestors used to manage life and affairs on the savannah lands, islands and sea they call home' (Bradley 2002:8; see also Bradley with Yanyuwa Families 2010). The resulting atlas (Yanyuwa Families, Bradley and Cameron 2003) is probably the most comprehensive counter-map yet to have been produced in Australia. It details the routes of the Yanyuwa songlines and incorporates illustrations of the stories and texts of the songs – but without music.[62]

---

58 As yet there have been no national surveys set up to assess the vitality of local Indigenous musical traditions and community attitudes to their revitalisation – comparable, for example to the two National Indigenous Language Surveys (McConvell, Marmion and McNicol 2005, Marmion, Obata and Troy 2014).
59 I have not been able to trace the origin of this term. It had been used as early as 2002 by ethnobiologist Cynthia Fowler in relation to 'thirdspace' on the island of Sumba, and shortly afterwards by the archaeologist Ian McNiven in relation to Australian Indigenous seascapes (2003; see also McNiven 2008). Since then it has been pressed into service by other archaeologists working in Australia (e.g. David 2006:137) and elsewhere (e.g. Fitzhugh 2014), as well as by conservationists (e.g. Studley and Jikmed 2016) and Indigenous activists, such as Navajo punk rock singer Jeneda Benally (2012:413). Greer, McIntyre-Tamwoy and Henry (2011:4) eschew 'spiritscape' in favour of 'cosmo-political landscape'.
60 In 2003, UNESCO held an international workshop on 'the importance of sacred natural sites for biodiversity conservation', which has been followed by a number of publications on 'integrating cultural and spiritual values in conservation management' (Verschuuren 2007; see also Mallarach and Papayanis 2007, Verschuuren, Wild, McNeely and Oviedo 2010, Brockwell, O'Connor and Byrne 2013). Some of the publications in this field (such as Verschuuren, Marika and Wise 2009) include studies of land management in Australia.
61 The term 'counter-mapping' was coined by Nancy Peluso (1995) and has been succinctly defined by Denis Byrne (2008a:609) as the 'tactical deployment of cultural mapping'. For an overview of subsequent developments in the theory and practice of counter-mapping, see Byrne (2008b) and Wood (2010:111–155). Compare also Turnbull (2000), in particular the section on Aboriginal mapping practices (pp. 33–39).
62 The project of which the atlas is a part includes other components as well, such as a sound archive and a website (Bradley with Yanyuwa families 2010:xiv). The website is incorporated in Monash University's 'Countrylines' archive, at http://artsonline.monash.edu.au/countrylines-archive/ [accessed 30 August 2017]. It includes a number of animations of Yanyuwa dreaming stories, which are narrated in Yanyuwa and incorporate some songs.

Nonetheless, the widespread adoption of digital technology in Indigenous communities means that future projects of this kind will not be limited to the visual dimension, but will be able to incorporate sound files as well.[63]

Such a development, desirable though it may at first seem for the purposes of song revitalisation, would not be without its own problems, some of which have been touched on by Denis Byrne (2008b:257) in his article on counter-mapping in New South Wales:

> Marginalised peoples are enjoying greater success in getting themselves and their interests onto maps but at the cost of an increasing volume of Indigenous knowledge becoming public domain. Another side effect is that maps are becoming increasingly embedded as privileged forms of spatial knowledge . . . as distinct, for example, from story-telling. A mud-map or sand-map is erased by nature soon after being inscribed; it 'belongs' to the map-maker in the sense that its materiality often lasts only for the duration of a performance. It belongs, in a sense, to the story which in turn belongs to the teller. A digital or printed map on the other hand can be reproduced at will and consumed without reference to the original knowledge-holder.

This cautionary note seems particularly relevant at the present point in time (early 2017), when the proportion of the world's population with internet connectivity is poised to pass 50%.[64] This means that 3.6 billion people now have access to any data that are publicly available online.[65] Peter Toner (2008: n.p.) has published a helpful article on some of the implications that the digital revolution has for Indigenous intellectual property, and notes the irony of the situation:

> . . . while advocates for the protection of indigenous cultural property may turn to Western intellectual property law for its protection, the classification of indigenous creations as a form of 'property' may itself undermine the cultural foundations on which those creations are predicated.[66]

These are just a few of the double binds inherent in the project of revitalising Indigenous singing practices in the second decade of the 21st century, and we can expect that there will be more as the consequences of current scientific experiments with sound as a form of weaponry begin to unfold. Our present period is witnessing the development of sophisticated sonic technologies in the service of warfare, 'military urbanism' and cybernetic capitalism. We are now all subject to what Steve Goodman (2010:131) has called 'audio virology', usually without even being aware of it.

> As predatory brand environments converge with generative music and consumer profiling, artificial sonic life-forms are released from the sterile viro-sonic labs of digital sound design into the ecology of fear (Goodman 2010:131).

It is hard to know whether Goodman's analysis is exaggeratedly paranoid or not paranoid enough! I include it here as a way of attempting to anticipate some of the pitfalls of the future sonic terrain in which Indigenous song revitalisation projects will be carried out.

---

63 In this context it is worth mentioning also the 'Songlines on screen' project (2016). This consists of 10 short films that provide a glimpse of the stories and performance practices associated with the songlines of ten different remote Aboriginal communities. The project was the result of a collaboration between Screen Australia and NITV (see *http://www.sbs.com.au/nitv/songlines-on-screen/article/2016/05/25/learn-indigenous-australian-creation-stories-songlines-screen-multimedia-features* [accessed 23 February 2017]).

64 Figures as at May 2017, from
http://www.internetworldstats.com/emarketing.htm; see also
http://www.itu.int/net/pressoffice/press_releases/2015/17.aspx#.WHV_SFw07IV [both accessed 20 May 2017].

65 Another way of putting this would be to say that half the world's population now lives in Cyburbia. I borrow this term from Michael Sorkin (1992:xii), although it has since been used by others. For insights into the human consequences of globalised cybercapitalism, see Berardi (2015).

66 This point has been elaborated ethnographically by Glaskin (2010, 2011).

Fortunately, Goodman's dystopian vision can be countered, or at least balanced, with more encouraging possibilities. I take heart, for example, from James Maffie's (2009) article on the future prospects of Indigenous knowledges,[67] which proposes a 'global polycentric epistemology'. This consists of:

> a variety of dialogues between mutual epistemological 'others'. Participants ask, 'how may this or that knowledge practice be brought into the service of human well-being?' It admits all varieties of knowledge practices ranging from rational argument and experimentation to dance, song, and ritual performance (Maffie 2009:53).

Maffie's paper was written as refutation of Charles Taylor's argument that 'the superiority of Western technology demonstrates the epistemological superiority of Western science over Indigenous knowledges'. Taylor had used a ditty that alludes to 19th century British imperial forces in Africa as a means of making his point: 'In the end, We have the Gatling gun, and they have not'.

Given the state of international politics at the present time,[68] Maffie's proposal for a global polycentric epistemology could perhaps seem unrealistically utopian. But we need hopeful visions of this kind, as alternatives to the epistemology of the Gatling gun. I suggest that the reclamation of Indigenous sonic spiritscapes could be one such alternative that has the potential to be realisable and effective in the local circumstances here in Australia. The present volume might be viewed, then, as a small step in supporting and furthering this reclamation.

Acknowledgements

This volume would not have been possible without the invaluable collaboration of my co-editor, Myfany Turpin, to whom I am grateful for more reasons than it would be possible to enumerate. In particular, I appreciate her major contribution to the recruitment of authors and reviewers, her feedback to contributors, her sourcing of material for the cover and her co-sponsorship of the print edition. My sincere thanks as well to Brenda Thornley, who drew the maps that appear in this introduction, and to the readers who have kindly provided feedback on the drafts, namely, Greg Bork, Grace Koch, Myfany Turpin and Petronella Vaarzon-Morel. I'm grateful also to Nick Evans and Jason Gibson for helpful correspondence.

Abbreviations used in the text

AIATSIS = Australian Institute of Aboriginal and Torres Strait Islander Studies
HRLM = Hunter River–Lake Macquarie language
NPN = non–Pama-Nyungan
NSW = New South Wales
NT = Northern Territory
PN = Pama-Nyungan
QLD = Queensland
SA = South Australia
TAS = Tasmania
TSI = Torres Strait Islands

---

[67] Maffie is a pioneer in the field of comparative world philosophy (see Maffie n.d., 1995, 2001, 2014). The article quoted above appears in a special issue of the journal *Futures* devoted to 'futures for indigenous knowledges'. See also the introduction to the special issue by David Turnbull (Turnbull 2009); Turnbull devotes specific attention to Aboriginal knowledge traditions in Turnbull (2000:33–38).

[68] This conclusion was written in January of 2017, and Mr D. Trump had just been inaugurated as president of the United States.

VIC = Victoria
WA = Western Australia

References

Agawu, Victor Kofi, 2014, Representing African music: postcolonial notes, queries, positions. New York: Routledge.

Amery, Rob, and Mary-Anne Gale, 2008, But our language was just asleep: a history of language revival in Australia. In William McGregor ed. Encountering Aboriginal languages: studies in the history of Australian linguistics, 339–82. Canberra: Pacific Linguistics.

Anderson, Jane E., 2009, Law, knowledge, culture: the production of indigenous knowledge in intellectual property law. Cheltenham UK: Edward Elgar.

Arthur, Bill and Frances Morphy, eds, 2005, Macquarie atlas of Indigenous Australia: culture and society through space and time. Sydney: Macquarie Library.

Bandt, Ros, 2014, Sonic archaeologies: towards a methodology for 're-hearing' the past – Lake Mungo, Australia and the Yerebatan Sarnici, Istanbul. In Linda C. Eneix, ed. Archaeoacoustics: the archaeology of sound (publication of proceedings from the 2014 Conference in Malta), 87–98. Myaka City, Florida: The OTS Foundation.

Bandt, Ros, Michelle Duffy and Dolly MacKinnon, 2007, Hearing places: sound, place, time and culture. Newcastle UK: Cambridge Scholars Press.

Barney, Katelyn ed., 2014, Collaborative ethnomusicology: new approaches to music research between Indigenous and non-Indigenous Australians. Melbourne: Lyrebird Press.

Bartleet, Brydie-Leigh, 2011, Stories of reconciliation: building cross-cultural collaborations between Indigenous musicians and undergraduate music students in Tennant Creek. Australian Journal of Music Education 2011(2):11–21.

Barwick, Linda, 2000, Song as an Indigenous art. In Sylvia Kleinert and Margo Neale, eds. The Oxford companion to Aboriginal art and culture, 328–334. Melbourne: Oxford University Press.

—— 2005, Performance, aesthetics, experience: thoughts on Yawulyu Mungamunga songs. In Elizabeth Mackinlay, Denis Collins and Samantha Owens, Aesthetics and experience in music performance, 1–18. Newcastle UK: Cambridge Scholars Press.

—— 2012, Including music and the temporal arts in language documentation. In Nicholas Thieberger, ed, The Oxford handbook of linguistic fieldwork, 166–179. Oxford: Oxford University Press.

Barwick, Linda, Grace Koch, Bill Arthur and Frances Morphy, 2005, Performing arts, sport and games. In Bill Arthur and Frances Morphy, eds. Macquarie atlas of Indigenous Australia: culture and society through space and time, 126–139. Sydney: Macquarie Library.

Barwick, Linda, and Allan Marett, 1995, Introduction. In Linda Barwick, Allan Marett and Guy Tunstill, eds. The essence of singing and the substance of song: recent responses to the Aboriginal performing arts and other essays in honour of Catherine Ellis, 1–10. Sydney: Oceania Monographs (University of Sydney).

—— 1996, Selected audiography of traditional music of Aboriginal Australia. Yearbook for Traditional Music 28:174–188.

Battiste, Marie Ann, and James [Sa'ke'j] Youngblood Henderson, eds, 2000, Protecting indigenous knowledge and heritage: a global challenge. Saskatoon, Canada: Purich.

Beckett, Jeremy, 2012, Returned to sender: some predicaments of re-indigenisation. Oceania 82(1): 104–112.

Benally, Jeneda, 2012, The holy San Francisco Peaks, Arizona: cultural and spiritual survival of south-western indigenous nations. In Gloria Pungetti, Gonzalo Oviedo and Della Hooke, eds. Sacred species and sites: advances in biocultural conservation, 409–413. Cambridge: Cambridge University Press

Bendrups, Dan, Katelyn Barney, and Catherine Grant, 2013, An introduction to sustainability and ethnomusicology in the Australasian context. Musicology Australia, 35(2):153–158.

Bennett, Andy, 2001, Cultures of popular music. Buckingham UK: Open University Press.

Bennett, Andy, and Steve Waksman, eds, 2015, The SAGE handbook of popular music. Los Angeles: SAGE.

Berardi, Franco Bifo, 2015, AND: phenomenology of the end. South Pasadena: Semiotext(e).
Bithell, Caroline, and Juniper Hill, 2014, The Oxford handbook of music revival. Oxford: Oxford University Press.
Blake, Barry, 1988, Redefining Pama-Nyungan: towards a prehistory of Australian languages. Aboriginal Linguistics 1:1–90.
Borthwick, Stuart and Ron Moy, eds, 2004, Popular music genres: an introduction. Edinburgh : Edinburgh University Press.
Bowern, Claire and Quentin Atkinson, 2012, Computational phylogenetics and the internal structure of Pama-Nyungan. Language 88:817–845. Online at *http://elischolar.library.yale.edu/ling_faculty/1* [accessed 6 April 2016]. 'Supplementary materials' online at *http://www.pamanyungan.net/papers/computational-phylogenetics-and-the-internal-structure-of-pama-nyungan/* [accessed 23 February 2017].
Bradley, John, 2001, Landscapes of the mind, landscapes of the spirit. In Richard Baker, Jocelyn Davies and Elspeth Young, eds. Working on country: contemporary Indigenous management of Australia's lands and coastal regions, 295–307. Melbourne: Oxford University Press.
—— 2002, Mapping the sacred. Cultural Survival Quarterly Magazine 26(2):8–10.
—— 2012, 'Hearing the country': Reflexivity as an intimate journey into epistemological liminalities. The Australian Journal of Indigenous Education 41(1):26–33.
Bradley, John, and Elizabeth Mackinlay, 2000, Songs from a plastic water rat: an introduction to the musical traditions of the Yanyuwa community of the southwest Gulf of Carpentaria. Ngulaig (Aboriginal and Torres Strait Islander Studies Unit, University of Queensland) 17: i–44.
Bradley, John, with Yanyuwa families, 2010, Singing saltwater country: journey to the songlines of Carpentaria. Crows Nest NSW: Allen & Unwin.
Breen, Marcus, ed., and Marylouise Brunton, 1989, Our place, our music. Canberra: Aboriginal Studies Press for the Australian Institute of Aboriginal Studies.
Brockwell, Sally, Sue O'Connor and Denis Byrne, 2013, Transcending the culture-nature divide in cultural heritage: views from the Asia–Pacific region. Canberra: ANU E Press.
Buckley, Ann, ed., 1998, Hearing the past: essays in historical ethnomusicology and the archaeology of sound. Liège: Etudes et recherches archéologiques de l'Université de Liège.
Byrne, Denis, 2008a, Counter-mapping in the archaeological landscape. In Bruno David and Julian Thomas, eds. Handbook of landscape archaeology, 609–616. Walnut Creek CA: Left Coast Press.
—— 2008b, Counter-mapping: New South Wales and Southeast Asia. Transforming Cultures eJournal 3(1):256–264.
—— 2010, The enchanted earth: numinous sacred sites. In B. Verschuuren, R. Wild, J. McNeely and G. Oviedo, Sacred natural sites: conserving nature and culture, 53–61. London: Earthscan.
—— 2012, Anti-superstition: campaigns against popular religion and its heritage in Asia. In P. Daly and T. Winter, eds. Routledge handbook of heritage in Asia, 295–310. London: Routledge.
—— 2013. The WCPA's natural sacred sites taskforce: a critique of conservation biology's view of popular religion. In S. Brockwell, S. O'Connor and D. Byrne, eds. Transcending the culture-nature divide in cultural heritage: views from the Asia–Pacific region, 157–169. Canberra: ANU E Press.
Capell, Arthur, 1963, Linguistic survey of Australia. Sydney: [prepared for the] Australian Institute of Aboriginal Studies.
Catt, Josh, and Helen Lancaster, 2005, Visionary encounters. Music Forum 11(4):8–11.
Centre for Imaginative Ethnography, 2016, Work in progress bibliography on sound and ethnography, online at *http://imaginativeethnography.org/soundings/all-about-sound-ethnography/* [accessed 26 December 2016].
Chadwick, Graham and George Rrurrambu, 2004, Music education in remote aboriginal communities. The Asia Pacific Journal of Anthropology 5(2):159–171.
Christen, Kimberly, 2005, Gone digital: Aboriginal remix and the cultural commons. International Journal of Cultural Property 12:315–345.
Christensen, Dieter ed., 1996, Yearbook for Traditional Music 28 (special issued devoted to intellectual property).

Clarke, Philip A., 2007, Indigenous spirit and ghost folklore of 'settled' Australia. Folklore 118(2):141–161.
Clunies Ross, Margaret, 1986, Australian Aboriginal oral traditions. Oral Traditions 1(2): 231–271.
—— 1987, Research into Aboriginal songs: the state of the art. In M. Clunies Ross, T. Donaldson and S. Wild, eds. Songs of Aboriginal Australia, 1–13. Sydney: Oceania Monograph 32 (University of Sydney).
—— 1989, The aesthetics and politics of an Arnhem Land ritual. TDR [The Drama Review] 33(4):107–127.
—— 1999, Ancestral songs: understandings of Aboriginal song since 1788. In The Australian Academy of the Humanities proceedings 1998, 93–113. Canberra: Australian Academy of the Humanities. Also published with the same title, in the same year and under the same imprint in Terry Smith, ed. First peoples, second chance: public papers from the 29th Annual Symposium of the Australian Academy of the Humanities, 81–103.
Coombe, Rosemary J., 2011, 'Possessing culture': political economies of community subjects. In Veronica Strang and Mark Busse, eds. Ownership and appropriation, 105–127. Oxford: Berg.
Coote, Jeremy, and Anthony Shelton, eds, 1992, Anthropology, art, and aesthetics. Oxford: Clarendon.
Corn, Aaron, 2013, Sustaining Australia's Indigenous music and dance traditions: the role of the National Recording Project for Indigenous Performance in Australia. Musicology Australia, 35(2):268–284.
Corn, Aaron, with Neparrnga Gumbula, 2007, Budutthun ratja wiyinmirri: formal flexibility in Yolngu manikay tradition and the challenge of recording a complete repertoire. Australian Aboriginal Studies 2:116–127.
Coronel-Molina, Serafín M., and Teresa L. McCarty, 2016, Indigenous language revitalization in the Americas. New York: Routledge.
Cotton, Hugh, 2011, Music-based language learning in remote Australian Indigenous schools. Bachelor of Music (Music Education) Honours thesis, Sydney Conservatorium of Music, University of Sydney.
Cowell, Andrew, 2016, Language maintenance and revitalization. In Nancy Bonvillain, ed. The Routledge handbook of linguistic anthropology, 420–432. New York: Routledge.
David, Bruno, 2006, Indigenous rights and the mutability of cultures: tradition, change and the politics of recognition. In Lynette Russell, ed. Boundary writing: an exploration of race, culture, and gender binaries in contemporary Australia, 122–148. Honolulu: University of Hawaii Press.
Deger, Jennifer, 2013, In-between. In Arnd Schneider and Christopher Wright, eds. Anthropology and art practice, 105–113. London: Bloomsbury.
Devlin, Brian, 2017, A glimmer of possibility. In Brian Devlin, Nancy Devlin and Samantha Disbray, eds. History of bilingual education in the Northern Territory: people, programs and policies, 11–25. Singapore: Springer.
Dirlik, Arif, 2011, Globalization, indigenism, social movements and the politics of place. Localities 1:47–90.
Disbray, Samantha, 2015, Indigenous language in education: policy and practice in Australia (edited by Mark Rose and Marnie O'Bryan). UNESCO Observatory Multi-Disciplinary Journal in the Arts 4(1). Online at *http://education.unimelb.edu.au/__data/assets/pdf_file/0009/1391652/005_DISBRAY_V2.pdf* [accessed 29 March 2016].
Donaldson, Tamsin, 1995, Mixes of English and ancestral language words in southeast Australian Aboriginal songs of traditional and introduced origin. In Linda Barwick, Allan Marett and Guy Tunstill, eds. The essence of singing and the substance of song: recent responses to the Aboriginal performing arts and other essays in honour of Catherine Ellis, 143–158. Sydney: Oceania Monographs (University of Sydney).
Dunbar-Hall, Peter, 1991, Aboriginal music: an annotated music education bibliography. Sounds Australian 42:6–7, 42.
Dunbar-Hall, Peter, and Chris Gibson, 2004, Deadly sounds, deadly places: contemporary Aboriginal music in Australia. Sydney: UNSW Press.
—— 2008, Singing about nations within nations: geopolitics and identity in Australian indigenous rock music. Popular Music and Society 24(2):45–73.

Dunbar-Hall, Peter, and Elizabeth MacKinlay, eds, 2011, special issue of The Australian Journal of Music Education (2011: issue 2) on 'issues related to the study and teaching of Aboriginal and Torres Strait Islander musics and cultures'.

Dunn, Kevin C., 2016, Global punk: resistance and rebellion in everyday life. New York: Bloomsbury Academic.

Dussart, Françoise, 2000, The politics of ritual in an Aboriginal settlement: kinship, gender, and the currency of knowledge. Washington, DC: Smithsonian Institution Press.

Ellis, Catherine J., 1979a, Present-day music of the Aboriginal student: a challenge for the educator. Australian Journal of Music Education 25:17–21.

—— 1979b, Developments in music education among Aboriginals of central and South Australia. In Jennifer Isaacs, ed. Australian Aboriginal music, 27–40. Sydney: Aboriginal Artists Agency.

—— 1984, Time consciousness of Aboriginal performers. In J. C. Kassler & J. Stubington, eds. Problems and solutions: occasional essays presented to Alice M. Moyle, 149–185. Sydney: Hale & Iremonger.

—— 1985, Aboriginal music: education for living. St Lucia: University of Queensland Press.

—— n.d., Central Aboriginal music. Section 2 of entry for 'Australia: 1. Aboriginal music'. In Deane Root, ed. Grove Music Online, n.p.: *http://www.oxfordmusiconline.com:80/subscriber/article/grove/music/40021* [accessed 21 August 2017].

Ellis, Catherine J., and Linda Barwick, 1987, Musical syntax and the problem of meaning in a central Australian songline. Musicology Australia 10(1):41–57.

Eneix, Linda C. ed., 2014, Archaeoacoustics: the archaeology of sound (publication of proceedings from the 2014 Conference in Malta). Myaka City, Florida: The OTS Foundation.

Evans, Nicholas, ed., 2003, The non-Pama-Nyungan languages of northern Australia: comparative studies of the continent's most linguistically complex region. Canberra: Pacific Linguistics.

—— 2005, Australian languages reconsidered: a review of Dixon (2002). Oceanic Linguistics 44:1.242–286.

Eyerman, Ron, and Andrew Jamison, 1998, Music and social movements: mobilizing traditions in the twentieth century. Cambridge: Cambridge University Press.

Falk, Catherine, and Catherine Ingram, 2011, From intangible cultural heritage to collectable artefact: the theory and practice of enacting ethical responsibilities in ethnomusicological research. Transmission of academic values in Asian Studies workshop. Canberra: The Australia–Netherlands Research Collaboration (ANRC). Online at *www.aust-neth.net/transmission_proceedings/papers/Falk_Ingram.pdf* [accessed 26 December 2016].

Farina, Almo, 2013, Soundscape ecology: principles, patterns, methods and applications. Heidelberg: Springer.

Farnell, Brenda, and Monica F. A. Wong Santos, 2014, A bibliography of the literature on Australian Aboriginal dancing (1987–2013). Journal for the Anthropological Study of Human Movement 21(2): n.p.

Feld, Stephen, 1982, Sound and sentiment: birds, weeping, poetics, and song in Kaluli expression. Philadelphia: University of Pennsylvania Press.

—— 1996a, Pygmy pop: a genealogy of schizophonic mimesis. Yearbook for Traditional Music 28:1–35.

—— 1996b, Waterfalls of song. In Steven Feld and Keith Basso, eds. Senses of place. Santa Fe: School of American Research Press, pp. 91–135.

—— 2001, The sound world of Bosavi. Online via the Acoustic Ecology Institute, at *http://www.acousticecology.org/edu/educurrbosavi.html* [accessed 10 October 2016].

—— 2003, A rainforest acoustemology. In Michael Bull and Les Back, eds. The auditory culture reader, 223–239. Oxford: Berg.

—— 2011, My life in the bush of ghosts: 'world music' and the commodification of religious experience. In Bob W. White, ed. Music and globalization: critical encounters, 40–51. Bloomington IN: Indiana University Press.

Feld, Stephen, Aaron Fox, Thomas Porcello, and David Samuels, 2004, Vocal anthropology: from the music of language to the language of song. In Alessandro Duranti, ed. A companion to linguistic anthropology, 321–345. Oxford: Blackwell.

Fitzhugh, William W., 2014, The Ipiutak spirit-scape: an archaeological phenomenon. In Charles E. Hilton, Benjamin M. Auerbach and Libby W. Cowgill, eds. The foragers of Point Hope: the biology and archaeology of humans on the edge of the Alaskan Arctic, 266–290. Cambridge: Cambridge University Press.

Fowler, Cynthia T., Altar rituals in thirdspace. In John R. Stepp, Felice S. Wyndham, and Rebecca Zarger, eds. Ethnobiology and biocultural diversity: proceedings of the Seventh International Congress of Ethnobiology, 152–170. Athens GA: International Congress of Ethnobiology.

Frishkopf, Michael, 2003, Authorship in Sufi poetry. Alif: Journal of Comparative Poetics 23: 78–108.

Gillespie, Kirsty and Ian Lilley, 2015, Transformations, transactions and technologies: new directions in Pacific heritage. International Journal of Heritage Studies, 21(2):115–116.

Glaskin, Katie, 2010, On dreams, innovation and the emerging genre of the individual artist. Anthropological Forum 20(3):251–267.

—— 2011, Dreaming in thread: from ritual to art and property(s) between. In Veronica Strang and Mark Busse, eds. Ownership and appropriation, 87–104. Oxford: Berg.

Goehr, Lydia, 1992, The imaginary museum of musical works: an essay in the philosophy of music. Oxford: Clarendon.

Goodman, Steve, 2010, Sonic warfare: sound, affect, and the ecology of fear. Cambridge, MA: MIT Press.

Gopinath, Sumanth, and Jason Stanyek, eds, 2014, The Oxford handbook of mobile music studies. New York: Oxford.

Grant, Catherine, 2010, The links between safeguarding language and safeguarding musical heritage. International Journal of Intangible Heritage 5:46–59.

—— 2011, Key factors in the sustainability of languages and music: a comparative study. Musicology Australia 33(1):95–113.

—— 2014, Music endangerment: how language maintenance can help. New York: Oxford University Press.

—— in press, A case for greater interdisciplinary collaboration in language and music revitalization. In Leanne Hinton, Leena Huss & Gerald Roche, eds. The Routledge handbook of language revitalization. Oxford: Routledge. Pre-press version available from *https://www.researchgate.net/publication/305331470_A_case_for_greater_interdisciplinary_collaboration_in_language_and_music_revitalization* [accessed 16 May 2017].

Grau, Andrée, 2000, Land, body, and poetry: an integrated dance aesthetic among the Tiwi. In Sylvia Kleinert and Margo Neale, eds. The Oxford companion to Aboriginal art and culture, 356–362. Melbourne: Oxford University Press.

—— 2004, Tiwi dance aesthetics. Yearbook for Traditional Music 35:173–178.

Grauer, Victor, 2011, Sounding the depths: tradition and the voices of history. Seattle: CreateSpace Independent Publishing Platform.

Green, Jennifer, 2014, Drawn from the ground: sound, sign and inscription in Central Australian sand stories. Cambridge: Cambridge University Press.

Greene, Paul D., and Thomas Porcello, 2005. Wired for sound: engineering and technologies in sonic cultures. Middletown CT: Wesleyan University Press.

Greenway, John, 1961, Folklore scholarship in Australia. The Journal of American Folklore 74(294):440–448. (Special issue: Folklore Research around the world: a North American point of view.)

Greer, Shelley, Susan McIntyre-Tamwoy and Rosita Henry, 2011, Sentinel sites in a cosmo-political seascape. In Refereed papers from the Seventh International Small Islands Cultures Conference (12–15 June 2011, Airlie Beach, QLD, Australia), 2–10. Online at *https://www.researchgate.net/publication/249008603_SENTINEL_SITES_IN_A_COSMO-POLITICAL_SEASCAPE* [accessed 30 January 2017].

Griffiths, Tom, 1996, Hunters and collectors: the antiquarian imagination in Australia. Cambridge: Cambridge University Press.

Guldi, Jo, n.d., The spatial turn in anthropology. Online at *http://spatial.scholarslab.org/spatial-turn/the-spatial-turn-in-anthropology/index.html* [accessed 29 January 2017].

Haenfler, Ross, 2015, Punk rock, hardcore and globalization. In Andy Bennett and Steve Waksman, eds. The SAGE handbook of popular music, 278–295. Los Angeles: SAGE.

Harkin, Michael E., 2004, Reassessing revitalization movements. Lincoln: University of Nebraska Press.
Harris, Stephen, 1990, Two way Aboriginal schooling: education and cultural survival. Canberra: Aboriginal Studies Press.
Harrison, Klisala, ed., 2016, Applied ethnomusicology in institutional policy and practice. Collegium: Studies across Disciplines in the Humanities and Social Sciences 21.
Harrison, Klisala, Elizabeth Mackinlay and Svanibor Pettan, eds, 2010, Applied ethnomusicology: historical and contemporary approaches. Newcastle UK: Cambridge Scholars.
Harrison, Rodney, and Deborah Rose, 2010, Intangible heritage. In T. Benton, ed. Understanding heritage and memory, 238–276. Manchester: Manchester University Press in association with the Open University.
Hayward, Philip, ed., 1998, Sound alliances: indigenous peoples, cultural politics, and popular music in the Pacific. London: Cassell.
Hinton, Leanne, 2011, Revitalization of endangered languages. In Peter Austin and Julia Sallabank, eds. The Cambridge handbook of endangered languages, 291–311. Cambridge: Cambridge University Press.
Hinton, Leanne, and Kenneth Hale, 2001, The green book of language revitalization in practice: toward a sustainable world. San Diego: Academic Press.
Hinton, Leanne, Leena Huss, and Gerald Roche, in press, The Routledge handbook of language revitalization. New York: Routledge.
Hobson, John, Kevin Lowe, Susan Poetsch and Michael Walsh, eds, 2010, Re-awakening languages: theory and practice in the revitalisation of Australia's indigenous languages. Sydney: Sydney University Press. Online at *http://ses.library.usyd.edu.au/handle/2123/6647* [accessed 29 March 2016].
Hogan, Linda, 2013, We call it *tradition*. In Graham Harvey, ed. The handbook of contemporary animism, 17–26. Durham: Acumen.
House of Representatives Standing Committee on Aboriginal and Torres Strait Islander Affairs, 2012, Our land our languages: language learning in Indigenous communities. Canberra: Parliament of the Commonwealth of Australia.
Hudson, Ray, 2006, Regions and place: music, identity and place. Progress in human geography 30(5): 626–634.
Hunter, Jessica, Claire Bowern and Erich Round, 2011, Reappraising the effects of language contact in the Torres Strait. Journal of Language Contact 4(1):106–140.
Impett, Jonathan, 2009, Making a mark: the psychology of composition. In S. Hallam, I. Cross and M. Thaut, The Oxford handbook of music psychology, 403–412. Oxford: Oxford University Press.
Janke, Terri, 2009, Intellectual property issues and arts festivals: preparing for the 11th Festival of Pacific Arts (Solomon Islands, 2012). Geneva: World Intellectual Property Organization.
Janke, Terri, and Robynne Quiggin, 2006, Indigenous cultural and intellectual property: the main issues for the Indigenous arts industry in 2006. Sydney: Aboriginal and Torres Strait Islander Arts Board.
Johnson, Vivien, 1996, Copyrites: Aboriginal art in the age of reproductive technologies. Sydney: National Indigenous Arts Advocacy Organization and Macquarie University.
Jones, Trevor A., 1965, Australian Aboriginal music: the Elkin collection's contribution toward an overall picture. In R. M. Berndt and C. H. Berndt, eds. Aboriginal man in Australia: essays in honour of Emeritus Professor A. P. Elkin, 285–374. Sydney: Angus & Robertson.
—— 1974, Ethnomusicological studies in Australia: a brief research report, list of courses and facilities available, select bibliography and discography. Australian Journal of Music Education 15:53–59.
—— 1980, The traditional music of the Australian Aborigines. In Elizabeth May, ed. Music of many cultures, 154–171. Berkeley: University of California Press.
Kartomi, Margaret J., 1988, 'Forty thousand years': Koori music and Australian music education. Australian Journal of Music Education (new series) 1:11–28.
Keeling, Richard, 1992, The sources of Indian music: an introduction and overview. The World of Music 34(2):3–21. (Special issue: Music and spiritual power among the Indians of North America.)
Kendon, Adam, 1988, Sign languages of Aboriginal Australia: cultural, semiotic and communicative perspectives. Cambridge: Cambridge University Press.

Kirkwood, Sandra and Adrian Miller, 2014, The impact of new technologies on musical learning of Indigenous Australian children. Australasian Journal of Early Childhood 30(2):94–101.

Klapproth, Danièle M., 2004, Narrative as social practice: Anglo-Western and Australian Aboriginal oral traditions. Berlin: Mouton de Gruyter.

Knox, Jim and Anthony Magen, 2009, Editorial. Soundscape: the Journal of Acoustic Ecology 9(1):1. (Special issue on 'changing soundscapes in the Australasian region'.)

Koch, Grace E. D., 1987, A bibliography of publications on Australian aboriginal music: 1975–1985. Musicology Australia, 10(1):58–71. Online at *http://dx.doi.org/10.1080/08145857.1987.10415180* [accessed 29 March 2016].

—— 1992, A bibliography of publications on Australian Aboriginal and Torres Strait Islander music: 1986–1992. Musicology Australia 15(1):87–95. Online at *http://dx.doi.org/10.1080/08145857.1992.1 0415208* [accessed 29 March 2016].

Koen, Benjamin D., Jacqueline Lloyd, Gregory Barz, and Karen Brummel-Smith, eds, 2008, The Oxford handbook of medical ethnomusicology. Oxford: Oxford University Press.

Kouvaras, Linda Ioanna, 2013, Loading the silence: Australian sound art in the post-digital age. Farnham, Surrey: Ashgate.

Kral, Inge, and Robert G. Schwab, 2012, Learning spaces: youth, literacy and new media in remote Indigenous Australia. Canberra: ANU E-Press.

Lane, Cathy and Angus Carlyle, eds, 2013, In the field: the art of field recording. Axminster UK: Devon Uniform Books.

Langlois, Tony, 2011, Non-Western popular music. Farnham UK: Ashgate.

Le Bomin, Sylvie, Guillaume Lecointre and Evelyn Heyer, 2016, The evolution of musical diversity: the key role of vertical transmission. PLoS ONE 11(3):e0151570. Online at *http://journals.plos.org/ plosone/article?id=10.1371%2Fjournal.pone.0151570* [accessed 6 April 2016].

Levine, Victoria Lindsay, 1993, Musical revitalization among the Choctaw. American Music 11(4):391–411.

Liebman, Elad, Eitan Ornoy and Benny Chor, 2012, A phylogenetic approach to music performance analysis. Journal of New Music Research 41(2):215–242. Online at *https://www.cs.utexas. edu/~eladlieb/paper.pdf* [accessed 6 April 2016].

Lo Bianco, Joseph, 1990, Making language policy: Australia's experience. In R. B. Baldauf, Jr. and A. Luke, eds. Language planning and education in Australasia and the South Pacific, 47–79. Clevedon UK: Multilingual Matters.

Lowitja Institute, 2015, Publications style guide v13 [PDF]. Carlton VIC: The Lowitja Institute. Online at *http://www.lowitja.org.au/publications* [accessed 25 May 2017].

Mackinlay, Elizabeth and Peter Dunbar-Hall, 2003, Historical and dialectical perspectives on the teaching of Aboriginal and Torres Strait Islander musics in the Australian education system. Australian Journal of Indigenous Education 32:29–40.

M[a]c – see under 'Mc'

Maffie, James, 1995, Towards an anthropology of epistemology. The Philosophical Forum 26(3):218–241.

—— 2001, Truth from the perspective of comparative world philosophy. Social Epistemology, 15(4):263–273.

—— 2009, 'In the end, we have the Gatling gun, and they have not': future prospects of indigenous knowledges. Futures 41:53–65 (special issue on 'futures for indigenous knowledges').

—— 2014, Aztec philosophy: understanding a world in motion. Boulder: University Press of Colorado.

—— n.d. Ethnoepistemology. In James Fieser and Bradley Dowden, eds. Internet Encyclopedia of Philosophy. Online at *http://www.iep.utm.edu/ethno-ep/* [accessed 14 June 2017].

Magen, Anthony, 2009, Australian Forum for Acoustic Ecology. Soundscape: the Journal of Acoustic Ecology 9(1):2. (Special issue on 'the investigation of changing soundscapes in the Australasian region.)

Magowan, Fiona, 1994, 'The land is our *märr* (essence), it stays forever': the *yothu-yindi* relationship in Australian Aboriginal traditional and popular musics. In Martin Stokes, ed. Ethnicity, identity and music: the musical construction of place, 135–155. Oxford: Berg.

—— 2007, Melodies of mourning: music and emotion in Northern Australia. Perth: UWA Press.
Magowan, Fiona, and Karl Neuenfeldt, 2005, Landscapes of Indigenous performance: music, song and dance of the Torres Strait and Arnhem Land. Canberra: Aboriginal Studies Press.
Mallarach, Josep-Maria, and Thymio Papayannis, eds, 2007, Protected areas and spirituality: proceedings of the first workshop of the Delos Initiative. Gland, Switzerland: The World Conservation Union.
Mansfield, John, 2014, Listening to heavy metal in Wadeye. In Amanda Harris, ed. Circulating cultures: exchanges of Australian Indigenous music, dance and media, 239–262. Canberra: ANU Press.
Marett, Allan, 2000, Ghostly voices: some observations on song-creation, ceremony and being in NW Australia. Oceania 71(1):18–29.
—— 2005, Songs, dreamings and ghosts: the Wangga of North Australia. Middletown CT: Wesleyan University Press.
Marett, Allan, and Linda Barwick, 2003, Endangered songs and endangered languages. In J. Blythe & R. M. Brown, eds. Maintaining the links: language identity and the land. Seventh conference of the Foundation for Endangered Languages, Broome WA, 144–151. Bath UK: Foundation for Endangered Languages.
Marmion, Doug, Kazuko Obata and Jakelin Troy, 2014, Community, identity, wellbeing: the report of the Second National Indigenous Languages Survey. Canberra: AIATSIS.
Martinelli, Dario, 2009, Of birds, whales, and other musicians: an introduction to zoomusicology. Scranton: University of Scranton Press.
McCollum, Jonathan and David G. Hebert, eds, 2014, Theory and method in historical ethnomusicology. Lanham MD: Lexington Books.
McConvell, Patrick and Laurent Dousset, 2012, Tracking the dynamics of kinship and social category terms with Austkin II. Proceedings of the EACL 2012 Joint Workshop of LINGVIS & UNCLH (Avignon, France, April 23–24 2012), 98–107. See *https://halshs.archives-ouvertes.fr/halshs-00694832/document* [accessed 21 February 2017].
McConvell, Patrick, Piers Kelly and Sébastien Lacrampe, in press, Kin, skin and clan: the dynamics of social categories in Indigenous Australia. To be published by ANU Press (Canberra). See *http://www.austkin.net/* [accessed 31 March 2016].
McConvell, Patrick, Doug Marmion and Sally McNicol, 2005, National Indigenous Languages Survey report 2005. Canberra: AIATSIS.
McNiven, Ian J., 2003, Saltwater people: spiritscapes, maritime rituals and the archaeology of Australian Indigenous seascapes. World Archaeology 35(3):329–349.
—— 2008, Sentient seas: seascapes as spiritscapes. In Bruno David and Julian Thomas, eds. Handbook of landscape archaeology, 149–157. Walnut Creek CA: Left Coast Press.
Mills, Sherylle, 1996, Indigenous music and the law: an analysis of national and international legislation. Yearbook for Traditional Music 28:57–86 (special issued devoted to intellectual property).
Mitchell, Tony, 2006, Blackfellas rapping, breaking and writing: a short history of Aboriginal hip hop. Aboriginal History 30:124–137.
Morphy, Howard, 1989, From dull to brilliant: the aesthetics of spiritual power among the Yolngu. Man (new series) 24(1):21–40.
Moyle, Alice M., 1966, A handlist of field collections of recorded music in Australia and Torres Strait. Canberra: Australian Institute of Aboriginal Studies.
—— 1967, Songs from the Northern Territory: companion booklet. Canberra: Australian Institute of Aboriginal Studies.
—— 1980, Aboriginal music and dance in northern Australia. In Stanley Sadie and John Tyrrell, eds. The new Grove dictionary of music and musicians, vol. 1:713–722. London: Macmillan.
—— 1984, Aboriginal music and dance: reflections and projections. In J. C. Kassler and J. Stubington, eds. Problems and solutions: occasional essays in musicology presented to Alice M. Moyle, 14–30. Sydney: Hale & Iremonger.
Moyle, Richard M., 1979, Songs of the Pintupi: musical life in a Central Australian society. Canberra: Australian Institute of Aboriginal Studies.
—— 2001, Observers observed: mutually changing perceptions at Balgo. Journal of Intercultural Studies 22(2):121–131.

Navas, Eduardo, Owen Gallagher and xtine burrough, eds, 2014, The Routledge companion to remix studies. New York: Routledge.

Nettl, Bruno, and Philip V. Bohlman, 1991, Comparative musicology and anthropology of music: essays on the history of ethnomusicology. Chicago: University of Chicago Press.

Neuenfeldt, Karl, 1998, Sounding silences: the inclusion of Indigenous popular music in Australian education curricula. Discourse: studies in the cultural politics of education 19(2):201–218.

Neuenfeldt, Karl, and Lyn Costigan, 2004, Negotiating and enacting musical innovation and continuity: how some Torres Strait Islander songwriters incorporate traditional dance chants within contemporary songs. Asia Pacific Journal of Anthropology 5(2):113–128.

Neuenfeldt, Karl, and Will Kepa, 2011, Indigenising the documentation of musical cultural practices: Torres Strait Islander community CDs/ DVDs. In Graham Seal and Jennifer Gall, eds. Antipodean traditions: Australian folklore in the 21st century, 72–90. Perth: Black Swan Press.

Nooshin, Laudan, 2009, Music and the play of power in the Middle East, North Africa and Central Asia. Farnham, Surrey: Ashgate.

Oien, Kathleen, 2000, Aboriginal contemporary music: rockin' into the mainstream? In Sylvia Kleinert and Margo Neale, eds. The Oxford companion to Aboriginal art and culture, 335–340. Melbourne: Oxford University Press.

Onnudottir, Helena, Adam Possamai and Bryan S. Turner, 2013, Religious change and indigenous peoples: the making of religious identities. Farnham, Surrey: Ashgate.

Ormond-Parker, Lyndon, Aaron Corn, Kazuko Obata and Sandy O'Sullivan, eds, 2013, Information technology and indigenous communities. Canberra: AIATSIS Research Publications.

Ottosson, Åsa, 2015, Making Aboriginal men and music in Central Australia. London: Bloomsbury Publishing.

Patrick, Wanta Steve Jampijinpa, 2015, *Pulya-ranyi*: winds of change. Cultural Studies Review 21(1):120–131.

Payne, Helen, 1978, The integration of music and belief in Australian Aboriginal culture. Religious Traditions 1(1):8–18.

—— 1993, The presence of the possessed: a parameter in the performance practice of the music of Australian Aboriginal women. In Kimberly Marshall, ed. Rediscovering the Muses: women's musical traditions, 1–20. Boston: Northeastern University Press.

Pedelty, Mark, 2011, Ecomusicology: Rock, folk, and the environment. Philadelphia: Temple University Press.

—— 2016, A song to save the Salish Sea: musical performance as environmental activism. Bloomington IN: Indiana University Press.

Peluso, Nancy Lee, 1995, Whose woods are these? counter-mapping forest territories in Kalimantan, Indonesia. Antipode 27(4):383–406.

Pettan, Svanibor, and Jeff Todd Titon, eds, 2015, The Oxford handbook of applied ethnomusicology. New York: Oxford.

Pinch, Trevor, and Karin Bijsterveld, eds., 2012, The Oxford handbook of sound studies. New York: Oxford University Press.

Pinney, Chris, and Nicholas Thomas, eds., 2001, Beyond aesthetics: art and the technologies of enchantment. Oxford: Berg.

Quiggin, Robynne, and Terri Janke, 2007, Music: protocols for producing Indigenous Australian music. Sydney: Australia Council for the Arts.

Rehding, Alexander, 2011, Ecomusicology between apocalypse and nostalgia. Journal of the American Musicological Society 64(2): 409–14.

Richards, Fiona, ed., 2007, The soundscapes of Australia: music, place and spirituality. Aldershot: Ashgate.

Russell, Ian, and Catherine Ingram, eds, 2013, Taking part in music: case studies in ethnomusicology. Aberdeen: Aberdeen University Press.

S[ain]t John – see under St

Samuels, David W., 2015, Music's role in language revitalization – some questions from recent literature. Journal of Linguistic Anthropology 25:346–355.

Samuels, David W., Louise Meintjes, Ana Maria Ochoa, and Thomas Porcello, 2010, Soundscapes: toward a sounded anthropology. Annual Review of Anthropology 39: 329–345.

Sanders, Julie, 2006, Adaptation and appropriation. London: Routledge.

Scarre, Christopher and Graeme Lawson, eds, 2006, Archaeoacoustics. Cambridge: McDonald Institute for Archaeological Research.

Schafer, R. Murray, 1968, The new soundscape: a handbook for the modern music teacher. Toronto: Berandol Music.

—— 1977, The tuning of the world. New York: Alfred A. Knopf.

Schippers, Huib, and Catherine Grant, eds, 2016, Sustainable futures for music cultures: an ecological perspective. New York: Oxford University Press.

Schneider, Arnd, and Christopher Wright, eds, 2010, Between art and anthropology: contemporary ethnographic practice. Oxford: Berg.

—— 2013, Anthropology and art practice. London: Bloomsbury.

Seeger, Anthony, 2005, Who got left out of the property grab again? Oral traditions, Indigenous rights, and valuable old knowledge. In Rishab Ghosh, ed. CODE: Collaborative ownership and the digital economy, 75–84. Cambridge MA: MIT Press, 2005.

—— 2015, Natural species, sounds, and humans in lowland South America: the Kĩsêdjê/Suya, their world, and the nature of their thought. In Aaron S. Allen and Kevin Dawe, eds. Current directions in ecomusicology: music, culture, nature, 89–98. New York: Routledge.

Seeger, Anthony, and Shubha Chaudhuri, eds, 2004, Archives for the future: global perspectives on audiovisual archives in the 21st century. Calcutta: Seagull Books.

Simpson, Moira, 2007, From treasure house to museum . . . and back. In Sheila Watson, ed. Museums and their communities, 157–170. London: Routledge.

Sinnreich, Aram, 2010, Mashed up: music, technology, and the rise of configurable culture. Amherst: University of Massachusetts Press.

Sloboda, John A., 1985, The musical mind: the cognitive psychology of music. Oxford: Clarendon.

Somerville, Margaret and Tony Perkins, 2010, Singing the coast. Canberra: Aboriginal Studies Press.

Sorkin, Michael, 1992, Introduction. In M. Sorkin, ed. Variations on a theme park: the new American city and the end of public space, xi–xv. New York: Hill and Wang.

Sterne, Jonathan, ed., 2012, The sound studies reader. New York: Routledge.

Stokes, Martin, ed., 1994, Ethnicity, identity and music: the musical construction of place. Oxford: Berg.

Stratton, Jon, 2015, Popular music, race and identity. In Andy Bennett and Steve Waksman, eds. The SAGE handbook of popular music, 381–400. Los Angeles: SAGE.

Strehlow, Theodor G. H., 1971, Songs of Central Australia. Sydney: Angus and Robertson.

Stubbs, Dacre, 1974, Prehistoric art of Australia. Melbourne: Macmillan.

Stubington, Jill, 1985, Traditional Australian Aboriginal music: a bibliography and discography of musicological writings. Unpublished paper, Monash University.

—— 2007, Singing the land: the power of performance in Aboriginal life. Sydney: Currency House.

Studley, John, and Awang Jikmed, 2016, Creating new discursive terrain for the custodians of the Tibetan spiritscapes of north west Yunnan. In Bas Verschuuren and Naoya Furuta, eds. Asian sacred natural sites: philosophy and practice in protected areas and conservation, ch. 21. London: Routledge.

Swijghuisen Reigersberg, Muriel, 2010, Applied ethnomusicology, music therapy and ethnographically informed choral education: the merging of disciplines during a case study in Hopevale, Northern Queensland. In K. Harrison, E. Mackinlay and S. Pettan, eds. Applied ethnomusicology: historical and contemporary approaches, 51–75. Newcastle upon Tyne: Cambridge Scholars.

Tait, Anja, Edel Musco, Megan Atfield, Leonie Murrungun, Catherine Orton and Tony Gray, 2010, Weaving new patterns of music in indigenous education. In Julie Ballantyne and Brydie-Leigh Bartleet, eds. Navigating music and sound education, 129–160. Newcastle upon Tyne: Cambridge Scholars.

Tanner, Fred, 2008, Land rights, native title and Indigenous land use agreements. In Martin Hinton, Daryle Rigney and Elliott Johnston, eds. Indigenous Australians and the law (2nd edn), 147–160. Abingdon UK: Routledge.

Taylor, Hollis, 2013, connecting interdisciplinary dots: songbirds, 'white rats', and human exceptionalism. Social Science Information 52(2):287–306.

—— n.d. Zoömusicology bibliography, online at *http://www.zoomusicology.com/bibliography.html* [accessed 18 November 2016].

Taylor, Hollis, and Andrew Hurley, 2015, Music and environment: a snapshot of contemporary and emerging convergences. Journal of Music Research Online: 1–18. *http://www.jmro.org.au/index.php/mca2/issue/view/7* [accessed 21 November 2016].

Taylor, Timothy D., 2012, World music today. In Bob W. White, ed. Music and globalization: critical encounters, 172–188. Bloomington IN: Indiana University Press.

Terkourafi, Marina, 2010. The languages of global hip-hop. London: Continuum.

Thompson, William Forde, 2014, Music in the social and behavioral sciences: an encyclopedia. Los Angeles: SAGE Publications.

Titon, Jeff Todd, 2009, Music and sustainability: an ecological viewpoint. The World of Music 51(1): 119–137 (special issue on 'music and sustainability').

Tomlinson, Gary, 1993, Music in Renaissance magic: toward a historiography of others. Chicago: University of Chicago Press.

—— 2007, The singing of the New World: indigenous voice in the era of European contact. Cambridge: Cambridge University Press.

—— 2015, A million years of music: the emergence of human modernity. New York: Zone Books.

Toner, Peter, 2008, Keeping places and the politics of repatriation. Critical World 17 September. Online at *http://criticalworld.net/cultural-property/* [accessed 29 January 2017].

Toner, Peter, and Stephen Wild, 2004, Introduction – world music: politics, production and pedagogy. Asia Pacific Journal of Anthropology (special issue) 5(2): 95–112.

Tonkinson, Robert, 1976, Australien. In Kurt Ranke et al., eds. Enzyklopädie des Märchens, 1:4 (cols 1065–1073). Berlin: De Gruyter.

Treloyn, Sally and Andrea Emberly, 2013, Sustaining traditions: ethnomusicological collections, access and sustainability in Australia. Musicology Australia 35(2):159–177.

Tsunoda, Tasaku, 2005, Language endangerment and language revitalization: an introduction. Berlin: Mouton de Gruyter.

Tunstill, Guy, 1995, Learning Pitjantjatjara songs. In Linda Barwick, Allan Marett and Guy Tunstill, eds, The essence of singing and the substance of song: recent responses to the Aboriginal performing arts and other essays in honour of Catherine Ellis, 59–73. Sydney: Oceania Monograph 46 (University of Sydney).

Turnbull, David, 2000, Masons, tricksters and cartographers: comparative studies in the sociology of scientific and indigenous knowledge. Amsterdam: Harwood.

—— 2009, Introduction: futures for indigenous knowledges. Futures 41:1–5 (special issue on 'futures for indigenous knowledges').

Turner, Margaret Kemarre, 2010, Iwenhe Tyerrtye: what it means to be an Aboriginal person. Alice Springs: IAD Press. (As told to Barry McDonald Perrurle, with translations by Veronica Perrurle Dobson.)

Turpin, Myfany, 2007, The poetics of Central Australian song. Australian Aboriginal Studies 2:100–115.

—— 2011, Song-poetry of central Australia: sustaining traditions. Language Documentation and Description 10:15–36.

Turpin, Myfany, and Mary Laughren, 2013, Edge effects in Warlpiri Yawulyu songs: resyllabification, epenthesis, final vowel modification. Australian Journal of Linguistics 33(4):399–425.

Vaarzon-Morel, Petronella, 2016a, Continuity and change in Warlpiri practices of marking the landscape. In Robert Whallon and William Lovis, eds. Marking the land, 201–230. London: Routledge.

—— 2016b, 'For a cultural future': re-figuring the Coniston Massacre. Unpublished paper presented at the December 2016 annual conference of the Australian Anthropological Society, University of Sydney, in the panel 'Cosmologies unbound'.

Verschuuren, Bas, 2007, Believing is seeing: integrating cultural and spiritual values in conservation management. Gland, Switzerland: International Union for the Conservation of Nature and Foundation for Sustainable Development.

Verschuuren, Bas, Mawalan II Marika, and Phil Wise, 2009, Power on this land: sacred sites management at Dhimurru Indigenous Protected Area in Northeast Arnhem Land, Australia. In Josep-Maria Mallarach and Thymio Papayannis, eds, 2007. Protected areas and spirituality: proceedings of the first workshop of the Delos Initiative. Gland, Switzerland: International Union for the Conservation of Nature.

Verschuuren, Bas, Robert Wild, Jeffrey McNeely and Gonzalo Oviedo, eds, 2010, Sacred natural sites: conserving nature and culture. London: Earthscan.

Walker, Clinton, 2000, Buried country: the story of Aboriginal country music. Sydney: Pluto Press.

Walker, Polly O., 2009, Singing a new song: the role of music in Indigenous strategies of nonviolent social change. In Ralph V. Summy, ed. Nonviolent alternatives for social change, 130–155. Oxford: EOLSS Publishers. Retrieved from *www.eolss.net/sample-chapters/c04/e6-120-07.pdf* [29 January 2017].

Wallace, Anthony F. C., 1956, Revitalization movements. American Anthropologist (new series) 58(2):264–281.

Wallach, Jeremy, Harris M. Berger, and Paul D. Greene, eds, 2011, Metal rules the globe: heavy metal music around the world. Durham, NC: Duke University Press, 2011.

Walsh, Michael, 2007, Australian Aboriginal song languages: so many questions, so little to work with. Australian Aboriginal Studies 2007 (2):128–144.

—— 2014, Indigenous language maintenance and revitalisation. In Harold Koch and Rachel Nordlinger, eds. The languages and linguistics of Australia, 329–362. Berlin: De Gruyter.

Warf, Barney, and Santa Arias, eds, 2008, The spatial turn: interdisciplinary perspectives. London: Routledge.

Waterman, Patricia Panyity, 1987, A tale-type index of Australian Aboriginal oral narratives. Helsinki: Suomalainen Tiedeakatemia.

White, Cameron, 2009, 'Rapper on a rampage': theorising the political significance of Aboriginal Australian hip hop and reggae. Transforming Cultures eJournal 4(1):108–130. *http://epress.lib.uts.edu.au/journals/TfC* [accessed 6 January 2017].

Wild, Stephen, 1986, Australian Aboriginal theatrical movement. In B. Fleshman, ed. Theatrical movement: a bibliographical anthology, 610–620. Metuchen NJ: Scarecrow Press. Republished as an appendix to Williams 2011 (see below) in Journal for the Anthropological Study of Human Movement 18(1 & 2):97–113.

—— 1987, Recreating the *jukurrpa*: adaptation and innovation of songs and ceremonies in Warlpiri society. In M. Clunies Ross, T. Donaldson and S. A. Wild, eds. Songs of Aboriginal Australia, 97–120. Sydney: Oceania Monograph 32 (University of Sydney).

Williams, Drid, 1991, Appendix 11: survey of Australian literature on Aboriginal dancing. In D. Williams, Ten lectures on theories of the dance, 322–378. Metuchen NJ: Scarecrow Press. Republished in 2011 in Journal for the Anthropological Study of Human Movement 18(1 & 2):75–113.

Wolfe, Jocelyn, Vincent Plush and Huib Schippers, eds, 2005, Encounters: meetings in Australian music. Essays, images, interviews. South Brisbane: Queensland Conservatorium Research Centre.

Wood, Denis, 2010, Rethinking the power of maps (with John Fels and John Krygier). New York: Guilford Press.

Yanyuwa Families, John Bradley and Nona Cameron, 2003, 'Forget about Flinders': a Yanyuwa atlas of the South West Gulf of Carpentaria. Brisbane: the authors (limited edition, copy held by AIATSIS as MS 3842).

1 Maaya waab (play with sound): song language and spoken language in the south-west of Western Australia

Clint Bracknell
Sydney Conservatorium of Music, University of Sydney

Abstract

Records of song performances in the endangered Nyungar language from the south-west of Western Australia offer examples of language usage by fluent speakers and are powerful symbols of cultural identity. These songs hold inherent potential for enhancing Nyungar language transmission and could also contribute to the objectives of Aboriginal empowerment often sought by language revivalists. However, as Aboriginal languages can sometimes be used with greater phonetic and morphological flexibility in song, an understanding of the differences between spoken and sung varieties of Nyungar language is vital to informing attempts to utilise traditional song texts in language maintenance activities. Nyungar words may be modified, extended or abbreviated in song. Analysis of such phenomena is complicated by the inconsistent nature of archival recordings and written records of the Nyungar language. Although a process of comparison and deduction may assist in interpreting song texts, Nyungar songs must also be understood and respected as powerful embodiments of culture and Country. As a Nyungar music researcher and language activist, I undertake the analysis and consolidation of a Nyungar song repertoire as a step toward the recirculation of Nyungar song traditions.

Keywords: revitalisation, singing, song, south-west, Western Australia, Noongar, Nyungar, cultural sustainability, endangered language, song language

1 Introduction

Nyungar (also spelled 'Noongar') is the endangered Aboriginal language of the south-west of Western Australia, an area stretching from Cape Arid National Park in the east, moving in a northwesterly arc to Dongara and encompassing Perth, the capital city of Western Australia (see Map 1.1). Over 30,000 people identify as Nyungar (SWALSC 2009), constituting one of the largest Aboriginal language groups in Australia. As is the case with many Aboriginal music styles, traditional Nyungar songs are primarily vocal music, featuring lyrics in the Nyungar language. This implies an inextricable link between Nyungar language and Nyungar

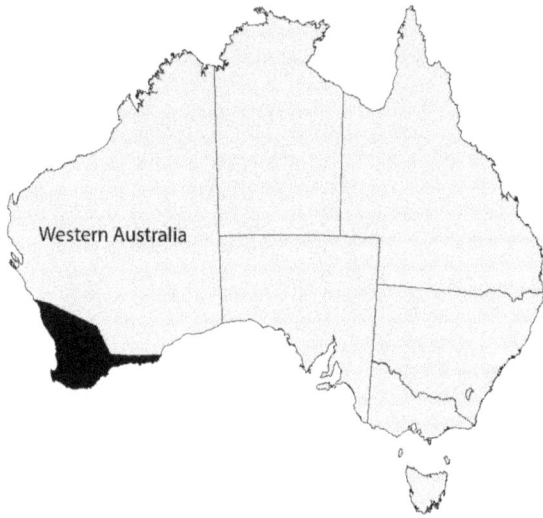

Map 1.1: The Nyungar language region

song traditions, a co-dependency that is critical for their vitality. Since 1829, various factors associated with colonisation have caused the intergenerational oral transmission of Nyungar language and song to diminish (Bracknell 2014a). The Australian Bureau of Statistics census lists Nyungar as a language spoken at home by 167 people in 1996 (McConvell and Thieberger 2001: 44); 196 people in 2001 (AIATSIS 2005: 75); 240 people in 2006; and, 369 people in 2011 (Australian Bureau of Statistics 2017), reflecting a slowly growing community of speakers, or at least a growing identification with the language. This small statistical increase is a likely result of Nyungar language revitalisation efforts undertaken over the past three decades. Walsh (2001) notes similar gains made by Aboriginal language revival movements elsewhere in 'settled' Australia. While a few senior Nyungar remember old songs, a significant number of song texts are also found in archival notes and audio recordings.

As a Nyungar of the Wirlomin clan from the south coast of Western Australia, I have participated in language revitalisation activities with the Wirlomin Noongar Language and Stories Project (Wirlomin Project) – a voluntary organisation with over 80 members – since 2010. Holding regular workshops, the Wirlomin Project combines archival data, the knowledge of senior Wirlomin people, and community development agendas to consolidate and enhance Nyungar cultural heritage, developing four illustrated, bilingual books since 2007 (Scott and Woods 2011; Scott and Roberts 2011; Scott and Nelly 2013; Scott, Brown and Winmar 2013). On the invitation of senior Wirlomin people, I undertook archival research on Nyungar song in 2013 and subsequently shared audio recordings and song transcriptions in subsequent Wirlomin Project workshops. In these workshops, we practiced reading stories we had developed in the Nyungar language, but found it more straightforward to sing the old songs. The songs were shorter and easier to remember, plus we could all participate at the same time.

As songs are of particular cultural importance across Aboriginal Australia, this should not have come as a surprise. Records of colonial interaction with Nyungar throughout the nineteenth century, including the journals of surveyor Sir George Grey (1841), suggest that the Nyungar language was once sung almost as frequently as it was spoken, with song constituting a primary domain of language use (Bracknell 2014b). Today, as rare examples of compositions by fluent language speakers and powerful symbols of cultural identity, old Nyungar songs have the potential to enhance the maintenance of Nyungar language and bolster cultural sustainability agendas. Clear links exist between singing and increased aptitude for second language learning (Jolly 1975), and teachers of threatened Aboriginal languages often rely on song as a mnemonic device (Hobson et al. 2010).

One of the greatest obstacles for the Aboriginal language revitalisation movement may well be the Australian accent, with its prominent near-open front unrounded vowel (æ), This sound is not found in the Nyungar language, but is common to the varieties of English most Nyungar speak as their first language today. To compensate, as Techmeier (1969) suggests, the repeated performance of songs in language learning promotes and reinforces correct pronunciation.

Edwards and Hobson (2013), moreover, assert that traditional Aboriginal song performances are valuable in language learning contexts as they reflect the correct stress and rhythmic patterns of Aboriginal languages. Nonetheless, terms and phrases in Aboriginal languages can sometimes undergo syllabic alteration when sung in order to meet the metrical requirements of various Aboriginal song genres (Turpin 2007a), often resulting in distortion of the patterns of syllabic prominence found in regular speech (Turpin and Laughren 2013). This kind of change is evident at the beginning of a Nyungar song performed by Charlie Traveller (Hercus 1965–1970):

Table 1.1: Comparison of sung phrase with spoken equivalent

	SUNG PHRASE				SPOKEN EQUIVALENT	
RHYTHM	♪ ♪ ♪	♪	♩ ♩		♪ ♪	♩ ♩
ACCENT		>		>	>	>
LYRIC	ma nga <u>rda</u>		-nga	<u>dwerd</u> a	<u>ma</u>ngardang	<u>dwerd</u>
GLOSS	jam.wattle		-COM	dog		

In this example, stress is placed on the third syllable of the first word, rather than the first syllable as is common to most spoken Aboriginal language. Aboriginal song language also may be variously distinguished from spoken language by its economy of expression, allusion or specialised vocabulary (Walsh 2007). Clearly, in light of the current need to consolidate Nyungar song texts both for potential use in language maintenance activities and to assist in ensuring the sustainability of Nyungar musical traditions, an understanding of the differences between spoken and sung Nyungar language is essential.

As Barwick (2006:57) observes, Aboriginal song texts 'may be short but they are often tricky' to analyse. The endangered state of the Nyungar language itself and the limited nature of archival resources available renders the task of interpreting meaning, form and function of the language used in Nyungar song particularly challenging. As a Nyungar person, my motivation to investigate Nyungar song traditions is Nyungar-centric, coalescing around individual and collective aims to consolidate and enhance a shared local cultural heritage (Bracknell 2015a). From the perspective of an ethnomusicologist and language activist with no formal linguistic training, this chapter will discuss the complexities associated with the interpretation of Nyungar song language, especially when dealing with written colonial records. The primary sources for this study consists of 102 public Nyungar song texts, including 80 fragmented and inconsistent written archival examples of lyrics collected between 1839 and 1930 and, additionally, audio recordings of 22 songs performed – sometimes multiple times – between 1965 and 2015 (see table 1.2).[1]

---

1 Additional Nyungar songs recorded by Wooltorton (1989) and McCabe (2004) are not considered in this brief study. Chauncy (1878) also notated a Nyungar melody with no text.

Table 1.2: Nyungar song text sources for this study

SOURCE	ORIGINAL DOCUMENTATION			REPEAT PERFORMANCES
	WRITTEN SONG TEXTS	TEXTS WITH MUSICAL NOTATION	AUDIO RECORDINGS	
Grey 1841	10			
Hassell and Davidson 1936	1			
Calvert 1894		3		
Bates, Daisy 1904–1912	65			
Laves 1931	1			
Hercus 1965–1970			2	
Tindale 1966–1968			5	
Douglas 1965–1967			1	
Tindale 1968			1	2
Brandenstein 1967–1970			8	
Brandenstein 1971–1976				2
Thieberger 1986			2	
McCabe and Miniter 2001			1	1
Bracknell 2015b			2	
Total per category	77		22	4
Total original song texts			102	

2 Spoken and sung language

The breadth of difference between language used in everyday speech and that used in song varies considerably across Aboriginal Australia. At one end of the spectrum, certain musical traditions may feature songs consisting entirely of non-lexical vocables, or employing spirit languages (Apted 2010), which may be incongruent with the local spoken language to the point of being completely un-translatable (Walsh 2007). At the other end, sometimes there is great similarity between song language and spoken language (Koch and Turpin 2008). A survey of archival records initially suggests reasonable correlation between spoken and sung Nyungar language. However, some song texts appear more economical than the spoken language, while others feature the embellishment or extension of comparable spoken terms.

Turpin (2005) demonstrates considerable differences in pronunciation between spoken and sung language in Central Australia, with language often changing in song as a result of particular rhythmic and structural constraints. However, in some Aboriginal language contexts, the omission of syllables, softening of consonants and the elongation or diphthongisation of vowels can be common in both singing and normal speech (Walsh 2007). In spoken Nyungar language, for example, Brandenstein (1988:1) defines 'a', 'i' and 'e' as 'filler vowels'. Additionally, Bates (1914:66) describes Nyungar speakers altering words purely for 'the sake of euphony'. Conversely, a similar range of variation exists in terms of the extent to which Aboriginal song language may employ the same morphemes and syntax as spoken language (Walsh 2007). When sung, certain Aboriginal languages may be simplified, with singers relaxing typical grammatical conventions (Koch and Turpin 2008). On the other hand, some insights on particular grammatical structures in endangered Aboriginal languages have only emerged as a result of examining song (Barwick, Birch, and Evans 2007).

Due to the small number of recorded song performances and the limited documentation of the language, an appraisal of Nyungar song language is challenging, particularly as the language has changed considerably in recent decades (Dench 1995). Few living speakers remember songs, let alone possess capabilities to 'straighten them out from the perspective of a participant' (Donaldson 1984:230). As Walsh (2007:132) observes, the rich expressive language commonly found in Aboriginal songs is usually one of the 'first casualties' of a 'rapid decline in language use'. Therefore, in the case of endangered and sparsely documented languages such as Nyungar, it can be extremely difficult to make distinctions between specialised poetic terms that were only used in song and vocabulary just rarely used – and thus undocumented – in spoken language. It is similarly problematic to recognise with certainty when spoken language is being altered in song.

3 Interpreting the archive

As with any oral tradition, Nyungar songs can only be recorded or transcribed from performance, and performances may vary in a range of ways. Rather than representing examples of singing within a traditional performance context, most audio recordings of Nyungar songs feature singers trying to remember or 'bring up' songs as they perform them, often for the first time in many decades. The singers on these recordings sometimes stop singing altogether at various points of a song to offer explanations to the researcher. While incredibly valuable in terms of providing melodic, rhythmic and lyrical information, the sparse and disjointed nature of most archival recordings of Nyungar song clouds analysis of the structural characteristics of particular song texts.

Written records of Nyungar song lyrics are even more problematic. Early transcribers rarely understood the complexities of Nyungar language, nor possessed formal linguistic training. As a result, Nyungar song lyrics are often written using a range of inconsistent, problematic orthographies. Even if the orthography can be interpreted, the text may or may not be properly split up into words. Indeed, misheard song lyrics – known as 'mondegreens' – are not uncommon in a range of language contexts (Turpin and Stebbins 2010). It follows that linguists, native speakers and even skilled Aboriginal music practitioners would struggle to consistently identify the exact intended terms in a given song text. Tomlinson (2007) goes so far as to suggest that the act of writing down and notating an Indigenous song is tantamount to its colonisation; reducing and enshrining it in written form according to an imperialist's narrow and perhaps erroneous interpretation, and consequently trapping it as an artefact of the past. Translations, transcriptions and notes provided by non-Nyungar researchers and writers can assist in the process of interpreting Nyungar song texts. However, relying exclusively on this material is problematic, as it is all refracted and possibly distorted through the lens of the colonial interpreter.

Audio recordings may offer much more veracity and contextual data than written records, although the existing archival audio recordings of Nyungar song mostly consist of poor-quality, frequently interrupted recordings of song performances, which are rarely accompanied by detailed explanations. Further complicating matters, it is not uncommon in any given region of Australia for singers to know songs in neighbouring languages or even languages far removed from the local area (Turpin 2011:33). Thus, a web of contingencies may obfuscate any understanding of Nyungar song based on archival examples alone. Given the potential for divergent understandings amongst singers, let alone the additional variables impacting on endangered song traditions, my interpretation of meaning in Nyungar song texts can by no means be considered authoritative, but may be better conceptualised as entering into dialogue with the archive, the endangered language and the song tradition.

Due to their poetic and sometimes abstruse nature, Nyungar song texts, like much Aboriginal music, may hold multiple meanings (Walsh 2007). As spoken Nyungar words may be elongated or abbreviated in song, the process of translating Nyungar songs needs to begin with the identification of Nyungar root-words within lyrics. As Nyungar is characterised by the complex use of functional suffixes, the secondary part is to establish whether these suffixes appear in song. The third step involves distinguishing 'poetic' or 'musical' alterations to spoken Nyungar language. This whole process must be underpinned by contextual understandings of Nyungar song. In efforts to ascertain the actual meaning of particular Nyungar song texts, rather than simply furnishing a literal translation, songs must be considered as constituting just one element of a 'package' of meaning, which may also include ownership, melody, rhythm, dance and performance context (Turpin 2005).

In his attempt to reconstitute an extinct language spoken by Indigenous people of the Californian coast, Broadbent (1957:287–279) asserts that the process of language 'reconstitution' involves the comparison of different versions of what various recorders of a language hear and transcribe. A diverse body of both scholarly and historical sources contains information about Nyungar language, with various investigators and observers employing a range of different, and somewhat unreliable, orthographies to document a number of similar-sounding Nyungar dialects (Thieberger 2004). English-speaking explorers and pastoralists with no linguistic training have compiled most of the primary sources of Nyungar vocabularies. However, Nyungar language includes a number of sounds not heard in English and difficult to represent using Roman script (Douglas 1968).

As is common in most Aboriginal Australian languages, the Nyungar language includes soft consonant sounds vocalised between 'b' and 'p'; 'd' and 't'; and, 'g' and 'k'. Generally, northern Nyungar speakers seem to favour the 'b' and 'd' sound, while southern speakers emphasise more of a 'p' and a 't'. Although perceivable to the point of identifying the local 'accent' of a speaker, these differences do not affect the interpretation of literal meaning. Hence, disagreement still exists among scholars and community members on the most appropriate orthography to use for writing Nyungar language, the definition and usage of particular words or phrases, and the degree of dialectic diversity in the south-west of Western Australia. The variety of spellings systems used across Nyungar language resources and in written archival examples of Nyungar song necessitates a flexible approach to word identification, in which various options are voiced and considered in a process of comparison to arrive at deduced, if not authoritative, interpretations. Employing this method, I have identified over 250 distinct Nyungar language root-words found in song texts.

Linguists offer explanations of Nyungar grammar and morphology (Laves 1931; Douglas 1968; Brandenstein 1988) but the pressures of language shift and the presence of few fluent speakers constrain efforts to fully document the Nyungar language and its linguistic conventions as applied in its original spoken form (Dench 1995). The Nyungar Language is similar to other Pama-Nyungan languages in that it is agglutinative, featuring root-words that can take on one or more suffixes. Dependent on context, these suffixes can serve various functions and may be slightly altered to achieve 'euphony' in spoken language (Bates 1914: 66). Table 1.3 lists some of the posited Nyungar suffixes found in the songs. One can reasonably conclude that spoken and sung Nyungar language employ similar morphology.

Table 1.3: A list of Nyungar suffixes found in song, illustrating some of their functions

SUFFIX	FUNCTIONS	EXAMPLE
-iny	Inceptive, Progressive	Waang (talk) > Waang**iny** (starting to talk, talking)
-idj	Completive	> Waang**idj** (just finished talking)
-an	Continuative	> Waang**an** (continuous or repetitive talk)
-l	Nominative, Locative	Kura (the distant past) > Kura**l** (in the distant past)
-ng	Possessive, Comitative	Wardan (sea) > Wardan**ang** (of or belonging to the sea)
-ak	Locative	> Wardan**ak** (on or by the sea)
-ak	Purposive	Kodj (axe) > Kodj**ak** (using an axe)
-ap	Associative	> Kodj**ap** (place associated with axes)
-min	Associative, Collective	Wirlo (curlew) > Wirlo**min** (group of 'curlew-associated' people)
-kar	Collective	Kulong (child) > Kulong**kar** (group of children)
-bərt	Negator	Dwongk (ear) > Dwongk**bərt** (without ears, deaf)

4 Poetic alterations

Describing Nyungar song language, Bates (1985:338) writes that ordinary terms 'undergo certain changes when they are utilised in song in order to ensure a certain harmonious equality of syllables'. Similarly, Gordon Locker, a singer from the Pilbara region of WA (cited in Brehaut, Stevens, and Vitenburgs 2001:63), notes that singers 'sometimes change the words a bit to make them fit in'. The phenomenon of aesthetic alteration of spoken vocabulary in Aboriginal song indicates that the translation of Nyungar songs requires a great deal more consideration than the comparatively straightforward translation of speech. Such changes to language imply the adherence to particular rhythmic structures or intended rhythmic, dynamic or poetic effects as found in Aboriginal song elsewhere in Australia (Barwick Birch and Evans 2007; Turpin 2007b; Treloyn 2009).

Using song lyrics performed by Nebinyan of Two Peoples Bay as examples, Bates (1904–1912) explains how a kind of '[p]oetic licence was indulged in when necessary', with the singer adapting words from their spoken context to better suit their sung context. In tables 1.4 and 1.5, I illustrate such differences between the language in each song text and the comparable spoken root words and suffixes, based on my interpretation of various excerpts of Nyungar songs.

Table 1.4: Five Nyungar song texts and comparable spoken text

PERFORMER/REFERENCE	SONG TEXT	SPOKEN EQUIVALENT
A. Nebinyan (Bates 1904–1912)	kaeb-uru kumbar-a	kaeb kumbar water large
	kaarl-a-iny-a yirra-ng-a	kaarl-iny yirra-ng fire-PROG above-COM
	kumbar warin	kumbar wardan large sea
	yirra-ng-a kumbar warin	yirra-ng kumbar wardan above-COM large sea
B. Ngilgian (Bates 1904–1912)	maang-arl-a maang-arl-a	mamang-al mamang-al whale-LOC whale-LOC
	warda baal	wardan baal sea it
	dawool ken ken ken	dawool ken ken ken thigh dance dance dance
	bard-i bard-i bard-i bard-iny	bard bard bard bard-iny dart dart dart dart-PROG

PERFORMER/REFERENCE	SONG TEXT	SPOKEN EQUIVALENT
C. C. Dabb (Brandenstein 1967–1970)	dely-bərt mando mandorn-ap	dely-bərt sea foam-NEG mandorn mandorn-ap Mondrain Isl. Mondrain Isl.-ASS
D. S. Dabb (Brandenstein 1967–1970)	kokandjeri waab-iny-eri	kokandjeri waab-iny Sheep play-PROG
E. L. Roberts (McCabe and Miniter 2001)	kurli maat waang-an-ang-a	kurli maat waang-an-ang bush-turkey leg talk-CONT-COM

Table 1.5: Poetic alterations in song texts A, B, C, D and E

DEVICE	EXAMPLES	CHANGE
Vowel epenthesis	A. kumbar > kumbara A. karliny > karlainya A. yirrang > yirranga B. mamangal > maangarla B. bard > bardi E. waanganang > waangananga	+ 'a' + 'a' x 2 + 'a' + 'a' + 'i' + 'a'
Whole syllable epenthesis	A. kaeb > kaeburu D. waabiny > waabinyeri	+ 'u' + 'ru' + 'e' + 'ri'
Consonant modification	A. wardan > warin B. mamangal > maangarla	'rda' > 'ri' 'l' > 'rl'
Consonant elision	B. mamang > maang B. wardan > warda C. mandorn > mando	– middle consonant 'm' – final consonant 'n' – final consonant cluster 'rn'

In analysis of Aboriginal song from the Kimberley in Western Australia, Treloyn (2009: 61) describes how the modification of spoken terms to fit particular semantic rhythmic structures in song can be used 'negotiate a fabric of relationships' between living and deceased composers, performers, ancestors and entities associated with the creation and maintenance of the universe. Indeed, at a deeper cultural level, ancestral Aboriginal songs can hold significant functional power. They can both heal or inflict injury, and are capable of creation and destruction, affecting changes in the physical world. In activities with the Wirlomin Project in the south-west of Western Australia, singing an ancestral Nyungar song about the *kurli* ('bush turkey', *Ardeotis australis*) for the first time in decades has coincided with increased sightings of the seldom-seen bird (Bracknell 2015c). Furthermore, senior Nyungar people remember their elders singing out to dolphins to bring salmon in to shore (Henderson et al. 2006). It is therefore not unreasonable to assume that changes to spoken terms in Nyungar song may function to imbue words with meaning and power.

4.1 Vowel and whole syllable epenthesis

Every Nyungar song considered in this study features either 'filler vowels' or other seemingly non-lexical word-extensions. In the songs provided as examples, a vowel is commonly added to the end of consonant-final words. Words ending with nasal sounds are less subject to this kind of vowel epenthesis, perhaps because nasals are sonorant sounds. One can sing holding a nasal sound, but cannot easily hold other consonants without adding a following vowel. Although 'filler vowels' are also common in spoken Nyungar language, this phenomenon is likely to be due to particular rhythmic or melodic considerations that require the extension of certain words to achieve an aesthetic or semantic intent. Whole-syllable epenthesis is less common, but follows a similar principle in the examples above, where a vowel plus an additional syllable is added to a consonant-final word.

4.2 Consonant modification and elision

Aesthetic and structural considerations may also be responsible for the abbreviation of spoken terms in almost half of the song texts analysed. In the case of *wardan > warin* in example A, the retroflex stop is sung as a rhotic. This change softens the enunciated rhythm of the second syllable, perhaps as to allow the singer to 'glide' over the substituted consonant or simply to sing the word faster.

The second-vowel 'a' also changes to 'i'. Dench (1994) alludes to the idea that second-vowel sounds in the Nyungar language are often interchangeable and sometimes indicative of regional dialect. Based on experiences listening to Nyungar speakers, I propose that this and many other unstressed second-vowel sounds occurring before consonants in the Nyungar language could be more accurately written using a schwa, e.g. *wardən > warən*.

In the alteration *mamangal > maangarla* in example B, an apical consonant is sung as a retroflex, suggesting a more emphatic or perhaps accentuated second syllable. The middle-consonant elision in this same item presumably results in the production of a long middle-vowel sound. Word-ending vowel epenthesis, along with these two alterations, suggests a change in rhythm:

♪ ♪ ♩ > ♩ ♩ ♪
mamangal > *maangarla*

This reflects a likely stylistic composition decision to alter and expand a word for a particular musical effect. The final-consonant elision of *wardan > warda* in example B allows for the word to retain two syllables but nonetheless suggests that the second syllable is sung more quickly than in normal speech, perhaps reflecting a new rhythmic pattern:

♪ ♩ ♩ > ♪ ♪ ♩
wardan baal > *warda baal*

Similarly, listening to the audio recording of Charlie Dabb's whaling song (example C in table 1.4), it is clear that the term von Brandenstein records as referring to Mondrain Island, '*mandornap*' is altered and partially repeated to suit the rhythmic setting:

♩ ♪ ♪ ♪ ♪
man-do man-dor-nap

Further analysis of rhythms implied by written Nyungar song lyrics and the stylistic differences between sung and spoken Nyungar language may well inform a process of grafting suitable rhythms and melodies onto songs with no recorded music.

4.3 Repetition and onomatopoeia

In addition to extension and abbreviation, Nyungar songs also employ other poetic devices. In Ngilgian's song (example B in Table 1.4), repetition of the terms *ken* ('dance or step') and *bard* ('jump, hop or dart') produces the effect of a person dancing on top of a whale whilst attempting not to lose balance. This kind of wordplay is reflective of a Nyungar term Bates records for 'singing' (1904–1912), *maaya waab*; literally, 'to play with sound'. So too is the prevalence of onomatopoeia in Nyungar song. One song described by Bates (1904–1912) and performed by Joobaitch (also known as George Ngoorweel) begins in Nyungar language and concludes with an imitation of the magpie's long morning call. Other onomatopoeic devices present in Nyungar songs include *baabur* (like 'babbling brook'), to describe water moving, and *dji-dji-dji-dji* ('drip, drip, drip, drip'), to describe blood dripping. Similarly, *wurangura wurangura* is the noise of a train approaching, and *nyu nyu nyu* is a ghostly cry (Bates 1904–1912).

Still, spoken Nyungar language is onomatopoeic in nature. Terms for birds such as *waardang* 'Western Australian raven' and *wirlo* 'bush stone curlew' are based on the calls of each bird. The sound of words like *bam* 'strike' or 'put' and *boony* 'kiss' is highly suggestive of their respective meanings. Spoken terms such as *wely-in-in-iny* to describe profuse weeping or water flowing (Brown 2002) also indicate some of the playfulness, flexibility and sensuality of the Nyungar language. As most archival recordings of fluent Nyungar speakers feature elicited wordlists rather than fluent speech, it is difficult to determine if onomatopoeia and repetition are more or less prevalent when the language is sung. Nevertheless, the boundaries between speech and song in Nyungar communicative culture were far less demarcated before the intrusion of English as the dominant language (Bracknell 2014a). I propose that the qualities of Nyungar language we might today consider playful, sensual or perhaps more befitting song than spoken language, are distinctive language characteristics worth retaining when undertaking language revitalisation.

5 Conclusion

Interpreting Nyungar song requires a significant degree of educated guesswork. Even with extensive and sometimes creative analysis of terms in song texts and comparison with word lists, many of the songs included in this study feature terms which defy identification, suggesting that they could possibly be: non-lexical vocables; archaic terms not used in speech; or imported terms from neighbouring Aboriginal languages. Unidentifiable words could also be the product of a writer's mistake or a singer's mispronunciation. In light of this, as much as I attempt to deploy rigour in the interpretation of Nyungar songs, the task is necessarily underpinned by a degree of speculation, albeit speculation informed by considering the cultural context around each song text. Of the difficulties in working with songs in endangered languages, Donaldson (1979: 74) explains that 'those who make translations from oral literature in languages which are neither widely spoken nor written have to prove that they really are translations'. In light of this, my interpretation of Nyungar song texts has necessarily involved cross-referencing with Nyungar language resources.

In examples of Nyungar song from the early twentieth century and more recent times, the vocabulary and morphology appears relatively consistent with that of spoken language. However, sung language may be more likely to feature epenthesis, elision, modification to consonants and changes in rhythmic speech patterns in order to fit the rhythmic setting of a given song. While repetition and onomatopoeia are prevalent in song, such poetic devices are also likely to have been common to regular speech in the past. The recirculation and performance of old Nyungar songs could be one way to promote and conserve the lyricism and artistry of Nyungar language in the present context of language revitalisation.

The interpretive translation and consolidation of Nyungar language song texts in collaboration with the Wirlomin Project is a first step towards the broader goal of recirculating Aboriginal-language songs in the south-west of Western Australia. Analysis of the ways in which language is used in these song texts provides a blueprint for the continuation of Nyungar oral literature and song traditions. The reliance of this interpretive process on language documentation, the potential for old songs to bolster language revitalisation and the inherently powerful nature of Nyungar song signifies the ongoing co-dependence of Nyungar language, song and cultural sustainability. The proliferation of similar projects focusing on the songs of endangered languages, as discussed in the following chapters, may prove increasingly critical to global language maintenance agendas.

References

AIATSIS, 2005, National Indigenous languages survey report. Canberra: Department of Communications, Information Technology and the Arts.

Apted, Meiki Elizabeth, 2010, Songs from the Inyjalarrku: the use of a non-translatable spirit language in a song set from north-west Arnhem Land, Australia. Australian Journal of Linguistics 30(1):93–103.

Australian Bureau of Statistics, 2017. Available at: *http://www.abs.gov.au* [accessed 4 April 2017].

Barwick, Linda, 2006, A musicologist's wishlist: some issues, practices and practicalities in musical aspects of language documentation. In Peter Austin, ed. Language documentation and description, 53–62. London: Hans Rausing Endangered Languages Project.

Barwick, Linda, Bruce Birch, and Nicholas Evans, 2007, Iwaidja *Jurtbirrk* songs: bringing language and music together. Australian Aboriginal Studies 2007 (2):6–34.

Bates, Daisy, 1904–1912, Papers of Daisy Bates in the south-west of Western Australia MS 365. J. S. Battye Library of Western Australian History.

—— 1914, A few notes on some south-western Australian dialects. The Journal of the Royal Anthropological Institute of Great Britain and Ireland 44:65–82.

—— 1985, The native tribes of Western Australia, edited by I. White. Canberra: National Library of Australia.

Bracknell, Clint, 2014a, Wal-walang-al ngardanginy: hunting the songs (of the Australian southwest). Australian Aboriginal Studies 1:3–15.

—— 2014b, Kooral dwonk-katitjiny (listening to the past): Aboriginal language, songs and history in south-western Australia. Aboriginal History 38:1–18.

—— 2015a, 'Say you're a Nyungarmusicologist': Indigenous research on endangered music. Musicology Australia 37(2):199–217.

—— 2015b, Workshop with the Wirlomin Noongar Language and Stories Project at Yardup, WA. Perth: Wirlomin Noongar Language and Stories Project [digital audio recording].

—— 2015c, Natj walanginy? What singing?: Nyungar song from the south-west of Western Australia. Perth: University of Western Australia.

Brandenstein, Carl Georg von, 1967–1970, Sound recordings collected by Carl von Brandenstein. Canberra: AIATSIS Audiovisual Archive, VON-BRANDENSTEIN_C04 [tape recording].

—— 1971–1976, Songs and narratives from Western Australia and New South Wales. Canberra: AIATSIS Audiovisual Archive, VON-BRANDENSTEIN_C05 [tape recording].

—— 1988, Nyungar anew: phonology, text samples and etymological and historical 1500-word vocabulary of an artificially recreated Aboriginal language in the south-west of Australia. Canberra: Pacific Linguistics.

Brehaut, Loreen, Peter Stevens, and Anna Vitenburgs, 2001, The Guruma story. Alice Springs: IAD Press.

Broadbent, Sylvia, 1957, Rumsen I: methods of reconstitution. International Journal of American Linguistics 23:275–280.

Brown, Hazel, 2002, Word list. Perth: Wirlomin Noongar Language and Stories Project.

Calvert, Albert, 1894, The Aborigines of Western Australia. London: Simpkin, Marshall, Hamilton, Kent and Company.

Chauncy, Philip, 1878, Notes and anecdotes of the Aborigines of Australia. In R. B. Smyth, ed. The Aborigines of Victoria, 221–284. Melbourne: Government Printer.

Dench, Alan, 1994, Nyungar. In N. Thieberger and W. McGregor, eds. Macquarie Aboriginal words, 173–192. Sydney: The Macquarie Library.

—— 1995, Comparative reconstitution. In J. C. Smith and D. Bentley, eds. Historical linguistics, 57–73. Philadelphia: John Benjamins.
Donaldson, Tamsin, 1979, Translating oral literature: Aboriginal song texts. Aboriginal History 3:62–83.
—— 1984, Kids that got lost: variations in the words of Ngiyampaa songs. In J. C. Kassler and J. Stubington, eds. Problems and solutions: occasional essays in musicology presented to Alice M. Moyle, 228–253. Sydney: Hale and Iremonger.
Douglas, Wilfred, 1965–1967, Sound recordings collected by Wilf Douglas. Canberra: AIATSIS Audiovisual Archive, DOUGLAS_W01 [tape recording].
—— 1968, The Aboriginal languages of the south-west of Australia. Canberra: AIAS.
Edwards, Jodi, and John Hobson, 2013, 'Head, shoulders, knees and toes' is not an Aboriginal song. Paper presented at 3rd International Conference on Language Documentation and Conservation (ICLDC) 2013: Sharing Worlds of Knowledge, Hawaii Imin International Conference Center, University of Hawaii.
Grey, George, 1841, Journals of two expeditions of discovery in north-west and western Australia: during the years 1837, 38, and 39. London: T. and W. Boone.
Hassell, Ethel, and Daniel S. Davidson, 1936, Notes on the ethnology of the Wheelman tribe of southwestern Australia. Anthropos 31(5/6):679–711.
Henderson, John, Hannah McGlade, Kim Scott, and Denise Smith-Ali, 2006, A protocol for Laves' 1931 Noongar field notes. Crawley: University of Western Australia.. Available at: *http://www.uwa. edu.au/__data/assets/pdf_file/0005/1355306/Protocol_for_Laves_1931_Noongar_Field_Notes.pdf* [accessed 06 October 2013]
Hercus, Luise, 1965–1970, Sound recordings collected by Luise Hercus. Canberra: AIATSIS Audiovisual Archive, HERCUS_L16 [tape recording].
Hobson, John, Kevin Lowe, Susan Poetsch, and Michael Walsh, eds, 2010, Re-awakening languages. Sydney: Sydney University Press.
Jolly, Yukiko S., 1975, The use of songs in teaching foreign languages. Modern Language Journal 59(1):11–14.
Koch, Grace, and Myfany Turpin, 2008, The language of Central Australian Aboriginal songs. In Claire Bowern, Bethwyn Evans and Luisa Miceli, eds. Morphology and language history: in honour of Harold Koch, 167–183. Amsterdam: John Benjamins.
Laves, Gerhardt, 1931, The Laves papers: text in Kurin. Canberra: AIATSIS.
McCabe, Timothy, 2004, Bid-waartiny (Looking for tracks) Cliff Humphries-Mai Kaadidjiny: The tracks and stories of Kellerberrin Noongar Cliff Humphries. Perth: Curtin University.
McCabe, Timothy and Jason Miniter, 2001, Interview with Lomas Roberts. Perth: Wirlomin Noongar Language and Stories Project Archive [cassette recording].
McConvell, Patrick, and Nicholas Thieberger, 2001, State of Indigenous languages in Australia 2001. Canberra: Department of the Environment and Heritage.
Scott, Kim, Hazel Brown, and Roma Winmar, 2013, Yira boornak nyininy. Crawley: UWA Publishing.
Scott, Kim, and Russell Nelly, 2013, Dwoort baal kaat. Crawley: UWA Publishing.
Scott, Kim, and Lomas Roberts, 2011, Noongar mambara bakitj. Crawley: UWA Publishing.
Scott, Kim, and Iris Woods, 2011, Mamang. Crawley: UWA Publishing.
SWALSC, 2009, South West Aboriginal Land and Sea Council. Available at: *http://www.noongar.org.au* [accessed 4 April 2017].
Techmeier, Mary, 1969, Music in the teaching of French. The Modern Language Journal 53(2):96.
Thieberger, Nicholas, 1986, Ngatju Project, language elicitation and songs, WA. Canberra: AIATSIS Audiovisual Archive, THIE-YOUNG_01 [cassette recording].
—— 2004, Linguistic report on the Single Noongar Native Title Claim. Beckenham WA: South West Aboriginal Land and Sea Council.
Tindale, Norman, 1966–1968, Site information, songs, cultural discussions from south-west WA. Canberra: AIATSIS Audiovisual Archive, TINDALE_N07 [tape recording].
—— 1968, Discussion with Murray Newman. Canberra: AIATSIS Audiovisual Archive, TINDALE_N08 [tape recording].
Tomlinson, Gary, 2007, The singing of the New World. Cambridge: Cambridge University Press.

Treloyn, Sally, 2009, Half way: appreciating the poetics of Northern Kimberley Song. Musicology Australia 31(1):41–62.

Turpin, Myfany, 2005, Form and meaning of *akwelye*: a Kaytete women's song series from Central Australia. PhD thesis, University of Sydney.

—— 2007a, Artfully hidden: text and rhythm in a Central Australian Aboriginal song series. Musicology Australia 29:93–108.

—— 2007b, The poetics of Central Australian song. Australian Aboriginal Studies 2007 (2):100–115.

—— 2011, Song-poetry of Central Australia: sustaining traditions. Language Documentation and Description 10:15–36.

Turpin, Myfany, and Mary Laughren, 2013, Edge effects in Warlpiri *yawulyu* songs: resyllabification, epenthesis, final vowel modification. Australian Journal of Linguistics 33(4):399–425

Turpin, Myfany, and Tonya Stebbins, 2010, The language of song: some recent approaches in description and analysis. Australian Journal of Linguistics 30(1):1–17.

Walsh, Michael, 2001, A case of language revitalisation in 'settled' Australia. Current Issues in Language Planning 2(2–3):251–258.

—— 2007, Australian Aboriginal song language: so many questions, so little to work with. Australian Aboriginal Studies 2007 (2):128–144.

Wooltorton, Sandra, 1989, Interviews for Nyungar Language Project: stories, oral history, songs, language elicitation. Canberra: AIATSIS Audiovisual Archive, BUNBURY_01 [tape recording].

2 Thabi returns: the use of digital resources to recirculate and revitalise Thabi songs in the west Pilbara

Sally Treloyn[1] and Andrew Morumburri Dowding[1]
University of Melbourne[1]

Abstract

Thabi is a public genre of song that records events and experiences that shaped the linguistic, cultural, economic and geographical landscapes of the west Pilbara region in the twentieth century. The genre, and its equivalents in neighbouring languages, thrived in the 1930s to the1960s in the social contexts of reserves, towns, missions, and stock and strike camps. However, today it is endangered, and there are only a few elders who recall songs. Over the last 10 years, members of a younger generation have sought to revive the tradition through preserving elders' knowledge and instigating performances. They have also been active in recovering recordings from archives and repatriating them to the contemporary family members of past singers, as well as circulating them in digital formats. The sense of urgency from younger men and women, as they begin to consider the potential consequences of losing these songs and the ability to perform them, has coincided with an explosion in connectivity through mobile devices, as more people are able to afford smartphones and tablets. This paper explores the repatriation and recirculation of digital recordings of Thabi in the west Pilbara, and the use of current archival tools and online platforms to maintain and transfer Aboriginal song heritage across generations. Specifically, it describes the early stages of a project to revitalise Thabi songs from two different perspectives: that of a musicologist; and that of a member of the Ngarluma and broader Ngarda-ngarli (west Pilbara) cultural heritage community.

Keywords: revitalisation, singing, song, Thabi, Pilbara, digital cultural heritage, repatriation

Introduction

Thabi (Ngarluma language) and its equivalents – *Jawi* (Yindjibarndi language), *Yirraru* (Ngarla language), *Dyabi* or *Jabi* (Nyamal and Kariyarra language) and *Nyirrbu* (Nyiyaparli language), henceforth *Thabi* for the purposes of this paper – is a public genre of song, sung by one or two singers without dance accompaniment. The genre is indigenous to the west Pilbara region, and is held by members of the Ngarluma, Yindjibarndi, Palyku, Martuthunira, Kurrama, Nyiyaparli,

Banyjima, Yinhawangka, Kariyarra, Nyamal and Ngarla language groups – collectively referred to as Ngarda-ngarli.[1] Anecdotal reports, legacy recordings held in the archive of the Australian Institute of Aboriginal and Torres Strait Islander Studies (AIATSIS), the spread of the genre, and the quantity and subject matter of the songs themselves, suggest that the Thabi genre thrived from at least the 1930s to the 1960s. Elders who lived on the outskirts of the port town of Roebourne recall regular Friday night gatherings, where composers (also known as 'fiddlers') would sing and share newly composed songs and those they had learned from others. The genre was shared widely and heard as far north as the Kimberley. Collections by Geoffrey O'Grady (1950s), Carl von Brandenstein (1960s), Helmut Petri (1960), Alice Moyle (1968), and Michael Burns (1980s), amongst others, indicate that some 500 unique songs were in circulation in the era.

Evidently, Thabi thrived in an era of massive cultural, social, linguistic and economic change, as the pastoral and mining industries boomed in the west Pilbara in the early to mid twentieth century. This musical response to social change is reminiscent of the way in which the Walakhanda Wangga repertory and the Djanba genre were created in Port Keats (Wadeye) in the 1950s and 60s, respectively, to accommodate the social changes brought by the new mission (Marett 2007, Barwick 2011). It also brings to mind a cultural boom – or 'efflorescence' – that occurred in the Kimberley in the 1940s (Redmond & Skyring 2010) and 1970s (Akerman 1979), and in the broader Aboriginal art scene from the 1970s (Altman 2005), as Indigenous peoples created innovative forms of artistic expression to adapt to changing economic and social environments. By the 1990s, however, possibly due to social changes that limited opportunities to practise and the availability of new entertainment technologies, Thabi had become endangered, with only a few elders recalling songs and performing rarely.

Interest in the Thabi legacy has increased over the last 10 years, via the circulation of archival recordings and the initiatives of emerging leaders, who have sought to revive and revitalise Thabi practice. These include one of the present authors, Dowding (through research and development), and his nephew Patrick Churnside (through research and performance). As a result, the song genre is making something of a comeback. Both emerging elders and younger people are utilising legacy recordings of Thabi to learn songs. Basil Snook, son of Nyamal singer Topsy Fazeldene, for example, has learnt and begun to perform a song about the Marble Bar to Port Hedland train line, recorded by Fazeldene with linguist Carl von Brandenstein in 1964 (Jebb and Marmion 2015). In the stage production *Hip bone sticking out*, Patrick Churnside sang one of his great-grandfather's Thabi songs, using legacy recordings to support his mastery of the tradition, and most recently performed the show *Tjaabi*, made up entirely of Thabi songs.[2]

The revitalisation of Thabi today is happening in a new period characterised by rapid environmental change and easy access to digital technologies that enable the recording, repatriation and circulation of song performances. There has also been an explosion in connectivity via devices such as phones, tablets, televisions and car radios. Ngarda-ngarli peoples are rapidly connecting to a range of online environments through mobile platforms, and there is an increasingly robust mobile infrastructure in both smaller communities, including Roebourne, Wickham, Wakathurni, Bellary, and Mingullatharndoo, as well as the larger regional centres, such as Karratha and Port Hedland. In many of these Aboriginal communities there is a younger

---

1   A map indicating the locations of Pilbara language groups and families referred to in this chapter can be viewed on the website of the Wangka Maya Pilbara Aboriginal Language Centre, 'Pilbara Language Families': *http://ap-southeast-2.static.modjula.com/wangkamaya/1Iwn9hqSzqG.jpg* [accessed 7 March 2017].
2   'Songs from the Pilbara – a living culture, a spectacle under the stars', *http://yijalayala.bighart.org/tjaabi/* [accessed 5 March 2017].

generation of people who use digital technologies daily. Their usage extends to accessing and sharing recordings of Thabi and other songs.

There is growing interest in the ways in which singers and song communities use and respond to new technologies. Most recently, for example, Barwick (2017:169–170) has shown how the dissemination and use of song recordings in Wadeye has:

> allowed a democratization of the means of making music, even a dispersal of the original social power and authority of the mob system, and possibly, a deprofessionalization of music making within the community. At the same time the funeral songs contribute to a strengthening of family and internal clan networks, and to a strengthening of relationships with institutions and outsiders who control the means of production of the songs.

The research project in which the authors are currently engaged seeks to examine the ways in which singers, songs, and song communities have responded to the environmental changes of their times, both in the period from the 1930s to the 1960s and today. The present chapter provides some details of the groundwork for this study. The chapter is in two parts. The first gives a brief introduction to the Thabi genre. In the second, Dowding contributes a first-person account of his experience as a member of the cultural heritage community, his discovery of Thabi recordings in a national archive, and his experience of returning these to his communities of elders and peers in a digital format.

Brief introduction to Thabi (Treloyn)

The Thabi genre (and its equivalents held by the various Ngarda-ngarli groups) has the following basic characteristics, which distinguish it from other song types performed in the west Pilbara and more widely:

- Performances are public, and there are no restrictions, whether by age or gender, on who may sing or hear songs.
- Songs are performed by a solo singer, or sometimes two singers.
- Singers accompany themselves with a rasp-like instrument that produces a scraping sound or, less frequently, with paired boomerangs.
- Songs are not accompanied by dance.
- The conventions of compositional structure are comparatively open. Songs may be through-composed, strophic, or cyclical; melodic, text and rhythmic patterns may be cyclical or non-repeating, coterminous or non-coterminous; and texts may be set isorhythmically or not.
- Songs may refer to contemporary events and experiences, as well as to ancestral beings and places.

These characteristics distinguish Thabi from other genres performed and held by Ngarda-ngarli peoples, such as Gunangu and Barlgabi. These are sometimes restricted by gender and age (or life stage); are performed by groups of singers; are accompanied only by paired boomerangs (with the occasional addition of clapping and lap-slapping); are accompanied by dance; and typically exhibit a Central Australian style that features cyclically repeating non-coterminous melodic, rhythmic, and textual units, and the isorhythmic performance of text. While these group genres are performed by both Ngarda-ngarli and Marlba (the collective term for peoples of the east Pilbara), our preliminary data suggest that Thabi and its equivalents are composed and performed for the most part only by Ngarda-ngarli.

From the collections of Brandenstein, O'Grady and others, and also from stories and explanations provided by elders, it is clear that Thabi songs proliferated among Ngarda-ngarli in the 1950s and 60s and were also shared to the north. For example, in 1967 Brandenstein recorded Ngarluma singer Robert Churnside (Dowding's maternal grandfather) singing the Thabi song 'Goodbye Mandabullangana'[3], attributed to the Kariyarra composer Maabin (Brandenstein and Thomas 1974:13, 64). Both Petri (in 1960) and Moyle (in 1968) recorded this same song at La Grange mission (now Bidyadanga), on the edge of the Kimberley, sung by a Karajarri man, Bronco (Moyle 1978:15). On Moyle's expedition in 1968, she recorded at least four different Thabi songs (as 'Dyabi') at La Grange: 'Goodbye Mandabulu [Mandabullangana]' and 'From this side of De Grey River', sung by Karajarri singer Tommy Dodd; and 'Aeroplane', 'Verandah' and 'The windmill at Wallanie plains' by Bronco[4], Possum, and Andy. Apart from 'Goodbye Mandabulu', we are yet to investigate the provenance of the La Grange songs. However, notes on Moyle's La Grange recordings suggest that a substantial amount of text may be in Nyangumarta, which is spoken to the north of the Ngarda-ngarli languages, along with Karajarri and Mangala.[5]

Moyle also recorded Dyabi further north in Broome (west Kimberley), including two songs sung by Yindjibarndi (Ngarda-ngarli) singer Henry Edwards: 'Aeroplane or Spitfire' and 'Pearling lugger', said to be in Karajarri, along with songs by two more singers, at least one of whom, Tommy Edgar, was Karajarri.[6] The other singer is listed as 'Paddy Rowe Djaguwan', who, according to Moyle's notes, is also Karajarri. At the time of writing, it is unclear whether this is Nyikina elder Paddy Roe, or Yawuru elder Paddy Djiagween (elsewhere recorded by Moyle as 'Paddy Djaguwin') or a different singer.[7] If the singer is either Roe or Djiagween, this is the first recorded instance of a Thabi song sung by a speaker from the west Kimberley. (Yawuru and Nyikina are both west Kimberley languages.)

While the uptake of Thabi by singers in the Kimberley is yet to be explored, the memories of Ngarinyin elders provide substantial detail of the spread and performance of Thabi in the northern Kimberley. Ngarinyin and Wunambal song custodian Matthew Dembal Martin recalls that, when he was a teenager in the 1960s, old singers from the Pilbara working as stockmen sang 'Jabi Jabi' (as Thabi is known amongst elder Ngarinyin), at both the Derby leprosarium known as Bungarun and at Kimberley Downs Station in Ngarinyin country.[8] A Karajarri man at Bungarun, known as Old Man Sugar, sang Jabi Jabi and accompanied himself with a tin, scraping it with a stick. While Jabi Jabi is not sung by Ngarinyin today, Martin relates how Ngarinyin man Campbell Allenbrae (born 1922, now deceased) brought Jabi Jabi from Anna Plains Station (Nyangumarta and Karajarri country) into the Kimberley, singing it as far north as Karunjie Station.

There are two major print collections of Thabi texts: Brandenstein and Thomas (1974), which includes transcriptions and translations of 65 Thabi songs; and Brown, Geytenbeek and Murray (2003), which does the same for 68 Yirraru songs. This selection from the broader repertoire provides an indication of the wide range of topics that song texts in the genre address. In Brandenstein and Thomas, these range over:

---

3   We use here the names that Brandenstein assigned to songs in *Taruru* (1974).
4   Bronco is also listed as the singer of 'Goodbye Mandabulu' in the recording made by Petri at La Grange in 1960.
5   This note, entitled 'Source 220 Djabi songs recorded at La Grange, 1968', is held at AIATSIS (Moyle_A07-002673_supplementary2.pdf).
6   Tommy Edgar, a Karajarri elder who lived in Broome and had close social and ceremonial ties to Yawuru (Glowcesski 1998:208), was recorded by Alice Moyle singing 'Shell divers', composed by Sandy Wigarangu in Karajarri (Moyle_A07-002678_supplementary2.pdf, p.12).
7   Glowczewski (1998:208) identifies Paddy Djiagween as one of the singers recorded by Moyle, but it is unclear if this applies to the Dyabi in the Moyle collection.
8   Personal communication, Matthew Dembal Martin, March 2017.

- descriptions of natural phenomena and animals; e.g. 'Waves'[9], in Ngarluma, by Dougall-Kudjardikudjardi (1974:10), and 'Stonefish', in Nyiyaparli, by Piniingu (1974:28)
- scenes from the pastoral and mining industries; e.g. 'Cattle loading', in Nyiyaparli, by Gordon Mackay-Wama (1974:14), and 'Gold-fever', in Yindjibarndi, by Cobbin Dale (1974:5)
- the police; e.g. 'Policeman', in Nyiyaparli and Nyamal, by Piniingu 1974:26)
- gambling; e.g. 'Card money', in Nyiyaparli, by Piniingu (1974:27)
- horse racing; e.g. 'To the Roebourne races', in Yindjibarndi, by Ned Tjinabii (1974:39)
- transport; e.g. 'The truck', in Nyiyaparli, by Dingo George (1974:5)
- the impact of development on the landscape; e.g. 'Development', in Kariyarra and Ngarluma, by Tjabi (1974:34).

There are also references to historical events, such as the bombing of Broome in World War 2 ('Air raid on Broome', in Kariyarra, by Billy Thomas-Wombi, 1974:29).

The books by Brandenstein (1974) and Brown et al. (2003) are both furnished with glosses and translations, as well as detailed contextual notes on the songs. There are also references to Thabi in an honours thesis by Anthony McCardell (1970), which provides an analysis of a selection of the recordings in the Brandenstein collection. This became a source of the musical notes and transcriptions in *Taruru* (Brandenstein and Thomas 1974). Alice Moyle (1977, 1978) also provides brief descriptions of Thabi, in addition to unpublished textual analyses that include transcriptions by Nora Kerr, held by AIATSIS.[10]

In spite of this comparatively ample body of earlier work, a substantial amount of analysis is still needed to create an accurate picture of the place of Thabi in the stylistic landscape of Australian Aboriginal music. Given the genre's proximity to the Western Desert, we might expect Thabi to display the typical characteristics of the Central Australian style, such as cyclical texts performed isorhythmically, and cyclical melodies with which the text has an independent relationship. But in fact the majority of texts are distinctly non-cyclical in structure. A preliminary examination of Thabi suggests that, as in the Wangga genre from further north, text and melody are for the most part coterminous and strophic, with clear alignment of melodic and textual boundaries. However, where the text displays a cyclical repetition pattern, typically at the beginning of a song performance, there may be some independence between melodic and textual units, as in Central Australian style song. Preliminary observations of melodic form suggest that melody may also operate as an identifiable signature of the owner and composer of a song (see also McCardell 1970:40), which is again reminiscent of Wangga.

The use of a rasp idiophone that the singer holds and scrapes with a smaller stick to accompany their singing is unique in Australia. The instrument – referred to as a *mirrimba* or *walbarra* in Ngarluma – occurs in a number of forms. Moyle provides a photo of an elder singer cradling a notched stick along his inner forearm, with a small stick held against it (Moyle 1977:5), suggesting that the instrument may be purpose-built for the genre. However, both Moyle and elders today tell how a spear-thrower with notches carved into it and scraped with a stick was also commonly used. Many variants are described in the notes accompanying the archival recordings, including the use of a comb, a metal file, serrated knives, and tobacco tins.

Innovation and individual creativity in the composition and performance of Thabi are evidenced by variations in instrument use as well as in text, rhythm, melody, semantic content,

---

9   We use here the names of both individuals and songs as they are transcribed by Brandenstein (1974).
10 Supplementary print material held with the audio collection at AIATSIS:
MOYLE_A07-002673_supplementary2.pdf, MOYLE_A07-002678_supplementary1.pdf, MOYLE_A07-002678_supplementary2.pdf.

and performance practice. In performances of the train song (see Jebb and Marmion 2015), the tempo of the rasp accompaniment (in Fazeldene's performance) and of the vocal rhythm and metre (in Piningu[11] Donald Norman's unaccompanied performance) features a distinctive slowing down as the train finally comes to a stop.[12] Gordon Lockyer, recorded by Michael Burns, accompanies himself with a guitar.[13] Tunes are equally innovative, featuring descending patterns as well as melodic contours that have what McCardell (1970:40) described as a 'central climax'. Thomas suggests that some tunes are 'slightly reminiscent' of European folksong and one tune has a 'Spanish-style' melody (Thomas, in Brandenstein and Thomas 1974, unpag.).

Based on preliminary descriptions of the musical system as well as studies that consider the use of musical systems to respond to social change, we hypothesise that clues as to how composers used Thabi to manage the changing social environments of the 1930s to the 1960s can be found in these instances of musical innovation and creativity. In the current project we will draw on the historical practices recorded in the collections of Brandenstein, O'Grady, Moyle and others, and the living knowledge of elders today, to identify and describe how Thabi composers and singers used music throughout that period. Our aim will be to understand the resilience of the Thabi musical system itself, and how this musical system played a role in the resilience of song custodians.

Today, new technologies, such as computers, media libraries, CDs, USB sticks, mobile phones, and so on, are also part of the environment in which Thabi is being practised and revitalised. In the second part of this chapter, Dowding gives an account of the role played by new technologies in the revitalisation of Thabi.

Thabi returns (Dowding)

I am an Aboriginal man with connections to the Ngarluma and Yindjibarndi communities in the Pilbara region. I follow the Ngarluma family line, as does my mother. In 2006 I completed a Bachelor of Arts (History/Anthropology) at Sydney University, and my family asked me to return to our community in the Pilbara to work in our newly-formed Native Title body, the Ngarluma Aboriginal Corporation.[14] This body was formed by the Ngarluma community to hold the rights and interests granted by their Native Title Determination (February 2005). Our small corporation had humble beginnings: our directors, who were elected representatives of the Ngarluma community, convened meetings in borrowed rooms and worked hard to manage the affairs of a Native Title organisation. By the end of 2005 the corporation had rented an office in the main street of Roebourne and grown in its capabilities, but it desperately needed staff to administer and run the office. I obliged, and left Sydney to work in the Pilbara.

My official job title at the Ngarluma Aboriginal Corporation (NAC) was Culture and Communications Officer, but my roles varied from day to day. Our language group was a relatively early beneficiary of the Native Title determination, but was slower to develop than the corporation itself. There were few models to emulate. Most days the corporation office was frequented by Ngarluma community members and elders, who enjoyed conversations about

---

11 Elsewhere transcribed by Brandenstein as Piniingu.
12 Carl von Brandenstein C05-0017578: 00:13:19 – c.00:24:00.
13 Michael Burns M01-016161: 00:25:38 – c.00:27:00.
14 When a determination recognising native title is made, the *Native Title Act* 1993 of the Commonwealth of Australia requires that native title holders (traditional owners whose native title interests in their country have been recognised by the determination) must establish a corporation to represent them. These organisations are known as Prescribed Bodies Corporate (PBCs), but become Registered Native Title Bodies Corporate (RNTBCs) when they are registered with the National Native Title Tribunal (NNTT). While RNTBC is the correct name for these organisations, they are most commonly known as PBCs.

their culture and their language. But there were few resources about culture and language in our premises, apart from the extensive federal court documents compiled for Native Title proceedings. So I began to engage in the creation of digital material to fulfil this need. We began working with the local language centre to make Ngarluma language-learning films. We also developed wordlists for early childhood learning and began to create maps of Country.[15]

I began searching the internet for any mention of the Ngarluma language and stumbled across a reference to my maternal grandfather, Bob Churnside (who had passed away in August 1977), in a text called *Taruru: Aboriginal song poetry of the Pilbara* (Brandenstein and Thomas 1974). I bought a copy of the text on amazon.com, and, when it arrived, I showed it to elders, who talked about my grandfather as a great singer of Thabi songs. I knew we had ceremonial songs that were talked about amongst initiated men, but I had only a shallow understanding of the Thabi tradition. As I continued to ask questions about these songs, however, I began to realise that this non-ceremonial, or public, genre of music was highly endangered and gradually slipping away from our community. The Ngarluma community did not perform this music regularly, and forums for the performance of Thabi had shrunk over the last few years to very limited public displays.

The initial discovery of the *Taruru* text led me to a search of the online catalogue of the Australian Institute for Aboriginal and Torres Strait Islander Studies (AIATSIS) archive in Canberra. The archive holds legacy recordings noted in Brandenstein's text, and I found many references to my maternal grandfather. In 2006, while in Canberra for a conference, I decided on the spur of the moment to go to the archive and see if I could obtain a copy of the recordings I had discovered. Once inside, I explained my family connection to Brandenstein's field tapes to the archive staff. In particular, I spoke about my grandfather and my desire to hear his recordings. The archive staff efficiently helped me to find a variety of resources that related to Roebourne and Thabi. The Brandenstein audio collection was of most interest to me, as the audition sheets, prepared by Grace Koch, included many entries that referred to my grandfather singing Thabi and, in some cases, explaining the songs in English.

It was an emotional experience, as I sat in the AIATSIS listening room, to hear my grandfather's voice and listen to the Thabi songs he composed. I was filled with pride and I marvelled at his creativity. His explanations of the songs in English touched me profoundly, as I spoke no Ngarluma at this point. I remember feeling that my grandfather had specifically left these recordings for me and the rest of our family to hold, as a legacy of his creative work, and as a vivid auditory display of his love for the cultural traditions of which he was so obviously a master. I spent hours listening through the collection, matching the recordings to the audition sheets, making notes on which tapes I would request. When I had finished, I asked the archivist for copies of the specific tapes, and was told I could not have copies until certain permissions where granted.

At that moment it felt insulting to be told I would not be able to take a copy of those recordings without someone else's consent. In hindsight, I can see the predicament of the archive, and as my experience in this field grows, I too face the complex challenges of individuals wanting access to and copies of audio and video that I record. But at the time I felt deflated and angry at being unable to have copies of my grandfather's songs immediately, particularly after the feelings I had experienced while listening to the tapes. I did a lot of explaining to the archival staff about my connection to the person on the tapes, and they seemed to be sympathetic.

---

15 Relevant publications include the *Ngarluma-English dictionary* (Port Hedland: Wangka Maya Pilbara Aboriginal Language Centre, 2008); *We are the Ngarluma people* (DVD) (Roebourne: Ngarluma Aboriginal Corporation, 2008); *Learning Ngarluma kinship names* (DVD) (Roebourne: Ngarluma Aboriginal Corporation, 2008).

Nonetheless, they maintained that there were protocols around access, that this collection contained culturally restricted information, and that there were multiple language groups and individuals singing on the tape. This meant that there were multiple layers of bureaucratic processes that needed to be dealt with before copies could be created.

Determined not to go home empty handed, I asked to see a manager and continued to plead for a copy of the specific tapes that featured my grandfather's songs. The manager had obviously had this experience before. Although he had some discretionary powers to allow community members to access recordings, he was still hesitant. There were additional complexities with this collection in particular. Brandenstein had died a number of years earlier and left the decisions about access to a family member, who for some reason, I understood, rarely granted it. My argument was then to assert cultural rights to these recordings, by virtue of being an heir (as the maternal grandson of Bob Churnside). However, I could see the difficult position of the manager. The manager suggested that a community copy of the material could be provided if I had written permission from the Native Title group. Fortunately, the NAC was able to confirm my identity and gave this permission for me to obtain copies of the tapes. All it took was a phone call and a fax to gain the required authority from the NAC chief executive officer. The archive then agreed to make community access copies, to which I, as a member of the community, would also have access. As it would take a week, I had to be content with the knowledge that the recordings would make it back to the Pilbara by the time I came home from the conference. On my return, a box of recordings on compact discs arrived at the NAC office in Roebourne, and I began to listen – with elders, who were immensely enthusiastic about their contents.

I think very fondly of this time. It seems to me, on reflection, that it marked a turning point – one that had a real and direct impact on the cultural continuity of our small language community. Ngarluma is a very endangered language, with less than 20 fluent speakers. The recordings created enthusiasm for many initiatives, in particular the recirculation of legacy recordings to encourage revitalisation of our language. I have always harboured hopes that the recordings would also activate a rejuvenation of the songs themselves, but this did not happen immediately. It came about through a slower process that evolved over a number of years of listening and talking about the recordings. What was occurring in the initial stages was a sense of reclamation, for things that were lost and had now found their way back home.

Over the years from 2006 to the present I observed elders listening to these recordings many times. The intimacy of their encounters with the songs varied greatly, but on the occasions that I watched their reactions I was always struck by the evocative power that the songs seemed to have for them. My own experiences were similar. Many times I would be listening attentively to the words of the song, but also to the very fine detail captured by the microphone, such as the murmur of a child in the company of the singer, the accidental rattle of an object near the performer, the barking of a dog, the sound of a performer shuffling uncomfortably while being interviewed. All these small details of the recordings gave colour and a vividness to the image of my grandfather that was conjured in my mind. Subtle noises on the recordings – not just the songs – created a sense of context in my imagination. They filled in details around the song and the stories. The context would then be mulled over with my own family: we would ask 'Who is that kid in the background?' or 'He must be sitting on the veranda'. There is power in this process. These legacy recordings became more than just the audio files of songs; they promoted social relatedness and connectedness across time. In my case, the recordings gave a feeling of connectedness to an elder I never met; a relatedness conjured internally to support the intergenerational transfer of knowledge from my grandfather to me.

As the initial euphoria of listening to the recordings wore off, the mechanics of community access to the tapes began to raise challenges. We encountered particular problems with the format and content of the recordings. For instance, the CDs contained hour-long files, each of which included the contents of a complete side of a source tape. To facilitate playback, I transferred these files into iTunes, still as hour-long tracks. The elders would ask me to play just the Ngarluma songs (as distinct from the songs in other languages that were also contained in the file). The first problem was that we were unable to locate the Ngarluma content from the file names. These followed a standard archive convention (e.g. C02-CVB-FT00045[16]) that meant very little to us. So, in order to find the particular Ngarluma content, we had to scan through the long audio files, trying to locate the singers or speakers of Ngarluma. The audition sheets provided some help, as they listed the time codes and typically the singer of each song item. This allowed us to skip to items that matched the elders' listening preferences. Elders would always sit and wait patiently for me to scroll through the hour-long tracks to the right spots in the recordings. Usually the time code on the archives' digitised copy was somewhat different to the time noted on the audition sheets, so there was always a delay in finding specific singers. This was always the major request, and it required visually scanning the audition sheets to find the name and timecode, finding the correct track, then navigating to the timecode, and finally locating the exact spot where the singer we were seeking started their performance.

The group of listeners expanded as community interest increased, and this is when the format of the files became increasingly problematic. Some of the files contained restricted men's business, either in the form of songs or conversations, mixed in with public material. In a few cases the audition sheets carried warnings of restricted content. But in other cases the recordist was not aware that the material was restricted or sensitive, so the audition sheets did not indicate when and where this content occurred. In one particular instance, very early after receiving the CDs, I sat with a group of elders listening. In a small, personal group it was easy to respond quickly to elders' comments about sensitive material and to skip the content promptly if required. On this particular day a group of elders came through the office door to join the listening session. As the singer in the recording was belting out many Thabi songs in a row, I went out of the room to make cups of tea for the new arrivals and left the recording running. When I returned, restricted material was being played, and the ladies present were very unhappy. The men were too, and asked for the recording to be stopped. This abruptly ended the listening for the day.

Instances like this served to create a degree of community apprehension around listening to the archival recordings, and the setback occurred largely as a result of my inexperience, combined with my enthusiasm for sharing the material and for making the archival file formats accessible. Soon after this incident, elders made it clear that we would need a process for sorting and separating restricted materials from those that were appropriate for a general audience, such as Thabi. We agreed that the senior men would sit and listen to each individual CD, to create a record of which ones contained restricted information. Once a CD was marked 'restricted', it was physically put into a box and held under lock and key in my office.

It was not just ceremonial information that we classified as restricted, but also stories recorded about controversial past events. In one instance we were listening to a recording of elders telling stories, and the two senior men present looked sternly at one another, one of them shaking his head. When I asked them what was being discussed, they said that the recording needed to be locked up, and no one was to listen: the elder on the recording was discussing

---

16   The naming convention translates to 'Collection 02, Carl Von Brandenstein, Field Tape Number 45'.

the exploits of *mabarngarda* ('witchdoctors'). They had realised that some of these recordings contained highly sensitive information.

Once these initial audition sessions were completed and the restricted data separated, the road became clearer for others to listen again. I used the application Audacity to 'cut' the hour-long files into smaller tracks and remove restricted data from the longer file. I also went through and cut single tracks for each song item. To these I gave preliminary names, such as '1_BOBCHURNSIDE_OLDCROW_K', indicating the position of the song item in the recording, the name of the singer, a rough title for the song, and a code indicating what language the song was being sung in. In this case, it was the first song item on the CD, and it was Bob Churnside singing a song about an old crow in the Kariyarra language (K).

I recall that much of my time in the office in this period was spent playing these tracks and creating CDs for people to play in their cars and at home. Once it became known in the Ngarluma community that we had a small collection of Thabi songs, it quickly sparked a lot of interest. Many different elders came to sit and listen, to laugh, to sing or to just enjoy the sound of their own elders' voices. It struck me often that these recordings were worth more than gold to the current generation of elders. They seemed to leave the present troubles of the town and find themselves back in an era that they described as a time of great cultural strength, when their own elders held definitive cultural knowledge and were never afraid to perform it.

As the Thabi iTunes collection grew, a small group of younger people (mainly late 20s up to mid 30s) came to get copies of songs. We began to receive requests for iPods to be filled and USB sticks to be loaded. Only from elders did I get requests to make CDs – the younger generation had already moved on to new media forms. I found that splitting the audio in the larger hour-long files into smaller track files made it more appealing to listeners. This packaged the material in the familiar formats of .mp3 and .wav that were compatible with the devices they used on a day-to-day basis. These devices displayed the titles for each track, indicating the song and the artist's name, which enabled the legacy recordings to be more easily located among the other genres, such as pop, country and rap music. In these early years people began to listen to Thabi songs in many places outside of the corporation offices. In private homes, USB sticks loaded with songs were plugged into the DVD player or the side of the TV, bringing Thabi into the lounge room. In cars, USB sticks were plugged directly into the car radio. Track names displayed on the console allowed easy selection. Numerous times a car full of young men would drive past and I would hear Thabi songs being played.

At this time, I had become a virtual custodian of the tapes, which led to the playing out of a small power dynamic. The computer with the iTunes catalogue was mine, it was located in my office, and I used it daily for all my other administrative tasks. If people wanted copies of recordings, they had to ask me. Initially this situation made sense to me, as we were housed within the walls of the NAC, and one of my designated roles was to generate cultural resources for our community. But the perception emerging in the community – that I had power over the catalogue of songs – could not be denied. It became clear that I needed to ensure the community viewed the corporation as the place that held and distributed these songs, not me as an individual. Later I bought a public computer and set it up in the foyer, so that people became free of the obligation to ask me for copies.

Today there exists a small group of younger Ngarluma men (including myself) and women who retain their interest in Thabi, and they have all had access to the original song catalogue we created at the NAC. There were some other recordings of Ngarluma songs circulating before the development of the NAC digital collection, but these were usually on cassette tape, created by individuals in the community who used tape recorders for the purpose. It seems to me that the digital format helped the proliferation of the Thabi songs. Moreover, the splitting of long archival recordings into separate tracks marked a new way for community members to access, navigate and select recordings. The ability to pick a specific composer and then download their songs onto a USB stick emerged as a vital part of the revitalisation of some composers' work. The examples are not numerous, but one particular young Ngarluma man, my nephew Patrick Churnside, has taken it upon himself to learn and sing his own great-grandfather's songs. He still performs today, in a variety of spaces and for wide variety of audiences; for example, during cultural tours for tourists, welcome to Country ceremonies, cultural awareness training sessions for mining and industry, NAIDOC week celebrations, various opening events for buildings and galleries, and a play that celebrates a Ngarluma Thabi composer. While this is a very positive result, founded on the community's possession of Thabi recordings, it is just one contribution to the objective of strengthening and revitalising the tradition in the broader Ngarluma community. How are we proceed from here in order to realise this aspiration?

As we begin 2017, there has been a major shift in my own thinking about the potential of the technology. In this chapter I have recalled my past experiences with the community's adaptation to new technologies: from reel-to-reel tape to cassette, then to digital platforms such as iTunes, and more recently to more mobile devices like iPods and USBs. The major innovation in recent years has been the smartphone that incorporates a music player (such as the iTunes application on iPhone). But even this is starting to seem out-dated, as services like Apple Beats and Spotify change the landscape of music listening.

To overcome the hurdles we have had in the past, we are beginning to explore a new format for streaming archival material. The Thabi genre seems to be suited to the new streaming platforms, as the songs are public and short in length (rarely longer that 2–3 minutes long), and the identification of composers and singers makes the process for sorting the songs much like the one used in mainstream music libraries hosted on platforms like Spotify. But the major consideration is that there exists a community of younger Ngarluma men and women who are already engaged with such streaming platforms. These are the same sorts of community members who drove the initial move from tape to USB and iPods, and today they drive the demand for the newer types of digital platform. The challenge is again laid before our community to ensure that the latest technology does not alter our traditions and our cultural values beyond recognition but rather enhances and strengthens them. Any innovations must support the resolve of our elders to achieve the revitalisation of Thabi.

Conclusion

There is an established body of research on the ways in which singers and song communities in Australia have used their musical systems to adapt to changing social environments. Our own preliminary research suggests that singers of Thabi in the period from the 1930s to the 1960s used that genre in the same way, as a means of responding to a range of novel environmental factors in the west Pilbara, including war, working conditions, new modes of transport, new settlements and new industries. Our ongoing research seeks to examine how the descendants of these singers are, today, revitalising the Thabi genre through the recirculation of their forebears' songs in order to adapt and respond to the new environments – social and digital – of the twenty-first century.

The case study provided by Dowding illuminates the process that communities go through when they access audio archives of their cultural heritage. It demonstrates the power of auditioning recordings for elders and younger generations alike, and the intimacy of the intergenerational knowledge transmission that this listening stimulates. It also shows how digital formats can be edited, and enhanced with metadata, to support cultural sensitivities and at the same time facilitate access to the material on personal mobile devices, car radios and in homes. In addition, Dowding's account makes clear how much care must be taken when auditioning unedited archival recordings. While the jarring experience of hearing sensitive material in an hour-long file led to community apprehension and a temporary halt to listening, responsive editing and the development of metadata enabled elders to restrict access to some material and users to select and listen to public materials via their personal devices. This made ongoing access possible and supported the beginnings of a revitalisation of the tradition. The intention now is to develop ways to feed the new metadata back to the archive, for ongoing use by Ngarluma and the broader audiences of Thabi.

References

Akerman, Kim, 1979, The renascence of Aboriginal Law in the Kimberleys. In R. M. Berndt and C. H. Berndt, eds. Aborigines of the west: their past and their present, 234–242. Perth, WA: University of Western Australia Press.

Altman, Jon, 2005, Brokering Aboriginal art: a critical perspective on marketing, institutions, and the state. Geelong, VIC: Deakin University.

Barwick, Linda, 2011, Musical form and style in Murriny Patha Djanba songs at Wadeye (Northern Territory, Australia). In Michael Tenzer and John Roeder, eds. Analytical and cross-cultural studies in world music, 303–342. New York: Oxford University Press.

—— 2017, Keepsakes and surrogates: hijacking music technology at Wadeye (northwest Australia). In Thomas Hilder, Shzr Ee Tan and Henry Stobart, eds. Music, indigeneity, digital media, 156–175. Rochester, NY: University of Rochester Press.

Brandenstein, Carl Georg von, and A. J. Thomas, 1974, Taruru: Aboriginal song poetry from the Pilbara. Adelaide: Rigby.

Brown, Alexander, Brian Geytenbeek, and Jilalga Murray, 2003, Ngarla songs. Fremantle, WA: Fremantle Arts Centre Press.

Glowczewski, Barbara, 1998, The meaning of 'one' in Broome, Western Australia: from Yawuru tribe to Rubibi Corporation. Aboriginal History 22:203–222.

Jebb, Maryanne, and Doug Marmion, 2015, Singing the train: a Nyamal song is heard again. In Nicholas Ostler and Brenda Lintinger, eds. The music of endangered languages (Proceedings of the 19th Foundation for Endangered Languages Conference), 122–127. Bath, UK: Foundation for Endangered Languages.

McCardell, Anthony, 1970, Thabi songs of the Pilbara: a musical survey. BA Honours thesis, University of Western Australia, Perth.

Marett, Allan, 2007, Simplifying musical practice in order to enhance local identity: the case of rhythmic modes in the Walakandha wangga (Wadeye, Northern Territory). Australian Aboriginal Studies 2007(2):63–75.

Moyle, Alice, 1977, Songs from the Kimberleys. Canberra: Australian Institute of Aboriginal Studies. Online at *http://aiatsis.gov.au/sites/default/files/docs/asp/song-from-the-kimberleys.pdf* [accessed 6 March 2017].

—— 1978, Aboriginal sound instruments. Canberra: Australian Institute of Aboriginal Studies. Online at *http://aiatsis.gov.au/sites/default/files/products/cd/aboriginal-sound-instruments.pdf* [accessed 6 March 2017].

Redmond, Anthony, and Fiona Skyring, 2010, Exchange and appropriation: the Wurnan economy and Aboriginal land and labour at Karunjie Station, north-western Australia. In Ian Keen, ed. Indigenous participation in Australian economies, 73–84. Canberra: ANU E-press.

3

Ngadiji: for women and men also.

A song and dance continuing to be performed by the Yanyuwa of the Gulf area of the Northern Territory

Margaret C. Sharpe
University of New England

Abstract

Ngadiji (also spelt *Ngadirdji*) is a song and dance cycle received in a dream in about 1935 by Elma Brown, a Yanyuwa woman from the Borroloola region, in the south-west of the Gulf of Carpentaria. It continues to be popular among the Yanyuwa people and is regularly performed. It is about the 'mermaid women', surreptitiously observed by the admiring male spirit Yirrinju (or Yurrunju). Traditionally, the melodic contour belonged to women's secret business, but was approved for public performance when this was legitimised by Elma Brown's dream. Ngadiji includes male dancers mimicking the peeping Yirrinju, and a verse where participating males dance both the men's and women's steps. Other writers, in particular Mackinlay and Bradley (2003) have dealt in detail with the dreaming background of Ngadiji. The present chapter complements the extant literature through an analysis of the rhythms and beating patterns, the melodic contours, the dance movements, and the song-texts. It is intended as a potential resource for the transmission of the Ngadiji cycle. Ngadiji continues to be performed as of 2015, sometimes danced, and used in processions in Borroloola on such occasions as NAIDOC Week.[1]

Keywords: Ngadiji, Yanyuwa, Borroloola, Australian Aboriginal, song, dance, sex roles

Introduction

The Yanyuwa people of the Borroloola area, in the south-west of the Gulf of Carpentaria, have an extensive body of compositions in their own song-dance styles (see particularly Mackinlay 1998), but a number of traditions from other places have been incorporated into their repertoires: *Yawulhu* from the Mount Isa area; *Malkirri* (fun dances) from the Mornington Island area; a song-dance from a Marra man; and *Ngadiji*, which is the focus of the present

---

1 Many thanks to my colleague Dr Cat Kutay, also interested in the preservation of Aboriginal languages and traditions, for her editing help and suggestions in revision of this chapter, and to Acacia Kutay for improving the presentation of the music and rhythms.

paper. *Ngadiji* (also spelt '*Ngadirdji*'), is based on a melodic contour from Central Australia, where it is used in women's secret/sacred songs and dances. The borrowing and trading of songs and their texts is a regular practice throughout Aboriginal Australia, but other cases I am aware of (from eastern Australia) suggest that the recipients of the new cultural elements may not be aware of the deeper significance of the songs, or even understand the meaning of the text.

In this chapter, I present an analysis of the 21 verses of the Ngadiji song cycle, in terms of their rhythms and beating patterns, melodic contours, texts and dance movements. With the texts I have included glosses and commentaries, where possible. (In some cases the words were unfamiliar to my Yanyuwa collaborators.) Ngadiji is well established in the Borroloola area, and was still being performed in 2015. Nonetheless, an analysis of the present kind may prove to be useful as an educational tool to assist with its transmission, or to revitalise it if the Ngadiji tradition were to decline.

Research context

In 1994–95, I was the chief investigator in a large ARC grant project on Aboriginal song and dance, which took me, Megan Morais (a dance ethnologist), and Elizabeth Mackinlay (then an ethnomusicology student under the late Catherine Ellis) to the south-west of the Gulf of Carpentaria, in the Northern Territory. Catherine Ellis was initially second chief investigator, the project being to study songs and dances among the Yanyuwa in the Borroloola area. Circumstances led to Mackinlay withdrawing from the team. However, she had begun and continued with valuable research (e.g. Mackinlay 1998) on the Yanyuwa women's song genres and song partners (who work together to compose songs). All three of us already had been given kin (or 'skin group') classification, Morais from her work on Warlpiri dance (Dail-Jones 1984, Ellis et al. 1990, Morais 1992), Mackinlay through her husband, a Yanyuwa man, and me from my work with the Alawa. I also had a reasonable fluency in Kriol, the lingua franca of that area of northern Australia.

At the time the project started, our aim was to look at the language of the texts of the songs, the melodic contours and rhythmic accompaniment, and the dance movements. Morais and I were planning to see how these three components contributed to the overall meaning of songs and accompanying dances.[2] The direction of our research was determined by what we were given access to. The community was welcoming and helpful to us, and one of the McDinny women gave us the use of her house for the project.

There were three doctoral theses known to me from researchers who had spent much longer times in the field with the Yanyuwa people and had been immersed in and had studied the social contexts: John Bradley (1997)[3], Richard Baker (1990) and John Avery (1985). Under the circumstances, our project focused on analysis of the language forms, melodic contour, rhythms and dance movements, and how each of these contributed to enrich the overall 'message' of the songs and dances. To an extent, I used the etic/emic methods described well by Pike (1947, 1967), which were also used by Chenoweth (1979:119ff) in analysing Usarufa music in Papua New Guinea. Although Morais (1994) made many notes about social context and so on, I do not touch on this here, except to note the circumstances of some performances, not all attended by me.

---

2   Some of Morais's findings have been published (e.g. Morais 1998).
3   See also Bradley (1988), Bradley with Kirton and the Yanyuwa community (1992), Bradley and Mackinlay (2000) and Mackinlay and Bradley (2003). Bradley spoke the males' form of the language fluently. See Kirton (1988) on the differences in the dialects.

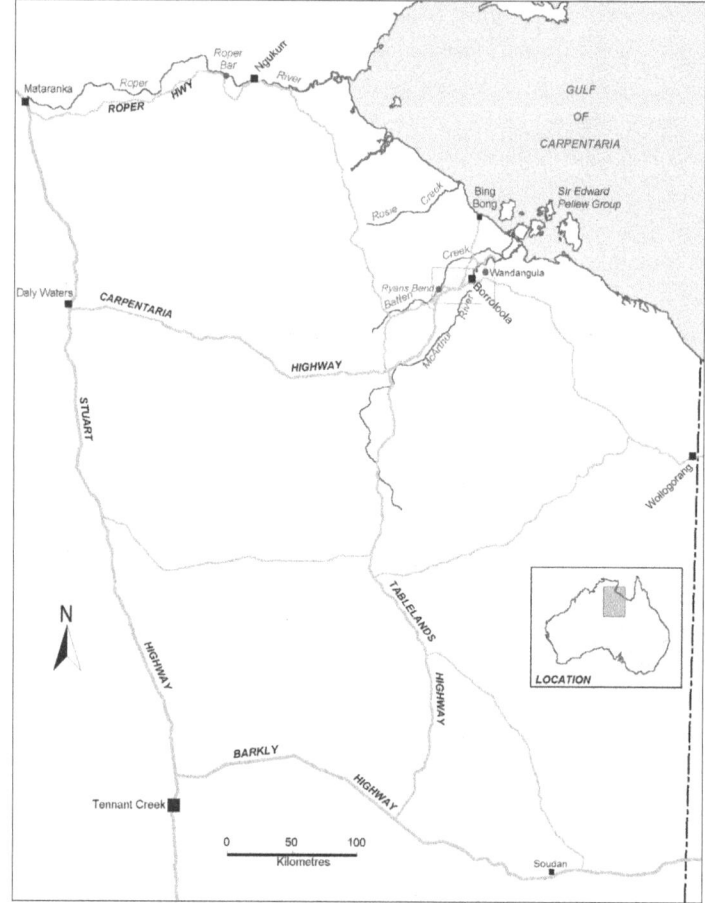

Map 3.1: Portion of the Northern Territory, showing Borroloola and the surrounding area (prepared by Michael Roach, Cartographer, UNE)

The discussion that follows falls into two main parts. In the first part, I present some background on Ngadiji, covering its history and reception as well as its significance for the Yanyuwa community. The second part incorporates my analyses of the various structural components of a Ngadiji performance, beginning with the musical (rhythmic and melodic) elements, moving on to dance movements and concluding with the song-texts. This last section includes a transcription of the texts of all 21 verses of the Ngadiji set, with glosses where available, and also notation of the rhythms and beating patterns.

The chapter is accompanied by a video recording of a Ngadiji performance that incorporates five of the 21 verses of the complete song cycle (some of them repeated a number of times). It is available here for viewing and download. A key to the verses being performed in the video is provided at the end of the paper.

  Video example 3.1 *'Ngadiji*. It's for women and men too.' Videoed at Wandangula by Megan Morais, 30 August 1994.

1 Ngadiji: origin, reception and history

Elma Bunubunu Brown (c. 1915–1987) received the Ngadiji song and dance sequence in a dream, around 1935 when she was about 19–20 years old. She was working on the Barkly Tablelands and living with her husband at Soudan Station, where she camped a bit apart from the other women (Sharpe 2003:69). When she returned to Borroloola, they stopped at Ryan's Bend, where she was reintegrated into Yanyuwa society. She taught other women the songs and dances. Elma later married Jerry Brown, who had composed another song-dance sequence, *Kalwangarra*. He became boss of *a-Ngadiji* after her death, until his own death some time after I was in the community.

During our time at Wandangula, an outstation some 13 kilometres from the Borroloola township (see Map 3.1), the Yanyuwa community performed Ngadiji and other songs and dances. They were accustomed to performing in other places as well, including Tennant Creek, Barunga, the Garma festival at Nhulunbuy and the University of Queensland, when Mackinlay was teaching there. Ngadiji, with its percussive beating, is a particular favourite for singing in procession on special occasions, such as NAIDOC Day in Borroloola. I saw this happen in 2002, and I found, in 2015, that it was still performed, and sometimes danced, on such occasions.[4]

Elma Brown's dream, which was given to her in the Wakaya language of the Tablelands, concerned a group of mermaid women who were taking part in a ceremony meant for women only. Unbeknownst to them, they were being spied on by a male spirit or merman in a 'wrong way' relationship to them (Bradley pers. com.), who was attracted by the beautiful dancing. The women caught sight of the merman, whose name was *Yirrinju*, and told him that it was a *Yawulyu* for women only. He begged to continue watching, and felt it was such a good song that it should be shared by both men and women. The Dreaming Women agreed to this suggestion. The performed sequences almost always begin with the dance for males only, which is a symbolic endorsement of their decision.

Bradley et al. (1992) give information that links the Ngadiji song cycle with Dreaming activities sung about in the *Kunapipi* ceremony (*a-Kunabibi* in Yanyuwa). The meeting between the *a-Ngadiji* Dreaming Women of the Barkly Tablelands and the *a-Mararabarna* Dreaming Women from the sea are sung about in both song cycles.[5] These *a-Mararabarna*[6] Dreaming Women are associated with the Rrumburriya semi-moiety, and are an important Dreaming for both men and women in the *Kunapipi* ceremony, as is also true of the *Walalu* whirlwind dreaming of the Mambaliya-Wawukarriya-Rrumburriya semi-moiety. On Wallhallow Station on the Tablelands is a long lagoon, Kalabirrngarni, where the Saltwater Dreaming women (the *a-Mararabarna*) entered into the ground after dancing *Kunapipi* ceremonies with the Ngadiji Dreaming women from the south. Bradley reported that the *a-Mararabarna* (or *a-Marrarrabarna*) 'established a charter for Yanyuwa women which gives strength and credence to their roles of hunting and nurturing' (Bradley et al. 1992:110). *Yirrinju* or *Yurrunju*,[7] the male spirit found spying on the Dreaming Women, is the bearer of fire (*buyuka* 'fire'), and also features in *a-Marndiwa* circumcision song and ceremony. The song in *a-Marndiwa* invokes him to

---

4   This wide diffusion of the ceremony is probably of recent date. Alice Moyle (1974:31) reported that 'Apart from the fact that it was a women's corroboree and had come from the south-east, from Borroloola, little was known at Rose River about the series called Ngadidji.'
5   The older pronunciation seems to have been *marrarrabarna* (Bradley pers. com. 2002).
6   *a-* is the most commonly used feminine prefix in Yanyuwa.
7   As sung and referred to in speech to me, the pronunciation was *yirrinju*; however, Bradley uses the variant form *yurrunju*. The stress is on the first syllable, unlike in its sung version.

help deaden the pain of circumcision that the boys will undergo in that ceremony (Bradley pers. com.).

Ngadiji thus brings together a number of contrary forces. Apart from juxtaposing men and women, its performance connects the Ngadiji women who come from the desert country on the Barkly Tablelands and the *a-Mararabarna* who have come from the sea just to the north of Borroloola. Both must be present to authentically tell the story of the two groups. The story embodies the tensions between the mainland and the sea in Yanyuwa thinking and movements, and this is illustrated by the dancers coming together and then moving away.

Ngadiji is a 'public' dance form, which means that participation as performer or audience is not restricted. Nonetheless, as Mackinlay (2000) and Mackinlay and Bradley (2003) discuss, this dance may also carry restricted meanings, because of the involvement of both the mermaid women and *Yirrinju* in initiation ceremonies. Moreover, Ngadiji uses a melodic contour that was from the women's secret tradition.[8] The esoteric significance is only accessible to those who have the relevant knowledge.

2 Formal analysis

As mentioned above, there are 21 sung texts, or 'verses', in the Ngadiji song cycle. In the research team's experience, these comprise the total number of verses. I have included below a transcription of all 21 of the texts we obtained and labelled them with a number and also with a key word from the text, usually the first word of the verse. For each of the verses, this transcription incorporates a gloss (where available), notation of the rhythms and beating patterns, and sometimes a commentary. It is followed by a table that correlates the song texts with the associated dance movements.

Although two of the senior women participating asserted there was a set order of verses in Ngadiji, the impression we had was there was not a fixed order in actual performance, although there were strong preferences. Anderson (1995) found order was not fixed in his Arnhem Land material, and Richard Moyle (1986:63) found that was also true of the Centralian music he worked on. The videoed performance that accompanies this chapter includes five distinct song texts, some of them repeated a number of times, but the order of verses differs somewhat from the sequence in my transcription. This is true also of the longer video made by the research team, which incorporates 14 of the verses (with dancing).

2.1 The percussive beat: rhythms and beating patterns

The percussive beats in Ngadiji are evenly spaced (see the sample musical transcription of Text 1, '*yirrinju*', in Musical example 3.3). Usually the leader begins beating after (s)he starts singing the text. Beats are always on the same syllables in the text, and beating continues for a short time after singing ceases. Leaders use clapping boomerangs when available.

I call the two speeds of beating 'single beat' and 'double beat'. (One of the performers also used the term 'double' for the latter.) If the timing of double beats is regarded as having crotchet spacing, single beats have minim timing. In the normal three-section melodic contour (see 2.2, below), beating usually ceases for two or more minims as the end of the second section approaches, and resumes on a breath intake or syllable /a/ before the leader launches into the third melodic section. During that break in beating, the dancers cease movement, to resume when the beating restarts. Beating tempo is of the order of 80 or 160 beats per minute. Usually

---

[8] Also used in a publicly released CD recording of Yawulyu Mungamunga of the Warumungu women, which is rhythmically annotated in Barwick et al. (2000).

there is a slight and gradual increase in tempo over the singing of a verse; performance of each verse lasts about 30 seconds.

Many verses may be accompanied by a single or double beat, except that no. 18 (*bijaja*) is always performed with a double beat. All texts except no. 9 (*nangala wadarimba*) and no. 16b (*yarukajikaji*) are a full number of minims in length; these texts have to be sung twice for the single beat to re-occur on the same syllable. Texts 5 (*bijaja*) and 19 (*wakaya*), with the form AABB, have a triple time effect and require repetition of lines to conform to the pattern of a full number of minims.

With little exception and with minor performance variation, each syllable in a text is sung over a quaver, a crotchet, a dotted crotchet or a minim. In a few cases a syllable may approach a dotted quaver followed by a semiquaver, and in text 10 (*yinjila*) this appears to be the norm at the beginning of the text.

The three-section melodic contour can be used for all verses, but the alternative four-section contour can only be used for texts 1, 7 and 8 (*yirrinju, nangala* and *ngadiji* respectively). In this case, the leader commences a rattled beat as (s)he begins singing (not later). The first and third sections are accompanied by the rattled beat, and the second and fourth by the single beat. There is no break in the beating in this contour, which is only used for the males dancing movements M2 and M3 (see section 2.3.2, 'Main movements used in Ngadiji').

2.2 The melodic contour

There are two related melodic contours used in Ngadiji. Both cover an octave or slightly more, beginning on an upper tonic and finishing on a lower tonic. Each of the contours can be separated into sections which begin with a breath intake and often a vowel /a/ (usually quaver-length) sung at a slightly higher pitch; in each section there is a fading of volume towards its end, this being most marked in the final section, which has a longer 'coda' on the lower tonic.

The most commonly sung contour, shown in Musical example 3.1, has three sections separated by breath intakes, and only the initial section descends over the range of an octave to the lower tonic. This contour is used for all verses. The 'x' in these examples indicates the clapped beat, and '– – – –' indicates that this pattern continues to a break indicated by '/'. The other two sections, similar to each other except that the final section ends in a longer time of singing on the lower tonic, range over about a sixth. In the initial section the leader begins singing on or near the upper tonic, and is joined by other singers before the descent begins. In its form, Ngadiji is a typical example of Centralian song patterns: at the start there is usually an extended segment of singing on or near the upper tonic, the singing then drops in pitch, finally coming to rest on a lower tonic, where singing fades out. After each breath intake within the contour there is a rise in pitch before singing again descends to the lower tonic. For this contour, single or double beats can be used, and the beating almost always starts after the upper tonic has been established. There is a pause in the beating pattern towards the end of the second section, and a resumption of beating with the breath intake for the third section. Dancers respond to the break by ceasing movement and straightening up and looking straight ahead if bent forward.

Musical example 3.1: The three-descent melodic contour and its clapped beat

The other contour, shown in Musical example 3.2, has four descents, again separated by breath intakes. Each descent is over an octave, or nearly so, beginning on the upper tonic, but descending quite rapidly from it towards the lower tonic. For this pattern, there is rattle-beating over the first and third descents (marked with ≈), and clapped beating over the second and fourth descents. This contour is only used for texts 1, 7 and 8, accompanied by the dance steps indicating the performance is for both males and females. For these verses, contour 1 is used when the dancers are kneeling and watching, and contour 2 when they are standing up with arms spread, doing men's or women's steps.

Musical example 3.2: The four-descent melodic contour and its rattled and clapped beat

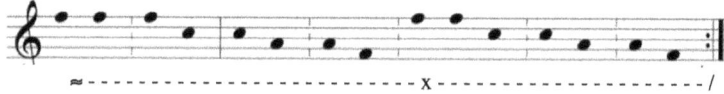

These two examples are notated in the emic pitches as I have analysed them. In both patterns, pitches of notes in the contour are far more variable than in Western music, and there can be glissandi between pitches. However, the pitches cluster around certain intervals in the 'scale' sung.

From my analysis, there are four emic scale steps in the melodic contour. Variation or inflection of these pitches can be accounted for by their position in the contour or section, by traditional conventions of singing this genre, by choices made by the leader(s) within these conventions as they lead the performance, by varying abilities of singers in pitching notes, and by the wider range of approximations to scale step in the singing of traditional-style music by a group which did not have strictly tuned instruments in use. Musical example 3.3 (below) shows a transcription of three different repetitions (a, b and c in the left margin of the transcription) of the three-descent contour for Text 1 (*yirrinju*). The variations as transcribed are typical of the various renditions of the melodic contour. The position of the transcriptions on the stave is chosen so the whole notation will fit within the treble clef stave, rather than to accurately reproduce actual pitch.

Lauridsen's discussion of the contours she was working on (Lauridsen 1983:37–38) should be kept in mind here:

1. The great majority of intervals fall within a fifth above the tonic. This is significant only in so far as it demonstrates the fact that many Aboriginal songs have a narrow range, often defining the limits of a melodic undulation.

2. There are a number of small, microtonal intervals above the tonic, intervals slightly larger than a half step (1.06) and smaller. This in part reflects the common practice of inflecting the tonic, particularly in songs consisting only of one main pitch with some inflection or embellishment marking phrase beginnings and endings.

3. The frequent occurrence of the frequency ratio 1.22 provides evidence for the presence of the 'neutral third' in Aboriginal music. This interval, falling halfway between a major and a minor third, has often been observed in Aboriginal music, and it is here shown to be among the most common of the intervals measured in this study.

4. The overall distribution of frequency ratios shows definite areas of high and low concentration, even in the area between 1.00 and 1.50, where the concentration is in general high. This suggests the existence of some system or systems of pitch preference operating within Aboriginal music traditions that determines which intervals are appropriate and which are not.

If there were a wider divergence of interval types in Aboriginal music, or if performers sang intervals arbitrarily or carelessly, a graph would show a more even distribution.

Musical example 3.3: Sample transcription of sung Text 1 ('Yirrinju')

It should also be kept in mind that in languages like Yanyuwa, where there are only three emicly distinct vowels, these can vary in ways which would not be possible for a language like English, where there are far more distinctions. (This is a bugbear to linguists working with old records of Aboriginal languages, and is complicated also by the English spelling system.) As in speech, so in musical pitches: a less finely divided system allows more variation in the allophones of an emic position. It is also clear that in singing, vowels can be distorted from vowels in the spoken text. The voice quality or timbre is different in singing than in speech due to the often wider mouth position (Sharpe 1970). Lauridsen also observed that the Yanyuwa have a more limited scale when the songs include didjeridu accompaniment, being constrained by the didjeridu fundamental and the hoot pitches.

Yanyuwa people distinguish between good and not-so-good singers, but those who are to any extent 'tone-deaf' are never excluded from performing.

2.3 The dance movements

In Warlpiri dance, Stephen Wild (1975) noted that men's dance movements were more clearly mimetic than women's. This would certainly apply to a number of the dances and dance genres I have seen performed by the Yanyuwa, but not to all. A number of the *Nguyulnguyul* (women's composition) items appear to have similar mimesis for both sexes; there may, however, be subtle distinctions.

In Ngadiji, there is a correlation between the meanings of certain texts and the dance movement of walking, shuffling forward or shuffling sideways (i.e. travelling,) but as meanings were not obtainable for all texts, and not all texts in our corpus had danced versions, this is tentative. For all doubled beat versions of texts, the most common movement was for the women and girls to bounce forward with knee-clapping. When knee-clapping and bouncing forward, the dancers' hands usually held skirts or an 'object', but the hands were not moved relative to the torso. For two verses a less common alternative 'movement' could also occur: kneeling and hand-clapping or kneeling and moving their 'boards'[9] in time with the doubled beat. There was also correlation between texts where the explanation included reference to sticks or a *daladala* board and women and girls holding a board, stick or a substitute (sometimes imaginary) in the dance.

When men and boys kneel and act as *Yirrinju* spying on the women, the reference is reasonably obvious, particularly, as Bradley informs me, when performed by adults!

There are about a dozen main dance movements or combinations of movements which were used in danced performances of Ngadiji in our recordings in 1994 and 1995, and for these we only have video records of dancing to 14 of the 21 texts.[10] For the women and girls there are variants of their nine or so movements, according to the style of locomotion (walking, shuffling, bouncing) and also according to whether dancers hold their skirts or pants, put hands behind backs, or hold a 'board' or 'stick' or 'bunch of feathers'[11], and so forth. The actual *daladala* boards which were illustrated by Bradley et al. (1992) were never seen in the performances we recorded. Shorter or longer sticks randomly picked up were used, as well as other props.

The main Ngadiji dance movements are classified below, in section 2.3.1[12], then listed in 2.3.2. Using principles of the emic method, I suggest how some movements group together or contrast. In my original work (Sharpe 2003:128 ff), I notated many of these movements with

---

9   Object names are put in quotes, such as 'boards', 'sticks', 'bunch of feathers', as frequently an imaginary object was manipulated, or a hat or cloth item, etc. substituted.
10 The 14 verses danced and video-recorded were: 1 (yirrinju), 3 (marrarraba), 6 (warrurldu), 7 (nangala), 8 (ngadiji), 10 (yinjila), 12 (yamala), 14 (ngadijarri), 15 (dibijang), 16 (yarukaji(kaji)), 18 (wadimba), 19 (wakaya), 20 (mungamunga), and 21 (yarrngijirri). Of these, Text 18 was only recorded with doubled beat, in both audio and video recordings.
11 See footnote 9.
12 The illustrative video clip that accompanies this chapter incorporates five of the Ngadiji verses, with some repetitions. There is a key to this video at the end of the chapter. The 'comments' column shows which movements were correlated with which verses.

Benesh Movement Notation (BMN), introduced to me by Morais, and I was able to check these with Joanne Page in Sydney. The help of these two experts has been invaluable in the analysis.

Some descriptions I use here to describe the movements are fairly transparent in meaning: terms such as 'walking' and 'clapping hands' are used in their everyday senses. I use the term 'shuffling' for a movement forward or sideways where it seems irrelevant whether the feet are in close contact with the ground or not, and where the forward or sideways movement seems determined by the placement and orientation of the dancers in the dance area. I have coined the term 'knee-clapping' for the movement of clapping knees together.

Some BMN terms are useful; I define them here:

> 'supporting an object' = holding an object
> 'supported' = when sitting, kneeling or lying the body is said to be supported by the part of the body bearing the weight
> 'contact' = touching a part of the body or another person
> 'skimming' = where the foot or feet are in contact, partial contact or close to contact with the ground while the movement is being executed
> 'sliding' = the foot is kept in contact with the ground and slid along the ground
> 'bouncing'[13] = describes forward jumping or skimming in the style described for Movement 7 (see 2.3.2 below); that is, bouncing forward with knee clapping.

In Yanyuwa dancing of Ngadiji (and also of other genres) there was considerable variation in renditions by different dancers. However, many of these were young children, some barely beyond toddler stage, some in their teens. Both Morais and I noticed some who more clearly knew what they were doing.

I use principles enunciated by Ken Pike (1947, 1967) to group some movements. Where very similar movements are used in the same positions in different performances, sometimes to the same verses, and they do not contrast within one danced item, a strong case can be made that they are emically the same movement. Where there is a clear contrast in similar movements within one dance by one dancer, there is a strong case that these movements are emically distinct.

2.3.1 Classification of movement types in Ngadiji

Dance movements, as I am analysing them here, are made up of choices from foot and leg movements or postures; hand and arm gestures including holding (supporting) things; and body torso and head positions. Ground pattern of movement is also relevant.

Foot and leg movements

For males there is:

> kneeling
> standing and sliding feet from side to side
> standing and stamping.

For females there is:

> kneeling and hand-clapping,
> standing and knee-clapping,
> jumping or bouncing forward with knee-clapping,
> walking forward (always in single file),
> shuffling forward, sideways or diagonally forward.

---

13 This term was also used by Morais, but in the older published resources available to me on BMN, this term is not defined.

The three shuffling movements could be regarded as variants of each other. They appear to be determined by the starting position of the dancer(s), where they chose to move towards, and the speed required to get there in the time allowed in singing the text. Walking or shuffling was also affected when more experienced dancers were towing learners with them. On the basis of the limited evidence, including that from texts, I have called these three movements 'travelling', a term which includes walking. Within the overall picture of the two groups travelling, this action is a reflection of the partly concealed restricted meaning, of which public explanations may not necessarily be given.

Hand and arm gestures

For boys and men there is

    hands behind back, and
    arms extended sideways when standing.

For women and girls there is

    hands behind roughly at pelvic level, or in pockets,
    hands holding their skirts or pants,
    holding a shorter or longer 'stick' close to waist,
    holding this item forward from waist, or
    holding this item at shoulder height
    holding a 'bunch of feathers' in one hand, holding skirt in the other.

Except when bouncing forward with knee-clapping, the 'stick' may be moved in a specified way. Clapping can be done while kneeling or sitting, by both males and females. At the temporary cessation of the percussive beat at the second lower tonic approach, dancers would cease movement, and often drop hands to their sides.

Head and torso movements

In all of the more vigorous movements (boys stamping or sliding feet, women except when kneeling), there was a tendency to bend the torso forward, more marked with some dancers than others. Competent female dancers bent their heads forward to direct their gaze towards the ground or their feet. However, at the cessation of the percussive accompaniment at the end of the second descent in the melodic contour, most women would straighten to an upright position, raise heads to look ahead, and often drop hands to their sides. With the women and girls also, and, particularly for some dancers, the torso was bent sideways (the head also bending in that direction), alternating direction every few beats. Dancers dancing in circles also inclined their heads towards the centre of the circle. Torso bending was particularly marked with the almost teenaged Cecilia (who performs solo in another videoed performance). Although quite badly hearing impaired, and lacking intelligible speech, Cecilia was an intelligent and apparently literate girl and one of the better dancers. One other excellent dancer was the late Annie Karrakayn (c. 1934–2008), who demonstrated a number of dance steps. In her performances, in many instances, she included a greater variety of movements than other dancers did.

2.3.2 Main movements used in Ngadiji

Men's and boys' movements

M1	kneeling and observing	boys kneeling and twisting from side to side
M2	sliding	boys standing and sliding feet from side to side
M3	stamping	boys stamping feet

Women's and girls' movements

M4	walking	moving forward in single file
M5	knee-clapping	standing clapping knees together with slight bounce
M6	shuffling forwards	moving forward in single file, shuffle step
M6a	shuffling sideways	moving sideways in a row
M7	bouncing forward	bouncing forward with knee-clapping
M8	displaying board	holding 'stick' and moving it up and down a little, with knee-clapping
M8a	displaying board	as M8, except hands move in vertical circles
M9	presenting the board	holding 'stick' well forward of body and moving it up and down a little, kneeling or with knee-clapping
M10	holding board close	holding 'stick' close to thighs or pelvic area, with knee-clapping, moving it back and forth horizontally
M11	arm swinging	swinging arms freely, with no 'stick', with knee-clapping
M12	displaying long 'stick'	holding 'stick' (usually a longer 'stick') level with or above shoulders and moving it diagonally sideways and back, again with knee-clapping
M12 a	using digging stick(?)	similar to M12 but with more pronounced 'digging' or 'spearing' motion
M13	bouncing forward	as in M7 (bouncing forward with knee-clapping), one hand holding bunch of 'feathers'
M14	clapping while seated	clapping while sitting or kneeling

2.3.3 Patterns of placement and progression of dancers

Figure 3.1 shows the general layout used in a performance. Dancing women enter from the back left or right of the performance area.

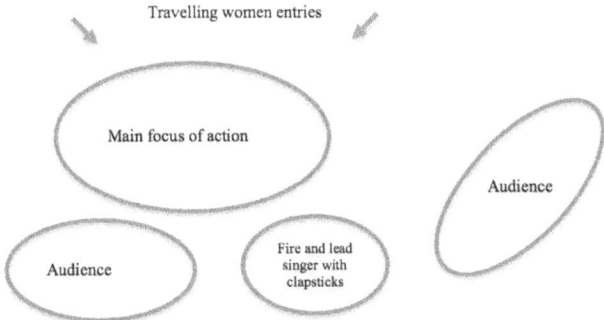

Figure 3.1: Ngadiji performance layout

Most commonly a group of dancers formed a line, where they either were in single file or shoulder to shoulder. However, in some items the dancers just formed a crowd with no or little clear pattern: this happened when all boys got up to dance movements 2 and 3 (sliding, stamping respectively) as a group, after all had danced in pairs. Dancing in a crowd also occurred for girls in some dancing of Movement 7 (bouncing forward with knee-clapping).

For boys and men, the only arrangement is in a row or rows shoulder to shoulder facing front (except as noted in the above paragraph). They knelt in a row for Movement 1 (kneeling and observing), and usually performed in pairs for movements 2 and 3.

For women and girls, single file was used for Text 18 (*wadimba*) when they walked in a zig-zagging forward movement across the performance area; for other items, they could be in a row (shoulder to shoulder) and perform movements together or move forward or sideways.

When bouncing with knee-clapping (M7), the ideal pattern seems to be for a pair to dance together, one progressing clockwise and the other counter-clockwise in a small circle, or if larger numbers are dancing together, for them to move in a curved path.

2.4 Texts in the corpus

Ngadiji singers drop their jaws considerably when they sing loudly and move the tongue forward. This can shift high vowels to a lower position. Often a vowel dictated as [i] is heard as [a] or [e]. The articulatory setting can also contribute to mis-hearing of consonants. The flap/trill /rr/ may be heard more as a liquid, and the different patterns of juncture between syllables can contribute to mis-hearing of a nasal-stop sequence as a stop or nasal, and vice versa.

In the transcription that follows, I show texts, rhythms and beating accompaniments used for the 21 Ngadiji verses, with the usual musical symbols for repeats. 'DW' marks words claimed to be in the Dreaming Women's language. I show also if we have no gloss for a verse, and note if we did not have a videoed recording. Glosses included are from knowledgeable women, as are comments. My own observations are incorporated under the heading 'Notes'.

1. *yirrinju* (no gloss for DW words)

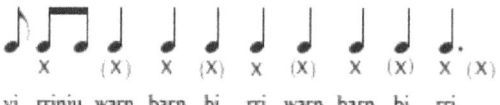

yi rrinju warn barn bi rri warn barn bi rri

Yirrinju warnbarnbirri   warnbarnbirri

Comment: *Yirrinju* spies on the Dreaming Women. He used to follow them to every camp, but they didn't see him.

2. *budburru* (no gloss, no video)

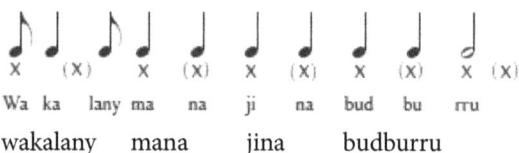

Wa ka lany ma na ji na bud bu rru

wakalany   mana   jina   budburru

Comment: *budburru* 'Women travelling, elders and young mob'.

3. *marrarraba*

wa ka lany ma na ji na marra rra ba

wakalany   mana   jina   marrarraba

Gloss: Dreaming Women call themselves Mararabarna or Marrarrabarna

4. *wulubarra* (not videoed)

wa ka lany ma na li la wulu ba rra

wakalany   mana   lila   wulubarra

Gloss: '*bin traveling*' (they) keep going

5. *bijaja* (no gloss obtained, not videoed)

|: bijaja jarrirri :| |: jarrirri la(m)bela bela(m)be :|

6. *warrurldu* (not videoed)

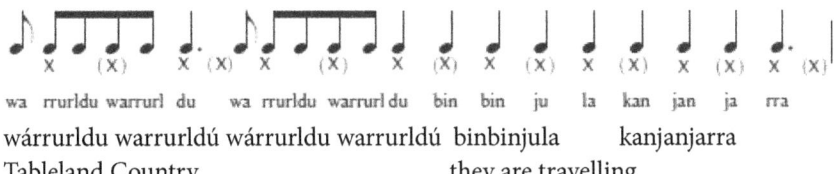

wárrurldu warrurldú wárrurldu warrurldú binbinjula   kanjanjarra
Tableland Country   they are travelling

Gloss: They are travelling in the Tableland plain country

7. *nangala* (no gloss given)

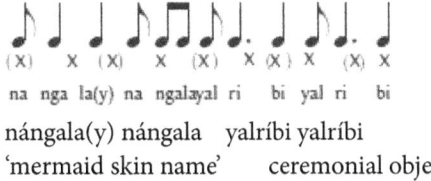

nángala(y) nángala   yalríbi yalríbi
'mermaid skin name'   ceremonial object

Comment: *Nangala* is the mermaid women's skin name

8. *ngadiji* (no gloss given)

ngadíji wárnbarnbalana   wárnbarnbalana   *ngádijé*

9. *nangala wadarimba* (no gloss given, not videoed)

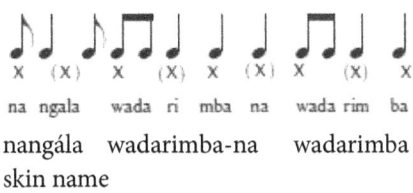

nangála wadarimba-na   wadarimba
skin name

10. *yinjila* (no gloss given)

(y)ínjilá   lawirnindi

11. *balungku* (no video)

balúngku balúngkú balúngku balungkú lhilhilhiya lhilhilhiya (balungku)
tree type   they bin travelling

Gloss: 'They bin travelling langa Barlungku country all the way down.'

12. *yamala* (no gloss given)

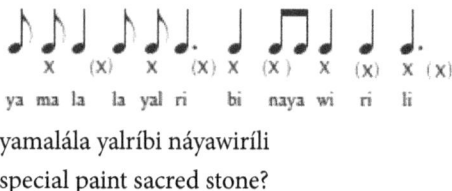

yamalála yalríbi náyawiríli
special paint sacred stone?

Comment: 'They kolim miselb dance skin name.' (They call themselves . . .)

13. *nginjarrarra* (no gloss given, no video)

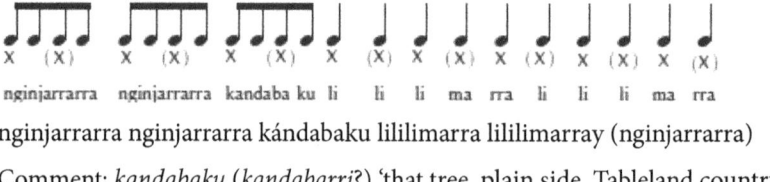

nginjarrarra nginjarrarra kándabaku lililimarra lililimarray (nginjarrarra)

Comment: *kandabaku* (*kandabarri*?) 'that tree, plain side, Tableland country'

14. *ngadijirri* (no gloss given)

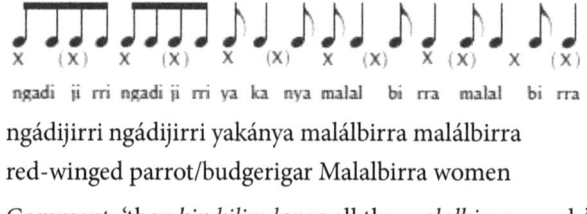

ngádijirri ngádijirri yakánya malálbirra malálbirra
red-winged parrot/budgerigar Malalbirra women

Comment: 'they *bin kilim langa* all the *malalbirra* people'

15. *dibijang* (no gloss obtained)

|: dibijáng árrarrarra :|: lángalángaláng arrarra :|

16a. *yarukaji* (no gloss obtained)

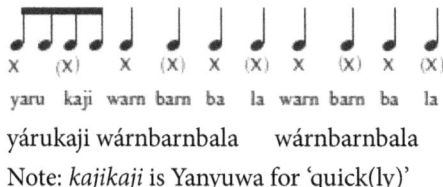

yárukaji wárnbarnbala wárnbarnbala

Note: *kajikaji* is Yanyuwa for 'quick(ly)'

16b. *yarukajikaji*

yarukajikaji warnbarnbala warnbarnbala

17. *arkalangala* (no gloss, no video)

arkalangakalang aríbibi aríbibi

18. *wadimba* (no gloss obtained)

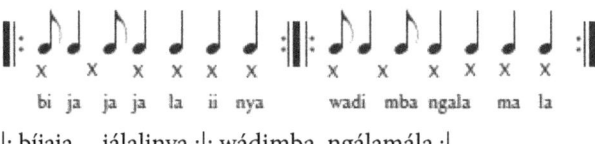

|: bíjaja jálalinya :|: wádimba ngálamála :|

19. *wakaya*

|: wakayá binalá jarrirri :|: mangarriji lá(m)belá béla(m)bé:|
Wakaya plain goanna

Comments: 'They're singing about two Waka women meeting up: Marra women and Wakaya women.'

20. *mungamunga* no gloss obtained

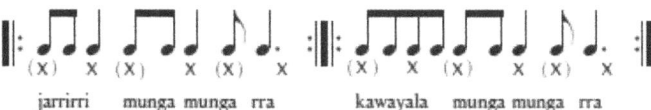

|: jarrirrí mungamúngarrá :|: káwayála mungamúngarrá:|
Mungamunga-? Mungamunga-?

Comment: 'They sing about the Mungamunga women from the Tablelands; women dance with small stick still.'

21. *yarrngijirri*

yárrngijirri yárrngijirri búyuka lá(m)belá béla(m)bé
fire

Gloss: 'Nakamarra or Nimala people light up fire, they sit down. They make fire and sit around.'
Comments: Fire belongs to *Wuyaliya* clan; 'They sing about the fire stick used to start fire.'
(Noted by Morais 1994.)

2.5 Correlation of texts, beats and dance movements

Table 3.1 charts the correlation of dance movements and beats with the texts of all 14 Ngadiji verses for which movements were recorded. (S = single beat, D = double beat, R = rattled beat.) In our observation, the other verses were not accompanied by dancing.

In most danced texts, one step is used throughout. However, there are some in which two or even three movements are used in sequence, as can be seen in the video. There are five such patterns, as shown below:[14]

Pattern 1: one movement throughout, except for stop when beating stops.
Pattern 2: one movement in Part 1, another movement in Part 2.
Pattern 3: sequence of 3 movements in Part 1, same sequence in Part 2.
Pattern 4: sequence of 3 movements in Part 1, 3 of these in sequence in Part 2.
Pattern 5: sequence of moving forward + arm action, same in Parts 1 and 2.

Table 3.1: Correlation of texts, beats and dance movements in Ngadiji performance

VERSE	BEAT	MOVEMENT	GLOSS
BOYS			
1 *yirrinju*	S R, S in turn	M1 M2, M3	*Yirrinju* spying includes women, men
7 *nangala*	R, S in turn	M2, M3	*Nangala* skin name
8 *ngadiji*	S R, S in turn	M1 M2, M3	*Ngadiji* Dreaming includes women, men, respectively
GIRLS			
1 *yirrinju*	S, R D	M14 (clapping) M7 (bouncing forward with knee-clapping)	
3 *marrarraba*	D	M7, M12a	Dreaming women call themselves *Marrarrabarna*.
6 *warrurldu*	S	M6, M11, M12a	travelling in *Warrurldu* country
7 *nangala*	D S	M7, M8 M6, M6A, M8, M11, M12, M12A, M6A + M6	*Nangala* skin name
8 *ngadiji*	D D S	M7, M7 + board, M8 M7 + stick held closed M14 (clapping)	
10 *yinjila*	S	M6 + stick, M6, M6a, M8, M8a, M10/M12	
12 *yamala*	D S	M7 with skirt or stick, M6a, M8, M11 (M6a with bounced arms) M6, M6a, M6a + M11, M11, M12a.	*marla* special paint, *yaribi* sacred stone

---

14 For more details, email me for my downloadable file with further information on dance patterns, including Benesh notations of these.

VERSE	BEAT	MOVEMENT	GLOSS
14 *ngadijirri*	D S	M7, M13 M6, M8, M12	*Malabirri* Tableland women dance as red-winged parrots.
15 *dibijang*	D S	M7 M6, M8 (M6 on last descending contour)	
16a *yarukajikaji*	D	M7, M6, M8, M6 + M8	
18 *wadimba*	D (always)	M4, M5, M6, M7, M8, M8a, M9, M10	
19 *wakaya*	S	M15 (patting)	*Waka(y)a* people were killing plain goanna all the way.
20 *munga*	D (rarely) S	M7 M5, M6, M8, M12a	They sing about the *mungamunga*.
21 *yarrngijirri*	D	M7	*Nakamarra* or *Nimala* people make a fire, and sit around. Fire belongs to *Wuyaliya* clan.

Conclusion

Music styles, as well as language, are liable to change with cultural change, especially when there is massive contact with a different musical culture. At the Lijakarda Festival at Wandangula in 1995, adults performed both traditional and contemporary songs, and since that first festival a Yanyuwa song in pop style first performed there has been choreographed by the women. There is very little evidence of mature younger men being seriously involved in (for example) the *Yalkawarru* funerary ceremony, except in the spectacular finale. More groups are producing new dances for special occasions, with influence from traditional dancing styles (as remembered or recalled) as well as from the current world around them. One is not justified in claiming that transmission of traditional styles is ceasing, but one is certainly justified in stating that such transmission is changing, perhaps being truncated. More contemporary styles are competing for audience, performers and mental space. However, it appears that Ngadiji is a fun dance-song with connections to some more serious ceremonies, and that this may help it to endure for a good while yet.

Table 3.2: Key to the videoed illustrations

TIME	TEXT	TEXT NAME	BEAT	COMMENT	STEP
0:14				Nancy McDinny lining boys up	
0.45	1	*yirrinju*	S	no beat pause, male(s) peeping	M1
1:54	1	*yirrinju*	R,S	2 boys: female-, then male-style dance in pairs	M2,3
3:30	7	*nangala*	R,S	2 boys: female-, then male-style dance in pairs	
4:00	7	*nangala*	R,S	all boys: female, then male dance	M2,3
4:40	5	*bijaja*	D	Women walk in line from back left, each verse changing direction and moving forward	M4
	5	*bijaja*	D	stand & knee clap in last part of contour	M5
6:33	5	*bijaja*		women return with same change of direction with each verse	M4,5
7:00	5	*bijaja*	D	Females sit in line, clap for a verse	
7:50	5	*bijaja*	D	2 girls at a time, jump circle	M7
	8	*ngadiji*	D	2 girls at a time, jump circle	M7
	7	*nangala*	D	2 girls at a time, jump circle	M7
	3	*marrarraba*	D	2 girls at a time, jump circle	M7

TIME	TEXT	TEXT NAME	BEAT	COMMENT	STEP
11:19	1 or 7	yirrinju or nangala	R,S	males stand and perform	M2,3
11:54, 12:20	20	mungamunga		girls from R from to L back to dance, diagonal line, shuffle, swinging arms; knee clapping, shuffle last section of contour	M6+11
13:30	8	ngadiji?	D	bouncing	M7
14:01	8	ngadiji	D	Annie Karrakayn, bounce forward with 'feathers'	M13
	8	ngadiji	D	bouncing	M7
14:45	–	–		interlude	
15:45	10	yinjala	S	shuffle in with 'sticks', knee clap while moving sticks	M8
17:15	10	yinjila		all sitting, singing and clapping	
17:50	1	yirrinju	S	all sitting, Dinny playing	
	1	yirrinju	R,S	hand clapping	
18:56				END	

References

Anderson, Greg, 1995, Striking a balance: limited variability in performances of a clan song series from Central Arnhem Land. In Linda Barwick, Allan Marett and Guy Tunstill, eds. The essence of singing and the substance of song, 12–25. Sydney: Oceania Monographs 46, University of Sydney.

Avery, John, 1985, The Law People: history, society and initiation in the Borroloola area of the Northern Territory. PhD thesis, University of Sydney.

Baker, Richard, 1990, Land is life: continuity through change for the Yanyuwa from the Northern Territory of Australia. PhD thesis, University of Sydney.

Barwick, Linda, with assistance of Papulu Apparr Kari and Jane Simpson, 2000, Yawulyu Mungamunga: dreaming songs of Warumungu women. Tennant Creek: Papulu Apparr Kari Language and Culture Centre.

Bradley, John, 1988, Men speak one way, women speak another Aboriginal Linguistics 1:126–134. (Dept of Linguistics, University of New England, Armidale, edited by Nicholas Evans and Steve Johnson.)

—— 1997, Li-Anthawirriyarra. People of the sea: Yanyuwa relations with their maritime environment. PhD thesis, Northern Territory University, Darwin.

Bradley, John, with Jean Kirton and the Yanyuwa Community, 1992, Yanyuwa wuka: language from Yanyuwa country. Bendigo: John Bradley.

Bradley, John, and Elizabeth Mackinlay, 2000, Songs from a plastic water rat: an introduction to the musical traditions of the Yanyuwa community of the southwest Gulf of Carpentaria. Ngulaig 17. (Brisbane: Aboriginal and Torres Strait Islander Studies Unit, University of Queensland.)

Chenoweth, Vida, 1979, The Usarufas and their music. Dallas, Texas: SIL Museum of Anthropology.

Dail-Jones (for later publications, see under 'Morais'), Megan Llinos, 1984, A culture in motion: a study of the interrelationship of dancing, sorrowing, hunting, and fighting as performed by the Warlpiri women of Central Australia. MA thesis, University of Hawaii.

Ellis, Catherine J., Linda Barwick and Megan Morais, 1990, Overlapping time structures in a Central Australian women's ceremony. In Peter Austin et al., Language and history: essays in honour of Luise A. Hercus, 101–136. Canberra: Pacific Linguistics C-116.

Kirton, Jean, 1988, Men's and women's dialects. Aboriginal Linguistics 1:111–125. Armidale: (Dept of Linguistics, University of New England, Armidale, edited by Nicholas Evans and Steve Johnson.)

Lauridsen, Jan, 1983, Musical scales in Australian Aboriginal songs: structure and social implications. PhD thesis, University of Maryland. (Ann Arbor: University Microfilm International.)

Mackinlay, Elizabeth, 1998, For our mother's song we sing: Yanyuwa women performers and composers of *a-nguyulnguyul*. PhD thesis, University of Adelaide.

—— 2000, Blurring boundaries between restricted and unrestricted performance: a case study of the Ngadirdji of Yanyuwa women in Borroloola. Perfect Beat 3(4):73–84.

Mackinlay, Elizabeth, and John Bradley, 2003, Of mermaids and spirit men: complexities in categorisation of two Aboriginal dance performances at Borroloola, Northern Territory. The Asia Pacific Journal of Anthropology 4(1–2):2–24.

Morais, Megan Llinos Dail-Jones, 1992, Documenting dance: Benesh movement notation and the Warlpiri of Central Australia. In Alice Marshall Moyle, ed. Music and dance of Aboriginal Australia and the South Pacific: the effects of documentation on the living tradition, 130–154. Sydney: University of Sydney.

—— 1994, Field notes recorded at Wandangula and Borroloola. MS.

—— 1998, Yanyuwa dance Gulf of Carpentaria. In Adrienne Kaeppler and K. W. Love, eds. Garland encyclopedia of world music, 460. New York: Garland Publishing.

Moyle, Alice, 1974, Songs from the Northern Territory: companion booklet for five 12 inch L.P.discs (revised edn). Canberra: AIAS.

Moyle, Richard, with the help of Slippery Morton, Alyawarra interpreter, 1986, Alyawarra music: songs and society in a Central Australian community. Canberra: AIAS.

Pike, Kenneth L., 1947, Phonemics: a technique for reducing languages to writing. Ann Arbor: University of Michigan Press.

—— 1967, Language in relation to a unified theory of the structure of human behavior (second revised edn). The Hague: Mouton & Co.

Sharpe, M. C., 1970, Voice quality: a suggested framework for description and some observations. In S. A. Wurm and D. C. Laycock, eds. Pacific linguistic studies in honour of Arthur Capell. Pacific Linguistics C-13, 115–134. Canberra: Pacific Linguistics, ANU.

—— 2003, Ngadiji, it's for women and men too: a study of a genre of Yanyuwa song and dance received in a trance. Thesis submitted for M.Phil. degree but withdrawn, University of Sydney.

Wild, Stephen, 1975, Wailbiri music and dance in their social and cultural nexus. PhD thesis, Indiana University. (Ann Arbor: University Microfilms International.)

4 Finding Arrernte songs

Myfany Turpin
University of Sydney

Abstract

Traditional Aboriginal songs are regarded by Arrernte people as the quintessential repository of their law, culture and family heritage. Knowledge of these songs and the dances and narratives that accompany them is a significant part of Aboriginal identity. However, the massive social upheaval since colonisation and the changes in lifestyle resulting from urbanisation have led to a decline in the performance of these songs. In 2015 a group of Arrernte women initiated a song revival that culminated in a five-week camp in Alice Springs. Here the women practised their songs with guidance from tradition-bearers, listened to audio recordings from the past and performed their songs. Amidst all the excitement and optimism of the project, further heritage recordings were located and shared amongst the relevant family members. A song inventory was created to assist in the documentation and retrieval of the songs on the recordings. In addition to producing the first ever audio-visual recording of many of these songs, other outcomes of the Arrernte camp included increased community involvement in traditional Arrernte singing; a corresponding increase in participants' understanding of the songs; and personal testimonies of an increased sense of identity and belonging. An ongoing issue is the long-term management of and access to both the legacy recordings and the newly created film from the camp.

Keywords: song, Aboriginal ceremony, women's ceremony, Arrernte

1 Introduction

Since the introduction of the first land rights legislation for Australia's Indigenous people in 1976, the legal processes for securing title to Aboriginal land have been heavily resourced. By contrast, far fewer resources have been put towards securing the knowledge and practices that underpin these systems of land tenure. Yet many types of traditional Aboriginal knowledge, including ceremonial songs, are close to being lost throughout Australia (Barwick & Turpin 2016). In this chapter I focus on the case of Central Australia, where Arrernte people have borne the brunt of non-Indigenous incursions into the region since 1871, when Alice Springs was established in the centre of their territory. For Arrernte people, holding onto their traditional songs is of vital importance.

Alice Springs is a town of some 35,000 people that services a vast area of inland Australia. It has an Aboriginal population of approximately 20% (2006 census), many of whom are not Arrernte. It is also the largest town in Australia where the Indigenous language is still being passed on as a first language. In 1994 there were said to be 1500–2000 speakers of the Eastern and Central Arrernte variety (Henderson and Dobson 1994); a more recent report finds 2444 speakers of Arrernte (AIATSIS and FATSIL 2005), but this conflates speakers of two quite different varieties: Western Aranda and Eastern & Central Arrernte (E&CA).

Eastern and Central Arrernte enjoys a relatively large speaker base, at least by comparison with other Australian Aboriginal languages today. However, the traditional songs are scarcely known, and those that are known are sung only by members of an older generation, who are mostly well into their 60s.[1] Like Aboriginal people elsewhere in Australia (Evans 2009:185), many Arrernte people are passionately interested in learning their hereditary land-based songs, even though some may be diffident about (or unable to use) the spoken language. While a number of younger Arrernte people participate in ceremonies in which they help assemble the necessary ritual items, join in the dancing and are frequently 'painted up' (Barwick and Turpin 2016), rarely do they participate in singing.[2]

In Arrernte society, as is often the case for Central Australian Aboriginal groups, participation in many activities, including singing, is divided along gender lines. In the 1950s, the anthropologist and linguist T. G. H. Strehlow (1971) recorded a vast corpus of Arrernte men's songs, but no Arrernte women's songs. It was not until the 1990s that a significant number of Arrernte women's songs were recorded (and archived) by Arrernte custodian M. K. Turner and linguist Jennifer Green (Green 1994). The fragility of these traditions was well recognised at the time, and, with the collaboration of two senior Arrernte singers (M. K. Turner and the late Edward Johnson), the team recorded 31 hours of Arrernte singing, and interpretation of songs, on audio cassette. As instructed by the singers, these tapes were archived at the Australian Institute of Aboriginal and Torres Strait Islander Studies (AIATSIS), with copies housed locally at the Central Land Council (CLC). The present chapter is concerned with the women's songs recorded in 2015 in a more recent project. This contributed to the earlier body of work with further recordings of some of the same songs and the addition of some hitherto unrecorded songs.

In the twenty-first century there has been increasing interest in reviving traditional songs. Partly inspired by the Yeperenye Festival in 2000, and partly by a growing awareness of the decreasing number of accomplished singers at the annual Women's Law and Culture meetings organised by the CLC, a number of Arrernte people and a few organisations have sought opportunities to re-engage with their singing traditions. The most notable of these is Akeyulerre, the Arrernte Healing Centre, which aims 'to sustain, develop and celebrate Arrernte cultural practices'. It is in the context of the extreme fragility of these traditions that the Arrernte Women's Project was inaugurated in 2014, resulting in in a five-week camp in 2015. This is described vividly in a personal account by Rachel Perkins (2016).

In the present chapter I elucidate the importance of traditional songs to Aboriginal people and the challenges involved in maintaining these songs today. I also detail the achievements of

---

1 Note that life expectancy for Aboriginal people in the NT is 14 years less than for non-Indigenous people.
2 It seems unlikely that traditional singing was ever only the domain of old people. In the areas to the north, where Northern Arrernte, Alyawarr and Anmatyerr are spoken, young people (i.e. under 60) join in the singing of the same types of songs that are sung by the Arrernte.

the women's camp. One of these was the bringing to light of a significant collection of recordings of Arrernte women's songs from the 1960s, which had not been archived or documented.

2 The value of traditional songs

The importance of traditional songs to Aboriginal people is amply attested throughout Australia. In regions where the intergenerational transfer of songs has been interrupted and legacy recordings exist, the audio material provides a critical link to once vibrant traditions. In 2002, jazz musician Judy Jacques issued a CD that commemorated the Aboriginal songs from a 1903 recording made in Tasmania. Of this project, she wrote that she 'needed, above all, to respect their utmost importance to the Palawa, the Indigenous people of Tasmania' (Jacques 2004:11). In this section I consider the role of song in traditional society, as a means of conveying how significant such legacy recordings are considered to be by contemporary Aboriginal people.

For Arrernte, as for other Aboriginal groups, traditional songs have mythological and religious significance. They honour particular ancestors and places through their allusion to creation stories, which M. K. Turner (2010:44) describes as 'precious like jewels'. The songs are performed with associated visual components: choreographed dance, body painting, costume and symbolic props, often representing places and totemic ancestors. The lean material culture of traditional Aboriginal society did not include portable forms of inscription (such as books), so oral tradition formed the repository of the community's history, religion, geography and genealogy, as well as many other types of knowledge. Songs could, under certain conditions, be performed to cause change; for example, to bring about rain, or create cohesion following a dispute, or heal the ill. Many songs were also performed at inter-cultural gatherings, where people came together for ceremonial events such as initiation, or the exchange of goods, or the sharing of particular foods in season. More broadly, songs express group solidarity and identity, celebrate the unique features of the relevant country, and provide the means of instruction for younger generations about sites, history, cultural practices and Aboriginal law more generally (Barwick and Turpin 2016).

Most Arrernte songs are the personal heritage of large family groups, and women's songs are no exception. Across Central Australia, women's songs (and ceremonies) are the principal means by which women demonstrate their patrilineal clan identity, as belonging to a defined clan estate (Peterson and Long 1986, Curran 2010). Clan groups are responsible for tracts of land and the associated *Altyerre* ('Dreamings') and creation stories. It is up to family heads to decide when, how and where their songs can be performed. Land Rights and Native Title have reinforced the value of Indigenous systems of land tenure, and claimants have often performed the songs of their estate as evidence of ownership of the land and responsibility for the Dreamings.

In the contemporary era, new forms of social activity and entertainment, often accessible through the internet, radio and television, have taken over many of the functions once fulfilled by traditional songs. Live music events in a variety of genres, including rock, pop and country, are all popular with Arrernte women, many of whom are also regular church-goers. As in other parts of Australia, Aboriginal teenagers are hooked up to their mobile phones, absorbing the commercial music that engages teenagers across the globe, as well as more local Aboriginal forms.

Given that traditional songs are associated with a vastly different way of life and economic basis, why are they so highly valued today? One explanation is that many Indigenous and minority peoples, while embracing the 'new' way of life, are at the same time anxious about losing their identity in the global melting pot. Cohen (1985:44) argues that 'as the structural bases of the boundary [of a culture] become undermined or weakened as a consequence of social change, so people resort increasingly to symbolic behaviour to reconstitute the boundary'. When it comes to reconstituting the boundaries of their cultures, for many Aboriginal people the learning of traditional songs and language – even if only in emblematic form – may be the obvious first choice. For some, the performing of traditional estate-based songs is also a way of demonstrating their opposition to the assimilation policies of mainstream Australian society.

Today the interest in family heritage and cultural identity extends well beyond the Indigenous minority. This is evidenced by the popularity of TV shows such as *Who do you think you are?* among other Australians, including those who have suffered far less dramatic social change. There is an increasing awareness that a strong sense of cultural identity is an important aspect of health and well-being, and the value placed on identity by the broader society is indicated by the cultural diversity visible at arts festivals and in the media. A number of studies have recognised that, for Aboriginal and Torres Strait Islander people, engaging in traditional practices and understanding one's connection to country are important aspects of identity (Phipps and Slater 2010:8, Dockery 2011:2, Kingsley et al. 2013:678, Guerin et al. 2011). Furthermore, Indigenous people themselves affirm that traditional dance and song, and the associated knowledge, are a key to achieving positive health outcomes (Abbott 2004:5). This is borne out by a statement by Arrernte woman Kumali Riley, one of the key instigators of the Arrernte Women's Project:

> ... learning how to sing and dance, being able to perform, makes me feel so good and proud of who I am; and that I am privileged to learn my grandmother's stories, our dances and our body designs which represent what the ceremony is about. I don't want to see it lost. It makes you feel so good about your belonging, where you belong (Kumali Riley pers. com. 2015).

Traditional Aboriginal performances are often used to represent Aboriginality in the media, the tourist industry, sporting events, arts festivals and politics, where they promote a variety of Indigenous, government and commercial ventures. Yet there are few opportunities for Aboriginal people to learn the performance practices that are so often called upon in these contexts, even though these activities are held in high esteem by Indigenous and non-Indigenous people alike.[3]

Amongst Arrernte today, the number of people who know how to perform their traditional songs is small. Generally, most people under the age of about 40 do not know them. Many people aged approximately 40–60 are familiar with the songs and dances, but not to the extent that they can lead a performance. Women who can lead performances and direct the activities tend to be older than 60. And there are even fewer people who claim to know the meaning of the songs.

The Arrernte Women's Project was set up to reverse the decrease in the number of singers. To this end, the Project aimed to provide opportunities for Arrernte women to perform and teach the songs and associated knowledge. Other goals included: to create recordings for future generations; to provide economic incentives for performing; to facilitate access to role models for younger Arrernte women; to assist in accessing archival recordings; and to create opportunities for Arrernte people to engage in songs in new ways.

This was never going to be an easy task, for reasons discussed in the next section.

---

3   Here a parallel can be drawn with what Heller (2003:486) describes as a commodification of minority identities (language and culture) coupled with a lack of institutional support for the maintenance of this identity in North America.

3 Overcoming the impediments to learning songs: some approaches

In the past, Arrernte songs were not taught explicitly. As elsewhere in Central Australia, song teaching is not formally recognised as a skill distinct from performing. Learning the songs, dances, paintings and meanings mostly occurs in performances, through constant repetition and (initially) imitation. Learning requires a solid relationship with a senior singer and the ability to overcome the fear of making a mistake (Barwick and Turpin 2016).

Yet traditional songs are not being performed as often as they once were, so the opportunities to learn them are far fewer now than in the twentieth century. This is partly the result of Arrernte people's movement away from country and into an urban lifestyle. Moreover, those in the diminishing pool of singers are often separated by vast distances, which means that logistical feats may be required to assemble the necessary performers. Additional transport is frequently needed to ensure the participation of younger people, for the sake of intergenerational learning.

Learning through exposure is not possible unless a long-term immersion context is created, but for Arrernte people there are few occasions when traditional songs are performed today. Such performances tend to be limited to one-off public events such as book launches, or the opening of a building, or the annual (but private) women's law and culture meetings organised by the CLC. In some other parts of Australia, funerals are a context for traditional singing (e.g. Brown 2014). But this is not the case in Central Australia, where the ways of learning these hitherto oral traditions may now involve the use of literacy – at least for those Arrernte people who grow up literate in both Arrernte and English. Some learners, especially those with little oral fluency in Arrernte, write down the song texts to practice and use as a prompt in their own performances.

One of the most obvious impediments to learning the traditional songs is that they are very different to the common English genres, such as rock, pop or folk. Many fluent speakers of Arrernte find they struggle with the songs, which require mastery of an esoteric language, an unfamiliar music and unfamiliar ways of meshing the lyrics with the melody. The songs employ a musical metre that disregards the stress patterns of everyday speech, and the vocal style makes use of microtonal ornamentation and diverse vocal timbres rarely encountered in western music. A singer must also be able to fit the uninterrupted repetition of lyrics into different parts of a melody that may be much longer than a single verse (Ellis 1985, Turpin 2011).

Apart from these technical difficulties, there are social impediments as well. The learning of songs cannot be separated from the maintenance of all the other social practices that surround their performance (Barwick and Turpin 2016), so a further challenge is to find ways of incorporating the relationships, knowledge and functions of songs (as alluded to above in section 2) into the learning process.

In addition to these complexities, there are broader contextual factors that make any learning activity difficult for many Arrernte people today. The statistics on Aboriginal social disadvantage and poverty in the NT are very sobering (Australian Indigenous HealthInfoNet, 2016). As a result of these liabilities, the pressures of everyday life – the number of funerals to attend, the time spent caring for relatives, raising children, circumventing violence and standing in welfare and housing queues – are greater for Aboriginal than non-Aboriginal people, and this leaves less time for concentrated learning.

The Arrernte Women's Project made a number of decisions to deal with these hurdles. The live-in camp that was the culmination of the Project provided a safe place and time for the intensive teaching and learning of ceremonial life. While the camp was focused on live intergenerational transmission, it also created recordings for future generations, and for the personal use of the participants. In addition, a number of songs from pre-existing recordings were identified and translated.

The Arrernte participants at the camp varied in their language fluency and educational background. For some, their first language was Arrernte, while for others it was English. Some had minimal experience with the Western education system and very little literacy, while others were highly literate and worked as teachers. It soon became apparent that these different experiences led to individual preferences in ways of learning. Some women memorised more by ear, while others used audio recordings and their own written versions of songs as back-up.

4 The Arrernte Women's Project camp

Over many years, discussions about how to support the practice of singing traditional songs had been ongoing between Arrernte film-maker Rachel Perkins and a number of senior Arrernte women. In 2013 Rachel secured a number of small grants to support a camp where Arrernte women could learn their traditional songs and the associated knowledge. This became known as the Arrernte Women's Project (Perkins 2016). It was made possible with the assistance of Arrernte members of Akeyulerre, (an Arrernte healing centre) and the present author. Under the direction of members of the broader Arrernte community, Rachel organised the camp, documented genealogies of the central Arrernte land-owning groups and appointed a recording crew of one video camera operator and one sound recordist.

My role in the Project was to document recordings of the songs.[4] I worked with undergraduate student Lana Henderson to create an inventory of all the public Arrernte songs that had been recorded to date (that is, prior to the recordings made in the course of this project). These included two major collections (recordings made by Green and Turner in the 1990s and my own recordings from the period 2007–09[5]), plus a recording held at the Central Australian Aboriginal Media Association (CAAMA), which was probably recorded by Philip Batty in the 1980s[6]. Our inventory lists 66 different audio files consisting of 937 song items. ('Song items' are the smallest stretches of uninterrupted singing in a performance, usually lasting between 30 and 90 seconds). A comparison of the rhythmic texts of these 937 song items revealed 291 different Arrernte verses. As is common in much traditional Aboriginal singing, a verse is performed two or three times (i.e. for two or three song items) before moving on to another verse. (In Arrernte this is explained as 'spreading out' the verse.) Thus, in any single performance there are always more song items than verses.

The culmination of the Project – the women's five-week song camp – began in April 2015, in Alice Springs. The camp was located just outside the town centre, so that the women could immerse themselves in ceremonial business unimpeded by the pressures of everyday life. Here they practised their songs under the guidance of tradition-bearers, listened to legacy audio recordings and discussed their meanings and significance. Their performance of the songs were filmed for posterity.

Once the camp was underway, the issues of ownership, privacy and access to the newly created recordings became topics for discussion. In most cases there was agreement over these issues within individual family groups, so the recordings were distributed on USB sticks

---

4   This work was part of a larger project on traditional songs across inland Australia, funded by the Australian Research Council (FT140100783, DP1092887).
5   Turpin's 2007 recordings were made possible from an Endangered Languages Documentation grant (IPF0100), funded by the Hans Rausing Foundation.
6   Philip Batty pers. com. 2015.

amongst the family members. In a few cases, however, there was an impasse, so the recordings at issue remain, at this stage, unarchived and undistributed.

The camp proved to be very popular, with over 100 Arrernte women of all generations participating in the course of the five weeks. Their ages ranged from the teens to the seventies. Many young people came because they found the camp an exciting place to be. They showed great respect for the senior women, the teachers and keepers of the songs, who allot the tasks involved in the performance. The order of verses, who should commence the song, the discussion of its meaning – these were all negotiated in the moment of performance, often with much hilarity and a blending of contemporary contextual events with matters of deep cultural significance. A performance is a group activity, and the younger women were courageous enough to participate fully, by being painted up and entering the dance arena.

On a practical level, the camp was run like a film set, with different family groups booked in for particular periods of time. This provided a chance for each of the groups to be the centre of attention, as the cameras focused on their learning and performance. The camp was big enough to have up to 40 people stay at one time, so women from some family groups would stay beyond their allocated time-slot to support the next family group. This facilitated continuity, provided encouragement for the next group and contributed to the atmosphere of a broader Arrernte women's network aiming to uphold their traditional singing practices.

The camp created its own momentum, and this led to the discovery of yet more legacy recordings. The Arrernte caretakers of these recordings requested assistance with digitisation and redistribution, so copies were provided on USB data sticks. One particularly significant collection of recordings that came to light was recorded by Aboriginal woman Ada Laughton in the 1960s and delivered to Rachel in two biscuit tins (Perkins 2016). This collection is discussed in detail below.

5 Ada Sylvia Laughton's collection of Arrernte women's songs

Ada Sylvia Laughton was born on Hodgson Downs Station around 1925. She was a member of the stolen generation and was raised in Alice Springs at the Bungalow, an institution for children of mixed descent. She married Herbert James Laughton ('Limpy'), an Arrernte man of mixed descent who worked for the Alice Springs municipal council and later the hospital. Ada was adopted by her Arrernte in-laws and spent most of her life in Alice Springs, raising her four children (see photos).

During the 1960s and up to the mid 1970s, Ada recorded her older Arrernte relatives singing traditional songs. It is not clear whether she made the recordings for the sake of posterity or because she wanted to learn the songs and intended to use the tapes as a memory aid. Ada's youngest daughter, Heather Laughton, who is now caretaker of these recordings, believes both motives were likely (pers. com. May 2016). Ada used a reel-to-reel audio tape recorder. It was perhaps an unusual appliance for an Alice Springs family at that time, but music was very much part of the Laughtons' life. Ada's husband Herbert played piano accordion and harmonica, and his nephew, Herbie (Patrick) Laughton, was a well-known country singer (Walker 2000).

Ada's husband's family were very dear to her, being the only family she knew.[7] It was with their permission that Ada took on the responsibility of recording and learning their songs – a task she did not undertake lightly. The trunk containing the reels was always kept under lock

---

7 According to her daughter Heather (pers. com. May 2016), at the age of 72 Ada discovered where she was originally from and met some of her family for the first time. This followed the federal enquiry into the Stolen Generation (Human Rights and Equal Opportunity Commission 1997).

4. FINDING ARRERNTE SONGS   95

Figure 4.1: The Laughton family (top: Herbert and Ada Laughton with their four children: L–R, Kenny, Keith, Jennifer and Heather, ca. 1960; below: Ada Laughton, ca. 1940; ca. 1990; photos courtesy of Heather and Sonya Laughton

and key. Heather recalls the first recordings taking place in the evenings at their Alice Springs backyard, on Gap Road, when she was eight years old. The women would make a fire and cook food, prepare medicines, sing and massage one another. It is worth recalling that at this time such an activity, however inoffensive and benign, was actually illegal. People of mixed descent, such as the Laughtons, were not allowed to socialise with their 'full-blood' relatives. Herbert's solution was to have his relatives listed as 'housekeepers'. Nevertheless, it was only under cover of darkness that the older women felt safe to sing, for fear of the authorities.

Ada was clearly unique. To my knowledge, no other person was recording Arrernte women's songs at that time – neither ethnographers nor community members. In 2008, M. K. Turner, with whom I had been working on the documentation of her own songs, informed me about Ada Laughton's recordings. She explained that she would like to access these, as some of her relatives, including her own mother, had sung on them. They would also be of great cultural significance to many Arrernte people. But the recordings were housed a considerable distance away, in Port Augusta, with Heather; and as I was a stranger, I left the matter in the hands of M. K. Turner.

The recordings did not materialise. This was not surprising, given the size of the task: how does one make copies of a group's 'crown jewels' (Marett and Barwick 2003:144), located some 1200 kilometres away, and distribute these in accordance with the appropriate cultural protocols? It was not until the Arrernte Women's Project that there was a viable process in place and a convergence of personnel who were capable of handling both the ethical and technical requirements of the task. In a conversation long after the camp, Heather mentioned that it was only because of the close relationship between Rachel Perkins's father and her own father (Herbert Laughton) that she decided to make the recordings available and have them archived for future generations.[8] As in traditional times, the sharing and trading of songs is grounded in close relationships between groups. In the past, this only ever happened as the outcome of live performances; but the contemporary use of audio recording technology means that this sharing now also occurs across time and space.

During the Arrernte Women's Project camp the recordings were entrusted to Rachel, with instructions for them to be digitised at the Pacific and Regional Archive for Digital Sources in Endangered Cultures (PARADISEC), and for M. K. Turner and I to transcribe and translate the songs. The collection consists of 12 reels, some recorded on both sides and others on one side only. Some of the recordings are interspersed with lengthy sections of radio, so the duration of the recording on any particular reel does not necessarily reflect the duration of the traditional Arrernte singing. Most of the song material consists of singing alone, but on a few recordings there are brief interpretations of the songs, and in some cases there are auditory hints of accompanying dancing (HL006). One reel is a recording of Ada herself practising the traditional songs (HL007, see Appendix).

The exact dates and the individual identities of the singers on the recordings are uncertain. However, Heather was able to recall the names of relatives involved in the night-time singing, who often stayed with them in Alice Springs. These senior Arrernte women, all of whom have passed away, were Tiny Webb (Penangke), Tilly Nelson Mulladad (Kngwarraye) and Maria Bird Cavenagh (Perrurle). Jessie Neale (Penangke), the mother of M. K. Turner, was also present on many occasions. In addition, Heather recalls Tilly's son, Louis Mulladad, and his wife, Doreen Palmer, visiting them in Adelaide, where further recordings were made (HL012).

---

8   Rachel's father was Charlie Perkins, an Aboriginal activist who was a key player in the 1965 Freedom Ride and the 1967 Referendum, which gave a number of rights to Aboriginal people.

The Appendix lists the digitised reels of the Arrernte singing in this collection.[9] There are 659 songs in total, comprising 84 unique Arrernte verses, many of which occur on multiple recordings. For example, Verse 20 can be heard on nine different recordings, incorporating a total of 26 renditions (song items). Verse 33 has a total of 35 renditions, again spanning nine recordings. The songs in the collection are mostly sung by women only, although Louis Mulladad was present with his mother, Tilly Mulladad, for the recording of some of them. He can be heard explaining the meanings of the songs in HL012, which was likely to have been recorded in Adelaide between 1968 and 1974.

On some of the recordings the songs are identified as being *ilpentye*. This is a genre that has a slightly different meaning in Arrernte to that in neighbouring languages. Its meaning is discussed below.

5.1 *Ilpentye* 'Arrernte women's songs'

Among the multiple meanings of the word *ilpentye*, the best known is 'love song' or 'charm'. According to the Arrernte dictionary (Henderson and Dobson 1994:361), *ilpentye* are songs people sing 'to make a particular person fall in [or out] of love with them, but ... not sung directly to that person'; men and women sing separate *ilpentye* songs. The dictionary also identifies another meaning of *ilpentye*, as 'women's singing and dancing (not necessarily love songs)'. For many Arrernte women, it is this second, broader sense that applies to their understanding of the term. Participation in *ilpentye* helps them develop a sense of pride in their own identity as Aboriginal women (Heather Laughton 2016 pers. com.).

An even broader meaning of *ilpentye*, as 'song', is evidenced in compounds such as *ilpentye-warre* 'singer'; moreover, in a closely related language (Kaytetye), *ilpentye-impentye* means 'singer; women's singalong' (Turpin and Ross 2012:391). Another phrase, *ilpentye artwe*, is encountered in six Arrernte verses, where it is said to refer to a male singer (*artwe* 'man'). This suggests that, depending on the context, the most general meaning of *ilpentye* may be 'song', unspecified for gender or function. It is also possible that *ilpentye artwe* refers to a male love-song singer. In a neighbouring language, Warlpiri, the cognate term *yilpinji* is a type of song performed by both men and women. When needing to distinguish love songs from women's singing in general, the latter can be disambiguated with the phrase *arrkene-kenhe* 'for fun' (as opposed to being for a specific purpose) or *arrartenhe-artenhe* 'for public display' (a nominalised form of the verb *arrarte-* 'to come out').

The semantic association between singing and romance is widespread, as is the association between music and special powers. Music is considered capable of invoking 'realms of knowledge to which we otherwise have little access' (Becker 1994:41). In Arrernte, the close connection between singing for fun and singing for causing effect (i.e. inducing romantic feelings) can be seen in the following exchange between the late Arrernte singer Maria Bird and M. K. Turner, who is seeking clarification of the function of these songs.

MB: Proper ilpentye. Number one.
These are real ilpentye songs and very powerful.
MKT: Arrkene-kenhe akweye?
Are they for fun?
MB: Arrkene-kenhe akwele-aye, ilpentye nhenhele akwele inerreke.
Of course they are fun, and you can change how a person feels with these songs.[10]

---

9   The Ada Sylvia Laughton collection is being prepared for deposit at AIATSIS.
10 AIATSIS archive tape JG02_019566, recorded in 1993, translated by M. Turpin 2016.

The broad range of meanings associated with the word *ilpentye* suggests an artistic practice that is flexible in its contexts and functions, yet its forms are remarkably fixed. The verses themselves show very little variation across time and context. Nonetheless, in private love songs, the style of vocal delivery and the associated actions may differ from those used in women's public performances.

Throughout Central Australia some songs are associated with particular places. But in the Laughton recordings there are only a few where the singers mention a connection with a specific locality. For example, on HL001_02, Verse 19 is said to relate to Ltyentye Apurte (Santa Teresa). In some cases we know of associated places because the songs exist on other recordings, where they are described in more detail. For example, M. K. Turner and linguist Jennifer Green recorded Maria Bird singing some of the same verses in 1993, where she describes them as *ilpentye* from Lyelthe [JG02_019594].[11] Lyelthe, a synonym for Unemarre, is an area northeast of Alice Springs that overlaps with parts of Huckitta cattle station.[12]

While some words in these verses are easily identifiable, others can refer to a broad range of phenomena, so their core meaning is not easily packaged in a single English word or phrase. Many of these words occur in multiple verses and thus become associated with the *ilpentye* genre. For example, *arlere-arlere* means 'something far away that appears to be close'. It is often used to describe a person or a hill coming into view. The word occurs in three verses in Ada Sylvia Laughton's collection (84, 35 and 41), and the first of these is translated below. (A verse is a repeating couplet, so two verses may create a quatrain, as in the present case.)

> *Intye palepale-ame ayenge arnpetyenhe*
>
> *Intye palepale-ame ayenge arnpetyenhe*
> *Ilewerre arlere-arlere-ame ayenge arnpetyenhe*
> *Ilewerre arlere-arlere-ame ayenge arnpetyenhe*
>
> *Through the grass, confidently I walk*
> *Through the grass, confidently I walk*
> *The mirage appears close but far as I walk*
> *The mirage appears close but far as I walk*
>
> (Verse 84, heard on HL005_02, HL004A, HL006_01, HL008_01and HL011. Transcribed and translated by M. K. Turner and the author.)

Mirages and other shining phenomena are frequently referred to in the songs. It may be that the word *ilewerre* 'mirage' is used symbolically here to refer to other, more subtle aspects of things that shimmer. Identifying the words, their meanings and the broader significance of the verses is a lengthy task. It requires the kind of specialist knowledge that is held today by only a few Arrernte elders.

6. Directions for the future

The Arrernte Women's Project was a rare opportunity for large intergenerational family groups to focus on the teaching and learning of their traditional songs, unimpeded by the pressures of everyday life. Rachel Perkins's presence, as a prominent media figure and an Arrernte woman, was no doubt one of the factors that helped to create a safe space. The fact that she wanted to

---

11 Verses 48, 26, 18, 20.
12 *Lyelthe* also means 'fragments of wood, wood-chips, debris' (Green, pers. com. 2016).

learn her own traditional songs encouraged other women to undertake the challenge of trying to acquire the necessary performance skills.

On the final day of the camp there were many personal testimonies about its significance in the women's lives. As an ethnomusicologist, it was a deeply moving experience to witness people expressing how much their songs and the camp experience meant to them. Perkins (2016) recalls one woman who, when her family sang the songs of her mother, said 'we are rich'. She also recounts that:

> (p)eople were expressing how their culture and songs connected them to their land and to their identity. Said one woman who had only just learned her local Dreaming song, 'Now no one can tell us we are not from here'.

Many participants wanted the camp to be an annual event, but finding funding for such a purpose is not easy, especially when the immediate output does not take a publicly accessible form; for example, as a film, a festival or an unrestricted performance. Some participants suggested the camp should be located even further from Alice Springs, to ensure full-time involvement from all participants and to prevent external interruptions. However, this would increase costs and reduce the number of people who could take part. For example, those in full-time employment would only be able to participate in the evenings. A number of participants suggested that the USB sticks of song recordings should be treated as ceremonial objects, with a formal handover based on established cultural practices. Reaching agreement on issues such as access to and distribution of recordings will require time, the experience of further camps and increased usage of the recorded songs. In spite of these concerns and different points of view, there is a consensus that the recordings must be treated with the utmost respect.

Since the camp I have encountered several of the Project participants in Alice Springs. Some have got together as a family group and sung on country for the first time; some requested further copies of their newly digitised recordings; and some described the experience of listening to the old recordings of their relatives singing as if they had spent the afternoon 'with Nanna'. Songs connect Arrernte people to their ancestors and their country, and they assist in the formation of identity and self-worth. The opportunity to restore these treasures that were on the brink of being lost forever is a rare and priceless gift.

Appendix

Table 4.1: The Ada Sylvia Laughton collection of Arrernte women's songs

RECORDING		NUMBER OF SONG ITEMS	NUMBER OF VERSES (FROM A TOTAL OF 84 UNIQUE VERSES)
DIGITAL FILE	ORIGINAL		
HL001_01	Reel 1 side A	18	7
HL001_02	Reel 1 side B	46	25
HL004_01	Reel 2 side A	94	21
HL005_02	Reel 3 side A	24	10
HL006_01	Reel 4 side A	38	14
HL006_02	Reel 4 side B	43	15
HL008_01	Reel 5 side A	20	11
HL009_01	Reel 6 side A	8	4
HL010_01	Reel 7 side A	24	8
HL010_02	Reel 7 side B	13	6

RECORDING		NUMBER OF SONG ITEMS	NUMBER OF VERSES (FROM A TOTAL OF 84 UNIQUE VERSES)
DIGITAL FILE	ORIGINAL		
HL007_01	Reel 8 side A	2	–
HL007_02	Reel 8 side A	15	–
HL011	Reel 9 side A	107	42
HL012	Reel 10 side A	49	20
HL013	Reel 11 side A	24	7
HL014	Reel 11 side B	58	19
HL015	Reel 12 side A	26	10
HL016	Reel 12 side B	50	23
Total songs		**659**	

References

Abbott, Kathy, 2004, Return to the heart. Aboriginal and Islander Health Worker Journal 28(2):4–5.

Australian Indigenous HealthInfoNet, 2016, Overview of Aboriginal and Torres Strait Islander health status, 2015. Perth, WA: Australian Indigenous HealthInfoNet.

Australian Institute of Aboriginal and Torres Strait Islander Studies and Federation of Aboriginal and Torres Strait Islander Languages (AIATSIS & FATSIL), 2005, National Indigenous languages survey report 2005. Canberra: Department of Communications, Information Technology and the Arts (DCITA). http://aiatsis.gov.au/publications/products/national-indigenous-languages-survey-report-2005. [Last accessed 12 September 2016.]

Barwick, Linda, and Myfany Turpin, 2016, Central Australian women's traditional songs: keeping yawulyu/awelye strong. In H. Schippers and C. Grant, eds. Sustainable futures for music cultures: an ecological perspective, 111–145. New York: Oxford University Press.

Becker, Judith, 1994, Music and trance. Leonardo Music Journal 4:41–51.

Brown, Reuben, 2014, The role of songs in connecting the living and the dead: a funeral ceremony for Nakodjok in western Arnhem Land. In A. Harris, ed. Circulating cultures: exchanges of Australian Indigenous music, dance and media, 169–202. Canberra: ANU Press.

Cohen, Anthony P., 1985, Symbolic construction of community. London: Routledge.

Curran, Georgia, 2010, Contemporary ritual practice in an Aboriginal settlement: the Warlpiri Kurdiji ceremony. Unpublished PhD thesis, Anthropology, Australian National University.

Dockery, Michael, 2011, Traditional culture and the wellbeing of Indigenous Australians: an analysis of the 2008 National Aboriginal and Torres Strait Islander Social Survey. Perth WA: Centre for Labour Market Research, Curtin University.

Ellis, Catherine, 1985, Aboriginal music: education for living. St. Lucia, QLD: University of Queensland Press.

Evans, Nicholas, 2009, Dying words: endangered languages and what they have to tell us. Hoboken, NJ: Wiley-Blackwell.

Green, Jennifer, 1994, Arrernte women's song project. Audio recordings held at the Australian Institute for Aboriginal and Torres Strait Islander Studies, Canberra. Accession number GREEN_J02 (019556-019561; 020300-020340).

Guerin, Pauline, Bernard Guerin, Deirdre Tedmanson, and Yvonne Clark, 2011, How can country, spirituality, music and arts contribute to Indigenous mental health and wellbeing? Australian Psychiatry 19(1):39–41.

Heller, Monica, 2003, Globalization, the new economy, and the commodification of language and identity. Journal of Sociolinguistics, 7(4):473–492.

Henderson, John, and Veronica Dobson, 1994, Eastern and Central Arrernte to English Dictionary. Alice Springs NT: IAD Press.

Human Rights and Equal Opportunity Commission, 1997, Bringing them home: National Inquiry into the Separation of Aboriginal and Torres Strait Islander Children from their Families. Sydney: Commonwealth of Australia.

Jacques, Judy, 2004, Passing the torch: commemorating the songs of Fanny Cochrane Smith. In D. Crowdy, ed. Popular music: commemoration, commodification and communication, 11–20. Proceedings of the 2004 IASPM Australia New Zealand Conference, held in conjunction with the Symposium of the International Musicological Society, 11–16 July, 2004, Melbourne.

Kingsley, Jonathan, Mardie Townsend, Claire Henderson-Wilson, and Bruce Bolam, 2013, Developing an exploratory framework linking Australian Aboriginal peoples' connection to country and concepts of wellbeing. International Journal of Environmental Research and Public Health 10(2):678–698.

Marett, Allan, and Linda Barwick, 2003, Endangered songs and endangered languages. In J. Blythe and R. M. Brown, eds. Maintaining the links: language identity and the land, 144–151. (Seventh conference of the Foundation for Endangered Languages, Broome WA.) Bath UK: Foundation for Endangered Languages.

Perkins, Rachel, 2016, Songs to live by. The Monthly 124: 30–35.

Peterson, Nicolas, and Jeremy Long, 1986, Australian territorial organisation: a band perspective.. Sydney: Oceania Monograph 30 (University of Sydney).

Phipps, Peter, and Lisa Slater, 2010, Indigenous cultural festivals: evaluating impact on community health and wellbeing. Melbourne: Globalism Research Centre, RMIT University.

Strehlow, T. G. H., 1971, Songs of Central Australia. Sydney: Angus & Robertson.

Turner, Margaret Kemarre, 2010, *Iwenhe Tyerrtye*: what it means to be an Aboriginal person. (Compiled by Barry MacDonald.) Alice Springs NT: IAD Press.

Turpin, Myfany, 2011, Song-poetry of Central Australia: sustaining traditions. Language Documentation and Description 10:15–36.

Turpin, Myfany, and Alison Nangala Ross, 2012, Kaytetye to English dictionary. Alice Springs, NT: IAD Press.

Walker, Clinton, 2000, Buried country: the story of Aboriginal country music. Sydney: Pluto Press.

5 Lone Singers: the others have all gone

Luise Hercus[1] and Grace Koch[2]
Australian National University[1] and Australian Institute of Aboriginal and Torres Strait Islander Studies[2]

Abstract

The Lone Singers and/or the Last Singers of songs from various Aboriginal traditions have a most important role to play in the preservation of knowledge. In areas of Australia where there are regular ceremonial performances, group singing provides the norm for analysis. However, in places such as Victoria, many songs sung by the elders have not been passed on, and only a few individual singers remember them. The Lone Singers on many occasions said that they were sorry for the verses because in the future there would be no one left to sing and remember them. Therefore, the recordings and the knowledge of these songs that may originally have been sung by more than one person are very precious. We will argue for the value of songs sung by Lone or Last Singers, showing their special merits and their place in contemporary Aboriginal society.[1]

Keywords: song, last singer, music notation, Aboriginal, ceremony, solo, Gippsland, South Australia, Native Cat, Seven Sisters

1 Group performances versus solo singers: the case for Central Australia

The ethnomusicologist Richard Moyle based his important studies on the recordings of performances from Central Australia of the music of the Pintupi, Alyawarra and Kukatja people. This involved group singing rather than renditions by solo performers. Aside from his exhaustive analyses of the melodic contours of various song series, he had an interest in the places in the melody where individual singers would break away from the group to sing a different pitch or pitches, referring to this practice as 'heterophony'. According to Moyle (1986:136), the ideal performance would be sung in unison, but this was not always the case. Referring to the way the Alyawarra men from the area around Ammaroo Station sang, he says:

---

1 We thank our anonymous referees for their comments on this paper.

> There does not appear to be any social situation in either sacred or secular realms in which groups of people speak in unison. However, there is a stated preference for singing in unison. Although this preference is worded either in terms of melodic unison ... or more generally ... it is apparent that the notion of rhythmic unison is implied ... When replaying recordings of certain songs, the *Agharringa* (name of their traditional estate) men would agree that the singers were *apata* (tangled) or *athirrithirrika* (broken in two) when either melodic or rhythmic unison foundered ... Despite explicit verbalisation that group singing should be in unison, it frequently occurs that more than one pitch is sounded simultaneously. There seems to be a clear distinction ... between what are regarded as simultaneous and minor variations of a [melodic] contour (which are acceptable) and vocal lines which are heard to depart from the established melodic contour (which are unacceptable). The [former] is considered as 'being the same' or '*irrkatja*' and [the latter as] separate (... 'broken in two' [or] '*athirrithirrika*') ... heterophony is acceptable but polyphony is not.

Moyle did his fieldwork in areas of Central Australia where songs and ceremonies, both for men and for women, were well known by large groups of people. Most of his work centres upon the long series of land-based songs that were being performed regularly by groups of singers and were fresh in their minds. His analyses were based upon the massed sounds of a group, emphasising how some singers departed from unison singing, and he considered that songs elicited from solo singers would not provide proper data for analysis. He checked with Grace Koch to see if her recordings of Kaytetye women from the Barrow Creek area of the Northern Territory were made with groups of singers. In other words, solo renditions were not the norm and would not provide an authentic performance.

Moyle's statement about the importance of group singing for a valid performance, however, cannot be applied to most of the recordings that were made by Luise Hercus since the 1960s. The recordings she made of some of the last speakers of Aboriginal languages from Victoria, South Australia, Queensland and New South Wales contain a wealth of songs performed mostly by solo singers. In this paper, we will consider the singers' feelings about their songs and their desire to preserve them for future generations; the special merits of working with Lone Singers (often the Last Singers); and the importance of the songs to the preservation of Aboriginal culture.

2 A brief comment about the songs and the notations[2]

Each of the songs referred to in this paper was recorded by Luise Hercus in the 1960s. Geographically, they range from Gippsland (Laurie Moffat's song) and Echuca (the Owlet Nightjar song) in Victoria to north-eastern South Australia and Finke, in the Northern Territory. All demonstrate the virtuosity of the performers, whether it be through ornamentation, use of percussion, or in vocal stamina.

Because they come from several areas, most of the songs have different musical styles. There are two exceptions: the song for the Karingala Waterhole, which is verse 5 of the Seven Sisters song line (Musical example 5.3), and the verse from the *Urumbula* song series (Musical example 5.4). Both of these have characteristics of Central Australian songs, such as a long melody

---

2   All musical examples, with full attributions, are located in the appendix at the end of this chapter. Notations of Indigenous music are often a work in progress. Linda Barwick (1990:60) writes about her own experience of musical analysis, in reference to her work on the Central Australian recordings of Catherine Ellis: 'What I know about this music is not a measurable quantity, but a constantly changing way of relating to the music. Each time I listen to or analyse a performance, I experience the music differently.' In accord with Barwick's observation, the notations in this paper (aside from minor revisions) are shown as Koch perceived them in 2015, when this paper was presented to the Aboriginal Languages Workshop held in Canberra.

Figure 5.1: George McDermott on the veranda of Bourke Hospital in 1970
(photo by Graham Hercus)

that descends to the lowest pitch, rising one or two times as the text is repeated. The final and lowest pitch contains a full reiteration of the text.

A brief musical analysis will be given for each notation. We have included the song texts only where they are clearly audible.

3 Feelings about song expressed by the Last Singers

There was great sadness about the loss of ceremonies, especially among those who had witnessed ceremonies and heard large groups of people from their areas singing together, as described by Richard Moyle for Central Australia. Those who were left as the Last Singers felt the loss most of all. For instance, George McDermott (Wangkumara), speaking at the Bourke Hospital in October 1970, stated:

> Good to see them dancing, good *mura*[3] that. That is the last *mura* I have seen, *Ngakaparáwarra*.[4]
> They all finished, no more about, nobody knows it, only me (Hercus field tape 356, 1970).

Maudie Naylon *Akawilyika* (Wangkangurru) spoke to Gavan Breen at Birdsville in June 1973 about a ceremony that had been lost:

> You wouldn't know this *kunkariya mura* [waddy tree Ancestral myth]. Only me know, I heard them singing. They was dancing it here, *Warrthampa* [name of the ceremony] (Breen field tape 373, 1973).

Moyle's statement about the importance of group singing for a valid performance pertains to past practices in many regions of Australia. However, it cannot be applied to most of the

---

3   *Mura* means 'History Time Ancestor'; it also means 'ceremony' and 'ceremonial song' in Diyari and other languages to the east and north-east of Lake Eyre.
4   The duck increase ceremony, which was centred on the Nockaburrawarry waterhole on the lower Wilson River.

recordings of the enormous repertoire of Mick McLean, a Wangkangurru man from the central Simpson Desert. Mick was the Last Singer of many song series, so most of the songs recorded were necessarily solo renditions.

Mick recalled the thrill of taking part in a rain ceremony:

> You come back [from the secluded place where you have been dressing up] looking just like a cloud[5] then, just like that. You come back as a white bank of cloud then, with other cloudbanks around (Hercus 2015:4.15).

Mick McLean on many occasions gave another reason why it was so sad to be the Lone Singer:

> When I am gone, there'll be nobody to sing my country!

This expression had a special meaning, as Reuther, in his great work on Diyari (1981, 1:200), long ago explained: 'when a man was dying, his mura-song was sung to him.' Among Wangkangurru people it was also sung after a death: it was the special song for a person's place of birth or for his closest totemic affiliation. Mick himself sang his sister's 'country', the Poolowanna Well in the central Simpson Desert, after her death. When relatives met for the first time after a person's death they would cry together and then sing that person's special song.

Even in Gippsland, where ceremonies had long gone, Laurie Moffat had memories of groups of people singing at Lake Tyers. Laurie was a distinguished spokesman for Aboriginal people in Victoria and an accomplished gum-leaf player.[6] On January 18 in 1963 at Lake Tyers he sang the one and only song Luise Hercus was able to record from Gippsland, and he went on to say:

> We'd all have a go at it. All the boys and the girls would sit down and hit [he clapped].

Audio example 5.1: Laurie Moffat's song (see appendix, Musical example 5.1)

The song is sung in a very legato, smooth tone within the range of a major third (F – A). There are four melodic phrases, all of which consist of a repetition of text on one pitch, with phrases 2 and 4 descending stepwise to a major third as shown on the notation. Phrases 3 and 4 are twice the length of the first two. The musical form can be shown as A B A1 B1, where the 'A1' and 'B1' phrases are the longer versions of A and B. The end of each phrase is marked by the syllables *ge*, *ne* or *ŋe*.[7] Laurie's vocal quality shows some slight vibrato on sustained notes.

The underlying rhythmic pulse tends to alternate between a triple and a duple metre. Phrase 4 includes an ornament that circles stepwise around the final pitch (F). A final descending trill, possibly a dance call, signals the end of the song. Laurie suggests that there would have been a handclapping accompaniment.

4 Special instances of songs where two or more singers were recorded

On the very rare occasions when it was possible for Luise Hercus to record two singers in a single session, they did not necessarily reinforce one another. This was the case when the Patterson

---

5 'Headdress of hair string entirely covered white down extending over shoulders and chest' (Spencer 1903:33).
6 He often played the gum-leaf outside the Myers store in central Melbourne, to draw attention to the Aboriginal cause.
7 The text has been transcribed phonetically by Stephen Morey, but the meaning is unknown.

brothers sang part of the Kuyani *Malkara* – the initial phase of the initiation ceremony, when the women were dancing. This was traditionally sung by a large group of men. Stuart Patterson, with a strong bass voice, knew the songs much better than his brother Percy, a weaker tenor. Percy gave up and concentrated on percussion. This recording was made by Cath Ellis and Luise Hercus by the Windy Creek, near Copley (South Australia), in January 1966.

Audio example 5.2: *Kuyani Malkara song* (see appendix, Musical example 5.2)

Melodically, this song consists of two pitches a major third apart, and the singers make some rhythmic variations where the rise or fall of a third occurs. There is only one variant where the vocal descent goes stepwise (see indication on notation). The song consists of two basic sections, each repeating a text line twice. The first bars of each section vary slightly at the beginning, both rhythmically and where the third leap appears, whereas the second bars of each section are identical, both in pitch and in rhythm.

Table 5.1: Kuyani *Malkara* song, basic sections

Handclapping in equal quavers underlies the melody, resulting in the handclaps coming between some of the notes.

The text consists of two lines[8]:

Nadidere deredi (rhythmic variation comes at the first iteration of this line)
Nadidere deredi
Nararanta rantari
Nararanta rantari

After the pause with a cough, the pitch drops approximately a semitone. This could reflect a strain on the singer or a mechanical issue with the tape recorder, as the melody is the same as at the beginning.

When two singers are equally matched they can be remarkably in unison, considering that they have not rehearsed and have not sung together for decades. This is shown by Tim Strangways and Mick McLean singing together verse 5 of the Seven Sisters. However, they

---

8   The song words are shown here as Koch heard them.

sounded almost as if they were in competition. This verse is about the Seven Sisters: they are camped at the Karingala waterhole on Peake Creek when the Ancestor Thunpila arrives carrying a decaying corpse. They tell him to take it away *awardaku*, 'a long way off'. Both singers were eager to explain all this immediately. Tim Strangways was Arabana and was mother's brother to Mick McLean's wife Kathleen: he was therefore senior to Mick. Tim died shortly after this recording was made in 1968 at Port Augusta, leaving Mick McLean as a Lone Singer for this and many other song cycles.[9]

Audio example 5.3: Tim and Mick's song (see appendix, Musical example 5.3)

For the first part of the melody (before the breath intake by Tim) Mick sings three pitches: F sharp, C sharp and B. Tim, however, slides down to the final B, thus touching upon more pitches. Tim begins the second iteration of the melody approximately a semitone higher than before. Mick keeps to three pitches (G, D and C) while Tim's melody includes a minor third leap (C – D sharp) four times, descending to the C at the end. Each singer chooses to vary the melody slightly, but the song is recognisable as basically the same. The slight variations in each singer's melody would account for the perception that they appear to be in competition during the performance.

There was only one occasion where Luise Hercus had the chance to record three knowledgeable singers together. In August 1974, when all the southern part of the Lake Eyre Basin was flooded, Mick McLean was taken to Finke by train from Marree to meet with Yumpi Jack (Antikirinya) and Archie Allen (Arabana/ Lower Arrernte). All were familiar with the southern part of the *Urumbula* series, the long song cycle concerned with *atyelpe* 'native cat'. It could be heard that three singers add extra depth to the song. This was partly because the individual singers sang some notes of the melody slightly differently, which corresponds to Moyle's notion of 'heterophony'. This was a unique occasion – normally Luise Hercus only had access to Lone Singers.

Audio example 5.4: *Urumbula* (see appendix, Musical example 5.4)

We do not have the words for this song, so the notation is approximate. The melody moves downward over an octave (C sharp – G). The bar lines show a rough indication of the musical phrases. Mick McLean and Archie Allen join in with Yumpi Jack where the melody falls to a D. Except for the G on the next system, where all three singers are in unison, Mick and Archie stay on the lower G for the measure, then sing again in unison until the last measure, where they stay a major fifth (C) below Yumpi Jack's G, joining in with him in unison on the next beat.

---

9   See the text for this song under section 5 of this paper, 'The special merits of the Lone Singer'.

There was one remarkable Lone Singer and percussionist who provided all parts of the accompaniment by himself. He stamped his foot to a steady rhythm and doubled that rate with a stick held in his hand. He was Arthur 'Igor' Reid, who was not a fluent speaker of Wangkumara, but was able to sing songs learnt from his stepfather King Frank Millar (Wangkumara). The recording in question was made at Dareton (NSW) in 1972.

Audio example 5.5: Igor Reid's song (see appendix, Musical example 5.5)

We do not have the words for this song but we can see a clear musical structure. This consists of two phrases; the first descends a minor third from middle C to A, then falls to G, rising through A to a B flat, ending on an A. On the repetition, the first phrase does not rise to a B flat, but remains on the A. The stick-against-tin accompaniment matches the quavers in the melody, while the foot stamp is in crotchets, with a ratio of 1:2. The percussion does not have any accented beats and runs steadily like clockwork. The melody is made up basically of 4 pitches: C, A, G, F (except for the one B flat, which seems to be a single variant.)

5 The special merits of the Lone Singer

Luise Hercus witnessed recording sessions by Catherine Ellis with groups of Western Desert women (see Buckley et al. 1967, and Ellis et al. 1968) and realised that her own work with Lone Singers was in fact easier in one respect: Lone Singers were ready to give whatever explanations were available to them, verse by verse, whereas when a group of Western Desert women sang together, it was a performance which could not be interrupted.

This is important because explanations of traditional songs are particularly difficult. They have been handed down through generations and therefore are likely to contain linguistic

Figure 5.2: Arthur 'Igor' Reid and his wife, Margaret, with her sister's grandchild, at Dareton in 1972

archaisms. This can be shown clearly in the Seven Sisters song recorded by Tim Strangways and Mick McLean (see appendix, Musical example 5.3). The notated verse contains the normal 1st person plural exclusive[10] form *arni*. In the same verse, however, we find *ngarnhinha* 'us', which is an archaic form preserving an initial *ng-* (as is found for instance in the Pitta Pitta first person plural *ngarna*).

> *Arnikarí Karílyanganha karí ngarninha*
> *Awardakú wanpardé*
> *Karilya Karilyánganha karí ngarninha*
> We are the ones from Mt Margaret, look at us
> Carry it a long way off!
> Mt Margaret, from Mt Margaret, look at us.

Songs can also be musically archaic. Songs that were composed after the original singers had passed away contain some of the musical features of songs that were documented much earlier. Although these are not really archaisms, they demonstrate the continuation of some aspects of song traditions. In 1886, the Rev. G. W. Torrance persuaded a solo singer, William Berak (or Barak), the last clan-head of the Woiwurung (Barwick 1998:52) to perform three songs for him, which he put into Western notation. These showed an 'intonation', or sounding of a single tone at the beginning of the song on a neutral syllable, such as 'ah', the sliding of a note at times into the following pitch and long sections of rapid repetitions of one note on different syllables (Torrance 1886:335–336).

These characteristics are marked on the notation of 'Owlet Nightjar', sung by Stan Day at Echuca in 1965.

Audio example 5.6: Owlet nightjar, Yerrateth-kurrk (see appendix, Musical example 5.6)

Such musical features appear also in songs composed by Stan Day's grandfather, David Taylor 'Marrerd' and Stan's great-uncle, Bob Taylor 'Nyawi'. The song has a range of an octave and a minor third. The word 'cook' appears at the beginning of 4 of the 14 musical phrases of the song. A leap of a minor 7th (F – E flat) occurs on the fourth system on the word 'bucket'.

6 The 'thing-a-mi-jig' and the importance of preservation of the songs

The Lone Singers Luise Hercus worked with wanted their songs recorded as part of their legacy; they wanted 'that machine' – known in Arabana as *pinti-kadnha* 'thing-a-mi-jig' – to store their songs and stories so that people could hear them in the future. In 1962 tape recorders were only just becoming available, and the older people could see that those machines would do exactly what they had wanted.

They perceived that the traditional ways of learning, which involved listening to and taking part in ceremonies and learning by repetition, were in many cases no longer viable. When

---

10 Exclusive means 'excluding the person addressed'. So if a group of people said amongst themselves, 'we (*arniri*) will all go away,' that 'we' would be inclusive; but 'we' is exclusive when it means 'we, not you' e.g. a Wangkangurru speaker might say to an enquiring linguist, 'we *arni* call the moon *ngarkani*'. That 'we' is exclusive because it implies 'we but not you'.

there were no more ceremonies, songs were passed on by older relatives, or even acquaintances, through persistent tuition. Mick McLean himself had learnt much in this way from his father. He had tried his hardest to pass on at least the rainmaker songs to a 'countryman', because this man was ritually most eligible and was also a friend. He was not an immediate relation, but he was a descendant of Markili, the rainmaker who was one of the six men who worked with Spencer and Gillen at Peake in 1903 (see Spencer 1903). The attempts at tuition didn't work: sadly his friend was too far removed from the traditions and the language to be able to learn. As Mick put it:

> I showed him one verse again and again and he got it, but next morning he couldn't remember anything.

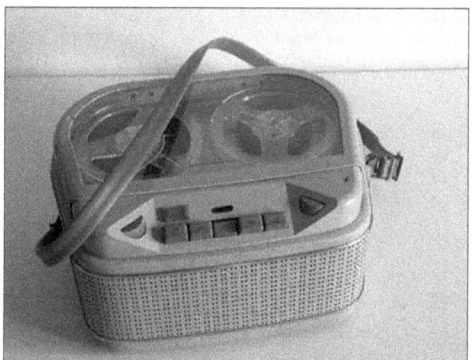

Figure 5.3: Butoba tape recorder, model MT511

The information was more than something merely deposited in the recorder: it could be put there to be amended later. Mick McLean was not feeling well when he recorded verse 27 of the Fire History (see Hercus 2013) and so he said:

> You know, if I am good one, I will give [it] you again one day, *walta nguru-nga,* [another time]: I just tell you, you keep'm in there so you can hear'm.

He wanted the song to stay there, in the right sequence, to be sung with a clearer voice on a later occasion: sadly this did not happen. But even when viewed as just a storage device, the 'thing-a-mi-jig' was welcomed by Lone Singers as it was impersonal, it simply kept the information they were so anxious to preserve.

This high esteem for modern technology as a storage device is carried into much younger generations. Luise Hercus often has to pacify descendants of Lone Singers who ask, 'why didn't you make a video of my grandad singing?' They don't realise that this technology did not exist half a century ago. As it was, tape-recorders only just came in time for many Lone Singers.

It seems that the singers were worried in a general way about their traditions and not necessarily with regard to their own immediate families or groups. Mick said on many occasions, speaking in English: 'I am telling you this so that people will know' – and he clearly said 'people' and not 'my people'.

7 Preserving links between land, ceremony, and culture

Reflecting the importance of 'telling you this so that people will know,' ceremonies were like major parties in celebration of song-lines, linking them back to the 'History Time'; that is,

---

11 *http://p.g.elec.pagespro-orange.fr/Le%20magnetophone.htm* [accessed 28/3/2016]

the Dreamtime. A party is not a party if one cannot invite others. So for a major ceremony people would come from far afield, learning in their travels about country new to them. At the ceremonies they would all sing together, including the verses from their own country; therefore song-lines and ceremonies formed links between people. It is thanks to the Lone Singers that people in the future will still be able to trace some of those links, although the unifying power of the ceremonies has disappeared.

It is through these links that many important verses, in languages no longer spoken, have been preserved. These include entire sections of the Fire History, of the Two Men and of the Seven Sisters. These sections are based in Wangkamadla country in far south-west Queensland. Wangkamadla people started being removed from their country from 1900 on. Mick McLean's father, a Wangkangurru/Lower Arrernte man, had been to ceremonies with them many years before, probably in the 1870s, and had learnt these verses. He passed them on to his son, who recorded them 100 years later. So these verses, along with geographical details from another country, from Wangkamadla country, were preserved via two Lone Singers, Mick McLean and his father.

An almost miraculous survival was that of the song for Lake Gregory, near Etadunna Station in South Australia. It belonged to the long song-line of the Swan History. It was an important verse because it was the last in the line. Wangkangurru – Yaluyandi people in Birdsville could still sing much of this line – but Lake Gregory was altogether too far away and the verse got lost. George McDermott recorded it in 1970 in Bourke, New South Wales. George had also learnt (presumably along with the song) where Lake Gregory was, even though it was far from his country. It seems that Grannie Moisey (Kurnu) had learnt that song in her youth and introduced it to Bourke, so people there started singing it. George McDermott explained it to the medical student[12] who was doing the recording:

> *George McDermott*: This old Moisey [Grannie Moisey's husband who was a patient in the same hospital] knows a bit about it too. His old woman used to sing it one time, she used to dance it one time, when they were dancing it.
> *Medical Student*: Which bloke was this?
> *George McDermott*: This old Moisey down here in the ward there.

There is no mistake about the verse: it is introduced with the word 'Paya-ngurru'. This is the actual name of Lake Gregory.

There is a moral to these survival stories: the verses were preserved via Lone Singers from a different area, speaking a different language. This could never have happened if the original people from that song-line had not been willing to share in the first place. So in these and other similar cases we can see that sharing and linking lead to preservation.

8 Re-learning culture through songs

Thanks to the recordings and to the increasingly keen desire to learn more about 'grandad and nanna', new links between people and culture are being forged. Although there may not have been interest in the old songs while the older generation was alive, the situation is changing. Along the Murray for instance, descendants want to relearn aspects of their heritage that had

---

12   Luise Hercus, when visiting Bourke in October 1970, met George McDermott for the first time and realised that this was a very knowledgeable man. He was in the hospital. Because she and Graham Hercus had to return to Melbourne most urgently, she lent her tape-recorder to two visiting medical students so that they could record George. They did a valiant job and George was more than willing to cooperate. They recorded 4.5 tapes, copies of which were subsequently deposited at AIAS by Dr Max Kamien, their supervisor.

been forgotten and they also want to compose new songs. They want to be heard, not just in their own townships, but all along the Murray Valley – and beyond.

Luise Hercus and Grace Koch aim to contribute towards this revitalisation by providing a large corpus of songs with music notations, mostly from Lone Singers, with as much background information as possible. Projects are continuing on documenting, notating, and analysing early songs from Victoria in collaboration with Stephen Morey and Ted Ryan, and from the Southern Lake Eyre Basin using Wangkangurru song cycles from Mick McLean. These projects would not have been possible if Lone Singers had not wanted to pass these precious songs on to future generations. To paraphrase Mick McLean, '[They] told us [these things] so that people will know.' This work will help to realise Mick's wish.

Appendix: Musical examples

Musical example 5.1: Laurie Moffat's song (Hercus field tape 94/2, 1963), sung by Laurie Moffat at Lake Tyers (VIC)

Range: Major third (F-A), with the ornament extending the range to a perfect 4th.

© Grace Koch

Musical example 5.2: Kuyani *Malkara* song (Hercus field tape 19, 1966); sung by Stuart Patterson and Percy Patterson by the Windy Creek (near Copley, SA)

Example 2
Kuyani Malkara

Musical example 5.3: Tim and Mick's song (Seven Sisters verse 5, 'Karilya'; Hercus field tape 193, May13, 1968); sung by Tim Strangways and Mick McLean at Port Augusta (SA)

Range: Major 6th (B - G)

5. LONE SINGERS 115

Musical example 5.4: *Urumbula* (Hercus field tape 673, 1974); sung by Mick McLean, Yumpi Jack and Archie Allen, at Finke (NT)

Example 4
Urumbula verse

Range: Octave and an augmented 4th (C# - G) © Grace Koch

Musical example 5.5: Igor Reid's song (Hercus field tape 104, 1972); sung by Igor Reid at Dareton (NSW)

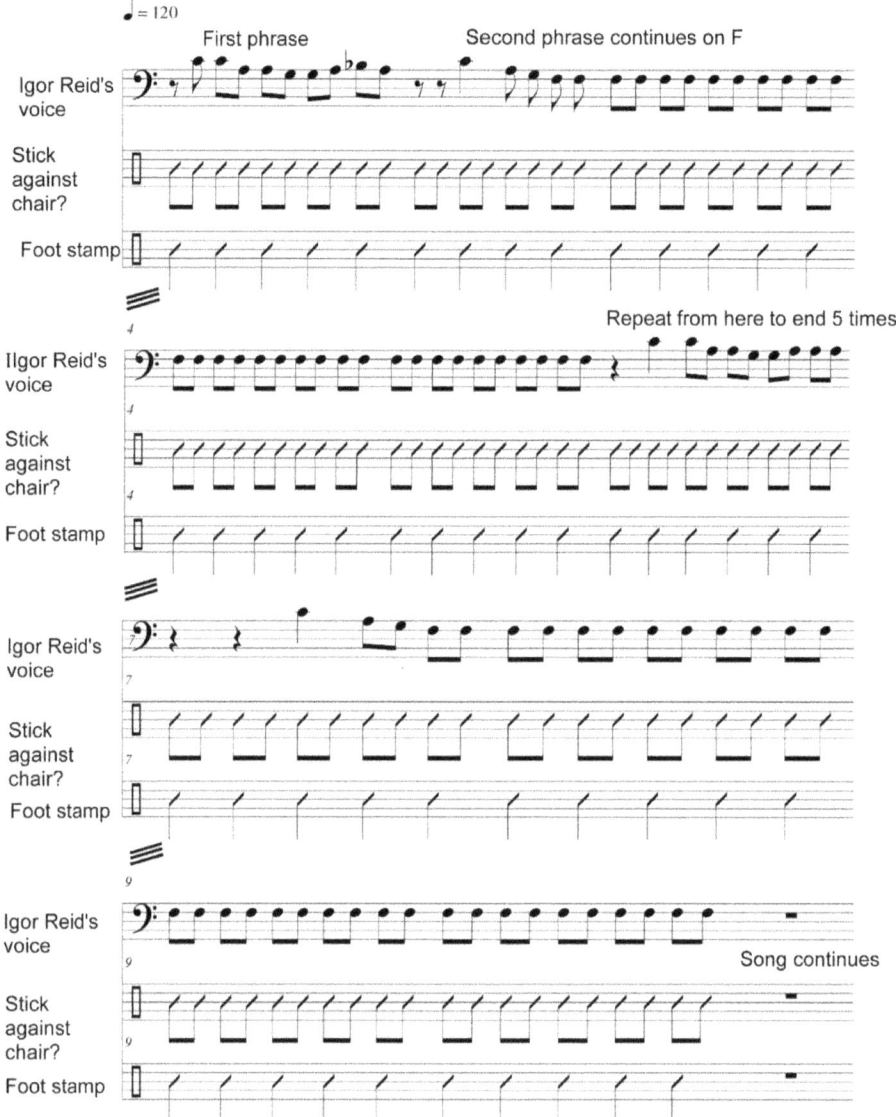

Musical example 5.6: Owlet nightjar, *Yerrateth-kurrk* (Hercus field tape 21/31, 1965); sung by Stan Day at Echuca (VIC)

References

Barwick, Diane, 1998, Rebellion at Coranderrk. Canberra: Aboriginal History (Monograph 5).

Barwick, Linda, 1990, Central Australian women's ritual music: knowing through analysis versus knowing through performance. Yearbook for Traditional Music 22:60–79.

Buckley, R., C. J. Ellis, L. A. Hercus, L. Penny and I. M. White, 1967, Group project on Andagarinja women vol.1. Adelaide: private publication [154 pp.] (for archive use exclusively because of extensive secret material).

Ellis, Catherine J., L. A. Hercus, R. Toussaint and I. M. White, 1968, Group project on Andagarinja women vol. 2. Adelaide: private publication [189 pp.] (for archive use exclusively because of extensive secret material).

Hercus, Luise Anna, 2013, The fire history, with musical notations by Grace Koch. Privately printed and deposited at AIATSIS.

—— 2015, The Rain from Peake (unpublished MS).

Moyle, Richard (with the help of Slippery Morton, Alyawarra interpreter), 1979, Songs of the Pintupi: musical life in a central Australian society. Canberra: Australian Institute of Aboriginal Studies.

—— 1986, Alyawarra music: songs and society in a central Australian community. Canberra: Australian Institute of Aboriginal Studies.

Reuther, Johann Georg, 1981, The Diari. Translated into English by P. A. Scherer. Canberra, AIATSIS (AIAS microfiche no. 2, from the original MS of 1904).

Spencer, Baldwin, 1903, Urabunna Old Peake Station. Museum Victoria (MS XM5863).

Torrance, George William, 1886, Music of the Australian Aboriginals. Journal of the Royal Anthropological Institute16:335–340.

Field tapes and AIATSIS Collection Numbers (where available):

BREEN_G20, June 1973, Birdsville, Qld. Field tape 373, AIATSIS archive tape number 2855.
HERCUS_L02, January 1963, Lake Tyers, Vic. Field tape 94/2.
HERCUS_L087, April 1965, Echuca, Vic. Field tape 21/31, AIATSIS archive tape number 998.
HERCUS_L15, May 1968, Peake Creek, SA. Field tape 193.
HERCUS_L16, January 1966, near Copley, SA. Field tape 19, AIATSIS archive tape number 2010.
HERCUS_L16, 1972, Dareton, NSW. Field tape 104, AIATSIS archive tape number 2051.
HERCUS_L21, October 1970. Field tape 356. AIATSIS archive tape number 2353.
HERCUS_L26, August, 1974, Finke, SA. Field tape 673.

6 Songs performed by Willie Rookwood at Woorabinda in 1965

Mary Laughren,[1] Myfany Turpin[2] and Gemma Turner[2]
University of Queensland[1] and University of Sydney[2]

Abstract

An understanding of traditional song forms that is based on the study of recorded song performances can inform a model for any revitalisation of song traditions. Recordings of songs sung in the south-eastern Queensland languages by mother tongue speakers are relatively rare. This paper analyses four songs sung by Mr Willie Rookwood at Woorabinda Reserve (central Queensland) in December 1965 that were recorded by Elywn Flint, lecturer at the University of Queensland. Willie Rookwood was born on Coogoon Station via Roma around 1890 and his language was Gunggari, a southern Maric language. We discuss the words and meanings of the songs, drawing on Rookwood's own explanations. We identify the structure of the text, rhythm and melody and the relationships between these. We compare these structural features of the songs with songs from Central Australia, a region where the traditional songs are better documented. Despite similarities in the placement of vocables in line-final position, the tendency for lines to consist of a noun plus a verb and the matching of word boundaries with bar boundaries, the verse structures of the Maric songs differ from the common AABB pattern of Central Australian songs.

Keywords: Aboriginal song, verse, Maric language, Gunggari, Woorabinda

1 Introduction

On the first of December 1965, at the Woorabinda Aboriginal Settlement in central Queensland, Elwyn Flint, a lecturer in the Department of English at the University of Queensland, recorded a number of Aboriginal people speaking their traditional Aboriginal languages. Flint used the fieldwork guide devised by Arthur Capell (1945) to elicit vocabulary items and a range of morphological paradigms and sentence types. Among the people Flint recorded at Woorabinda were three elderly men and a woman who had been born and raised in different locations within the Maric-speaking area of Queensland (see Barrett 2005, Beale 1975 and Walsh and Wurm 1981). Judging by their conversations with Flint recorded during these elicitation sessions, the people interviewed also spoke English, the language they used in their everyday life. Other Aboriginal countrymen of these speakers were also present during some recording sessions and they participated in singing a traditional song; they were referred to from time to time in the course of the recording sessions but were not formally interviewed by Flint as part of his language elicitation.

Flint was at Woorabinda as part of his long-term research project known as the Queensland Speech Survey (QSS), the primary aim of which was to record and analyse the varieties of English spoken in Queensland, including those spoken by Aboriginal people.[1] He was also interested in ascertaining the knowledge of traditional Aboriginal languages in Queensland at that time. He was very excited by and supportive of the research program of the then recently established Australian Institute of Aboriginal Studies (AIAS)[2] situated in Canberra. He used his access to Aboriginal people living on the missions and government settlements he visited to meet people who had knowledge of their traditional languages, with whom other linguists might eventually work in order to document these languages for posterity. Flint was also in contact with anthropologists wanting to conduct research on various aspects of Aboriginal culture and encouraged them to contact those Aboriginal people he had met who had shown interest in explaining aspects of their culture and languages to researchers in order to have them recorded. These motivations emerge in his conversations with the Aboriginal people recorded at Woorabinda, and elsewhere.

The main three men from the Upper Warrego and Maranoa regions of Queensland whom Flint interviewed and recorded at Woorabinda on the first of December 1965 were Eddie Conway (EC) who was born at Springsure, Vivian Solomon (VS) who was born at Mount Playfair Station east of Tambo, and Willie Rookwood (WR), born at Coogoon Station near Roma around 1890.[3] Flint also interviewed Sadie Coombra (SC), whom he records in his notes as coming from Mitchell.[4]

While there is a striking similarity between the recorded vocabularies of these four speakers, there are differences in lexicon, pronunciation and some grammatical forms. This is compatible with the long-standing claim that these languages form part of a dialect chain stretching from the Springsure area in the north-east to the Roma and Mitchell area in the south (see Dixon 2002 and references therein). The vocabulary of Willie Rookwood – and of Sadie Coombra – is clearly very similar to that of the two more northerly speakers, Eddie Conway and Vivian Solomon. However, as is evident in the language recorded by Flint, the northern and southern varieties are distinguished by one striking phonological difference. Apart from a few terms, including the language name, Gunggari, words beginning with a velar stop (written *k* in song texts documented below) in the speech of the northern speakers (Eddie Conway and Vivian Solomon) lack an initial consonant in the speech of the southern Gunggari speakers (Willie

---

1 Flint's QSS documents and recordings are archived in the Elwyn Flint Papers, Fryer Library, at the University of Queensland. Flint's recordings of traditional Aboriginal languages have been digitised, and analogue copies of his original tapes are held in the AIATSIS collection. See Flint Papers catalogue at *https://www.library.uq.edu.au/fryer-library/ms/Flint/flint_catalogue.html* with cross references to materials held by AIATSIS.
2 Now known as the Australian Institute of Aboriginal and Torres Strait Islander Studies (AIATSIS).
3 Flint kept meticulous recording logs. Each speaker (or group of speakers) was assigned a group number: EC = R. 329, VS = R.330, WR = R. 331 and SC = R. 332. Willie Rookwood may have gained his surname from Rookwood Station, established in the nineteenth century on the Maranoa River. Both he and Sadie Coombra were among the original inhabitants of Woorabinda (Clements 1977), Rookwood being moved there from the Taroom settlement when it was closed down.
4 Flint records Sadie's surname as 'Cumbera'. In a personal communication to Mary Laughren on 24/11/2015, Mr Des Crump informed Laughren that both his great aunt Effie and her sister Sadie were from Coombra Station via Bollon, south of Mitchell, hence the origin of their surname. See also Clements (1977) for further information on both Willie Rookwood and Sadie Coombra.

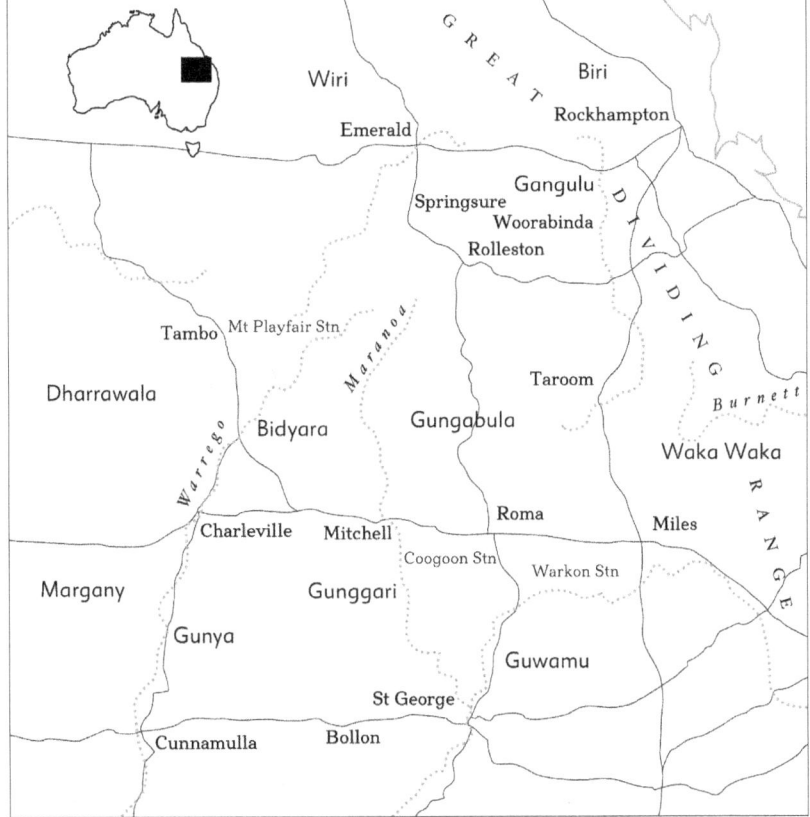

Map 6.1: The Upper Warrego-Maranoa region of Queensland. (Names of languages are in large font, towns in smaller font, stations in smallest font and rivers in italics.)

Rookwood and Sadie Coombra).[5] This loss of initial *k/g is reflected in the name Ungorri (corresponding to Ungkari in the writing system used in this study) recorded by Howitt (1904:108) as the name of the language spoken 'in the country comprising Saint George, Charleville, Nive, Taroom, Surat and Condamine', which Breen (n.d.) judges to be derived from Gunggari by the loss of the initial consonant.[6]

Willie Rookwood refers to his language as Gunggari.[7] He gives his Aboriginal (or 'bush') name as Wunkulala and explains that he is a *dhangurd mardi* or Possum (Dreaming) man. Referring to *dhangurd*, Willie Rookwood explains, 'That's not my name, that's my religion that's

---

5   Breen (1973a:2) notes that this feature marks the distinction between the Warrego and Maranoa languages.
6   Given the pervasive nature of the dropping of the initial velar stop in the speech of Willie Rookwood and Sadie Coombra, it is clear that the language name 'Gunggari' entered the language after this change had occurred, from a language which preserved the word-initial velar stop. As Breen (n.d.) points out, this term derives from a cardinal direction term, meaning 'east' in some languages and 'north' in others. Thus it is possible that people to the west of the Gunggari-speaking (and Ungkari-speaking) areas used this term to refer to their eastern neighbours. In support of this claim, *kungkari* 'east' is recorded in Wangkumara, which is spoken to the west of the Gunggari speaking area.
7   There are distinct western Queensland languages called by the same name which are usually distinguished by different spellings: Kungkari versus Gunggari (see Breen 1990, Breen n.d.). The Maric language of the Maranoa area spoken by Willie Rookwood and Sadie Coombra is typically written as 'Gunggari' while the more westerly language is written as 'Kungkari'. Although we use *k* as the symbol for a dorso-velar stop in our documentation of Flint's Maric data, we retain 'Gunggari' as the spelling of the language name in a bid to avoid confusion with Kungkari – which Dixon (2002:xxxiii) includes in the Je subgroup of his Greater Maric Group – and to maintain continuity with established practice.

Figure 6.1: Willie Rookwood, aged 48 (taken by Norman Tindale, 1938, © South Australian Museum)

come through the bora ground'.[8] He also explains that the Dreaming of his countrywoman Sadie Coombra, whose Gunggari name is Mankulanyi, is *dhakany* 'sand goanna'.[9]

At a certain point in Flint's interview with Willie Rookwood, the latter starts to question Flint about his religious affiliation and beliefs and the two men establish their mutual association with the Anglican denomination.[10] Rookwood then asks Flint if he would like to listen to and record a traditional song that the former would sing. Flint enthusiastically agrees that he would like to do so and Rookwood proceeds to sing a series of four songs. Other people join in the singing of the song 'Red Kangaroo', which we discuss in section 3. Rookwood's initiation of this discussion of religion and song would seem to reflect the significance he attached to these subjects and the fact that singing and theological beliefs and practices are very much intertwined in Australian Aboriginal culture. Rookwood explains the meaning of the song texts and the more general context in which they were traditionally sung, laying out the cultural conceptual framework in which the song texts are to be understood, as will be demonstrated in the following sections.

Our primary aim here is to document the four songs sung by Willie Rookwood that were recorded by Flint in 1965. In the following sections we set out the lyrics and music of each song starting with *Dyindidyindi* 'Willy wagtail', for which Rookwood gave the most detailed explanation of the words and their meaning. In our discussion of the formal properties of the songs

---

8   Breen (1973a:154) records *wunku* as a Bidyara section name, which suggests that *Wunkulala* is built on the root *wunku*.
9   For a detailed account of the contents of Flint's 1965 recordings made at Woorabinda (and a comparison with other sources which document these and closely related languages), see Laughren (2013).
10 Flint, a non-Indigenous man from Brisbane, was ordained an Anglican priest in 1938 and served as an army chaplain during World War 2 (Edwards 1997).

and the ways in which the lyrics are matched to music, we make some comparisons between the four songs and also with other Australian Aboriginal song traditions that we are familiar with, particularly Arandic and Warlpiri songs from Central Australia (henceforth 'Central Australian song style').

The structure of the remainder of this article is as follows: in §2 we discuss the 'Willy wagtail' song, the text of which is fairly transparent. In §3 we discuss the Red Kangaroo song and in §4 the Two Men Fighting song. In §5 we discuss the Farewell song, which is actually the first song on the recording but also the most different. In §6 we compare the four songs, noting that the different verse structures correspond to the different linguistic-geographic origins of the songs. We conclude by comparing the songs performed by Rookwood with the broader Central Australian musical style, as described by Alice Moyle (1966: xvii; 1974:i) and in our own research (Turpin & Laughren 2013, 2014). Note that the musical examples for each section are to be found in Appendix B.

2 Dyindidyindi 'Willy wagtail' (song 2)

This song is said to be about a man who appears in the form of a willy wagtail. From the singer's interpretation of the song, we get a sense of how beings straddle the physical and spiritual dimensions and how an experience situated at the intersection of these realms can be encapsulated in a song.

> It come up to you. He come up as a bird. When he come up as a bird, then he turn into a human. Human, spiritual way. He come in spiritual way, you see. In the early days of Aboriginal people, well they come like that in a bird, image of a bird, image of a dog, image of a kangaroo, image of an emu. When they come up close to you, if they want to, they'll turn into a man then. That's how that corroboree come about (Willie Rookwood to Elwyn Flint 1/12/1965, 8'06–8'25).[11]

2.1 The rhythmic text

As in many traditional Aboriginal songs, the song is made up of a short rhythmic text that repeats over the course of a much longer melody. The singer gives a word-for-word translation of this text. This is shown in (1) with a broad rhythmic transcription.

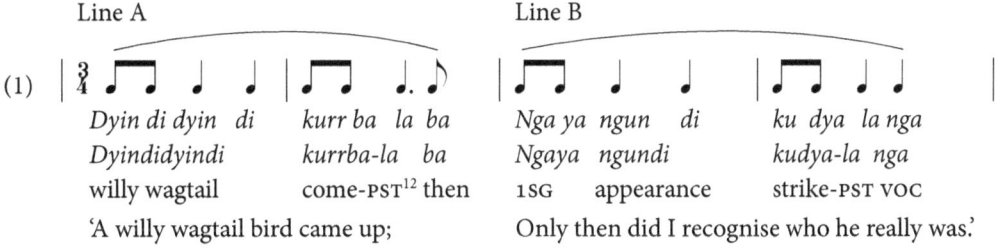

(1)

Line A	Line B
Dyin di dyin di kurr ba la ba	Nga ya ngun di ku dya la nga
Dyindidyindi kurrba-la ba	Ngaya ngundi kudya-la nga
willy wagtail come-PST[12] then	1SG appearance strike-PST VOC
'A willy wagtail bird came up;	Only then did I recognise who he really was.'

The rhythmic text consists of 16 syllables spanning 4 bars of ¾ metre. Triple metre is evident from the accompanying clap beat (represented by crosses in Musical example 6.1, Appendix B). Each bar has a similar rhythmic pattern. Based on parallel rhythm and syntax (noun + verb), the text can be divided into two lines, each of two bars.

The song is in a Maric language, although it is not clear which particular variety. The word *dyindidyindi* 'willy wagtail' is found in Gunggari, Gunya and Margany and similar words are

---
11 The time code refers to the archival recording UQFL173_b54_R311_332A_sideB.
12 The following abbreviations are used in linguistic glosses: 1SG=1 person singular, 3DU=3 person dual, IMPF=imperfective, INST=instrumental, NEG=negative, PST=past, REC=reciprocal, REF=reflexive, VOC=vocable.

found well beyond this region. The word may in fact be onomatopoeic. *Ngaya* 'I' is similarly widespread across the region. The phrase *ngundi kudya-* 'appearance strike' probably means 'recognise'. *Kudya-* is a verb meaning 'to hit with a missile'. According to Willie Rookwood *ngundi* 'appearance, gait, image' is a Gunggari word.

Other words in the song, however, appear not to be Gunggari. The 'k' initial words *kurrba-la* 'came up' and *kudya-la* 'struck' occur only in the northern Maric languages, while in the southern varieties such as Gunggari, these are *urrba-la* and *udya-la* respectively. We do not know whether the song is from a northern variety, or whether it originated in one of the southern varieties before these languages lost their initial velar stop. Perhaps the northern variety words were deliberately chosen to signal a northern origin of the bird; or, alternatively, to create a poetic rather than everyday sounding word. Another possibility is that, in this song tradition, syllables must be consonant-initial, especially if they fall on the beat. These ambiguities mean that it is best to think of the language of the song as Maric, rather than a more specific language variety.

The last syllable *nga*, for which no speech equivalent was given, is almost certainly a vocable.[13] A vocable is a sequence of speech sounds from a given language which form one or more syllables, but does not represent a word of the language (cf. Fabb 1997:104). The evidence for this analysis is that *nga* is a vocable in other songs on this recording and beyond (Austin 1978: 531); also it is in line-final position, and in songs from Central Australia rarely do such vocables occur in any other metrical position. Furthermore, the *nga* syllable is omitted when a breath is taken at this point in the text cycle. This can be seen in bars 4, 16 and 20, for example, in Musical example 6.1.

2.2 Song structure and melody

The song consists of 16 cycles of the rhythmic text, ending at the penultimate syllable, omitting the vocable *nga*. There is very little variation of the rhythmic text throughout the course of the song. In the transcription of the song in Musical example 6.1, each repetition of the rhythmic text is signalled with a boxed number and the circled number represents each iteration of the melody. The melody consists of four sections, each of which maps on to one statement of the rhythmic text and so the melody as a whole is 16 bars. From Musical example 6.1 it can be seen that the first section of the melody is a descent from the 3rd to a repeating tonic, E (e.g. bars 1–4). The downward movements are characterised by glissandi, as is the case throughout all the songs. The second section is an ascent from the 4th to the 6th descending back to the 3rd (e.g. bars 5–8). The third section is only minimally different from the first section, with a step down to the second, F#, and back to the third (e.g. bar 9). The final section is a repeated tonic (e.g. bars 13–16). The melody spans four lines and so can be likened to a stanza.

This melody is sung four times over the course of the song (indicated by the numbers in circles in Musical example 6.1). The third stanza (iteration of the melody) is interrupted by the singer's coughing (bar 46). It seems reasonable to assume that without interruption, the underlying structure of the song is 64 bars.

2.3 A comparison with Central Australian song style

As is common in the songs of inland Australia, the 'Willy wagtail' song consists of two lines, with the number of rhythmic notes determined by the number of syllables (Ellis 1968). The

---

13 Holmer (1983) analyses the Gunggari verbal suffix *-nga~ -na* as variants of the imperfective aspect inflection which contrasts with the perfective suffix *-la*. In the song *nga* follows *-la*, ruling out this option.

song also has a repeating melody that is much longer than the rhythmic text, which is a feature of songs from 'a vast area of the continent, from western Cape York to most of inland WA' (Moyle 1966:xvii).[14] The song departs from the Central Australian style, however, in its fixed relationship between rhythmic text and melody: the melody always corresponds to four cycles of the text, and each melodic section is one statement of the text, beginning and ending at the same point. In contrast, Central Australian songs show variability in the alignment of the rhythmic text and melody in the course of a single song (and also across multiple performances of a song).[15]

3 Bawurra 'Red kangaroo' (song 3)

Following the 'Willy wagtail' song, Willie Rookwood, accompanied by others, sings a song that is said to be about a red kangaroo (*Macropus rufus*). The kangaroo wakes up at the sound of a happy family bird (*Struthidea cinerea*)[16], who heralds the approach of a hunter. Rookwood explains the event that the song portrays as follows:

a. Well this here, that's Happy Family now see, that kangaroo asleep see, so there's a person sneaking for it see, so he heard this bird singing out now, you know them happy family birds? They singing out now. Well that fella got up now with a fright, he see that fella, he look around, he see that *mardi* [man] coming for him to kill him see. No good, he went. (Willie Rookwood to Elwyn Flint 1/12/1965, 12:09–12:38).

In an explanation of the song's theme Rookwood provides the phrase '*bawurra, ngula yurdi kuthi-kuthi*' (red kangaroo, that red animal). *Bawurra* is a widespread term for this macropod in Maric languages. The speech equivalents of the rest of the text remain somewhat of a mystery. However, we can say much about the structure of the song, which is similar to 'Willy wagtail' in many respects.

3.1 The rhythmic text

As in the song 'Willy wagtail', the rhythmic text of 'Red kangaroo' consists of two lines of four bars, as shown in (2).

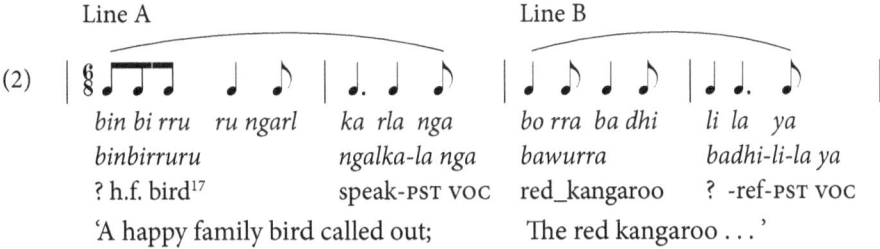

Unlike 'Willy wagtail', there is no accompanying clap beat, yet the metre of this song feels as if it is a duple compound metre (6/8); that is, the beat subdivides into three quavers rather than two. This song has a much slower tempo than the other three songs, which are all in simple metre.

---

14 Moyle qualifies this by noting that 'north-western central Australia, Cape York and inland NSW have not been studied in detail' (Moyle 1966:xvii).
15 Another feature of much Central Australian music is that either text line may commence a song. But without other performances for comparison, it is not possible to determine if this might apply to the song under consideration here.
16 Also commonly known as an apostlebird.
17 Breen (1981:351) glosses *binbira* and *binbida* as 'budgerigar' in the related Maric languages Gunya and Marrgany.

The rhythmic text can be divided into two lines based on parallel rhythm and the syllables *nga* and *ya*, which occur in bar final position, and so are prime candidates as vocables. The rhythmic text has 15 syllables, one less than 'Willy wagtail', and so its two lines differ rhythmically in that Line A sets a three-syllable unit to the first beat ♩♩♩, whereas Line B sets a two-syllable phonetic unit to the first beat ♩♪.[18] There is a tendency for musical phrases to end in a long note (this is not unique to Aboriginal songs), so on purely musical grounds the division into phrases can be perceived as in (3) in which the vocables are phrase initial while still at the end of a bar. A similar mismatch between units of text and units of rhythm is also encountered in some Arandic songs (see, for example, Figure 1 in Turpin in press).

(3) [musical notation]

ya bin bi rru ru ngarl ka rla nga bo rra ba dhi li la

3.2 Song structure and melody

Like 'Willy wagtail', 'Red kangaroo' consists of 16 cycles of the rhythmic text, plus an extra half. The song commences with the second syllable *bi* and ends with Line A. The repetitions of the verse throughout the course of the song show little variability in the text; only the final syllable of Line A, *nga*, is sometimes sung *ya* (three times, bars 18, 34 and 46 in Musical example 6.2, Appendix B) and sung once as *ka* (bar 10).

The melody of 'Red kangaroo' is sung four times, summarised in Table 6.1. Each iteration of the melody aligns with the start of the rhythmic-text. The length of the melody is not fixed; each time it varies by either repeating the final tonic for an extra line or half-line (as in the 3rd and 4th iteration) or it omits the first melodic phrase (as in the 1st iteration). In this way the melody expands and contracts to accommodate different lengths of rhythmic text, in a similar way to Central Australian songs (Barwick 1989, Treloyn 2007, Turpin & Laughren 2013). However, unlike Central Australian songs, expansion and contraction in 'Red kangaroo' always accommodates the entire rhythmic text and never just a section of it.

Table 6.1: Text-melody setting 'Red kangaroo' (song 3)

MELODY	DURATION	TEXT
1st iteration, bars 1–12	12 bars	rhythmic text x 3
2nd iteration, bars 13–28	16 bars	rhythmic text x 4
3rd iteration, bars 29–48	20 bars	rhythmic text x 5
4th iteration, bars 49–66	18 bars	rhythmic text x 4.5

We describe the melody drawing on its second iteration, bars 13–28 in Musical example 6.2. The melody consists of four phrases, defined by where a breath is usually taken. The first phrase is a descent from the fifth to the second (bars 13–14). The second phrase is a repeated upper tonic descending to the tonic (bars 15–21). The third phrase is characterised by ornamentation on the 4th and then 5th pitch after which it descends to the tonic (bars 21–25). The exact point at which the breath occurs varies. The fourth phrase is a repeated tonic.

---

18 The first syllable [bo] derived from the underlying two syllables [ba-wu] is linked to the longer of the notes making up the first beat. We have noted the same reduction of two monomoraic syllables separated by a glide to a single syllable linked to a relatively long note in Warlpiri *yawulyu* songs (Turpin & Laughren 2013:404).

Breaths sometimes replace the final syllable *ya* (e.g. bar 12) and *nga* (e.g. bar 14). An additional point at which a breath is taken is before the fifth syllable of the verse (*ngal*); however, this syllable is never omitted (providing further evidence of our interpretation of *ngalka-la* 'speak-PAST' as the speech equivalent). This said, the failure to align the first (stressed) syllable of *ngalkala* with the rhythmically prominent left boundary of a bar distinguishes this song from the other three, as well as from Central Australian songs. In the spoken form, it is the word-initial syllable which is prominent, whereas in this song the initial syllable of the verb is aligned with the weakest rhythmic position.

The ornamentation in 'Red kangaroo' is more complex than that of the other three songs and implies a higher level of difficulty, in particular by comparison with songs 2 and 4, which are executed quite simply. Bars 6 to 8 demonstrate this, as complex melisma is combined with portamento to provide one long flowing line (reminiscent of Indian classical sung ornamentation). The same passage repeated in bars 22 to 24 shows the same level of complexity but a different melismatic pattern (omitting the final vocable *nga* of Line A), indicating that ornamentation is an important vehicle for variation and expression on the part of the singer. The technical execution of these passages indicates a high level of vocal expertise, which raises the question as to why Mr Rookwood sang this song so differently. This could imply either that he was more secure in the song style, that he had learnt it from a singer with a higher level of skill, that the song itself was in a different genre to the others or that he had simply sung it more often, so that the variety of melismatic figures was more easily recalled.

4 Unimila 'Two men fighting' (song 4)

The last song sung by Willie Rookwood is said to be about a white policeman walking towards two men who are in a fist fight, to see what they are fighting over: '*Buliman mandala* [Policeman went]. He wanna catch them two *mardi* [man], see what they fighting over' (16'32"). Flint goes on to ask what happened, and Rookwood replies that it 'came to nothing, it just came to that corroboree' (16'46). Rookwood explains the meaning of the song using a few Maric words and phrases, including the following:

(4a) *Mardi   bula   uni-mi-la*
man   3DU   hit-REC-PST
'Two men fought one another.' (15'06")

(4b) *Murra-ngku,   that means knuckles.*
fist-INST
'with (their) fist.' (15'18")

(5) *Widhu-wula   manda-lala*
Whiteman-two   go-PST:IMPF
'Two Whitemen (policemen) were going.'[19] (16'02")

4.1 The rhythmic text

Only two words in his explanations can be tentatively matched with words in the song: *uni-li* 'hit each other' and *marda* 'hand', although *mardi* 'man' is also a possibility for this same portion of the song text. For some parts of the text we could find no speech equivalents with meanings

---

19 It is not clear whether both the Whitemen are policemen or just one of them.

compatible with those provided by the singer. The rhythmic text and putative speech equivalents are shown in (6).[20]

(6)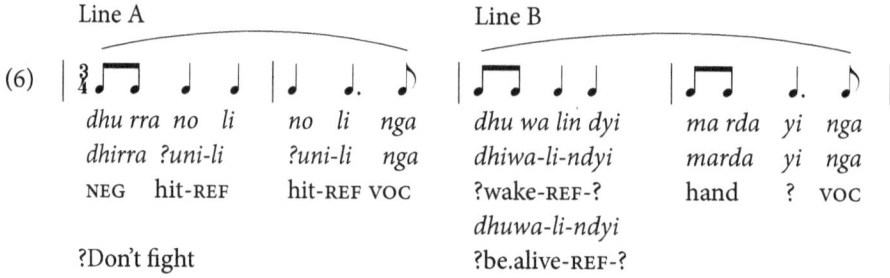

Line A			Line B		
dhu rra no li	no li	nga	dhu wa lin dyi	ma rda	yi nga
dhirra ?uni-li	?uni-li	nga	dhiwa-li-ndyi	marda	yi nga
NEG hit-REF	hit-REF	VOC	?wake-REF-?	hand	? VOC
			dhuwa-li-ndyi		
?Don't fight			?be.alive-REF-?		

Like 'Red kangaroo', this song consists of 15 syllables spanning four bars. Its rhythm is almost identical to that in the 'Willy wagtail' song. Triple metre is again evident from the accompanying clap beat (see Musical example 6.3, Appendix B). The text can also be divided into two lines, based on parallel rhythm and the recurring syllable *nga*, which, as we have seen in previous songs, is a line-final vocable. The only rhythmic difference between the two lines is that in Line A, the first beat of bar 2 is occupied by a single syllable, *no*, whereas in Line B the first beat of bar 2 is divided into two syllables – *marda*. The long syllable *no* suggests a speech equivalent with an internal glide initial syllable that has been elided, such as *nawuli*; however, we can find no speech equivalents for such a postulated form.

As in the previous song, on musical grounds the division between lines A and B could also be made before the upbeat *nga*. Such a division is illustrated in (7).

(7)

Line A: nga dhu rra no li no li
Line B: nga dhu wa lin dyi ma rda yi

4.2 Song structure and melody

The song consists of 19 cycles of the rhythmic text, which is three more repetitions than in the previous songs. This is also the longest song, and its tempo is similar to that of the 'Willy wagtail' song. Unlike the previous songs, this song commences and ends with the final bar of the verse, *mardayi*.[21] From Musical example 6.3 we can see that throughout the course of the song the verse shows consonant variability in three places:

- the final syllable of both lines varies between *nga ~ ba ~ ma ~ ka*
- bar 4 varies between *mardayi ~ marlayi*
- the interdental sound *dh* in both lines is pronounced as a fricative, stop or nasal

The variability in the rhythmic text may reflect the uncertainty surrounding the phonology of words in this song.

The melody of 'Two Men Fighting' is sung six times, summarised in Table 6.2. In most cases the melody lasts for three cycles of the verse; however, the fifth iteration of the melody is longer, as the tonic extends for an extra cycle of the verse. As mentioned in relation to 'Red Kangaroo', such an extension of the melody to accommodate more rhythmic text is reminiscent of Central Australian songs, although there it is much more common and variable. In this song

---

20 *Dhuwa-* 'be alive'; *dhiwa-* 'wake' (*vt*) and *dhirra* 'NEG' are documented by Breen (1973a & b) in Bidyara.
21 It appears that the recording began after the singing had commenced.

the rhythmic text and verse are always coterminous (with the exception of the first iteration of the melody), unlike much Central Australian song. Expansion of the melody occurs, but as in 'Red kangaroo', only for the duration of the entire verse and never for just a section of it.

Table 6.2: Text-melody setting in 'Two men fighting' (song 4)

MELODY	DURATION	TEXT
1st iteration, bars 1–9	9 bars	rhythmic text x 2.5
2nd iteration, bars 10–21	12 bars	rhythmic text x 3
3rd iteration, bars 22–33	12 bars	rhythmic text x 3
4th iteration, bars 34–45	12 bars	rhythmic text x 3
5th iteration, bars 46–61	16 bars	rhythmic text x 4
6th iteration, bars 62–73	12 bars	rhythmic text x 3

The melody itself consists of two simple phrases. The tonic is A. The song makes no use of the 7th, so we don't know whether it is sharp or not, or in fact whether the scale is hexatonic. Here we describe the melody drawing on its second iteration, bars 10–21. The first section is a descent from the 6th to the 2nd over three bars (e.g. bars 10–12) and the second section is a descent from the 5th to the tonic, with the descent over two bars and the tonic over seven bars (e.g. bars 13–21). Breaths are taken at the end of the first melodic section in place of the syllable *dyi*.[22] Breaths are also taken in the second melodic section, in place of the verse-final vocable *nga*, both during and at the end of the repeated tonic. This provides further evidence that this syllable is a vocable.

5 'Farewell' (song 1)

The first song sung by Willie Rookwood on the recording is the one that is the most different. It is said to belong to the Burnett River district, and to be in a language different to that spoken by the singer. We suggest that it may be in the Wakawaka language, which belongs to a different subgroup (Wakka-Kabic), to the east of the Maric languages (see Laffan 2003). Rookwood sings through the lines of the song, trying to catch a hint of its meaning. After singing the second line he says, 'It's just like there is a person going away', so Flint calls it a 'Farewell corroboree'. The rhythmic text of this song is shown in (8).

5.1 The rhythmic text

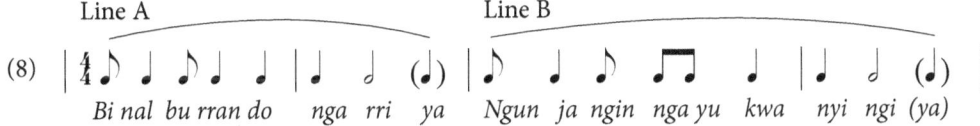

We could find no sure speech equivalents with meanings compatible with those provided by the singer.[23] The rhythmic text consists of 17 syllables, one more than in the 'Willy wagtail' song. Like the other songs, this one consists of four bars which divide into two lines: eight syllables in Line A and nine syllables in Line B. In Line B the third beat is divided into two syllables (*ngayu*),

---

22 With one exception in bar 27 where no breath is taken and the syllable is sung to a melody that steps upwards from the 2nd to the 3rd.
23 *Burrando* may be an inflected form of verb *burra* 'get up, go away' documented in Maric languages by Holmer (1983:231 & 331) and Breen (1973a:§6.12). Breen (1981:358) records *ngundya* 'face' in Maric language Gunya, which may correspond with *ngunja* at start of Line B.

whereas it is only one syllable in Line A (*rran*). A significant difference in the song 'Farewell' can be seen in the patterning of the two lines throughout the song, as shown in Table 6.3. Each line repeats either four, six or seven times before moving on to the alternate line, which also repeats before moving back to the other line. Only the last line of the song, Line B, is not repeated.

Table 6.3: Verse structure of 'Farewell' (song 1)

A1	*Binal burrando ngarri ya '* *Binal burrando ngarri '* *Binarl burrando ngarri* *Binal burrando ngarri ' **ngaya***	A2	*Binal burrando ngarri ya* *Binal burrando 'ngarri ya* *Binarl burrando ngarri '* *Binal burrando ngarri ya* *Binarl burrando ngarri '* *Binarl burrando ngarri* *Binal burrando ngarri ' **ngaya***
B1	*Ngunja nginngayukwa nyingi* *Ngunja nginngayukwa nyingi '* *Ngunja nginngayukwa nyingi* *Ngunja nginngayukwa nyingi ya* *Ngunja nginngayukwa nyingi '* *Ngunja nginngayukwa nyingi ' **ngaya***	B2	*Ngunja nginngayukwa nyingi*

Before repeating a line, a breath can be taken replacing the last syllable, (e.g. bar 4); or alternatively, the singer can continue without taking a breath, either singing *ya* or extending the duration of the previous syllable (*rri* or *ngi*). Bar 2 has both *ya* and a breath, and consequently it has an extra beat.

Unlike the other songs, 'Farewell' has a two-syllable 'bridge' that always leads into the alternate verse – *ngaya* ♫ , and this is always preceded by a breath (e.g. bars 8 and 20). This creates an anacrusis, as if *ngaya* '1sgNOM'[24] were part of the following line, as illustrated in (9).

(9)

nga ya Ngu nja ngin nga yu kwa | nyi ngi |

nga ya Bi nal bu rran do | nga rri |

5.2 Song structure and melody

The melody of this song is sung three times, summarised in Table 6.4. As in 'Red kangaroo', the length of the melody is not fixed; each time it varies in length by either repeating the final tonic for an extra line (as in the 2nd iteration) or omitting the line of repeated tonic (as in the 1st iteration).

Table 6.4: Text-melody setting in 'Farewell' (song 1). '|' represents a melodic phrase boundary

MELODY	DURATION	TEXT
1st iteration, bars 1–12	12 bars	AA|AA|BB
2nd iteration, bars 13–26	14 bars	BB|BB |AAA
3rd iteration, bars 27–36	10 bars	AA|AA|B

The melody itself can be divided into three phrases based on where a breath *always* occurs. We illustrate this with the 3rd iteration of the melody in Musical example 6.4 (Appendix B). The

---

24 *Ngaya* '1sgNOM' in the relevant Maric languages, but *ngay* or *ngee* in Wakka-Kabic languages (Laffan 2003).

first phrase is a 2-bar descent from the fourth to the tonic followed by two bars of repeated tonic (bars 27–30).[25] The second phrase is a 2-bar stepwise passage 5–6–5 followed by a 2-bar descent to the tonic (bars 31–34). The third phrase commences on the fifth (with the upbeat *ngaya*) leading into the same 2-bar descent to the tonic as in the second phrase. In the first and second iterations, this is followed by two bars of repeated tonic, although not in this final iteration.

5.3 Summary of 'Farewell'

The verse structure of this song differs dramatically from that of the other three songs. In this song, line repetition occurs before moving on to the alternate line (AAA…BBB… rather than ABAB etc.). While this resembles Central Australian song style to some extent, a major difference is that the number of line repetitions is fixed in Central Australian songs (usually once, i.e. AABB). The 'Farewell' song has no set number of line repetitions. It is perhaps for this reason that the melody involves an upbeat *ngaya* to herald the change of line, in the way a cue from an improvising soloist in a jazz band might herald the return to the head. The insertion of a disyllabic unit (i.e. *ngaya*) at the end of the melody is rarely, if ever, encountered in Central Australian song.

There are, however, other aspects of the rhythmic text of this song that resemble the other three songs sung by Willie Rookwood, as well as the broader Central Australian song style. First, the verse consists of two lines with the number of rhythmic notes determined by the number of syllables. Second, the relative lengths of the verse and melody differ in that the melody is longer than the rhythmic-text. Finally, in relation to pitch, 'Farewell' has an ascending phrase within a melodic section, similar to 'Willy wagtail' and 'Red kangaroo'.

6 Conclusion

In this chapter, we have tried to show how an understanding of the structural features of song can inform efforts to revitalise ancestral song traditions. For example, the placement of vocables in line-final position, the tendency for recurring noun + verb line structure, and the matching of word boundaries with bar boundaries, can help weigh up the arguments in favour or against proposed speech equivalents. The style of ornamentations used are also noteworthy. We have also suggested that different verse structures, particularly as A/B versus AA+/BB+, and different degrees of ornamentation may reflect differences in the origins of songs, and thus their linguistic-geographic affiliation.

To date, nothing has been published on the songs of this region. However, linguists Gavan Breen and Margaret Sharpe recorded both speech and a few songs from this part of Queensland. Breen recorded Bob Toogler singing a song said to be in the Margany language, traditionally spoken to the west of the Gunggari language (Breen_G10-001586A). Margaret Sharpe recorded Willy Rookwood, Sadie Coombra and Eddie Conway in April 1966 (ms1353). Her recordings include *Bawurra* 'Red kangaroo' by Willie Rookwood (AIATSIS SHARPE_M02-003086A, 7'51") and one additional song about an old blind woman searching for something she has dropped on the ground (5'45").[26]

Since working on these songs, we have compiled them onto a CD that has been circulating in the descendant community since 2015 (Figure 6.2), mostly through Tom Kirk and Aunty Ruth Hegarty. Some community members were unaware of the existence of these recordings, and the Fryer library at the University of Queensland is currently working to connect the Flint recordings with descendants of the speakers on the collection.[27] The analysis and recirculation

---

25   The first bar of the song starts somewhat differently, centred around the 3rd pitch rather than the 4th.
26   Willie Rookwood passed away later that same year (Clements 1977).
27   https://www.library.uq.edu.au/fryer-library/indigenous-voices/.

of the recordings have inspired moves to revive songs of the Warrego-Maranoa region.[28] Tom Kirk, who is involved with language revitalisation, spent time in the emotion-laden task of analysing and engaging with the songs. A descendant of Aunty Ruth Hegarty has been working on a version of 'Willie wagtail' for performance. It is hoped that such performances will bring the songs of this region into the contemporary world.

Acknowledgements

We thank Elizabeth Alvey at the Fryer Library for locating the digitised versions of these recordings and Kathy Seton and Andrew Fahey for helping us connect with descendants of Mr Rookwood. We also thank Des Crump, as well as Mr Rookwood's descendants Aunty Ruth Hegarty and Tom Kirk, for providing contextual information about Willie Rookwood and Sadie Coombra, feedback on an earlier draft of this article, and for granting permission to reproduce the photo. We thank Ben Foley for production of the CD cover and map. We gratefully acknowledge the Australian Research Council for funding this research (FT140100783, DP1092887).

Figure 6.2: CD cover of Willie Rookwood's songs from the Flint recordings

Appendix A: Recording details

Table 6.5: Details of recordings analysed in this chapter (Flint Collection, University of Queensland UQFL173_b54_R311_332A_sideB)

Song 1	*Burrandu* 'Farewell'	2'32 – 3'41	1'09 seconds
Song 2	*Dyindidyindi* 'Willy wagtail'	5'09 – 6'24	1'15 seconds
Song 3	*Bawurra* 'Red kangaroo'	9'51 – 11'31	1'41 seconds
Song 4	*Unimila* 'Two men fighting'	13'05 – 14'36	1'29 seconds

---

28 There was a sheet music publication based on five traditional songs of this region titled 'Australian Aboriginal songs: melodies, rhythm and words truly and authentically Aboriginal / collected and translated by H.O. Lethbridge, accompaniments arranged by Arthur S. Loam' (originally published 1937. For further details, see the Skinner and Wafer 'checklist', entry 27, online at *http://sydney.edu.au/paradisec/australharmony/checklist-indigenous-music-1.php#027*). We have been unable to identify any similarities between this sheet music and the songs discussed here. We thank Aunty Ruth Hegarty for bringing this to our attention.

Appendix B: Musical examples

Musical example 6.1: *Dyindidyindi* 'Willy wagtail' (song 2) (MM ♩ = 152) 1'15"

Musical example 6.2: *Bawurra* 'Red kangaroo' (song 3) (MM ♩. = 80) 1'39"

6. SONGS PERFORMED BY WILLIE ROOKWOOD AT WOORABINDA IN 1965

Musical example 6.3: *Unimila* 'Two men fighting' (song 4) (MM ♩ = 149) 1'28"

Musical example 6.4: 'Farewell' (song 1) (MM ♩ = 109) 1'29"

References

Austin, Peter, 1978, A grammar of the Diyari language of north-east South Australia. PhD dissertation, Australian National University, Canberra.

Barrett, Bevan, 2005, Historical reconstruction of the Maric languages of Central Queensland. MA thesis, Department of Linguistics, Australian National University, Canberra.

Barwick, Linda. 1989. Creative (ir)regularities: The intermeshing of Text and Melody in Performance of Central Australian Song. Australian Aboriginal Studies 1:12–28.

Beale, Anthony, 1975, The Maric language(s). BA (Hons) thesis, Department of Linguistics, Australian National University, Canberra.

Breen, J. Gavan, 1973a, Bidyara and Gungabula: grammar and vocabulary. Linguistic Communications 8. Monash University, Melbourne.

—— 1973b, Supplement to Bidyara and Gungabula: grammar and vocabulary. Melbourne: unpublished manuscript. (Copy held by AIATSIS as PMS 231.)

—— 1981, Margany and Gunya. In R.M.W. Dixon and Barry Blake, eds. Handbook of Australian languages, vol. 2, 275–393. Canberra: The Australian National University Press.

—— 1990, Salvage studies of western Queensland Aboriginal languages. Pacific Linguistics Series B-105. Canberra: Pacific Linguistics.

—— n.d. Thoughts about the names Mandandanyi and Gunggari. Ts, 4p. (Received from Gavan Breen 6th November 2000.)

Capell, Arthur, 1945, Methods and materials for recording Australian languages. Oceania 16(2):144–176.

Clements, J., ed., 1977, Woorabinda 1927–1977: golden jubilee year. Rockhampton, QLD: Woorabinda Golden Jubilee Committee.

Dixon, R. M. W., 2002, Australian languages: their nature and development. Cambridge: Cambridge University Press.

Edwards, Peter, 1997, Elwyn Henry Flint (1910–1983): some reflections on Elwyn. *https://www.library. uq.edu.au/fryer-library/ms/Flint/flint_cat_edwards.html* [accessed 20/10/2016].

Ellis, Catherine J., 1968, Rhythmic analysis of Aboriginal syllabic songs. Miscellanea Musicologica 3:21–49.

Fabb, Nigel, 1997, Linguistics and literature: language in the verbal arts of the world. Oxford: Blackwell.

Flint, Elwyn Henry, 1965, Indigenous languages recorded as part of the Queensland Speech Survey. The University of Queensland. Collection. doi:10.14264/uql.2015.467.

Holmer, Nils, 1983, Linguistic survey of south-eastern Queensland. Pacific Linguistics Series D-54. Canberra: Pacific Linguistics.

Laffan, Kate, 2003, Reconstruction of the Wakka-Kabic languages of south-eastern Queensland. BA (Hons.) thesis, Australian National University, Canberra.

Laughren, Mary, 2013, Elwyn Flint's 1965 recordings of Maric languages of the Warrego-Maranoa region of Queensland. *https://www.researchgate.net/publication/236119081_Elwyn_Flint's_1965_ recordings_of_Maric_Languages_of_the_Warrego-Maranoa_region_of_Queensland* [accessed 25 Jan 2016].

Lethbridge, H. O., 1937, Australian Aboriginal songs: melodies, rhythm and words truly and authentically Aboriginal. Collected and translated by H. O. Lethbridge, accompaniments arranged by Arthur S. Loam. Melbourne: Allan & Co. (Republished 1960.) See also *http://sydney.edu.au/ paradisec/australharmony/checklist-indigenous-music-1.php#027*.

Moyle, A. M., 1966, A handlist of field collections of recorded music in Australia and Torres Strait. Canberra: Australian Institute of Aboriginal Studies.

—— 1974, Songs of the Northern Territory. Companion booklet for the set of five long-playing discs (or cassettes). Canberra: Australian Institute of Aboriginal Studies.

Treloyn, Sally, 2007, Songs that pull: jadmi junba from the Kimberley region of northwest Australia. PhD dissertation, University of Sydney.

Turpin, Myfany, in press, Parallelism in Arandic song-poetry. Oral Tradition 31(1).

Turpin, Myfany, and Mary Laughren, 2013, Edge effects in Warlpiri yawulyu songs: resyllabification, epenthesis and final vowel modification. Australian Journal of Linguistics 33(4):399–425.

—— 2014, Text and meter in a Lander Warlpiri song series. Selected papers from the 44th Conference of the Australian Linguistic Society, *2013*, ed. by Lauren Gawne and Jill Vaughan. *http://hdl.handle. net/11343/40974* [accessed 27/01/2016].

Walsh, M. J., and S. A. Wurm, 1981, Maps of Australia and Tasmania. In S. A. Wurm and S. Hattori, eds, Language atlas of the Pacific area, part 1 (New Guinea area, Oceania, Australia), maps 20–23. Canberra: Australian Academy of the Humanities.

7 A survey of traditional south-eastern Australian Indigenous music

Barry McDonald
Independent researcher

Abstract

This chapter comprises a discussion of south-eastern Australian traditional Aboriginal music, based on the evidence of features that have been described by observers and researchers since the beginning of European occupation in the late eighteenth century.

The accounts canvassed cover subjects such as instrumentation, dance forms, song types, song creation, and musical education. An examination of recorded musical forms follows this survey, with the results of selected scholars' analyses summarised in order to determine if stylistic homogeneity can be discerned within the sample.

Further discussion contends that the attempt to isolate regional styles for Australian Indigenous musics is hampered by the fact that much of the data around south-eastern practice and production were gathered well before similar work began in other areas of the continent, by which time European attitudes and scholarly technologies and methodologies had undergone considerable and significant development. On the other hand, where south-eastern studies have been undertaken more recently, it is not known how far the music recorded has been modified by protracted European influence.

Keywords: regionalism, instrumentation, performance styles, composition, education.

Introduction

This chapter originally formed part of a much larger study examining change in south-eastern Australian Aboriginal music between 1830 and 1930 (McDonald 2001; see also McDonald 1996a, McDonald 1996b). Its purpose there was to provide a foundational description of Aboriginal music from which the direction, quality, and extent of subsequent change in the south-east could be discerned. The study found that, while musical structures altered radically in response to European innovation, various important, essential, Indigenous elements endured.

The present, revised, version of the chapter retains the focus on the early records but, by and large, omits discussion of the nature of the musical changes that took place in the colonial period and subsequently. Nonetheless, it casts light on the predilection of many early researchers for the collection and analysis of 'unadulterated' musical expression. It is argued that this was a consciously cultivated political attitude that ignored the actual historical situation, where Aboriginal music was already developing in significantly interesting ways in its continuing relationship with the European mainstream.

The chapter opens with a discussion of the problems inherent in defining regional styles in the music of Indigenous Australia (section 1). This is followed by an examination of available evidence for musical features of the region known as 'the south-east' (section 2). The argument moves on to consider the formal analyses of song texts and musical data, and provisionally explores the stylistic relationship of the south-east with other Australian regions (section 3). The last major segment deals with musical meaning systems and includes an investigation of the aesthetics of sound and tone and an overview of melodic, rhythmic, gestural, and visual performance languages (section 4). The chapter concludes with a brief sketch of the musical features that the south-east clearly shares with other parts of Australia, then provides some pointers for future research into those aspects of the regional comparison that remain obscure.

1 Issues regarding regional identity

In compendia of traditional Indigenous musical styles, the Australian continent is typically divided into the following regions: Arnhem Land; the central desert; the Kimberley; the south-west; Cape York; and south-eastern Australia and Tasmania (Jones 1972, 1980; Moyle 1966, 1992). While there are special musical characteristics that do partly distinguish some of these areas, others may be largely classifications of convenience. Logically, it is necessary to demonstrate that two conditions obtain in any argument for regionality: that the area in question is essentially culturally homogeneous; and that it presents recognisably different characteristics to other divisions. Furthermore, these premises require that evidence drawn from the different regions will be directly comparable. There are impediments to meeting all these conditions in any assessment of pre-contact cultural regionality for south-eastern Australia; these are summarised below.

The musical region dealt with here is, unlike the others, essentially an historical categorisation, rationalised chiefly on the ground that Indigenous performance traditions in the south-east had ceased to operate by the time the more remote geographical areas were being studied in depth. As a consequence, the broad thrust of comparative research into the region's Indigenous music has been historical, rather than taking recent or current performance into consideration. The picture that such an analysis presents has of course been determined by the available evidence, which mainly comprises scattered European-settler observations and analyses, the musical products of cultural 'salvage' operations undertaken systematically here since the mid 1950s, and the rare and recently elicited musical reminiscences of Aboriginal people themselves. In turn, the nature of this pool of evidence reflects, to a large degree, both the theoretical leanings of those who elicited it, and the state of development of contemporary musical research methodologies.

Nineteenth-century mainstream approaches to ethnological research were informed, as Russel McGregor has convincingly demonstrated, by the various tenets of what he terms the 'doomed race theory' (McGregor 1998). This is seen to have dictated both the selection of information considered relevant, and the way in which it was collected and presented. Furthermore, much of the evidence was gathered by non-experts using research tools that are now considered insufficient for the accurate recording and analysis of Indigenous song. Combined with a typically non-relational, 'objective' approach to interlocutors, these conditions ensured that many of the more subtle technical and meaning-based aspects of south-eastern Aboriginal music escaped coherent European documentation.

Ironically, given the core research programme's exclusive focus on the collection of 'pure' Indigenous music of a pre-contact nature, it is quite possible that by the time more reliable recording techniques such as the gramophone were introduced, much south-eastern Indigenous expression was already significantly modified by European influence. To the extent that such influence may well have pervaded Indigenous musical systems in the most fundamental ways, some of its original features are probably now quite indiscernible. This methodological confusion has particularly affected analysis of the Indigenous south-eastern tonal system, eroding confidence in the ability of nineteenth-century research results to accurately reflect the south-eastern musical situation. This not only renders comparison with other regions very difficult, but also hampers any attempt to chart more recent local developments, as Aboriginal music has continued to respond to European innovation. Thus, differences between the empirical methodologies employed in the south-east, and the more sophisticated techniques used in localities only later intensively occupied by Europeans, have resulted in the former region presenting as indeed discrete – but perhaps for reasons related more to changing European styles of cultural analysis than to any particular mode of Indigenous expression.

Not only do doubts shadow the question of the south-east exhibiting unique musical characteristics, it is uncertain whether cultures within the region were sufficiently homogeneous to suggest it was ever a true cultural entity. Some justification for questioning regional homogeneity lies in the following example of local language distribution, which shows that significant cultural discontinuities could occur within a restricted geographical area, while at the same time similarities obtained between widely dispersed and isolated communities. This concerns the central New England language Anaiwan, which is superficially so different to the languages surrounding it that for many years it was considered by European linguists to be an essentially non-Australian tongue (Crowley 1976:23). Terry Crowley demonstrated that Anaiwan is in fact related to its neighbours, but had been modified to a point of near-unrecognisability by the application of what he describes as a set of extreme phonological rules (Crowley 1976:41). Interestingly, while very similar rules have 'altered' such widely separated languages as Anaiwan, the Mbabaramic group of Cape York (Crowley 1976:23), and the Arandic languages of Central Australia (Crowley 1976:45), most of the languages lying between these regions have remained unaffected. The Anaiwan case is typical of other evidence used to question the concept of 'culture regions' in Australia. Les Hiatt's study of themes in Australian anthropological discourse highlights considerable and significant cultural diversity amongst Aboriginal groups within geographical regions (Hiatt 1996), and Bob Reece asserts that the assumption of cultural homogeneity before the European era was largely an invention of nineteenth-century scholarship (Reece 1996:29).

Any examination of regionalisation is of course a discussion about sameness and difference, two fundamentally relative concepts. As seen below, there are coherent objections to the proposition that the south-east showed marked musical differences to other regions, and also to any assertion that it did not. As one might expect, close musical analysis has produced results which could be used to support either position, negating the possibility of a simple conclusion.

2 Instruments, song and dance

2.1 Introduction

There are a number of possible approaches to the analysis of early south-eastern Indigenous music, their selection depending largely on the understandings one wishes to educe. Two of these are suggested by the following comment:

> A large task for the future is to correlate a synthesis of what diverse early observers have to say about Aboriginal song and dance with the results of recent research into extant traditions (Clunies Ross 1987:3).

One of the suggested paths (interpreting 'extant traditions' to mean only those of north, west, and Central Australia), involves the descriptive survey of characteristic south-eastern features such as musical form and content, performance contexts, and the nature of composition and instrumentation. Overall findings could be used for comparison with those for other regions, to determine stylistic similarities and contrasts across the continent, and to perhaps flesh out the historical picture with modern evidence. A second strategy (interpreting 'extant traditions' to include those of the south-east itself), is more complex, and seeks to reveal in greater depth the meaning that music has had for Aboriginal people in the south-east, the relationship between music and other Aboriginal cultural/spiritual entities there, and the dynamic procedure of Indigenous musical practice through its continuing relationship with non-Aboriginal innovations. This strategy presumes a quite different treatment of the historical material (much of which is *prima facie* unsupportive, having been designed for the first approach), and is based on the proposal that Aboriginal musical history displays significant continuity between older and more recent formal expressions. The ideal approach to analysis would combine these suggested treatments, and to some extent this is what is attempted below. After presenting a brief survey of the documented evidence concerning older south-eastern Indigenous music, some details of the less-visible aspects of music-making will be discussed, with reference to the findings of modern scholars in other parts of the continent.

Commentators generally agree that when Indigenous Australian Aboriginal music is spoken of, what is meant is predominantly vocal music. In fact, Trevor Jones and other scholars consider that there was no performance of strictly instrumental music in 'old style' Aboriginal society (Jones 1965:368). This seems to be borne out for the south-east, sound instruments probably being used in an integrated role only. Following a short historical survey of instrumentation, examination in this section will be made of musical contexts, types of song, composition, and learning.

2.2 Musical instruments

The foremost musical instrument of the south-east comprises a pair of hand-held clapsticks, struck together to provide a highly percussive accompaniment to singing. These sticks were often 'purpose made' in a variety of slender cylindrical shapes, although boomerangs, clubs, and other wooden implements were also commonly pressed into service. Hardwood seems to have been the favoured material of manufacture, Leonard de Silva saying that in his area on the mid-north coast of New South Wales, sticks were made of ironbark or bloodwood. 'Easy wood' was also used however, with newly cut sticks being placed in a fire to 'take the dead sound out and put the (right) sound into them' (de Silva 1994). Leonard said that it was important to have each member of the clapstick pair sounding the same: loud and resonant (de Silva 1994; also Gummow 1992:171). It seems that clapsticks were generally played either solo or *ensemble* for corroboree dancing, and provided performers with some opportunity to display instrumental virtuosity

(McKenzie 1961; Gummow 1983:204). Gumbaynggirr musicians gathering at Corindi Beach in northern New South Wales customarily accompanied singing with yellow-bean war-shields, which produced a deep, hollow, powerful tone when struck together, and sometimes used small rocks and unworked driftwood sticks for percussion, these latter apparently in preference to manufactured items (Perkins 1998).

There is reason to believe that the stick-pair was predominantly a man's instrument (Gummow 1992:171), women using possum-skin 'bundles' for idiophonic (percussive) expression:

> When the possum skin is rolled into a bundle the hair surface is turned inwards, and, of course, the tighter the bundle, the better the sound it makes. The bundle is struck with the hand, and is solely a women's instrument (Kennedy 1933:148).

Apparently small shells were sometimes included in these bundles, so that when struck, 'they made a jingling sound' (Kennedy 1933:148). Closely related was an instrument Jimmy Barker described as a 'pillow made of kangaroo skin and stuffed with possum fur' that was 'used as a drum' in western New South Wales corroborees (Barker & Mathews 1977:37). In later years, ordinary kapok pillows and blankets were adapted for the same purpose (Gummow 1992:174). Evidence from the north coast of New South Wales indicates that a further type of pillow-drum was used there, consisting of a woven reed covering stuffed with grass (Margaret Somerville 1998: pers. comm.).

The use of shell-string rattles has been inferred from the examination of rock engravings in the Sydney region (Kennedy 1933:153), and rattles made of small bunches of leaves seem to have been widely used, either held in the armpit, tied around the ankles of dancers, or shaken by hand (Fraser 1892:n.p.; Kennedy 1933:154; Meston n.d.:n.p.; Oates 1985:118.).

Body percussion was common in Indigenous society, mainly taking the form of thigh-slapping and hand-clapping. In both cases, the character of the sound produced could be varied, cupped hands resulting in a hollow 'thud', the flat of the hand eliciting a 'crisper' tone (Maggie Morris 1994; Kennedy 1933:148). John Hunter of the First Fleet made particular note of the use of body percussion in the Sydney region:

> he was assisted by several young boys and girls who sat at his feet, and by their manner of crossing the thighs, made a hollow between them and their belly, which they beat time with the flat of their hand, so as to make a kind of sound which will be better understood from the manner of its being produced than from any verbal description (Hunter 17/2/1791, quoted in Egan 1999:227).

Tony Perkins details another form of body percussion where, in his youth, seated Gumbaynggirr men would tap their feet against the ground while singing certain ceremonial songs (Perkins 1998).

The integration of instrumental- and body-percussion techniques has also been documented, and seems to have been a technique used by both men and women:

> Their music consisted of two sticks of very hard wood, one of which the musician held upon his breast in the manner of a violin and struck it with the other in good and regular time ... (Hunter 17/2/1791, quoted in Egan 1999:227).

This example is extremely interesting, in that it most likely demonstrates the appropriation of the chest cavity as a resonating chamber, in precisely the same manner as did old-time country fiddlers. A similar approach to percussive resonance can be seen to inform a practice employed by women throughout the south-east, the following instance recorded from the western fall of New England in the 1850s:

> The women sat round in an admiring circle, chanting in chorus a sort of wild recitation, all the singers beating time, and admirable time too, with their 'paddy melon' sticks on a sort of drum made by a fold of their opossum skin cloaks, which was stretched between their knees (quoted in Gummow 1992:81; see also Kennedy 1933:148, and Mundy 1852, vol. 1:216).

While the drum proper is considered by scholars to have had no pre-contact Australian distribution outside Cape York, there is some evidence for its use further south, although this may indicate European influence. Part of Harry Buchanan's description of a Gumbaynggirr corroboree contains the following information: 'One man and one woman singer sit at each of the two end fires, and a drummer sits at the middle fire' (Eades 1979:346).

Mr Buchanan gave the Gumbaynggirr lexeme *buljurr* for 'drum', neither the word nor its components apparently having any other meanings in the language (Steve Morelli 1995: pers. comm.). Indeed, Gumbaynggirr elder Leonard de Silva considered the drum, which he also called *buljurr*, to have been an Indigenous instrument, describing it as a possum hide stretched over one end of a small hollow log (Emily Walker and Steve Morelli 1994: pers. comm., also see Morelli 2008:25). In the second half of the twentieth century, Keith Lardner inherited from his old Yarrawarra people the art of manufacturing drums by forming a circular resonator from stripped bark and then stretching a kangaroo skin over one of its ends (Lardner 1998). Keith did not know how venerable this practice was, however. Other more-or-less supportive evidence exists – Victorian pioneer John Bulmer translates the word *boorinya*, drawn from a Gippsland creation myth, as 'beat the drum' (Campbell & Vanderwal 1994:41), Gummow records the Bundjalung word *bulbing*, normally glossed as 'drum' (though it may refer exclusively to the possum-skin pillow), and Bell cites Taplin's *tartengk* as a Ngarrindjeri word for drum (Gummow 1992:172; Bell 1998:177).

There is also considerable uncertainty about whether the 'bush leaf', a reed aerophone (blown instrument) commonly played by Aboriginal people in recent times, was used in Australia before European invasion. The evidence seems to be so far fairly evenly balanced (Bradley 1995:10). Dick Donnelly and other Bundjalung people (Gummow 1992:176, 177) considered that corroboree music was played on the instrument by Aboriginal people in pre-European times, as did Tony Perkins (1998), Leonard de Silva (1994), and Maisie Kelly (1994).

Residents of the Oban district of New South Wales have described the local performance of Aboriginal music, heard at a distance, as a drone-like 'humming' (Ellis 1984; Newbury 1995). Of course this may have been the sound, not of the leaf, but of the bullroarer, that most sacred initiatory instrument whose name in south-eastern Aboriginal languages is often cognate with the term for 'God' or 'the first man'. It is doubtful that the *yuludarra*, to use its Gumbaynggirr name, was ever used musically, *sensu stricto* (Berndt & Berndt 1988:371).

2.3 The corroboree

It appears that the south-eastern Aboriginal musical occasion *par excellence* was the corroboree. This word entered Australian English very early via the language of the Dharuk people of Sydney, for whom *ca-rab-ba-ra* signified 'dance' (Donaldson 1987:20). Although a more incisive semantics is probably no longer possible, the word has a long pedigree of subsequent use, amongst both Aboriginal and white people, as referring to chiefly non-sacred Indigenous dance gatherings (Donaldson 1987:20). The Victorian ethnologist A. W. Howitt describes the situation succinctly:

> The songs and dances of the Australian Aborigines are usually spoken of by our own people as '*corroborees*,' and this word is also even frequently applied to any of their social gatherings. This application is, however, not correct, for the songs, the song and dances, and the assemblies for

social and other purposes have each their own distinctive name. The word '*corroboree*' has been adopted by the settlers from some tribal dialect in the early settled districts, probably of New South Wales, and has been carried by them all over Australia. It may now even be regarded as an addition engrafted upon the English language. The word '*corroboree*' probably meant originally both the song and the dance which accompanied it, as is the meaning of the word '*gunyeru*' in the Kurnai languages (Howitt 1887:327).

Typical descriptions of corroborees portray men dancing and clapping sticks, with women providing vocal and percussion accompaniment (White 1934:226). Most other possible permutations of this organisation have been recorded, however (Eades 1979:346; Oates 1985:117; Barker & Mathews 1977:36, 37; Mathews 1985:105), and both women and men had their own closed ceremonies which featured music and dance (Mathews 1901:62; Maggie Morris 1994). Detailed descriptions of these closed ceremonies are, by definition, either non-existent, unavailable, or their discussion respectfully suppressed.

It seems to have been common for a 'song leader' to direct corroborees in the south-east. This was no doubt necessary, given the recorded complexity of Indigenous music in performance. According to Catherine Ellis, a song leader in Central Australia would undergo many years of rigorous training, not only in the manipulation of musical structures, but also in the proper understanding of mythology associated with the songs (Ellis 1997b:75). One description of a Victorian song leader in action is here provided from the experience of William Buckley:

> The man seated in front appeared to be the leader of the orchestra, or master of the band – indeed I may say master of ceremonies generally. He marched the whole mob, men and women, boys and girls, backwards and forwards at his pleasure, directing the singing and dancing, with the greatest decision and air of authority (quoted in Hill 1993:32).

Another observer wrote that:

> the dancers . . . are arranged in one or more lines at a suitable distance, their bodies ornamented by designs in pipeclay . . . In front, and facing them stands a man called the 'fiddler,' who acts as conductor or leader. He keeps the most admirable time by beating his boomerang with a piece of stick . . . (Mann 1885:42, 43).

A trait commonly ascribed to corroborees by both white and Aboriginal commentators was theatricality (Donaldson 1987:20; Gardner 1854; Gummow 1992:82, 92), a characterisation that underlined both the close connection between music and dance, and the programmatic nature of the performances. Song and dance were often said to be organised 'act by act', each one presenting a stage in the event or process described. Margaret Gummow cites singers who state that corroborees from the north coast of New South Wales might contain up to 13 such acts (Gummow 1992:92). Taking an alternative view in his critique of persistent European failure to respond sensitively to Aboriginal communication, Paul Carter regards white observers' theatrical analogies as an intentional trivialisation of the corroboree's political meanings (Carter 1992a:166).

Occasions for 'getting up' a corroboree were no doubt sometimes politically motivated, but their functions, individual characters, and group composition appear to have exhibited great variety. Although corroborees might involve a quite localised gathering of individuals or family camps within the one language group, commentators often emphasised their 'inter-tribal' nature. This aspect is well supported by the following paraphrased origin story from the Richmond River:

> Long ago there were three brothers, all influential men, who had a difference about their sway in those parts. They were named Birrung, Mum-mor-ni, and Yab-brine. Having had a dispute,

Birrung went north, Mummorni south and Yabbrine west. The latter introduced the corroboree and it was the means of uniting them all again (Hewitt 1936:24).

What Hewitt's account of the myth fails to mention is that the initial separation of the brothers represents, for the Bundjalung, the creation of Australian tribal groupings – the institution of social difference (also see Gummow 1992:30, 31). It is significant that the corroboree is described there as having been created at the same time as the tribal unit, to provide a site for future productive relations between the groups. That corroborees were generally considered integrative is suggested by the following description, from the *Northern Star*, of a dance performed in northern New South Wales in 1910:

> It may be interesting to those who were present last evening that the man depicted was a representation of Yabbrine, who, according to aborigines' tradition, introduced the corroborees. He was the youngest of three brothers, the others being named Birrung and Mummoonie, among whom a better end arose. Yabbrine, by introducing the corroborees, brought all the people together in harmony. Hence, it is always a meeting of goodwill, and when, in old times tribal fights were engaged in, and disputes were settled, the corroboree was the finale, and then all dispersed in peace, so the meeting yesterday signified more than a mere performance... (quoted in Gummow 1992:87).

Isabel McBryde demonstrates that songs and dances were indeed customary articles of intertribal trade in the south – often exchanged for material goods – and that corroborees were important and prominent features of trading occasions (McBryde 1984:135,143; see also Clunies Ross 1986:232; Wyndham 1889). R. H. Mathews attests to their use whenever tribes met at initiations (Mathews 1898:58), and frequent mention is made of corroborees occurring at large gatherings arranged for feasting, fighting or the settling of disputes (White 1934:227; Gardner 1854). Dick Donnelly describes how such a gathering might be conducted in northern New South Wales:

> Well, different tribe would show their corroboree you see, we finish ours first, tonight say. Oh, we'd show ours, *Bundjalung*. Well, *Gungari* tomorrow night, see? Somebody else next night. They might be there a month putting all these dances through. That's the way it was... Anyway, very fond... I am of a few of these dances I'd seen, and I learnt some of these songs belongin' to them (Gummow 1992:189).

In this fashion, individual songs and song-styles could travel right throughout the south-east, often over very long distances. Howitt instances the spread of one song between South Australia, Victoria and the far north coast of New South Wales, involving a journey of perhaps thousands of kilometres (Howitt 1904:414). It is clear that the trade aspect of corroborees endured for many years after white contact, and there are numerous reports of south-eastern Aboriginal people holding public corroboree performances to which admission was charged, and of performing for whites at the annual government blanket distribution, an important event in the cold south of the continent (de Silva 1994; *Armidale Express*, 28-2-1874:4; *Glen Innes Examiner*, 17-5-1881:6, 29-5-1888:3). This exchange dimension to the corroboree is positively identified in Carter's portrayal of an incident involving the Victorian squatter John Cotton:

> He observed how, shortly after he gave one of the Devil's River tribe a suit of European clothes, 'One of the tribes performed a corroboree or native dance' (Carter 1992b:169).

2.4 Types of Indigenous song

> They are numerous, and vary both in measure and time. They have songs of war, of hunting, of fishing, of the rise and set of the sun, for rain, for thunder, and for many other occasions...
> (Tench 1999:262, 3).

While there has been a great deal more collection than analysis of the songs of south-eastern Australia, the occasions on which songs were performed and the uses to which they were put have been reasonably well recorded. Diane Bell provides a handy introduction to this general discussion in saying:

> Music, Cath Ellis... contends, is the main intellectual medium through which Aboriginal people conceptualise their world. She writes:
>
> Through song the unwritten history of the people and the laws of the community are taught and maintained; the entire physical and spiritual development of the individual is nurtured; the well being of the group is protected; supplies of food and water ensured through musical communication with the spiritual powers; love of homeland is poured out for all to share; illnesses are cured; news is passed from one group to another (Ellis 1985:17, quoted in Bell 1998:180).

The following outline of song types, which reinforces Ellis's view by demonstrating just how pervasive singing was in south-eastern Aboriginal life, does not attach great importance to any putative taxonomic scheme. In this regard, Diane Bell discusses typologies of Ngarrindjeri music, commenting that while different researchers have identified different categories:

> all the... researchers admit that their typologies of Ngarrindjeri songs are less than satisfactory, that there are variations within areas, and that they are frequently contradicted by their informants (Bell 1998:177).

Whilst also acknowledging deficiencies in any attempt at constructing an accurate and multi-purpose taxonomy, Margaret Gummow does take the process further in recording eight categories of Bundjalung songs which are recognised more-or-less consistently by the singers themselves:

> *Yawahr*, Shake-a-Leg and *Burun* songs are all identified by their dances; Sing-You-Down, Blessing for Babies and Lullaby are identified by the functions for which they were performed; Djingan is identified by the content of the songs; and Jaw Breaker is identified by the language of the song (Gummow 1992:74ff.).

Norman Tindale was another researcher who divided the songs he gathered (from South Australia) into eight categories, none of which corresponds to Gummow's examples, however (Berndt & Berndt 1988:369).

Given below is a summary – comprehensive but not exhaustive – of the recorded evidence for south-eastern song-types. It must be said at the start that this outsider's grouping-by-function fails to adequately consider essentially opaque levels of meaning in either the songs themselves (Gummow 1983:205), or their performance contexts (Ellis 1980:725). That particular topic will be discussed in greater detail in section 3, below.

Corroboree-singing was only one aspect of Aboriginal group musical activity, and as a category represents a cover-all description masking a number of distinct genres. Some of these primarily action-type pieces include: songs composed to describe and celebrate significant events such as frontier conflict with Europeans (Vale 1996; Norton 1907:101); the first sightings of horses (Horton 2000:47), sailing ships (Armitage 1933:96), or railway locomotives (Archibald 1964, Dixon 1980:53; Bell 1998:179; Hercus and Koch 1996:148); songs to make white men go away from Aboriginal country (Goddard 1934:245; Carter 1992a:166; Swain 1993:124); songs composed with a didactic social aim (especially McKenzie 1961, where a corroboree song depicts the unlawful actions of killing game after sunset); songs related to the dance itself, such as the many 'shake-a-leg' or 'shivery-legs' songs (Gummow 1992; Archibald 1964; de Silva 1994); and drinking and gambling songs (Gummow 1983:249; de Silva 1994).

A rather more difficult genre is that of the song-series or mythical song-cycle, celebrating the creation and re-creation of life and landscape by animal or human ancestors (Ellis 1980:722). Strictly speaking, one should not assume, merely by analogy with cultures from elsewhere on the continent, that mythical cycles or 'songlines' must have been performed in the south-east. However, Radcliffe-Brown's evidence that mythical landscape creation was an Australia-wide phenomenon (Radcliffe-Brown 1929b:415) is salient here, and is supported by the present author's happening upon references to creation stories that seem to cross tribal boundaries in northern New South Wales (Cohen 1980; Laves 1929:1250).

Isolated songs about significant animals, unfortunately without helpful Aboriginal exegesis, have certainly been collected in the region (Gordon 1968b:14; Howitt 1887:333; Gummow 1983:205). While these may be interpreted as generally pertaining to totemic or ancestor relationships, they need not imply song-cycles, and could instead represent rituals for species increase, totem assignation at initiation (Radcliffe-Brown 1923:440–443), or a number of alternative forms. However, Jones (1965), Gummow (1983), and Donaldson (1987) have all argued that the propensity for 'cycle-building' towards longer accretions, typical of songlines, is inherent in the structure of southern music, and the admittedly slender record of mythological story-cycles for the region can be seen to at least provide occasion for its utilisation.

In the absence of clear evidence, it is of course possible to conclude that south-eastern Aboriginal society sang no mythological series. On the other hand, there is ample reason to consider that their existence had been entirely overlooked by early researchers. A parallel situation concerns Radcliffe-Brown's apparent failure to discover convincing local evidence for increase-singing (Radcliffe-Brown 1929b:409), while other more relationship-oriented researchers were to fare much better in the region 50 years later (Gummow 1992). Tellingly, Radcliffe-Brown made so bold as to assert at the time that, while he did not discover certain determining particulars pertaining to totemism in his lightning survey of north-east New South Wales:

> it is of course possible that an intensive study of the mythology (which it is now too late to carry out) might have revealed some connection (Radcliffe-Brown 1929b:414).

The irony here is that Gerhardt Laves was canvassing for mythological data, with considerable success, in the very same general area and at the very time that Radcliffe-Brown wrote (Laves 1929). Radcliffe-Brown's failure in the field seems due, in large measure, to his commitment to a personal version of the Doomed Race Theory:

> It must be remembered that these researches can now cover only a part of the continent. There are many tribes which it would have been possible to study twenty or even ten years ago that are now forever lost to us, all memory of their former customs having gone (Radcliffe-Brown 1929b:415).

The failure to record the occurrence of recognisably mythological singing should not be ascribed merely to ignorance or prejudice of course. R. H. Mathews made no specific mention of it in his researches into New South Wales ceremonials 30 years earlier (Mathews n.d., 1897, 1898, 1899, 1900a, 1900b, 1902, 1903), and while this may well have been caused by oversight, it is conceivable that, even by his time, the performance of local song-cycles had effectively ceased. Evidence from Central Australia shows that for these to be properly performed, there is a need for the relatively peaceful and uninterrupted occupation of land by a lineage of hereditary ceremonial managers. The process is therefore extremely sensitive to social disruption. One consequence of the 1928 Coniston massacre in the Northern Territory was that the murder of ceremonial managers left gaps in kinship lines that continued to confound ritual observance for many decades thereafter (Vaarzon-Morel 1998:44; C. Ellis 1993: pers. comm.).

The phenomenon of social singing without dancing – in the form of inter-tribal song 'competitions' – has been recorded for the south-east by Radcliffe-Brown and Bootle (Radcliffe-Brown 1929a, notebook 6:148; Bootle 1899:4–5). Other 'non-corroboree' social genres include: funeral and mourning songs (Martin 1961; Howitt 1904:418; Gunson 1970:47); marriage songs (apparently used to keep relations between celebrating families 'calm' – Laves 1929:1269; Medhurst 1895; Holmer 1969:63); songs sung in connection with 'feasting' (especially the *widji-widji* or 'grace' songs of the New England tablelands – Jay 1995); songs sung during initiations by ceremonial managers (Mathews 1899:69; Gummow 1983:90; Gunson 1970:52; Perkins 1998); songs sung by mothers and other relatives during the process of separating from initiands (Mathews 1901:62; Morris 1994); entertainment songs, including 'gossip' songs and others composed to pillory or provide social comment (Martin 1961; Dixon 1980:85; Clunies Ross 1986:244; Hercus and Koch 1996:148; Berndt & Berndt 1988:369); songs of pleading used during 'judicial hearings' (Gunson 1970:58); and finally, songs which express some form of group solidarity or identity (Buchanan 1973; Gummow 1983:26).

Most other attested song categories indicate solo performances, characterised in the main by their potential to directly influence people, events and processes (Ellis 1993). Chief among these are songs or incantations used by 'clever fellers', the Aboriginal 'doctors' found throughout the Australian continent. Their performance highlights the Indigenous transitive use of the verb 'to sing', and types include: songs to cure wounding, disease, disorders, or to ensure future health (Elkin 1977:39; Laves 1929:1239; Howitt 1887:334; Gummow 1992:134–135; Perkins 1998); songs for ritual killing (Elkin 1977:152; Gummow 1992:138); songs 'to make dead men rise' (Laves 1929:1246); songs to put individuals or whole groups to sleep (Laves 1929:1243); songs to change from human form to that of an animal or bird for the expedition of travel (Perkins 1998); songs to communicate directly with spiritual ancestors (Elkin 1977:129; Donaldson 1987:26); songs connected with the sacred and very powerful quartz crystals (Laves 1929:1222); and songs to start or stop wind and rain (Gordon 1968b:14; Barker & Mathews 1977:32). Rain-making songs could sometimes have been sung by whole groups directed by the 'clever feller' (Enright 1934:240), while associated songs to hasten the advent of spring may have been sung chiefly by women (Goddard 1934; Milson 1840; Moyle 1960). Further solo songs represent a seemingly random variety of categories, some perhaps used only for personal expression, while others retained powers similar to 'doctors' songs, but were presumably accessible to a wider group.[1]

One very important song-class is that for species increase. Although Radcliffe-Brown, in his published survey of south-eastern totemism, denies the occurrence of increase-singing there (Radcliffe-Brown 1929b:409), his own field notes seem to contradict him (Radcliffe-Brown 1929a), as does evidence collected by Laves (1929:1123), W. J. Enright (1934:241), Tindale (Berndt & Berndt 1988:369), Callaghan (Martin 1961) and Margaret Gummow (1992). Increase songs were said to be like 'hymns' to totem creatures (Radcliffe-Brown 1929a, notebook 6:37), normally sung only by the individual to whom belonged both the creature and its increase site, and who was accordingly responsible for their management. Remaining song types include those to stop a thief (Laves 1929:1223; McDougall 1901:63); songs to stop a kangaroo (or duck)

---

[1] It should be noted here that it is unlikely that power resided solely in songs themselves, but in the relationship between country, spiritual Ancestors, singer, song and 'sung'.

while hunting (Perkins 1998; Radcliffe-Brown 1929b:409); songs to cause dolphins to herd fish into shallow waters (Perkins 1998); songs to paralyse a man being pursued (Gummow 1992:139); 'love magic' songs (Laves 1929:1225); lullabies (Kartomi 1984:70); and love songs 'to sweethearts' (Laves 1929:1225; Howitt 1887:334). Bill Cohen speaks of one such love song composed early in the twentieth century by his father Jack:

> He then started to sing an Aboriginal song in Aboriginal language. The understanding of this Gumbangarri song: a young Aboriginal lad courting an Aboriginal girl and lifting her, with her long black hair dangling, onto a saddle and taking her home to his tribe (Cohen 1988:10).

Also recorded are songs rejecting a suitor (Laves 1929:1274; Gordon 1968b:24); songs sung to express emotional or religious states, including songs to 'God' (Goddard 1934 246; Howitt 1887:331; Eades 1979:346; Hoddinott n.d.; Thomas 1905:50); songs inviting tribes to initiation (Radcliffe-Brown 1929a, notebook 6:141); and songs celebrating the coming home to one's people (Martin 1961; McKenzie 1961).

2.5 Song creation

Most modern researchers involved with Indigenous Australian tribal musicians record the bequest of new material, by Ancestors, to living song-makers via dreams (see Stubington 1979 and Ellis 1985). This is also well documented for the south-east, perhaps representatively so by A. W. Howitt:

> The makers of the Australian songs, or of the combined songs and dances, are the poets or bards of the tribe and are held in great esteem . . . the songs . . . are obtained by the bards from the spirits of the deceased, usually their relatives, during sleep in dreams . . . The bard who composed this song came of a poetic stock. His father and his father's father before him are said to have been 'makers of songs which made men sad or joyful when they heard them' . . . There are other poets who composed under what may be called natural influences as distinguished from supernatural. Umbara, the bard of the Coast Murring told me that his words came to him 'not in sleep as to some men, but when tossing on the waves in his boat with the waters jumping up round him' (Howitt 1887:329–31).

Margaret Gummow provides several instances of such dream composition from the Bundjalung area, and cites similar accounts from elsewhere in northern New South Wales (Gummow 1992:181–182). Howitt also notes the complementary process of composing under more mundane circumstances, and this is again supported by Gummow, who details how Raymond Duncan and Jack Barron composed Bundjalung songs in the 'ordinary' way (Gummow 1992:179). This apparently sometimes involved the composer lying on the ground, which may have an analogue in the compositional technique of Milerum of the Ngarrindjeri who, 'by lying on his back on the land . . . could make contact with the power of his country' (Bell 1998:193).

An interesting variation to composition-through-Ancestors – that of songs being given by God – intersects with discourse relating to the existence or otherwise of a pre-contact south-eastern belief in a Supreme Being. Archdeacon Gunther of the central-western New South Wales Wellington mission made the following observation early in the nineteenth century:

> Nor must I omit to mention that there has been from time to time, *i.e.* every three or four years, a curious ceremony performed among the blacks, several tribes being assembled, which appeared to be a remnant of some religious rites. A song was sent for the occasion by Baiami or his son, which was sung by those assembled; a solemn procession took place, certain mysterious figures painted on pieces of bark of men and other objects were displayed at the time (quoted in Thomas 1905:51).

The mention of Baiami indicates that this may have been an early example of a *bora* ceremony, which the historian of religion Tony Swain regards as a post-contact phenomenon (Swain 1993). It may therefore be interesting to speculate whether Gunther's observation could illustrate the subtle re-fashioning of compositional protocol (or its discourse) in response to the European presence. On the other hand, the learning of songs following the visitation of 'God' was also documented by A. C. McDougall for Gumbaynggirr culture, which seems to have left no analogous record of *bora*. Speaking of the Gumbaynggirr *ngulungurr* or 'clever men', McDougall explains that they were visited by Yuludarra when it was necessary for them to learn certain healing songs:

> The Ulun-garras leave camp and retire to the tops of the mountains at certain seasons of the year ... They are believed to actually swallow the bingi-burra (quartz stone) given to them by Uli-tarra, who visits them in their retirement and teaches them how to use the stone and to chant the necessary songs ... (McDougall 1901:64).

Another way that new songs and corroborees could be composed in south-eastern Aboriginal society involved the composer either travelling, or being taken to a special place to be 'shown' the song by spiritual beings. The following shorthand account was found in R. H. Mathews' field notes, and relates to the Wiradjuri of New South Wales:

> The Wah-wee [and songmakers] – little creature lives in deep waterholes. Clever man can go and see him and get a new song. First must paint himself all over with red ochre. He follows after the rainbow some day when there's a shower, and the end of the rainbow rests over the waterhole in which is the wah-wee's abode. He contacts wah-wee who sings him a new song for the corroboree. He repeats the song after the wah-wee until he has learnt it sufficiently and then starts back to his own people. When they see him coming, painted red all over and singing, they know he has been with the wah-wee. This 'doctor' [bard] then takes a few of the other headmen with him into the bush and <u>they strip pieces of bark off trees</u>, and paint different devices on them with coloured clays. These pieces of bark, ornamented in this way are then taken to the corroboree ground and all the men dance and sing the new song. This is how new songs and corroborees are obtained (Mathews, field-notebooks Series 3 Folder 13; original emphasis and superscript; cf. Mathews 1905 [1904]:162).

In another instance, the composer is taken under the sea to be taught the song and dance:

> my old man, grandfather, made a corroboree song there, you know ... he was sort of a clever man, he was ... Yeah you see, he was under the sea for a week ... They come down here lookin' for him. They didn't know where he went, but, when they come back to Evans Head ... they're feeding him on brandy ... he was cold ... They were feeding him on brandy, when he come back, and he got all right then and he made that song. ... You see, he seen 'em corroboreeing, all the women ... he must have been under the sea – they must have took him – all the witches from the seaside like – under the sea (Gummow 1992:115).

That this basic situation could be further ramified is shown by the following example of alternative practice in the Hunter Valley, which seems to combine all the previously discussed elements of dream-visits, God, and travelling to a special place to learn a song:

> Wallatu was the god who presided over poetry. He also composed music. He came in dreams and transported the individual to some sunny hills, where he inspired him with supernatural gifts (Goddard 1934:244, condensed from Dunlop 1848).

It is clear from the evidence given above that song-makers occupied a special place in Aboriginal society, and may have had powers akin to those of 'clever fellers'. Such an exalted status probably extended to song-owners generally, although this subject remains obscure for the south-east.

It is quite possible that the local situation paralleled that obtaining in Central Australia, where profound song-knowledge brought with it 'private wealth, supreme social prestige, and political power' (Ellis 1997b:60).

2.6 Musical education

Unfortunately, very little is known of Indigenous music education in the south-east, beyond the Wah-wee's evidence that the most fundamental mechanism involved in learning songs was probably imitative. However, it would be mistaken to characterise musical education as merely mimetic, and Ellis argues that while rote learning might characterise the earliest steps in a Pitjantjatjara child's musical education, the overall learning process:

> is not one of memorising innumerable individual items and learning their appropriate groupings, but it is one of knowing the structural principles that are being deliberately and creatively manipulated in order to produce a living and energised performance (Ellis 1997b:61).

Ellis emphasises that this process takes many years of sustained effort, often lasting into advanced adulthood. The well-attested role of song-leaders in south-eastern musical practice highlights the importance of correct performance, and suggests that the learning of music was complex and protracted there also. The following description of musical skill in modern Anbarra society seems to fit very well with the observations recorded above of south-eastern corroboree song leaders:

> These performers are real specialists. First they have to keep in mind all the customary song words and melodic phrases appropriate to between twenty and thirty song subjects. Then they must be able to perform them, often for long periods, improvising their choice of customary phrases, rather like a jazz singer does, in short verses of set structure... Another skill the singer has to master is the creation of a continuous but variable rhythm for each subject, which he beats out on a pair of hardwood clapsticks... In some situations these singers may also be directing a group of dancers (Clunies-Ross 1994:76).

The lack of detailed information regarding music education in the south-east is due chiefly to the structural shifts local Aboriginal society has experienced over the last century. However, it can be inferred, from the abundant evidence of music's significance in Aboriginal social life, that learning must have been a most important social process there. Something of the nature of that process might be gleaned by examining stated reasons for its presumed cessation. Diane Bell flags this heuristic strategy in her analysis of Ngarrindjeri history:

> The attacks on language and the attack on ceremonial life struck at the core of certain sorts of knowledge in an oral culture. While the songs were sung, the places and their stories were secure. But it was a long process by which one learnt the songs, and gained sufficient status to be able to sing them. It required time spent with the old people, time on site at sacred places, time in the country learning while doing (1998:182).

Gummow says much the same thing when she canvasses reasons for what is described as a decline in old-time Aboriginal cultural expression:

> Singers often need to be at specific sites or places to perform the... songs that they... remember. Performance prerequisites and contexts for performances are, however, constantly changing as European influence increases... suitable performance contexts are becoming increasingly difficult to arrange, and this may be one factor in the decline in performances (Gummow 1995:130).

Given the orality of Aboriginal musical culture and its orientation towards place and purpose, certain conditions must have been absolutely necessary for effective education to continue relatively unchanged. As Bell and Gummow both suggest, these would presumably have included some security of tenure in or near one's own country, the opportunity for repeated hearings of particular performances, and most importantly, sufficient reason to perform music, whether for ceremonial or other purposes.

3 Formal analysis
3.1 Texts
The main published textual work for south-eastern songs has been carried out by Tamsin Donaldson, who has explored both the nature of language-change in selected Ngiyampaa songs from western New South Wales, and the structural variation experienced by these songs during the process of their transmission. Donaldson has identified textual cues for dancers in songs from the far-west of the state (Donaldson 1987:36ff), while Margaret Gummow has done the same for the east (1985, 1992). The latter has also isolated rhyme and rhythm patterns in New South Wales Aboriginal songs, including those with macaronic texts, and demonstrates that similar patterns were applied to lines in both English and Aboriginal languages (Gummow 1983:99, 249). This indicates that English textual elements were able to be incorporated smoothly into basically Indigenous musical structures, a reverse of the better documented process whereby purely Aboriginal texts have been set to common European airs (Donaldson 1984a:231; Buchanan 1973; Donaldson 1995). 'Macro' textual structures have also been examined by Donaldson and Gummow, and both researchers identify the two-section form as being typical of south-eastern Aboriginal song. Singers have been shown to sometimes manipulate certain textual mechanisms, so that these typically short verses may be extended, by repetition, according to the demands of performance (Donaldson 1987:36; Gummow 1987).

From the time of first European contact in south-eastern Australia, singers have told researchers that they do not understand the words to some of their songs (Dixon 1980:54; Howitt 1887:329; Gordon 1968b:13). This textual opacity may be attributed to a number of factors. As already mentioned, the wide diffusion of songs throughout the region must have resulted in their performance by 'foreign' language speakers (Gummow 1992:89). On the other hand, some songs are considered to employ archaic words from the home language (Dixon 1980:54) or a special song-language whose meaning is purposely obscured from the uninitiated (Ellis 1980:725; Clunies Ross 1986:242). R. H. Mathews posits a further possible cause, based on a proposition popular with researchers up until quite recently. In presenting the transcriptions of several songs noted from performers on the south coast of New South Wales, Mathews comments that:

> It may be mentioned that the words of these chants possess no meaning to the present natives, having been handed down from one generation to another. They were probably in the language of conquering tribes in the past (Mathews 1901:63).

In addition, it should be emphasised that the typically abbreviated and highly allusive expression of Aboriginal songs must rely, for effective communication, on a very closely shared cultural experience (Clunies Ross 1986:242; Radcliffe Brown 1923:440). Over the course of time, factors relating to transmission may introduce enough variation into a text – or social circumstances might change sufficiently – so as to reduce the transparency of an otherwise-plain meaning, even to members of the same or a very closely related language group (Donaldson 1984a:240ff.).

On the other hand, because meaning in songs could possibly have been conveyed by tone-production, gesture, pitch and rhythm (subjects which will be dealt with below) as well as by words (Ellis 1997b:59), perhaps there was a greater intuitive understanding of foreign-language songs than has been commonly supposed. In spite of a general tendency towards obscurity, there is evidence that the language of imported songs was sometimes knowingly modified to accommodate local dialects, perhaps even investing them with a new and invigorated meaning (Jones 1965:289; Donaldson 1984:247; Howitt 1904:414).

3.2 The relationship of song and dance

Regarding the relation of song to dance here, it is not known how far the immediate demands of the dance influenced song composition itself. It has been said that dancers, at the level of the individual step, took their immediate rhythmic cues from percussionists, not the singers (de Silva 1994). While this would make sense when it is taken into account that sung melodic rhythms were normally much more complex than the single-beat rhythm of women's percussion, the patterns produced in Willie Mackenzie's recorded performances show that clapstick rhythms may at times have been quite intricate (Mackenzie 1961).

The case could have been different, however, from the perspective of the subject-matter and structure of the dances, which may have, to some extent, directed the technical aspects of the making of songs (this observation of course does not apply to situations where songs and dances were given together in dreams or other circumstances). For example, just as Aboriginal languages contain names for birds and animals constructed on principles of onomatopoeia (Dixon 1980:106; Ellis 1985:68–70), so might song-texts and melodies reflect, in their technical (including rhythmic) construction, local perceptions of creatures they portrayed. There is at least one recorded example of a south-eastern corroboree song known to contain onomatopoeic allusions to dance steps (Gummow 1987:3), while this and other songs are recognised as utilising verbal and musical cues related closely to the *structure* of the dance they accompanied (Donaldson 1984:37, Gummow 1992:92–94). In this way, dancers may well have taken their cues from singers, but presumably only at the structural level.

3.3 Music

The oldest accounts of contact suggest that it was occasionally possible for the first Europeans to appreciate and to a limited extent understand the differentiated structures of south-eastern Aboriginal music. The following description, by New South Wales Judge-Advocate David Collins, must surely comprise the earliest published English-language musical analysis of Australian Indigenous singing:

> A party who went to the eastern shore to procure fire-wood, and to comply with the desire the natives had so often expressed of seeing them land among them, found them still timorous; but being encouraged and requested by signs to sing, they began a song in concert, which actually was musical and pleasing, and not merely in the diatonic scale, descending by thirds, as at Port Jackson, the descent to this was waving, in a rather melancholy soothing strain. The song of *Bong-ree*, which he gave them at the conclusion of theirs, sounded barbarous and grating to the ear: but *Bong-ree* was an indifferent songster, even among his own countrymen. These people, like the natives of Port Jackson, having fallen to the low pitch of their voices, recommenced their song at the octave ... their singing was not confined to one air; they gave three (1789, quoted in Gummow 1992:78, 79).

There has since been a moderate amount of musical analysis undertaken of south-eastern songs, the main works being those of Torrance (1887), Moyle (1960), Jones (1965), Kartomi (1984) and Gummow (1983, 1985, 1987, 1992). After each of these studies is considered in its turn, some comparison will be made of their findings. It must be said at this point that, as there is no consensus as to whether the use of fixed pitches operated in old-style Aboriginal society, and as Ellis considered Jones and Moyle to have assumed an adherence to a western-style tonal system, references to scale organisation in the following analyses should be treated with caution.

While Margaret Gummow's major opus comprises a detailed analytical survey for the Bundjalung group of northern New South Wales (1992), the work most relevant to the present context concerns her close study of 69 separate song-performances recorded from four widely separated areas of New South Wales (1983). After analysing her material, Gummow made certain broad conclusions, summarised briefly as follows.

Melodies were found to be generally descending, exhibiting definite tonal plateaux and regular 'intoning' of the final keynote. Pentatonic, heptatonic and hexatonic scales predominated. Melodic progression was basically by step – both ascending and descending – and although some leaps of as much as an octave were found, these were typically placed between, rather than within phrases. Two types of tonal organisation occurred, one where the tonic was the lowest and final note of the song, and the second – considered by Gummow to be a special feature of the sample she examined – where material was arranged centrically around the tonic. Songs were found to adhere to two basic structures, the 'varied repeat' and strophic forms, while a minority appeared to be through-composed. Rhythmically, the sample was described as predominantly syllabic, occasionally isorhythmic, and as containing numerous documented examples of both isometre and heterometre. Gummow noted the occurrence of some rhapsodic, melismatic, highly ornamented material from the Bundjalung area, which she believes may represent a women's style. Otherwise, the most common rhythmic types found were simple- and compound-duple, simple- and compound-triple, with additive rhythms occurring occasionally (Gummow 1983:270ff; see also Gummow 2001).

Margaret Kartomi's analysis of one Bundjalung lullaby produced features agreeing in principle with Gummow's findings. This song displayed a stepwise-descending melodic contour, followed a heptatonic scalar progression, but had no distinct tonic. Rhythmic organisation was isometric and isorhythmic (Kartomi 1984:70–73).

Alice Moyle has analysed the music of two Tasmanian songs recorded from the singing of Mrs Fanny Cochrane-Smith in 1899 and 1903. Moyle recognised each as belonging to a different genre, distinguished by her as 'corroboree' and 'legato' styles. The former she found to have a melody which first ascended before descending to a 'reiterated ground tone', with an anhemitonic pentatonic scalar structure set within the compass of an octave. Rhythm was syllabic and isometric, and notated in triple time. The legato song she analysed as having a basically downward-pushing ornamented melody, though organised centrically around the tonic, and bearing the same scalar structure as the corroboree. Its rhythm was found to be rhapsodic and melismatic. Moyle compared the two Tasmanian songs with corroboree songs recorded along the southern coasts of South and Western Australia, and found significant difference in the area of melodic procedure: where the Tasmanian examples both ascended and descended, the mainland songs all exhibited descending melodies. After briefly surveying early historical descriptions of Tasmanian music, including James Bonwick's comment-in-passing that 'songs do not exceed the compass of a third', Moyle carefully concluded that:

> Tasmanian song styles were widely varied. It seems that they ranged from monotone reiterations to songs of a relatively sophisticated nature, such as the 'legato' or 'Spring' song (Moyle 1960:75).

In 1887, G. W. Torrance conducted a cursory analysis of the performances of William Berak (or Barak), a Victorian Aboriginal singer. Torrance found that melodic compasses in Berak's songs rarely exceeded a third, minor intervals predominating in a step-wise descent to an intoned keynote tonic. A brief melodic ascent was noted for one song in his sample. Rhythm was strongly marked and apparently heterometric, alternating 'suddenly' between 'duple and triple' times. Some explanation for the preponderance of narrow compasses noticed by Torrance (and perhaps by others, for example Bonwick in Tasmania) occurs in the following note appended to two of his transcriptions:

> This song was repeated ... a third lower, and sung through to the same sound ... This drone or chaunt is repeated *ad lib.* as long as the ceremony lasts, a tone lower each time, and accompanied throughout with clapping of hands and stamping of feet (Torrance 1887:339).

It seems obvious that what Torrance classed as entire melodies, merely repeated a tone or a third lower, modern analysts would likely regard as verses or sections of a larger whole. Berak's material is therefore likely to have exhibited wider tonal compasses than Torrance allowed for, bringing them into line with other southern Australian examples.

The present author has undertaken summary analyses of the music of some Gumbaynggirr songs, for the sole purpose of increasing slightly the available south-eastern analytical sample. While his findings did not vary from those described above, the songs of Granny Florence Ballengarry of the New South Wales central-north coast were interesting in the light of previous descriptions of a 'legato' style of singing (Ballengarry 1974). Granny Ballengarry's songs are sung slowly, in free rhythm, and their melodies, ornamented by portamenti and single and double grace notes, proceed melismatically. Considering the comments of Moyle and Gummow *supra*, it may be that the suggestion of a characteristic south-eastern women's style can be further supported, although the evidence for it remains slight. Again, while her seemingly European-influenced melodies may not render much further assistance on this point, the songs of another Gumbaynggirr woman, Junie Mercey, suggest the possible existence of a discrete and integrated women's repertoire (Mercey n.d.). It seems a short step only from the recognition of a women's repertoire, to the confident consideration of a women's style of performing it.

Trevor Jones has analysed the bulk of the sound recordings housed in the archives of the University of Sydney as 'The Elkin Collection' (Jones 1965). Like Gummow, he arranged his sample according to geographical area, and of the 12 'micro-regions' he examined throughout the continent, two occur in the south-east. Jones' results do not differ materially from those of his fellow analysts, although something further will be said of his comparison of south-eastern with other Australian styles.

A very basic picture of the most general technical features of south-eastern Australian song can be traced from the foregoing descriptions. Although there is some evidence for micro-regionalisation within the south-east, particularly in the occurrence of certain isorhythms in songs from the Corner Country of New South Wales (Gummow 1983:274), it seems to be suggestive only, and, as Ellis comments, regional stylistic unity is perhaps the more dominant feature: 'tribal music has broad similarities through a region where there are many differentiations of style' (Ellis 1980:727).

Generally speaking, most south-eastern melodies have been characterised as descending step-wise, through intoned tonal plateaux, to rest on an extended final tonic. Scales used are described as predominantly pentatonic and hemitonal diatonic, the latter consisting mainly of six or seven tones. Melodic compasses were perceived as typically moderately-wide (mostly around an octave), and melodic rhythm as primarily syllabic. Syncopation was noted to have been achieved through the use of various technical components (including glottal-stopping), and isorhythm and isometre seem to have been stable features. Simple times were most commonly transcribed – in two, three or four – with compound two and three occurring less frequently. Percussion accompaniment was characteristically 'four-square', with some evidence of stick-beating styles that employed considerable rhythmic variation. Songs normally comprised short sections, most often two, that were presumably extendable to form longer cycles. Vocal styles may have varied widely. Features of a sub-genre that might be considered special to, without necessarily defining the south-eastern region, comprise centric tonal organisation, heterometre, and a 'legato' singing-style characterised by free-rhythm and a melismatic, ornamented melodic procedure.

3.4 Comparison between the south-east and other Australian regions

The basically comparative results of Trevor Jones' survey found that diatonic hemitonal scales predominated in the south-east and in many other areas, particularly in the north of the continent. Overall, Jones found six- and seven-note scales to be reasonably well dispersed throughout, as were melodic compasses of around an octave. A generally descending contour was found in all 166 melodies analysed, the vast majority finishing on the tonic, with a few showing centric tonal organisation. In common with areas all over Australia, Jones found that the south-eastern region used duple and quadruple metres, with triple times (especially compound triple) being rare everywhere. Australian songs were classed as overwhelmingly isometric, with heterometre occurring only once in his sample, in north–central Australia. Rhapsodic rhythm was also found to be very rare, while isorhythm predominated in all areas. Sectionalised structures were the universally found norm, and Jones interpreted the predominant structural type to be strophic, assuming a tendency in even short sung examples towards repetition and 'cycle building'. Finally, Jones observed that there appeared to be little difference in vocal quality or technique demonstrated from one area to another (Jones 1965:285ff).

After Jones published his findings, Alice Moyle prepared a general map of Australian song-features which illustrated significant stylistic similarities for the whole continent, really isolating only Cape York in the north-east (Moyle 1966:xv–xvii). This seeming homogeneity could reflect methodological problems in research such as the lack of a unified 'micro' analytical approach sensitive enough to pick up more subtle differences, the difficulty in obtaining Indigenous taxonomies for all regions, or the bias of dominant analytical techniques towards eliciting stylistic similarity rather than difference (Nettl 1983:320). It is clear, however, that there are also non-technical continuities, such as those relating to performance contexts, the circumstances regarding song composition (Stubington 1979:20; Howitt 1887:330), and the 'power-laden' qualities of songs throughout the country (Ellis 1993). The comparative situation is probably accurately described by Gummow when she says:

> the music of New South Wales has general characteristics in common with music from the rest of Aboriginal Australia (Gummow 1983:277).

4 The context of musical meaning

4.1 Introduction

As mentioned throughout this chapter, some undoubtedly important aspects of south-eastern Aboriginal music-making either escaped the attention of early European observers, or were recorded with little understanding of their possible significance. This deficit can be made somewhat good by referring the more simplistic European observations to the findings of researchers, most notably Catherine Ellis, who have worked with modern Aboriginal musicians in northern and Central Australia. Although this type of comparative research runs a risk of drawing uncritical or careless analogies, there is some justification for its limited use here, given both the lack of directly relevant local evidence, and the provisional conclusions arrived at above regarding Australian musical homogeneity.

In the earlier discussion of the opacity of song-texts, the idea was mooted that language may not have been the sole medium through which music imparted its 'message' to south-eastern Aboriginal people. Catherine Ellis here characterises the Pitjantjatjara experience of musical communication as a complex layering of meanings:

> The music cannot be fully understood without reference to the meaning of the extramusical information with which it is related ... In this way many pieces of information are presented simultaneously. The rhythmic pattern and songtext can refer directly to one event in the story, and to others by implication. The body design on the dancers can signify a different aspect of the story. The dance step, which is tied to musical structure through the beating accompaniment, may depict yet another piece of information, while the dancers themselves represent the personality attributes and characteristics of those whom they portray. Melody, as well as indicating the nature of events taking place in the ceremony (painting, dancing etc.) acts as a constant reminder of the essence, the 'taste' of the ancestor (Ellis 1985:92–94).

This description may well apply to an historical south-eastern situation only dimly perceived by nineteenth-century European observers. Before moving on to a fuller discussion of aspects of south-eastern musical meaning-systems, something should first be said of local Aboriginal aesthetic attitudes to sound.

4.2 The aesthetics of sound

There is very limited evidence available for how south-eastern Aboriginal people may have perceived musical sound. Almost nothing is known of the singing styles, tone production or aesthetic preferences of south-eastern Aboriginal corroboree singers, although Leonard de Silva stated that it was important for performers to be well synchronised, and that the singers make a good, strong, unified sound (de Silva 1994; see also sub-section 4.3 below). The situation is a little clearer for sounds produced by musical instruments. Many published vocabularies include words for particular sounds of all sorts, and Margaret Gummow has abstracted those that relate to musical percussion from various Bundjalung glossaries. These include: words for the noise made by hitting two hard objects together; knocking sounds; clapping sounds; rhythmic sounds (e.g. of footsteps or boomerang-tapping); and rattling sounds (Gummow 1992:172). It is not clear whether these Bundjalung words were formed on onomatopoeic principles, but that Bundjalung people did possess an acute appreciation of percussive sound and its production is suggested by Charlotte Page's description of the pillow-drum of Gidabal women:

> the sound it used to make – the sound used to go a long way. You wouldn't think it was a pillow, but they just knew how to do it. They clap that see – they held it like that and they hit it with their hand and it used to make some lovely noise. *A real sound you know* (Gummow 1992:174, emphasis added).

The overwhelming importance of percussion to south-eastern Aboriginal musicians is evident from the discussion of instruments at the start of this chapter. These could produce a sophisticated array of percussive sounds that, working in concert, would evoke richly-layered rhythmic and tonal textures. In the basic attested musical organisation of a south-eastern ceremonial occasion, combined percussion would be provided by the stamping of the dancers' feet upon a specially-hardened earth 'dancing-floor' (Gummow 1992:176), by stick-players, and by pillow-drum beaters. Add to these the ensemble singing of men and women, the optional sounds of rattle and body-percussion, and – all these practices contributing their own unique qualities – an impressive sonic picture results.

4.3 The language of sound

Elder Tony Perkins has considerably expanded the available core of evidence for an Aboriginal sound aesthetic in his discussion of the meanings of non-percussive tone in his own Gumbaynggirr society. Mr Perkins spoke of the different relative emotional valencies borne by high-pitched and low-pitched tones: the former typically engaging with feelings of fear, worry, grief or despair; the latter evoking reassurance, peace and a feeling of control. Further, Mr Perkins instanced the always-negative connotations of the death-bird's 'high screech', and told of being taught never to throw a pipi shell, as the high-pitched whistle that resulted could generate harmful consequences (Perkins 1998).

That south-eastern Aboriginal women sang in a significantly higher register than men was remarked by John Currie, a pioneer settler in Bundjalung country, in a description of a corroboree he witnessed in 1875:

> First of all the men lead off with sonorous tones. Then the women, with their shrill voices, joined in at intervals (quoted in Gummow 1992:168).

While there is no necessary correlation being made here between women's vocal range and intense emotional states, it may be the case that women were especially well equipped to express these when required. Consider the following incident from Central Australia recorded by Catherine Ellis, where she describes the women's 'keening' that accompanied the death of a member of the group with whom she was working:

> It sounded unlike any other Aboriginal vocal production that I had heard. The pitch was very high ... and great prominence was given to the top note of the wail ... two years after the original incident, this wailing occurred during [a] ... totemic ceremony. In the midst of a thrilling performance ... one woman began to wail. I could hardly continue recording, so great was the shock I felt (Ellis 1985:66).

Further emphasising his point that there were messages or meanings in the quality of sounds, Tony Perkins told of witnessing his elders singing to dolphins from a headland, directing the creatures to herd sea-mullet into shallow waters to render the fish easily caught. He stated that when this occurred, it was obvious to him that the communication's power and meaning resided in the *sound* of the singing, and that the words, if merely recited, would not have had the required effect (Perkins 1998). In another case, Sylvester Ellis, who shared close relationship with Aboriginal people in eastern New England, stated that he knew there was some sort of 'signal' in the sound of the bull-roarer (S. Ellis 1984).

Despite Trevor Jones' conclusion that Indigenous vocal production demonstrated uniformity across the country, historical descriptions indicate that it may have varied between language groups and even amongst individuals within groups. While this evidence is fragmentary, individual south-eastern vocalisations have been variously described as soft and musical (Tench 1999:98), harsh, grating, soothing (Gummow 1992:168), sonorous, and finally, shrill (Gummow 1992:168). Ben Cherry enjoyed the 'soft' quality of Aboriginal singing on New England (Cherry 1987), while Watkin Tench demonstrates that Bennelong was capable of producing a variety of vocal timbres:

> It was observed that a soft gentle tone of voice which we taught him to use, was forgotten, and his native vociferation returned in full force (Egan 1999:198).

In applying all this information to what was said earlier in regard to the learning of songs by Aboriginal people – despite a frequent lack of understanding of their texts – it is likely that the sound of the song itself may have resonated across language boundaries. George Taplin offers strong support for this view in his observation that:

> The Narrinyeri are skilful in the utterance of emotion by sound. They will admire and practise the corrobery (ringbalin) of another tribe merely for the sounds of it, although they may not understand a word of the meaning. They will learn it with great appreciation if it seems to express some feelings which theirs does not. They may not be able to define the feelings, but yet this is the case (quoted in Carter 1992b:36).

That the semantics of south-eastern Aboriginal languages may have been generally mediated by context and pitch-production, is suggested by the following nineteenth-century account from the New England region:

> The various expressions conveyed by the peculiar 'Ay, ay,' so constantly used by the natives in speaking, is perfectly indescribable. It is used doubtfully, positively, interrogatively, or responsively, as the case may be, and contains in itself a whole vocabulary of meanings, which a hundred times the number of words could not convey in writing (quoted in Carter 1992b:34).

This observation is extended specifically to musical situations by the opinion of Mrs Eliza Dunlop, who glossed her translations of the texts of a number of songs she collected at Wollombi, in the Hunter Valley, in the early 1840s, with these words:

> Very much more is contained in the few words they repeat so often than I can properly explain. I understand them, but it is impossible to convey their full meaning (Goddard 1934:245).

4.4 Melodic and rhythm languages

Although there is no record of specific melodic or rhythm languages existing for south-eastern Australian music, their use has been marked in research with certain Central Desert cultures. Catherine Ellis points out that there, particular melodies or rhythmic patterns may retain an unvarying meaning even though sung to different language texts (Ellis 1985:106). The example given below explains this in more detail, and incidentally demonstrates the difficulty with which such insights are elicited, even for the experienced scholar:

> Rhythm may carry factual information. I have gathered, from field experience, that performers may learn the specific meaning of a song from the rhythm of the text so that either the text or the rhythm can convey the same information. The suggestion that this is possible arose when I was recording a long Dreaming songline which crossed a number of tribal boundaries, and I was playing back a recording of an earlier portion of the song to a singer who lived in a more northern area and who did not know the dialect of the recorded performance. He constantly maintained that a particular small song on the recording was about a claypan and that he knew it quite well. It was only careful analysis of his version which determined that he was drawing his conclusions on rhythmic and not linguistic grounds (Ellis 1985:103, 4).

There is no reason to reject the possibility that specific rhythmic patterns had certain meanings for south-eastern Aboriginal people also, especially given the sophistication of the rhythmic dimension to their musical culture. Tony Perkins certainly allowed for this possibility when he described a special foot percussion used to accompany particular Gumbaynggirr ceremonial songs, and which he said indicated rhythmically that initiands had now passed into manhood (Perkins 1998).

4.5 Gestural and visual languages

Gesture was a commonly used means for conveying musical understandings to an audience. From the following, and other known descriptions, it is clear that south-eastern Aboriginal singing was very often accompanied by a parallel gestural expression, which, as Howitt demonstrates, was learned together, with or without dance, as part of a whole-song 'package':

> With some songs there are pantomimic gestures or rhythmical movements, which are passed on from performer to performer, as the song is carried from tribe to tribe ... A very favourite song of this kind has travelled in late years from the Murring to the Kurnai. It was composed by one Mragula, a noted song maker of the Wolgal, describing his attempt to cross the Snowy River in a leaky bark canoe during flood. The pantomimic action which accompanies this song is much fuller than the words, and is a graphic picture ... (Howitt 1887:330–332).

It appears that even the newly arrived Europeans could sometimes glean meaning from Aboriginal singing, and David Collins' account shows his sensitivity to communication by both tone and gesture in a reasonably volatile contact situation:

> These people, like the natives of Port Jackson, having fallen to the low pitch of their voices, recommenced their song at the octave ... which was accompanied by slow and not ungraceful motions of the body and limbs, their hands being held up in a supplication posture, and the tone and manner of their song and gestures seemed to bespeak the goodwill and forebearance [sic] of their intentions (quoted in Gummow 1992:78, 79).

Lending support for the assertion that gesture was indeed important in local Aboriginal society, Adam Kendon attests to the currency of sophisticated sign languages in much of south-eastern Australia in the nineteenth century. He cites relevant historical references that include most of the New England language groups, one white resident of Tenterfield saying: 'They also spoke on their fingers similar to the deaf and dumb' (quoted in Kendon 1988:41).

But musical gesture should be given an extended definition here, one not restricted to the upper-body movement that presumably comprised sign language. John von Sturmer makes the claim for the whole-body significance of Aboriginal dancing in the north of Australia: 'Here the body speaks – directly and in its totality' (quoted in Carter 1992a:183), and Watkin Tench describes the passion of Indigenous dance movement closer to home:

> Some dances are performed by men only, some by women only, and in others the sexes mingle. In one of them I have seen the men drop on the ground and kiss the earth with the greatest fervour, between the kisses looking up to Heaven. They also frequently throw up their arms, exactly in the manner in which the dancers of the Friendly Islands are depicted in one of the plates of Mr. Cook's last voyage (Tench 1999:263).

G. C. Mundy was similarly alive to the vibrant communicative potential of the dancers' movements in a corroboree he witnessed in Sydney in 1846 (Mundy 1852, vol. 1:216ff). The fact that gesture interacted there in a particularly dynamic fashion with designs painted on the performers' bodies, introduces the last category of 'musical' communication I wish to discuss, that of painted decoration. Ellis and others have documented the close relationship of song to body paint for Central Australia, and both the Wah-wee and Wellington Mission stories related above describe designs for painting on bark being given to the songmaker along with new songs and dances. Illustrations and photographs of south-eastern ceremonial occasions overwhelmingly attest to the importance of body design to music (Sayers 1994), but there is unfortunately very little other information to which one can refer this evidence in order to gain a deeper understanding. It would be reasonable to assume that the dramatic dimension to the use of paint and other decoration was of prime significance. It has been often recorded that once painted-up, performers could no longer be recognised as their former selves. The transformative potential of body painting may well have enhanced the power of ceremonies to transcend the mundane constraints of the present, to cement identification with Ancestors and their stories, and to otherwise generate maximum emotional effect. Watkin Tench's description of the richness of dancers' body decoration captures some of that ambience:

> I have already mentioned that white is the colour appropriated to the dance, but the style of painting is left to everyone's fancy. Some are streaked with waving lines from head to foot; others marked by broad cross-bars, on the breast, back and thighs, or encircled with spiral lines, or regularly striped like a zebra. Of these ornaments, the face never wants its share, and it is hard to conceive anything in the shape of humanity more hideous and terrific than they appear to a stranger – seen, perhaps, through the livid gleam of a fire, the eyes surrounded by large white circles, in contrast with the black ground, the hair stuck full of pieces of bone and in the hand a grasped club, which they occasionally brandish with the greatest fierceness and agility (Tench 1999:263).

This section has hopefully provided positive evidence that tone, melody, rhythm, gesture, and design all combined to support song-texts in presenting multi-layered meanings in south-eastern Australian Aboriginal musical performance. One important dimension to the analysis of these meaning-oriented aspects resides in its potential to cast light on how south-eastern Aboriginal music, right up to the present, has developed in response to European influence. Where textual and musical characteristics have undergone great change over time, it is in these more subtle areas that significant continuities could be discerned, and where consequently, a 'truer' regional Indigenous musical identity might be found to lie. This however, is a subject beyond the scope of the present examination.

Conclusion

The foregoing survey has attempted to provide a broad yet reasonably detailed picture of late eighteenth-, nineteenth-, and early twentieth-century Aboriginal music-making in south-eastern Australia. It has suggested that this culture, while diverse, exhibits many similarities with Indigenous Australian music generally. Music and dance were seen to occupy the very core of Aboriginal social existence, the integration of various meaning systems into the musical paradigm resulting in a cultural experience of considerable subtlety and complex richness. Unfortunately, political bias, defective methods of enquiry, and a lack of research interest in certain areas have resulted in serious gaps in this musical narrative. Many of the less concrete and more sophisticated dimensions of music-making escaped the often very limited notice of European observers altogether, and even some major musical entities such as song-cycles remain unrepresented. This partial obscurity will perhaps be illuminated to some degree by subsequent research. Catherine Ellis' assertion that any understanding of Indigenous Aboriginal music must refer to both musical and integrated extra-musical information, seems to be well borne-out for south-eastern Australia, and this approach perhaps offers the best prospects for future studies in the historical ethnomusicology of this region.

Glossary of musical terms and concepts
(all websites last viewed on 2 August 2015)[2]

Ad lib. An abbreviation from Latin meaning 'as much and as often as desired, freely' *(https://www.google.com.au/search?q=glossary+of+musical+terms&ie=utf-8&oe=utf- 8&gws_rd=cr&ei=L8a-VeP XIKS3mAWw_5WIBA#q=ad+lib.+definition).*

---

[2] A good source of definitions for terms that have been used for rhythmic analysis of Aboriginal music is Ellis (1968).

Additive rhythms: Additive rhythm is much used in folk music, especially in Africa and Eastern Europe, and has been standard in Western concert music since the beginning of this century. In music using non-additive rhythm, or 'divisive rhythm' (which is the most common form used in Western music) the rhythm is the product of binary or ternary divisions of a larger unit of time. (A waltz, for example, makes rhythmic patterns based on groups of three equal beats repeated regularly, with the main accent on the first beat; in 'common time', the main accent occurs on the first of every four equal divisions or beats.) In additive rhythm, by contrast, instead of large time-units being subdivided into regular beats, the beat, metre and melodic rhythm are all fashioned from multiples of the smallest unit *(http://www.encyclopedia69.com/eng/d/additive-rhythm/additive-rhythm.htm)*.

Air: an instrumental tune, or, more commonly, the melody of a song (See also *https://www.google.com.au/search?q=glossary+of+musical+terms&ie=utf-8&oe=utf- 8&gws_rd=cr&ei=L8a-VePXIKS3mAWw_5WIBA#q=air+in+music)*.

Anhemitonal: Musicology commonly classifies note scales as either hemitonic or anhemitonic. Hemitonic scales contain one or more semitones and anhemitonic scales do not contain semitones *(https://www.google.com.au/search?q=glossary+of+musical+terms&ie=utf- 8&oe=utf-8&gws_rd=cr&ei=L8a-VePXIKS3mAWw_5WIBA#q=anhemitonic+scale+definition)*.

Centric tonal organisation: Where the tonic or keynote occurs in the middle of a melody rather than at the end, and where typically the tune, through its progression, moves both below and above the tonic.

Compass (or range): In music, this word describes the interval between the lowest and highest note of a melody (See *http://www.thefreedictionary.com/compass)*.

Diatonic: In music theory, a diatonic scale…is a scale composed of seven distinct pitches. The diatonic scale includes five whole steps and two half steps for each octave, in which the two half steps are separated from each other by either two or three whole steps, depending on their position in the scale (See *https://en.wikipedia.org/wiki/Diatonic_scale*).

Drone: In music, a drone is a harmonic or monophonic effect or accompaniment where a note or chord is continuously sounded throughout most or all of a piece *(https://www.google.com.au/search?q=glossary+of+musical+terms&ie=utf-8&oe=utf-8&gws_rd=cr&ei=L8a-VePXIKS3mAWw_5WIBA#q=drone+in+music)*.

Fixed pitches: Pitch can be understood here as another name for 'note'. 'Fixed pitch' in this sense refers to a system that follows the Western practice of using recognisable, predictable, and stable tones in melody, tones more likely to be separated by Western-style intervals of a tone or semitone than by micro-intervals. When early European observers wrote down the Aboriginal melodies they heard, standard Western notation was used. This is a very clumsy tool for the purpose, and one which presupposes the utilisation of Western pitch in performance. No-one knows whether the Aboriginal singers from whom the melodies were taken really sang like this, or sang microtonally (Also see *https://en.wikipedia.org/wiki/Pitch_%28music%29)*.

Glottal-stopping: The glottal stop is a type of consonantal sound used in many spoken languages, produced by obstructing airflow in the vocal tract or, more precisely, the glottis. In English, the glottal stop is represented, for example, by the hyphen in uh-oh! *(https://en.wikipedia.org/wiki/Glottal_stop)*.

Grace notes: Grace notes are ornaments, embellishments, or musical flourishes that are not necessary to carry the overall line of the melody, but serve instead to decorate or 'ornament' that line. Many ornaments, particularly grace notes, are performed as 'fast notes' around a central note (See *https://en.wikipedia.org/wiki/Ornament_%28music%29)*.

Heptatonic: A heptatonic scale is a musical scale that has seven notes per octave *(https://en.wikipedia.org/wiki/Heptatonic_scale)*.

Heterometre: A mixed metre; a metre that combines different elements, like triple and duple time (See *https://www.google.com.au/search?q=glossary+of+musical+terms&ie=utf-8&oe=utf-8&gws_rd=cr&ei=L8a-VePXIKS3mAWw_5WIBA#q=heterometre+in+music)*.

Hexatonic: A hexatonic scale is a scale with six pitches or notes per octave *(https://www.google.com.au/search?q=glossary+of+musical+terms&ie=utf-8&oe=utf-8&gws_rd=cr&ei=L8a-VePXIKS3mAWw_5WIBA#q=hexatonic)*.

Intervals: In music theory, an interval is the difference between two pitches. An interval may be described as horizontal, linear, or melodic if it refers to successively sounding tones, such as two adjacent pitches in a melody, and vertical or harmonic if it pertains to simultaneously sounding tones, such as in a chord. In Western music, intervals are most commonly differences between notes of a diatonic scale. The smallest of these intervals is a semitone. Intervals smaller than a semitone are called microtones (*https://en.wikipedia.org/wiki/Interval_%28music%29*).

Isometre: In music theory, isometre indicates the use of pulse without recognised metre. Some scholars referenced here (e.g. Gummow) seem to have used the term in this strict sense, while others (e.g. Jones) seem to have employed it to characterise melodies that proceed with a regular pulse that, once discerned, may or may not be able to be subdivided into discernable rhythmic patterns. In other words, Jones seems to have used it in contradistinction to 'free' or 'rhapsodic' rhythm (See *https://en.wikipedia.org/wiki/Isometre*).

Isorhythm: (From the Greek for 'the same rhythm') is a musical technique that arranges a fixed pattern of pitches with a repeating rhythmic pattern *https://www.google.com.au/search?q=isorhythm&ie=utf-8&oe=utf-8&gws_rd=cr&ei=suS-VancK6G0mAXSgoWoCQ*). Alternatively, Merriam-Webster defines isorhythm as: a single fixed rhythmic pattern … that is reiterated throughout the whole of a sung voice part (*http://www.merriam-webster.com/dictionary/isorhythm*

Keynote: The keynote is the main note of a musical scale; the note upon which a musical key is based. It has the same meaning here as the word 'tonic' (Also see *http://piano.about.com/od/musicaltermsa1/g/GL_keynote.htm*).

Legato: In music performance and notation, legato (Italian for 'tied together'), indicates that musical notes are played or sung smoothly and connected. That is, the player or singer transitions from note to note with no intervening silence. (See *https://www.google.com.au/search?q=glossary+of+musical+terms&ie=utf-8&oe=utf-8&gws_rd=cr&ei=L8a-VePXIKS3mAWw_5WIBA#q=legato+in+music*).

Macaronic: A song text using a mixture of languages (*https://en.wikipedia.org/wiki/Macaronic_language*).

Melismatic rhythm: Melisma (Greek: μέλισμα, melisma, song, air, melody; from μέλος, melos, song, melody), plural melismata, in music, is the singing of a single syllable of text while moving between several different notes in succession (*https://www.google.com.au/search?q=glossary+of+musical+terms&ie=utf-8&oe=utf-8&gws_rd=cr&ei=L8a-VePXIKS3mAWw_5WIBA#q=melismatic+in+music*).

Melodic progression: A melody (from Greek μελῳδία, melōidía, 'singing, chanting') also tune, voice, or line, is a linear succession of musical tones that the listener perceives as a single entity (*https://en.wikipedia.org/wiki/Melody*).

Monotone reiterations: Monotone refers to a sound that has a single unvaried tone, here repeated (See *https://en.wikipedia.org/wiki/Monotone*).

Octave: Many Western musical scales are typically written using eight notes, and the interval between the first (lowest) and last (highest) notes is an octave. (See *https://en.wikipedia.org/wiki/Octave*).

Onomatopoeia: is a word that phonetically imitates, resembles or suggests the source of the sound that it describes. Onomatopoeia (as an uncountable noun) refers to the property of such words (*https://en.wikipedia.org/wiki/Onomatopoeia*).

Pentatonic: A pentatonic scale is a musical scale or mode with five notes per octave in contrast to a heptatonic (seven note) scale such as the major scale and minor scale (*https://www.google.com.au/search?q=glossary+of+musical+terms&ie=utf-8&oe=utf-8&gws_rd=cr&ei=L8a-VePXIKS3mAWw_5WIBA#q=pentatonic+scale*).

Portamento (plural portamenti): In music, portamento is a gradual slide in pitch from one note to another (*https://www.google.com.au/search?q=glossary+of+musical+terms&ie=utf-8&oe=utf-8&gws_rd=cr&ei=L8a-VePXIKS3mAWw_5WIBA#q=portamento+in+music*).

Reiterated ground tone: The repeated final note (often the tonic or keynote) of a melody.

Rhapsodic rhythm: Rhapsodic rhythm is non-metric or irregular rhythm. Unlike metric rhythms where the rhythm can be counted, rhapsodic rhythms are often random (*https://sites.google.com/site/thredgolddance/word-of-the-week/schadenfreudeshah-dn-froi-duhnoun*).

Scale organisation: In music theory, a scale is any set of musical notes ordered by fundamental frequency or pitch. A scale ordered by increasing pitch is an ascending scale, and a scale ordered by decreasing pitch is a descending scale (*https://www.google.com.au/search?q=glossary+of+musical+terms&ie=utf-8&oe=utf-8&gws_rd=cr&ei=L8a-VePXIKS3mAWw_5WIBA#q=scale+in+music*).

Simple and compound time signatures: Time signatures are the rhythmic patterns that any song or tune is cast in. The terms duple, triple, and quadruple refer to the number of beats in a measure. The term simple means that each of these beats can be broken into two notes. For example, 2/4 time is classified as simple duple. 'Duple' refers to the two beats per measure, and 'simple' states that each of these beats can be divided into two notes. 3/4 time is classified as simple triple. 'Triple' refers to the three beats per measure. Again, 'simple' states that each of these beats can be divided into two notes. 4/4 time is classified as simple quadruple due to its four beats which can be divided into two notes. While beats in simple metre are divided into two notes, beats in compound metre are divided into three. 6/8 time can be used to demonstrate this. Where six eighth notes make up a measure, they can either be grouped into two beats (compound duple) or three beats (simple triple). Since the simple triple pattern already belongs to 3/4 time, 6/8 is compound duple. (See *http://www.musictheory.net/lessons/15*).

Step: In music, a step, or conjunct motion, is the difference in pitch between two consecutive notes of a musical scale. In other words, it is the interval between two consecutive scale degrees. Any larger interval is called a skip (also called a leap), or disjunct motion (*https://www.google.com.au/search?q=glossary+of+musical+terms&ie=utf-8&oe=utf-8&gws_rd=cr&ei=L8a-VePXIKS3mAWw_5WIBA#q=step+in+music*).

Strophic Form: (also called 'verse-repeating' or chorus form) is the term applied to songs in which all verses or stanzas of the text are sung to the same music. The opposite of strophic form, with new music written for every stanza, is called through-composed (*https://en.wikipedia.org/wiki/Strophic_form*).

Syllabic Rhythm: Song music in which each syllable of text is matched to a single note. This is the opposite of melismatic rhythm, which describes the singing of a single syllable of text while moving between several different notes in succession (See *https://www.google.com.au/search?q=glossary+of+musical+terms&ie=utf-8&oe=utf-8&gws_rd=cr&ei=L8a-VePXIKS3mAWw_5WIBA#q=melismatic+in+music*).

Syncopation: In music, this indicates the displacement of the usual rhythmic accent away from a strong beat onto a weak beat (*http://www.thefreedictionary.com/syncopation*).

Through-Composed: The term through-composed means that the music is relatively continuous, non-sectional, and/or non-repetitive. A song is said to be through-composed if it has different music for each stanza of the lyrics. This is in contrast to strophic form, in which each stanza is set to the same music (*https://en.wikipedia.org/wiki/Through-composed*).

Tonal Plateaux: Tone here can be understood as another name for 'note'. A tonal plateau is where a note will rest for a while before the melody starts moving again (Also see *https://www.google.com.au/search?q=glossary+of+musical+terms&ie=utf-8&oe=utf-8&gws_rd=cr&ei=L8a-VePXIKS3mAWw_5WIBA#q=tone+in+music*).

Tonic: In music, the tonic refers to the main note of a melody, the tonal centre or final resolution tone. (See *https://www.google.com.au/search?q=glossary+of+musical+terms&ie=utf-8&oe=utf-8&gws_rd=cr&ei=L8a-VePXIKS3mAWw_5WIBA#q=tonic+in+music*).

References

A. Bibliographic resources

Armidale Express, 28-2-1874, p. 4.

Armitage, E., 1933, Corroborees of the Aborigines of Great Sandy Island. Journal of the Royal Geographical Society (Queensland Branch) 48:96.

Austin, Peter, R. M. W. Dixon, Tom Dutton and Isobel White, eds. 1990, Language and history: essays in honour of Luise A. Hercus, Canberra: Pacific Linguistics, series C116.

Barker, Jimmy and Janet Mathews 1977, The two worlds of Jimmy Barker. Canberra: Australian Institute of Aboriginal Studies.

Barwick, Linda, Allen Marett and Guy Tunstill, eds, 1995, The essence of singing and the substance of song. Sydney: Oceania Monograph 46.
Bell, Diane, 1998, *Ngarrindjeri wurruwarrin*: a world that is, was, and will be. Melbourne: Spinifex.
Berndt, Ronald M., and Catherine H. Berndt, eds, 1965, Aboriginal man in Australia. Sydney: Angus & Robertson.
—— 1988, The world of the first Australians. Canberra: Aboriginal Studies Press.
Bootle, F. J. E., 1899, Aboriginal words and meanings. Science of Man 2(1):3–5.
Bradley, Kevin, 1995, Leaf music in Australia. Australian Aboriginal Studies 1995/2:2–14.
Campbell, A. comp., and R. Vanderwal ed., 1994, Victorian Aborigines: John Bulmer's recollections 1855-1908. Melbourne: Museum of Victoria.
Carter, Paul 1992a, Living in a new country: history, travelling and language. London: Faber and Faber.
—— 1992b, The sound in between: voice, space, performance. Kensington: New South Wales University Press.
Chapman, Valerie and Peter Read eds, 1996, Terrible hard biscuits. Sydney: Allen & Unwin.
Clunies Ross, Margaret, 1986, Australian Aboriginal oral tradition. Oral Tradition 1(2):231–271.
—— 1987, Research into Aboriginal songs: the state of the art. In M. Clunies Ross, T. Donaldson and S. Wild, eds. Songs of Aboriginal Australia, 1–13. Sydney: Oceania Monograph 32.
—— 1994, Songs from Djambidj. In R. M. W. Dixon and Martin Duwell, eds. The honey-ant men's love song and other Aboriginal song poems, 75–76. St. Lucia: University of Queensland Press
Clunies Ross, Margaret, T. Donaldson, and S. Wild, eds, 1987, Songs of Aboriginal Australia. Sydney: Oceania Monograph 32.
Cohen, Bill, 1988, To my delight. Canberra: Aboriginal Studies Press.
Crotty, Joel, 1995, Musicological readings of selected 19th-century textual and iconographic representations of Aboriginal Music in Victoria. Unpublished MS, University of Melbourne.
Crowley, Terry, 1976, Phonological change in New England. In R. M. W. Dixon, ed. Grammatical categories in Australian languages, 19–50. Canberra: Australian Institute of Aboriginal Studies.
Dixon, Robert M. W., 1980, The languages of Australia. Cambridge: Cambridge University Press.
Dixon, Robert M. W., and Martin Duwell, eds, 1994, The honey-ant men's love song and other Aboriginal song poems. St. Lucia: University of Queensland Press.
Donaldson, Tamsin, 1984, Kids that got lost: variations in the words of Ngiyampaa songs. In Jamie C. Kassler and Jill Stubington, eds. Problems and solutions, 228–253. Sydney: Hale & Iremonger.
—— 1987, Making a song (and dance) in south-eastern Australia. In Margaret Clunies Ross, Tamsin Donaldson and Stephen Wild, eds. Songs of Aboriginal Australia, 14–42. Sydney: Oceania Monograph 32.
—— 1995, Mixes of English and Ancestral language words in southeast Australian Aboriginal songs of traditional and introduced origin. In Linda Barwick, Allen Marett and Guy Tunstill, eds. The essence of singing and the substance of song, 143–158. Sydney: Oceania Monograph 46.
Dunlop, Eliza Hamilton, 1848, Native poetry. Sydney Morning Herald, 11 October, 3.
Eades, Diana, 1979, Gumbaynggir. In R. M. W. Dixon and B. J. Blake, eds. Handbook of Australian languages 1, 245–361. Canberra: Australian National University Press.
Egan, Jack, 1999, Buried alive. Sydney: Allen & Unwin.
Elkin, A. P., 1931–1936, unpublished field notebooks, Box 11, item 1. University of Sydney Archives, Sydney.
—— 1977, Aboriginal men of high degree (2nd ed.). St. Lucia: University of Queensland Press.
Ellis, Catherine J., 1968, Rhythmic analysis of Aboriginal syllabic songs. Miscellanea Musicologica 3:21–49.
—— 1980, Aboriginal music and dance in southern Australia. In Stanley Sadie, ed. The new Grove dictionary of music and musicians, vol. 1, 723–729. London: Macmillan.
—— 1984, Time consciousness of Aboriginal performers. In Jamie C. Kassler and Jill Stubington, eds. Problems and solutions, 149–185. Sydney: Hale & Iremonger.
—— 1985, Aboriginal music: education for living. St. Lucia: University of Queensland Press.
—— 1993, Powerful songs: their placement in Aboriginal thought. The World of Music 36(1):3–20.

—— 1997, Understanding the profound structural knowledge of Central Australian performers from the perspective of T. G. H. Strehlow. Strehlow Research Centre Occasional Papers 1:57–78.

Enright, W. J. 1934, Notes on Kumbangerai. Mankind 1(10):239–240.

Fraser, J. 1883, The Aborigines of New South Wales. Proceedings of the Royal Society of New South Wales 16:193–233.

Gardner, William, 1854, Productions and resources of the northern and western districts of New South Wales. Mitchell Library, Sydney (ML A176).

Glen Innes Examiner, 17-5-1881, p. 6.

Glen Innes Examiner, 29-5-1888, p. 3.

Goddard, R. H., 1934, Aboriginal poets as historians. Mankind 1(10):234–236.

Gordon, John, 1968a, Survey of Aboriginal music in N.S.W.: Brief report on second and third field trips. Australian Institute of Aboriginal and Torres Strait Islander Studies, Canberra (PMS 2197).

—— 1968b, Transcriptions of Aboriginal songs of N.S.W. Australian Institute of Aboriginal and Torres Strait Islander Studies, Canberra (MS 548).

Gummow, Margaret J., 1983, Aboriginal music of New South Wales: an exploratory study. Unpublished honours diss., University of New England, Armidale.

—— 1985, Cueing in several performances of a song from the Bandjalang tribal area of N.S.W. Paper presented to the 9th National Conference of the Musicological Society of Australia, Monash University, Melbourne.

—— 1987, The square dance as an Aboriginal performing art. Paper presented to the 'Popular Music' seminar at the University of New England, Armidale.

—— 1992, Aboriginal songs from the Bundjalung and Gidabal areas of south-eastern Australia. Unpublished Ph.D. diss., University of Sydney, Sydney.

—— 1993, The power of the past in the present: singers and songs from northern New South Wales. The World of Music 36(1):43–49.

—— 1995, Songs and sites/moving mountains: a study of one song from northern NSW. In Linda Barwick, Allen Marett and Guy Tunstill, eds. The essence of singing and the substance of song, 121–132. Sydney: Oceania Monograph 46.

—— 2001, South-eastern Aboriginal music. In Stanley Sadie and John Tyrrell, eds. The new Grove dictionary of music and musicians (2nd edn), n.p. London: Grove. In Grove Music Online [electronic resource]: *http://www.oxfordmusiconline.com/*

Gunson, Niel, ed., 1974, Australian reminiscences and papers of L. E. Threlkeld, Canberra: Australian Institute of Aboriginal Studies.

Harper, Walter R., 1902, A corroboree song. Science of Man 5(11):175.

Hercus, Luise and Grace Koch, 1996, A native died sudden at Lake Allallina. Aboriginal History 20:133–150.

Hewitt, T. G., 1936, Aboriginal words and names, upper Clarence River district. Mitchell Library, Sydney (ML B857):23–24.

Hiatt, Lester R., 1996, Arguments about Aborigines. Cambridge: Cambridge University Press.

Hill, Barry, 1993, Ghosting William Buckley. Melbourne: William Heinemann.

Hoddinott, William G., n.d., Gumbaynggirr song texts. Australian Institute of Aboriginal and Torres Strait Islander Studies, Canberra (MS 2126/1, item 10).

Holmer, Nils M. and V. E. Holmer, 1969, Stories from two native tribes of eastern Australia. Uppsala: A.-B. Lundequistska Bokhandeln.

Horton, David, 2000, The pure state of nature. St. Leonards: Allen & Unwin.

Howitt, Alfred W., 1887, Notes on songs and songmakers of some Australian tribes. Journal of the Anthropological Institute 16(3):327–335.

—— 1904, The native tribes of south-east Australia. London: Macmillan.

Isaacs, Jennifer, ed., 1979, Australian Aboriginal music. Sydney: Aboriginal Artists Agency.

Jones, Trevor A., 1965, Australian Aboriginal music: the Elkin Collection's contribution toward an overall picture. In R. M. Berndt and C. H. Berndt, eds. Aboriginal man in Australia: essays in honour of Emeritus Professor A. P. Elkin, 285–374. Sydney: Angus & Robertson.

—— 1972, The nature of Australian Aboriginal music. Hemisphere 6(12):2–6.

—— 1980, The traditional music of the Australian Aborigines. In Elizabeth May, ed. Music of many cultures, 154–171. Berkeley: University of California Press.

Kartomi, Margaret J., 1984, Delineation of lullaby style in three areas of Aboriginal Australia. In Jamie C. Kassler and Jill Stubington, eds. Problems and solutions, 59–93. Sydney: Hale & Iremonger.

Kassler, Jamie C., and Jill Stubington, eds, 1984, Problems and solutions: occasional essays in musicology presented to Alice M. Moyle. Sydney: Hale & Iremonger.

Kendon, Adam, 1988, Sign languages of Aboriginal Australia. Cambridge: Cambridge University Press.

Kennedy, K., 1933, Instruments of music used by the Australian Aborigines. Mankind 1(7):147–157.

Laves, Gerhardt, 1929, unpublished field notebooks. Australian Institute of Aboriginal and Torres Strait Islander Studies, Canberra (MS 2189).

Longman, Murray J., 1960, Songs of the Tasmanian Aborigines as recorded by Mrs. Fanny Cochrane-Smith. Papers & Proceedings of the Royal Society of Tasmania 94:79–86.

McBryde Isabel, 1984, Exchange in south eastern Australia: an ethnohistorical perspective. Aboriginal History 8(2):132–153.

McDonald, Barry, 1996a, The idea of tradition examined in the light of two Australian musical studies. Yearbook for Traditional Music 28:106–130.

—— 1996b, Evidence of four New England corroboree songs indicating Aboriginal responses to European invasion. Aboriginal History 20:176–194.

—— 2001, 'You can dig all you like, you'll never find Aboriginal culture there': relational aspects of the history of the Aboriginal music of New England, New South Wales, 1830–1930. Unpublished Ph.D. dissertation, University of New England, Armidale.

McDougall, A. C., 1901, Manners, customs and legends of the Coombangaree tribe. Science of Man 4(4):63–64.

McGregor, Russell, 1998, Imagined destinies. Aboriginal Australians and the doomed race theory, 1880–1939. Melbourne: Melbourne University Press.

Mann, J. F., 1885, Notes on the Aborigines of Australia. Proceedings of the Royal Geographical Society of Australasia (New South Wales and Victorian Branch) 1:27–63.

Manning, J., 1883, Notes on the Aborigines of New Holland. Proceedings of the Royal Society of New South Wales 16:155–173.

Mathews, Janet, 1985, Lorna Dixon. In Isobel White, D. Barwick and B. Meehan, eds. Fighters and singers, 90–105. Sydney: George Allen & Unwin.

Mathews, Robert Hamilton, n.d., unpublished field notebooks. National Library of Australia, Canberra (MS 8006).

—— 1897, The Keepara ceremony of initiation. Journal of the Anthropological Institute 26:320–337.

—— 1898, Initiation of Australian tribes. Proceedings of the American Philosophical Society 37:54–68.

—— 1899, The Walloonggurra ceremony. Queensland Geographical Journal 15:67–74.

—— 1900a, The Murrawin ceremony. Queensland Geographical Journal, NS, 16:35–41.

—— 1900b, The totemic divisions of Australian Tribes. Queensland Geographical Journal, NS, 16:164–175.

—— 1901, The Thoorga and Yookumbill languages. Queensland Geographical Journal, NS, 17:49–73.

—— 1902, The Burbung of the New England tribes, New South Wales. Proceedings of the Royal Society of Victoria, NS, 9:120–136.

—— 1903, Wandarral of Clarence and Richmond River tribes. Proceedings of the Royal Society of Victoria, NS, 10:29–42.

—— 1904 [1905]. Ethnological notes on the Aboriginal tribes of New South Wales and Victoria. Journal of the Royal Society of New South Wales 38: 203–381. (Republished in 1905 as a monograph, under the imprint of F.W. White, General Printer, Sydney.)

Medhurst, J., 1895, Letter to R. H. Mathews. Mathews Collection, Australian Institute of Aboriginal and Torres Strait Islander Studies, Canberra (MS 1606/2, item 18).

Meston, Archibald, n.d., Meston collection. John Oxley Library, Brisbane (OM 64-17).

Milson, Rachel, 1840, Kamilaroi vocabulary and songs. Mitchell Library, Sydney (ML A1668).

Morelli, Steve, n.d., Gumbaynggirr song texts. Unpublished MS.

—— 2008. Gumbaynggirr dictionary and learner's grammar. Nambucca Heads NSW: Muurrbay Aboriginal Language & Culture Co-operative.
Moyle, Alice M., 1960, Two native song-styles recorded in Tasmania. Papers and Proceedings of the Royal Society of Tasmania 94:73–78.
—— 1966, A handlist of field collections of recorded music in Australia and Torres Strait. Canberra: Australian Institute of Aboriginal Studies.
—— ed., 1992, Music and dance of Aboriginal Australia and the South Pacific. Sydney: Oceania Monograph 41.
Mundy, Godfrey Charles, 1852, Our Antipodes (3 vols). London: Richard Bentley.
Nettl, Bruno, 1983, The study of ethnomusicology. Chicago: University of Illinois Press.
Norton, Albert, 1907, Stray notes on our Aboriginals. Science of Man 9(7):101–103.
Oates, Lynette F., 1985, Emily Margaret Horneville of the Muruwari. In Isobel White, D. Barwick and B. Meehan, eds. Fighters and singers, 106–122. Sydney: George Allen & Unwin.
Radcliffe-Brown, Alfred R., 1923, Notes on the social organization of Australian tribes (part 2). Journal of the Royal Anthropological Institute 53:424–447.
—— 1929a, unpublished field notebooks. Australian Institute of Aboriginal and Torres Strait Islander Studies, Canberra (MS 995).
—— 1929b, Notes on totemism in eastern Australia. Journal of the Royal Anthropological Institute 59:349–415.
Reece, Bob, 1996, Inventing Aborigines. In Valerie Chapman and Peter Read, eds. Terrible hard biscuits, 28–41. Sydney: Allen & Unwin.
Riley, W. E., 1831, The corobberie. Riley Papers, Mitchell Library, Sydney (ML A295).
Roth, H. Ling, 1887, Australian tunes. Journal of the Anthropological Institute 16(4):425.
Sayers, Andrew, 1994, Aboriginal art of the nineteenth century. Melbourne: Oxford University Press.
Stubington, Jill, 1979, North Australian Aboriginal music. In Jennifer Isaacs, ed. Australian Aboriginal music, 7–19. Sydney: Aboriginal Artists Agency.
Swain, Tony, 1993, A place for strangers: towards a history of Australian Aboriginal being. Cambridge: Cambridge University Press.
Tench, Watkin, 1999, 1788. Melbourne: Text Publishing Co.
Thomas, Northcote W., 1905, Baiame and the bell-bird. Man 5:49–51.
Threlkeld, Lancelot, n.d., Songs of the natives of New South Wales to the north of Sydney. Threlkeld Papers, Mitchell Library, Sydney (ML A382), p. 129.
Torrance, George W., 1887, Music of the Australian Aborigines. Journal of the Anthropological Institute 16(3):335–340.
Vaarzon-Morel, Petronella, comp., 1998, Warlpiri women's voices: our lives our history. Alice Springs: IAD Press.
Von Sturmer, John R., 1987, Aboriginal singing and notions of power. In M. Clunies Ross, T. Donaldson and S. Wild, eds. Songs of Aboriginal Australia, 63–76. Sydney: Oceania Monograph 32.
Walker, William, 1821, Letter to R. Watson. In Bonwick, J. Transcripts, Mitchell Library, Sydney, (B.T. 52), 1040–1042.
White, H. O'Sullivan, 1934, Some recollections of the Aborigines of New South Wales in the years 1848, 1849 and 1850. Mankind 1(9):226–227.
Wyndham, W. T., 1889, The Aborigines of Australia. Proceedings of the Royal Society of New South Wales 23:36–48.

B. Interview-based resources

Archibald, Frank, 1964, Armidale, audio tapes, Hoddinott Collection, A.T. 1395, Australian Institute of Aboriginal and Torres Strait Islander Studies, Canberra.
Ballengarry, Florence, 1974, Nambucca Heads, audio tapes, Eades Collection, A.T. 4499, Australian Institute of Aboriginal and Torres Strait Islander Studies, Canberra.
Buchanan, Harry, 1973, Nambucca Heads, audio tapes, Crowley Collection, A.T. 2763 Australian Institute of Aboriginal and Torres Strait Islander Studies, Canberra.

Cherry, Ben, 1987, Kingstown, audio tapes, McDonald Collection, TRC 2720/10/1–5; TRC 2720/11, National Library of Australia, Canberra.
Cohen, George, 1980, audio tapes, Creamer Collection, A.T. 05048, Australian Institute of Aboriginal and Torres Strait Islander Studies, Canberra.
De Silva, Lenny, 1994, audio tapes, Armidale. McDonald Collection, D3223/7–13, Australian Institute of Aboriginal and Torres Strait Islander Studies, Canberra.
Ellis, Sylvester, 1984, Ward's Mistake. McDonald Collection, TRC 2720/23/1–7; TRC 2720/24/1–3, National Library of Australia, Canberra.
Jay, Norma, 1995, Ebor, audio tapes, McDonald Collection, D3223/5,6, Australian Institute of Aboriginal and Torres Strait Islander Studies, Canberra.
Kelly, Maisie, 1993–1996, Armidale, audio tapes, McDonald Collection, D3223/1–4, Australian Institute of Aboriginal and Torres Strait Islander Studies, Canberra.
Lardner, Keith, 1998, Corindi Beach, uncatalogued audio tapes, author's collection.
Laurie, Bing, 1998, Corindi Beach, uncatalogued audio tapes, author's collection.
Laurie, Bruce, 1998, Corindi Beach, uncatalogued audio tapes, author's collection.
Martin, M., 1964, audio tapes, Callaghan Collection, TRC 2920/2, National Library of Australia, Canberra.
McKenzie, Willy, 1964, Brisbane, audio tapes, Callaghan Collection, TRC 2920/2, National Library of Australia, Canberra.
Mercey, Junie, n.d., Nambucca Heads, audio tapes, Muurrbay Language Centre, Sherwood.
Morris, Maggie, 1994, Kempsey, audio tapes, McDonald Collection, D3223/30, Australian Institute of Aboriginal and Torres Strait Islander Studies, Canberra.
Morris, Queenie, 1994, Macksville, audio tapes, McDonald Collection, D3223/26, Australian Institute of Aboriginal and Torres Strait Islander Studies, Canberra.
Newberry, Royce, 1995, Guyra, audio tapes, McDonald Collection, D3223/17, Australian Institute of Aboriginal and Torres Strait Islander Studies, Canberra.
Perkins, Tony, 1998, Corindi Beach, uncatalogued audio tapes, author's collection.
Vale, Hazel, 1994–1996, Armidale, audio tapes, McDonald Collection, D3223/31, Australian Institute of Aboriginal and Torres Strait Islander Studies, Canberra.

8 Applying multilingual knowledge to decipher an historical song of change

Raymond Kelly[1] and Jean Harkins[1]
University of Newcastle[1]

Abstract

Aboriginal songs from the Mid North Coast of New South Wales have been audio recorded since the 1930s, following on from previous written accounts of songs and verse by Threlkeld (n.d. [1820s?]) and others. Here we examine a song recorded at Armidale, in the 1960s, preserved in the AIATSIS sound archive, but not hitherto transcribed and analysed. Although it contains only six lines, the complex interplay of words and phrases from traditional language (primarily Thangatti~Dhanggati) and Aboriginal English (with some NSW Pidgin), had made it difficult for previous researchers to ascertain the meaning even at the surface level.

By employing a combination of local cultural background knowledge and Indigenous-led linguistic investigation, we aim to:

- explore some of the richness of the song's cultural meaning from an Indigenous perspective
- show how the features of the song connect with a contemporary understanding, as a multilingual and multicultural welcome to youngsters of an age to commence formal education
- argue that the potential for re-evaluating, re-analysing and revaluing such cultural material is worth facing the many analytical challenges it presents.

By tracing relationships of structure and meaning, we can discern many of the elements that open up such understandings for 'enculturated listeners' (Turpin and Stebbins 2010:2). The patterned code-switching between language varieties further illustrates features of multilingual discourse at the crossroads of intergenerational language shift.

Keywords: Aboriginal song, sound archives, transcription, multilingualism, language contact, Dhanggati, south-eastern Australia, NSW Pidgin, Aboriginal English

Introduction

We focus here on a single, short song from the Mid North Coast of New South Wales (NSW), where Aboriginal songs were first recorded in the 1930s on wax cylinder, and subsequently with increasingly sophisticated audio recording technologies. Prior to the advent of sound recording, there was some written documentation of songs and poetry in south-eastern Australia (see Skinner and Wafer, this volume). These and subsequent tape recordings made through the 1960s and 70s illustrate song traditions surviving, and to varying degrees thriving, through times of cultural change. At least some of these traditional musical forms continue to flow into the work of today's songmakers and performers (Gummow 1995; McDonald, this volume).

This particular song was recorded in Armidale, NSW, by the linguist Nils Holmer (1964), along with mostly spoken language elicitation and texts; the song has not hitherto been transcribed and analysed, although accompanying spoken material is transcribed in Holmer's field notes and by Lissarrague (2013). In a mere six lines of song text, there is a complex interplay of words and phrases from traditional language (primarily Thangatti)[1], NSW Pidgin (Troy 1993), and Aboriginal English (Harkins 2008). This, along with the usual difficulties of puzzling out words in songs, had made it difficult for previous researchers to ascertain the meaning even at the surface word level, let alone its more abstract and contextual significances. Similar issues of transcription and analysis have been noted in other NSW languages (Donaldson 1979, 1984, 1995; McDonald 1996), as well as elsewhere on the continent (e.g. Hale 1984:257; Alpher and Keeffe 2001; Bracknell, this volume; Jebb and Marmion 2015). Only through an Indigenous-led process of synthesising local cultural and historical knowledges with deep linguistic investigation (Kelly 2015, Barney 2014), can we begin to open up an understanding of the depth of cultural meaning for Indigenous inheritors of such archived material.[2] Our aim is to demonstrate how this kind of approach can generate potential new insights into what emerges as a multilingual[3] welcome addressed by a senior man to members of a younger, multicultural generation who are soon to be put through the first stages of formal traditional education.

To give some background to the performer of the song and the circumstances of its recording, we note that the singer was Mr Lachlan Vale (nicknamed Locky), who was at the time living on the Aboriginal reserve at East Armidale. The large Vale family extended through Bellbrook and Kempsey as well as Armidale, and are identified principally with Thangatti language and country. This recording was made in February–March of 1964 and is archived as Holmer's Field Tape 4 in the sound archive of the Australian Institute of Aboriginal and Torres Strait Islander Studies (AIATSIS). Mr Vale also recorded two Thangatti narratives for Holmer in April–May 1964, archived as Field Tape 1. Professor Nils Holmer, from the University of Lund in Sweden, was funded by the then Australian Institute of Aboriginal Studies to collect language material from northern NSW and south-east Queensland between January and August of 1964. He contributed some, not all, of his field recordings to the AIATSIS archive in the form of four sound tape reels (Holmer 1964). His analyses and vocabularies of Thangatti and Gathang were published in Holmer (1966, 1967), and some texts were published in Holmer and Holmer (1969).

---

1   While the established spelling is 'Dhanggati' in the excellent grammar by Lissarrague (2007), variant spellings are also used on the basis of personal and family identification and preference.
2   We express warm thanks to Amanda Lissarrague and Jim Wafer for clarifying several linguistic points; two anonymous reviewers for prompting us to refine our discussion; and John Maynard and the Purai Global Indigenous and Diaspora Research Studies Centre for encouraging and supporting this research.
3   Many Aboriginal people identify more with the words 'bilingual/bicultural' than 'multilingual/ multicultural', based on the highly salient contrast between Aboriginal and non-Aboriginal cultural contexts. In using the latter terms, we recognise the multilingual and multicultural reality of traditional Aboriginal societies as well as those that came to Australia more recently.

The 1964 recordings were probably made in one of the small tin houses that were built on the East Armidale reserve to replace the tents and makeshift shacks, after concerns were raised about poor health among the Aboriginal population in the early 1960s (Kelly 2015). It is important to note that two other respected language speakers, Mr Doug Scott and Mr Frank Archibald, were present during the song recording. Their approving chuckles can be heard at the end of the song, followed by several minutes of conversation in Thangatti between Mr Vale, Mr Scott and Mr Frank Archibald. All three men were in their late sixties to early seventies at that time.[4] The voices of children playing and speaking in the language can also be heard in the background on the tape.[5]

Before proceeding to analyse the song itself, we offer an experimental sketch of the kind of intuitive, encultured understanding of the audio material that emerges for a *gurri* 'Aboriginal person of this region' who grew up at the intergenerational crossroads between traditional cultural practices, and contemporary continuities and discontinuities of language, education, cultural memory, oral tradition, and song. Our aim here is to draw the reader into the conceptual world in which this seemingly opaque jumble of mixed language begins to make perfect sense, before we go on to identify specific textual and linguistic features that anchor these understandings in the process of extracting meaning from a highly complex and elliptical textual form.

2 Listening between the lines

In this section I, Ray Kelly, am writing in the first person, as one who grew up on the East Armidale Aboriginal reserve in daily contact with the speakers recorded on this tape. The singer, Lachlan Vale, is the father-in-law of my mother's auntie, Hazel Vale *née* Archibald; my siblings and I grew up as classificatory brothers and sisters to our generation of the Vale family. Doug Scott is a great-uncle of my father. I may well be among the children playing in the background on the tape, as I would have been three years old at the time, and was the kind of child who hung around listening to the elders as much as possible. I present the full song text here, as I understand it, followed by an account of its cultural resonances from my perspective as an 'encultured listener' (Turpin and Stebbins 2010:2).

My current understanding of this song is formed through some decades as an inheritor and student of this cultural material, through a learning process very like the traditional one described by Hale (1984:259–60). But even within the shared cultural knowledge of a community, each listener brings a unique set of knowledge and experience to the text, and each person's interpretation and response to it will be their own. No doubt my present understanding will deepen as lifelong learning unfolds. Nothing like an absolute or definitive interpretation is being suggested here, but I try to explain where my understanding is coming from, both in

---

4   Doug Scott was recorded as being eight years old in 1903, as a pupil at the Nulla Nulla Aboriginal Reserve school, so in 1964 he would have been 69. Lachlan Vale's two younger sisters are on the same school roll, aged 10 and 12, and Frank Archibald lived 1884–1975, so Mr Vale was probably at least five years older than the other two men. Birth date records are not fully consistent, but indicate that Mr Vale was born around 1888, Mr Scott between 1890–94, and Mr Archibald between 1884–91. Mr Vale was also called Bubba Vale (from *babaang* 'grandfather', in recognition of his status as an elder), and sadly, passed away in 1965. (Referring to those who have passed away by title plus surname, with first name only if needed for clarification, is frequent in Aboriginal English to show respect for the departed. This convention probably arose from widely documented traditional practices of not speaking the personal name of the deceased.)
5   After these tapes were digitally remastered in 2008, as described in Kelly (2015), the greatly improved sound quality facilitated a more thorough analysis of both the language material and contextual background sounds. Modern remastering of all such material is urgently needed to improve language inheritors' access to it.

terms of my cultural background knowledge and in the song text itself. Here is my transcription of the song as I hear it:[6]

You an' me, tiny man, maaguraalu galay,
You an' me, tiny man, maaguraalu galay.
Do you see? No, no sabi;
Caught in bingaay yirruu,
Caught in a bingay yaarripirringu.
The top lady to the bottom say:
An' sting you bun, yaarriurrikayi!

For me, this song evokes the voice of a *Thupara* 'knowledge holder'[7] whose role was to serve as a guide or mentor for younger members of the Aboriginal communities in and around the Mid North Coast of New South Wales. As each child grew, the senior women would make regular assessment of their readiness to progress through the stages of growth as a person. This song references one of the important periods of growth for Aboriginal children: the transition from tiny people into the world of the *guraa* or *guraamun* 'big boy' or 'big girl'.[8]

Against the backdrop of the Aboriginal Welfare Board, as a child living on the Aboriginal reserve at East Armidale during the 1960s, I was extremely lucky to be raised in a communal environment that still practised leadership and personal development within culturally defined cohorts or age groups. In my childhood community, Aboriginal children were encouraged to embrace stages of proper behaviour and leadership appropriate to their age. Our words for age-groups and social roles were not only labels and meanings, but also guideposts for how young people acted – good, bad and indifferent.

For a young person in their formative years, as a *guraa* or *guraamun*, the expectation is that they are now community members who can be relied upon to think of the safety, health and actions of those younger than themselves. They might take action to prevent dangerous behaviour, or they might simply act as the voice of the grown-up in the absence of anyone older.

Family kinship played an enormous part in how some community members saw their roles. Uncles and aunties on your mother's line at times seemed way too strict, and would whenever the opportunity arose remind you where you stood in the family structure. *Dhalayi* 'younger children'[9] were keenly watched over by the community at large; any child found to be acting inappropriately or abusive to others or property could be marched home to face the music.

For a little *gurri* like the 'tiny man' in this song, to be escorted away by older male members of his family for training or instruction could be a new and potentially frightening experience. However, the women in his family would have reinforced that his time was approaching and that he would be expected to change, he would need to modify his behaviour, he would need to grow up. When I listen to Lachlan Vale sing about a 'tiny man' I hear a song of compassion and solidarity, of hope and remembrance, as if the song was sung by an old man who remembered that he was once a little *gurri* himself.

---

6   My representation of the sounds agrees in most respects with Lissarrague's (2007) orthography, apart from a few words that are discussed individually below.
7   *Thupara* is formed from the same root as *dhupiyn* 'know, understand' (Lissarrague 2007:134); probably a verb stem *thupa-* 'know' plus a nominalising suffix *-ra*. As in the language name, the digraphs th/dh can be used according to individual preference, as can the symbols for stops p/b, t/d, k/g.
8   *Guraa/mun* is related to *gurraarr* 'long, tall, straight' (Lissarrague 2007:145); Holmer (1967) wrote that *gurruman* (as he spelt it) meant 'uninitiated boy or youth', while his language consultant Mr Len Duckett said 'a big boy' (Holmer 1964; Lissarrague 2007:146). The first rhotic in *guraa* and *guraarr* is spelt here as approximant rather than trill, from my perception of multiple instances of these words.
9   *Dhalayi* 'child, girl, boy, baby' (Lissarrague 2007:129–130).

3 So much meaning, so few words

We turn now to the challenge of unpacking and analysing the song text, with a view to identifying what are the textual and linguistic features that signal or correspond with the enculturated understanding expressed above. We want to explore how the words, phrasing and structure of the text itself contribute to Ray's interpretation, while also recognising other possible understandings. Although in one sense there is 'so little to work with' (Walsh 2007), there is so much meaning here that the question for us has become not 'What does it mean?' but 'How is so much meaning packed into so few words?'

3.1 Rhyme and metre

Looking first at the text structure as a whole, we can see that despite its brevity, the song displays remarkable complexity in its structural organisation, with strong correspondences of rhythm and text (Turpin 2007a, b). It has rhyme both within and between lines, though not in the specific formal structures of European poetry (Walsh 2010:125). The first two lines are identical, but the other lines are not repeated, giving a six-line structure of AABCDEF:

*You an' me, tiny man, maaguraalu galay_*	A
*You an' me, tiny man, maaguraalu galay_*	A
Do you see? No, no sabi	B
Caught in binga-ay yirruu	C
Caught in a bingay yaarripirringu	D
The top lady to the bottom say	E
An' sting you bun, yaarriurrikayi!	F

This sequence can be repeated cyclically, in the 'timeless' manner described by Turpin (2007b:100) for Central Australian song.

The rhyme scheme operates both between lines and within them. Lines A, E and F all end with the sequence [ai], while C and D end in the high back vowel [u]. The usual pronunciation of the long variant [uː] is lower and more open (approaching [ɔ]) than for short [u]; in lines C and D this difference is reduced, probably because of the rhyming effect. The only line that otherwise doesn't participate in the rhyme scheme, line B, has an internal rhyme with high front [iː] on the stressed syllables. The metrical structure is regular, with nine sets of four beats each (indicated by underlining of the vowel/diphthong on which the beat falls). While not as complex as the rhythmic structure described by Turpin (2007b), similar principles can be seen in the alignment of rhythm and text. Examples include: a 'rest' beat at the end of line A; lengthening of *bingay* in C; and stress on the second syllable of *lady* in line E (producing a rhythmic structure closer to that of line B).

3.2 Code-switching

The pattern of code-switching is remarkably regular in relation to both the rhythmic structure and the grammatical structure. Each line starts off in English, and switches into traditional language (or NSW Pidgin in B) at roughly the halfway point. In line A there are four beats in English and four in Thangatti. Line B has two beats in English and two beats in Pidgin. Lines C and D are distinguished by a change in the pattern, with one beat in English and three in Thangatti. The effect of this is to highlight the words most central to the song's message, as will be explained in the next section. There is no switch in line E, and F returns to the two-plus-two pattern of line B.

Audio example 8.1: *Tiny man* sung by Raymond Kelly

You an' me, tiny man,	*maaguraalu galay _*	A
You an' me, tiny man	*maaguraalu galay _*	A
Do you see? No,	*no sabi*	B
Caught in	*binga-ay yirruu*	C
Caught in a	*bingay yaarripirringu*	D
The top lady to the bottom say:		E
An' sting you bun,	*yaarriurrikayi!*	F

Grammatically, most of the switches are at phrase boundaries (MacSwan 2013). In line A, the subject noun phrase (NP) is English and the verb phrase (VP) is Thangatti. In B, the interrogative clause and its answer are in English, and the VP is in Pidgin. Lines C and D have subject ellipsis, with the first part of the VP in English and the postverbal NP in Thangatti. There is no switch in line E, and F has a main clause in English and subordinate clause in Thangatti.

Structurally impressive as this is, its pragmatic effect is most striking, in relation to the context and purpose of the song. The singer, the traditional knowledge holder, whose first language is Thangatti, is addressing the song to young multilinguals, who may be more familiar with English (and Pidgin) than with the full traditional language. So he[10] begins each line at their level, with simple English structures, before switching to more traditional language (Auer 2013). In effect, he is meeting the youngsters in their linguistic space before gently drawing them into the traditional language domain of the educational process that is to come. In today's educational terms of developmentally appropriate practice, and translanguaging in language teaching (García and Wei 2014), the pedagogical sophistication of the *Thupara* could hardly be bettered. A young listener with limited traditional language proficiency could still perceive messages of caring solidarity ('you and me, tiny man'), an impending if mysterious gathering ('caught') involving elders ('top lady') and a jocular but pointed warning of behavioural regulation ('sting on the bum').

3.3 Phonological, semantic and grammatical features

Having shown how these various text-level structures support the purpose and message of this song in its social and cultural context, we turn now to the analysis of each line, examining phonological processes, morphosyntactic structure, and semantic content. The aim of this is not to advance an interpretation intended to be definitive, particularly in the light of the many obstacles to a full interpretation of elliptical, opaque and thoroughly 'tricky' (Hale's loan-translation of Warlpiri *yajiki*, 1984:259) text. Instead, we want to open up some space for well-grounded and critically aware hypothesising about how linguistic aspects of song point toward and lead us into multiple layers of meaning and possibilities for deeper linguistic and cultural understanding.

---

10 The song is gender-specific in regard to the addressee (tiny man), but there is nothing specifically indicating a male singer. While this seems a reasonable inference from the broader social context in which older men educate boys, and from its being sung by Mr Vale, the point remains open to consideration.

For each line, we present our current morpheme-by-morpheme gloss, and comment on the salient features of phonology, morphology, syntax and semantics that guided us to these interpretations. This is not an exercise in starting from a cultural understanding and then hunting for language evidence to support it; rather, we think we can point to at least some of the pieces of language that prompted this interpretation within its cultural context. Songs, however, have the power to generate many possible interpretations, of which, as Michael Walsh points out, 'it is simply wrong to enquire which of these explanations is the "right" one, any more than sifting through the numerous accounts of James Joyce's *Ulysses* would reveal a single, "right" one' (Walsh 2007:129).

(1) *You an'   me,   tiny man,   maa-guraa-lu-galay.*
              me   get-big.boy-let's-many

'You and me, tiny man, it's time to get [you big boys] together.'

In the English part of this first line, we see some Aboriginal English features familiar to Aboriginal people in this region. The final stop of *an(d)* is lenited, as in many colloquial varieties of English, and the first sound in *me* sounds more like [n] than [m] on the tape, possibly by assimilation[11] to the preceding alveolar nasal. The semantic scope of *tiny* is extended to the collocation *tiny man*, where *little* would be more likely to occur here in contemporary Aboriginal and non-Aboriginal English.[12]

The Thangatti verb phrase has the transitive verb *maa* 'get' followed by several suffixes for which we can offer at least two possible analyses. Our first impression was of a sequence with purposive *gu* (*-gurayi* if it follows a nominaliser, Lissarrague 2007:70) followed by what appears to be the locative suffix *-ra*, probably with a nominalising function before the hortative *-lu* and plural suffix *galay*.[13] All of these suffixes are attested in Lissarrague (2007), but not in this particular order and sequence. We need more evidence to be sure if we are identifying them correctly. Our alternative analysis (shown in the gloss above) is that *maa* is followed by *guraa* 'big boy' before *-lu* and *-galay*. Both analyses accord with the listener's understanding of the meaning as, essentially, 'it's time to get all you big boys together [for ceremony]'. The second analysis could involve a kind of noun-incorporation, not identified elsewhere for Thangatti. Both analyses indicate more complex verbal morphology than seen in analyses of spoken Thangatti. This morphological complexity could be related to the high information density of the song text compared with everyday spoken language, and/or to the tendency of song to preserve more archaic, and often more complex, forms of language. Nonetheless, there is no individual element here that is not found in the recordings of Thangatti speech as well as song.

This line could be seen as rather opaque, in that the verb indexes an unstated agent or agents with the purpose of getting many unstated entities together. The verb *maa* itself is richly polysemous, as indicated in Lissarrague's (2007:148) glosses of 'get, fetch, take, catch, grab'. The words inserted in square brackets in the gloss are inferred on the basis that, in the social context of an

---

11 There is a faint, sibilant-like sound at the end of *me*, producing something that sounds more like *nirr* with devoiced trill [nir̥], but could be an effect of the tongue moving toward the initial sound of the following word, *tiny*. We mention this detail as an illustration of the auditory challenges in the taped material.
12 Ray Kelly finds himself singing *little man*, as often as *tiny man*, to his grandsons.
13 Lissarrague's (2007:18) spelling is *-galayi* based on her analysis of a VCV sequence *ayi;* but we think there may be a difference in the sound files between a disyllabic sequence /a.yi/ and a monosyllabic sequence /ay/, based on our observation that the latter is often realised as a monophthong [eː], while the former remains [a.yi]. We are seeking more evidence on this point, but for now we are spelling this *galay*. On the identification in this line of *guraa* 'big boy' versus *-gu-ra* 'PURP-LOC', the difference in vowel length isn't sufficient to make a firm determination, because it could be a rhythmic effect within the song.

older mentor addressing a young boy or boys about such a potential event, this is likely to be preparing the youngsters for the prospect of being gathered by senior men into a 'young men's camp' for education in the next stage of their progress toward manhood. This degree of subject and object ellipsis, or surface referential opacity, is not at all unusual in Australian languages (as highlighted by Garde 2013). The intense community interest in cultural, educational and ceremonial activity ensure that this is the first thing people would think of in relation to an unspecified someone intending to get together many unspecified others, despite the apparent contextual vagueness (Garde 2006, Donaldson 1979). This understood inference puts a clearer perspective on the solidarity expressed in the phrase 'you and me', reassuring the youngster that he will not go through this experience alone: that he will have a mentor's guidance and support.[14] Nonetheless, the elliptical structure combined with polysemy requires so much interpretive effort from the listener that we would not present our interpretation as definitive.

(2) *Do you see? No,   no   sabi.*
                         NEG   know
     'Do you see? No, [I/you] don't know.'

The English part here is fully standard, with *see* used in the sense of 'understand'. The question and answer sequence has at least two possible readings because of the subject ellipsis. It may be a switch of voice, with the *Thupara* asking the question, then answering it in the voice of the addressee saying 'I don't know'. Or it could be a rhetorical question, where the *Thupara* asks and then answers his own question: 'No, you don't know'. The switch to Pidgin for *no sabi* might be motivated by the need for a rhyme here.[15] Or it could be the adult framing the child's reply in Pidgin, seen as a simplified, childlike or 'light' form of language. Code-switching to signal change of speaker in Aboriginal storytelling has been noted elsewhere (Klapproth 2004).

(3) *Caught in   binga-ay   yi-rruu,*
                  brother   be-transformation
     'Caught [gathered] into brother [hood] [at daybreak *or* to be transformed],'

The English verb 'caught' echoes its Thangatti equivalent *maa* 'get' in line (1), with reference to the same prospective event. In Aboriginal English, 'caught' and 'got' are often perceived as interchangeable, because the voicing distinction between English /k/ and /g/ is non-phonemic in most Aboriginal languages. The vowel distinction between /ɔ/ and /ɒ/ is likewise non-phonemic for languages with the rounded back vowels /u/ and /uː/. The Thangatti phrase is semantically and referentially opaque without the cultural knowledge that the young men being passed through the Rules are regarded as a cohort of brothers, and that the gathering up of the youngsters was traditionally done just before daybreak. This gathering into the men's camp for commencement of instruction was sometimes spoken of in Aboriginal English as *breakaway from daylight*.

---

14 It will be noticed that we are not using the term 'initiation', which has been rightly critiqued for its connotations of occultism, anthropological exoticisation and othering of traditional educational practice. Its European cultural baggage does not fit comfortably with a traditional intellectual environment where hierarchical behaviour, individual credentialism, and ritual abuse of power are discouraged on a principled basis. Aboriginal people of this region usually speak of mature men as having 'gone through the Rules', or having been 'put through' (with unspecified object, understood as transition to manhood).
15 Of course the second *no* could be just a repetition of the English negator; our interpretation of it as part of the Pidgin verb phrase *no sabi* is not dogmatic.

Lengthening of the final syllable in *bingay* is almost certainly due to a rhythmic constraint, where this word carries two beats and is thus extended into three syllables [pi.ŋai → pi.ŋa.ai], as the melody moves upward by four notes on the second syllable. This places great metrical and melodic emphasis on *bingay*, which is a cultural keyword and core cultural concept governing men's relationships and obligations to each other, in everyday life as well as in ceremonial activity.

The word *yirruu* poses an analytical puzzle to which we can only offer some points we think are worth considering. The word is not in the dictionary (Lissarrague 2007), nor have we found it in the written documentation by Holmer or others. Originally we thought it was *yingu* or *yinguu*; Ray remembers this as a word of cultural importance, signifying or connected with a place of traditional education and/or a 'cohort' or 'brotherhood' of those involved in ceremonial activity. On closer investigation in the audio files, a sound like a devoiced rhotic can be heard before the nasal, more like [jiɽŋuː] or *yirrnguu*. This may simply be a hitherto undocumented word, of sufficient cultural importance that one can hope it might be remembered by others. However, we would also like to point to possible connections with two other words, as indicated in our gloss of 'be-transformation'. The form *yi* is mentioned by Lissarrague (2007:169) only as a variant of the suffixes *-kayi* (subordinator) and *-tayi* (nominaliser). In some of the sound files, however, *yi* seems able to function independently with existential sense, though not as a syntactic copula; hence our tentative gloss 'be'. The second syllable is even harder to pin down, but we suggest a possible connection with *rruu*, which conveys sudden transformation or illumination.[16] We gloss this tentatively as 'transformation', to leave open the possibility that it refers to either or both the transformation to daylight, and the transformation of boys into men.

This does not explain the velar nasal. An epenthetic nasalised onset to the back vowel [jiɽⁿuː] is one possibility; another is that the word *yirrnguu* is unsegmentable and the cultural association with transformation is noncompositional. The only other evidence for our suggestion of epenthesis comes from the placenames Euroka and Euroka Creek, in Thangatti country, near Burnt Bridge. Euroka Creek, pronounced *yirruu-ka*, is also known locally as Sunrise Creek, which suggests an identification of *yirruu* with sunrise or daybreak (followed by locative suffix *-ka*).

(4) *Caught in a   bingay   yaa-rri-pi-rri-ngu.*
     brother   enter-PROG-him-PL-THRU
     'Gathered into a brotherhood going through [the Rules] together.'

The English portion is parallel to the previous line, except for the addition of the indefinite article, possibly for rhythmic variation in a line where the melody does not rise as dramatically as in the previous line. The Thangatti portion is also parallel, with only the last word changing. This word poses an analytical challenge because of its polysemy, morphological complexity and very rapid pronunciation in the song. *Yaa* 'enter' occurs frequently in the sound files, and is represented in the dictionary as *yalaa* 'enter' (Lissarrague 2007:168). There is also some fortition of word-initial [j], such that it sounds more like [ʲj] or even [ɟ]; initially we thought we were hearing something like *djampingu* [ɟaɽ.ᵐpi.ŋu], but we are fairly sure the verb is *yaa* 'enter' with another series of suffixes. This verb has many meanings related to its core sense of 'go into', depending on what is entered, hence the derived forms *yalaati* 'swim', *yalaanya* 'bury (transitive)'. In this line the listener can discern who is entering, i.e. a group of brothers, but

---

16   When *rruu* appears as an independent morpheme, the trill is fricativised (a phonological process noted by Lissarrague 2007:5), sounding more like [ʐuː], usually with exaggerated intonation: *Rruuuu!* as an interjection akin to *Lo and behold!* or *Abracadabra!* This sense probably accounts for its appearance as *Djuwa* 'a magic word' in Lissarrague (2007:135), in a narrative context of sudden transformation of a carpet snake into a shark.

what they are entering is left unspecified. This ellipsis is also seen in Aboriginal English, where *going through* in such a context would so clearly signal 'going through the Rules' that there is no need to state this overtly.

The first suffix is *-(i)rri*, often heard in the sound files in a context of ongoing action; that is, progressive or continuous aspect. This does not correspond exactly to Lissarrague's (2007:45–46) account of aspect, but the continuous suffix that she identifies as *-tiyn* could possibly be our *-(i)rri* with non-future suffix *-n* (Lissarrague 2007:43–46). We think that *-(i)rri* loses its initial vowel by assimilation to the preceding vowel of the verb *yaa*, and its rhotic is devoiced on the recording.

Perhaps the most tentative of our suggestions here is the association of *-pi-rri* with third person reference plus plurality. Lissarrague (2007:29–30) notes examples of first person kin-possession markers as possible remnants of a larger system of bound pronouns. We are very tentatively suggesting that *-pi* might be a third person bound pronominal form (agreeing with the ellipsed third-person subject of *caught*). This is something we are investigating further in previously unanalysed data. One possible piece of evidence for this comes from the placename *Yarrahapinni*, which commemorates a koala ancestor rolling down the mountainside, analysed by Lissarrague (2007:168–169), following Gerhard Laves, as *yarri* 'koala' *yapani* 'rolls down' (Lissarrague 2007:168–169). However, in a recording by Mr Doug Scott, his pronunciation is more like *piyaarri yaarripirrni*, which we think may correspond to *pi-yaa-rri yaa-rri-pi-rri* '3sg-go-PROG go-PROG-3sg-PROG'. That is, the understood subject (the koala, known locally as *guula* rather than *yarri*) was going [i.e. rolling]: the gloss in Aboriginal English would be 'he went over and over, he did'. Obviously, we need more evidence before advancing this as more than a tentative hypothesis.

Also tentatively, but with firmer support, we identify a pluralising suffix *-(u)rri*, not to be confused with the progressive suffix *-(i)rri* because it follows a pronoun, not a verb, although it also loses its initial vowel by assimilation. This *-(u)rri* is attested several times in the sound files, possibly related to the plural suffix *-kurr* identified by Lissarrague (2007:19)[17]. The form *-ngu* at the end of *yarripirringu* is likewise not listed by Lissarrague, but this form also occurs frequently in songs, in contexts of someone or something entering and travelling through (or along) something else. A perlative case (Dixon 2002:532) has not been described for Thangatti; further investigation of *-ngu* in the sound files may yield more evidence for or against this possibility. Our tentative gloss of *-ngu* as 'THRU' reflects an Aboriginal English gloss of this line (i.e. *going through* or *being put through*).

(5) *The top lady to the bottom say:*
 'The senior woman says to those under [her authority]:'

In local Aboriginal English, *top lady* (or *boss lady*) refers to a senior woman, holding cultural authority in a family and/or ceremonial context. This corresponds to the cultural role of *buulaa*, or *baluwa* in Lissarrague (2007:120), where this role is described in terms of age: 'a very old woman, a great-grandmother'. Oral tradition tells of senior women's authority in the days when traditional ceremonies were still maintained. Such women were recognised with the title of *buulaa* (or *granny)*, as with 'Bolar' Callaghan, also known as 'Bolla' Pearce, who is still well remembered.[18] The standard Aboriginal English uninflected third-person singular verb form, *say* without inflection *-s*, is also seen here.

---

17 *-kurr* is a nominal suffix, while *-rri* on a verb stem is found where a group of actors are performing the verb action together (i.e. plural subject marking, glossed in Aboriginal English as *all together*); this also requires further investigation.
18 Two Thangatti elders, speaking with Barry Morris (pers. com.) in 1980–81, described the crucial role of women at

(6) An' sting you   bun,   yaa-rri-urri-kayi!
                    bum   enter-PROG-PL-SUB

'that you'll be chastised [i.e. you'd better behave], when you mob go in there.'

Several Aboriginal English features can be observed here. The conjunction *an(d)* shows cluster reduction as above, but here it functions as a complementiser rather than a coordinating conjunction, signalling an indirect quotation of the *top lady*'s instructions. Subject ellipsis produces a passive-like effect: the *top lady* tells those under her authority 'that you are to get a sting on the bum' to regulate behavior. A shift in place of articulation of the final nasal of *bum* (backside) to *bun* is a politeness feature to avoid attributing a potentially offensive word to a senior woman (a strategy that can be seen as related to traditional etiquette or avoidance register). Inalienable possession of that body part is signalled by unmarked *you* rather than possessive *your*. This is also observed in first-person usage, as in *me eyes* versus *my glasses*, in some Aboriginal English of this region.

In the Thangatti word *yaarriurrikayi*, we see the same array of non-future and simultaneous suffixes *-rr-i* on *yaa* 'go', followed in this case by the plural subject marker *-(u)rri* and subordinator *-kayi*. This subordinating suffix, described by Lissarrague (2007:67–70), functions similarly here to the English subordinator *when*, as in the gloss '*when* you mob go [there]' (i.e. to the men's camp). An alternative possibility is that the addressees here could be women and girls being warned by the elder woman not to go there (i.e. you'll be chastised *if* you go there).[19] Phonologically, the five syllables here are reduced to sound more like three. The trills are devoiced, and epenthetic alveolar nasals appear syllable-finally: [jaː.ɾi.u.ɾi.kai → jaɾⁿ. aɾⁿ.kai]. The morphological complexity in lines (4) and (6) is greater than in the recordings on which Lissarrague's analysis was based, and our analysis here is more speculative than hers. Our intention is to encourage and promote a broader community interest in this line of enquiry, as well as making case for deeper investigation of this rich material and what it means to its inheritors.

4   Reflections on form and meaning

While we have been discussing these six lines as a 'song', in keeping with Turpin and Stebbins' (2010:3) definition as a sequence of syllables that is sung, from an Aboriginal perspective this stretch of text is *not* in itself a song, and most definitely not *bayirati* 'singing' (clearly also related to *baayati* 'dance', Lissarrague 2007:123, 119).[20] Turpin has pointed out that Aboriginal song is a multimedia package (Turpin 2005:90, quoted in Walsh 2007:137), seamlessly interweaving text, rhythm and melody, solo and choral performance, with dance, story, percussion, instrumental and sound effects, visual design (body painting, costume, sand patterns), staging and lighting, props, associated ceremonial and/or recreational practices – all grounded in Country, kinship, language, and Dreaming. Most of these multimedia elements were absent on the occasion of Mr Vale's 1964 recording session, but the pleasure expressed in his and Mr Scott's laughter no

---

various points in the *Murrawon~Marrwan* ceremonies: 'They['d] dance every night. If they didn't dance every night, according to the Law, brothers'd get sick out in the bush. They had to dance' (John Quinlan). 'Granny Callaghan nickname *Bulaw*: had to do it her way' (Ellen Quinlan Davis).

19   We think that, culturally speaking, it is a little more likely that the addressees are the boys, because of the traditional practice of women ritually and often playfully chasing or 'hunting away' the boys from the women's camp, sending them off to the men with their mothers' and aunties' encouragement.

20   Vocabulary, semantic structure, and categorisation of song, dance, and related aspects of performance are well worth exploring in this and related languages, as recommended by Walsh (2007:132–133); but that further project is beyond our scope here.

doubt derived from the old men's rich memories of the full performances that were so central to traditional intellectual and cultural life.

Alongside the important caveat that songtext does not equal *bayirati* or capital-S Song in an Aboriginal sense, we reiterate that our tentative attempts toward enculturated (Kelly) and intercultural (Kelly–Harkins) understandings of meaning do not equal assertions about Meaning in any essentialist sense. They are simply the hypotheses that we two individuals can make at this present moment, bringing our current resources of knowledge, experience, analysis and (perilously) intuition to the task of assigning meaning to cultural material. Trying to do this in a scholarly way, we welcome the challenge and rigour of presenting the evidence that underpins our current hypotheses, in hope of encouraging others to engage in their own hypothesising, while avoiding as best we can the pitfalls of selective interpretation and over-enthusiastic reconstruction so rightly warned against by others (Moyle 1986, Walsh 2007).

On our voyage around this song, it has been most encouraging to meet others writing about the same kinds of questions and intellectual challenges posed by the information density and structural underspecification of song language. We can offer a few reflections on the above, prompted by the marvellously pertinent questions posed by Michael Walsh (2007:130–135). Although we are far from satisfying his linguist's wish list (pp.136–139), or even formulating our own intercultural educators' wish list, we have at least tentatively proposed some morpheme-by-morpheme glossing, and have tried to provide explanations with as much explicitness and candour as we can.

In this particular song, the relation of the song language to spoken language (Thangatti, Aboriginal English, and NSW Pidgin) is very close, as befits the song's educational purpose and addressees. The fact that it is addressed to young boys also, obviously, places it in the domain of public rather than culturally restricted song, notwithstanding its implied references to impending ceremonial business. There is an interweaving of language structure and song rhythm, metre, and melody, but no strong influences of one upon the other, apart from phonological lengthening of metrically stressed vowels (especially in line 3), and contraction of unstressed syllables (especially in line 4, where the five syllables of *yaarripirringu* are contracted to sound more like three syllables [ˈjaɽ.ᵐpiɽ.ŋu]. Phonological processes of fortition, lenition, epenthesis, and unstressed syllable reduction heard in this and other Thangatti songs are the same as those found in the rapid connected speech of fluent speakers in the audio recordings.

We have noted above the morphological complexity and information density of the Thangatti structures in lines (1), (4) and (6). We have sketched the barest outline of this complexity, hoping to promote more discussion rather than suggest that our current speculations could be final. More investigation of the unanalysed portions of archived spoken language in the audio files will be needed before we can say whether or not this complexity is greater than in the connected speech of the fluent speakers. Syntactically, the Thangatti parts of the song, while highly elliptical, are no more so than the spoken language. They seem to show little syntactic simplification (cf. Koch and Turpin 2008), in light of the clausal subordination in (6) above, and the indirect quotation structure in (5)–(6). High semantic density and extensive polysemy are characteristic of spoken Thangatti, in ways very similar to what is seen in this song. It might be assumed that the polysemy of words like *maa* 'get, fetch, take, catch, grab' and *yalaa* 'enter, go into, put under, bury, swim, dive' (as glossed in Lissarrague 2007:148, 168) is attributable to the hyperpolysemy seen in language attrition (Schmid 2011). However, corresponding semantic elaboration exists alongside it, for example in different verbs for different ways of 'going': e.g. go along, go inside, go into, go on, go upwards (Lissarrague 2007:177). Extensive polysemy among affixes in Australian languages is also well documented (Bowern, Evans and Miceli 2008).

Considering the non-traditional language elements from Aboriginal English and NSW Pidgin, in our view these in no way diminish this song's authenticity. Rather, they demonstrate the strength of cultural continuity (Walsh 2007:134) in the practice of drawing on any and all available linguistic resources in the service of Aboriginal communicative purposes, as well as in the educationally deft use of multilingual strategies to engage young multilingual addressees. In regard to the functions and purposes of the song, we look forward to increasing discussion and awareness of the educational uses of traditional and contemporary song, not only in language teaching but across the curriculum as advocated by Papen (2016, chapter 8), as well as in community building, as demonstrated by the sadly now disbanded Gumbaynggirr Elders Choir (2014).

In exploring the interplay of form and meaning in this song, we have found ourselves dealing with each of the levels of meaning identified by Turpin and Stebbins (2010:8–14). Meanings of individual words and grammatical morphemes required interpretation in their context within the song, including cultural knowledge and potential for multiple meanings. Interactional meanings were central to understanding the relationship of performer to addressees and audience. Connotative meanings were involved in discerning the contextual meanings of *maa, caught, bingay,* and *yaa*. Emotional meanings were particularly rich in this example of a song concerned with highly valued cultural events, evoking solidarity, humour, remembrance, and intellectual pleasure. Linguistic imagery (Curran 2010) was highly salient, in the metaphorical associations of *caught, top lady, bottom,* and *sting you bum*; and the image-schemata of the *bingay yirruu,* passage 'through' the Rules, and ceremonial authority from *top lady* to *the bottom*.

5 Conclusions

All of the form-meaning relations touched upon here contribute to an almost limitless meaning-potential of this little song, for those with eyes to see and ears to hear. The layered nature of Aboriginal cultural meaning is such that anyone willing to have 'skin in the game' can extract satisfying meaning from song and performance, each at their own level of education and understanding. From the young and foolish to the old and wise, from senior knowledge holders and elders to stolen children, visitors from afar and even complete cultural outsiders: every person brings some resources with which to construct meaning in relation to the cultural richness on offer. This applies to contemporary Indigenous performance as much as ancestral cultural practice, though in different ways. The underlying pedagogical principle, requiring the learner to assign meaning on the basis of limited evidence, was insightfully described by Ken Hale, who recognised the thrill of discovery and 'intellectual joy' (Hale 1984:259) to be gained from this style of autonomous learning (Nunan and Richards 2015).

In a time of preoccupation with the troubles faced by our young people, we may lose sight of the fact that all children deserve to live in a society that thinks about and plans for their personal and interpersonal development free from bigotry, violence and shame. If we fail to think critically and act decisively in this crucial development period for the young *dhalayi gurri* in our family and our broader communities, we will continue to see the planning and building of new prisons and correctional, instead of educational, institutions for our disenfranchised Indigenous youth.

Meaningful access to cultural heritage is essential to young Australians' right to an education that is culturally affirming, an education that values and respects the place of Aboriginal people in building our nation and our identity for the future. We think that cultural heritage materials like this song and others like it can be reclaimed and revalued by their inheritors in ways that will be valuable to them, despite challenging issues in interpretation. In exploring this little song to a tiny *gurri,* we hope to have given some indications, both experiential and analytical, of how the deceptively simple, time-honoured but evolving textual, metrical and linguistic structures of this song demonstrate some of the broader power of song as a genre, to support linguistic and cultural resilience across the intersections of Aboriginal multicultural experience.

References

Alpher, Barry and Kevin Keeffe, 2001, Playing songs can be dangerous. In Jane Simpson et al., eds. Forty years on: Ken Hale and Australian languages, 465–476. Canberra: Pacific Linguistics.

Auer, Peter, 2013, Bilingual conversation: language, interaction and identity. Hoboken: Taylor and Francis.

Barney, Katelyn, ed., 2014, Collaborative ethnomusicology: new approaches to music research between Indigenous and non-Indigenous Australians. Melbourne: Lyrebird Press.

Bowern, Claire, Bethwyn Evans and Luisa Miceli, eds, 2008, Morphology and language history: in honour of Harold Koch. Amsterdam: John Benjamins (Current Issues in Linguistic Theory, 298).

Curran, Georgia, 2010, Linguistic imagery in Warlpiri songs: Some examples of metaphors, metonymy and image-schemata in Minamina Yawulyu. Australian Journal of Linguistics 30(1):105–115.

Dixon, Robert M. W., 2002, Australian languages: their nature and development. Cambridge: Cambridge University Press.

Donaldson, Tamsin, 1979, Translating oral literature: Aboriginal song texts. Aboriginal History 3:62–83.

—— 1984, Kids that got lost: variation in the words of Ngiyampaa songs. In Jamie C. Kassler and Jill Stubington, eds. Problems and solutions: Occasional essays in musicology presented to Alice M. Moyle, 228–253. Sydney: Hale & Iremonger.

—— 1995, Mixes of English and ancestral language words in southeast Australian Aboriginal songs of traditional and introduced origin. In Linda Barwick, Allan Marett and Guy Tunstill, eds. The essence of singing and the substance of song: recent responses to the Aboriginal performing arts and other essays in honour of Catherine Ellis, 143–156. Sydney: University of Sydney.

García, Ofelia and Li Wei, 2014, Translanguaging: language, bilingualism and education. Basingstoke: Palgrave Macmillan.

Garde, Murray, 2006, The language of kun-borrk in western Arnhem Land. Musicology Australia 28:59–89.

—— 2013, Culture, interaction and person reference in an Australian language. Amsterdam: John Benjamins.

Gumbaynggirr Elders Choir, 2014, Yarri yarrung! CD produced by Gumbaynggirr Elders Choir, Nambucca Heads, NSW (limited community distribution).

Gummow, Margaret, 1995, Songs and sites/ moving mountains: A study of one song from northern NSW. In Linda Barwick, Allan Marett and Guy Tunstill, eds. The essence of singing and the substance of song: recent responses to the Aboriginal performing arts and other essays in honour of Catherine Ellis, 121–131. Sydney: University of Sydney.

Hale, Kenneth L. 1984, Remarks on creativity in Aboriginal verse. In Jamie C. Kassler and Jill Stubington, eds. Problems and solutions: occasional essays in musicology presented to Alice M. Moyle, 254–262. Sydney: Hale & Iremonger.

Harkins, Jean, 2008, NSW contact languages. In Jim Wafer and Amanda Lissarrague, eds. A handbook of Aboriginal languages of New South Wales and the Australian Capital Territory, 402–412; 810–815. Nambucca Heads, NSW: Muurrbay.

Holmer, Nils M., 1964, Language elicitation, stories and songs from northern NSW and Queensland. 4 audiotape reels. AIATSIS Sound Archive (accession no. 001755–001756, call no. Holmer_N01; open access).

—— 1966, An attempt towards a comparative grammar of two Australian languages. Canberra: Australian Institute of Aboriginal Studies.

—— 1967, An attempt towards a comparative grammar of two Australian languages, Part 2. Indices and vocabularies of Kattang and Thangatti. Canberra: Australian Institute of Aboriginal Studies.

Holmer, Nils M., and Vanja E. Holmer, 1969, Stories from two native tribes of eastern Australia. Uppsala: Lundequistska Bokhandeln.

Jebb, Maryanne, and Doug Marmion, 2015, Singing the train: a Nyamal song is heard again. In Nicholas Ostler and Brenda Lintinger, eds. The music of endangered languages (Proceedings of the 19th Foundation for Endangered Languages Conference), unpag. Bath, UK: Foundation for Endangered Languages. Online at *https://www.academia.edu/30210846/Singing_the_Train_a_Nyamal_song_is_heard_again* [accessed 27 May 2017].

Kelly, Raymond F., 2015, Dreaming the Keepara: New South Wales Aboriginal perspectives, 1808–2007. PhD thesis, University of Newcastle, Australia.

Klapproth, Danièle, 2004, Narrative as social practice: Anglo-western and Australian Aboriginal oral traditions. Berlin: Walter de Gruyter.

Koch, Grace and Myfany Turpin, 2008, The language of Central Australian Aboriginal songs. In Claire Bowern, Bethwyn Evans and Miceli Luisa, eds. Morphology and language history: in honour of Harold Koch, 167–183. Amsterdam: John Benjamins.

Lissarrague, Amanda, 2007, Dhanggati grammar and dictionary with Dhanggati stories. Nambucca Heads, NSW: Muurrbay.

—— 2013, Interlinearised text of Holmer [1967]. Unpublished manuscript. AIATSIS Library (call no. pMS 6603, open access).

MacSwan, Jeff, 2013, Code switching and grammatical theory. In Tej K. Bhatia and William Ritchie, eds. Handbook of bilingualism and multilingualism, 223–250. Oxford: Blackwell.

McDonald, Barry, 1996, Evidence of four New England corroboree songs indicating Aboriginal responses to European invasion. Aboriginal History 20:176–194.

Moyle, Richard, 1986, Alyawarra music: songs and society in a Central Australian community. Canberra: Australian Institute of Aboriginal Studies.

Nunan, David and Jack C. Richards, eds, 2015, Language learning beyond the classroom. London: Routledge.

Papen, Uta, 2016, Literacy and education: policy, practice and public opinion. New York: Routledge.

Schmid, Monika S., 2011, Language attrition. Cambridge: Cambridge University Press. (Key Topics in Sociolinguistics.)

Threlkeld, Lancelot Edward [attrib.], n.d. [1820s?], Songs of the natives of New South Wales to the north of Sydney (manuscript). In Threlkeld, Rev. Lancelot Edward – Papers, 1815–1862 (Z A382), p. 129. State Library of NSW, Sydney. (Microfilm held as CY 820 [frames 777–909].)

Troy, Jakelin, 1993, Language contact in early colonial New South Wales 1788–1791. In Michael Walsh and Colin Yallop, eds, Language and culture in Aboriginal Australia, 33–50. Canberra: Aboriginal Studies Press.

Turpin, Myfany, 2007a, Artfully hidden: phonological and rhythmic correspondences in a Central Australian Aboriginal song series. Musicology Australia 29:93–107.

—— 2007b, The poetics of Central Australian Aboriginal song. Australian Aboriginal Studies 2007 (2):100–115.

Turpin, Myfany, and Tonya Stebbins, 2010, The language of song: some recent approaches in description and analysis. Australian Journal of Linguistics 30(1):1–17.

Walsh, Michael, 2007, Australian Aboriginal song language: so many questions, so little to work with. Australian Aboriginal Studies 2007 (2):128–144.

—— 2010, A polytropical approach to the 'Floating Pelican' song: an exercise in rich interpretation of a Murriny Patha (Northern Australia) song. Australian Journal of Linguistics 30(1):117–130.

9 Ghost-writing for Wulatji: incubation and re-dreaming as song revitalisation practices

Jim Wafer
University of Newcastle

> There is a god of Poesy, Wallatu, who composes music, and who, without temple, shrine, or statue, is as universally acknowledged as if his oracles were breathed by Belus or Osiris: he comes in dreams, and transports the individual to some sunny hill, where he is inspired with the supernatural gift.
>
> Eliza Hamilton Dunlop, 'Native Poetry' (1848a)

Abstract

This chapter elaborates a rationale for revitalising Aboriginal singing practices by means of the traditional but endangered technique of composition through dreams. It is based on exegesis of a song in the language of the Hunter River and Lake Macquarie that was published in 1848 by Eliza Hamilton Dunlop. Her transcription of the song text was accompanied by a commentary that associated the name of the composer with a 'god of Poesy' called 'Wallatu'. I argue, on the basis of a comparative overview of 'dream composition' in Aboriginal Australia, that this mythical being was plausibly responsible for 'song incubation' in this region, and conceivably both ancestor and inspirer of the poet who was Mrs Dunlop's informant.

My reconstruction of the text and metrical pattern of the song provides the foundation for an analysis of its stylistic devices, and this in turn may have implications for understanding both mnemotechnical practices ('arts of memory') and kin classification in the region in question. For the sake of contextualising the notion of 'song incubation', the chapter includes also a brief survey and listing of relevant ethnographic and historical observations from Australia and other parts of the world.

Keywords: musical dream, dream composition, song incubation, re-dreaming, arts of memory, Wallatu, Eliza Hamilton Dunlop, Wollombi, Hunter Valley, Lake Macquarie

1 Introduction

A. W. Howitt's late-nineteenth century account of Aboriginal song-making in south-eastern Australia includes an observation about what we might call 'dream composition' that has since been replicated, with minor modifications, in many, perhaps even most, of the other regions of the continent. According to Howitt (1887a:329; cf. 1904:416), 'the songs are obtained by the bards from the spirits of the deceased, usually their relatives, during sleep in dreams'.[1]

We could compare this with Jill Stubington's (2007:102) succinct summary of the relevant Australianist research from the intervening 120 years: 'the most commonly reported experience of new songs entering a repertoire is that of a musician being taught a song in a dream by a spirit familiar'. Stubington (2007:102) also observes that 'there seems to be a continuum between songs which were taught by ancestral heroes, songs taught by spirit familiars, songs taught by recently deceased ancestors, and songs which are recognised as being the invention of a living person'.

In the same period, there have been accounts of dream composition from many other parts of the world, but no attempts to survey them for the purpose of developing a comparative theoretical framework. The little theorising there has been comes mainly from sleep scientists, who treat the matter under such rubrics as 'the musical dream' (e.g. Massey 2006; see also Streich 1980, Willin 1999:92, Barrett 2001:66–81, Sacks 2008:307–311, Grace 2012[2]).

It would take us well beyond the limited scope of the present paper to review this body of literature. Nonetheless, I hope to be able to provide here some relevant preliminary observations, as background to my analysis of a song published in 1848 in the language of the Hunter River and Lake Macquarie[3] (New South Wales). Recent language work in this region has made the reconstruction of the words to this song fairly straightforward, and its history, too, is relatively transparent. But what remains mysterious is the identity of the 'god of Poesy', whose name, 'Wallatu', published in conjunction with the song (as reproduced above in the epigraph), suggests that he was its inspirer. My efforts to understand him are intended to support the notion of 'dream composition' as a song revitalisation practice, not just in regions where it is an ongoing tradition, but also in those parts of Australia, such as the Hunter Valley, where Indigenous musical life has suffered a period of interruption.

2 The musical dream

The frequency of occurrence of the musical dream varies widely between cultures. At the low end of the scale, dream sounds of any kind were reported by only 1.5 per cent of the American tertiary students surveyed in one study (Barrett 2001:67). But in many Indigenous cultures of North America, dream composition is considered to be not just the norm, but also a responsibility – at least for certain sections of the population (Massey 2006:42). There have been ethnographic reports of this phenomenon among American Indians since the late nineteenth

---

1 This is not the earliest reference to the oneiric origin of song in Indigenous Australia, but it has the advantage of explicitness. Appendix A of the present chapter provides a fairly comprehensive listing of relevant references in the Australianist literature, with a brief introduction. The Australian list (Table 9.2) is followed by a representative sample of references from other parts of the world, organised by region (Table 9.3).
2 The broader neglect of this topic in the psychological literature is epitomised by the lack of any reference to it in *The Oxford handbook of music psychology* (Hallam, Cross and Thaut 2009). It is also largely absent from the general psychological discourse on dream theory, and there is no mention of it in the pioneering contribution by Hunt (1989). The anthropological literature tends to comment on it only in passing, as an ethnographic curiosity, and it has eluded specific attention in the recent cross-cultural surveys of dream research, such as Tedlock (1991), Goulet (1994), Lohmann, ed. (2003), Stewart, ed. (2004) and Laughlin (2011).
3 Hereafter abbreviated to 'HRLM'.

century, and the following passage by the pioneering ethnomusicologist Frances Densmore (1926:77–78) is representative:

> The first song received by an individual in a dream was the boy's 'vision song.' Later in life he might also receive songs in dreams. Every Indian boy, at the age of about twelve years, was expected to fast for several days and watch for the dream or 'vision' in which he saw his individual 'spirit helper,' and usually received a song from that source. In later years, when he wished to receive 'spirit help,' he sang the song and also performed certain prescribed acts. Sometimes the boy fasted at home, with his face blackened with charcoal; more often he went away and remained alone, night and day, waiting for his vision, while in some tribes the vigil was ceremonial in character.[4]

This summary reflects the practices of a large number of North American Indian cultures, but not all. One of the differences between Pueblo and Pima musical traditions, for example (according to Herzog 1936:318–320), is that the Pueblo recognise some songs as the product of human creativity, while the Pima attribute all songs to supernatural intervention in dreams.

Australian Aboriginal cultures are similarly divided, between those (the majority) in which dream composition is the standard practice, and those, such as the Tiwi, among whom 'the designs, songs, and dances are attributed to the creative individual artist or performer' (Goodale 2003:153).[5] It is hard to know whether the Tiwi are unique in this regard, because information about song traditions is scanty or non-existent for many other Aboriginal groups. But the available data suggest a widespread ideology of passivity in the composition process. As Ian Keen (writing of the Yolngu) puts the matter (2003:138): 'creativity in ritual is the result of dreaming and reverie *happening* to a person [emphasis added]'; that is, without the person's volition or agency. 'Yolngu downplay individual creative powers, at least in the domain of religion, displacing agency onto creative ancestors' (Keen 2003:133).[6]

This presents an obvious paradox for any treatment of composition as a factor in the revitalisation of Aboriginal singing practices, since it implies, broadly speaking, that new songs in the ancestral tradition can only be 'found' in dreams, rather than made or composed. Whether musical dreams can be actively sought, in the manner of the North American vision quest or the ancient practice of 'dream incubation'[7], is a question rarely addressed in the Australianist

---

4 This passage is taken from a book that Densmore wrote for a general audience. There is greater ethnographic nuance in her specialised studies of particular groups, such as the Chippewa (1910:126–165), Teton Sioux (Densmore 1918:157–204) and Menominee (Densmore 1932:77–98). See also Densmore 1953 and the Densmore bibliography by Hofmann (1968). On the widespread distribution of the vision quest or 'guardian spirit quest' in North America, see Benedict (1922), Hultkrantz (1979:74) and Keeling (1992:18, n. 6).

5 Nonetheless, two qualifications are necessary. First, there is documentation of Tiwi receiving musical inspiration from the Nyingawi (the mangrove-dwelling hairy beings who were the first teachers of the Kulama rituals). Campbell (2013:242), for example, mentions the case of the late Enrail Munkara, who, according to family tradition, 'first sang Nyingawi to revere his deceased father Munkara, having heard the Nyingawi themselves singing and so incorporating some Nyingawi language'. (The Nyingawi are worth comparing with the mangrove-dwelling, song-giving dwarves called *warranguridjakud* in western Arnhem Land, as mentioned by Brown and Evans in their Chapter 12 in the present volume.) Second, Tiwi initiation practices parallel the Amerindian 'vision song' scenario by requiring the composition of new songs. 'To become a fully initiated Tiwi and able to participate in adult ritual life one must learn to compose many new and original songs to be sung, without any faltering or mistakes in the poetic form of the language, throughout the three day Kulama' (Goodale 2003:161). The crucial difference from those parts of Indigenous Australia (and Indigenous America) where human agency is downplayed in the composition process is that 'Tiwi value individual achievement and originality' (Goodale 2003:163).

6 Metcalfe and Game (2010:170) have theorised this kind of ambiguity around the question of agency as an intrinsic part of the creative process: 'creative experiences are those in which there is a giving and receiving that is neither sequential nor locatable, experiences where a gift occurs, but not through the desires of any subject, however decentred, and not in a way that allows giving to be distinguished from receiving.'

7 This term refers to the rituals of dream induction practised in ancient Greece, Rome, Egypt and Mesopotamia. In the Greek world, they took the form of healing rites carried out in the *asklepieia*, or temples of Asclepius, the god of medicine, and had as their objective the prompting of a dream in which the god himself would appear, in person or by means of a

literature, and then only in passing. Still, there are enough examples to suggest that what we might call 'song incubation' does occur in at least some parts of Aboriginal Australia, and probably also in other regions where it has simply not been observed or recorded.

One good example comes from the Kimberley, in the north-west, and dates back to Andreas Lommel's field work with the Frobenius expedition in 1938-39. In an ethnography of the Wunambal published some time later (Lommel 1952:55-56[8]), Lommel wrote as follows:

> But it also happens that a medicine man who possesses the gift of *miriru* loses it again. He is suddenly incapable of making contact with the spirits and his poetic gift for creating songs and dances dies.
>
> In such a case all the men then get together in order to resume the broken connections with the dead ancestors.
>
> They lay the medicine man on the ground, all the men sit down in a circle around him. The men begin to sing, and as they do so slowly massage the medicine man's body. The men sing for hours in an even rising and falling tone:
>
> > Mmmmmm nnnnnn mmmmmm nnnnnn
>
> (it is a humming such as is found in many Russian folksongs). The medicine man slowly goes into a trance, his soul finally leaves the body and now, so it is said in the accounts, wanders aimlessly around in order to find the spirit of a dead ancestor. After long wanderings it will finally meet such a one.
>
> You see, the dead ancestors themselves send out one from their midst to look for the medicine man. They have themselves already sorely felt the absence of the medicine man and the broken contact with their living descendant and they wish to resume relations with the living.
>
> The medicine man reports to the spirit of the dead that he no longer knows the way to the underworld and is not 'finding' songs any more. The spirit of the dead – often it will be the spirit of his father or grandfather – promises to help him and to fetch him in a few days.
>
> After a time – it is perhaps in the evening and the people are sitting there quietly and conversing – the medicine man suddenly hears a distant call. It is his spirit familiar who is asking for him. He goes aside and converses with it for a while.
>
> But a few days later his soul then leaves the body. His body lies there quietly and he sleeps. Led by the spirit familiar, many spirits now come from the underworld and take possession of the medicine man's soul that they want to see among them again. They dismember the soul, and each spirit carries one of the pieces into the underworld. There, deep beneath the ground, they put the medicine man's soul together again.
>
> They again show him dances and sing songs to him. Thenceforth, such a medicine man again has the gift of *miriru*.

---

message. Meier's account of this practice includes the observation (2009:74) that 'Asclepius commanded many persons to write odes or mimes and to compose certain songs'. See also Jayne (1925), Laufer (1931:210–211), Lincoln (1935:4–5, 22), Reed (1977); Watkins (1977:14–30); Morinis (1982); Miller (1994:109–117); Bulkeley (1995:120–130); Kingsley (1999); Patton (2004); Harrisson (2009); Nielsen (2012). Mrs Langloh Parker (1905:132) used the term 'incubation' for the 'hatching' of songs by Aboriginal songpersons, which quite possibly indicates that she was familiar with the term's ancient usage. J. S. Lincoln (1935:22), in his early comparative study, includes Australia among the regions of the world where the 'division into unsought and sought dreams' occurs. (The other regions he mentions are Melanesia, Polynesia, Africa and North America.) He notes that the dream-seeking practised in these regions is 'similar to the ancient temple incubation'. His evidence for Australia comes from Roth (1903:29): 'The Boulian of North Queensland, after starving for three days, is rewarded by the fancied apparition of a *malkari* or nature-spirit, which proceeds to stick pebbles or bones or quartz crystals into his body, and thus makes him a medicine man'.

8   Lommel published a number of versions of this account, which appeared originally in German, in Lommel (1952:55–56). The English version reproduced here is from the Campbell translation (Lommel 1997:64–65) of this work. Other versions (in English) include Lommel (1967:138–140); Lommel (1989:33–34); Lommel and Mowaljarlai (1994:283). Lommel defines *miriru* as 'the ability to separate the soul from the body ... The people have received *miriru* from the spirits of the dead' (Lommel 1952:53, 1997:63).

In this case, the communal nature of the activity, as well as the fact that it is precipitated by an affliction, gives it a strong similarity to the dream incubation practices of antiquity. But the alternative scenario, in which an individual who has no therapeutic motive undertakes a 'spiritual exercise'[9] for the purpose of acquiring a song, is also represented in the literature. A fine example comes from New South Wales. In 1904 and 1909, R. H. Mathews published two accounts of the song-inspiring function of a being called 'the Wahwee'. I reproduce here the 1909 version, since it is preceded by some contextual information lacking in the earlier account:

> The story of the Wahwee is current among the Wiradjuri, Kamilaroi, Wailwan, and other tribes of New South Wales. It was related to me by an old Kamilaroi black-fellow, named 'Jimmy Nerang', whom I met at the Bora ceremony held at Tallwood in 1895. The Rev. Wm. Ridley mentions the Wawi (my Wahwee) as a monster living in deep waterholes. I gave a drawing of the Wahwee represented on the ground at the Burbung ceremonies of the Wiradjuri tribe in 1893 (1909:485).[10]
>
> *The Wahwee.*—The Wahwee, a serpent-like monster, lives in deep waterholes, and burrows into the bank beneath the level of the water, where he makes his den. He has a wife and a son, but they camp in a different place. A 'doctor' or clever blackfellow can sometimes go and see a Wahwee, but on such occasions he must paint himself all over with red ochre. He then follows after the rainbow some day when there is a slight shower of rain, and the end of the rainbow rests over the waterhole in which is the Wahwee's abode. On reaching this waterhole, the man dives in under the bank, where he finds the Wahwee, who conducts him into the den, and sings him a song which he never heard before. He repeats this song many times in the presence of the Wahwee, until he has learnt it by heart, and then starts back to his own people. When they see him coming, painted and singing a new song, they know he has been with the Wahwee, and a few of the other head-men and clever fellows take him into the adjacent bush, where they strip pieces of bark off trees, on which they paint different devices in coloured clays. All the people of the tribe are then mustered, and these ornamented pieces of bark are taken to the corroboree ground, where everyone sings and dances. This is how new songs and corroborees are obtained (1909:487).

The clever man's visit to the Wahwee[11] is liable to be read as pure fantasy, even a tall tale, unless one is able to approach it as an account of purposeful activity. If we treat it as the record of a deliberately undertaken private ritual, akin to the practice that C. G. Jung (1968:190–193; 1997) called 'active imagination'[12], then it suggests quite strongly that Aboriginal people have

---

9   To apply cross-culturally a term that Pierre Hadot has recycled to refer to aspects of the Western philosophical tradition. He sets out his rationale for this usage in Hadot (1995:81–82). There is, as yet, no standard terminology for the comparative study of what others (e.g. Samuels 2010) have called 'inner work'. There are helpful insights in the cross-cultural studies of meditation (e.g. Eifring 2015), but the term 'meditation' is not broad enough to encompass the full range of solo practices that entail directed strategies for modifying subjectivity. In the ethnographic literature there is no lack of studies on institutionalised group activities (such as rituals) intended to alter consciousness (as surveyed, for example, by Bourguignon 1973:3–33), but little attention has been paid to what Foucault (1988) has called 'technologies of the self' in small scale societies. There is some overlap with the literature on 'creative practice', as theorised, for example, by Metcalfe and Game (2010).

10   The references here are to Ridley (1875:138) and Mathews (1896:301, 315 and plate XXVI, between 295 and 296). See also my account of the 'Waway' in Wafer (2017). Donaldson (1997:6–7) provides two short texts about the 'Waaway' in Ngiyampaa, and from these we learn that 'Waaway made the Lachlan and the Barwon (Darling) [Rivers]'. My thanks to David Nash for drawing my attention to this document, and also to Honery (1872:250). Both of these references are additional to the Waway bibliography included in my article 'Why Waway?' (Wafer 2017:294).

11   Although the Wahwee may be one of the main inspirers of song, he has 'attendants and messengers', called *barinma* in Wiradjuri (Günther in Fraser 1892:72; cf. Grant & Rudder 2010: 299), who probably also functioned as instigators of song incubation. For avian and mythological associations of the term *barinma* (in Gamilaraay and related languages), see Giacon (2013:273).

12   For a history and overview of Jung's development of the concept, see Chodorow's introduction (1997:1–20) to her compilation of Jung's writings on the subject. Jung wrote little on either music or sound, but the relevance of his notion of 'active imagination' to these fields is sketched out in Kittelson (1996:82, 85). This work also provides a useful overview of the Jungian literature on sound, but only mentions the musical dream (1996:67–68) in passing.

techniques for inducing dreams or visionary states in which songs are expected to be manifested – in other words, methods of 'song incubation'. These are not necessarily as elaborately formalised as the examples from Lommel and Mathews. Among Warlpiri, for example, there is an understanding that 'the position of one's body, in relation to both the land and one's kin, must be configured in specific ways' in order to facilitate 'dreams of ceremonial relevance'. The requirements are that one must sleep 'on one's side and in close proximity to the kin with whom one has a *kirda-kurdungurlu*[13] relationship' (Dussart 2000:140–141).

The elementariness of this incubatory practice is probably related to the democratic nature of song acquisition among the Warlpiri, who 'claim that dreams containing ceremonial content can be dreamt by anyone, including the uninitiated' (Dussart 2000:143).[14] Another contemporary incubation procedure comes from western Arnhem Land. There, according to the account by Reuben Brown and Nicholas Evans in the present volume (Chapter 12), a musical dream may be incubated by placing under one's pillow the clapsticks that once belonged to a deceased mentor. In other parts of Australia, the incubation procedure is sometimes even more basic: a composer intent on receiving a song may simply lie on the ground, to make contact with the power inherent in the soil (cf. Bell 1998:193, McDonald this volume, Chapter 7)[15], and this can happen not just at night, but also in broad sunshine (Gummow 1992:179).

The distribution of the ability and opportunity to incubate songs clearly varies between Aboriginal cultures. If the practice is open to anyone among the Warlpiri of Yuendumu, it is more restricted for the Western Desert people of Jigalong, where women are told not to undertake dream-spirit journeys, and 'it is also safer for ordinary people ... to be taken on dream-spirit trips by native doctors' (Tonkinson 1970:280). The special association that 'doctors' or 'medicine persons' or 'clever blackfellows'[16] have with dream (and song) incubation appears to be very widespread, as we see from the fact that the examples from Lommel and Mathews come from opposite sides of the continent.[17]

These considerations provide some clues that may be helpful in establishing the identity of the 'god of Poesy' who is mentioned in the epigraph that heads this essay.

---

13 *Kirda* are the members of an individual's own patrimoiety, *kurdungurlu* those of the opposite patrimoiety. For a fuller explanation, see Dussart 2000:28–35.
14 Nonetheless, the author notes that 'in my decade-long research at Yuendumu I have never registered cosmologically significant dreams emerging from the sleep of the young' (Dussart 2000:143).
15 A similar principle may apply in the case of the sea. As Howitt (1887a:329–31) points out, 'there are other poets who composed under what may be called natural influences as distinguished from supernatural. Umbara, the bard of the Coast Murring told me that his words came to him "not in sleep as to some men, but when tossing on the waves in his boat with the waters jumping up round him".'
16 These individuals have been referred to by a number of other terms (such as listed by Glaskin 2008:39–40; see also Elkin 1977 [1945], Hume 2002:108–163), including 'sorcerers', 'magicians', 'wizards', 'men of high degree', 'shamans', and so on. There is as yet no consensus about the nomenclature. In light of the argument I am putting forward in this chapter, I might suggest calling them 'oneironauts' – a term invented by sleep scientist Stephen LaBerge (1985:71) to refer to people who have the ability to travel within a dream on a conscious basis. Such a definition fits well with what Glaskin says of the *jarlngungurr* ('shamans', in her translation) of the north-west Kimberley: 'Through dream travel, *jarlngungurr* can access metaphysical dimensions of the real world that others cannot so readily access, and it is this capacity that lies at the core of their power' (2008:60). Nonetheless, for the sake of not compounding the terminological clutter, I have generally preferred to use the older (and more widely understood) terms. A readily comprehensible alternative would be 'dreaming specialists'.
17 Such an association is common in other parts of the world as well. 'Basilov [1995] notes the close relationship between bard and shaman among many Central Asian groups' (Sumegi 2008:29).

3 Wulatji: patron of song incubation?

On 11 October 1848, Eliza Hamilton Dunlop, wife of David Dunlop, the police magistrate and Protector of Aborigines in the frontier settlement of Wollombi, on a tributary of the Hunter River[18], published an item of 'Native Poetry' in the *Sydney Morning Herald* (Dunlop 1848a). She had been a poet herself, in her native Ireland, and continued to publish verse after she and her husband arrived in Australia in 1838.[19] Her transcription of the words of the song was followed by a very freely versified translation (probably better called an 'adaptation'), as well as a glossary of individual terms. Between the transcription and the translation, there was a brief account (as reproduced above in the epigraph) of a 'god of Poesy' called 'Wallatu'.

There are unsolved mysteries in this passage. As John O'Leary (2004:91) has already pointed out, the name that Mrs Dunlop applied to this 'god' was, according to her contemporary Lancelot Threlkeld, in fact the name of Dunlop's human informant, who was both the composer and singer of the song. Threlkeld – the missionary linguist whose work provides the foundation for our understanding of the language in which the song was composed – transcribed the published poem (and some of the associated material) in his own reminiscences (Gunson 1974, 1:58), and added the following observations:

> This very individual, Wúllati, or as the white folks used to call him, Woolaje, always confounding the sound of a t with a j, lived near to our establishment, he was esteemed highly by the tribes, and in an increasing ratio as they were nigh or distant from this individual. No doubt he formed the delightful subject of their evening Soirees, and also of their midnight dreams. He favored me several times with his company, and perhaps thought it an honor when he made proposals to me for a matrimonial alliance with one of the members of my family, much to the amusement of us all. He was a very old, thin, small headed, bald man, of a most cheerful disposition, with a smile always on his countenance, except in the presence of strangers; and whenever he came to our tribe, his company was much enjoyed, an evening feast was provided, and the choicest tit-bits were set before the toothless guest. Oft were his gibes wont to set their table, on the green grass, in a roar of laughter, and their festive board, generally the bark of a tree, was enlivened before it ended in the midnight hour with his song and dance, assisted with his own voice and musical accompaniment of two sticks, beating time to the divine inspiration of the sacred muse.

I deduce from these texts that the poet's name was probably 'Wulatji' (as it would be spelt in the orthography developed for HRLM by Amanda Lissarrague 2006),[20] and that he was named

---

18 Wollombi Brook. I conjecture that the Indigenous name for this watercourse is 'Mala' (see appendix D, 'Notes on some placenames mentioned in the text'). In the year of Dunlop's publication, the Aboriginal population of the district was already much reduced: 'the Wollombi tribes, which in the thirties could be counted in the hundreds... in 1848 numbered 54' (Squire 1896:83). For a history of relations between Aboriginal people and colonists in the Hunter Valley in this time period, see Dunn (2015).
19 Their story, which I can do no more than skim over here, holds considerable interest in itself. Relevant publications include Gunson (1966); De Salis (1967, 1972); Webby (1980:50–52); Dunlop (1981); Vickery (2002:34–35); O'Leary (2004, 2011:39–44). For a more extensive list of pertinent literature, see Austlit (http://www.austlit.edu.au/) under 'Eliza Hamilton Dunlop' (page A31624) and 'Native poetry' (page C696511) [accessed 13 September 2016]. The last of these sources lists two modern editions of 'Native poetry', in Dunlop (1981:7–8) and Kinsella (2009:34–35). The poem has also appeared in *The Band of Hope Journal and Australian Home Companion* (Sydney, Saturday 5 June 1858, 179–181); *Evening News* (Sydney, Tuesday 11 February 1908, 2); Goddard (1934: 245); and Gunson (1974, 1:58).
20 The form of Wulatji's name ('Wallatu') that was published in the *Sydney Morning Herald* is probably a misprint. In Threlkeld's transcription of the relevant passage, he rendered the opening words as 'There is a god of Poesy, Wallati' (Gunson 1974, vol. 1:58). In other words, he interpreted the final vowel of the name as *i*. But it is also clear that he regarded Dunlop's interpretation of the first vowel as a mishearing, since he proceeds to spell the name, in his own orthography, as 'Wúllati'. (The accented *u* was his convention for representing /u/. Without an accent, his *u* generally means /a/. See the 'Key' to his Australian spelling book [1836:4].) Threlkeld and Dunlop appear to be in agreement about the consonants. But the fact that 'the white folks' heard the last consonant in 'Woolaje' as a *j* suggests strongly that the phoneme was in fact the laminal stop (represented in the Lissarrague orthography as /tj/), probably realised as the dental allophone, [t̪]. The

after a spirit regarded as the ancestral prototype of the songman, something like an Aboriginal Orpheus (to draw a classical analogy that is probably more appropriate than Belus or Osiris). We might speculate, for example that the human Wulatji inherited the name, perhaps through a chain of succession, from a deceased teacher or kinsman. This would make the relationship between Wulatji and his namesake a close personal one, involving perhaps the kind of identification of the singer with his predecessor that Marett (2000:23–24) discusses in relation to the *wangga* song traditions of north-western Australia.[21]

On the other hand, Dunlop's reference to this spirit entity as 'a god of Poesy' and her comparison with gods of ancient Egypt and the Near East suggest rather a more universal figure, one whose role is to inspire song in all those capable of receiving the 'supernatural gift'. Such figures are certainly not common in Aboriginal Australia, where most spirit entities are localised and incorporated into the kinship system. Still, the south-east is one of the regions where 'transcendental powers' are known, and these 'stand in equal relation to all things, including men' (Jones 1980:156; see also Parker 1905:7). Jones cites the 'All-Father' of the south-east – probably most widely known by his Wiradjuri name, 'Baayami'[22] – as an example. Moreover, Baayami is reported by a number of sources (e.g. Thomas 1905:51 and Berndt 1947:336) to be a giver of song. So it seems at least plausible that there could be others (one of which might be the Wahwee) who are specifically associated with song incubation.

The notion that Wulatji (as spirit) could be a 'transcendental power' responsible for song incubation is possibly supported by the etymology of his name. My hypothesis is that the name comes not from HRLM, in which Wulatji's poem was composed, but rather from Wiradjuri, where *wula* is glossed by the Wiradjuri dictionary (Grant & Rudder 2010:473) as 'sound, voice, a call', and *-dyi* is a form of the ablative suffix (Grant & Rudder 2010:345, 353). So the whole name could be interpreted to mean something like 'origin of sound'. Apart from the appositeness of the gloss, this interpretation is supported by two other factors: there is no plausible etymology of the name in HRLM; and Wulatji's poem includes another Wiradjuri word that, like *wula*, doesn't occur in the HRLM dictionary.[23]

While Wulatji and the Wahwee have in common that they both inspire song, there is one immediately obvious difference between the incubation procedures associated with them. In the case of the Wahwee (and also of the unnamed 'helping spirit' in Lommel's account from the other side of the continent), there is a dream journey to the underworld. But dreams inspired by Wulatji entail being transported upwards, to a 'sunny hill'. One might compare here a different dream from the same region, as recorded by the missionary Threlkeld (Gunson 1974, 1:134). It has become known in the literature (e.g. van Toorn 2006:47–52, Keary 2009:143) as 'Biraban's dream':

> M'Gill [Biraban] came, and related to me as follows:– 'The night before last, when coming hither, I slept on the other side of the Lake, I dreamed that I and my party of blacks were up in the Heavens; that we stood on a cloud; I looked round about in the Heavens; I said to the men that were with me, there He is? there is He who is called Jehovah; here he comes flying like fire with a great shining – this is He about whom the whites speak. He appeared to me like a man with clothing of fire, red like a flame. His arms were stretched out like the wings of a bird in the act of flying. He did not

---

apical and laminal stops (/t/ and /tj/, respectively) are contrastive in HRLM, but Threlkeld rarely differentiated between them.
21 To elaborate the classical parallel: in the Renaissance, Orpheus was regarded as the spiritual forebear of a lineage of singer-composers, from Homer to Marsilio Ficino (Warden 1982:86).
22 As spelt in the contemporary Wiradjuri orthography developed by Grant and Rudder (2010:290). See also Appendix D of the present chapter.
23 Specifically, *yambi* – see below, and Grant & Rudder (2010:479).

speak to us, but only looked earnestly at us as he was flying past. I said to the blacks with me, let us go down, lest he take us away; we descended on the top of a very high mountain ... we came to the bottom, and just as we reached the level ground, I awoke. We often dream of this mountain, many blacks fancy themselves on the top when asleep.'

Possibly this mountain is the same 'sunny hill' to which Wulatji transports his songmen.[24] In any case, the two locations have in common that they are associated with high places and thus probably with a mythology in which the distinction between sky and earth is significant (as it is in other parts of Australia, see e.g. Morton 1989:281).

Before we come to the song itself, let me return, for a moment, to the identity of the human Wulatji. He may well be the poet mentioned by Horatio Hale (1846:110) in the account of his visit to Australia with the United States Exploring Expedition in 1839: 'In the tribe on Hunter's River, there was a native famous for the composition of these songs or hymns, which, according to Mr. Threlkeld were passed from tribe to tribe, to a great distance, until many of the words became at last unintelligible to those who sang them.'[25] In support of this conjecture, I note that his song is fame-worthy in a number of ways: it is by far the longest of any of the song texts from the colonial period, with the exception of another song in the same language, which (as I argue below) is probably the work of the same songman. The two songs are also, clearly, the compositions of a highly accomplished poet, and (rather rare) examples of what could be thought of as the 'lyric' genre in Aboriginal poetry.[26]

The other poem that I suggest is attributable to Wulatji is the one that Percy Haslam published in 1984 and 1986, the first time under the title 'Awabakal poem'. The only information about its provenance that Haslam furnishes is that it was 'recorded by a family south of Swansea in the 1850s' (1984:71).[27] This fits fairly neatly with the evidence that Threlkeld provides about Wulatji, in his commentary on the song published by Dunlop:

> Such is a fair specimen of Song, translated with a little poetic licence. The orthography, although different from the system laid down in my Australian Grammar, sufficiently conveys the sound to enable me at once to discover the dialect of Wúllati the Poet who resided, near our residence on the sea shore, close to moon Island, until he died. The word 'Nung-ngnún' means a song, and when attached to the verbalizing affix *wit-til-li-ko* becomes *Nung-ngún wit-til-li-ko*, according to the idiom of the language, For to song a song, – English, to sing a song.

Moon Island[28] lies opposite Swansea Channel, at the entrance to Lake Macquarie. Geoff Ford (2010:350, note 85) writes that Wulatji 'retired' to this location, which might suggest that the poet came from Wollombi – the small Hunter Valley settlement where Mrs Dunlop was living at the time she recorded the words of Wulatji's song. But as far as I have been able to determine,

---

24 I conjecture that the mountain in question is probably Mount Yango, in both cases. (See appendix D, 'Notes on some placenames mentioned in the text'.)
25 There is at least a suggestion, in Hale's account, that this 'famous native' composed a song (or songs) that was sung in honour of Baayami, and also that he may have been part of the group of 'strange natives, who went about teaching it' (Hale 1846:110). This conjecture is necessarily somewhat speculative. Like Katie Parker (1905:80), who transcribed the song in question half a century later, I have been unable to translate it (or even identify the language).
26 For a discussion of Aboriginal song genres, see the introduction to this volume, and also C. H. Berndt (1978a) and Clunies Ross (1986).
27 Haslam died in 1987, and I have been unable to trace an original manuscript from the 1850s in his papers – or, at least, among those held in the Haslam Collection at the University of Newcastle (see Cultural Collections 2016). The absence of an original version leaves Haslam open to the suspicion that he has forged the text. Still, the poem has been composed with a level of technical skill that would be very surprising to find in a non-Indigenous person living long after the language ceased to be spoken. (The song has been interlinearised in Lissarrague 2006:272–273.)
28 This islet appears on Google Maps under the name 'Green Island'. However, according to the website of the Geographical Names Board of NSW, the official name is 'Moon Island'. The website notes that 'Green Island' was the 'previous name' (see Geographical Names Board of New South Wales n.d.).

there is no evidence as to where this original documenting took place. In the likely event that it did indeed happen at Wollombi, Wulatji was most probably a visitor, whether long or short term, since the language of both of his poems is that of HRLM, not the language of Wollombi, which is generally accepted to be Darkinyung.[29]

Other works have also been ascribed to Wulatji, at least by implication. Roy Hamilton Goddard, great-grandson of Eliza Hamilton Dunlop, attributes one of the four songs he has transcribed (1934:245–46) from the Milson manuscript (Milson c. 1840+) to 'the Wollombi poet' (1934:245). In the context, this appears to imply (erroneously, in my view) that the poet was Wulatji, and could be read as suggesting that he composed the other songs in the manuscript (images 9, 15, 19, 20) as well.

The manuscript is written in various hands, and Goddard attributes its authorship to 'Mrs. E. H. Dunlop and her daughter (Mrs. Rachel Milson) and granddaughter (Mrs. J. H. Bettington)' (1934:244).[30] It includes a vocabulary entitled 'Words of the Wollombi Tribe of Aboriginal Natives New South Wales' (images 16–18), of which Caroline Jones (2008:96) says, 'these pages are recognizably Eliza Dunlop's handwriting, not Mrs Milson's'. Authorship of the other sections of the manuscript is not so clear. The document includes vocabularies in several different languages and a comparative table (image 14), but the heading 'Murree gwalda or Blacks Language of Comileroi' (image 5) evidently applies at least to the pages that occur as images 5–13 of the online version[31], and probably to other parts of the manuscript as well.

In any case, the 'spring song' ('Curreele yananay curreelba') that Goddard attributes to 'the Wollombi poet' has been partly reconstituted by John Giacon (2010), and, even with gaps, the language is clearly Gamilaraay or a related dialect. The style is also so different from the HRLM song transcribed by Dunlop that there appears to be no good reason for attributing it to Wulatji. This probably applies to the other songs in the Milson manuscript[32] as well. Giacon has been able to recognise Gamilaraay words in some of them, and I have not been able to find any positive indication that the language is HRLM.

4 Wulatji's song: the text

Here is the first published version of the song, as it appeared in the *Sydney Morning Herald* in 1848.

Nung-Ngnun
Nge a runba wonung bulkirra umbilinto bulwarra;
Pital burra kultan wirripang buntoa

---

29 The Milson manuscript (Milson c. 1840+) includes a vocabulary entitled 'Words of the Wollombi Tribe of Aboriginal Natives New South Wales' (images 16–18), which has been attributed to E. H. Dunlop by Caroline Jones (2008:7, 96) and is recognisably Darkinyung. The manuscript is unpaginated, so I have referenced it according to the image numbers in the online version, made available by the State Library of NSW at *http://acmssearch.sl.nsw.gov.au/search/itemDetailPaged.cgi?itemID=950311* [accessed 20 January 2016]. (This incorporates frames 35–57 of the microfilm version.)
30 See appendix C of the present chapter ('Sketch genealogy of E. H. Dunlop's descendants and affines') for clarification of these relationships. Goddard himself was the son of Rachel Milson's youngest daughter, Mrs Thalia Dunlop Goddard, and therefore presumably the person who donated the manuscript to the Mitchell Library, referred to in the attribution at the head of the manuscript: 'by Mrs Milson grandmother of the donor'. He was also the author of a number of publications on the rock carvings and material culture of the Wollombi region (e.g. Goddard 1937a, 1937b). Oddly, the Mitchell Library's bookplate (Milson c. 1840+: image 2) refers to the donor as 'D. Goddard'. Since none of Goddard's siblings had names with the initial letter 'D', this is possibly an error.
31 John Giacon (2010) has confirmed that the vocabulary in the wordlists on these pages comes predominantly from Gamilaraay and the related language Yuwaalaraay.
32 See also O'Leary (2011:40–41).

Nung-Ngnun
Nge a runba turrama berrambo, burra kilkoa:
Kurri wi, raratoa yella walliko,
Yulo Moane, woinya, birung poro bulliko,

Nung-Ngnun
Nge a runba kan wullung, Makora, kokein,
Mip-pa-rai, kekul, wimbi murr ring kirrika:
Nge a runba mura ke-en kulbun kulbun murrung.

Dunlop included her own verse translation (or adaptation), which, although extremely free, at least provides some guidelines for the reconstitution of the original song.

Our home is the gibber-gunyah,
Where hill joins hill on high;
Where the turruma and berrambo,
Like sleeping serpents lie; –
And the rushing of wings, as the wangas pass,
Sweeps the wallaby's print from the glistening grass.

Ours are the makoro gliding,
Deep in the shady pool;
For our spear is sure, and the prey secure ...
Kanin, or the bright gherool.
Our lubras sleep by the bato clear,
That the Amygest's track hath never been near.

Ours is the koolema flowing
With precious kirrika stored;
For fleet the foot, and keen the eye,
That seeks the nukkung's hoard; –
And the glances are bright, and the footsteps are free,
When we dance in the shade of the karakon tree.

Dunlop divides the poem into three unequal sections and precedes each one with the word 'Nung-Ngnun', which we know from Threlkeld (in Gunson 1974, vol. 1:58) means 'song'.[33] It is unclear whether these headings have been supplied by Dunlop or whether such 'announcements' formed part of the actual performance of the song. This latter possibility seems unlikely, since the interpolations break the song into three unequal sections. It is more plausibly analysed as falling into four equal sections, each consisting of eight measures, as below, where I treat each of the four sections as a 'verse', and each half verse of four measures as a 'line'.[34]

---

33 Lissarrague (2006:125) reconstructs the word as *NanguN*; I hypothesise rather *nannguyn*.
34 For present purposes, I define 'line' (of a song) as the smallest metrical unit with a boundary cue (such as a pause or a lengthened final note). In this context, a verse is a group of lines based on a metrical schema that recurs in the course of the song.

Table 9.1 (part 1): Reconstitution of 'Nung-Ngnun' ('Song'), based on Dunlop's 'Native poetry' (1848a)

Nung-Ngnun (*nannguyn*, 'song')

VERSE 1, LINE 1			
Measure 1	2	3	4
ngayaran -pa	wanang	palkirr[i] yampi[ii] -li-n -tu[iii]	pulwarra
1PL -GEN	where	mountain live.with -CT-PRS -ERG	high.place
VERSE 1, LINE 2			
Measure 5	6	7	8
pital para	ka -tan[iv] wiri >[v]	pang pantu >	wa[vi]
happy 3PL.NOM	be -PRS eaglehawk	wallaby	
VERSE 2, LINE 1			
Measure 9	10	11	12
ngayaran -pa	tarama pi >	rampu[vii] para	-kiluwa[viii]
1PL -GEN	war.boomerang waddy	3PL	-SEMB
VERSE 2, LINE 2			
Measure 13	14	15	16
kariway	ngaratuwa[ix]	yalawa	-li -ku
snake	asleep	sit	-DVB -PURP
VERSE 3, LINE 1			
Measure 17	18	19	20
yulu[x] muwayn	wuyu -nya >[xi]	pirang puru >	pa -li -ku
dance kangaroo	grass -MT -ABL	smooth	-DVB -PURP
VERSE 3, LINE 2			
Measure 21	22	23	24
ngayaran -pa	ka -n walang[xii]	makurr kukuyn	miparay
1PL -GEN	be -PRS head	fish water	honeycomb
VERSE 4, LINE 1			
Measure 25	26	27	28
kaykal wimpi	marrarring[xiii]	kiri >	ka
sweet coolamon	inside	honey	
VERSE 4, LINE 2			
Measure 29	30	31	32
ngayaran -pa	marrakiyn	kalpankalpan	marrang
1PL -GEN	girl	beautiful	good

My glosses are almost all taken from Lissarrague's HRLM wordlist and grammar (2006). The few exceptions are noted in Table 9.1 (part 2) below. A list of abbreviations used in the glosses is provided at the end of this chapter, before the appendices.

Table 9.1 (part 2): notes to the reconstitution of 'Nannguyn'

i The final *a* in Dunlop's 'bulkirra' is probably not a separate syllable but rather a superfluous element of her orthographic convention for representing the alveolar rhotic /rr/ at the end of a word. She has used the same convention in the case of 'makora' (*makurr*, 'fish').

ii I have assumed that this word has the same form and meaning as Wiradjuri *yambi*, 'live with, stay together as a man with a woman (as husband and wife)' (Grant and Rudder 2010:479), and that the initial consonant, *y*, has been elided in Dunlop's transcription (and possibly in Wulatji's rendition as well).

iii The only sense I can make of -*tu* is as a likely example of poetic licence. I take it that *yampi* must be a transitive verb, in which case the ergative suffix required on the noun (here, *palkirr*) has been displaced to follow the verb (and observes the same morphophonemic rule as with a noun).

iv The source form is 'kultan'. This can only be a misprint for 'kuttan'.

v Where a morpheme crosses the boundary between two measures, I have indicated this by using the right-facing chevron symbol (>) after the first part. This permits the hyphen to be reserved for suffixes.

vi HRLM *pantarr*, 'kangaroo' (Lissarrague 2006:130); Gathang *bandaarr*, 'wallaby' (Lissarrague 2010:176). I have adopted Mrs Dunlop's interpretation of the meaning ('wallaby'), and also of the phonology (/pantuwa/). This apparently aberrant form may be dialectal, or possibly a poetic convention is in play. While it would be possible to treat Dunlop's version as a mishearing, it is actually a better fit with the rhyme scheme and metre.

vii I have found two sources for the translation of this word. One is the 'Comileroi' wordlist in the Milson manuscript (c. 1840+), where 'Birrambo' occurs with the meaning 'Waddy' (image 11 of the online version). The other is the glossary that accompanies E. H. Dunlop's adaptation of Wulatji's poem in Isaac Nathan's *Southern Euphrosyne* (1848:94), where Dunlop spells the word as 'berramboo' and glosses it thus: 'the waddy or war-club, similar to those of New Zealand'. Wulatji's original poem is not included with this version, which is headed 'Pialla Wollombi', rendered as 'the poetry or language of Wollombi'. 'Pialla' is probably borrowed from the Sydney language, where the verb *baya*- means 'to speak' (Troy 1994:73). Dunlop does not include Wulatji's original song text in this version, and her adaptation differs in a number of ways from the version published in the same year in the *Sydney Morning Herald*. But both versions include a number of 'Aboriginal' words that are not actually in Wulatji's original, and the two sets of such words (and their glosses) are not identical. Appendix B ('E. H. Dunlop's glossaries', at the end of the present chapter) provides a comparative table (Table 9.4) of these words, with likely language affiliations.

viii The source form appears to be 'kilkoa'. I have assumed this is a misprint for 'killoa'; that is, the HRLM semblative suffix *kiluwa* (Lissarrague 2006:62). If this supposition is correct, and the usage here is not an example of poetic licence, it suggests that the suffix can be used with free pronouns (otherwise only attested on nouns and demonstratives).

ix Since there are no words in HRLM that begin with a rhotic, Dunlop's 'raratoa' is clearly a mishearing, and the most likely basis of the word is HRLM *ngarapu*, 'asleep' (Lissarrague 2006:126). The distortion of the usual form of the word follows a pattern very similar to the one noted above in relation to *pantuwa*. In other words, it is possible that the same poetic convention (omitting the last syllable of the word and substituting it with -*tuwa*) is being applied.

x Gamilaraay, Yuwaalaraay, Yuwaalayaay: *yulu-gi*, 'dance, play' etc. [intransitive verb] (Ash, Giacon and Lissarrague 2003:156).

xi I am obliged to treat -*nya* as a metrical element or some other kind of poetic convention. The usual ablative case suffix here would be -*kapirang*.

xii The significance of 'head' in this context is unclear, since the three words *walang*, 'head', *makurr*, 'fish' and *kukuyn*, 'water', are juxtaposed without any indicators, apart from the sequence, of their syntactic relationship.

xiii HRLM *marrarring*, 'inside' (attested in Threlkeld's translation of Luke 9:34, e.g. in Fraser 1892:153).

The literal translation is as follows:

Ours is the place where the mountains cohabit with the heights
The eaglehawks and wallabies are happy

Ours are the boomerangs and waddies, they are like
Snakes lying asleep

The kangaroos dance on the grass to smooth it down
Ours is the head of the fish in the water

The sweet honeycomb, the nectar inside the wooden bowl
Ours are the splendid and beautiful young women.

5 Wulatji's song: formal analysis

This reconstruction treats the song as divided into 32 measures with a value of 4 beats each. These are grouped into lines of 4 measures, each of which is divided into 2 hemistichs (half-lines) of two measures each. The underlying pattern for each line is 16 quarter notes, lengthened to half notes or whole notes when required by the metre, often at or towards the end of a line. The main ambiguity in my reconstruction is the placement of the caesuras (which is relevant to where the long notes occur in the line). The major caesuras occur between the two halves of each line, and the minor caesuras between each measure (or, to put it another way, between the two halves of each hemistich). I have based my decisions about the caesuras largely on the premise that the composer of this song puts the stress in the normal position on a word – that is, on the first syllable – when this is possible. (This contrasts with some practices in other parts of Australia, where the stress is intentionally distorted.) A noteworthy thing about this song is its use of metrical breaks in the middle of words. This occurs across (major) caesuras in line 2 (*wiri- // pang*), line 3 (*pi- // rampu*), and line 5 (*wuyu-nya // -pirang*).

If my analysis holds good, the song shows a quite remarkable symmetry, consisting as it does of 8 lines of 16 beats each. The structure can be conceptualised in terms of powers of 2. Each measure consists of 2^2 beats; each hemistich consists of 2^3 beats; each line consists of 2^4 beats; each verse consists of 2^5 beats; and the song as a whole consists of 2^7 beats. This suggests that there is probably also an implicit grouping of 2^6 beats, which divides the song into halves – two groups of two verses each.[35] This is hinted at also by a change in the metrical pattern. In the first half of the song, two short notes followed by one long note is the underlying pattern for the last measure in each line; in the second half of the song, it is the underlying pattern for the last (i.e. second) measure in each hemistich. The only deviation from this pattern occurs in the last verse, where the metre needs to accommodate an aberrant number of syllables in both lines. The syllable count for the whole song is 15/12/15/12/14/14/10/13, which suggests a metrical schema of AABB (or possibly AABC).

This may also have implications for the melodic structure. There are no repetitions in the song text, but the metrical similarities with songs from other parts of Australia suggest that the melody is likely to be strophic (rather than through-composed). Moreover, the relationship between melody and text is likely to be mainly syllabic, although the irregularities in the syllable count could be indicative of melismas. Beyond that, we can speculate that the melodic contour might plausibly follow a descending pattern covering an octave. I base this conjecture not just on the premise that this contour is common (and perhaps the commonest) in Aboriginal music in most parts of Australia (Jones 1965:371–372), but also on the fact that we know it was used in the immediate linguistic region in which Wulatji was active. Threlkeld wrote, of Indigenous singers he heard in Newcastle, that 'their tune is rather dismal; they begin high and end in about an octave below the pitch' (Gunson 1974, 1:86).[36] While the metrical variations suggest that

---

35 We could perhaps call these two units 'stanzas', although this would imply either that they have distinctive formal properties that are recognised in the relevant literary tradition (as in the stanzas of a Petrarchan sonnet), or that they represent distinct iterations of the melody. In neither case do we have the evidence to apply the usage to the present song.
36 This is Threlkeld's most specific account of melody. He also makes a number of less informative comments on Aboriginal singing and dancing (e.g. Gunson 1974:56–59, 63). There are no audio recordings or transcriptions of the Indigenous music of this region, and very few reports that attempt to describe it verbally. Apart from Threlkeld's passing references, there is also an account (Anon. 1869), by an anonymous journalist from the *Maitland Mercury*, of an 'Aboriginal corroboree' performed in 1869, in Maitland. This took place on Nicholson Racecourse, in front of a paying public. (My thanks to Stephen Wye for drawing this article to my attention.) By contrast with the poverty of the written accounts, at least two of the most detailed early images of Aboriginal ceremonies come from this region – Joseph Lycett's painting known as 'Corroboree at Newcastle', dating to about 1818, and the engraving attributed to Walter Preston called 'Corrobborree, or Dance of the Natives of New South Wales, New Holland'. (See *https://coalriver.files.wordpress.*

the melody is unlikely to be the same for every verse, it is impossible to know how the melodic sections and repetitions might be aligned with metrical units.

Throughout the song, we find a clever use of end rhyme, internal rhyme, alliteration and assonance. There are only a few linguistic ambiguities, where I have had to resort to 'poetic licence' as the justification for my reconstruction.

1. *-tu* in measure 3.
2. *pantuwa* (instead of *pantarr*) in measures 7–8.
3. *ngaratuwa* (instead of *ngarapu*) in measure 14.
4. *-nyapirang* (instead of *-kapirang* in measures 18–19.

This kind of 'aesthetic alteration of spoken vocabulary in Aboriginal song' (Bracknell, this volume[37]) is very common throughout Australia.

The 'foreign' words (by which I mean the words that don't occur in Lissarrague's 2006 HRLM wordlist and have to be reconstructed on the basis of words from other languages) are:

1. *yampi* (measure 3). Dunlop translates this as 'joins', which almost certainly indicates that the Wiradjuri meaning, 'live together as man and woman' (Grant and Rudder 2010:479) applies here. The fact that it is used with HRLM tense suffixes suggests that the word is likely to have occurred in HRLM as well as Wiradjuri.

2. *yulu* (measure 17). This is a verb root meaning 'dance, play' in Gamilaraay, Yuwaalaraay and Yuwaalayaay (Ash, Giacon and Lissarrague 2003:156). It is used here without tense suffixes, which suggests that the word is being treated as a nominal (so either 'the dancing of the kangaroos' or 'the dancing kangaroos'). The occurrence of this word in HRLM is possibly attested also by the first line of the second of two songs that Threlkeld published in 1826: 'Yulo burrah mirre'. My tentative interpretation of this line is as *yulu para mirri* (play 3PL.NOM dog) 'the dogs (are) dancing/playing'. If this is correct, it means that in HRLM *yulu* is a nominal, not a verb, and means not just 'a dance/play' but can also be used adjectivally: 'dancing', 'playing', 'at play' etc.

3. *pirampu* (measures 10–11). We know from the Milson manuscript (c. 1840+: image 11) that the word spelt there, in the 'Comileroi' section, as 'Berrambo' is translated as 'Waddy'. This gloss is confirmed in the notes to the poem that Dunlop (1848b) published under the title 'Pialla Wollombi' in Isaac Nathan's *Southern Euphrosyne* (1848:94). I have not been able to trace it in other Gamilaraay sources (such as Ash, Giacon and Lissarrague 2003).

6 Kinship and Aboriginal 'arts of memory'

In many parts of Aboriginal Australia songs function as mnemonic devices for memorising placenames and/or their associated stories and features (Hercus and Simpson 2002:12; Payne 1984:265, 1989:46–47). Indeed, certain categories of song constitute what we might call 'audible maps'. There is good evidence to support this in the areas where a substantial song corpus has been preserved (see e.g. Strehlow 1971 and cf. Ellis 1984:152). But it needs to be emphasised that songs of this type (such as the travelling song cycles that narrate mythical journeys) codify more than just topography. They are also social maps, in which the individual localities constitute the nodes in a vast kinship network.

---

com/2013/03/a928350u.jpg;
    https://downloads.newcastle.edu.au/library/cultural%20collections/images/PrestonCorroboree1820.jpg;
    and *https://hunterlivinghistories.com/2014/01/20/corroboree-wickham/* [all accessed 29 August 2017].

37 Chapter 1 (see section entitled 'Poetic alterations').

Each site is associated with a mythical being who stands in a particular kin relationship to all the relevant components of its environment: other places and their ancestral beings, as well as humans, animals, plants and some natural phenomena, such as moon and rain. The geographical features (and some celestial features – see Johnson 1998:103–114) provide the focal components of a mnemotechnical system in which the 'loci' (Yates 1966:18–19 and *passim*) or 'topoi' (Carruthers 1990:29 and *passim*) are *literal* (as distinct from, or perhaps in addition to being, metaphorical or mythical) 'places'. These places are related to each other not just by the routes of travel that connect them, but also by a taxonomic schema that is based primarily on kinship.

In the south-east, where the documentation of Aboriginal music is fragmentary, there are no records of songs of this 'cartographic' type.[38] Nonetheless, the surviving song material has the potential to illuminate other relevant aspects of the cultures of the region. In the case of Wulatji's song, for example, there appear to be implicit references to a particular type of kin classification that is known from other parts of the country (in central NSW) but not from the Hunter River and Lake Macquarie, where the language of the song was spoken. So little is known about the kinship system of this region that the poem may well prove to be one of the only relevant sources.[39] At the same time, it can possibly tell us something about mnemotechnical practices in this culture area.

In 2012 Carlo Severi published an article that drew attention to the relevance of the 'arts of memory' discourse to anthropology. He also provided a helpful definition of an 'art of memory' (or 'mnemotechnic'): 'the use of taxonomic thought and the creation of a visual form of salience' (Severi 2012: 475). While I question the need for the 'forms of salience' to be visual (and propose that in Australia they are predominantly auditory[40]), the main point is that 'arts of memory' are intimately linked to a language's classification system, its organisation of all cultural knowledge into semantic domains. Wulatji's poem suggests that the same kind of 'binarising' taxonomic thinking that is common throughout Australia may have been characteristic of the Hunter River and Lake Macquarie region as well.

The opening line of the poem includes the word *yampi*. As mentioned above, this is probably a loan from Wiradjuri, where it is glossed as 'live with, stay together as a man with a woman (as husband and wife)' (Grant and Rudder 2010:479). This word is applied to the relationship between *palkirr*, 'the mountain(s)' and *pulwarra*, 'the high place(s)'. My suggestion is that there are two specific peaks or ranges involved, and that the relationship between them has something to do with intermarrying groups.[41]

It seems likely that the theme of cohabitation that is introduced in the first line is continued in at least the second, and possibly in later ones as well. In the second line the eaglehawk is paired with the wallaby. The eaglehawk is mythologically significant in many parts of Australia,

---

38 But note that McDonald (this volume, Chapter 7) argues persuasively that songs of the travelling song cycle type probably did occur in the south-east.
39 Sources from the late-nineteenth century (Fawcett 1898:180; Fison and Howitt 1880:280) indicate that the inland dialects of HRLM, such as Wanarruwa and Kayawaykal, used the same section system as the speakers of Gamilaraay (see also Wafer and Lissarrague 2008:449–450). But Threlkeld's substantial body of work on the coastal dialects makes no mention of this system (nor, for that matter, of any other).
40 This runs contrary to the standard assumptions of the 'arts of memory' discourse. Mary Carruthers (1990: 18), for example, has said that 'material presented acoustically [must be] turned into visual form' to be mnemotechnically useful. This is not the place to debate the point; but I refer the reader to Walter Ong's (1983:281) observations about the shift 'toward the visual throughout the whole cognitive field' that happened in fifteenth and sixteenth century Europe; and also to Gary Tomlinson's (1993:135) and Murray Schafer's (1994:10–11) comments on the same subject.
41 Wollombi, where Mrs Dunlop probably heard this song from Wulatji, is the closest settlement of any size to Mount Yango. Since Yango is a site of major significance, I conjecture that it could be one of the peaks implied. (See appendix D, 'Notes on some placenames mentioned in the text'.)

and is often partnered with another creature. Most famously, in the Upper Murray region there was a widespread matrimoiety system that treated the eaglehawk and the crow as emblematic of the two moieties (see Wafer and Lissarrague 2008:420).[42] This is not to imply necessarily that the eaglehawk and wallaby had a function as straightforward as this in the Hunter district.[43] I suggest that the more likely import of their pairing in this song has to do with a principle of kin classification about which we know very little. It is a form of dual classification that appears not to be based on any of the three types of moiety that are fairly well understood in Australia (matrimoieties, patrimoieties and generation moieties), but on some other principle of recruitment that has never been adequately explained in the literature. It is vaguely known as 'totemism', but in its manifestations in NSW, it is sometimes called 'bloods', 'shades' or 'winds'. The moieties are based on contrasting properties of these terms – quick and slow blood, shade of branch and trunk, hot wind and cold wind (Testart 1980:76–79; Wafer and Lissarrague 2008:442–445).

The relevant form of totemism in the present case is based on a distinction between creatures that have fur and those that have scales or feathers, as occurs in Wangaaypuwan (Radcliffe-Brown 1923:425) and other languages of central NSW. It seems at least plausible that this type of binary classification could underlie Wulatji's pairing of the eaglehawk and the wallaby, as well as the juxtaposition of some of the other creatures (and artefacts) in the poem. It is applicable, for example, in the case of 'snake' and 'kangaroo', and probably also of 'fish' and 'honeycomb'.[44] It could also be metaphorically applied in the case of the two different kinds of weapons.[45] This does not necessarily mean that this type of totemism was in use in the Hunter region. Its appearance in the poem might be an exotic reference that Wulatji picked up on his travels. On the other hand, we have absolutely no information at all about kin classification in the coastal dialects of HRLM, so there are no a priori reasons for not considering the fur/scale system as a possibility.

It could perhaps be argued that the structural features I have pointed out are merely a result of the *parallelismus membrorum* that characterises Aboriginal song. This term was invented in 1788 for the study of Hebrew poetry, but as Jakobson (1987) has shown, the stylistic device it designates is common in poetic-linguistic traditions around the world. Sachs (1943:92) defines the term as follows: 'the half-verse is answered by another half-verse that expresses either an intensification or an antinomy'. Strehlow (1971:109–117) has drawn attention to the use of this

---

42 The pairing of Eaglehawk and Crow is widespread in Australia (see, for example, Waterman (1987:38, 54, 62, 78, 107). Some representative interpretations include Mathew (1899:15–22), Blows (1975, 1995), and van Toorn (2006:31–34).

43 Such an obvious moiety system is unlikely to have escaped the attention of Lancelot Threlkeld. In spite of his general disinterest in and disdain for Indigenous mythology, he did impart some precious details about the place of the Eaglehawk in the lore of the Hunter Valley–Lake Macquarie region to W. Augustus Miles (1854:23–25). 'These tribes believe that the world was created by the diamond-tailed eagle, and that he brought in his beak, and deposited, the stones which form the mystic stone circles on many of the hill tops . . . The Rev. L. Threlkeld informs me that he has seen them on the very summits of the mountains at Lake Macquarrie [sic]; and the legend is, that they were brought there by the eaglehawk, a bird of mysterious omen, and much reverenced by the blacks.' Threlkeld himself wrote of the Eaglehawk's role in the creation of the stone circles in his reminiscences (Gunson 1974, 1:66, cf. 73 n. 29, 78 n. 114). He had come across a group of these structures on an unspecified 'high hill', and his description (Gunson 1974, 1:66) bears comparison with that given by McDonald (1993:85) of the stone arrangements she and her party found on top of Mount Yango in 1987. It is worth noting as well that Threlkeld provided the HRLM name 'Bo-ro-yi-róng' for Pulbah Island (Threlkeld 1834:84), and I have argued elsewhere (Wafer 2017:295 n. 4) that this placename is probably derived from HRLM *puruyi*, 'eaglehawk' (Lissarrague 2006:135). For further relevant associations of the Eaglehawk, see Appendix D of the present chapter.

44 Fish obviously belong with the creatures that have 'scales and feathers', and there is evidence (admittedly from a location far from the Hunter Valley) that bees (and therefore honeycomb) are more likely to be aligned with those that have 'fur'. In the kinship system of the Annan River (near Cooktown), the section names are based on a distinction between (types of) bees and (types of) eaglehawks (Howitt 1904:118; see also McConvell and McConvell, forthcoming).

45 C. H. Berndt (1978b:76) notes the opposition of digging stick and spear as symbolic of the division of the sexes, both in everyday life and in rituals (see also Payne 1993:16–17 on the ritual significance of the digging stick). My suggestion is that an analogous opposition may underlie the juxtaposing of boomerangs and waddies in the present poem – a distinction based not on gender, however, but on a different cosmological division, such as fur as opposed to scales and feathers.

device in Arrernte songs from Central Australia, and to the range of musical and textual means Arrernte song-persons deploy to achieve it. It appears to be common throughout the continent (cf. Donaldson 1987:36).

The relevant linguistic techniques include various kinds of word-play, such as the use of homonyms and words with a similar phonology but different meanings. We probably see an example of this in the last verse, where *marrakiyn* ends the first line and *marrang* the second. But in the rest of the poem, the parallelism seems to be semantic rather than phonological. And if it is semantic, then it is reasonable to hypothesise that the fur/scale division furnishes the principles according to which the antinomies are organised – even though the relevant paired terms are not systematically distributed in alternating half-verses.

A. P. Elkin (1970:705) observed that 'the dual division is an essential feature of Aboriginal ritual, comprising aspects of opposition and co-operation'. There is evidence from many parts of Australia to support this generalisation (see also Radcliffe-Brown 1958, Durkheim and Mauss 1963:6–15); but there are also large gaps in the data, particularly in the south-east. If, as I speculate here, the semantic pairings in the poem do indeed reflect social divisions, this not only extends our understanding of the distribution of dual classification in Australia, but also indicates the fundamental nature of the role this binary principle plays in Australian taxonomic thinking and arts of memory.

7 Conclusion: song revitalisation through dreams

'In ancient Greek religion... the Earth was believed to engender dreams', according to Kimberley Patton (2004:205). I have not come across a formulation as explicit as this from Aboriginal Australia, but it is certainly implied in observations such as the following, by Arrernte speaker Margaret Kemarre Turner (2010:66–67):

> This is a story that was told to me: We'd taught dancing to all these *Pertame*, Southern Arrernte girls, they were doing *anthepe*, women's-side song and dance. And on that *anthepe* songs, it had all *Arrernte* people singing, old men singing. And when they took it down to Canberra – they did that dance traditional down there – well, they reckon all those Little People from that country, when they went to sleep they heard them singing! All these People from that country came talking to them in the Dream they reckoned, *akwele angketyekewe, apetyewarreke, alyelhewarreke, alyewerle*, talking, and singing their own songs in that country. That's how people learn their own songs, you know, when people go and dance. *Irrerntarenye mape*, the People of that Land gives you them songs from your own place, wherever it might be. Anyhow, they could just hear all the Old People singing, and dancing, sitting around. But those young women didn't understand the language. It wasn't any of their language, so I think that the other language must still be alive *itethe ahelhele*. They couldn't understand them because it was different. And it's still there, the language and those songs and dances are definitely alive in the ground somewhere 'round there, Canberra-*thayate*. It's good to know that.

The *irrerntarenye*[46] are essentially spirits of place, 'People of that Land'.

> *Irrerntarenye mape*, the People of that Land gives you them songs from your own place, wherever it might be (2010:67). *Irrerntarenye's* everywhere, all over this country, and overseas as well... And some people may not know that there's these Little Spirit People. But you've got to talk to the Little Spirit People, they're waiting for you to talk to them and tell them who you are (2010:118).

---

46 Defined by the Arrernte dictionary as 'spirits in the shape of small people that live in the ground in some places' (Henderson and Dobson 1994:404). There is a more comprehensive account of these beings in Róheim (1972:124–126). For further references to Australia's 'Little People', see Clarke (2007:146, 150).

The notion that at least some songs have their origins in 'Country'[47] is widespread and possibly universal in Aboriginal Australia, though the land is generally understood to operate through intermediaries – such as the *irrerntarenye* (and other kinds of spirit beings), who communicate their messages to humans via songs that are received in dreams or visions.

Patton points out that 'dream incubation', in the ancient Mediterranean world, originally meant '"going to sleep in a sacred place" . . . In other words, the starting point in a given incubation tradition could be the belief that the place "does" many things of metaphysical value, including sponsor iconic dreams for those who sleep there' (Patton 2004:195 n. 2). This belief appears to be fundamental in Aboriginal cultures as well.[48] To give one clear example: Marett (2005:42) cites the case of John Dumoo, who 'received a *wangga* song from a group of Walakandha [ghosts] while sleeping near their *kigatiya* Dreaming site at Wudi-djirridi'.

But the dreamer does not need to be physically present in the vicinity of a sacred site to receive a song from a spirit entity associated with that location. Bob Tonkinson (1970:276) notes that Western Desert people who live in the settlement of Jigalong, at some distance from their traditional homelands, nonetheless 'claim to maintain continuous contact by making journeys to and from their home territories in dream-spirit form.' It is in the course of these dream-spirit journeys that new songs are received (Tonkinson 1970:284).

Another strategy for maintaining the continuity of traditional practices in a changed physical environment is the dreaming of songs inspired by the spirits who inhabit the new location. Stephen Wild (1987) describes this process of ritual adjustment at Lajamanu, and Allan Marett (2000:27; 2005:4–5) gives an analogous account from Belyuen. Marett (2000:27) also observes that 'in the aftermath of the displacements suffered by Aboriginal societies in the course of European settlement, the phenomenon of song dreaming has arguably become one of the principal mechanisms by which displaced social groups adapt to changing patterns of residence.'[49]

The underlying logic of this adjustment procedure is that every Aboriginal person has a duty to take care of Country (understood in the distinctively Aboriginal sense of the word, as referring to both ancestral land and the land in general[50]). This responsibility is not limited to issues of environmental management (as often interpreted by non-Aboriginal people), but requires

---

47 When the noun 'country' is used in its distinctively Aboriginal sense, I capitalise it, in conformity with a convention that is becoming increasingly common among Aboriginal people themselves. For an example of this usage, and the reasons behind it, see *http://www.visitmungo.com.au/aboriginal-country* [accessed 9 May 2017].

48 There are undoubtedly cases in Aboriginal Australia where the sonic properties of a place constitute a major factor in its mythological associations and metaphysics. Lake Alexandrina, for example, is mentioned by George Taplin (1879:62–63) as emitting a booming sound that local Aboriginal people attribute to a 'water-spirit . . . called Mulgewanke'. (See also Clarke 2007:145.) The whirlpool of Jindirrabalgun, near Sunday Island in the Kimberley (Glaskin 2008:53–54), is another likely example. But the investigation of 'soundscapes' (Schafer 1994) is at such an early stage in Australia (see for example Richards ed. 2007) that it is too soon to make generalisations or draw conclusions. Whether the emerging fields of archaeoacoustics (Scarre and Lawson 2006; Eneix 2014) and acoustic ecology (Feld 2001) will be able to contribute to our understanding of Aboriginal musical traditions remains to be seen. Certainly, archaeologists in other parts of the world have reported good results from 'treating the landscape as an intelligent interlocutor' (Devereux 2013:61). This is also the approach that Australian sound artist Ros Bandt (2014) has used at Lake Mungo.

49 Commenting on a similar situation among the Pintupi, Fred Myers (1986:53) observes 'that historical change can be integrated, but . . . is assimilated to the pre-existing forms'. See also Redmond (2001).

50 Deborah Bird Rose (2013:100) provides a good summary (based on fieldwork with people of the Victoria River District) of the concept of Country: 'Australian Aboriginal people have picked up the word "country" and remade it into a powerful signifier of local, multispecies belonging. In Indigenous country there is no nature/culture divide. One could say that country is all culture, but the more interesting point is that it is all sentient, communicative, relational and inter-active. In this sense, culture is not something you have, but rather is the way you live, and by implication, the way your knowledge arises and is worked with. Country is both the context of life and the emergent result of life being lived.' Elsewhere (2004:153–154) she observes as follows: 'A fundamental proposition . . . is that the living things of a country take care of their own. All living things are held to have an interest in the life of the country because their own life is dependent on the life of their country.'

entering into a communicative relationship with the land, which may then send dream songs via the spirits who inhabit the place. The composition of new songs (of the ancestral kind) is not an end in itself, but is subordinated to the need to fulfill an obligation to the land by creating public performances of its messages.

Revitalisation strategies based on this principle could perhaps be summed up under the concept of 're-dreaming', which I borrow from an article by Ursula McConnel (1935:66[51]) on totemic rituals in Cape York:

> One man said he had 'dreamed' the ritual of which he was in charge, but that his father had also 'dreamed' it before him. The ritualistic procedure is apparently handed down from one generation to another relatively intact, but it seems that a man 're-dreams' the ritual and so acquires the necessary mystical qualifications for carrying it on.[52]

If the incubation of new songs is considered an appropriate response to displacement in those regions where ancestral singing practices are ongoing, perhaps it can also serve to restore relationships to Country in the places where the song traditions have suffered serious disruption. The conclusion I draw from M. K. Turner's story is that the land itself has the potential, everywhere, to inspire contemporary Aboriginal people with musical dreams.

But how can the potential inherent in Country be realised in places where intergenerational ritual transmission has been disrupted? Does it require an understanding of traditional incubation techniques and performance practices? If so, can these be taught; for example, by veteran songpersons recruited from those parts of the country where the song traditions are still active?[53] These are the kinds of questions that can only be addressed by Aboriginal people themselves, as they face the multiple challenges of cultural renewal.

To leave the matter there would be to treat song revitalisation as a purely technical matter, and thus to neglect the broader philosophical issues that this discussion raises. If scholars, both Indigenous and non-Indigenous, are to take seriously James Maffie's (2009) call for a 'global polycentric epistemology', we are obliged to face the task of developing the necessary conceptual tools. In the present case, for example, we have to find a 'bridging' language for discussing propositions like '*irrerntarenye*'s everywhere, all over this country, and overseas as well' – a language that avoids, on the one hand, the ethnocentric trap of dismissing such statements as superstition, and, on the other, the New Age trap of simplifying Indigenous culture to the point where it can be appropriated and marketed.

---

51   See also Róheim (1945:6 and note 10).
52   Two other chapters in the present volume also discuss re-dreaming. Nancarrow and Cleary (Chapter 10) mention that Lardil songmen re-dream songs not just in their own Country, but also when travelling (see note 53, below). Similarly, the account of 'dream-conceived songs' in Brown and Evans's Chapter 12 suggests that, in western Arnhem Land, musical dreams often entail a re-dreaming (although the authors do not use this term), rather than a creation *ex nihilo*. These accounts come from quite diverse locations, which suggests that the practice is very widespread in Aboriginal Australia. It is probably a familiar occurrence in Indigenous cultures of other continents as well. Linda Hogan (2013:23–24), for example, writes of 'a Northern Cheyenne man who said that some of their songs were lost during the times when the Americans chased Black Kettle's band back and forth across the continent ... But, he said, the songs of those they lost during those painful times were held in trust for them by the wolves who taught them back to the people.' The presumably oneiric nature of this transmission suggests a plausible counterpart to 're-dreaming'.
53   Nancarrow and Cleary, in the present volume, document a number of cases where Lardil songmen have dreamt songs during visits to places in southern Australia, including Jenolan Caves, Robinvale, a beach near Adelaide, and Morialta Falls. They make a couple of points that are worth noting here: 'These songs are regarded by the songmen as belonging to the country where they are dreamt, and are not necessarily meant for Lardil people ... On one occasion Lardil songman Kenneth Jacob dreamt a red kangaroo song after visiting Morialta Falls near Adelaide. In the following days we returned to the falls to film him singing the song in situ. The footage and the song were passed on to Kaurna people as they were regarded as the true owners of the story.'

Towards an ethnography of listening to silence

My attempt to sketch some of the elements of such a bridging language begins with the contention that 'dreaming', in the sense in which Aboriginal people use the term, has a semantic range that overlaps, in some ways and to some extent, with 'listening'. The Indigenous concept, I suggest, extends beyond what the word 'dream' means in English to include waking forms of attentiveness to Country. Thus Wulatji, as 'god of Poesy', speaks to the song-seeker on a 'sunny hill', where he (or she) might, indeed, be having a dream or daydream – or they might just be listening to the land. Perhaps song incubation can, in some cases, be as simple as that.

This is a bit speculative, and could do with better ethnographic support. Unfortunately, the 'ethnography of listening'[54] is still relatively undeveloped, and the kinds of auditory attention it deals with usually involve the human voice. It is rare to find any mention of the arts of listening to silence.[55] There is, however, one 'ethnography of listening' that offers a number of relevant observations. Donal Carbaugh, in his article on 'listening and landscape' among the Blackfeet of northern Montana, notes that 'at least for some people, places can (and do) "speak," if only we – citizens and scholars alike – take the time to "listen" accordingly' (1999:252). This kind of listening is 'a non-linguistic mode of learning from, and inhabiting places' (Carbaugh 1999:257).

> Such acts are ... not so much internally focused on one's meditative self, but externally focused on one's place through an active attentiveness to that scene, to the highly active powers and insights it offers. In the process, one becomes a part of the scene, hearing and feeling with it (Carbaugh 1999:259).

Further, 'there is an 'important cultural sense in which sacredness, place and listening are interrelated' (Carbaugh 1999:258). This means that listening 'can be doubly placed as a cultural attentiveness to a known sacred place, and to the sacredness in just about any place' (Carbaugh 1999:259).

> There is the potential for mystery in this 'listening' process that is important to emphasize. One does not make 'listening' happen through an assertion of one's own will. In fact, efforts to 'listen' this way will likely fail. In other words, one can put oneself in a proper place to 'listen,' but the success and quality of the process is something that issues forth from the place, coming along of its own. On special occasions, and if good fortune permits, the spirits in the world can come in ways that defy normal expectations, and reveal sacred truths (Carbaugh 1999:262).

Much of what Carbaugh says of Blackfeet practice applies also to Aboriginal understandings of listening, place and sacredness. In the Australian context, however, we would need to add that not only do places speak – they themselves also listen (Povinelli 1995:505–506). Moreover, the communication between place and person that happens in silence is not limited to the (metaphorical) 'inner ear' but involves all the senses. Places are particularly sensitive to smell, to the extent that they have the ability to differentiate between humans on the basis of their distinctive sweat (Povinelli 1995:509–514).

The ability to listen is based on the skills of the hunter:

> Snowy's story [about hunting porcupine] tells us that there are many active intelligences out there paying attention. Indeed, within a context of hunting, killing and eating, creature-culture intelligence can be highly charged ... Consider the crocodile: its silent and concealed attentiveness is very far from passive! Often it exercises its intelligence precisely by paying attention without

---

54 The concept was probably first formulated by Bendix (2000). For other relevant literature, see also Purdy (2000) and Back (2007).
55 But see Glenn (2004), Voegelin (2010). It is important to note that listening to silence is not always or necessarily an individualised activity. Le Clézio (1993:77), for example, mentions an Aztec ritual in which 'for eight days, people danced in silence, without songs or music, without moving their feet, merely lifting and lowering their arms'.

drawing attention. Good hunters (nonhumans and humans) do this: they know others are paying attention, they know the ways in which others pay attention, and they find ways to circumvent that attention. The exercise of agency calls for both communication and attention; one is not so much an actor as an inter-actor or participant. Let us think that to participate is to be attentive, to be knowledgeable, to act on knowledge, or to refrain from acting (which is also a form of intelligence). Snowy was explaining all this in relation to porcupines: part of what makes porcupines intelligent and hard to hunt is that they are actively paying attention, actively knowing what is going on in their world, and inter-acting on the basis of that knowledge (Rose 2013:101–103).

If the skills required to listen to animal life have developed as a survival mechanism, they have done so through a cultural process that has linked them closely to the kinds of listening that occur between humans, and between humans and the manifestations of the unknown, such as spirits and dreams.

Beyond hauntology

The lack of a clear boundary between 'listening to Country' and dreaming has two significant implications. It means, first, that dreams have a special relationship with place (cf. Hacking 2001:246, 256), and, second, that attentiveness to the 'voice' of a place opens it to the emergence of images and sounds from the 'dream world'.[56]

It is important to recognise that this 'voice' is necessarily layered, multiple and mediated. If we assume that Wulatji's song had its origin in the place that Mrs Dunlop referred to as the 'sunny hill', and that he received it by listening to the voice of his metaphysical namesake, we are already dealing with at least three layers (the hill, the 'god of Poesy', and the human Wulatji). I say 'at least' because the spirit being was probably the apical ancestor of a lineage of songmen who were Wulatji's forebears and/or teachers, and their voices were no doubt present, to varying degrees, in the voice that Wulatji heard. In the process of reaching its present 'projection' in this chapter, the voice behind the song has accrued further layers, contributed by the likes of Eliza Hamilton Dunlop and Lancelot Threlkeld, as well as by the Indigenous and scholarly ghosts[57] I have invoked to assist with the hatching of my interpretation.

As a way of approaching this kind of literary layering, from 'there' and 'then' to 'here' and 'now', Jacques Derrida has made use of various Gothic tropes, including the neologism 'hauntology':

> Repetition and first time: this is perhaps the question of the event as question of the ghost. What is a ghost? What is the effectivity or the presence of a specter, that is, of what seems to remain as ineffective, virtual, insubstantial as a simulacrum? ... Let us call it a hauntology (Derrida 1994:10).

Jodey Castricano elucidates Derrida's hauntological preoccupations in terms of '*transgenerational haunting*, that manifestation of the voices of one generation in the unconscious of another' (2001:16). '[Thus] ... *to be* is to be *haunted*, if not by the dead, then by ... "their lives' unfinished business [that] is unconsciously handed down to their descendants"' (2001:39).[58]

---

56 This is less a world in any kind of spatial sense than a dimensionless solution that sometimes crystallises into forms (or at least emergent forms) of varying intelligibility. Some of these become coherent enough to be recognisable as (culturally constituted) entities, such as narratives, answers to problems, ghosts, texts, songs, spirits, mathematical formulae, pictures, scenarios, dance steps – occasionally even scholarly articles (Hunt 2014:20), books (Wolf 2014:xiii), and game-changing theories (Hacking 2001).
57 My use of this term is not intended to imply that all of these entities are deceased, but rather that my relationship to most of them is virtual and therefore, if not literally 'disembodied', at least 'decorporealised' (Calise 2015), or perhaps 'heterotopian' (Foucault 1986).
58 The internal quotation is from Nicholas Rand, in his editorial introduction to section V ('Secrets and posterity: the theory of the transgenerational phantom') of Abraham and Torok (1994:167).

While this transgenerational haunting is inevitably a part of everyone's lives, Australia's colonial history means that Indigenous and non-Indigenous people experience its impact differently. My task in this paper, then, has necessarily entailed an attempt to develop a language that does justice to two distinct (but historically mingled) kinds of transgenerational haunting.

There are other potential kinds of bridging language that could be used for this discussion, some of them more scientific and less directly associated with 'popular' and 'folk' notions of the supernatural. But the more technical the language, the more it sacrifices something in terms of both comprehensibility and 'experience-nearness'.[59] As I see it, the task that lies ahead is to develop a language that goes beyond hauntology[60] and still 'has the effect of protecting traditional beliefs and accounts from mere translation into the cultural idiom and tacit beliefs of scholars' (Hufford 1995:34). At this point in time, such a language is still in the process of being (collectively) dreamt.[61]

The main task I have given myself in the present chapter is the more modest one of drawing attention to some possibilities that are rarely considered in the prevalent discourses on Aboriginal cultural renewal. Nonetheless, the argument I have presented has broader implications. The one which I want to highlight, in conclusion, is that the musical dream appears to be one of those 'anomalous' human experiences (Cardeña, Lynn and Krippner 2014) that have a universal distribution 'independent of prior belief or knowledge' (Hufford 1995:14). But this is not the place to develop the point.

A more personal conclusion I draw from Indigenous philosophy (as presented, for example, by people like M. K. Turner and Deborah Rose) is that every human has an obligation to care for Country. As part of my own attempts to exercise this responsibility, I have tried to demonstrate how much a single song can reveal about traditional culture and singing practices in the 'sacrifice zone' of the Hunter Valley region (Cottle 2013[62]), which I call home. Another way of putting this would be to say that I have made an effort to care for the region's ghosts.

In the last decade or so there has been a 'multispecies turn' in a number of fields of scholarship, including the human sciences:

---

59 To give an example invented for the purposes of the present discussion: one might frame the experience of receiving songs from a ghost in terms of 'a comparative ethnometapragmatics of emergent coherence'. (I borrow 'ethnometapragmatics' from Michael Silverstein, 1992:60.) This formulation is not intended as satire (least of all on the work of the generations of scholars who have contributed to it), rather as an illustration of the point that, to the sceptical non-specialist, technical language can sound like (mere) scholarly glossolalia. Victor Turner (1969:141) enunciates the problem succinctly when he says, 'abstractions appear as hostile to live contact'.

60 This is actually implied in the notion of hauntology itself. As Colin Davis (2005:378–379) puts the matter, 'For Derrida, the ghost's secret is not a puzzle to be solved; it is the structural openness or address directed towards the living by the voices of the past or the not yet formulated possibilities of the future. The secret is not unspeakable because it is taboo, but because it cannot not (yet) be articulated in the languages available to us. The ghost pushes at the boundaries of language and thought.' Davis's article is part of a growing body of literature on hauntology – see, for example, Sprinker ed. (1999), Sword (2002), Weinstock ed. (2004), Davies (2007), McCorristine (2010), Trigg (2012), Blanco and Peeren eds (2013). 'Hauntology' and 'the spectral turn' have also gained some traction in Australia, and Indigenous spirit beliefs figure prominently in many of the relevant studies (e.g. Gelder and Jacobs 1998, P. Clarke 2007, Turcotte 2007, Althans 2010, Finegan 2014, R. Clarke 2016, Waldron ed. 2016). In other pertinent works, these beliefs still haunt the background (e.g., Turcotte 2009a, Turcotte 2009b). Music, musicology and sound studies have also experienced the 'spectral turn', to the extent that 'hauntology' is now established as a genre, or 'musical movement' (though the usage of the term in this context is not quite the same as in textual studies – see Sexton 2012:562–566). The literature includes such works as Young (2010), Reynolds (2011), Elferen (2012), Fisher (2013), Reid (2017).

61 There are signs that point towards the development of such a language in fields like comparative philosophy (e.g. Maffie 2013) and what we might call 'comparative ethnohistoriography' (e.g. Le Clézio 1993, Landes 2011).

62 Cottle makes no mention of the impact that living in this 'sacrifice zone' has on its Aboriginal residents (such as the members of the Wonnarua Nation with whom I have been collaborating for a number of years). But see Hooks and Smith (2004) on 'national sacrifice areas and Native Americans'.

Creatures previously appearing on the margins of anthropology – as part of the landscape, as food for humans, as symbols – have been pressed into the foreground in recent ethnographies. Animals, plants, fungi, and microbes . . . have started to appear alongside humans in the realm of *bios*, with legibly biographical and political lives' (Kirksey and Helmreich 2010:3).

While this approach is a welcome corrective to an earlier anthropocentrism, it tends to overlook the invisible inhabitants, the ghosts (if you like) who are an intrinsic part of the ecology. Even in the 'eroded and disowned no-places' that Donna Haraway (2014:247) calls 'unexpected country', we have a responsibility towards them; for they, too, have 'legibly biographical and political lives', as I have tried to show through the modality of ghost-writing for Wulatji.

Acknowledgements

This chapter has benefited from the feedback of a number of colleagues and friends, in particular, Petronella Vaarzon-Morel, Barry McDonald and Greg Bork, who were kind enough to read several different drafts. It originated as two separate papers, presented at the meetings of the Australian Linguistics Society in December of 2014 ('Verbal "arts of memory" in south-eastern Australia') and the Aboriginal Languages Workshop in March of 2015 ('The politics of restoration in the era of the absent original'). Other readers who have provided helpful comments on sundry preliminary versions of the article include Marie Makinson, David Nash, Tony Newman, Bernard Newsome, Deborah Bird Rose, Jill Stowell, John Stowell, Myfany Turpin, and two anonymous (but insightful) peer reviewers. I owe a large debt of gratitude to all of these, as well as to Wonnarua language-keeper Sharon Edgar-Jones for encouraging my work on this song; to Mark Dunn, Amanda Lissarrague, Steve Morelli and John Giacon for helpful correspondence; and to Muurrbay Aboriginal Language and Cultural Co-operative for practical and in-kind support. Thanks also to Donna Snowdon and Colin Hawkshaw for their hospitality at the Gibber Gunyah, and for their help in obtaining the photograph that occurs as Figure 9.1.

The chapter is dedicated to my parents, Eric and Beryl Wafer, whose benevolent presence has sustained me throughout this project.

Abbreviations used in the text

1PL = 1st person plural
3PL = 3rd person plural
3PL.NOM = third person plural nominative
ABL = ablative case
CT = continuous aspect
-DAT = dative case
-DVB = deverbaliser
-ERG = ergative case
-GEN = genitive case
HRLM = the Hunter River–Lake Macquarie language
-KIN = kin term suffix
-MT = metrical element
NSW = New South Wales
-PRS = present tense
-PURP = purposive case
-SEMB = semblative suffix

References follow the Appendices.

Appendix A: The oneiric origin of song in the literature from Australia and beyond   p. 211
Appendix B: E. H. Dunlop's glossaries   p. 214
Appendix C: Sketch genealogy of E. H. Dunlop's descendants and affines   p. 217
Appendix D: Notes on some placenames mentioned in the text   p. 219
References   p. 227

Appendix A: The oneiric origin of song in the literature from Australia and beyond

The musical dream in Indigenous Australia

Table 9.2 (below) includes all the references I have been able to find that allude, with a reasonable degree of explicitness, to the oneiric origin of song in Indigenous Australia. The requirement for a 'reasonable degree of explicitness' means that the earliest item on the list is E. J. Eyre's account of 1845 (Eyre 1845, vol. 2:367):

> He then told me, that occasionally individuals had been up to the clouds, and had come back, but that such instances were very rare; his own mother, he said, had been one of the favoured few. Some one from above had let down a rope, and hauled her up by it; she remained one night, and on her return, gave a description of what she had seen in a chaunt, or song, which he sung for me...

It is possible that some earlier sources may be relevant, but they have been omitted as requiring too much interpretation to be regarded as 'reasonably explicit'. To give just one example: Judge-advocate Collins, writing of the early days of the Colony of New South Wales (Collins 1798, vol. 1:595–596), reported as follows:

> We were told by him and others, ... that by sleeping at the grave of a deceased person, they would, from what happened to them there, be freed from all future apprehensions respecting apparitions; for during that awful sleep the spirit of the deceased would visit them, seize them by the throat, and, opening them, take out their bowels, which they would replace and close up the wound. We understood that very few chose to encounter the darkness of the night, the solemnity of the grave, and the visitation of the spirit of the deceased; but that such as were so hardy became immediately car-rah-dys,[63] and that all those who exercised that profession had gone through this ceremony.

Collins does not refer to this rite as a means for acquiring songs, but it is clear from later accounts (e.g. Lommel 1952:55–56, quoted in the main body of this chapter) that the equivalents of the 'car-rah-dys' in other parts of Australia undertook similar practices for the sake of receiving 'corroborees' from the ghosts of the dead. There are relevant data from outside Australia as well. Chadwick (1946:61–62), for example, has assembled records from mediaeval Scandinavia of analogous procedures for acquiring the ability to compose skaldic panegyric verse. (Cf. also Laufer 1931:211.)

The musical dream beyond Australia

Much of the literature cited in Table 9.3 – a listing of references to the musical dream outside of Australia – treats the subject only in passing, though there are a few cases (such as Roseman

---

[63] Elkin (1977 [1945]:79–80), who cites this episode, uses the more recent (and now more common) spelling *karadji* and defines the term as 'clever man'. See also Troy (1994:38) and Clarke (2007:155 n.11).

1993, Graham 1995) where the topic constitutes a major ethnographic focus. There may be a degree of overlap with the research on music and trance (Rouget 1985, Becker 1994) in some places, particularly in Africa (see for example Friedson 1996:27, Olivier 1998:364), and also in the literature on 'musical mediumship' (e.g. Parrott 1978, Willin 1999:72–90), but as a general rule these two phenomena (trance and the musical dream) appear to be fairly clearly distinguishable.[64]

Table 9.2: Reports of the musical dream in Indigenous Australia, by date

1845	Eyre, vol. 2:367	1986	Myers: 51
1848a	Dunlop	1987	Berndt: 171–172
1876	Smyth, vol. 1:473	1987	Clunies Ross: 5
1880	Kühn: 287	1987	Wild: 105–112
1884	Howitt: 195	1989	Keogh: 3
1884	Palmer: 291	1989	Lommel: 33–34
1885	Howitt: 310, n. 1	1989	Payne: 46–47
1887a	Howitt: 329	1992	Gummow: 179–185
1887b	Howitt: 39, 44–45	1992	Marett: 195
1896	Gillen: 175	1995	Evans: 23
1897	Roth: 117	1995	Gummow: 123
1899	Spencer and Gillen: 278, 294	1995	Keogh: 39
1902	Roth: 20	1995	Marett and Page: 27–28
1904	Howitt: 436–437	2000	Bradley and Mackinlay: 13
1904	Spencer and Gillen: 451	2000	Dussart: chapter 4 (139–176)
1905	Parker: 132	2000	Marett
1905	Thomas: 51	n.d. (2001?)	Ellis
1924	Horne and Aiston: 137	2001	Magowan: 275–276
1927	Spencer and Gillen: 563	n.d. (2001?)	Marett
1933	Elkin: 267–268	2001	Redmond: 121, 126
1933	Róheim: 221, 227, 259 and *passim*	2003	Keen: 128–129
1935	McConnel: 66	2003	Mackinlay and Bradley: 2, 5–7, 10–13, 21(n.2)
1935	Tennant-Kelly: 469	2003	Marett and Barwick: 145, 147, 149
1935	Tindale: 223	2003	Tonkinson: 94
1939	Kaberry: 257	2003	Treloyn: 209–211
c. 1940	Bates [published 1985:339–340]	2005	Barwick: 5, 12
1945	Reay: 323	2005	Glaskin: 299, 305
1945	Róheim: 6, 98	2005	Marett: chapter 2 (39–54)
1947	Berndt: 336	2005	Poirier: 178, 207
1949	Reay: 96 (cf. 92, 103,105)	2006	Garde: 86
1951	Berndt and Berndt: 211–214	2006	Treloyn: 153–154
1952	Lommel: 53–56	2007	Barwick, Birch and Evans: 9, 11

---

64 See also Bourguignon (1973:12–15) for a discussion of the distinction between dreams and (types of) trance. There are occasional references to trance-like phenomena in the Australianist literature (e.g. Threlkeld in Gunson 1974:63; Elkin 1977 [1945]:24–26, 184 and *passim*; Petri 2014 [1952]:173 and *passim*; Petri 1965; Lommel 1952:55; Strehlow 1971:557–558; Payne 1993; Glaskin 2008), but this is a potential field of research that remains largely undeveloped.

1952	Róheim: 106–107	2007	Magowan: 289–290
1953–1957	Elkin and Jones: 12, 63, 77, 136 (single volume edition)	2007	San Roque: 153
1953	Petri [trans. 2014:101–104 and *passim*]	2007	Stubington: 102
1954	Elkin [3rd edn]: 259	2007	Turpin: 103
1961	Pentony: 146	2008	Glaskin: 61
1963	Stanner: 259, n. 9	2008	McCaul: 140
1965	Hiatt: 58	2010	Apted
1965	Petri: 285	2010	Glaskin
1969	Schneider and Sharp: 65	2010	Reid: 320, 325
1970	Berndt and Berndt: 561	2010	Turner: 67
1970	Tonkinson: 284–285	2011a	Glaskin: 87–88
1971	Strehlow: 244, 640	2011b	Glaskin: 44–48
1973	Munn: 145–149	2013	Campbell: 242
1978	Payne: 9	2013	Marett, Barwick & Ford: 25
1979	Moyle, R.: 58–59	2013	Tonkinson: 134–136 and *passim*
1980	Moyle, A.: 717	2014	Brown: 173, 180
1984	Ellis: 151–152	2014	Treloyn: 214, 215, 232
1984	Payne: 269	2015	Glaskin: 670–671
1986	Moyle, R.: 52–63, 132–134	2016	Glowczewski: 201–206.

Table 9.3: Reports of the musical dream outside Australia, by region, then date

NORTH AMERICA			
1895	Boas: 645, 649	1953	Densmore
1900	Teit: 320	1958	Ewers: 163, 166
1902	Kroeber: 279–280	1964	Smithson and Euler: 6 and *passim*
1904	Dixon: 23	1966	Hallowell: 283
1907–1930	Curtis, vol. 7:81–83, 129, 133; v. 8: 184; v. 10:83–84; v. 13:84–85; v. 14:96	1967	Merriam: 3–24
1910	Densmore: 126–165	1971	Ridington 1971
1912	Wissler: 100, 263 and *passim*	1979	Hultkrantz: 77
1918	Densmore: 157–204	1980	Hinton: 276, 278–279
1922	Benedict: 1, 17	1981	Spaulding: 335
1922	Lowie: 321, 323 and *passim*	1983	Nelson: 172
1925	Kroeber: 670, 754	1985	Flannery and Chambers
1926	Densmore: 77–78	1989	Nettl: 56–57 and *passim*
1926	Gifford: 59	1991	Beaudry
1930	Teit: 384	1992	Beaudry
1931	Forde: 127–128	1992	Keeling: 8–9
1932	Densmore: 77–98	1992	McClintock: 146, 430
1934	Park: 101–103	1994	Bahr
1935	Demetracopoulou: 483–488	1994	Irwin: 143–150
1935	Lincoln: part 3, 311 and *passim*	1999	Tedlock: 87, 96
1936	Herzog: 318, 320		

EUROPE			
731	Bede: book 4, ch. 24; tr. 2008: 215–218	1999	Willin: 72–136
1929	Pound	2009	Davis: 49–50
1946	Chadwick: 61–62	2009	Meier: 74
1978	Parrott	2015	Faery Folklorist
1992–93	Uí Ógáin: 200, 202 and *passim*		
LATIN AMERICA			
1976	O'Brien: 40–41	1998	Orobitg: 47(n.16), 128 and *passim*
1978	Grebe: 91	1999	Augé: 33–35
1990	Ereira: 128	2007	Kracke: 112
1992	Perrin	2009	Beyer: chapter 6 (63–80)
1994	Graham	2010	Labate & Pacheco: 68
1995	Graham: 114–128	2013	Piedade: 317, 319
1996	Olsen: 40, 205–206, 242, 251	2014	Cemin: 46
AFRICA			
1967	England: 61	1996	Friedson: 27, 99, 114, 147
1978	Fischer: 16, 18	1998	Kisliuk: 177
1979–1980	Garfias: 213–214 and *passim*	1998	Olivier: 364–366
1982	Yonker: 246–247	2005	Waugh: 163
1992	Charsley: 161	2011	Grauer: 99
ASIA			
1959	Stein: 332–334	1996	Roseman: 234, 237, 240
1965	Emeneau	1998	Roseman
1979	Ellingson: 83–84, 335–338, 767	2000	Franke: 285–287
1986	Roseman: 67–70	2000	Roseman
1988	Wagner: 15	2003	Green: 290, 300, 305
1993	Roseman: 80, 82 and *passim*	2005	van Lint: 346, 374, 376
1995	Basilov: 238 and *passim*	2008	Sumegi: 29–30, 130 note 81
1996	Baptandier (para. 34 of online edition)		
OCEANIA			
1917	Landtman: 196	1979	Stephen: 8–9
1927	Ivens: 14		

Appendix B: E. H. Dunlop's glossaries

There are two versions of Eliza Dunlop's English adaptation of Wulatji's poem. The one published under the title of 'Native poetry' (*Sydney Morning Herald* 11 October 1848, p. 3) has been reproduced above in section 4. This was probably the first of the two, and it was preceded by a transcription of the original song-text, in the Hunter River–Lake Macquarie language. The other version (Dunlop 1848b, transcribed below) appeared in Isaac Nathan's miscellany *The southern Euphrosyne* (p. 94) and is probably later, since this publication is variously dated to 1848 (most sources) and 1849 (e.g. in AustLit, see References, below). The transcription of Wulatji's original was omitted in this case.

PIALLA WOLLOMBI.*[65]
The poetry by Mrs. E. H. Dunlop – inscribed to William Hamilton Maxwell,[66] Esq., author of 'Stories of Waterloo,' &c

Our home is the *gibber-gunyah*,
    Where hill joins hill on high:
There *berramboo* and *boomerang*
    Like sleeping serpents lie!
There our *lubras* can look on the *battwan* clear,
That the track of a white man hath never come near.

Ours are the *wascera* gliding –
    Deep in the shady creek;
Where bright *gerool* and *cooperra* tell
    How sure the prey we seek:
While the rushing of wings, as the *wangas* pass,
Sweeps the *wallaby's* print from the glist'ning grass.

Ours is the *coole-man* flowing,
    With fragrant *contiyon* stored:
For fleet the foot, and keen the eye,
    That seeks the *conindin's* hoard!
But dearer the glance, and the footsteps to me,
Of the *lubra* who laughs by the *kurrijong* tree!

The two versions share the same overall structure and content, but in the second one (as transcribed here) some lines have been transposed, some phrases and sentences modified, and a number of vocabulary items changed. These include both English words and lexemes from a number of different Aboriginal languages. Dunlop provided glossaries for both versions of her adaptation, and Table 9.4 (below) sets out the contents of these glossaries in a format that enables them to be compared with each other and with other (mostly modern) linguistic sources.

The comparison permits a number of observations about Dunlop's use of words from Aboriginal languages. In the first version of her adaptation, most of these words come from the Hunter River–Lake Macquarie language (HRLM); — that is, the language in which Wulatji's poem was composed. Nonetheless, a number of them (*bato, kanin, karrakun, nukkung*) do not in fact occur in Wulatji's original song-text. In the second version, almost all of these words have been omitted and replaced with words that have been borrowed into English from other Aboriginal languages (the majority from the Sydney language). The first version, with its mixture of HRLM, Darkinyung, Gamilaraay and NSW Pidgin probably reflects the linguistic situation at Wollombi better than the second one, where my conjecture is that Dunlop has preferred common English loans from Aboriginal languages because they would be more familiar to her audience.

There are three words for which I am unable to suggest a source form: *amygest, contiyon* and *wascera* (spelt 'wascerra' in the glossary). The form '*contiyon*' is consistent with the phonology of Aboriginal languages of the region, but the other two forms (*amygest, wascera*) are not. (The /s/ phoneme is rare in Aboriginal languages generally, and does not occur in those of New South Wales.) This does not necessarily mean that these words have not been borrowed from

---

[65] The asterisk refers to a footnote in the original source, which reads '* The poetry or language of Wollombi'. This is presumably intended as a translation of the poem's title, 'Pialla Wollombi'. See 'Pialla' in Table 9.4.
[66] The Scots–Irish novelist William Hamilton Maxwell (1792–1850) was Eliza Dunlop's cousin, and the presumed namesake of Eliza and David Dunlop's third child (and second daughter) Wilhelmina Hamilton Maxwell Dunlop. W. H. Maxwell's novel *Stories of Waterloo* was published in 1829.

Aboriginal languages, since they could be phonologically hybrid forms influenced by English. But their etymology remains a mystery.

In Table 9.4, the first column includes the items in the glossary that Dunlop appended to 'Native poetry', listed alphabetically. Where the same or a similar term occurs in the glossary of 'Pialla Wollombi', it is listed in column 2, next to the relevant item in column 1. The balance of the items in this second glossary then follow in column 2, in alphabetical order. The third column lists the language from which each vocabulary item is presumed to come, and the fourth column provides references to the sources on which this presumption is based. Abbreviations used for these sources are as follows:

A: Ash, Giacon and Lissarrague 2003
D: Dixon, Ramson and Thomas 1990
J: Jones 2008
L: Lissarrague 2006
M: Milson c. 1840+
T: Troy 1994

Table 9.4: Vocabulary items from E. H. Dunlop's glossaries

'NATIVE POETRY'	'PIALLA WOLLOMBI'	LANGUAGE	REFERENCES
Amygest – White-fellow.			
Bato – Water.	**Battwan**[67]: spring water	HRLM[68], Darkinyung	paTu: water (fresh) (L 132); badhu: water (J 148)
[Turruma and] **Berrambo** – War arms.	**Berramboo**: the waddy or war-club, similar to those of New Zealand	Gamilaraay?	birrambo: waddy (M 9)
Gheerool – Mullet.	**Gerrool**[, and Cooperra]: the mullet and eel.	Darkinyung	djirul: mullet (J 156)
Gibber-gunya – Cave in the rock.	**Gibber-gunyah**: cave-of-the-rock	Sydney, English loan	giba: stone or rock (T 50); gunya: house or hut (T 44); gibber-gunyah: a shallow cave used as a dwelling or for shelter (D 200; see also 192–193 and 199–201)
Kanin – Eel.		HRLM	kaNiyn: eel (L 114)
Karrakun – The oak-tree.		HRLM	karakan: swamp oak (L 114)
Kirrika – Honey.		HRLM	kiR[i]ka: honey, white (L 118)
Makoro – Fish.		HRLM, Darkinyung	makurr: fish (L 121); magur: fish (J 164)
Nukkung – Wild bee.		HRLM	Nakang: small, stingless native bee (L 125)
Turruma [and Berrambo] – War arms.		HRLM	TaRama: war boomerang (L 137)
Wanga – A species of pigeon.	**Wanga-wanga**: a wild pigeon of the largest kind, of most exquisite plumage.	Darkinyung, Sydney, English loan	wangawanga: wonga wonga (pigeon) (J 172); wungawunga: wonga pigeon (T 56); wonga-wonga: the ground-feeding grey and white pigeon (D 95)

---

67 I reconstruct this word as HRLM /patu-wan/ and conjecture that -wan is an augmentative suffix. Compare Yuwaalaraay and Yuwaalay*aay -wan*, 'prominent (big)' (Ash, Giacon and Lissarrague 2003:138).
68 The Hunter River–Lake Macquarie language.

'NATIVE POETRY'	'PIALLA WOLLOMBI'	LANGUAGE	REFERENCES
	Boomerang: striking-weapon – from *boomallee*, to strike.	Sydney, English loan	bumarang: boomerang for fighting (T 43); boomerang: a crescent-shaped wooden implement used as a missile or club (D 175–177)
	Conindin: the small native honey-bee easily tracked through the air by a white down adhering to it, which is strewed by the natives on the sweet yams, on which the insect loves to feed.	Gamilaraay	guni: native bee (A 96)
	Contiyon: honey		
	The **coole-man** is a bowl, hollowed with great ingenuity by the aborigines, from an excrescent substance of a semi-circular form, found growing on the iron-bark, apple, and other gumiferous trees; the inner wood is rather more porous and fibrous than that on which it grows; but the bark (which is the cooleman) is hard and smooth, one or two inches in thickness, and containing from a pint to two gallons. On a first examination I was inclined to the opinion of an author (Professor Rennie,) on 'Insect Architecture,' who believes that 'such growths may be caused by the juncture of the *Iynips*,' but admitting, with that authority, that these excrescences are 'pseudo-galls,' I rather infer them to be like wens on animals, 'produced by too much nourishment.'	Gamilaraay English loan	guliman: coolamon, dish (A 94); coolamon: a basin-like vessel of wood or bark (D 184)
	[Gerrool, and] **Cooperra**: the mullet and eel.	Darkinyung	gubira: eel (J 160)
	Kurrijong: a tree, from the inner rind of which nets are woven.	Sydney English loan	garradjun: fishing line – lines were made from bark of trees such as the kurrajong (T 44); kurrajong: a name given to any of several plants yielding a useful fibre (D 119)
	Lubra: female or daughter – young females of a tribe.	English loan (origin uncertain, possibly Tasmanian)	lubra: a derogatory term for an Aboriginal woman (D 170)
	Pialla: poetry or language	Sydney	baya: to speak (T 73)
	Wallaby: a small species of the kangaroo, which is also called *barwan*, and *billoo* – they are yet found in thin herds in the mountanous [sic] ranges of the Wollombi.	Sydney English loan	wulaba: rock wallaby (T 50); wallaby: any of many smaller marsupials of the family Macropodidae (D 80–81)
	Wascerra: fish		

Appendix C: Sketch genealogy of E. H. Dunlop's descendants and affines

The genealogical chart that appears below as Table 9.5 is intended mainly to provide an overview of the kin relationships between the various members of Eliza Hamilton Dunlop's family mentioned in the text. It incorporates as well all of her children (from both marriages)[69], but only a selection of their descendants.

---

69 Gunson (1966) mentions another child (a son) from Dunlop's first marriage, but no further information about this individual is currently available.

Table 9.5: Sketch genealogy of E. H. Dunlop's descendants and affines

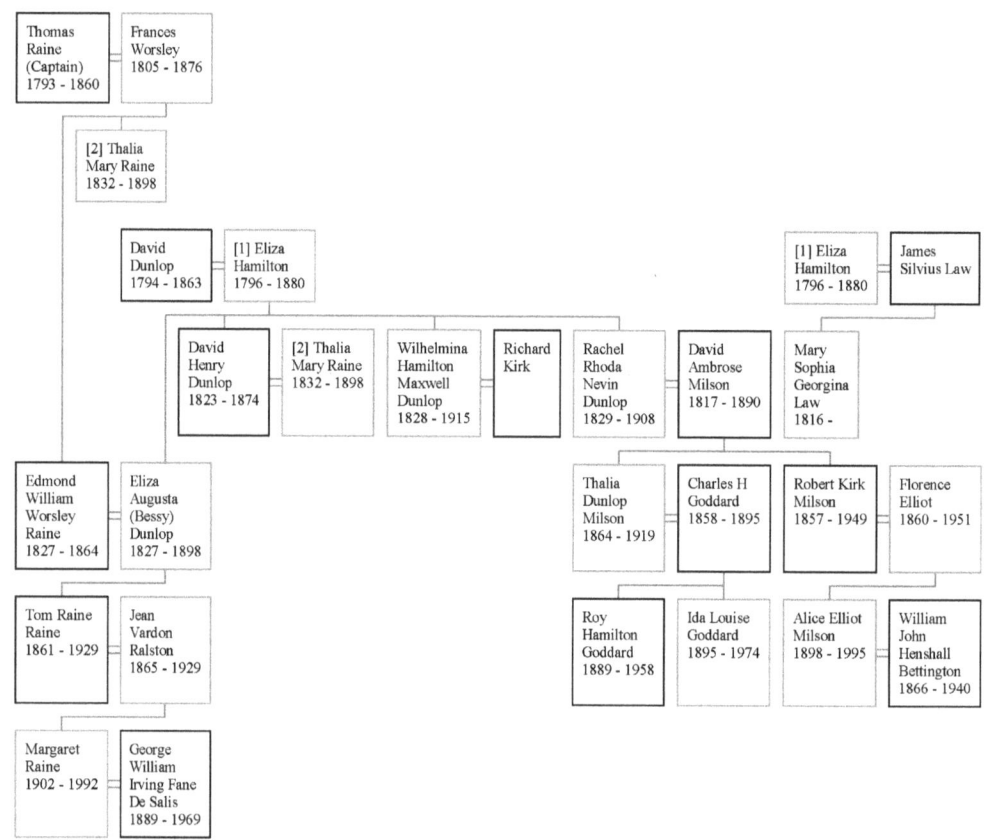

Dunlop's name appears twice on the third row of the chart, distinguished by the number [1]. The first occurrence, on the left of the chart, relates to her second marriage (to David Dunlop) and her descendants from that marriage. The second occurrence, on the right, refers to her first marriage (to the Irish astronomer James Silvius Law).

The other individual whose name appears twice is Thalia Mary Raine, distinguished by the number [2]. In the second row she appears as the daughter of Captain Thomas Raine and Frances Worsley, and in the fourth row as the wife of David Henry Dunlop. This layout has been necessitated by the fact that two of the Raine children married two of the Dunlop children. (Thalia's brother Edmond William Worsley Raine married David Henry's sister, Eliza Augusta Dunlop.) It is for the same reason that Eliza Augusta's name precedes (that is, occurs to the left of) David Henry's, even though he was the eldest child. (The other Dunlop children occur in the correct birth order.)

The two Dunlop descendants who have published works relevant to the present chapter are Roy Hamilton Goddard (sixth row, middle of page) and Margaret De Salis (*née* Raine) (seventh row, far left). Goddard's work on Aboriginal poetry (1934) and rock carvings of the Wollombi district (1937a, 1937b) are included in the list of references below, and he was presumably the person who donated the Milson manuscript (Milson c. 1840+) to the Mitchell Library. The attribution at the head of the manuscript reads, 'by Mrs Milson grandmother of the donor'. (Rachel Rhoda Nevin Milson, *née* Dunlop, was Eliza Dunlop's daughter and Goddard's grandmother.) But in his article on Aboriginal poetry, Goddard credits authorship of the manuscript to 'Mrs. E. H. Dunlop and her daughter (Mrs. Rachel Milson) and granddaughter (Mrs. J. H. Bettington)' (1934:244). The last named of these is presumably Goddard's cousin, Alice Elliot Bettington (*née* Milson), who was in fact the the *great* granddaughter of Eliza Dunlop, but the granddaughter of Rachel Milson.

Margaret De Salis published a monograph on the lives of David and Eliza Dunlop in 1967 and a newspaper article summarising this book in 1972. The black and white portrait of Eliza Hamilton Dunlop facing the book's title page is 'by courtesy of Miss I. L. Goddard'; that is, Roy Goddard's sister, Ida Louise (sixth row). (A colour print of this portrait currently hangs in the Wollombi Museum.) Margaret De Salis also wrote a book about her other pioneering ancestor, Captain Thomas Raine, which was published in 1969.

David and Eliza Dunlop's second daughter, Wilhelmina Hamilton Maxwell Dunlop, was presumably named after Eliza's cousin, the Scots-Irish novelist William Hamilton Maxwell (1792–1850).

Appendix D: Notes on some placenames mentioned in the text

Wollombi Brook

I have assumed that the Indigenous name for Wollombi Brook is 'Mala', based on De Salis's 1972 reference to a poem by Eliza Hamilton Dunlop with the title 'The Mulla (or Wollombi) Creek'. I have been unable to trace this poem, but Dunlop uses 'Mulla' in the same sense in a poem called 'Erin Dheelish', published in 1865. I conjecture that the name may be related to the Gamilaraay word *mala*, which means 'fork', in the sense of 'something that branches into two' (Ash, Giacon and Lissarrague 2003:106). This would be appropriate for the location of Wollombi, which sits in the fork created by the junction of Wollombi Brook and Congewai Creek (also known as the North Arm of Wollombi Brook). Indeed, Needham (1981:8) gives the meaning of 'Wollombi' itself as 'place where the waters meet'. (I have been unable to confirm this gloss.)

According to the map in Gordon, Crousen and Jones (1993:44), Wollombi lies at the place where three distinct groups (Darginung, Wonarua and Awabagal) converge. In other parts of Aboriginal Australia, the merging of watercourses has symbolic implications that could possibly be relevant in the present case. Fiona Magowan writes that, among Yolngu of eastern Arnhem Land, 'the confluence of two rivers may unite different clans of the same moiety through the meanings of the song texts' (1994:141), because 'waters ... represent the spiritual essence of each clan's identity' (1994:140).

The Dunlops' residence (built with convict labour in 1841 and still standing) was called 'Mulla Villa'. De Salis (1967:98) speculates that this name owes its origin to the Irish toponym 'Mullavilly'. If this is the case, then the name is likely to have been adapted to 'Mulla Villa' precisely because of the duplication of referents.

The mountains and the heights

I suggest that the *palkirr* ('mountain') and *pulwarra* ('high place') mentioned in Wulatji's song are probably specific peaks or ranges, and that their identity would have been readily apparent to his Aboriginal audience. The fact that they are not specified by name is probably a feature shared with song traditions in many other parts of Australia.[70] Because Mount Yango is both

---

[70] For example, in Arrernte song traditions, according to T. G. H. Strehlow (1971:159), 'very few of the placenames mentioned in the myths have found their way into the songs ... the "secret name" of a place is very frequently a couplet which describes the scenic setting of the sacred site without actually naming it.'

the highest[71] and also the most mythologically significant summit in the vicinity of Wollombi, I speculate that it is likely to be one of the elevations in question.

R. H. Goddard (1937b:4) mentions the relevant myth in his account of a spirit called 'Wa-boo-ee', who 'was supposed to have sprung from Devil's Rock[72] and landed on Yango, in the West (Yango, or Yengo dilla, meaning "caught by the foot" or "stepping over"). Wa-boo-ee was of great stature – he thought nothing of stepping up to the sky for a change of residence and of throwing a few rocks, in the shape of mountains, down to the earth as stepping stones.'

'Wabbooee' receives the longest entry in the section of the Milson manuscript (1840+: image 9) devoted to 'Gods and goddesses', where he is described as 'The greatest spirit of all; he commands the seasons and weather, his residence is in the North'. He is the god of the daylight, and his wife, Malamala, is goddess of the south and the night. Both are also apocalyptic deities. When he dies,[73] 'the world will be destroyed by huge rocks which fall from Heaven.' When Malamala dies, 'darkness rests upon the earth until her husband removes it'. (See as well Ash, Giacon and Lissarrague 2003:135, under *wabuwi*.)

There is also a more recent account of Wabuwi, as told by Uncle Paul Spearim[74], in 'the story of Buwadjarr and the six Wandabaa spirits' (2014). 'Buwadjarr' means 'father' in Gamilaraay (and related languages), and is also the term used by women and the uninitiated to refer to the 'All Father', Baayami.[75] According to Spearim, Wabuwi is a 'weather spirit' who, along with five other spirits, was punished by Buwadjarr for his disobedience. In this account, Buwadjarr shuts Wabuwi away in a cave near Yetman (on the Macintyre River, in far northern NSW). When the initiation season arrives and the weather changes, Wabuwi escapes from the cave, leaves behind a single footprint and 'tries to snatch away the girls and young boys'.

The story points up an interesting contradiction in the data. Some writers[76] have identified the presiding spirit of Mount Yango as Baayami (variously spelt[77]) rather than Wabuwi. But in the Spearim narrative, these two personae are represented as enemies. So what are we to make of their relationship to the mountain and to each other?

Frederic Slater (1937:13) avers that Wabuwi is 'another name' for Dharramalin,[78] who is variously regarded as 'a sort of half brother or near relative' of Baayami (Mathews 1904:343), his 'agent' (Ridley 1875:137) or his son (Howitt 1904:585). In one report (Howitt 1904:407) there

---

71 'Between the Hawkesbury River and the Hunter Range, elevation is consistently between 250–350m AHD. Mt Yengo, in the north-west of the region, has the highest elevation at 386m. Closer to the coast, the elevation is between 100–150m AHD' (McDonald 2008:11).
72 Burragurra. (See Enright 1898:182; Needham 1981:8; Macqueen 2004:125.)
73 The Milson manuscript has 'whenever he died', which suggests that this happens periodically.
74 *http://kindigenous.weebly.com/about-paul-spearim.html* [accessed 11 August 2017].
75 Ash et al. (2003:52). I borrow the term 'All Father' from K. Langloh Parker (1905:4–10). The collective name 'Wandabaa' is no doubt derived from *wanda*, 'ghost; white man' and the suffix *baa*, 'time of; place of' (Ash et al. 2003:138, 25). Apart from Wabuwi, two of the other Wandabaa spirits (Yarayawu and Bagii) are mentioned in the Milson manuscript (1840+: image 9), as 'Yarree yarwoo' and 'Buggee'. 'Nguruma' is defined in Ash et al. (2003:127) as 'spirit-haunted stone'. I have not been able to find an earlier source for 'Mardu'.
76 For example, Slater (1937:12–13), Needham (1981:11), McDonald (1993:85), Jones (2009:4–5).
77 In the standard orthography of both Gamilaraay and Wiradjuri, it is 'Baayami' (Ash et al. 2003:27; Grant and Rudder 2010:290). The most common earlier spellings are 'Baiamai', 'Baiame', 'Baiami' and 'Byamee'. The word occurs only once in the early HRLM sources, in Fawcett (1898:181), who spells the name as 'By-a-me' (in Wonnarua).
78 There is good support for this in Gamilaraay (and related languages), where 'Dharramalan' is analysed as *dharra*, 'thigh, leg' plus *maal*, 'one' (Ash et al. 2003:57). The fact that this entity is represented iconographically as having only one leg (cf. Slater 1937:13 and Plate III) confirms his identification with Wabuwi, who is said to leave behind only a single footprint (Spearim 2014). In Wiradjuri the name is spelt 'Dharramalin' (Grant and Rudder 2010:344), and this supports an alternative etymology based on the verb *dharra*, 'to eat, swallow'. I have adopted the Wiradjuri spelling, on the grounds that (as I conjecture below) the name is more likely to have originated in Wiradjuri country. Other spellings of the name include Turramūlan (Ridley 1875:136–137), Dhuramoolan (Mathews 1896:297–298), Daramulun (Howitt 1904:555), Dharramulan (Matthews 1904:343–344) and Turramullan (Slater 1937).

is a plurality of Dharramalins, who are collectively regarded as Baayami's sons. This is not the place for a systematic analysis of the pertinent sources,[79] but I summarise below the points that relate to the association of these figures with Mount Yango.

All of the earliest references to Baayami come from Wiradjuri country. These include Henderson (1832:147–148), Hale (1846:110) and Günther (1892:70, 94).[80] Moreover, in Wiradjuri there is a plausible etymology for Baayami's name. According to Günther (1892:94), Baayami has 'emu's feet', which suggests an etymological link to *baayi* ('a footprint') and *baaya* ('tread') (Grant and Rudder 2010:290).[81] I note also that, among Wiradjuri, the Emu is not just under Baayami's direct protection (Berndt 1947:353); in the symbolism of the Bora ritual he is also Bayaami's intended prey (Mathews 1896:300). This perhaps provides some evidence for the purported link of Baayami with Mount Yango, since there is an abundance of emu footprints carved into the rock platforms in the surrounding area, as detailed by Goddard (1937:3–5; see also Slater 1937:11).

This association with the Emu makes Baayami potentially a relative of the 'so-called "high god"' of the Western Aranda (Róheim 1974:111; cf. Róheim 1934:74–75), the great emu-footed one, first mentioned in print (as 'iliinka') by Carl Strehlow (1907–1920, 1:1–2). T. G. H. Strehlow (1971:614–620) has devoted a longish discussion to this being, whose name he spells as 'Iḻiŋka'. Although the accounts by Róheim and the two Strehlows differ in some details, they all grant that Emu-foot's domain was the sky (see also Morton 1989:283).

Astronomer Ray Norris (with his collaborator Cilla Norris) observes that 'this Emu in the Sky[82] features in the songs and stories of Aboriginal groups right across Australia, from Western Australia to New South Wales,[83] although it's not universal, and detailed interpretations differ' (Norris and Norris 2009:5). Among the Warlpiri neighbours of the Arrernte, the Emu in the Sky is known as 'Wanya-parnta',[84] the Flying Emu (Corn and Patrick 2014:156). The Gamilaraay associate the emu with earthly waterholes but also with a celestial waterhole, located in the Coalsack (Fuller, Norris and Trudgett 2014:3).

It is interesting to note, in connection with the discussion of incubation in the main body of this article, and with K. Langloh Parker's reference (1905:132) to the 'hatching out' of songs among the Yuwaalayaay, that 'in real life it is the male emu which patiently sits on the eggs and hatches them' (Strehlow 1971:619). In the Bora ceremony of south-eastern Australia, this unusual avian practice provides the basis for the Emu's important symbolic role: 'male emus care for emu chicks, and elder men take young men through the knowledge ceremony that is

---

79 The literature is fairly substantial because of the 'Australian High God controversy' that took place in the late nineteenth and early twentieth centuries. (For a succinct overview, see Cox 2014:21–26).

80 Günther's work on the Wiradjuri language dates back to 1838, but was not published until late in the century.

81 See also Grant and Rudder (2010:452), under '*nguruwiny dyinanggarang*'. Ridley (1875:17) cites C. C. Greenway as the source of an etymology that derives 'Baia-me' from a putative verb 'baia', translated as 'to make or build'. But Parker (1905:4–5) notes that this verb 'is not known to me in Euahlayi [Yuwaalayaay]. Wirádjuri has *bai*, a footmark, and Byamee left footmarks on the rocks'. Admittedly, she adds that this 'is probably a chance coincidence.' (The evidence at Mount Yango could indicate otherwise.) Mathews (1904:340) suggests a derivation of Baayami's name from the word *bai*, which he translates as 'the semen of men and animals'. The Wiradjuri dictionary (Grant and Rudder 2010:303) only lists *bayiin*, glossed as 'semen of animals'.

82 An Indigenous constellation that stretches along the southern Milky Way, from the Southern Cross and the Coalsack (the head) through Scorpius to Scutum (the feet). See also Norris 2007–2011, 'Australian Aboriginal astronomy', online at *http://www.emudreaming.com/index.html* [accessed 29 August 2017].

83 According to Doug Williams, the Githabul people of northern NSW associate the site of Julian Rocks with '*wayo jalgumboonj*, the fairy-emu' (quoted in McClean 2013:88). The first part of this expression is probably related to the verb *wayah*, 'to fly' (Sharpe 1995:97) and the second to the placename Jalgambuyn (Mount Lindesay; Sharpe 1995:187).

84 *Wanya*, 'emu down'; *-parnta*, associative suffix: 'having, possessing'. (See Swartz 2012, Interactive Warlpiri-English dictionary, at *http://ausil.org/Dictionary/Warlpiri/aboutwarlpiri.htm* [accessed 10 May 2017].)

the Bora' (Fuller, Norris and Trudgett 2014:3).[85] There is good evidence for Baayami's association with initiation ceremonies (e.g. Ridley 1873:269, Mathews 1896: 297–298, Parker 1905:5–7), and also for his function as a giver of song (e.g. Thomas 1905:51, Berndt 1947:336).

Dharramalin enters the written record a little later than Baayami. The earliest source I have been able to trace is Ridley (1861:445): 'They also believe in the existence of many demons, of whom Turramullun is the chief. They say that Turramullun is the author of disease and of medical skill, of mischief and of wisdom also; that he appears in the form of a serpent at their great assemblies.' This summary is based on stories from people of the Namoi and Barwon Rivers (speakers of Gamilaraay and the related languages Yuwaalaraay and Yuwaalayaay).

Late in the nineteenth century, Dharramalin's name begins to appear in the Wiradjuri literature too (for example in Mathews 1896:297–298). The following definition is provided by the Wiradjuri dictionary: 'guardian spirit responsible for metaphorically swallowing young men by taking them "inside" the burbang [initiation ceremony] and then regurgitating them trained and transformed as men' (Grant and Rudder 2010:344).

Nonetheless, the earliest Wiradjuri allusion to Dharramalin may come from the same source as that in which Baayami appears for the first time, namely, John Henderson's account (1832:147) of his visit to the Wellington Valley mission in 1830. The passage is worth quoting at length:

> Piame is the name of the god of the black people of New South Wales; he is the father of their race, and formerly appears to have sojourned amongst them. Mudjegong, on the other hand, is an evil spirit, who after having derived his existence from Piame, declared war upon him, and now endeavours with all his power to frustrate his undertakings. The offspring of Piame were numerous; but the whole, with the exception of two, were destroyed by Mudjegong, who converted them into different wild animals. A number of the devices on the trees are intended to represent these transmigrations; such as the snakes, the oppossum, the emu, the kangaroo, the cockchaffer, &c.; while others were stated to indicate the forked lightning, warlike instruments, and falling meteors. The evil spirit seemed to be described under the form of the eagle-hawk; an imitation of his erie forms a conspicuous object at the upper extremity of the grove.

There are two entries for *mudyi-gang* in the Wiradjuri dictionary: one of them glosses the term first as 'elders who train and accompany novices preparatory to initiation' and then as 'an old man'. The other defines the word as 'bull-roarer' (Grant and Rudder 2010:414).

The interpretations given for the name 'Dharramalin' in early sources also link the initiator (who is actually and symbolically an 'old man') with the bull-roarer (Howitt 1904:541, 493; Mathews 1896:298). Moreover, according to Howitt (1884:192), it was Dharramalin who made the original *mudyi* (an alternative name for the *mudyi-gang* bull-roarer). What this suggests fairly clearly is that 'Mudyigang' was the public (or 'exoteric') name for 'Dharramalin' (Thomas 1905:52). The latter word, was, in fact not supposed to be spoken outside the ceremonial ground of the Bora (Howitt 1904:528).

If this conjecture is correct, it implies that the supposed enmity between Baayami and Dharramalin (Mathews 1896:297–298) and the demonisation of Dharramalin in public accounts (see e.g. Ridley 1875:137; Henderson 1832:147) are additional exoteric features of the

---

85 Variations in gender role and 'leggedness' are crucial factors in the distribution of characteristics between Baayami and Dharramalin and their close associates. Baayami has a wife who is sometimes figured as an emu (Blows 1995:61); in Dharramalin's case, the emu is sometimes his wife (Howitt 1904:560) and sometimes his mother (Howitt 1884:456). As for the possession of only a single leg: this is generally attributed to Dharramalin (e.g. Greenway 1878:242, Greenway 1901:114, Mathews 1904:343, Howitt 1904:585) but sometimes to Baayami (e.g. Slater 1937:12–13).

story.⁸⁶ To the uninitiated, Dharramalin is the fearful being who makes himself known in the sound of thunder and the bull-roarer (Howitt 1904:431). It is he who, either as serpent (Ridley 1861:445) or as eaglehawk (Henderson 1832:147), swallows the boys undergoing initiation. No doubt his association with these two species is founded on their propensity for snatching and eating the young of other species (cf. van Toorn 2006:31), since this parallels the ritualised snatching of young men from their mothers for the purpose of putting them through the Law.

In fact, the very distinction between Baayami (as benevolent All Father) and Dharramalin (as Baayami's demonic or at least tricksterly agent) may be exoteric (Howitt 1904:499–500). In any case, the way their relationship is explained, as well as the associated terminology and symbolism, varies from group to group – and no doubt from one time-period to another. Their association with Mount Yango, as represented in the literature, appears to be based largely on Gamilaraay stories about the mountain. Among Darkinyang, in whose country Mount Yango is said to lie, the relevant entities are called 'Dhurramoolun' and 'Ghindaring' (Mathews 1897:3, 6), and the latter takes on the demonic characteristics associated elsewhere with Dharramalin. For speakers of the Hunter River–Lake Macquarie language, who also have an interest in the mountain, the All Father is known as 'Kuwiyn' (Lissarrague 2006:120; Threlkeld, in Gunson 1974, 1:62; Howitt 1904:499),⁸⁷ and his more ambiguous exoteric aspect is probably Patjikan, 'the Biter' (Threlkeld in Gunson 1974, 1:50, 61; Lissarrague 2006:132).

I suspect that the distinction between the benevolent All Father and his ambiguous agent is based not just on the need to sustain separate exoteric and esoteric perceptions of these entities, but also on more fundamental cosmogonic principles. If it is true, as Parker (1905:7) says, that Baayami stands outside the kinship system, he then represents a primordial unity that existed prior to the differentiation of species, humans and places. According to Parker (1905:7), he is 'the original source of all totems, and of the law that people of the same totem may not inter-marry.' He 'had a totem name for every part of his body, even to a different one for each finger and toe. And when he was passing on to fresh fields, he gave each kinship of the tribe he was leaving one of his totems' (Parker 1905:7). In other words, humans and their social groups constitute a fragmentation of the undivided wholeness represented by Baayami. This perspective makes it easier to understand the darker aspects of such paradoxical figures as Wabuwi and Dharramalin: they are representatives of the dualistic world of division and multiplicity.⁸⁸

The import of this discussion is that Baayami may be associated with Yango as its original creator, while Wabuwi is the part of himself with which he invested it before moving on to create other places. Wabuwi could also (like Dharramalin) have links to the Eaglehawk. There are stone circles on top of the mountain (McDonald 1993:85), and Threlkeld wrote, of other such structures he found in the Hunter Valley, 'the tradition was, that the Eagle-Hawks brought these stones and placed them together in the form in which they were found' (in Gunson 1974, 1:66). Moreover, according to W. A. Squire's account of 'Baiamai' (1896:50), 'the eagles are his emissaries, who overlook the tribal rites and report to their master any error or slip in the ceremonial.'

---

86 One might compare the Book of Job. See Stanley Diamond's introductory essay ('Job and the trickster') to the 1972 edition of Paul Radin's classic book on the trickster.

87 In other sources this name is spelt as Koun (Threlkeld, in Gunson 1974, 1:62), Koin (Hale 1846:111, Howitt 1904:496–499), Koen (Hale 1846:111), Goign (Mathews 1897:328–334), Coen (Howitt 1904:431, 496), and Kohin (Howitt 1904:498–500).

88 The relationship between the one and the many is a universal theme of metaphysical systems and their mythological elaborations, including those of the contemporary world. Richard Coyne (2001), for example, has analysed the manifestations of this motif in the theoretical literature of information technology.

The fragmentary stories about Mount Yango that have survived appear to be attempts to reconcile the differing kinship systems and ritual practices of the various groups from the local region and beyond who used the site. Tony Swain (1993:145) has argued that the introduction of 'All Father' figures like Baayami into Aboriginal beliefs was a millenarian innovation that resulted from the invasion of Australia. While it may indeed have been an innovation, I see no need to interpret it as a specific reaction to the arrival of the English and their religion.[89] Even if it did post-date the invasion (and the evidence for this is weak), I am more inclined to see it as a normal step in the ongoing Aboriginal practice of reinterpreting kinship categories and their associated mythology in the light of changing political contingencies, particularly in areas such as marriage alliances and succession. In other words, the genesis of Baayami was probably due to a broader set of relevant social changes, many of them already taking place before colonisation. Surely we must also allow that pre-invasion Aboriginal history may have had its own pattern of home-grown 'apocalyptic episodes' (Landes 2011:16 and *passim*).

If Baayami's association with Mount Yango is indeed of recent origin, this implies that there are layers of earlier stories there; so it is possible that the stories about Wabuwi originated in a different stratum of the narrative palimpsest. Goddard (1937:7) notes that Wabuwi is represented by the sun, and is said to have leapt to Mount Yango from Burragurra (otherwise known as 'Devil's Rock').[90]

No doubt further research may be able to extend and refine these preliminary interpretations of the available knowledge about Mount Yango. For example, Wabuwi could possibly be associated with the stories of the sun's origin as an emu egg, as reported from many other parts of eastern Australia (Haynes 2000:57).[91] But to pursue this attempt at cosmogonic reconstruction further would take us well beyond the limited purposes of the present appendix.

So let me conclude with some observations on the mountain's name. The term 'Yango' was probably first recorded by William Parr[92] on 7 November 1817, in the field book of his expe-

---

89 See Ian Keen's review of Swain, in particular the section headed 'The "All-Father"' (Keen 1993:102–103); also Blows (1995:67, n.5).
90 According to Goddard (1937:7), the mountain lies due west of the place from which Wabuwi undertook his leap. This implies that the location is actually much closer to 'Finchley Aboriginal Site' than to Burragurra. Mount Yango is *almost* due west from Finchley (actually slightly south of west), whereas it lies at about 40 degrees north of west from the site today known as 'Burragurra Aboriginal Site'. (See the map in National Parks and Wildlife Service 2004 for the contemporary location of both sites). In other words, there appears to be a discrepancy in Goddard's account. Later writers (e.g. Sim 1966:16, 18; Needham 1981:27, 29–32) have consistently identified Burragurra ('Devil's Rock) and Finchley ('Flat Rock') with the sites that today go by those names. Still, Goddard may have been using the name 'Burragurra' in a broad sense, to refer to the whole of the north-south ridge that joins Finchley and Burragurra. The orientation of these two sites, and of other rock carving sites along the same track, is of particular interest because it is likely to have astronomical and calendrical significance. To give just one example: from the point on this ridge that lies due east of Yango, the sun would be seen setting directly over the mountain at the vernal equinox. This can hardly be coincidence, though I am obliged to leave it up to the archaeoastronomers to elaborate the ramifications. There is a small body of older literature on Aboriginal stone alignments (see Lane and Fullagar 1980:146–151) and a few recent studies that interpret some of these structures in terms of their probable function as astronomical measuring devices (see e.g. Hamacher and Norris 2011:4–7). But I have not been able to locate any research into Aboriginal alignment of *sites* for the purpose of astro-calendrical observations.
91 Haynes (2000:57) is worth quoting at length in this regard: 'Amongst the Boorong people of western Victoria, it was believed that Gnowee, the sun, was made by Pupperimbul, one of the Nurrumbunguttias, or old spirits, who were removed to the heavens before the advent of *homo sapiens*. The earth was in perpetual darkness until Pupperimbul prepared an emu egg which he threw into space, where it burst, flooding the sky with light. Variations of this story are found in many areas of eastern Australia, but in Boorong mythology, Gnowee is closely related by kinship to other celestial bodies: Chargee Gnowee, Venus, is the sister of the sun and wife of Ginabongbeart, Jupiter (Stanbridge, 1861:301). Thus the celestial bodies reflect family relationships, thereby both dignifying the latter as an integral part of the cosmos and familiarising the sky.' Variants of this story are summarised by Waterman (1987:31, 56), who provides references to the relevant sources. Cameron (1903:47) gives a NSW (Wangaaypuwan) version (in English).
92 Nonetheless, Andy Macqueen (2004:26) speculates that Benjamin Singleton may have been the first English speaker to ascertain it.

Figure 9.1: Sunset over Mount Yango, vernal equinox, 2017 (photograph by the author)

dition in search of a route from the Hawkesbury to the Hunter (Macqueen 2004:142.) A week later, on 15 November, he made a sketch of the mountain from a hill north of Putty (Macqueen 2004:49, 148). The mountain is mentioned by name again a couple of years later, in John Howe's journal of his first expedition through the same country. On 1 November 1819 he took his bearings from two peaks, one of which he referred to as 'Yango' (Macqueen 2004:168[93]) – 'so called by the Natives'. Then in 1833 the site was mapped by the surveyor Frederick Robert D'Arcy, who spelt the name as 'Yungo' (see map detail reproduced in Jones 2009:32[94]). But none of these

---

93   Howe also mentioned Mount Yango, in passing, on his return journey (Macqueen 2004:173). His journal of the expedition was originally published in *The Surveyor*, in the issue of 30 June 1917 (pp. 71–86), where it was mis-attributed to James Meehan. More recent (and correctly attributed) versions occur as Howe (1989) and in Macqueen (2004:165–174).
94   Online at *https://www.wollombi.org/wp-content/uploads/2016/02/yengo.pdf* [accessed 29 September 2017]. Jones provides no source for the map, which is captioned as '*Yengo* recorded as "*Yungo*" by Darcy in 1833'. But it is presumably a detail from F. R. D'Arcy's map held by State Records of NSW under the title 'Plan McDonald River (then spelt Macdonald) from Yango Creek to Warren Creek, showing ranges & Mounts Bulgalben, Yungo, Moruben' (SRNSW, SG Maps & Plans, Item 3034), dated 1833. D'Arcy made several expeditions to the Wollemi Creek region, just to the west of Mount Yango and the Macdonald River, in the years 1833–1835 (Macqueen 2010:59–87). Macqueen's account of the expedition of June–July 1833 mentions that D'Arcy's party was camped at 'Putty Creek near its junction with Wollemi Creek' (Macqueen 2010:62)

explorers provided a gloss; nor did they give any indication of how to interpret their spelling for the purpose of correct pronunciation.

It is hard to reconcile Goddard's interpretation of the meaning ('caught by the foot' or 'stepping over') with other evidence. Two of the responses to the Anthropological Society of Australasia's 1899 questionnaire concerning 'native names of places' mention Yango (~Yengo),[95] and in both cases the meaning has to do with mountains or rocks. These glosses are at least plausible, given that the word *yuyn.gu* means 'mountain' in Gathang (Lissarrague 2010:285; see also Sim 1966:38, n. 14[96]) and that there is an equivalent form in HRLM, spelt by Threlkeld as *yúnku* in his translation of Luke 23:30 (in Fraser 1892:190), where it applies to 'the hills'. Moreover, there are no words for 'foot' or 'step over' that provide a likely etymology in any of the relevant languages.

If the toponym 'Yango' is indeed derived from an Indigenous word that means simply 'mountain', I conjecture that the place may also have had a more distinctive name that was less commonly used, either because it was esoteric or because Yango was significant enough to be referred to simply as '*the* mountain', without requiring further specification.

Nonetheless, the concept of 'stepping down' could well be etymologically linked to the names of other sites associated with Yango, in particular Barraba and Burragurra. Needham (1981:8)[97] glosses 'Barraba' as 'place of descent', so it is plausibly interpreted as consisting of two HRLM morphemes: *para*, meaning 'down' (Lissarrague 2006:131) and *pa*, 'place of' (Lissarrague 2006:63). In this case, the available evidence seems to support Needham's interpretation. The etymology of 'Burragurra' is less straightforward. Needham (1981:8) glosses it as 'place where the spirit walked'; and this site, too, is plausibly associated with the descent of the presiding spirit of Mount Yango and thus with the word *para*, 'down'. The meaning of the second part of the name (presumably *-kara*) is less obvious, but it could well be the same morpheme that occurs in the two principal words for 'clever person' in this region, namely, *kara-kal* and *kara-dji*.[98]

---

in June of that year. This location is close enough to Yango to suggest that D'Arcy may have drawn the map while he was in the vicinity. The map in question is listed in the online repositories of Tim Sherrat (wragge) at *https://github.com/wragge/srnsw-indexes/blob/master/data/list-of-maps-and-plans-and-supplement-.csv* [accessed 29 September 2017].

95   In 1899, the Anthropological Society of Australasia distributed a questionnaire to police stations, mainly in NSW and Queensland, requesting information for a 'Collection of Native Names of places with their meanings'. A compilation of the responses was microfilmed in 1991 by W & F Pascoe Pty Ltd, as the first of five rolls of the Society's manuscript material. A digital version (PDF and TIFF files) of all five rolls was made available on compact disc by the Geographical Names Board of NSW in 2003 (see References, below). The Society gained the prefix 'Royal' in 1901, so the original documents, now held by the Mitchell Library, State Library of NSW, Sydney, are catalogued under 'Royal Anthropological Society of Australasia – Records, 1885–1914, with additional material, 1921–1926, ca. 1991, and papers of Alan Carroll, 1886–1892' (MLMSS 7603). But the most practicable method for referencing the individual responses to the questionnaire is probably to use the roll and image numbers of the PDF files (which are the same for the TIFF files) as they are listed on the CD. In the present case, the scanned responses are included in roll 1 as image 010384 and image 010401. Neither response includes the name of the author or the location of the police station, but there are enough recognisable words in both lists to be able to ascribe language affiliations with a fair degree of certainty. The language of the wordlist in image 010384 is HRLM, and the relevant entry in this list reads, 'Yengo: Big Rocks'. The language of the other wordlist (image 010401) is Gathang, and there the relevant entry reads, 'Yango: small mountain'. This is followed by 'Milly buring [?] Yango': Large mountain'. (My thanks to Amanda Lissarrague for assistance with identifying the language of this list.)

96   Sim interprets the name to mean 'mountain', based on the Kutthung vocabulary of W. J. Enright (1900:114) and an anonymous article on Aboriginal placenames that was itself based on the Anthropological Society of Australasia's questionnaires mentioned above. Lissarrague (2010:285) cites even more sources, including Scott, Branch and Holmer.

97   Admittedly, Needham and his sources need to be treated with some caution. To give just one glaring example: the myth he recounts in the section on the so-called 'defloration cave' (Needham 1981:18–20) is borrowed from Andreas Lommel's work (1949:160–161) on the Wunambal of Western Australia, but treated as being of local (Darkinyung) origin.

98   *Karakal* comes from HRLM (Lissarrague 2006:114); *karadji* appears to have been widespread in the languages of coastal NSW (Elkin 1977 [1945]:79–80).

I have left till last a conjecture that ties this appendix back to the chapter's beginning, specifically to the 'sunny hill' mentioned in the epigraph. Earlier I suggested that this hill could be Mount Yango. There is possibly support for this in a small book published by W. A. Squire in 1896, called *Ritual, myth, and customs of the Australian Aborigines*. Squire was a solicitor in the Hunter Valley town of Maitland, a member of the Maitland Scientific Society, a friend of amateur ethnologist W. J. Enright, and at least an acquaintance of R. H. Mathews and John Fraser (Squire 1896:5).[99] In addition, he collaborated with A. J. Prentice[100] on an article about Aboriginal use of quartz crystal (Prentice and Squire 1896).

Much of Squire's book is a generalised sketch of Aboriginal culture derived from earlier published ethnographic material. But some of his observations are evidently based on his own experience, including a trip he made to the Wollombi region with Enright and Prentice (Squire 1896:79). There is one passage in particular that is relevant to the issue at hand. In it Squire (1896:60) remarks as follows: '... in his primitive observatory the Karaji kept a three days' and three nights' solitary vigil within a stone circle on a mountain top, communing with *Wanda*, the Unknown Spirit'.

This is unlikely to be an eyewitness account, and Squire provides no source for it. Still, if we accepted it as well founded, it could supply a number of pieces of the puzzle that are otherwise missing from this narrative; in particular: the function of the stone circles on top of Mount Yango; the identity of the 'sunny hill' that songmen frequent to seek the inspiration of the 'god of Poesy'; and a motive for Wulatji's visit to Wollombi.

References

Abraham, Nicolas, and Maria Torok, 1994, The shell and the kernel: renewals of psychoanalysis (edited, translated, and with an introduction by Nicholas T. Rand). Chicago: University of Chicago Press.

Althans, Katrin, 2010, Darkness subverted: Aboriginal Gothic in Black Australian literature and film. Göttingen: V & R Unipress.

Anon., 1869, Aboriginal corroboree. Maitland Mercury and Hunter River General Advertiser, 1 July 1869:2.

Apted, Meiki Elizabeth, 2010, Songs from the Inyjalarrku: the use of a nontranslatable spirit language in a song set from north-west Arnhem Land, Australia. Australian Journal of Linguistics 30(1): 93–103.

Ash, Anna, John Giacon, and Amanda Lissarrague, comps & eds, 2003, Gamilaraaay, Yuwaalaraay and Yuwaalayaay dictionary. Alice Springs: IAD Press.

Augé, Marc, 1999, The war of dreams: exercises in ethno-fiction. London: Pluto Press.

AustLit, 2011, Native poetry. *http://www.austlit.edu.au/austlit/page/C696511* [accessed 13 September 2016].

—— n.d, Eliza Hamilton Dunlop. *http://www.austlit.edu.au/austlit/page/A31624* [accessed 13 September 2016].

Back, Les, 2007, The art of listening. Oxford: Berg.

Bahr, Donald, 1994, Native American dream songs: myth, memory and improvisation. Journal de la Société des Américanistes 80:73–93.

Bandt, Ros, 2014, Sonic archaeologies: towards a methodology for 're-hearing' the past – Lake Mungo, Australia and the Yerebatan Sarnici, Istanbul. In Linda C. Eneix, ed. Archaeoacoustics:

---

99 Enright and Mathews are well known (both have entries in the *Australian Dictionary of Biography*). For biographical sketches of Fraser, see Barcan (2011:72), Roberts (2008:107–108) and
   https://downloads.newcastle.edu.au/library/cultural%20collections/awaba/people/fraserjohn.html [accessed 11 August 2017]. I have based my brief account of Squire partly on his own publications, and partly on an obituary that appeared in the *Newcastle Morning Herald* on 25 January 1908 p. 6
   (*http://nla.gov.au/nla.news-article138393809* [accessed 11 August 2017]).

100 Also, like Squire, a lawyer. See his obituary in the *Maitland Daily Mercury* 30 July 1936 p. 4 (*http://nla.gov.au/nla.news-page13540762* [accessed 12 August 2017]).

the archaeology of sound (publication of proceedings from the 2014 Conference in Malta), 87–98. Myakka City, Florida: The OTS Foundation.

Baptandier, Brigitte, 1996, Entrer en montagne pour y rêver: Le Mont des Pierres et des Bambous. Terrain 26:99–122. *http://terrain.revues.org/3160* [accessed 3 September 2016].

Barcan, Alan, 2011, Education for a liberal democracy, 1856–1866: the Hunter Valley. Journal of the Royal Australian Historical Society 97(1):66–83.

Barrett, Deirdre, 2001, The committee of sleep. New York: Crown Publishers.

Barwick, Linda, 2005, Performance, aesthetics, experience: thoughts on yawulyu Mungamunga songs. In Elizabeth Mackinlay, Denis Collins and Samantha Owens, eds. Aesthetics and experience in music performance. Newcastle UK: Cambridge Scholars Press.

Barwick, Linda, Bruce Birch, and Nicholas Evans, 2007, Iwaidja *Jurtbirrk* songs: bringing language and music together. Australian Aboriginal Studies 2007/2:6–34.

Basilov, Vladimir N., 1995, Blessing in a dream. Turcica 27:237–246.

Bates, Daisy, 1985, The native tribes of Western Australia (ed. Isobel White). Canberra: National Library of Australia.

Beaudry, Nicole, 1991, Rêves, chants et prières dènès: une confluence de spiritualités. Recherches amérindiennes au Québec 21(4):23–36.

—— 1992, The language of dreams: songs of the Dene Indians (Canada). The World of Music 34(2):72–90.

Becker, Judith, 1994, Music and trance. Leonardo Music Journal 4:41–51.

Bede, the Venerable, Saint, 2008, The ecclesiastical history of the English people (trans. Bertram Colgrave and R. A. B. Mynors). With the Greater chronicle and Letter to Egbert (trans., ed., intro. by Judith McClure and Roger Collins). Oxford: Oxford World's Classics. (Translation of Bede, *Historia ecclesiastica gentis Anglorum*, completed in 731.)

Bell, Diane, 1998, *Ngarrindjeri wurruwarrin*: a world that is, was, and will be. Melbourne: Spinifex.

Bendix, Regina, 2000, The pleasures of the ear: toward an ethnography of listening. Cultural Analysis 1:33–50.

Benedict, Ruth Fulton, 1922, The vision in Plains culture. American Anthropologist (new series) 24 (1):1–23.

Berndt, Catherine H., 1978a, Categorisation of, and in, oral literature. In L. R. Hiatt, ed. Australian Aboriginal concepts, 56–67. Canberra: Australian Institute of Aboriginal Studies Press/ New Jersey: Humanities Press.

—— 1978b, Digging sticks and spears, or, the two sex model. In Fay Gale ed. Woman's role in Aboriginal society, 64–84. Canberra: Australian Institute of Aboriginal Studies.

Berndt, Ronald M., 1947, Wuradjeri magic and 'clever men'. Oceania 17(4):327–365.

—— 1987, Other creatures in human guise *and* vice versa: a dilemma in understanding. In M. Clunies Ross, T. Donaldson and S. A. Wild, eds. Songs of Aboriginal Australia (Oceania Monograph 32), 168–191. Sydney: University of Sydney.

Berndt, Ronald M. and Catherine H. Berndt, 1951, Sexual behavior in western Arnhem Land. New York: Viking Fund.

—— 1970, Time for relaxation. In S. A. Wurm and D. C. Laycock, eds. Pacific Linguistic studies in honour or Arthur Capell, 557–591. Canberra: Pacific Linguistics (series C, no. 13).

Beyer, Stephan V., 2009, Singing to the plants: a guide to Mestizo shamanism in the Upper Amazon. Albuquerque: University of New Mexico Press.

Blanco, Maria del Pilar, and Esther Peeren, eds, 2013, The spectralities reader: ghosts and haunting in contemporary cultural theory. London: Bloomsbury Academic.

Blows, Johanna M., 1975, Eaglehawk and crow: birds, myths and moieties in south-east Australia. In L. R. Hiatt, ed. Australian Aboriginal mythology: essays in honour of W. E. H. Stanner. Canberra: A.I.A.S.

—— 1995, Eagle and crow: an exploration of an Australian Aboriginal myth. New York: Garland.

Boas, Franz, 1895, The social organization and the secret societies of the Kwakiutl Indians. Washington DC: Report of the U.S. National Museum for 1895, pp. 311–737.

Bourguignon, Erika, ed., 1973, Religion, altered states of consciousness and social change. Columbus: Ohio State University Press.

Bradley, John, and Elizabeth Mackinlay, 2000, Songs from a plastic water rat: an introduction to the musical traditions of the Yanyuwa community of the southwest Gulf of Carpentaria. Ngulaig (Aboriginal and Torres Strait Islander Studies Unit, University of Queensland) 17:i–45.

Brown, Reuben, 2014, The role of songs in connecting the living and the dead: a funeral ceremony for Nakodjok in western Arnhem Land. In Amanda Harris, ed. Circulating cultures: exchanges of Australian Indigenous music, dance and media, 169–201. Canberra: ANU Press.

Bulkeley, Kelly, 1995, Spiritual dreaming: a cross-cultural and historical journey. New York: Paulist Press.

Calise, Santiago Gabriel, 2015, A decorporealized theory? considerations about Luhmann's conception of the body. Pandaemonium Germanicum: Revista de Estudos Germanísticos 18(26):104–125. *http://dx.doi.org/10.1590/1982-88371826104125* [accessed 4 July 2017].

Cameron, A. L. P., 1903, Traditions and folk-lore of the Aborigines of New South Wales. Science of Man 6(3):46–48.

Campbell, Genevieve, 2013, Sustaining Tiwi song practice through Kulama. Musicology Australia 35(2):237–252.

Carbaugh, Donal, 1999, 'Just listen': 'Listening' and landscape among the Blackfeet. Western Journal of Communication 63(3):250–270.

Cardeña, Etzel, Stephen Jay Lynn and Stanley Krippner, 2014, Varieties of anomalous experience: examining the scientific evidence (2nd edn). Washington DC: American Psychological Association.

Carruthers, Mary, 1990, The book of memory: a study of memory in Medieval culture. Cambridge: Cambridge University Press.

Castricano, Jodey, 2001, Cryptomimesis: the gothic and Jacques Derrida's ghost writing. Montréal: McGill-Queen's University Press.

Cemin, Arneide, 2014, The rituals of Santo Daime: systems of symbolic constructions. In Beatriz Labate and Edward MacRae, eds. Ayahuasca ritual and religion in Brazil, 39–64. Abingdon UK: Routledge.

Chadwick, Nora K., 1946. Norse ghosts: a study in the *Draugr* and the *Haugbúi* [part 1]. Folklore 57(2):50–65.

Charsley, Simon, 1992, Dreams in African churches. In M. C. Jędrej and Rosalind Shaw, eds. Dreaming, religion and society in Africa, 153–176. Leiden: E. J. Brill.

Chodorow, Joan, 1997, Introduction. In C. G. Jung, Jung on active imagination (edited and with an introduction by J. Chodorow). Princeton: Princeton University Press.

Clarke, Philip A., 2007, Indigenous spirit and ghost folklore of 'settled' Australia. Folklore 118(2):141–161.

Clarke, Robert, 2016, Travel writing from black Australia: utopia, melancholia, and aboriginality. New York: Routledge.

Clunies Ross, Margaret, 1987, Research into Aboriginal songs: the state of the art. In M. Clunies Ross, T. Donaldson and S. A. Wild, eds. Songs of Aboriginal Australia (Oceania Monograph 32), 1–13. Sydney: University of Sydney.

Collins, David, Philip Gidley King and George Bass, 1798, An account of the English colony in New South Wales: with remarks on the dispositions, customs, manners, &c. of the native inhabitants of that country. To which are added, some particulars of New Zealand; compiled, by permission, from the MSS. of Lieutenant-Governor King by David Collins. London: Printed for T. Cadell, Jun., and W. Davies.

Corn, Aaron and Wantarri Jampijinpa Patrick, 2014, Singing the winds of change: ethnomusicology and the generation of new collaborative contexts for the teaching of Warlpiri knowledge across generations and cultures. In Katelyn Barney, ed. Collaborative ethnomusicology: new approaches to music research between Indigenous and non-Indigenous Australians, 147–168. Melbourne: Lyrebird Press.

Cottle, Drew, 2013, Land, life and labour in the sacrifice zone: the socioeconomic dynamics of open-cut coal mining in the Upper Hunter Valley, New South Wales. Rural Society 22(3): 208–216.

Cox, James, 2014, The invention of God in Indigenous societies. Durham: Acumen.

Coyne, Richard, 2001, Technoromanticism: digital narrative, holism, and the romance of the real. Cambridge MA: MIT Press.

Cultural Collections, University of Newcastle, 2016, The Percy Haslam Collection. *http://libguides.newcastle.edu.au/dreamtime/haslam* [accessed 20 January 2016].

Curtis, Edward S., 1907–1930, The North American Indian (20 volumes). Seattle: E. S. Curtis. Online at *http://curtis.library.northwestern.edu/index.html* [accessed 29 August 2017].

Davies, Owen, 2007, The haunted: a social history of ghosts. Basingstoke: Palgrave Macmillan.

Davis, Colin, 2005, État présent: hauntology, spectres and phantoms. French Studies 59(3):373–379.

Davis, Patricia M., 2009, Discerning the voice of God: case studies in Christian history. In Kelly Bulkeley, Kate Adams and Patricia M. Davis, eds. Dreaming in Christianity and Islam: culture, conflict, and creativity, 43–56. New Brunswick NJ: Rutgers University Press.

Demetracopoulou, D., 1935, Wintu songs. Anthropos 30(3/4):483–494.

Densmore, Frances, 1910, Chippewa music. Bureau of American Ethnology Bulletin 45. Washington DC: Smithsonian Institution.

—— 1918, Teton Sioux music. Bureau of American Ethnology Bulletin 61. Washington DC: Smithsonian Institution.

—— 1926, The American Indians and their music. New York: Woman's Press.

—— 1932, Menominee music. Bureau of American Ethnology Bulletin 102. Washington DC: Smithsonian Institution.

—— 1953, The belief of the Indian in a connection between song and the supernatural. Bureau of American Ethnology Bulletin 151:217–223. Washington DC: Smithsonian Institution.

Derrida, Jacques, 1994, Specters of Marx: the state of the debt, the work of mourning, and the New International (trans. Peggy Kamuf). New York: Routledge.

De Salis, Margaret Fane, 1967, Two early colonials: by a great granddaughter. Sydney: the author.

—— 1969, Captain Thomas Raine, an early colonist. Sydney: the author.

—— 1972, David and Eliza Dunlop. [Address given to the Greater Cessnock City Historical Society, 12 May 1972.] Cessnock Eagle 16 May: 4. Available online at *http://cessnock.spydus.com/cgi-bin/spydus.exe/ENQ/OPAC/BIBENQ?BRN=16536* [accessed 17 August 2016].

Devereux, Paul, 2013, Dreamscapes: topography, mind, and the power of simulacra in ancient and traditional societies. International Journal of Transpersonal Studies 32(1):51–63.

Diamond, Stanley, 1972, Job and the trickster. Introduction to Paul Radin, The trickster, xi–xxii. New York: Schocken.

Dixon, Robert M. W., W. S. Ramson and Mandy Thomas, 1990, Australian Aboriginal words in English: their origin and meaning. Melbourne: Oxford University Press.

Dixon, Roland B., 1904, Some shamans of northern California. Journal of American Folklore 17(64):23–27.

Donaldson, Tamsin, 1987, Making a song (and dance) in south-eastern Australia. In Margaret Clunies Ross, Tamsin Donaldson and Stephen Wild, eds. Songs of Aboriginal Australia, 14–42. Sydney: Oceania Monograph 32.

—— 1997, Ngiyampaa wordworld. Canberra: AIATSIS.

Dunlop, Eliza Hamilton, 1848a, Native poetry. The Sydney Morning Herald 11 October: 3.

—— 1848b, Pialla Wollombi. In Isaac Nathan, ed. The southern Euphrosyne and Australian miscellany, 94. London & Sydney: Whittaker & Co. [The poem is entitled 'The gibber gunyah' in the table of contents.]

—— 1865, Erin Dheelish. The Empire [Sydney] 8 July:5.

—— 1981, The Aboriginal mother and other poems (ed. Elizabeth Webby). Canberra: Mulini Press.

Dunn, Mark, 2015, A valley in a valley: colonial struggles over land and resources in the Hunter Valley, NSW 1820–1850. PhD thesis, University of NSW, Sydney. Online at *http://handle.unsw.edu.au/1959.4/55057* [accessed 5 July 2017].

Durkheim, Émile and Marcel Mauss, 1963, Primitive classification (trans. Rodney Needham). London: Cohen & West.

Dussart, Françoise, 2000, The politics of ritual in an Aboriginal settlement: kinship, gender, and the currency of knowledge. Washington, DC: Smithsonian Institution Press.

Eifring, Halvor, 2015, Meditation and culture: the interplay of practice and context. London: Bloomsbury Academic.

Elferen, Isabella van, 2012, Gothic music: the sounds of the uncanny. Cardiff: University of Wales Press.

Elkin, Adolphus Peter, 1933, Totemism in north-western Australia: the Kimberley Division. Oceania 3(3):257–296.

—— 1954, The Australian Aborigines: how to understand them (3rd edn). Sydney: Angus and Robertson.

—— 1970, The Aborigines of Australia: 'one in thought, word and deed'. In S. A. Wurm and D. C. Laycock, eds. Pacific Linguistic studies in honour or Arthur Capell, 697–716. Canberra: Pacific Linguistics (series C, no. 13).

—— 1977, Aboriginal men of high degree (2nd edn). St Lucia QLD: University of Queensland Press. (Originally published 1945, Australasian Publishing Co., Sydney.)

Elkin, Adolphus Peter, and Trevor Jones, 1953–1957, Arnhem Land music. Sydney: Oceania Monograph 9. (Single volume edition, continuously paginated; reprinted from separate editions of Oceania over the period 1953–1957. Equivalent page numbers listed in table of contents.)

Ellingson, Terry J., 1979, The mandala of sound: concepts and sound structures in Tibetan ritual music. Ph.D. thesis, University of Wisconsin, Madison. (2003 edition published by Cambridge University Press.)

Ellis, Catherine J., 1984, Time consciousness of Aboriginal performers. In J. C. Kassler & J. Stubington, eds. Problems and solutions: occasional essays presented to Alice M. Moyle, 149–185. Sydney: Hale & Iremonger.

—— n.d., Central Aboriginal music. Section 2 of entry for 'Australia: 1. Aboriginal music'. In Deane Root, ed. Grove Music Online, n.p.:
http://www.oxfordmusiconline.com:80/subscriber/article/grove/music/40021 [accessed 21 August 2017].

Emeneau, M. B., 1965, Toda dream songs. Journal of the American Oriental Society 85(1):39–44.

Eneix, Linda C. ed., 2014, Archaeoacoustics: the archaeology of sound (publication of proceedings from the 2014 Conference in Malta). Myaka City, Florida: The OTS Foundation.

England, Nicholas M., 1967, Bushman counterpoint. Journal of the International Folk Music Council 19:58–66.

Enright, W. J., 1898, Aboriginal rock carvings in the Wollombi district, New South Wales. Science of Man and Journal of the Royal Anthropological Society of Australasia 1(8):181–183.

—— 1900, The language, weapons, and manufactures of the Aborigines of Port Stephens, New South Wales. Journal of the Royal Society of NSW 34:103–118.

Ereira, Alan, 1990, The heart of the world. London: Jonathan Cape.

Evans, Nicholas, 1995, A grammar of Kayardild: with historical-comparative notes on Tangkic. Berlin: Mouton de Gruyter.

Ewers, John C., 1958, The Blackfeet: raiders on the Northwestern Plains. Norman: University of Oklahoma Press.

Eyre, Edward John, 1845, Journals of expeditions of discovery into Central Australia, and overland from Adelaide to King George's Sound, in the years 1840–1 (two vols). London: T. and W. Boone. (Facsimile edition published 1964, Libraries Board of South Australia, Adelaide.)

Faery Folklorist, 2015, The Trows of Orkney and Shetland. Online at *http://faeryfolklorist.blogspot.com.au/2015/10/the-trows-of-orkney-and-shetland.html* [accessed 25 September 2017].

Fawcett, J. W., 1898, Customs of the Wannah-ruah tribe, and their dialect or vocabulary. Science of Man and Journal of the Royal Anthropological Society of Australasia 1(8):180–181.

Feld, Stephen, 2001, From ethnomusicology to echo-muse-ecology: reading R. Murray Schafer in the Papua New Guinea rainforest. Online via the Acoustic Ecology Institute, at *http://www.acousticecology.org/writings/echomuseecology.html* [accessed 5 September 2016].

Finegan, Samuel Patrick, 2014, Broken gates and leaky graves: spectral language and Australia's ghost stories. PhD thesis, Queensland University of Technology, Brisbane. Online at *https://eprints.qut.edu.au/71189/* [accessed 6 July 2017].

Fischer, Eberhard, 1978, Dan forest spirits: masks in Dan villages. African Arts 11(2):16–23.
Fisher, Mark, 2013, The metaphysics of crackle: Afrofuturism and hauntology. Dancecult: Journal of Electronic Dance Music Culture 5(2): 42–55.
Flannery, Regina, and Mary Elizabeth Chambers, 1985, Each man has his own friends: the role of dream visitors in traditional East Cree belief and practice. Arctic Anthropology 22(1):1–22.
Ford, Geoffrey Eric, 2010, Darkiñung recognition: an analysis of the historiography for the Aborigines from the Hawkesbury–Hunter ranges to the northwest of Sydney. M.A. thesis, University of Sydney.
Forde, C. Daryll, 1931, Ethnography of the Yuma Indians. Berkeley: University of California Publications in American Archaeology and Ethnology 28(4):83–278.
Franke, Patrick, 2000, Begegnung mit Khidr: Quellenstudien zum Imaginären im traditionellen Islam. Stuttgart: Franz Steiner.
Fraser, John ed., 1892, An Australian language as spoken by the Awabakal, the people of Awaba or Lake Macquarie (near Newcastle, New South Wales): being an account of their language, traditions and customs, by L. E. Threlkeld; re-arranged, condensed and edited with an appendix by John Fraser. Sydney: Charles Potter, Govt. Printer.
Foucault, Michel, 1986, Of other spaces (trans. Jay Miskowiec). Diacritics 16(1):22–27.
—— 1988, Technologies of the self (edited by Luther H. Martin, Huck Gutman and Patrick H. Hutton). Amherst: University of Massachusetts Press.
Friedson, Steven M., 1996, Dancing prophets: musical experience in Tumbuka healing. University of Chicago Press.
Fuller, Robert S., Ray P. Norris and Michelle Trudgett, 2014, The astronomy of the Kamilaroi and Euahlayi peoples and their neighbours. Australian Aboriginal Studies 2014/2:3–27.
Garde, Murray, 2006, The language of *Kun-borrk* in western Arnhem Land. Musicology Australia 28:59–89.
Garfias, Robert, 1979–1980, The role of dreams and spirit possession in the *Mbira Dza Vadzimu* music of the Shona people of Zimbabwe. Journal of Altered States of Consciousness 5(3):211–234.
Gelder, Ken, and Jane M. Jacobs, 1998, Uncanny Australia: sacredness and identity in a postcolonial nation. Carlton South VIC: Melbourne University Press.
Geographical Names Board of New South Wales, n.d., Moon Island (reference 39040). http://www.gnb.nsw.gov.au/place_naming/placename_search/extract?id=anwGWyWAGH [accessed 3 November 2016].
—— 2003, Royal Anthropological Society of Australasia manuscripts dated 1900 (4¾ in. computer optical disk). Bathurst: NSW Government, Dept. of Lands.
Giacon, John, 2010, Transcription of Milson's Kamilaroi vocabulary 2000. Unpublished digital typescript, revised 22 June, 2010.
—— 2013, Etymology of Yuwaalaraay Gamilaraay bird names. In Robert Mailhammer, ed. Lexical and structural etymology: beyond word histories, 251–291. Berlin: De Gruyter.
Gifford, Edward Winslow, 1926, Yuma dreams and omens. Journal of American Folklore 39(151): 58–69.
Gillen, Francis J., 1896, Notes on some manners and customs of the Aborigines of the McDonnell Ranges belonging to the Arunta tribe. In Baldwin Spencer, ed. Report on the work of the Horn Scientific Expedition to Central Australia, vol. 4 (Anthropology), 161–196. London: Dulau.
Glaskin, Katie, 2005, Innovation and ancestral revelation: the case of dreams. Journal of the Royal Anthropological Institute 11(2):297–314.
—— 2008, Dreams and memory: accessing metaphysical realms in northwest Kimberley. Journal of the Anthropological Society of South Australia 33:39–73.
—— 2010, On dreams, innovation and the emerging genre of the individual artist. Anthropological Forum 20(3):251–267.
—— 2011a, Dreaming in thread: from ritual to art and property(s) between. In Veronica Strang and Mark Busse, eds. Ownership and appropriation, 87–104. Oxford: Berg.
—— 2011b, Dreams, memory, and ancestors: creativity, culture, and the science of sleep. Journal of the Royal Anthropological Institute 17(1):44–62.
—— 2015, Dreams, perception, and creative realization. Topics in Cognitive Science 7: 664–676.

Glenn, Cheryl, 2004, Unspoken: a rhetoric of silence. Carbondale: Southern Illinois University Press.
Glowczewski, Barbara, 2016, Desert dreamers. Minneapolis: University of Minnesota Press.
Goddard, Roy H., 1934, Aboriginal poets as historians. Mankind 1(10):91–92.
—— 1937a, Aboriginal rock carvings, Wollombi district, N.S.W. Mankind 2(4):91–92.
—— 1937b, Certain observations of Aboriginal rock-carvings in the Wollombi district. (Paper read before ANZAAS meeting, 14 January 1937, 1–9). Sutherland NSW: S.C.A.M. Print.
Goodale, Jane C., 2003, Tiwi Island dreams. In Roger Ivar Lohmann, ed. Dream travelers: sleep experiences and culture in the western Pacific, 149–167. New York: Palgrave Macmillan.
Gordon, Paul, Peter Crousen, and Garry Jones, 1993, Yengo country: some ancient sandstone art in south-eastern Australia. Pacific Arts 7:43–49.
Goulet, Jean-Guy, 1994, Dreams and visions in other lifeworlds. In David E. Young and Jean-Guy Goulet, eds. Being changed by cross-cultural encounters: the anthropology of extraordinary experience, 16–38. Peterborough, Canada: Broadview Press.
Grace, Nancy, 2012, Music and dreams. In Deirdre Barrett and Patrick McNamara, eds. Encyclopedia of sleep and dreams 430–432. Santa Barbara CA: Greenwood.
Graham, Laura R., 1994, Dialogic dreams: creative selves coming into life in the flow of time. American Ethnologist 21(4):723–745.
—— 1995, Performing dreams: discourses of immortality among the Xavante of Central Brazil. Austin: University of Texas Press.
Grant, Stan, and John Rudder (comps), 2010, A new Wiradjuri dictionary. O'Connor, ACT: Restoration House.
Grauer, Victor, 2011, Sounding the depths: tradition and the voices of history. Seattle: CreateSpace Independent Publishing Platform.
Grebe, María Ester, 1978, Relationships between music practice and cultural context: the kultrún and its symbolism. The World of Music 20(3):84–106.
Green, Nile, 2003, The religious and cultural roles of dreams and visions in Islam. Journal of the Royal Asiatic Society (3rd series) 13(3):287–313.
Greenway, Charles C., 1878, Kamilaroi language and traditions. Journal of the Anthropological Institute of Great Britain and Ireland 7:233–246.
—— 1901, The borah, 'boohra' or 'boorbung'. Science of Man 4(7):117–118.
Gummow, Margaret, 1992, Aboriginal songs from the Bundjalung and Gidabal areas of south-eastern Australia. PhD thesis, University of Sydney.
—— 1995, Songs and sites/moving mountains: a study of one song from northern NSW. In Linda Barwick, Allan Marett and Guy Tunstill, eds. The essence of singing and the substance of song: recent responses to the Aboriginal performing arts and other essays in honour of Catherine Ellis, 121–131. Sydney: Oceania Publications (University of Sydney).
Gunson, Niel, 1966, Dunlop, Eliza Hamilton (1796–1880). In Australian Dictionary of Biography, National Centre of Biography, Australian National University, *http://adb.anu.edu.au/biography/dunlop-eliza-hamilton-2007/text2455* [published first in hard copy 1966, accessed online 6 January 2016]
—— 1974, Australian reminiscences and papers of L. E. Threlkeld, vol. 1. Canberra: AIAS.
Günther, James, 1892, Grammar and vocabulary of the Aboriginal dialect called the Wirradhuri. In John Fraser, An Australian language as spoken by the Awabakal, Appendix D, 56–120. Sydney: Charles Potter, Govt. Printer.
Hacking, Ian, 2001, Dreams in place. Journal of Aesthetics and Art Criticism 59(3):245–260.
Hadot, Pierre, 1995, Philosophy as a way of life: spiritual exercises from Socrates to Foucault. Oxford: Blackwell.
Hale, Horatio E., 1846, Ethnography and philology. Vol. 6 of United States exploring expedition, during the years 1838, 1839, 1840, 1841, 1842, under the command of Charles Wilkes, U.S.N. New York: Lea and Blanchard.
Hallam, Susan, Ian Cross and Michael Thaut, 2009, The Oxford handbook of music psychology. Oxford: Oxford University Press.

Hallowell, A. Irving, 1966, The role of dreams in Ojibwa culture. In G. E. von Grunebaum and Roger Caillois, eds. The dream and human societies, 267–289. Berkeley: University of California Press.

Hamacher, Duane, and Ray P. Norris, 2011, 'Bridging the gap' through Australian cultural astronomy. In Clive Ruggles, ed. Oxford IX: International Symposium on Archaeoastronomy and Astronomy in Culture. Proceedings of the International Astronomical Union Symposium 278:1–9. Online at *http://www.atnf.csiro.au/people/rnorris/papers/n268.pdf* [accessed 18 September 2017].

Haraway, Donna, 2014, Speculative fabulations for technoculture's generations: taking care of unexpected country. In Eben Kirksey, ed. The multispecies salon, 242–261. Durham NC: Duke University Press.

Harrisson, Juliette, 2009, The Classical Greek practice of incubation and some Near Eastern predecessors. Online via Academia at *https://newman.academia.edu/JulietteHarrisson* [accessed 28 July 2016].

Haslam, Percy, 1984, Awabakal poem. In Department of Education (Hunter Region), Aborigines of the Hunter Region, 71. Newcastle: NSW Department of Education. Republished in 1986 under the heading 'Aboriginal Songs from the 1850s' in Les Murray, The New Oxford Book of Australian Verse, 36–37. Melbourne: Oxford University Press.

Haynes, Roslynn, 2000, Astronomy and the Dreaming: the astronomy of the Aboriginal Australians. In Helaine Selin, ed. Astronomy across cultures: the history of non-western astronomy, 53–90. Boston: Kluwer.

Henderson, John, 1832, Observations on the colonies of New South Wales and Van Diemen's Land. Calcutta: Baptist Mission Press.

Henderson, John and Veronica Dobson, 1994, Eastern and Central Arrernte to English dictionary. Alice Springs: IAD Press.

Hercus, Luise, and Jane Simpson, 2002, Indigenous place names: an introduction. In Luise Hercus, Flavia Hodges, and Jane Simpson, eds. The land is a map: place names of Indigenous origin in Australia, 1–23. Canberra: Pandanus Books in association with Pacific Linguistics.

Herzog, George, 1936, A comparison of Pueblo and Pima musical styles. The Journal of American Folklore 49(194):283–417.

Hiatt, Lester R., 1965, Kinship and conflict: a study of an Aboriginal community in northern Arnhem Land. Canberra: Australian National University.

Hinton, Leanne, 1980, Vocables in Havasupai song. In Charlotte J. Frisbie, ed. Southwestern Indian ritual drama, 275–305. Albuquerque: University of New Mexico Press.

Hofmann, Charles, 1968, Frances Densmore and American Indian Music: bibliography. In C. Hofmann, Frances Densmore and American Indian music: a memorial volume. New York: Museum of the American Indian, Heye Foundation. Online at
http://news.minnesota.publicradio.org/features/199702/01_smiths_densmore/docs/hofmannbiblio.shtml [accessed 27 July 2016].

Hogan, Linda, 2013, We call it *tradition*. In Graham Harvey, ed. The handbook of contemporary animism, 17–26. Durham: Acumen.

Honery, Thomas, 1878, Wailwun language and traditions. Journal of the Anthropological Institute of Great Britain and Ireland 254–7:246.

Hooks, Gregory, and Chad L. Smith, 2004, The treadmill of destruction: national sacrifice areas and Native Americans. American Sociological Review 69(4):558–575.

Horne, George A., and George Aiston, 1924, Savage life in Central Australia. London: Macmillan.

Howe, John, 1989, Hunter journey: the diary of John Howe (with an introduction by D. B. Waterson and T. G. Parsons). Sydney: St. Mark's Press.

Howitt, Alfred William, 1884, On some Australian beliefs. Journal of the Anthropological Institute of Great Britain and Ireland 13(2):185–198.

—— 1885, The Jeraeil, or initiation ceremonies of the Kurnai tribe. Journal of the Anthropological Institute of Great Britain and Ireland 14(4):301–325.

—— 1887a, Notes on songs and songmakers of some Australian tribes. Journal of the Anthropological Institute, 16(3):327–335.

—— 1887b, On Australian medicine men; or, doctors and wizards of some Australian tribes. Journal of the Anthropological Institute of Great Britain and Ireland 16(1):23–59.
—— 1904, The native tribes of south-east Australia. London: Macmillan.
Hufford, David J., 1995, Beings without bodies: an experience-centred theory of the belief in spirits. In Barbara Walker, ed. Out of the ordinary: folklore and the supernatural, 11–45. Logan, UT: Utah State University Press
Hultkrantz, Åke, 1979, The religions of the American Indians. Berkeley: University of California Press.
Hume, Lynne, 2002, Ancestral power: the dreaming, consciousness, and Aboriginal Australians. Melbourne: Melbourne University Press.
Hunt, Harry T., 1989, The multiplicity of dreams: memory, imagination and consciousness. New Haven: Yale University Press.
—— 2014, Implications and consequences of post-modern philosophy for contemporary transpersonal studies III. Deleuze and some related phenomenologies of felt meaning: psychosis and mysticism as inherent 'structures of thought'. International Journal of Transpersonal Studies 33(2):16–32.
Irwin, Lee, 1994, The dream seekers: Native American visionary traditions of the Great Plains. Norman OK: University of Oklahoma Press.
Ivens, Walter George, 1927, Melanesians of the south-east Solomon Islands. London: Kegan Paul, Trench, Trübner.
Jakobson, Roman, 1987, The poetry of grammar and the grammar of poetry. In K. Pomorska and S. Rudy, eds. Language in literature, 121–144. Cambridge MA: The Belnap Press of Harvard University.
Jayne, Walter Addison, 1925, The healing gods of ancient civilizations. New Haven: Yale University Press.
Johnson, Dianne, 1998, Night skies of Aboriginal Australia: a noctuary. Sydney: Oceania.
Jones, Caroline, 2008, Darkinyung grammar and dictionary: revitalising a language from historical sources. Nambucca Heads: Muurrbay.
Jones, Garry, 2009, Yengo country: a source of cultural and spiritual awakening. *http://wollombi.nsw.au/documents/doc-94-yengo.pdf* [accessed 29 August 2016].
Jones, Trevor A., 1965, Australian Aboriginal music: the Elkin collection's contribution toward an overall picture. In R. M. Berndt and C. H. Berndt, eds. Aboriginal man in Australia: essays in honour of Emeritus Professor A. P. Elkin, 285–374. Sydney: Angus & Robertson.
—— 1980, The traditional music of the Australian Aborigines. In Elizabeth May, ed. Musics of many cultures: an introduction, 154–171. Berkeley: University of California Press.
Jung, Carl Gustav, 1968, Analytical psychology: its theory and practice. New York: Random House.
—— 1997, Jung on active imagination (edited and with an introduction by Joan Chodorow). Princeton: Princeton University Press.
Kaberry, Phyllis M., 1939, Aboriginal woman: sacred and profane. London: Routledge and Kegan Paul.
Keary, Anne, 2009, Christianity, colonialism, and cross-cultural translation: Lancelot Threlkeld, Biraban, and the Awabakal. Aboriginal History 33:117–155.
Keeling, Richard, 1992, The sources of Indian music: an introduction and overview. The World of Music 34(2):3–21.
Keen, Ian, 1993, Ubiquitous ubiety of dubious uniformity. [Review of Tony Swain, 1993, A place for strangers.] The Australian Journal of Anthropology 4(2):96–110.
—— 2003, Dreams, agency, and traditional authority in Northeast Arnhem Land. In Roger Ivar Lohmann, Dream travelers: sleep experiences and culture in the western Pacific, 127–147. New York: Palgrave Macmillan.
Keogh, Ray, 1989, Nurlu songs from the west Kimberley: an introduction. Australian Aboriginal Studies 1:2–11.
—— 1995, Process models for the analysis of *nurlu* songs from the western Kimberleys. In Linda Barwick, Allan Marett and Guy Tunstill, eds. The essence of singing and the substance of song: recent responses to the Aboriginal performing arts and other essays in honour of Catherine Ellis, 39–51. Sydney: Oceania Publications (University of Sydney).
Kingsley, Peter, 1999, In the dark places of wisdom. Point Reyes CA: The Golden Sufi Center.
Kinsella, John, 2009, The Penguin anthology of Australian poetry. Camberwell, VIC: Penguin.

Kirksey, S. Eben, and Stefan Helmreich, 2010, The emergence of multispecies ethnography. Cultural Anthropology 25(4):545–576.

Kisliuk, Michelle Robin, 1998, Seize the dance! BaAka musical life and the ethnography of performance. New York/Oxford: Oxford University Press.

Kittelson, Mary Lynn, 1996, Sounding the soul: listening to the psyche. Einsiedeln: Daimon.

Kracke, Waud H., 2007, To dream, perchance to cure: dreaming and shamanism in a Brazilian indigenous society. In Jadran Mimica, ed. Explorations in psychoanalytic ethnography, 106–120. Oxford: Berghahn.

Kroeber, Alfred Louis, 1902, Preliminary sketch of the Mohave Indians. American Anthropologist 4(2):276–285.

—— 1925, Handbook of the Indians of California. Bureau of American Ethnology Bulletin 78. Washington DC: Smithsonian Institution.

Kühn, Wilhelm Julius, 1880, The Turra tribe. In Lorimer Fison and A. W. Howitt, Kamilaroi and Kurnai, appendix H, 284–287. Melbourne: George Robertson.

Labate, Beatriz Caiuby and Gustavo Pacheco, 2010, Opening the portals of heaven: Brazilian ayahuasca music (trans. Matthew Meyer). Münster: Lit Verlag.

LaBerge, Stephen, 1985, Lucid dreaming. New York: Ballantine.

Landes, Richard, 2011, Heaven on Earth: the varieties of the millennial experience. Oxford: Oxford University Press.

Landtman, Gunnar, 1917, The folk-tales of the Kiwai Papuans. Helsinki: Societas Scientarum Fennica.

Lane, L., and R. L. K. Fullagar, 1980, Previously unrecorded Aboriginal stone arrangements in Victoria. Records of the Victorian Archaeological Survey 10:134–151.

Laufer, Berthold, 1931, Inspirational dreams in eastern Asia. Journal of American Folklore 44(172):208–216.

Laughlin, Charles D., 2011, Communing with the gods: consciousness, culture and the dreaming brain. Brisbane: Daily Grail.

Le Clézio, Jean-Marie Gustave, 1993, The Mexican dream, or, The interrupted thought of Amerindian civilizations (trans. Teresa Lavender Fagan). Chicago: University of Chicago Press.

Lincoln, Jackson Steward, 1935, The dream in primitive cultures. London: Cresset Press. (Reprinted 1970, Johnson reprints.)

Lint, Theo Maarten van, 2005, The gift of poetry: Khidr and John the Baptist as patron saints of Muslim and Armenian Āšiqs–Ašułs. In J. J. van Ginkel, H. L. Murre-van den Berg, T. M. van Lint eds. Redefining Christian identity: cultural interaction in the Middle East since the rise of Islam, 335–378. Leuven: Peeters.

Lissarrague, Amanda, 2006, A salvage grammar and wordlist of the language from the Hunter River and Lake Macquarie. Nambucca Heads: Muurrbay.

—— 2010, Gathang grammar and dictionary with Gathang stories. Nambucca Heads: Muurrbay.

Lohmann, Roger Ivar, ed., 2003, Dream travelers: sleep experiences and culture in the western Pacific. New York: Palgrave Macmillan.

Lommel, Andreas, 1949, Notes on sexual behaviour and initiation, Wunambal Tribe, north-western Australia. Oceania 20(2):158–164.

—— 1952, Die Unambal: ein Stamm in nordwest-Australien. Hamburg: Museum für Völkerkunde.

—— 1967, The world of the early hunters. London: Evelyn, Adams & Mackay. (Translated by Michael Bullock. American edition published as *Shamanism: the beginnings of art*.)

—— 1989, Shamanism in Australia. In M. Hoppál and O. J. von Sadovszky, eds. Shamanism past and present: part 1, 25–34. Los Angeles: International Society for Trans-Oceanic Research.

—— 1997, The Unambal: a tribe in northwest Australia (trans. Ian Campbell). Carnarvon Gorge QLD: Takarakka Nowan Kas Publications.

Lommel, Andreas, and David Mowaljarlai, 1994, Shamanism in northwest Australia. Oceania 64(4): 277–283.

Lowie, Robert H., 1922, The religion of the Crow Indians. New York: Anthropological Papers of the American Museum of Natural History 25 (part 2).

Mackinlay, Elizabeth, and John Bradley, 2003, Of mermaids and spirit men. The Asia Pacific Journal of Anthropology 4 (1/2): 2–24.
Macqueen, Andy, 2004, Somewhat perilous: the journeys of Singleton, Parr, Howe, Myles and Blaxland in the northern Blue Mountains. Wentworth Falls NSW: the author.
—— 2010, Frederick Robert D'Arcy: colonial surveyor, explorer and artist. Wentworth Falls NSW: the author.
Maffie, James, 2009, 'In the end, we have the Gatling gun, and they have not': future prospects of indigenous knowledges. Futures 41:53–65 (special issue on 'futures for indigenous knowledges').
—— 2013, Aztec philosophy: understanding a world in motion. Boulder: University Press of Colorado.
Magowan, Fiona, 1994, 'The land is our *märr* (essence), it stays forever': The *yothu-yindi* relationship in Australian Aboriginal traditional and popular musics. In Martin Stokes, ed. Ethnicity, identity and music: the musical construction of place, 135–155. Oxford: Berg.
—— 2001, Syncretism or synchronicity? Remapping the Yolngu feel of place. Australian Journal of Anthropology 12(3):275–290.
—— 2007, Spirit, place and power in Arnhem Land traditional and Christian music. In Fiona Richards, ed. The soundscapes of Australia: music, place and spirituality, 282–296. Aldershot: Ashgate.
Marett, Allan, 1992, Variability and stability in Wangga songs from north-west Australia. In Alice M. Moyle, ed. Music and dance of Aboriginal Australia and the South Pacific: the effects of documentation on the living tradition, 193–212. Sydney: Oceania Monographs 41.
—— 2000, Ghostly voices: some observations on song-creation, ceremony and being in NW Australia. Oceania 71(1):18–29.
—— 2005, Songs, dreamings, and ghosts: the wangga of north Australia. Middletown, CT: Wesleyan University Press.
—— n.d., Northern Aboriginal music. Section 1 of entry for 'Australia: 1. Aboriginal music'. In Deane Root, ed. Grove Music Online, n.p.:
http://www.oxfordmusiconline.com:80/subscriber/article/grove/music/40021 [accessed 21 August 2017].
Marett, Allan, and Linda Barwick, 2003, Endangered songs and endangered languages. In Joe Blythe and R. McKenna Brown, eds. Maintaining the links: language, identity and the land. (Proceedings of the Seventh FEL Conference, Broom, Western Australia, 22–24 September 2003.) Bath: Foundation for Endangered Languages.
Marett, Allan, Linda Barwick and Lysbeth Ford, 2013, For the sake of a song: *wangga* songmen and their repertories. Sydney: Sydney University Press.
Marett, Allan, and JoAnne Page, 1995, Interrelationships between music and dance in a Wangga from northwest Australia. In Linda Barwick, Allan Marett and Guy Tunstill, eds. The essence of singing and the substance of song: recent responses to the Aboriginal performing arts and other essays in honour of Catherine Ellis, 27–38. Sydney: Oceania Publications (University of Sydney).
Massey, Irving J., 2006, The musical dream revisited: music and language in dreams. Psychology of Aesthetics, Creativity, and the Arts 5(1):42–50.
Mathew, John, 1899, Eaglehawk and crow: a study of the Australian aborigines, including an inquiry into their origin and a survey of Australian language. London: Nutt.
Mathews, Robert Hamilton, 1896, The Burbung of the Wiradthuri tribes. Journal of the Anthropological Institute of Great Britain and Ireland 25: 295–318.
—— 1897, The Burbung of the Darkinung tribes. Proceedings of the Royal Society of Victoria 10(1):1–12.
—— 1904 [1905], Ethnological notes on the Aboriginal tribes of New South Wales and Victoria. Journal of the Royal Society of New South Wales 38, 203–381. [Republished in 1905 as a monograph, under the imprint of F. W. White, General Printer, Sydney.]
—— 1909, Australian folk-tales. Folklore 20(4):485–487. (This article also appears in a modern edition in part 3 of Martin Thomas's Culture in translation: the anthropological legacy of R. H. Mathews, 143–145. Canberra: ANU E Press and Aboriginal History Inc.)
McCaul, Kim, 2008, The persistence of traditional healers in the 21st century and of anthropology's struggle to understand them. Journal of the Anthropological Society of South Australia 33:129–166.

McClean, Nick, 2013, Being on country: Githabul approaches to mapping culture. In Sally Brockwell, Sue O'Connor and Denis Byrne, eds. Transcending the culture-nature divide in cultural heritage: views from the Asia–Pacific region, 83–99. Canberra: ANU E Press.

McClintock, Walter, 1992, The Old North Trail, or, life, legends, and religion of the Blackfeet Indians. Lincoln: U of Nebraska Press. 146, 430

McConnel, Ursula H., 1935, Myths of the Wikmunkan and Wiknatara tribes: bonefish and bullroarer totems. Oceania 6(1):66–93.

McConvell, Patrick, and William McConvell, forthcoming, The birds and the bees: the origin of sections in Queensland. To appear in Piers Kelly, Patrick McConvell and Sebastien Lacrampe, eds. Skin, kin and clan: the dynamics of social categories in Indigenous Australia. Canberra: Australian National University Press.

McCorristine, Shane, 2010, Spectres of the self: thinking about ghosts and ghost-seeing in England, 1750-1920. Cambridge: Cambridge University Press.

McDonald, Josephine, 1993, Dreamtime superhighway: an analysis of Sydney Basin rock art and prehistoric information exchange. Canberra: ANU E Press.

—— 2008, On a clear day, you can see to Mount Yengo. Or: investigating the archaeological manifestations of culturally significant foci in the prehistoric landscape. In Paul Faulstich and Paul S. C. Taçon, eds. Spatial considerations in rock art (proceedings of Symposium E). In Australian Rock Art Research Association, Time and space: dating and spatial considerations in rock art research, 84–91. Melbourne: Archaeological Publications (papers of the second AURA congress, Cairns 1992).

Meier, Carl Alfred, 2009, Healing dream and ritual: ancient incubation and modern psychotherapy. Einsiedeln, Switzerland: Daimon Verlag.

Merriam, Alan P., 1967, Ethnomusicology of the Flathead Indians. Chicago: Aldine.

Metcalfe, Andrew, and Ann Game, 2010, Creative practice: the time of grace. Time and Society 19(2):165–179.

Miles, W. Augustus, 1854, How did the natives of Australia become acquainted with the demigods and daemonia, and with the superstitions of the ancient races? Journal of the Ethnological Society of London 3:4–50.

Miller, Patricia Cox, 1994, Dreams in late antiquity: studies in the imagination of a culture. Princeton: Princeton University Press.

Milson, Rachel, c. 1840+, Mrs. David Milson Kamilaroi vocabulary and Aboriginal songs, 1840 (manuscript). State Library of NSW, Sydney. ML A1608, CY Reel 2355. Online at *http://acmssearch.sl.nsw.gov.au/search/itemDetailPaged.cgi?itemID=950311* [accessed 20 January 2016]

Morinis, E. A., 1982, Levels of culture in Hinduism: a case study of dream incubation at a Bengali pilgrimage center. Contributions to Indian Sociology 16(2):255–270.

Morton, John, 1989, Singing subjects and sacred objects: a psychological interpretation of the 'transformation of subjects into objects' in Central Australian myth. Oceania 59(4):280–298.

Moyle, Alice M., 1980, Aboriginal music and dance in northern Australia. In Stanley Sadie and John Tyrrell, eds. The new Grove dictionary of music and musicians, vol. 1:713–722. London: Macmillan.

Moyle, Richard, 1979, Songs of the Pintupi: musical life in a Central Australian society. Canberra: Australian Institute of Aboriginal Studies.

—— 1986, Alyawarra music: songs and society in a central Australian community. Canberra: Australian Institute of Aboriginal Studies.

Munn, Nancy, 1973, Walbiri iconography: graphic representation and cultural symbolism in Central Australian society. Ithaca and London: Cornell University Press.

Myers, Fred R., 1986, Pintupi country, Pintupi self: sentiment, place, and politics among Western Desert Aborigines. Washington DC: Smithsonian Institution.

Nathan, Isaac, ed., 1848, The southern Euphrosyne and Australian miscellany: containing oriental moral tales, original anecdote, poetry and music. London & Sydney: Whittaker & Co.

National Parks and Wildlife Service (NSW), 2004, Yengo National Park and Parr State Conservation Area. Sydney: Department of Environment and Conservation (NSW). (Pamphlet with map.)

Needham, William J., 1981, A study of the Aboriginal sites in the Cessnock–Wollombi region of the Hunter Valley, N.S.W. Cessnock: W. J. Needham. (Cover title: Burragurra, where the spirit walked: the Aboriginal relics of the Cessnock–Wollombi region in the Hunter Valley of N.S.W.)
Nelson, Richard K., 1983, Make prayers to the raven: a Koyukon view of the northern forest. Chicago: University of Chicago Press.
Nettl, Bruno, 1989, Blackfoot musical thought: comparative perspectives. Kent OH: Kent State University Press.
Nielsen, Tore, 2012, Dream incubation: ancient techniques of dream influence. Revised version of T. Nielsen, 1988, Ancient methods of dream incubation: bodily methods of inducing spiritual presence. Bulletin of the Montreal Center for the Study of Dreams, Université de Montréal 3(3-4):6–10. Online at *http://dreamscience.ca/en/documents/New%20content/incubation/Incubation%20 overview%20for%20website%20updated.pdf* [accessed 20 January 2016].
Norris, Ray, 2007–2011, Australian Aboriginal astronomy. Online at *http://www.emudreaming.com/index.html* [accessed 17 December 2016].
Norris, Ray, and Cilla Norris, 2009, Emu dreaming: an introduction to Australian Aboriginal astronomy. Sydney: Emu Dreaming.
O'Brien, Linda L., 1976. Music in a Maya cosmos. The World of Music 18(3):35–42.
O'Leary, John., 2004, Giving the Indigenous a voice: further thoughts on the poetry of Eliza Hamilton Dunlop. Journal of Australian Studies 82:85–93 (notes on 187–189).
—— 2011, Savage songs and wild romances. Amsterdam: Rodopi.
Olivier, Emmanuelle, 1998, Bushman vocal music: the illusion of polyphony. In Mathias Schladt, ed. Language, identity and conceptualization among the Khoisan, 359–370. Cologne: Rüdiger Köppe.
Olsen, Dale A., 1996, Music of the Warao of Venezuela: song people of the rain forest. Gainesville: University Press of Florida.
Ong, Walter J., 1983, Ramus: method and the decay of dialogue (2nd edn). Cambridge MA: Harvard University Press.
Orobitg, Gemma, 1998, Les Pumé et leur rêves: étude d'un groupe indien des Plaines du Venezuela. Paris: Éditions des Archives Contemporaines.
Palmer, Edward, 1884, Notes on some Australian tribes. Journal of the Anthropological Institute of Great Britain and Ireland 13(3):276–347.
Park, Willard Z., 1934, Paviotso shamanism. American Anthropologist 34:98–113.
Parker, K. Langloh, 1905, The Euahlayi tribe: a study of Aboriginal life in Australia. London: Constable.
—— 1930, Woggheeguy: Australian Aboriginal legends. Adelaide: Preece.
Parrott, Ian, 1978, The music of Rosemary Brown. London: Regency Press.
Patton, Kimberly, 2004, 'A great and strange correction': intentionality, locality, and epiphany in the category of dream incubation. History of Religions 43:194–223.
Payne, Helen, 1978, The integration of music and belief in Australian Aboriginal culture. Religious Traditions 1(1):8–18.
—— 1984, Residency and ritual rights. In J. C. Kassler & J. Stubington, eds. Problems and solutions: occasional essays presented to Alice M. Moyle, 264–278. Sydney: Hale & Iremonger.
—— 1989, Rites for sites or sites for rites: the dynamics of women's cultural life in the Musgraves. In Peggy Brock, ed. Women, rites and sites: Aboriginal women's cultural knowledge, 41–59. Sydney: Allen & Unwin.
—— 1993, The presence of the possessed: a parameter in the performance practice of the music of Australian Aboriginal women. In Kimberley Marshall, ed. Rediscovering the Muses: women's musical traditions, 1–20. Boston: Northeastern University Press.
Pentony, Brian, 1961, Dreams and dream beliefs in north western Australia. Oceania 32(2):144–149.
Perrin, Michel, 1992, Appendix: the poetic vision of Setuuma, Guajiro shaman. Diogenes 158(Summer):181–184.
Petri, Helmut, 1965, Traum und Trance bei den Australiden. Bild der Wissenschaft 4:277–285.
—— 2014, The Australian medicine man (trans. Ian Campbell, ed. Kim Akerman). Perth: Hesperian Press. [Originally published in 1953 as *Der australische Medizinmann* (Vatican City: Annali Lateranensi, vol. 17).]

Piedade, Acácio Tadeu de Camargo, 2013, Flutes, songs and dreams: cycles of creation and musical performance among the Wauja of the Upper Xingu (Brazil). Ethnomusicology Forum, 22(3):306–322.

Poirier, Sylvie, 2005, A world of relationships: itineraries, dreams, and events in the Australian Western Desert. Toronto: University of Toronto Press.

Pound, Louise, 1929, Caedmon's dream song. In Kemp Malone and Martin B. Ruud, eds. Studies in English philology: a miscellany in honor of Frederick Klaeber, 232–239. Minneapolis: University of Minnesota Press.

Povinelli, Elizabeth A., 1995, Do rocks listen? The cultural politics of apprehending Australian Aboriginal labor. American Anthropologist 97(3):505–518.

Prentice, A. J., and W. A. Squire, 1896, The murruba gibbers of the Australian Aborigines. Maitland Weekly Mercury 8 August 1896 p. 11 (online at *http://nla.gov.au/nla.news-article132400011* [accessed 11 August 2017]).

Purdy, Michael W., 2000, Listening, culture and structures of consciousness: ways of studying listening. International Journal of Listening 14(1):47–68.

Radcliffe-Brown, Alfred Reginald, 1923, Notes on the social organisation of the Australian tribes (Part II). Journal of the Royal Anthropological Institute of Great Britain and Ireland 53:424–447.

—— 1958, The comparative method in social anthropology. In A. R. Radcliffe-Brown, Method in social anthropology: selected essays (ed. M. N. Srinivas), 108–129. Chicago: University of Chicago Press.

Radin, Paul, 1972, The trickster: a study in American Indian mythology. New York: Schocken.

Reay, Marie, 1945, A half-caste Aboriginal community in north-western New South Wales. Oceania 15(4):296–323.

—— 1949, Native thought in rural New South Wales. Oceania 20(2):89–118.

Redmond, Anthony, 2001, Places that move. In A. Rumsey and J. F. Weiner, eds. Emplaced myth: space, narrative, and knowledge in Aboriginal Australia and Papua New Guinea. Honolulu: University of Hawai'i Press.

Reed, Henry, 1977, Dream incubation. In Joseph K. Long, ed. Extrasensory ecology: parapsychology and anthropology, 155–192. Metuchen NJ: Scarecrow Press.

Reid, Lindsay Ann, 2017, To the tune of 'Queen Dido': the spectropoetics of early modern English balladry. In Helen Dell and Helen M. Hickey, eds. Singing death: reflections on music and mortality, 139–153. Abingdon: Routledge.

Reid, Nicholas, 2010, Social identity and recurrent themes in the Djanba repertory. In Brett Baker, Ilana Mushin, Mark Harvey and Rod Gardner, eds. Indigenous language and social identity: papers in honour of Michael Walsh, 319–331. Canberra: Pacific Linguistics.

Reynolds, Simon, 2011, Retromania: pop culture's addiction to its own past. London: Faber and Faber.

Richards, Fiona, ed., 2007, The soundscapes of Australia: music, place and spirituality. Aldershot: Ashgate.

Ridington, Robin, 1971, Beaver dreaming and singing. In P. Lötz and J. Lötz, eds. Pilot not commander: essays in memory of Diamond Jenness. Anthropologica (new series) 13(1/2):115–128.

Ridley, William, 1861, Journal of a missionary tour among the Aborigines of the western interior of Queensland, in the year 1855. In J. D. Lang, Queensland, Australia, 435–445 (Appendix I). London: Edward Stanford.

—— 1873, Report on Australian languages and traditions. Journal of the Anthropological Institute of Great Britain and Ireland 2(2):257–291.

—— 1875, Kámilarói, and other Australian languages (2nd edn). Sydney: Thomas Richards, Government Printer.

Roberts, David Andrew, 2008, 'language to save the innocent': Reverend L. Threlkeld's linguistic mission. Journal of the Royal Australian Historical Society 94(2):107–125.

Róheim, Géza, 1933, Women and their life in Central Australia. Journal of the Royal Anthropological Institute of Great Britain and Ireland 63:207–265.

—— 1934, Primitive high gods. Psychoanalytic Quarterly 3(1) part 2:62–133.

—— 1945, The eternal ones of the dream: a psychoanalytic interpretation of Australian myth and ritual. New York: International Universities Press.

—— 1952, The gates of the dream. New York: International Universities Press.
—— 1972, The panic of the gods and other essays. New York: Harper.
—— 1974, The riddle of the Sphinx: or human origins. New York: Harper.
Rose, Deborah Bird, 2004, Reports from a wild country: ethics for decolonisation. Sydney: University of New South Wales Press.
—— 2013, Val Plumwood's philosophical animism: attentive interactions in the sentient world. Environmental Humanities 3:93–109.
Roseman, Marina, 1986, Sound in ceremony: power and performance in Temiar curing rituals. PhD dissertation, Cornell University, Ithaca.
—— 1993, Healing sounds from the Malaysian rainforest: Temiar music and medicine. Berkeley: University of California Press.
—— 1996, 'Pure products go crazy': rainforest healing in a nation-state. In C. Laderman and M. Roseman, eds. The performance of healing, 233–269. New York: Routledge.
—— 1998, Singers of the landscape: song, history, and property rights in the Malaysian rain forest. American Anthropologist (new series) 100(1):106–121.
—— 2000, The canned sardine spirit takes the mic. The World of Music 42(2):115–136.
Roth, Walter E., 1897, Ethnological studies among the North-West-Central Queensland Aborigines. Brisbane: Edmund Gregory, Government Printer.
—— 1902, Games, sports and amusements. North Queensland Ethnography: Bulletin no. 4. Brisbane: Home Secretary's Department. (Facsimile edition published 1984 by Hesperian Press, Victoria Park, WA.)
—— 1903, Superstition, magic and medicine. North Queensland Ethnography: Bulletin no. 5. Brisbane: Home Secretary's Department.
Rouget, Gilbert, 1985, Music and trance: a theory of the relations between music and possession. Chicago: University of Chicago Press.
Sachs, Curt, 1943, The rise of music in the ancient world: east and west. Mineola NY: Dover.
Sacks, Oliver, 2008, Musicophilia: tales of music and the brain. London: Picador.
Samuel, Geoffrey, 2010, Inner work and the connection between anthropological and psychological analysis. In J. Weinhold and G. Samuel, eds. Body, performance, agency and experience (Ritual dynamics and the science of ritual, vol. 2), 301–316. Wiesbaden: Harrassowitz.
San Roque, Craig, 2007, On *Tjukurrpa*, painting up, and building thought. In Jadran Mimica, ed. Explorations in psychoanalytic ethnography, 148–172. Oxford: Berghahn.
Scarre, Chris and Graeme Lawson, 2006, Archaeoacoustics. Cambridge: McDonald Institute for Archaeological Research.
Schafer, R. Murray, 1994, The soundscape: our sonic environment and the tuning of the world. Rochester VT: Destiny Books.
Schneider, David M., and Lauriston Sharp, 1969, The dream life of a primitive people: the dreams of the Yir Yoront of Australia. Washington DC: American Anthropological Association.
Severi, Carlo, 2012, The arts of memory: comparative perspectives on a mental artefact. HAU: Journal of Ethnographic Theory 2(2):451–85.
Sexton, Jamie, 2012, Weird Britain in exile: Ghost Box, hauntology, and alternative heritage. Popular Music and Society 35(4):561–584.
Sharpe, Margaret, 1995, Dictionary of Western Bundjalung including Gidhabal and Tabulam Bundjalung (2nd edn). Armidale: the author.
Silverstein, Michael, 1992, The indeterminacy of contextualization: when is enough enough? In Peter Auer and Aldo Di Luzio, eds. The contextualization of language, 55–76. Amsterdam: John Benjamins.
Sim, Ian M., 1966, Rock engravings of the MacDonald River district, N.S.W. Canberra: Australian Institute of Aboriginal Studies.
Slater, Frederic, 1937, Intepretation of the drawings at Burragurra and Yango. (Paper read before ANZAAS meeting, 14 January 1937, 10–15). Sutherland NSW: S.C.A.M. Print.
Smithson, Carma L., and Robert Euler, 1964, Havasupai religion and mythology. Salt Lake City: University of Utah Press.

Smyth, Robert Brough, 1876, The Aborigines of Victoria: with notes relating to the habits of the natives of other parts of Australia and Tasmania compiled from various sources for the Government of Victoria. Melbourne: John Ferres, government printer.
Spaulding, John, 1981, The dream in other cultures: anthropological studies of dreams and dreaming. Dreamworks 1(4):330–342.
Spearim, Paul, 2014, The story of Buwadjarr and the six Wandabaa spirits. National Indigenous Times 13(346):16 (19 February 2014).
Spencer, Baldwin, and Francis James Gillen, 1899, The native tribes of Central Australia. London: Macmillan.
—— 1904, The northern tribes of Central Australia. London: Macmillan.
—— 1927, The Arunta: a study of a stone age people. London: Macmillan.
Sprinker, Michael, ed., 1999, Ghostly demarcations: a symposium on Jacques Derrida's *Spectres of Marx*. London: Verso.
Squire, W. A., 1896, Ritual, myth, and customs of the Australian Aborigines: a short study in comparative ethnology. Maitland: Mercury Print.
Stanbridge, William Edward, 1861, Some particulars of the general characteristics, astronomy and mythology of the tribes in the Central part of Victoria, Southern Australia. Transactions of the Ethnological Society of London (new series) 1:286–304.
Stanner, William E. H., 1963, On Aboriginal religion VI: cosmos and society made correlative. Oceania 33(4):239–273.
Stein, Rolf-Alfred, 1959, Recherches sur l'épopée et le barde au Tibet. Paris: Presses Universitaires de France.
Stephen, Michele, 1979, Dreams of change: the innovative role of altered states of consciousness in traditional Melanesian religion. Oceania 50(1):3–22.
Stewart, Charles, ed., 2004, Anthropological approaches to dreaming. Dreaming (special issue) 14(2–3).
Strehlow, Carl, 1907–1920, Die Aranda- und Loritja-Stämme in Zentral-Australien. Frankfurt am Main: Joseph Baer & Co.
Strehlow, Theodor G. H., 1971, Songs of Central Australia. Sydney: Angus and Robertson.
Streich, Hildemarie, 1980, Musik im Traum. Musiktherapeutische Umschau 1:9–19.
Stubington, Jill, 2007, Singing the land: the power of performance in Aboriginal life. Strawberry Hills NSW: Currency House.
Sumegi, Angela, 2008, Dreamworlds of shamanism and Tibetan Buddhism: the third place. Albany: State University of New York Press.
Swain, Tony, 1993, A place for strangers: towards a history of Australian Aboriginal being. Cambridge: Cambridge University Press.
Swartz, Stephen M., 2012, Interactive Warlpiri–English dictionary: with English–Warlpiri finderlist (2nd edn). Darwin: Australian Society for Indigenous Languages. Online at *http://ausil.org/Dictionary/ Warlpiri/aboutwarlpiri.htm* [accessed 29 August 2017].
Sword, Helen, 2002, Ghostwriting modernism. Ithaca: Cornell University Press.
Taplin, George, 1879, The Narrinyeri. In James D. Woods, ed. The native tribes of South Australia, 1–156. Adelaide: E. S. Wigg & Son.
Tedlock, Barbara, 1991, The new anthropology of dreaming. Dreaming 1:161–178. (Reprinted in Kelly Bulkeley, ed., 2001, Dreams: a reader on religious, cultural, and psychological dimensions of dreaming, 149–164. New York: Palgrave.)
—— 1999, Sharing and interpreting dreams in Amerindian nations. In David Shulman and Guy G. Stroumsa, eds. Dream cultures: explorations in the comparative history of dreaming, 87–103. New York: Oxford University Press.
Teit, James A., 1900, The Thompson Indians of British Columbia (ed. Franz Boas). New York: Memoirs of the American Museum of Natural History 2 (part 4).
—— 1930, The Salishan tribes of the Western Plateaus (ed. Franz Boas). Bureau of American Ethnology, 45th annual report (1927–28), 23–396. Washington DC: Smithsonian Institution.
Tennant-Kelly, Caroline, 1935, Tribes on Cherburg Settlement, Queensland. Oceania 5(4):461–473.

Testart, Alain, 1980, Some puzzling dualistic classifications in New South Wales. Bijdragen tot de Taal-, Land- en Volkenkunde 136(1):64–89.
Thomas, Northcote W., 1905, Baiame and the bell-bird. Man 5:49–51.
Threlkeld, Lancelot E., 1826, Australian Aboriginal song. Sydney Gazette, 5 January, 4. [This item actually includes two songs, the second of which (cited in the present text) is subtitled simply 'Another' (sc. 'Australian Aboriginal song').]
—— 1834, An Australian grammar comprehending the principles and natural rules of the language, as spoken by the Aborigines, in the vicinity of Hunter's River, Lake Macquarie, &c. New South Wales. Sydney: Stephens & Stokes, Herald Office.
—— 1836, An Australian spelling book in the language as spoken by the Aborigines in the vicinity of Hunter's River, Lake Macquarie, &c. New South Wales. Sydney: Stephens & Stokes, Herald Office.
Tindale, Norman B., 1935, Initiation among the Pitjandjara natives of the Mann and Tomkinson Ranges in South Australia. Oceania 6(2):199–224.
Tomlinson, Gary, 1993, Music in Renaissance magic: toward a historiography of others. Chicago: University of Chicago Press.
Tonkinson, Robert, 1970, Aboriginal dream-spirit beliefs in a contact situation: Jigalong, Western Australia. In R. M. Berndt ed. Australian Aboriginal anthropology, 277–291. Perth: University of Western Australia Press, for the Australian Institute of Aboriginal Studies.
—— 2003, Ambrymese dreams and the Mardu Dreaming. In Roger Ivar Lohmann, ed. Dream travelers: sleep experiences and culture in the western Pacific, 87–105. New York: Palgrave Macmillan.
—— 2013, Dream spirits and innovation in Aboriginal Australia's Western Desert. International Journal of Transpersonal Studies 32(1):127–139.
Treloyn, Sally, 2003, Scotty Martin's *Jadmi Junba*: a song series from the Kimberley region of northwest Australia. Oceania 73(3):208–220.
—— 2006, Songs that pull: composition/ performance through musical analysis. Context: Journal of Music Research 31:151–164.
—— 2014, Cross and square: variegation in the transmission of songs and musical styles between the Kimberley and Daly Regions of Northern Australia. In Amanda Harris, ed. Circulating cultures: exchanges of Australian Indigenous music, dance and media, 203–238. Canberra: ANU Press.
Trigg, Dylan, 2012, The memory of place: a phenomenology of the uncanny. Athens OH: Ohio University Press. Online at *https://muse.jhu.edu/book/14350* [accessed 6 July 2017].
Troy, Jakelin F., 1994, The Sydney language. Canberra: the author (with the assistance of the Australian Dictionaries Project and AIATSIS).
Turcotte, Gerry, 2007, Ghosts of the Great South Land. The Global South 1(1):109–116.
—— 2009a, The kangaroo gargoyles: footnotes to an Australian Gothic script. In A. Sarwal and R. Sarwal, eds. Reading down under: Australian literary studies, 352–364. New Delhi: SSS Publications.
—— 2009b, Peripheral fear: transformations of the Gothic in Canadian and Australian fiction. Brussels: P.I.E. Peter Lang.
Turner, Margaret Kemarre, 2010, Iwenhe Tyerrtye: what it means to be an Aboriginal person. Alice Springs: IAD Press. (As told to Barry McDonald Perrurle, with translations by Veronica Perrurle Dobson.)
Turner, Victor, 1969, The ritual process: structure and anti-structure. Chicago: Aldine.
Turpin, Myfany, 2007, The poetics of central Australian song. Australian Aboriginal Studies 2007/2:100–115.
Uí Ógáin, Ríonach, 1992–93, Music learned from the fairies. Béaloideas: The Journal of the Folklore of Ireland Society 60–61:197–214.
van Toorn, Penny, 2006, Writing never arrives naked: early Aboriginal cultures of writing in Australia. Canberra: Aboriginal Studies Press.
Vickery, Ann, 2002, A 'lonely crossing': approaching nineteenth-century Australian women's poetry. Victorian Poetry 40(1):33–54.
Voegelin, Salome, 2010, Listening to noise and silence: towards a philosophy of sound art. New York: Continuuum.

Wafer, Jim, 2017, Why Waway? The Proctor map and the getting of song in New South Wales. In Peter Austin, Harold Koch and Jane Simpson, eds. Language, land and song: studies in honour of Luise Hercus, 287–303. London: EL Publishing.

Wafer, Jim, and Amanda Lissarrague, 2008, A handbook of Aboriginal languages of New South Wales and the Australian Capital Territory. Nambucca Heads: Muurrbay.

Wagner, Rudolf G., 1988, Imperial dreams in China. In Carolyn T. Brown, ed. Psycho-Sinology: the universe of dreams in Chinese culture, 11–24. Lanham MD: University Press of America.

Waldron, David, ed., 2016, Goldfields and the Gothic: a hidden heritage and folklore. North Melbourne: Australian Scholarly Publishing.

Warden, John, 1982, Orpheus and Ficino. In John Warden, ed. Orpheus: the metamorphoses of a myth, 85–110. Toronto: University of Toronto Press.

Waterman, Patricia Panyity, 1987, A tale-type index of Australian Aboriginal oral narratives. Helsinki: Suomalainen Tiedeakatemia.

Watkins, Mary, 1977, Waking dreams. New York: Harper.

Waugh, Earle H., 2005, Memory, music, and religion: Morocco's mystical chanters. Columbia SC: University of South Carolina Press.

Webby, Elizabeth, 1980, The aboriginal in early Australian literature. Southerly 40(1):45–63.

Weinstock, Jeffrey Andrew, 2004, Spectral America: phantoms and the national imagination. Madison: University of Wisconsin Press/Popular Press.

Wild, Stephen, 1987, Recreating the *jukurrpa*: adaptation and innovation of songs and ceremonies in Warlpiri society. In M. Clunies Ross, T. Donaldson and S. A. Wild, eds. Songs of Aboriginal Australia (Oceania Monograph 32), 97–120. Sydney: University of Sydney.

Willin, Melvyn J., 1999, Paramusicology: an investigation of music and paranormal phenomena. PhD thesis, University of Sheffield. Online at *http://etheses.whiterose.ac.uk/14778/* [accessed 6 July 2017].

Wissler, Clark, 1912, Ceremonial bundles of the Blackfoot Indians. New York: Anthropological Papers of the American Museum of Natural History 7 (part 2).

Wolf, Richard K., 2014, The voice in the drum: music, language, and emotion in Islamicate South Asia. Urbana: University of Illinois Press.

Yates, Frances A., 1966, The art of memory. London: Routledge and Kegan Paul.

Yonker, Dolores M., 1982, Dream as validator in traditional African cultures. Dreamworks 2(3):242–250.

Young, Rob, 2010, Electric Eden: unearthing Britain's visionary music. London: Faber & Faber.

10 Finding laka for burdal: Song revitalisation at Mornington Island over the past 40 years

Cassy Nancarrow[1] and Peter Cleary[2]
James Cook University, Cairns, Australia[1]
and independent researcher[2]

Abstract

The Lardil song tradition known as *burdal* has never really been lost. However, its history is not necessarily an unbroken linear narrative. There have been times when some songs have been 'forgotten', only to come back though dreams at a later date. This timelessness, or the idea that songs can be re-dreamed unpredictably at any time, is seen as an ongoing confirmation of the veracity and power of important stories.

The authors have been closely involved in the maintenance and revitalisation of *burdal* and other song traditions at Mornington Island over several decades. This article is written from our collective experience in collaboration with four generations of Lardil songmen and women, and incorporates reflections on past practices and contemporary situations. We break down the myth of songs being handed down from a 'misty ancient past', and look instead at key issues of song ownership, creation, authenticity and sustainability in a modern context.

Lardil concepts of *burdal* 'song', *laka* 'way' and *mirndiyan* 'dreaming' are explored, and song practices of recent times considered in terms of cultural shift and commercialisation of song culture. A description of conscious attempts at recording and revival activities is given, including archive repatriation, 'culture camps', touring and mentoring programs. We also discuss various methods of archiving and cataloguing song material and what has worked best in different circumstances. We conclude by identifying possible strategies for the future.

Keywords: Mornington Island; Lardil songs; burdal; dreaming songs

1 Introduction

Lardil people are the traditional owners of Mornington Island in the Gulf of Carpentaria. The Lardil language is part of the language family known as Tangkic, which includes Gangalidda (of the neighbouring mainland) and Kayardild (of nearby Bentinck Island), and could be considered critically endangered. Descendants of many other traditional owner groups also live at Mornington Island, which has a population of about 1100, of which around 900 identify

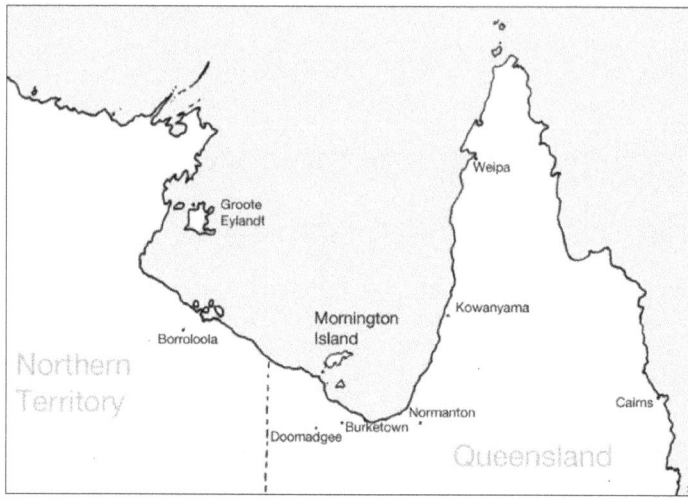

Map 10.1: Geographical location of Mornington Island

as Aboriginal. Most people on Mornington Island these days speak as their first language a creole that, while largely English-lexified, also utilises many Lardil words and phrases, and has a sound system and intonation pattern similar to Lardil and other Australian languages.

Lardil people have always had links with other mainland and coastal communities, especially to the west, where most traditional stories are said to have come from. By the 1860s there were sizeable non-Indigenous populations in Burketown and nearby Sweers Island, and in 1914 the first Presbyterian mission was established on Mornington Island. The mission went through a number of identifiable eras, with varying levels of control over the cultural lives of Lardil and mainland Aboriginal people, until its closure in the 1970s. Between 1944 and 1952, a particularly strict regime was in place, characterised by extreme repression of traditional cultural practices, including song and dance.

A concept persists in Australia of Aboriginal songs originating in time immemorial and being passed down from generation to generation unchanged. This belief has been exploited at times by Lardil people and promoters; for example, in a 1972 Sydney newspaper advertisement, 'Authentic legend and corroboree dances. See ancient and unchanged tribal legend performed. See the Brolga and the Honeybee dance with Australia's most authentic portrayal from the Lardil tribe'.[1] Although there are some valid elements in this stereotype, overall it is not a true picture of the dynamic process by means of which Lardil songs come into being, belong to people and place, and are collaboratively worked to create performance.

Many remote communities in Australia retain cultural knowledge and skills deriving from traditional performance practices. This knowledge is closely integrated with social structure and relationships to land, both of which have been seriously affected by colonisation. Survival has been a matter of ongoing resistance and adaptation, as a response to the continuing nature of colonisation (see Cleary 2006:2).

There are a number of traditional Lardil song genres: *kujika* and *marndar* are men's (initiation) ceremony songs; *jarada* belong to a different men's ceremony associated with 'love magic'; *jawala* are funeral songs; and *wankabel* are women's hunting songs. There are also other song

---

[1] Advertisement for a performance at the Sydney Town Hall as part of the Waratah Festival, 1972 (*Sydney Morning Herald*, Saturday, 23 September 1972, p. 30: *https://www.newspapers.com/newspage/119743490/* [accessed 22 October 2017]).

types that could be used for healing, birthing, and singing the weather. The *burdal* songs that are the focus of this chapter are public 'corroboree' songs, usually accompanied by dance. They are performed outside of any ceremonial context, although there can be crossovers with other genres in both meaning and musical style. *Burdal* come to people in dreams and may then have the accompanying *laka* ('dance') negotiated by the dreamer's group.

The loss and revival of men's ceremony practices, including *kujika* and *marndar* songs, is an important story in itself, but one that is outside the scope of the present chapter.[2] Nonetheless, it is worth noting, in this context, the close relationship that Lardil songmen have with other Gulf communities, especially the Yanyuwa people of Borroloola, through ceremony and stories. The Yanyuwa song traditions, summarised by Bradley and Mackinlay (2000), have much in common with those at Mornington Island, except that Lardil *burdal* (currently over 160 distinct songs dreamt by at least 40 individuals) are always received through dreams.

Within the *burdal* genre there are two subclasses: *kirdi burdal* ('small burdal'), fun dances that children are encouraged to participate in; and *mutha burdal* ('big burdal'), which relate important stories and are danced by adults at the end of an evening of dance (see Memmott 1979:112). Most *burdal* are danced by both men and women (with defined roles), although there are a handful that are for either just men or just women to dance. While *burdal* can be dreamt by either men or women, the public singers for *burdal* are always men.

The term *laka* in Lardil has a complex range of meanings. Its most general English gloss would be something like 'way', as in the 'way to do something'. But it also has a deeper sense as 'the way you conduct yourself'. The late Kenneth Jacob composed a Lardil motto for the local school, *Thaldi bana merri kuba laka*, roughly calquable as 'Come and listen (learn) good-way'. In the context of dance, *laka* simply refers to the movements made by dancers, and the verb *layiwurri* means 'to find *laka*'. It is used to refer to the process of dance creation, as described in the account by Nancy Wilson that begins the next section.

An important distinction can be made between the passive way in which songs are received in dreams and the active process of 'finding' or developing an appropriate dance to go with the song. This need for active development applies even when the dream contained elements of dance. Putting song and dance together in waking reality is still a collaborative process between songmen and dancers.

2 Dreaming of songs

Nancy Wilson recorded the following account of events from the 1940s:

> We used to go out bush for holidays ... our camps round about each other. And when I go to bed now I can hear person singing ... singing in his sleep. It's a dream, like, his dream ... he might have two or three lines of that song what he dream. And he get up in the early morning and he sing ... then he might forget couple of lines. He ask them other mates bla him now, 'Hey, youfella bin hear me singing last night?' They said, 'Yeah'. 'Ah, what this song, what this line here, this *burdal*, this part here, now? I singim two line, and what that other line I singim?' ... That other man say, 'Well, you bin sing like that'. Alright, he putim in that third line bla that song. And he might put in the fourth line. So that song mightbe got four lines of song ... Another lot come sing from nother end of their camp ... them ladies they sit down sing too, with them men ... Alright they sing, sing, sing.
>
> Alright, when that song finish, they might have something to eat ... then this boss fella now what bin dream the dance, he singout now, '*Thaldi* now, we go *layiwurri*'. That mean, 'we get up, we go

---

2   For further discussion of the revival of men's ceremony at Mornington Island, see Paul Memmott's recently published account (2016).

> now, make up this song what I bin dream last night.' So they all get up and they go long way from the camp ... just the men themselves ... And they sit down now, 'Where *laka* now?'. That mean, 'Where's the action now? Any action?'. 'Yeah'. One man might get up, do his action ... they agree with it. Then another man get up, action. Mightbe they disagree, they don't wantim ... They ask, 'Well, what that meaning of that dance?'. Well, he must be for either bird, or fish, or ... bushfire ... or mightbe shake-a-leg ... So that corroboree go on and on. They agree with it then. That's how they get their dance (in Nancarrow 1999:65–6).

The dreaming of songs is regarded by Lardil people as a gift from deceased ancestors, *karnanganmenda* 'sky people'[3], various 'unseen people', or the *mirndiyan* associated with story places on country. The Lardil term *mirndiyan* is usually translated into English as 'dreaming', but also incorporates the senses of 'story' and 'totem' (see McKnight 1999:229). *Mirndiyan* are the underlying stories associated with place that can make themselves known through dreams. The experience of stories emerging thus unexpectedly is an ongoing confirmation of their timeless veracity and power, even though the actual representations of story through *burdal* are situated in time as well as place.

The same song may be dreamt by two different people. Fred Jarrarr explained how a story spirit first gave Fred's classificatory son Kenny Roughsey a song in a dream, which Kenny forgot upon waking. Fred then dreamt the same song the following night, remembered it, and a dance was made to go with it.

> One song, that bla walba[4]. Well mefla bin go that time from here, [...] Mefla bin go round ... to that story now, there where they stand up la water, that Maarnbil story. That man from Sydney Island, Warambay[5], bin follow mefla right up langa Meekiyan. Then that fella gaveim [the song to] this fella. Everything e bin dream about e bin loseim again, then I bin dreamim that night ... This song no more from olden time, this one bin dream from this time ... if e bin only song from olden time, mightbe forget about all thatun, mifella. This song, alright, from this time (Jarrarr 1975).

He goes on to describe how they subsequently performed the *walba* song with its paddle dance on tour in the Gold Coast, Brisbane and Sydney, even transporting a full *walba* and paddles down from Mornington Island for the purpose.

Jarrarr's recount implies that songs can exist independently of individual memory, and that the forgetting of songs is no barrier to their appearance in dreams at later times. This concurs with a broader Lardil experience of *mirndiyan* existing independently of the knowledge of individuals. For example, it has been reported (e.g. by Lindsay Roughsey in Memmott (1979:213) and by Cecil Goodman (pers. com. 2013)) that much of the Lardil story of *Thuwathu* 'Rainbow Serpent' was lost during the late nineteenth and early twentieth centuries. This was a time of great upheaval in the southern Gulf – as in other parts of Australia (see Trigger 1992). Knowledge of the *Thuwathu* story and associated songs was re-dreamt by Sandy Goodman and Paddy Marmies in the 1930s, bringing the *Thuwathu* story back into the consciousness of Lardil people. Further *Thuwathu* songs have subsequently been dreamt by several other men, mostly in the 1940s to 1960s, but also a handful in the 1970s and one in the 1980s.

Lardil songmen have on occasion dreamt new songs when travelling outside Mornington Island. These songs are regarded by the songmen as belonging to the country where they are dreamt, and are not necessarily meant for Lardil people. On one such occasion, songman Stanley

---
3 There is an account of analogous Yanyuwa sky people in Mackinlay and Bradley (2003). These authors present a detailed account of Yanyuwa man Jerry Brown Rrawajinda's reception of a song from the Ngabaya Spirit Man of the sky. This story is familiar to Lardil songmen also.
4 A *walba* is a bark raft. The words of the song begin *yakinba rangu biyara rama*.
5 *Warambay* was a black stingray and warrior.

Chong was with a group that detoured to Jenolan Caves, near Sydney. He and most of the other Lardil people waited near the mouth of the cave while some went inside. That night he was staying in a flat in Bondi, with the rest of the group, and dreamt the song of the Rainbow Serpent, who came down through the cave and swirled around the pool in front. Stanley recalled that the song was sung for him by old men sitting around the waterhole and then translated into his own language (Cleary 1984:51).

Following this experience, several songmen expressed the intention of putting a dance together for the new song when they returned to Mornington Island. That process did not ever happen, however. No recordings were made, and, as far as the authors know, no one can now remember how the song went. Resources and equipment were very limited in those years, so this event just remains as a story. There were other cases, involving different songmen, where songs were dreamt outside Lardil country; for example, at Robinvale, on the Murray River, and at a dingo story site on a beach south of Adelaide. On one occasion, Lardil songman Kenneth Jacob dreamt a red kangaroo song after visiting Morialta Falls, near Adelaide. In the following days we returned to the falls to film him singing the song *in situ*. The footage and the song were passed on to the local Kaurna people, as they were regarded as the true owners of the story.

3 Touring and public performance

Gordon Watt made the following observations in an interview with the authors:

> When we first go out [on tour in the late 1960s] ... can't be frightened of people, even children. You got to face them when you dancing. You can't be dancing with you head down all the time, nothing. You feel a lot better when you doing something, dancing ... thats bin how I feeling when I first dance ... I just love it. Some week we mightbe do two or three schools in one day ... I feel really tired, but we had to do it ... it's our culture. We gotta keep the culture going (Watt, 18 July 2012).

Lardil songmen and dancers first performed to mainstream Australian audiences in 1965. Because of the remote island location of the community, substantial organising and expense were involved then, as now, in travelling to mainland urban centres to perform. The first tours were facilitated by mission administration in conjunction with festival organisers and entrepreneurs. From about 1973 Lardil people became more involved in the organisation of touring activities, and in 1977 incorporated into Woomera Aboriginal Corporation (henceforth referred to here are 'Woomera'[6]) with the joint aims of sharing culture through touring and reviving culture on Mornington Island. Over the next 25 years, more than 120 tours were conducted in almost every part of Australia. As well, there were in excess of 20 international tours.

In response to the availability of funding and a burgeoning 'market' in mainland Australia, touring proliferated in the 1980s and 1990s. It steadily expanded so that by the late 1990s over 150 individuals left the island in any one year for periods of four to eight weeks, mostly in the form of educational performances in schools, but also in the context of folkloric festivals and, occasionally, staged theatre performances. One effect of this process was daily exposure to and practice of songs. Because touring involved such intense and organised routines it proved to be an excellent learning time. Some experienced dancers were able to reskill as emerging singers, and some younger people were mentored by older songmen, allowing them to step up as singers in the context of a focus on youth-only performances.

---

6   In 2010 Woomera had a name change to Mirndiyan Gununa Aboriginal Corporation ('Mirndiyan Gununa').

There was sufficient flexibility in the touring schedules that new singers could practice before live audiences. Nonetheless, while there were many men on tour who took on a singing role from time to time, it was always recognised that the source of authority lay with a small number of the elder songmen. Between these men there were many tensions over issues such as ownership of particular *burdal*, performance rights, and creative or conservative interpretations of song meanings. These frictions created the potential for rivalry and jealousy (Memmott 1979:197). Family politics and differences in style have played a role in fostering and/or stifling the developing talent of younger performers.

One effect of national and international touring and public performance was a growing awareness of the issues surrounding 'authenticity'. Casey (2011:60) uses the term 'epistemic violence' to describe the separation of Aboriginal performance practices into 'authentic' and 'contaminated'. She argues that 'authenticity' in some schools of thought, especially those deriving from Durkheim, is improperly reserved for ritual and ceremony, but that such a division does not take account of cultural contexts and historical performance practices, and may lead to the impression that 'authentic' practices are static and unchanging 'museum-pieces'. Casey's argument also has relevance to the epistemic division implied by the often used terms 'traditional' and 'contemporary'.

The realities of working cross-culturally immediately require some artistic compromises, but these are not intrinsically incompatible with the 'authentic' or 'traditional' cultural practices, such as song dreaming and *layiwurri* (described above), which have always incorporated the elements of creativity and dynamism.

Lardil *burdal* are regarded as being primarily owned by the person who dreams them. However, there is a complex, broader web of ownership based on factors such as the family of the dreamer, the people who helped remember the song and 'find' the dance, and the country to which the story or meaning of the *burdal* belongs. Even more broadly, there is a strong sense of ownership today by Lardil people of the entire *burdal* repertoire, and, to a degree, sharing is encouraged within the Mornington Island community.

The main concern for Lardil people has been the use of the songs by other, non-Lardil, Aboriginal people. This has occurred on a number of occasions, and in some cases can be traced back to 'permission' being granted by a Lardil individual to an external group to use a particular song and/or dance. Some of these cases occurred through programs organised by Woomera, but others involved Lardil individuals who were engaged to teach and perform throughout the mainland.

Such acts of bestowing cultural rights however hold little validity back in the community. They are generally regarded as theft, and provoke outrage. Despite the depth of feeling, such affronts are nevertheless dealt with by quiet diplomacy, to bring about a cessation of the offending activity. Approaches are made on a personal level, sometimes by an intermediary, and usually result in immediate redress, with word spreading through Aboriginal networks. Reputations are important enough for protocol to be enforced. Nonetheless, Lardil people see vigilance as important, to protect both the integrity of original song words and the connection of song to people and country.

From the 1970s, Woomera tried to establish a protocol with other Aboriginal performers, such as students from the Aboriginal/Islander Dance Theatre (AIDT), to limit the performance of Lardil song and dance to occasions where a Mornington Island performer was involved. At first the protocols were followed, but in more recent times this has not always been the case. Songs and dances easily become trade products, and guidelines are not always easily enforced in situations of scattered leadership. Protocols are still evolving, to deal with the complexity of situations that have been created by ongoing historical developments (see Cleary 2006).

Lardil song culture has been exposed to potential appropriation not just by travel but also by the commercial availability of song recordings. In 1985 a recording project by Woomera created cassette tapes of *burdal* songs for distribution in the community and for giving away as special gifts on tour.[7] These recordings were subsequently made into a CD (Cleary 1993) that was produced and distributed commercially (as *Budal Lardil*), with a contract giving royalties back to Woomera on behalf of the performers. Ironically, the existence of this CD later created a crisis that led to more intense scrutiny and research into song protocols and intellectual rights. In 1998 it was discovered that songs from *Budal Lardil* were being distributed in Europe on compilation CDs, without any connection back to Mornington Island. Legal action eventually resolved this matter, but it took two years and resulted in a heightened awareness that appropriation of songs could be happening at any time.

This was not the first time a commercial recording of Lardil *burdal* had been produced. In 1966 W&G Records released an LP recorded by George Kransky and coordinated by the Reverend Douglas Belcher. In 1977 the Australian Institute of Aboriginal Studies (AIAS) released a compilation tape that included recordings of *burdal* made by Alice Moyle. While we are not aware that these recordings involved any misappropriation of songs, their existence, in an absence of clear protocols around ownership, is seen as a potential risk.

4 Archives and records

In 1992, Peter Cleary and Sam Pilot began collating information about Lardil songs in a typed document they called a 'songs register', arranged as a set of different fields. These included a Lardil name for the song; an English name; the 'country' the song belonged to; the 'owners/dreamers'; a rough transcript of the song text; and a summary of the 'meaning'. At that time the document's main purpose was to inform the development of presentation material to explain *burdal* for a non-Lardil audience. This was a creative process involving both songmen and lead dancers, who decided which *burdal* they were going to perform and what was to be said (and not said) about each item.

A few performers rotated in the role of 'presenter', and gradually particular ways of explaining the meanings of dance and story became routine. These explanations were repeated many times on tours that lasted for weeks. Such ways of presenting *burdal* were created in a cross-cultural setting, but made their way back into Mornington Island culture through school classes taught by performers back from tour.

From the late 1990s, the songs register also played a role in documenting ownership of songs for copyright discussions, as discussed above. The committee of the Woomera organisation saw the need to create a more formal and thoroughly researched register of songs, which was accomplished with the help of an AIATSIS research grant. The first task was to access documentation of *burdal* from archival collections, such as that of Paul Memmott, at the Aboriginal Data Archive. Memmott had audio recordings and a card file of Lardil songs, similar in form to the Woomera register (see Memmott 1979:520 for an example layout). Much of the information on Memmott's cards was able to be matched with contemporarily known songs. Other archival material sourced from AIATSIS included recordings of Lardil songs by Tindale (1960, 1963),

---

7   Recordings of some *kujika*, *wankabel* and other sacred songs were also made at the time, but these recordings were never publicly available.

Trezise (1965), Moyle (1966), Woolston (1966), and Keen (1969–70). Many of these recordings contained invaluable commentary on and discussion of song origins and associations.

A photocopied book was produced containing a page or two on each of about 90 *burdal*. Overall it was similar to the original 'songs register', but with the innovation of a multi-sourced commentary. This acknowledged a multiplicity of interpretations and historical points of view, as recorded from dancers and songmen at different times. All the elder songmen were given copies. The organisation kept some, but it was clear that songmen did not want the book or its contents made more widely available.

This book became the basis for a number of 'culture camps'. These began in 1997, with up to 100 participants over three days at a time. People sat around cassette players listening, discussing and remembering *burdal* from their own childhood. These journeys of discovery in the daytime further unfolded in the evenings, when old songs and dances were reconstructed. Some of these resurrected *burdal* later made their way into public performance back in Gununa or out on tour.

Over the next few years this research continued, both formally and informally. It involved further archival work and more interviews with songmen, which revealed many more *burdal* than had previously been documented. As a result, instead of just aiming to collect and document extant recordings, we also began to make new recordings of all known songs. In many cases this required a significant amount of practice and teaching by the elder songmen, which contributed to the momentum for several more camps.

In 2002 the software program FileMaker Pro was chosen as a database platform, because of its ability to allow many-to-many relationships between songs and recordings. An iTunes library was also used to organise digitised recordings referred to in the FileMaker database. This method was dropped after a year or so, because of difficulties with maintaining the iTunes library in the face of computer upgrades and crashes. Informally, however, dancer Renee Wilson, in her organisational role, continued to use iTunes, as a means of organising song recordings on her MP3 player. She was able to make use of these easily accessible and portable recordings on numerous occasions, in rehearsal and performance, as a memory-jogger for elder songmen.

When a further update of the song book was printed in 2007, it included around 150 songs. Some songmen did look at the book from time to time, and were aware of the information in it (as all had contributed to various degrees), but they have not used it directly as a resource for learning songs. Listening to recordings and singing along with elder songmen has been a much more effective learning strategy, although the document is still valued as a reference point.

In 2012 the Mirndiyan Gununa Corporation began using the Ara Irititja digital archive program[8] (now known as 'Keeping Culture') to archive photographs, slides, film and audio material. This database is arranged around digital 'artefacts', which facilitates a focus on sound and video recordings. Some custom modifications were made to allow the FileMaker song data to be transferred across. Currently, both the FileMaker and Keeping Culture platforms are being maintained. They include over 160 *burdal* and 70 other songs, many performed on multiple recordings. Nonetheless, further work could be done to make the information accessible and usable in the community.

---

8 See *http://www.irititja.com/* [accessed 9 April 2017].

5 Cultural revival at Mornington Island

> The old people . . . taught us the songs and dances we must learn to keep strong with; to stay part of us and of our dreaming and our land. Without that we cannot live.
> – Larry Lanley, *The problem of preserving traditional values in a changing cultural context* (1978)

The first contemporary dance festival was held at Mornington Island in 1979, as a public affirmation and rekindling of cultural identity and pride. At that time there were at least 20 elder songmen with the knowledge and skills to lead dance performance. Around nine of these men were recognised as dreamers of songs. Over the following three decades the numbers dwindled, especially the number of *muyinda* – elder men with knowledge and experience dating from the period before colonial incursions. Currently at Mornington Island there is one songman in his 70s, two in their 40s, one in his 30s and four in their 20s. There are other men (and women) who have a passive knowledge or latent ability to sing some songs, but those just enumerated are recognised as the main people who sing for public events. It is worth considering the reasons for the generational gaps in this list.

From the late 1950s, after a period of mission-led suppression, a cultural revival of sorts began. From then until the early 2000s, the role of songman was left to those men who were already at the time regarded as 'experts', and younger men were not encouraged or supported to take on apprentice roles. For instance, the four men now in their 40s and 50s were all dancers for many years, relying on increasingly elderly senior men to sing for them. Although the transition from dancer to songman was probably a 'traditional' pathway, it was not automatic. More recently it has been recognised that, without intervention, there might come a time when there are no expert songmen left in the community. So these men have been given explicit support to learn from their elders.

The loss of key songman Ian James in 2002 was further impetus for a mentoring program at Mornington Island. In this case, Cecil Goodman, Gordon Watt and Kenneth Jacob were assigned as mentors for younger men in their 30s. The program was intended to address not just the obvious matter of a decline in songman numbers, but also issues around 'elitism'. These had begun to arise from the professional touring program. At its most general, the aim of the program was to broaden the skill base out beyond a handful of people. The mentoring arrangement was relatively informal. Mentees were given access to recordings of songs on CD for private study and sat next to elder songmen at rehearsals and performances.

Around the same time, some songmen and dance leaders were engaged to give regular dance lessons in the primary school. One or two boys would be chosen by the songmen to sit beside them. When there were spare boomerangs, these 'apprentices' would play along. Otherwise they would clap in time. This was the first deliberate effort to mentor boys as future songmen, even though at first they were only expected to keep the rhythm. Today, many years later, some of those same boys have become the main songmen in the community.

There are a number of technical challenges young songmen face in learning to sing *burdal* songs with the level of skill required for public performance. A knowledge of spoken Lardil is only partially adequate for recognising terms in the language of *burdal* songs, and their meanings are, to an extent, open to interpretation (see Nancarrow 1999, 2010). Some words are specific 'song words', some are borrowed from neighbouring languages, and others are regarded as the language of 'unseen people'. There are also differences between different songmen in pronunciation, rhythm and placement of text. It can also be a challenge if there are too few participants at rehearsals. Sometimes the singers are required to dance, so the task of keeping the song words and rhythm going falls to one or two people. The singers also need to respond to the dancers. It is up to the *wijungu* ('lead dancer') to signal a change, or to 'break' the dance, and the songmen have to follow.

In addition, singers need to adjust the quality of their voice when singing for dancers. While a quiet voice is sufficient for individual or small group singing practice, a 'belting register' (Henrich 2006) is necessary for projecting over the noise of dancers and in large spaces. Maintaining the rhythm of boomerangs and/or clapsticks can be another challenge, especially when this is different to the rhythm of the song text. All of these skills must be managed simultaneously.

The most recent dance festivals at Mornington Island, in 2012 and 2013, provided an updated overview of cultural maintenance in the Lardil community. The few previous years were marked by a notable lack of community dance activity and organised (funded) touring projects. In 2012, only two elder songmen performed (Cleary 2012), and by 2013 both of these men were unavailable due to illness. This was a crisis point, and it was uncertain whether the festival could take place at all. A week before the planned opening night of the 2013 festival, people gathered in the dance ground with the intention of practising. Six men had come forward to sing and, equipped with boomerangs and clapsticks, they sat in a line ready. Elders sat on the side. It was about 5pm, after a long hot day, and nobody could find their voice. It took a painful 90 minutes before the six could find a rhythm together and their voices became stronger and resonant. The sun had set and more and more people came in to dance. Eventually more than 60 people were on their feet. Nobody wanted to stop, and keys had to be found to switch on the floodlight. The 90 minutes of waiting had been an essential part of the process, which led to a successful festival the following week.

Even more recently, in April 2015, a group of young men recreated the dance for a jabiru *burdal* that had not been danced for at least 50 years. There were two main catalysts: an approaching book launch at the school; and the uncovering of a recording from 1976 of songmen singing and discussing the song. Over two days, the young men got together with elder songmen and dancers who helped interpret the Lardil language on the recording and assist with the *layiwurri* process. One of the eldest men remembered seeing the dance as a boy. His memories of the jabiru *laka* were incorporated, but the final result was a collaboratively created choreography. The *burdal* was performed with dance on the third day of practice, to an audience of about 300 people.

6 Conclusions: expectations for cultural survival

They still need to sit with me.

– Cecil Goodman (pers. com. 2015)

There are many factors in contemporary life that work both for and against the maintenance of song culture. One of these is that dance events are often commissioned by non-Lardil stakeholders, who control the financial rewards. Cultural and commercial values are competing in the community all the time. The role of money cannot be ignored in strategies for song maintenance, and yet, alone, it cannot sustain the culture. Similarly, access to archival sources can be invaluable if combined with effective ways of organising the material and sharing it with the right people, but it is not an end in itself. Beyond locating and repatriating this material lies the more onerous task of using it in such a way that it will have an ongoing life in the community. This has been and still is a great challenge.

In the end, no amount of organisational structuring of projects and activities will replace an individual's commitment to a face-to-face teaching relationship with an elder songman. Underlying this learning of songs there can be a revitalisation of the ability to dream songs and 'bring them out' as *burdal*. A song may be given to anyone, but the receiver must feel that it is right and proper to bring that knowledge into the public domain, either themselves as a singer or by passing the song on to recognised songmen. This is an inner, personal responsibility, but is also one requiring sanction from the community. This is not an organisational matter, because the support has to be expressed communally.

It is time to reflect on the rising generation, in whose hands the future of the culture is held. In spite of fears of cultural loss within the Lardil community, it is a measure of success that there are now a number of young songmen. They, and the families who support and encourage them, create and maintain the social fabric in which the song culture may survive.

We are writing this article not long after the funeral of one of our elder songmen. Many young men came forward at the ceremony, to sing and dance and pay him respect. There remains after him only one other songman over 60, whose words we have quoted above as an epigraph to this section. He was in hospital at the time he spoke them He has lived through all those disrupted years of religious indoctrination, 'grog wars'[9] and the many family and social upheavals that have gripped the community. He is well aware of his own limitations, in terms of his ability to pass on everything the rising generation needs to know about the song traditions; but there is still much they can learn from him.

References

Bradley, John, and Elizabeth Mackinlay, 2000, Songs from a plastic water rat: an introduction to the musical traditions of the Yanyuwa community of the Southwest Gulf of Carpentaria. Brisbane: Aboriginal and Torres Strait Islander Studies Unit, University of Queensland.

Casey, Maryrose, 2011, Performing for Aboriginal life and culture: Aboriginal theatre and Ngurrumilmarrmiriyu. Australasian Drama Studies 59:53–68.

Cleary, Peter, 1984, Woomera Aboriginal Corporation, Annual report. Townsville: Woomera Aboriginal Corporation.

—— 1993, Budal Lardil: songs of Mornington Island. Accompanying notes to recording made at Slim's Creek in 1988 by Harry Waterson. Larrikin Records CD LRF 285.

—— 2006, On two feet: initial research into the potential of Indigenous dance in North Queensland. Commissioned report for the Director of Dance and Music, Arts Queensland. Brisbane: Arts Queensland.

—— 2012, Gulf festival Mornington Island. Unpublished report to Mirndiyan Gununa Aboriginal Corporation and funding bodies.

Cleary, Peter, and Sam Pilot, 1992, Songs of M.I. Unpublished data file, Woomera Aboriginal Corporation, Townsville.

Henrich, Nathalie, 2006, Mirroring the voice from Garcia to the present day: some insights into singing voice registers. Logopedics Phoniatrics Vocology 31(1):3–14.

Jarrarr, Fred, 1975, Larumben songs. Interview recorded by Paul Memmott. Unpublished field tape F4, 25 September 1975.

Lanley, Larry, 1978, The problem of preserving traditional values in a changing cultural context. Address given at the UNESCO Regional Seminar on the Role of Museums in Preserving Indigenous Cultures, Adelaide.

Mackinlay, Elizabeth, and John Bradley, 2003, Of mermaids and spirit men. The Asia Pacific Journal of Anthropology, 4(1–2):2–24.

---

9 David McKnight (2002) has written extensively about the effects of alcohol at Mornington Island.

McKnight, David, 1999, People, countries and the rainbow serpent: systems of classification among the Lardil of Mornington Island (Oxford Studies in Anthropological Linguistics). Oxford: Oxford University Press

—— 2002, From hunting to drinking: the devastating effects of alcohol on an Australian Aboriginal community. London: Routledge.

Memmott, Paul, 1979, Lardil properties of place: an ethnological study in man-environment relations. PhD thesis, University of Queensland, Brisbane.

—— 2016, Reviving culture on Mornington Island. In Mark Moran, ed. Serious whitefella stuff: when solutions became the problem in Indigenous affairs, 73–101. Melbourne: Melbourne University Press.

Nancarrow, Cassy, 1999, Burdal Lardil: creation and communication of meaning in Mornington Island songs. Unpublished Honours thesis, University of Sydney.

—— 2010, What's that song about?: interaction of form and meaning in Lardil burdal songs. Australian Journal of Linguistics, 30(1):81–92.

Trigger, David, 1992, 'Whitefella comin': Aboriginal responses to colonialism in northern Australia. Cambridge: Cambridge University Press.

11 Maintaining song traditions and languages together at Warruwi (western Arnhem Land)

Reuben Brown[1], David Manmurulu[2], Jenny Manmurulu[3], Isabel O'Keeffe[4] and Ruth Singer[1]
University of Melbourne[1], Inyjalarrku songman (Warruwi Community)[2], Warruwi School & Yagbani Aboriginal Corporation[3], University of Melbourne / University of Sydney[4]

Abstract

As Indigenous musicians, language activists, scholars, educators, and others from around Australia undertake a variety of approaches in their efforts to revitalise song and language, in this chapter we provide a snapshot of the situation in Warruwi community, western Arnhem Land. Here, sustaining the local performance tradition of *manyardi* ceremonies and songs relies on maintaining diversity, and the task of documenting both linguistic and musical diversity has relied on intercultural collaboration and an interdisciplinary approach.

Warruwi is a highly multilingual community where multiple small languages are still being spoken, and individually-owned songsets (distinct repertoires of songs) continue to be performed in public ceremony and passed on to children. In this chapter, we suggest that it is the maintenance of this diversity of languages and songs – rather than just maintaining individual languages or songsets – which is highly valued by the community.

For over a decade, a team of linguists, musicologists, Indigenous ceremony holders and educators has been working together on aspects of language and song at Warruwi. This collaboration has produced new insights into the social practices and ideologies that underpin the creation and maintenance of linguistic and musical diversity, and has led to the documentation of new expressions, particularly in the Mawng language. Interdisciplinary research on *manyardi* has expanded the documentation of lexical resources, such as patterns of polysemy and idiomatic expressions, and contributed to a more complex understanding of the meanings expressed through music and dance. From the perspective of David and Jenny Manmurulu – ceremony holders and educators for the Inyjalarrku (mermaid) songset – this collaborative research has reinforced the ways in which performing *manyardi* not only expresses important aspects of their language, but also has the potential to unite the ancestral past with the future, as they draw on spirits of the country, while teaching the next generation to carry on singing and dancing.

Keywords: idioms, Inyjalarrku, language transmission, manyardi, Mawng, multilingualism, music education, music diversity

Linguistic and musical diversity in western Arnhem Land and Warruwi community

Across western Arnhem Land multilingualism is the norm, and in the community of Warruwi, on Goulburn Island, adults typically speak between three to eight languages, while most children speak at least two Indigenous languages from birth (Singer and Harris 2016:1–2). Up to 10 different languages are spoken at Warruwi, in spite of its small population of around 400 residents. There are many small languages in the area, which people continue to maintain through complex patterns of multilingualism within families. These include the Iwaidjan languages of Mawng (tied to clan estates on Goulburn Island and along the coast of the mainland opposite Goulburn Island) and Iwaidja (from the Cobourg Peninsula). Also spoken at Warruwi are the Gunwinyguan languages Bininj Gunwok (a *lingua franca* for the mainland community of Gunbalanya, associated with clan estates located on or around the Arnhem Land escarpment or 'stone country') and Kun-barlang (Warlang); Maningridan languages such as Ndjébbana (Gunavidji), Burarra, Nakara; and varieties of Yolŋu-matha from northeast Arnhem Land, as well as English (Singer and Harris 2016:7). Map 11.1 shows the pre-contact location of Aboriginal languages in the Top End, according to their associated clan estates. Languages that are today spoken at Warruwi are underlined.

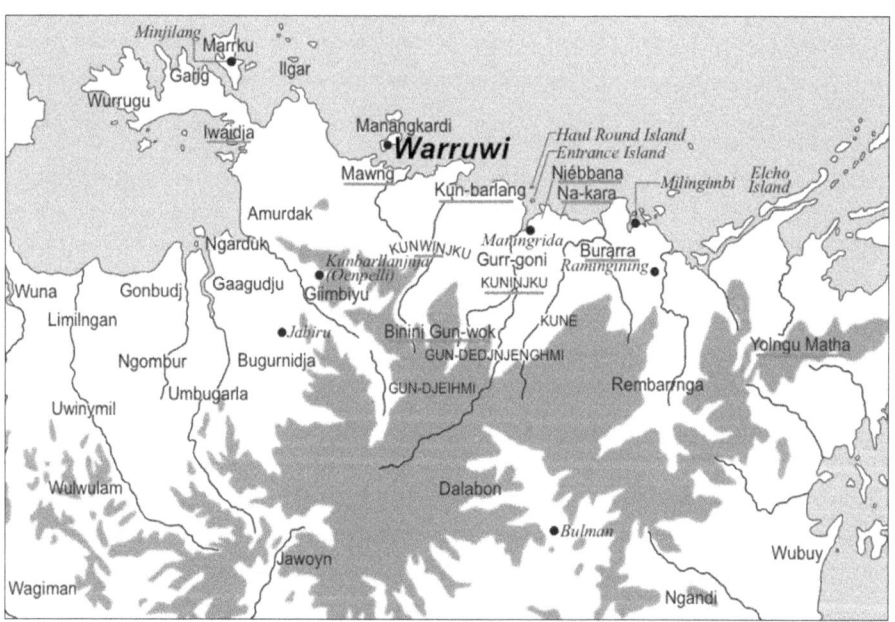

Map 11.1: A reconstruction of pre-contact language-land associations in western Arnhem Land, Northern Territory. (Shaded area shows Arnhem Plateau.[1])

Just as Warruwi is recognised for its linguistic diversity, so too can it be considered a hub of musical diversity for the region (see Barwick et al. 2007:9). *Manyardi* (or *kun-borrk* in Bininj Gunwok) are clapstick- and didjeridu-accompanied songs which are performed for both formal occasions involving dance – such as funeral ceremonies, *Mamurrng* (diplomacy) ceremonies, *Inyimany ja najaman* (girls' puberty) ceremonies, local festivals and celebrations – and also

---

1 Map by Chandra Jayasuriya (University of Melbourne) commissioned by Isabel O'Keeffe and edited by David Bickerdike; based on various linguistic data compiled by Mark Harvey as well as Bininj Gunwok dialect information by Evans (2003). The Bininj Gunwok dialects are indicated by upper case lettering.

informal occasions, such as trips to one's clan estate, or song documentation and elicitation sessions (which may not involve dancing) with scholars from outside of the community. As they have done for many generations, numerous singers at Warruwi regularly perform songs from their named *manyardi* repertoires or 'songsets' (Barwick, O'Keeffe, Singer 2013:47; Garde 2006:61; O'Keeffe 2007:48). These songsets have been handed down to singers by their male relatives, and are associated with particular languages from the region, including dialects that are no longer spoken, such as Manangkardi (once spoken by people on North and South Goulburn Island and associated with the Mirrijpu/Yalarrkuku songset) and Ngurtikin (a variety of Mawng spoken by people living on the western side of the mainland and associated with David Manmurulu's Inyjalarrku songset). Recordings of *manyardi* over the past decade made by ceremony holders at Warruwi in collaboration with musicologists and linguists reflect this diversity, as do earlier recordings made in Warruwi in the 1940s to 1960s by anthropologist Ronald Berndt and Sandra Le Brun Holmes.[2] Table 11.1 shows a total of 14 distinct western Arnhem Land songsets recorded in Warruwi, associated with nine different languages from the region, as well as three different clan song series belonging to the *manikay* genre from northeastern Arnhem Land (shaded).[3] The main singers resident at Warruwi today are custodians of the Inyjalarrku (mermaid), Milyarryarr (black heron) and Mirrijpu/Yalarrkuku (seagull) songsets.

Table 11.1: *Manyardi/kun-borrk* and *manikay* recorded at Warruwi from 1940s to 2013, showing the songset name, singer/s, associated language/s, recordist and recording details[4]

SONGSET	(LEAD) SINGER/S	LANGUAGE ASSOCIATION	RECORDING DETAILS
Diyama (cockles)	Anjawartunga Maxwell	Burarra	Birch and A. Brown (2006), Barwick et al. (2011–2015)
Inyjalarrku (mermaid)	David, Rupert and Renfred Manmurulu	Mawng (Ngurtikin)	Le Brun Holmes (1965), Barwick et al. (2011–2015), Brown (2013)
Itpiyitpi (grasshopper)	David Gameraidj, Magundili Nungalomin [Nangaluminy]	Mawng, Kunwinjku and Kun-barlang	Berndt & Berndt (1970), Berndt & Phillips (1973) (recorded in 1964), Le Brun Holmes (1965)
Kaddikkaddik (oyster catcher)	Ngaloman [Ngalorlman], Mangulugulu, Andrew Nadumalu	Kun-barlang	Berndt (1987) (recorded in 1961 and 1964)

---

2   More recent researchers who have collaborated with Warruwi ceremony holders and other songmen from western Arnhem Land include Meiki Apted, Linda Barwick, Bruce Birch, Reuben Brown, Nicholas Evans, Murray Garde, Allan Marett, Isabel O'Keeffe and Ruth Singer. Relevant research projects include 'The West Arnhem Land Song Project' funded by Hans Rausing's Endangered Languages Project, Singer's DECRA research project 'What makes a multilingual community?' as well as an honours thesis by Apted (2007) and PhD dissertations by Brown (2016) and O'Keeffe (2017).
3   Associated languages include both spoken languages and spirit languages, which share similarities with their spoken counterparts but are not translatable (see Apted 2010, O'Keeffe 2017).
4   Brown's fieldwork recordings are in the process of being deposited under collection RB1 in PARADISEC's archive, while Singer's recordings are under collection RS1 in PARADISEC and also at ELAR and AIATSIS. Further details of these recordings can also be found in Brown's (2016) and O'Keeffe's (2017) dissertations. For citations in this chapter that are derived from Brown's and O'Keeffe's fieldwork recordings, a footnote provides details of the speaker's name, recording ID (including the date of recording [YYYYMMDD] and recordist ID – Reuben Brown [RB], Isabel O'Keeffe [IO] or with maiden surname Bickerdike [IB], Ruth Singer [RS]), and relevant time code where available. For details of published material by Birch and A. Brown (2006), Le Brun Holmes (1965), Berndt & Berndt (1951), Berndt & Berndt (1970), Berndt & Phillips (1973) and Berndt (1987) see the list of references at the end of the chapter. The *manikay* clan songs from Eastern Arnhem Land are indicated with shading at the end of Table 11.1.

SONGSET	(LEAD) SINGER/S	LANGUAGE ASSOCIATION	RECORDING DETAILS
Kalajbarri (frigate bird)/ Ldhaha (sea)	Archie Brown	Iwaidja	Barwick et al. (2011–2015)
Kunbarlang (love songs)	Balilbalil [Barlirlbarlirl]	Kun-barlang	Berndt & Berndt (1951) (written texts only)
Marrwakara (goanna)	John Guwadbu 'No. 2' and Joseph Gamulgiri; Harold Warrabin	Mawng	Berndt (1987) (recorded in 1961 and 1964), Le Brun Holmes (1965), Barwick et al. (2011–2015), Brown (2012)
Milyarryarr (black heron)	Johnny Namayiwa, Henry Guwiyul	Marrku, Manangkardi and Ilgar	Barwick et al. (2011–2015), Brown (2013)
Mirrijpu/Yalarrkuku (seagull)	Solomon Ganawa, Solomon Nangamu, Russell Agalara	Manangkardi	Barwick et al. (2011–2015), Brown (2013)
Nakurrututu (mudfish)	Malangawa/Malangkawa	Mawng	Berndt & Berndt (1970) (written texts only, recorded in 1961)
Ngarnarru	Billy Nawaloinjba	Manangkardi	Barwick et al. (2011–2015)
Nginji ('giant')/Ngili ('mosquito')	Frank Nabalamirri	Mawng	Le Brun Holmes (1965), Barwick et al. (2011–2015)
Ulurrunbu (floating island)	Archie Brown	Manangkardi	Barwick et al. (2011–2015)
Yanajanak (stone country spirits)	Charlie Mangulda	Amurdak	Barwick et al. (2011–2015)
Galpu clan songs	Fred Mathaman	Galpu clan variety of Dhangu	Barwick et al. (2011–2015)
Gumatj clan songs	Johnny Burrwanga	Gumatj clan variety of Dhuwal	Barwick et al. (2011–2015)
Murrungun clan songs	Joe Moscow and Terry Gandadila	Murrungun clan variety of Djinang	Barwick et al. (2011–2015)

2 'Different together': maintaining diversity

What does the presence of both musical and linguistic diversity at Warruwi tell us about Arrarrkpi (Aboriginal) society? As Barwick, Birch and Evans suggest, 'linguistic diversity clearly does not arise in a social vacuum. It is cultivated and maintained by sociolinguistic practices, and supported by cultural beliefs' (2007:7). Nowhere else are these sociolinguistic practices and cultural beliefs more clearly enacted than in the ceremonial performance of *manyardi*. In response to a question about the difference in musical style between *manyardi* and *manikay*, James Gulamuwu (Inyjalarrku singer and brother of David Manmurulu) answered: 'Yeah, like we all different together. Yolŋu people [of northeastern Arnhem Land] they play different, we [of western Arnhem Land] play us mob different.'[5] Gulamuwu's characterisation of 'different together' alludes to a 'conscious differentiation' (Barwick 2011:348) – both within western Arnhem Land repertories and within musical genres of the Top End region – that occurs 'together' in a shared ceremonial social space and within a unified musical framework. Such dialogism accords with Nicholas Evans' (2010:14) characterisation of western Arnhem Land languages and multilingualism, which he suggests is supported by the 'constructive fostering of variegation'. Indeed, the constructiveness of language variegation is a theme of the story of the ancestress Warramurrungunji (told in multiple languages), who travelled from Croker Island, over Warruwi and over the mainland toward Gunbalanya and the stone country, depositing different languages as she went (Evans 2010; O'Keeffe 2017).[6]

---
5   James Gulamuwu, 20110903RBMPMRIL07, 00:26:12.555–00:26:23.977.
6   The idea that performance enacts complementary phenomena pertaining to both the human and ancestral worlds

While western Arnhem Land songmen are responsible for leading the singing of their particular songs in ceremony, they rely on each other for didjeridu accompaniment and vocal 'back up', and therefore must be familiar with one another's songs and their particular clapstick and didjeridu rhythms, in order to carry out the performance. As David Manmurulu (Brown et al. 2013) suggests, the success of a ceremonial performance is highly dependent on whether everyone comes together to take part:

> When we have like funeral ceremonies and all that, if we [Inyjalarrku group] come and sing and nobody gets up and dance . . . then we feel no good again, we feel bad, and then our song will go bad again. But if we all happy, like dance all the ladies and even the young kids, children, dance, that makes us happy, and we can get the song going very good, very well. We sing happily, get together, dancing, good. We say *karryaryakpakpa ja manyardi*[7], then it comes back good again, then we feel like, especially me when I sing, I feel good.

Equally, while female ceremony holders are responsible for preparing aspects of the ceremony (painting themselves and younger girls with white ochre in the body design that evokes the animal or spirit after which their associated songset is named) and ensuring that the dancing fits with the ceremonial action, they must also be familiar with the full repertoire of songs, and sensitive to their male counterparts who are dancing as well as leading the singing. Jenny Manmurulu (Brown et al. 2013) described the extensive process through which she and her family together learnt a 'farewell song' that David Manmurulu received in a dream, then taught it to other members of the community:

> With this song, the farewell song, it took us a while to practise, because when David's dad [George Winunguj] passed away in 1994, when David dreamt about this song, and then it took us two or three years . . . he was saying 'oh, Jenny, we have to try this', and he was telling the boys [David and Jenny's sons Rupert, Renfred and Reuben] 'we have to try [singing] this song'. So when [they all] start singing this song about a couple of month later, he said to me, 'well Jenny, I'll have to show you, I'll have to perform you the dance, so you can teach the other ladies and young girls, doing this goodbye song.'

Just as speakers at Warruwi might 'code-switch' or address one another in different languages such as Mawng and Bininj Gunwok (Singer and Harris 2016), so too do singers take turns in leading the ceremony, so that songs from each group's repertoires are interspersed throughout the performance (Brown 2016). With careful attention to song ordering, ceremony leaders highlight particular songs which resonate with particular stages in the ceremony, or with an aspect of the identity of the main recipient of the ceremony (such as a recipient of the Mamurrng diplomacy ceremony, or a deceased spirit for whom a funeral ceremony is being held). Such is the multi-modality of western Arnhem Land performance that all of the occasions when *manyardi* was recorded at Warruwi (represented in Table 11.1) involved two or more different songs-sets performed together (apart from one solo performance of Milyarryarr for an *Inyimany ja najaman* ceremony).

One of these occasions was a Mamurrng (diplomacy) ceremony performed in 2012 for Reuben Brown and research collaborators (including Barwick, Marett, O'Keeffe, Birch, and others), as well as Brown's adopted Bininj (Aboriginal) family from Gunbalanya.[8] The perfor-

---

has also been explored in relation to *manikay* of north-east Arnhem Land. See, for example, Fiona Magowan's (2007) analysis of the situated knowledge involved in learning and performing *manyikay*, and Franca Tamisari's (2002) phenomenological analysis of the anthropology of *manikay* performance.

7   The meaning of this word might be translated: 'support and energise the musicians [in the same way that water refreshes the thirsty and parched]'.

8   Brown carried out extensive fieldwork in Gunbalanya from 2011–2013 for his PhD thesis. Like many other *Balanda* 'non-Indigenous people' who live in or have ongoing ties with members of the community, he was given a place within

mance involved an elaborate dance staged over two nights in which each performer enacted the handing over of a wooden pole (decorated with brightly coloured tassels of wool, with the hair of the recipient woven into the central tassel with beeswax). As Jenny Manmurulu (JM) and David Manmurulu (DM) explain in conversation with Isabel O'Keeffe (IO) (Brown et al. 2013):

> JM: [The Mamurrng] it's a gift ceremony where, when a person say 'oh I like to give this thing to maybe a hair or a shell, or maybe a bone of fish, or anything', and it's like a concert thing where people ask to come and sing and dance, perform
>
> …
>
> DM: to see the dancing and the song …
>
> JM: … different style of dancing and the songs
>
> IO: And so it brings people together sometimes from Warruwi and lots of different communities?
>
> JM: Lots … if this family member [is] based at Warruwi, he'll bring other people that lives maybe Maningrida, Oenpelli, Minjilang, Croker Island or [Warruwi], you know, they give us time to get those people there and then we do a big performance there for them …

As 'givers' of the *mamurrng* in the 2012 ceremony, both the Inyjalarrku and Yanajanak groups had to support one another to carry out the performance:

> the two songs joins together – combine together, and we all share the dancing, no matter … We had to paint Inyjalarrku body paint, but we still had to dance the Yanajanak [songset].[9]

Therefore, although ceremonies such as the Mamurrng are about residents – such as those from Warruwi and neighbouring communities – articulating their particular language and clan identities by performing their 'different styles', such differences are clearly inclusive and complementary, rather than exclusive or divisive.

3 Deepening lexical documentation through musical documentation and vice versa

All languages are rich in idiomatic expressions with meanings that are not the sum of their parts; for example, 'to take somebody's side' (Pawley 2007; Wray 2012). However, initial work on little-documented languages such as Mawng, Kunbarlang or Kunwinjku tends not to dwell on these kinds of expressions. The basic morphosyntactic machinery is more often the focus of initial fieldwork, along with commonly used nouns and verbs. In addition, language speakers may avoid using as many idiomatic expressions as usual with linguists whose language proficiency is still developing.

One risk for field linguists is to inadvertently document a simple version of the language being researched, which may bypass more sophisticated expressions with idiomatic meanings. For example, the smaller a dictionary, the fewer the senses that tend to be listed per lexeme. In any language, however, most lexemes are used in many different ways. Given the limitations on linguists in terms of time and range of contexts in which to capture the use of a word, collaboration with ceremony holders and musicologists can provide a way to access quite complex expressions in a language. New senses of words and new idiomatic expressions tend to develop through metaphorical extension of meanings from the concrete realm to the abstract realm

---

the extensive kinship network in western Arnhem Land, and adopted by Donna Nadjamerrek as her sibling. Nadjamerrek attended the Mamurrng ceremony, along with other family members, and sat with the recipient group. For a further account of this ceremony, see Brown (2017). For accounts of other diplomacy ceremonies from the region, see Wild and Hiatt (1986) and Borsboom (1978).

9   Jenny Manmurulu, 20121103RB01, 16:38–17:46

(Evans and Wilkins 2000). Haviland (2006) demonstrates how ethnographic research such as musicology really underpins lexical documentation. What he calls 'context-free linguistics' only gets us so far: it may not necessarily allow us to access those parts of a language in which unique concepts and metaphorical, abstract ideas are expressed. The expressions that came up in the musicological research with Mawng-speaking musicians contained few new words that had not previously been documented by linguists, but instead fleshed out the range of senses for known words, and brought up many new idioms and complex verb constructions.

3.1 Documenting lexical knowledge

Although it has been critiqued, the Boasian ideal of a grammar, a dictionary and a text corpus still persists in the new field of language documentation (Gippert, Himmelmann & Mosel 2006). However, constructing a diverse and well-annotated corpus is increasingly seen as more important than a fuller grammatical description. For example, in Himmelmann (1998) and Gippert et al. (2006), the 'sketch grammar' appears to have taken the place of the full grammar. Despite this shift, the dictionary nevertheless holds its ground, as a collection of lexical knowledge. But what do linguists document when documenting lexical knowledge? They document individual lexemes (i.e. words), the different senses that the lexemes have, the different ways they can be used and also idioms and other multi-word lexical units such as complex verbs. Typical methods for extending a dictionary are domain-based elicitation and corpus expansion, as well as participating in and documenting particular activities, such as house-building (Haviland 2006; Mosel 2004).

Much of the expressive resources of a language lie in the polysemous senses of words and in their idiomatic combinations with other words, such as those shown in Table 11.2 and examples (1) to (3). However, multi-word combinations are often only listed in endangered language dictionaries when it is unavoidable for the linguist – such as when complex verbs composed of two lexemes are common (cf. Pawley 1993). Some examples of these kinds of complex verbs in Australian languages are coverb constructions in Mawng and Murrinhpatha complex verb stems. Noun-verb idioms can be harder to pick, as they do not have strict rules (for example, governing the order of the noun and the verb). In Mawng for example, a coverb must directly follow its verb with no intervening words, but a noun that forms a noun-verb idiom with a verb can be positioned quite freely in the sentence. Three examples of idioms involving the word *wirrngak* are shown in examples (1) to (3) and summarised in Table 11.2.

In example (1) the word *wirrngak* combines with the verb *-maju* 'suffer, be sick, die' to create an idiom meaning 'be hungry'. Both words that comprise the multi-word construction are shown in bold.

(1)[10] 'Ngawu ka-ta-nyi wiwi la **wirrngak** marrik an-**maju**-ng'
come 2sg/3ED-eat-I2 DC CONJ hunger NEG 2sg-suffer-I1

'Wiwi come and eat so you won't be hungry (later on).'[11]

In example (2) the word *wirrngak* combines with a complex verb, a coverb construction, which already involves two separate words, *-ma* 'get' and the coverb '*rturrk*'. In combination these

---

10 Abbreviations used in the interlinear glosses are listed at the end of this chapter. The pronominal prefixes of transitive verbs are glossed by giving the features of the subject followed by the object, separated by a forward slash (/). Coverb constructions are presented by displaying the meaning of the coverb construction as a whole under the coverb. The inflecting verb has a gloss in capitals. Articles are glossed simply with their gender, e.g. ja 'MA' is the Masculine gender.
11 The text was found by Singer in written and edited form, in the early 2000s at Warruwi School, with no author or date listed. It was then archived with the Northern Territory Archive Service. 'MS Text 1 Yinkarnarrk1:37' is Singer's reference, as used in her archive deposit of the transcription file.

words form a coverb construction meaning 'pull'. This two-word construction can then further combine with the word *wirrngak* to create an idiom meaning 'make (someone) upset' as in example (2).

(2) La anima-j **rturrk-pu** **wirrngak**.
 and 3MA/3LL-GET-PP make.upset -3pl.OBL life
 He really upset them.[12]

Another commonly used idiom involving *wirrngak* combines the word with the verb *-aka* 'throw' to mean 'breathe' as in example (3).

(3) Juka jita warranyngiw marrik ang-**aka**-y mira ta **wirrngak**.
 DEM.P.FE FE child NEG 3GEN/3LL-throw-I1 EMPH2 LL breath
 This child is not breathing properly.[13]

Table 11.2: Idiomatic expressions that involve the word *wirrngak* 'breath, life force'

	NOUN-VERB IDIOM	MEANING	DESCRIPTION OF MULTIWORD COMBINATION
1	-maju wirrngak	be hungry	With verb -*maju* 'suffer'
2	-ma rturrk [OBL] wirrngak	make really upset	With coverb construction -*ma rturrk* meaning 'pull'
3	-aka ta wirrngak	1.breathe 2.rest 3.take a holiday	With verb -*aka* 'throw' and Land gender article *ta*

3.2 Deepening lexical knowledge through musical documentation

Ceremonial performance temporarily unites the concrete and abstract. Spiritual beliefs, stories and language are joined to the physical performance of music and dance. Franca Tamisari has shown how for Yolngu 'the act of naming is made powerful and performative through externalisation and suggests a complex series of transformations in which body, language and place constitute each other' (Tamisari 2002:96). Tamisari gives examples of nouns associated with dance movements that capture and reproduce movement and motion at particular places and in the body (2002: 97–98).The following three expressions were first recorded by Linda Barwick and Isabel O'Keeffe in discussion with David Manmurulu. These expressions similarly deepened the lexical documentation of the Mawng language, despite the fact that a lot of documentation had already been done on Mawng.[14]

Expression 1: new sense of -aruki *'climb'*
The verb -*aruki* 'climb' was originally recorded being used in a concrete sense, to refer to physical movement upwards in space, but it also refers to a rise in pitch in a song. The verb can also be nominalised to refer to a particular part of a song where the pitch changes, as shown in example (4).

---

12 This text was recorded by Heather Hinch and archived by Arthur Capell at AIATSIS. It is on AIATSIS tape HINCH_H01_00599A. Singer transcribed and translated it with Mawng speakers, 'HH Text 6 Giant 019' is Singer's code, used in her archive deposits to refer to the transcription file.
13 Example is from Hewett et al. (1990) – the Mawng dictionary, in the form it was before Singer began working on it.
14 For example, a dictionary of 3500 words (Singer et al. 2015), a thesis (Singer 2006) and two books (Capell and Hinch 1970, Singer 2016) on the language, and the collection of texts by various linguists from 1964 to the present (see Singer 2006: Appendix 2).
15 David Manmurulu, 20070424IB01, 00:08:52.874–00:08:54.344

(4)   *ja*   *k-arr-**aruki**-n*
      MA   PR-1pl.in-rise.in.pitch-NP
      the part [of the song] where we rise up in pitch[15]

At least one Inyjalarrku song also links the abstract and physical through the arm actions of the women's dance (O'Keeffe 2017). In one section of the Inyjalarrku 'farewell song' (WALSP song ID IL18), the height of the women's arm actions correlates with the descending pitch. Most of the song is accompanied by the women's *wumarrk* 'low' dance action, in which women sway from side to side on the spot with their arms swinging by their sides. However at the start of line D (50) on the high vocal drone (an octave above the tonic), the women sway holding their arms at head height, performing the *wanji* 'head' dance action. As the melodic contour descends from the 8th degree of the scale to the 6th, the women move their arms to the *kumpil* 'chest' dance action, then as the melodic contour descends from the 8th to the 5th, the women perform the *arka* 'halfway' dance action. Finally as the melodic contour hovers around the 5th degree of the scale, the women return to the *wumarrk* 'low' dance action that accompanies most of the song (see Musical example 11.1 and Figure 11.1).

Musical example 11.1: Musical transcription of line D (50) of *Inyjalarrku* song IL18 and associated dance actions (listen to Audio example 11.1). Musical transcription by Isabel O'Keeffe; song word transcription by Isabel O'Keeffe with David Manmurulu.[16]

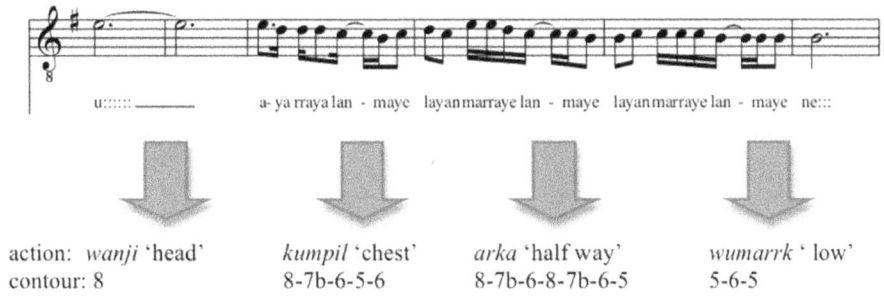

Audio example 11.1: *Inyjalarrku* song IL18; David Manmurulu and Rupert Manmurulu (lead singers); Albert Narul (didjeridu player)

Expression 2: Metaphor (nigi 'mother', -lijpularr 'child' and nulakpi 'heavy')
The mother–child metaphor is productive in Mawng and is also found in neighbouring languages Kun-barlang and Bininj Gunwok. The use of the term *ja nigi ja manyardi* 'the mother song' adds to our understanding of this.[17] The use of *nigi* 'mother (formal)' to refer to the largest

---

16 Refer to recording 20061114IB-24-IL18_19, where Line D (50), transcribed in Musical example 11.1, occurs at 00:00:38.09–00:00:48.45 and at 00:01:12.04–00:01:22.70.
17 The Mawng term *nigi* 'mother' is a term of reference (rather than address) and it is not used by children. When referring to the mother song (rather than a person) the masculine article *ja* is used, agreeing with 'song' or 'dance', which are classified as masculine gender in Mawng (*ja nigi* could also be used to refer to a mother's brother). Similarly, the term *ja nu-lakpi* 'the heavy one' (in Mawng) includes the masculine article and prefix. Similar agreement can be seen with the

Figure 11.1: *Inyjalarrku* dance actions *wanji* 'head' (top left), *kumpil* 'chest' (top right), *arka* 'halfway' (bottom left), *wumarrk* 'low' (bottom right), performed by Jenny Manmurulu at Marrinymarriny ('Fraser Beach'), Goulburn Island (photo by Beth Luck, used with permission)

example of something and *lijpularr* 'child' as the smaller counterparts was already documented. For example, to refer to the thumb in Mawng we say *nigi* 'mother' and to refer to the fingers we say *wi-lijpularr* (pl-child) 'the children'. The term *nigi* 'mother' is also used to refer to the largest of the three types of louse, and to the larger clapstick of a clapstick pair. The use of the term *nigi* 'mother' to refer to a particular song provides an example of this metaphor being used in a more abstract sense.

Most songsets in western Arnhem Land have at least one important song that is considered the *nigi* 'mother song' and is also referred to as *ja nu-lakpi* (MA MA-heavy) 'heavy one'. Its heaviness refers to its emotional impact, and the fact that it has the slowest tempo of all the songs in the songset (often with numerous changes in the tempo and clapstick beating). Since it often draws a stage of the ceremony to a close, the *nigi* typically has the longest duration of all the songs in the songset. As David Manmurulu points out, whereas the rest of the songset is generally performed in no fixed order, the *nigi* is different: 'We can start off with any song, as long as the *nigi* always be the last'. Particularly for funeral ceremonies, he says, 'we always finish off with the *nigi* song'.[18]

Figure 11.2: Rupert Manmurulu (left) and David Manmurulu (right) dancing the giant dance (photo from still by Isabel O'Keeffe 2006, left, and from still by Manmurulu and Nabalamirri 2001, right)

This comment alludes to another abstract quality of the *nigi* song: when performed with women's ceremonial dancing at the end of the funeral, as the coffin is interred in the grave, it reinforces the carrying of the deceased spirit home to their ancestral country (Brown 2014:179, O'Keeffe 2017). The Inyjalarrku *nigi* song (listen to Audio example 11.1),[19] along with the penultimate song (often called the 'farewell song'), is sometimes accompanied by a special *yumparrparr* ('giant dance'), danced by a single male dancer (David Manmurulu or his son Rupert Manmurulu – see Figure 11.2). This dance has further abstract significance, as *yumparrparr* 'giants' are associated with death and are said to fight over the bodies of the deceased and take the spirit of deceased people to the land of the dead (Berndt and Berndt 1988, Lamilami 1974).[20]

---

term in Kun-barlang: *na-rdulmuk* (ma-heavy) 'the heavy one'.
18 David Manmurulu, 20070529LB01A 00:09:44.735–00:09:55.055; 20070818MA.
19 Refer to recording 20061114IB-24-IL18_19, where the *nigi* song starts at 00:01:38.52
20 Also discussed by David Manmurulu in conversation with Isabel O'Keeffe, 20060724IB01.

Expression 3: Insights into the origins of the noun amurl

The term *amurl* is used to refer to a women's dance action that is part of the dance accompanying the Inyjalarrku 'mermaid' songset. For this action, the dancers raise one arm to their forehead and place the other on their hip and dip their heads slightly. They then switch over the position of their arms in time with the next gapped clapstick beat. The dance actions, including the *amurl* action, are regarded as having been given to the songman George Winunguj (David Manmurulu's father) by *Inyjalarrku* 'mermaids' (O'Keeffe 2017).

The term *amurl* can be used as a noun to refer to this dance action, or as part of a putative complex verb construction to refer to the performance of these poses, as illustrated in example (5). Singers can call out *ma amurl!* ('ok amurl') to remind women to do the dance action at the appropriate time in the song.

(5)   *kangp-i-n*   ***amurl***
      3pl/3LL-pierce-NP   amurl
      they do *amurl* dance actions[21]

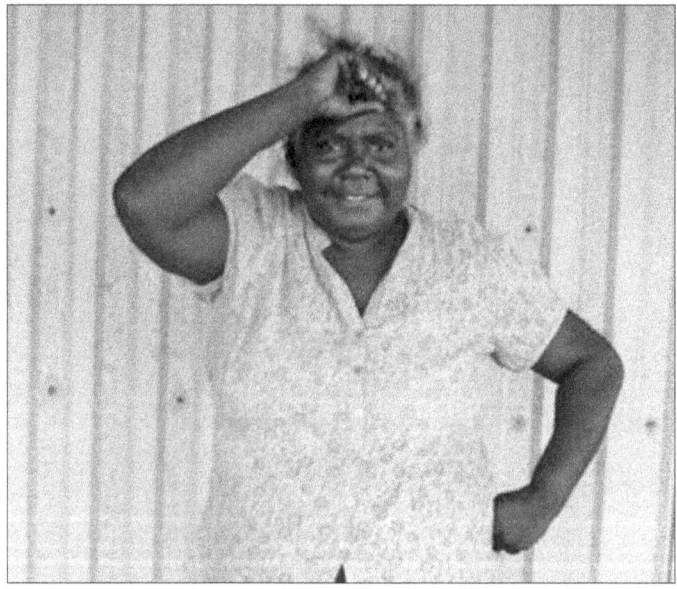

Figure 11.3: Jenny Manmurulu demonstrating the *amurl* dance action (photo by Ruth Singer)

When O'Keeffe and Barwick first recorded the term *amurl*, David Manmurulu had said that the word 'means something to the song' and that the action was related to the *Inyjalarrku* beings who passed it on to people to dance.[22] However, it was not clear to O'Keeffe and Barwick what the dance action represented or where the term may have originated. Singer's recording of the coverb construction for 'dive', which uses a similar term *murlmurl*, as illustrated in example (6), provided further clues.

(6)   *kangp-i-n*   ***murlmurl***
      3pl/3LL-pierce-NP   dive
      they dive in[23]

---

21 20070405LB01, 01:03:55.120–01:03:57.040.
22 David Manmurulu, 20070420IB03 00:18:49.174–00:18:52.654 and 00:58:11.787–00:59:12.307.

Given that the expression *kangp-i-n amurl* ('to do *amurl* dance movements') uses the same verb as the coverb construction *-e murlmurl* ('to dive'), this suggested a link between the two coverb constructions. This led O'Keeffe and Barwick to ask further questions of David and Jenny Manmurulu about the link between the *amurl* dance action and diving. It emerged that the *amurl* dance action represents the actions of the *Inyjalarrku* mermaid beings diving into the water. In performing the *amurl* action in ceremony, the women embody the *Inyjalarrku* 'mermaids' – who originally gave the dance actions – and express their connection with these mermaid beings. Jenny Manmurulu expressed this as, 'it's like being an *Inyjalarrku* – I can feel they are in me'.[24] The physical and metaphorical connection between the *amurl* dance movement and the way people – and *Inyjalarrku* – use their arms when diving into water, demonstrates the way in which performed and embodied knowledge arising from ceremonial contexts enriches our understanding of language.

4 Maintaining 'different together' for the next generation

Intergenerational engagement in the social activities and performances around ceremony are a crucial part of maintaining the diversity and vitality of the *manyardi* song tradition of western Arnhem Land. As David Manmurulu suggests, most young people learn *manyardi* through a long-term process of participation and observation, until their older relatives feel that they are ready to take on the responsibility of leading ceremony:

> When I was a little boy, then my father's singing. I used to follow him around. Then when I grow up to 10 or 11 years old, or 12, I started practising, singing with my dad. Yeah, and that's how I learned. Then when I grew up, my old man was getting old and I used to sing with him, all the way, then he seen me and he said 'ok my son, it's all yours, I'm too old, then I hand it over.' So he hand it over to me and I start singing it. He was teaching me for Mamurrng, or teaching me to take young boys for circumcise, then he taught me everything then, that's how I still follow the track from my father taught me. I'm teaching my three boys . . . then when I die, then my sons will take over, then it will go on and on . . . from generation to generation. Then when they die they pass it to their kids.[25]

This intergenerational learning has been facilitated by the integration of aspects of *manyardi* performance and associated knowledge into the mainstream education at Warruwi School, where Jenny Manmurulu is senior Indigenous teacher:

> I've been dancing Inyjalarrku all my life and I'm teaching the young kids now . . . I teach other kids in the community on funerals or any special occasions that we have at Warruwi. And when we have cultural activities at school, I usually ask my husband to come and sing, and I do a lot of the dancing, instructing with all the girls from age 5 to 17 year old students at Warruwi School (Jenny Manmurulu, in Brown et al. 2013).

Although the *manyardi* song tradition is strong at Warruwi, it nevertheless remains vulnerable without support structures around intergenerational learning. David and Jenny's son Rupert Manmurulu is proud of the strength of the Inyjalarrku group – which often has three or four singers singing in unison (whereas other groups tend to have one or two). However, he is also conscious of a lack of engagement among other younger people with their *manyardi*, and the implications of this:

---

23 Singer et al. (2015).
24 Discussion between Isabel O'Keeffe and Jenny Manmurulu, RS1-377.
25 David Manmurulu interviewed by Isabel O'Keeffe, 20100403EC, 00:36:14.320–00:38:01.255.

Apart from my dad there's a lot of families back there [in western Arnhem Land], they've got their own songs and they've got sons, nephews and whatever else, y'know and their sons and nephews they don't look forward y'know towards what their father been doing, and their grandparents. They just want to go separate road, y'know. But for us, y'know, proud of my dad y'know he's been there, done it, so y'know if, one day, his days might go on, me and my brother here, we'll still be singing and all that, continuing on. We're showing our kids and we're even showing more of that our age – me and Reuben [Manmurulu's] age – like at home, and we're making all the other people, like old people, really very proud of us and they turning around and saying 'ah well, you look what them boys are doing, they carrying it on, they're singing and whatever, because their father really taught them well.'[26]

Researchers also have an important role to play in supporting and maintaining diversity and vitality of language and music in western Arnhem Land and beyond. Experts such as Jenny Manmurulu and David Manmurulu have discussed their song tradition on numerous occasions alongside researchers in public forums.[27] This has generated greater interest and prestige for language and songs, not only among the wider public, but also within Aboriginal communities such as Warruwi.[28] Digital copies of audio and video recordings of *manyardi* made by researchers over the years are in constant circulation in the community, where they have been used as a teaching aid for learning songs, and as inspiration for new performances.[29] Unique events such as the 2012 Mamurrng ceremony at Warruwi for Brown (which was initiated with the ceremonial giving of a lock of Brown's hair to Manmurulu in 2011 and commissioned with funding from an ARC Discovery grant led by Barwick, Marett and historian Martin Thomas)[30], have also ensured that intercultural research collaborations are articulated within Arrarrkpi cultural ceremonial practices that reinforce ongoing and reciprocal relationships and principles of diversity and complementarity.

5 Conclusion

In western Arnhem Land, systems that maintain and foster diversity are reflected in sociality and underpin not only language but also *manyardi* (ceremony/song). Warruwi community is possibly unique in terms of both its multilingualism and the diversity of its songsets. These express connections not only to spoken languages but also to languages or dialects no longer spoken, as well as to spirit languages belonging to ancestral spirits of the country. These different songs, representing different clan estates and language groups, are juxtaposed in ceremonial performance, where performers must rely upon one another to achieve a common goal (i.e. good relations between neighbouring groups, or grieving and saying goodbye to deceased family members). Being 'different together' means articulating one's unique identity – tied to

---

26 Rupert Manmurulu, 20070818MA.eaf.
27 David Manmurulu and Jenny Manmurulu have given public presentations and performances of *manyardi* at numerous symposia for Indigenous Music and Dance, conferences of the Musicological Society of Australia, as well as the AIATSIS 50th Anniversary conference 2014.
28 Barwick, Birch and Evans (2007:7) similarly found that the publication of a CD on *Jurtbirrk* songs led to a greater interest in documentation of Iwaidja language and song in Minjilang on Croker Island.
29 See for example a video of a dance performed in Darwin in 2014 by students at Warruwi School who were taught by Sophie Kinnane and inspired by a recording of Inyjalarrku and *manyardi* ritual performance (Warruwi Community School 2014).
30 The occasion in 2011 was the Annual Symposium for Indigenous Music and Dance in Darwin (where Brown was the youngest attendee), while the ARC Discovery Project (DP1096897), led by Barwick, Marett and historian Martin Thomas, was titled 'Intercultural inquiry in a trans-national context: exploring the legacy of the 1948 American-Australian Scientific Expedition to Arnhem Land'.

Figure 11.4: David Manmurulu and his sons (including Rupert on didjeridu) and grandsons perform and record Inyjalarrku at Warruwi (photo by Beth Luck, used with permission)

particular melodies, body designs, song words, rhythms, and movements that are passed on to family members – in a space where such differences are constructive and complementary.

The examples discussed in this chapter, which have led to deeper lexical understanding of Mawng and musical understanding of *manyardi*, have arisen from similarly synergistic three-way conversations between linguists, musicologists, and performers with specialist knowledge, in particular Jenny Manmurulu and David Manmurulu. Such collaborations follow in the footsteps of other research carried out together by linguists and musicologists on Australian song, as discussed in Barwick, Birch and Evans (2007:7). Based on these experiences, we suggest that the ideal of 'constructive variegation' or maintaining 'different together' can not only be applied to language and music from this region, but can also be conceived of as an interdisciplinary methodological principle for examining aspects of music and language together, as part of an intercultural approach involving both Arrarrkpi (Indigenous) and Balanda (non-Indigenous) working in both ceremonial and academic environments.

There are a number of benefits to such an approach. For linguists who want to extend the documentation of a language's lexical knowledge, a consideration is not only to add more lexemes, but also to elaborate on what is known about each lexeme: its senses and uses. Collaboration with specialists of song, such as performers and musicologists, can offer a way to record and understand expressions with more abstract meanings in the lexicon. These include more abstract senses of already recorded lexemes, noun-verb idioms and complex verbs. The pursuit of such work is also a good way of accessing emotion vocabulary, which for Australian Indigenous languages is often absent from traditional narratives. Deeper meanings of words such as *-marranguli* 'be emotionally moved by weather, place, song' can come out through discussions of how people feel about songs, rituals and working together to put ceremonies on. In the case of the documentation of Mawng, simply extending the corpus through collecting texts would probably not have deepened our understanding to the same extent, as most multi-word idioms are quite rare in texts.

The collaborative approach we have described has also been constructive for musicological documentation of *manyardi*. As Michael Walsh points out, for Indigenous Australian song traditions in general 'we know too little about how people actually talk about song, and about local aesthetics. Too often Aboriginal musical nomenclature is absent or poorly documented in accounts of Aboriginal song traditions' (2007:133). Without in-depth knowledge of the multiple languages in western Arnhem Land, it is difficult for musicologists to work out whether particular terms are specialised musical terms, everyday expressions, or special idiomatic expressions. Singer's specialist knowledge of Mawng has also lent greater understanding of musical terminology documented by Barwick, Brown and O'Keeffe in collaboration with ceremony leaders such as David and Jenny Manmurulu, revealing richly layered meanings and symbolism behind *manyardi*.

Finally, this state of being 'different together' – of keeping diversity in both language and song – has been shown to rely upon the maintenance of three particular factors: the intergenerational learning and participation in *manyardi* by people of all ages; support for such learning; and the recognition, particularly among Balanda both within and outside the immediate community, that one's unique ties to country, ancestry, and language, are articulated through ceremonial performance.

Abbreviations used in Mawng examples: 1 First person, 2 Second person, 3 Third person, CONJ Conjunction, DC Daughter's child, DEM Demonstrative, P Proximal, D Distant, ABS Abstract (i.e. discourse demonstrative), ED Edible gender, EMPH2 Emphatic postverbal particle, FE Feminine gender, GEN Non-Masculine gender (i.e. any gender but Masculine), I1 Irrealis 1 tense-aspect-mood suffix, I2 Irrealis 2 tense-aspect-mood suffix, in Inclusive pronominal category, KRDP K-reduplication suffix: encodes iterative or durative tense-aspect-mood, LL Land gender, MA Masculine gender, NEG Negative preverbal particle or prefix, NP Nonpast tense-aspect-mood suffix, OBL Oblique pronoun, pl Non-singular number (restricted mainly to humans), PP Past punctual tense-aspect-mood suffix, sg Singular number (restricted mainly to humans).

Other abbreviations used in this text: AIATSIS Australian Institute of Aboriginal and Torres Strait Islander Studies, ARC Australian Research Council, DECRA Discovery Early Career Research Award, ELAR Endangered Languages Archive, PARADISEC Pacific and Regional Archive for Digital Sources in Endangered Cultures, WALSP Western Arnhem Land Song Project.

References

Apted, Meiki, 2007, Songs from the Inyjalarrku: an investigation of non-translatable spirit song language from north-western Arnhem Land. Honours thesis. Melbourne: University of Melbourne.

—— 2010, Songs from the Inyjalarrku: the use of non-decipherable, non-translatable, non-interpretable language in a set of spirit songs from north-west Arnhem Land. Australian Journal of Linguistics, 30 (1): 93–103.

Barwick, Linda, 2011, Musical form and style in Murriny Patha Djanba songs at Wadeye (Northern Territory, Australia). In Michael Tenzer and John Roeder, eds. Analytical and cross-cultural studies in world music, 316–354. Oxford: Oxford University Press.

Barwick, Linda, Bruce Birch, and Nick Evans, 2007, Iwaidja Jurtbirrk: bringing language and music together. Australian Aboriginal Studies 2007 (2):6–34.

Barwick, Linda, Bruce Birch, Nicholas Evans, Murray Garde, Alan Marett, Isabel O'Keeffe and Ruth Singer, 2011–2015, The west Arnhem Land song project metadata database, 2011–2015. *https://elar.soas.ac.uk/Collection/MPI1013566* [accessed 7 September 2017].

Barwick, Linda, Isabel O'Keeffe and Ruth Singer, 2013, Dilemmas in interpretation: contemporary perspectives on Berndt's Goulburn Island song documentation. Occasional Paper No.12, 46–72. Perth: Berndt Museum of Anthropology.

Berndt, Ronald 1987, Other creatures in human guise and vice versa: a dilemma in understanding. In Margaret Clunies Ross, Tamsin Donaldson, and Stephen Wild, eds. Songs of Aboriginal Australia, 169–191. Sydney: University of Sydney.

Berndt, Ronald, and Catherine Berndt, 1951, Sexual behavior in western Arnhem Land. New York: Viking Fund.

—— 1970, Time for relaxation. In Stephen A. Wurm and Donald C. Laycock, eds. Pacific Linguistic Studies in honour of Arthur Capell, 557–591. Canberra: Linguistic Circle of Canberra.

—— 1988, The world of the first Australians (5th edn). Canberra: Aboriginal Studies Press.

Berndt, Ronald, and Eric Phillips, 1973, The Australian Aboriginal heritage: an introduction through the arts. Sydney: Australian Society for Education through the Arts in association with Ure Smith.

Birch, Bruce, and Archie Brown, 2006, Ngarnji Mamurrng [DVD]. Minjilang: Iwaidja Inyman.

Borsboom, Adrianus Petrus, 1978, Maradjiri: A modern ritual complex in Arnhem Land, North Australia. PhD dissertation, Katholieke Universiteit, Nijmegen.

Brown, Reuben, 2014, The role of songs in connecting the living and the dead: a funeral ceremony for Nakodjok in Western Arnhem Land. In Amanda Harris, ed. Circulating cultures: exchanges of Australian Indigenous music, dance and media, 169–201. Canberra: ANU Press.

—— 2016, Following footsteps: the kun-borrk/manyardi song tradition and its role in western Arnhem Land society. PhD dissertation, University of Sydney, Sydney.

—— 2017, A different mode of exchange: the Mamurrng ceremony of western Arnhem Land. In Kirsty Gillespie, Don Niles, and Sally Treloyn, eds. A distinctive voice in the Antipodes: essays in honour of Stephen A. Wild. Canberra: ANU Press.

Brown, Reuben, David Manmurulu, Jenny Manmurulu, and Isabel O'Keeffe, 2013, Music and wellbeing in western Arnhem Land. Symposium on Aboriginal and Torres Strait Islander Music and Wellbeing. Melbourne: University of Melbourne.

Capell, Arthur, and Heather E. Hinch, 1970, Maung Grammar. The Hague: Mouton de Gruyter.

Evans, Nicholas, 2003, Bininj Gun-wok: a pan-dialectal grammar of Mayali, Kunwinjku and Kune. Canberra: Pacific Linguistics.

—— 2010, Dying words: endangered languages and what they have to tell us. West Sussex: Wiley-Blackwell.

Evans, Nicholas, and David Wilkins, 2000, In the mind's ear: the semantic extensions of perception verbs in Australian languages. Language 76(3): 546–592.

Garde, Murray, 2006, The language of Kun-borrk in western Arnhem Land. Musicology Australia 28:59–89.

Gippert, Jost, Nikolaus Himmelmann, and Ulrike Mosel, eds., 2006, Essentials of language documentation. Berlin: Mouton de Gruyter.

Haviland, John B., 2006, Documenting lexical knowledge. In J. Gippert, N. Himmelmann and U. Mosel, eds. Essentials of language documentation, 129–162. Berlin: Mouton de Gruyter.

Hewett, Heather, Anne Dineen, David Stainsby and Robin Field, 1990, Maung dictionary. Archived as electronic file at the Australian Institute of Aboriginal and Torres Strait Islander Studies.

Himmelmann, Nikolaus, 1998, Documentary and descriptive linguistics. Linguistics 36:161–195.

Lamilami, Lazarus, 1974, Lamilami speaks, the cry went up: a story of the people of Goulburn Islands, North Australia. Sydney: Ure Smith.

Le Brun Holmes, Sandra, 1965, Land of the morning star: songs and music of Arnhem Land [LP record]. Sydney: HMV/EMI Australia.

Magowan, Fiona, 2007, Melodies of mourning: music & emotion in Northern Australia. Crawley WA: University of Western Australia Press.

Manmurulu, David and Frank Nabalamirri, 2001, Nginji giant dance, unpublished video recording, filmed and edited by Stephen Teakle and Lucy Eames, presented by David Narul.

Mosel, Ulrike, 2004, Dictionary making in endangered speech communities. Language Documentation and Description 2:39–54.

O'Keeffe, Isabel, 2007, Sung and spoken: an analysis of two different versions of a Kun-barlang love song. Australian Aboriginal Studies 2007 (2):45–62.

—— 2017, Multilingual manyardi: manifestations of multilingualism in the manyardi/kun-borrk song traditions of western Arnhem Land. PhD dissertation, University of Melbourne, Melbourne.

Pawley, Andrew, 1993, A language which defies description by ordinary means. In William Foley, ed. The role of theory in language description, 87–129. Berlin: Mouton de Gruyter.

—— 2007, Developments in the study of formulaic language since 1970: a personal view. In P. Skandera, ed. Phraseology and culture in English, 3–48. Berlin: Mouton de Gruyter.

Singer, Ruth, 2006, Agreement in Mawng: productive and lexicalised uses of agreement in an Australian language. PhD dissertation, University of Melbourne, Melbourne.

—— 2016. The dynamics of nominal classification: productive and lexicalised uses of gender agreement in Mawng. Berlin: Mouton de Gruyter (Pacific Linguistics 642).

Singer, Ruth, Nita Garidjalalug, Heather Hewett, Peggy Mirwuma and Phillip Ambidjambidj, 2015, Mawng dictionary v. 1. *http://www.mawngngaralk.org.au/main/dictionary.php* [accessed 15 March 2017].

Singer, Ruth, and Salome Harris, 2016, What practices and ideologies support small-scale multilingualism? A case study of Warruwi community, northern Australia. International Journal of the Sociology of Language 241: 163–208.

Tamisari, Franca, 2002, Names and naming: speaking forms into place. In L. Hercus, F. Hodges and J. Simpson, eds. The land is a map: placenames of Indigenous origin in Australia, 87–102. Canberra: Pandanus Books.

Walsh, Michael, 2007, Australian Aboriginal song language: so many questions, so little to work with. Australian Aboriginal Studies 2007 (2):128–144.

Warruwi Community School, 2014, GBI Super Crew (BEAT Festival Performance, 2014). YouTube video, uploaded by Warruwi Community School, September 17, 2014, *https://www.youtube.com/watch?v=0QK3wE3xyNc* [accessed 1 May 2016].

Wild, Stephen, and L. R. Hiatt, eds, 1986, Rom, an Aboriginal ritual of diplomacy. Canberra: Australian Institute of Aboriginal Studies.

Wray, Alison, 2012, What do we (think we) know about formulaic language? An evaluation of the current state of play. Annual Review of Applied Linguistics 32:231–254. doi:10.1017/S026719051200013X.

12 Songs that keep ancestral languages alive: a Marrku songset from western Arnhem Land

Reuben Brown[1] and Nicholas Evans[2]
University of Melbourne[1] and Australian National University[2]

Abstract

When songs are performed in socially meaningful and memorable contexts, they can act as vehicles that carry aspects of an individual's language and identity, sometimes long after that person dies and his or her language is no longer spoken. In this chapter we present an illustrative case study from western Arnhem Land: the Milyarryarr ('black heron') songset, which is associated with the 'extinct' languages of Marrku, Manangkardi, and Ilgar but continues to be performed by songman Johnny Namayiwa.

Before his death in 2003, the late Charlie Wardaga, who spoke these languages, handed over the songs to Namayiwa. While the languages were not part of Namayiwa's linguistic repertoire, he was able to identify some song words in order to work up translations in Marrku with Nicholas Evans, who had previously worked with Wardaga.

Namayiwa performs and teaches his inherited songset in a variety of public ceremonial contexts. These include funeral ceremonies, *Mamurrng* (diplomacy) ceremonies, local festivals and celebrations. He has also added to the songset some new compositions that were given to him in dreams. Public ceremony is prominent in western Arnhem Land, and songsets such as Milyarryarr are performed alongside others in order to enact important social transitions and transactions. We suggest that it is this performance context that has enabled the transmission of knowledge of ancestral languages that are no longer spoken, which otherwise might not have been passed on.

Keywords: Bininj Gun-wok, Ilgar, Iwaidjan, language documentation, language transmission, Milyarryarr, Manangkardi, Marrku, spirit language, song ownership

1 Introduction

The phenomenon of song transmission across linguistic boundaries is found in many parts of Indigenous Australia. Treloyn (2006:48–50), for example, notes that many *junba* repertories originating from the Kimberley have been passed on as far as Port Keats (Wadeye) in the Daly region to the north-east, and as far south-west as the Pilbara region, along a network of trade paths known as the *wurnan*. In the present chapter, we focus on western Arnhem Land, a region where great linguistic and musical diversity has been maintained and fostered over time, in spite of relatively small language populations (see Brown, Manmurulu, Manmurulu, O'Keefe & Singer, this volume, Evans 2006, Evans 2010). In the public song tradition of western Arnhem Land – known as *manyardi* in Iwaidjan languages and *kun-borrk* in Bininj Gunwok – songs are individually owned and passed on to male relatives (Garde 2006; Barwick et al. 2007). What happens if the individual who inherits the songset does not speak the language or languages employed in it?

Many western Arnhem Land songsets feature words entirely or partly in ancestral 'spirit languages', which have a 'recognisable vocabulary of words and phrases which resemble a natural/spoken/everyday language of the region, but which are not associated with meaning in any conventional sense' and for which the singer may not be able to offer a translation (Apted 2010:102). Given the variety of linguistic expertise in western Arnhem Land, occasionally song words will be assigned by some speakers to 'spirit language', while other speakers can furnish translations. Koch and Turpin (2008:167) suggest a number of other factors which can make the task of translating unfamiliar song words difficult, including:

> the multi-dialectal nature of song, the presence of metrical requirements which force phonological alteration of words, as well as the methods of song transmission and interpretation.

In this chapter we examine a case where words that initially appeared untranslatable turned out to come from another language after all – and indeed to preserve, in a small but poignant way, words from a language that is on the verge of being lost. When Linda Barwick, Bruce Birch and Nicholas Evans began recording and transcribing music on Croker Island in the 2003–05 period as part of their DoBeS[1] project 'Iwaidja and other endangered languages of the Cobourg Peninsula (Australia) in their cultural context', they were given language affiliations for all songsets performed in the region. The Milyarryarr set was 'closed' at the time – it could not be performed or recorded due to the death of Charlie Wardaga in September 2003. Performances of another songset, Manbam, were able to be recorded, and it was said to be associated with the Marrku language; but the singers recorded at that time could not assign meanings to the linguistic material.

The Milyarryarr songs we discuss below had to wait for another decade to be recorded and interpreted, and this entailed transposition to another place (Warruwi) and another performer – songman Johnny Namayiwa. Namayiwa is a resident of Goulburn Island, where he speaks a number of languages, in particular Mawng (belonging to the Iwaidjan family, and not too distantly related to Ilgar).[2] He composes and performs both contemporary and traditional styles of *manyardi* (song), crucially including the Milyarryarr songset, which he learned from composer/owner Charlie Wardaga. Wardaga was a Namangalara clan man who spoke Ilgar, Manangkardi and Marrku. Namayiwa describes how Wardaga taught him Milyarryarr by singing the songs over and over with him until he got the song right, and how Wardaga would correct his pronunciation of the song words within the context of a ceremonial performance:

> This old man used to tell me 'I'll sing about two or three times, see if you can pick up this word – [I'll sing] three times, and the fourth time you gotta sing yourself. Like he sing behind, you know,

---

1 Dokumentation bedrohter Sprachen (Documentation of Endangered Languages), Max Planck Institute for Psycholinguistics.
2 As well as Mawng, Namayiwa speaks the closely related language Iwaidja, also from the Iwaidjan family, plus Kunwinjku and Kun-barlang from the Gunwinyguan family (Evans 2003).

like keep his voice down, and I used to sing up . . . and we used to sing along together, when I used to make mistake in there, he used to sing loud to show me that word, that next word. Like, he was a teacher.³

Namayiwa describes how Wardaga would also ritually scrape the tongue of Namayiwa and his relatives with a large cockleshell, to help them with the languages he spoke:

> Well he had his Dreaming [site], he asked me to go with him, but we didn't have any boat to go across ... And he asked me to take me over there to thing my tongue, with, um, some kind of a cockleshell, but it's big ones. That's a sacred place there where they go and he scrape their tongue. He did it to one young fella, and that young fella he's talking all kind of language.⁴

Towards the end of his life, Wardaga passed on the responsibility for leading the performance of his Milyarryarr songset in public ceremony to both his son Henry Guwiyul and to Namayiwa. This handover was formalised in a ceremony in which Wardaga gave his clapsticks to Namayiwa. At Minjilang on Croker Island, where Wardaga lived, the songs were not performed during the period of dormancy that occurred after his death in 2003 (Barwick et al. 2011-15).

Guwiyul, who lives at Minjilang and often leads the songs in ceremony with Namayiwa, informed Namayiwa that the songset had 'all mixed languages – Ilgar, Manangkardi and Marrku'⁵; it is worth noting that many traditional stories in the region likewise deploy a polyglot palette (Evans 2011). Like Namayiwa, Guwiyul is not a fluent speaker of these languages, though he learned some Ilgar from his father, who spoke it regularly. He also learned the songs through the same method as Namayiwa – that is, by performing under Wardaga's tutelage. Before he passed away, Wardaga had shared some of his knowledge of Ilgar and Marrku with Nicholas Evans, as had other Marrku speakers (now deceased) such as Mick Yarmirr and Joy Williams (Evans 2001, Evans et al, 2006). Nonetheless, our knowledge of all these languages remains fragmentary (Evans 2016). When, in 2013, Evans and musicologist Reuben Brown came together with Namayiwa to document his songs and elicit the words of the song text, no fluent speakers of any of these languages remained. What meanings could be made from the Milyarryarr song text, and what remnants of the languages might it offer?

2 Text analysis of the language in Milyarryarr song MR07

Although he could not speak Wardaga's languages or understand the meaning of the Milyarryarr song texts, Namayiwa could clearly recite it for Evans and Brown, and had picked up some context for the song words along the way: 'the only one [that I can translate] is that Marrku one (WALSP song ID MR07)' he offered, 'I know a few things, few meanings there, but the rest of the songs, I don't know.'⁶ It is on this song, MR07, that we focus here, since we did not succeed in identifying recognisable words from languages of the region in the other songs of the set.

As we worked through the song, Namayiwa sung it phrase by phrase, getting us to sing it after him. (As with most singers of Aboriginal Australian songs we have worked with, the normal teaching mode is to sing the song piece by piece, rather than to speak the text without the music.) In the process, Evans recognised a number of words, on the basis of his previous linguistic work in the region, mostly from Marrku but in one case from Ilgar. In some cases these

---
3   Johnny Namayiwa, 20131107RB01, 55:36–56:13. Brown's fieldwork recordings are referenced throughout this chapter listing the speaker, file name (YYYYMMDD, Recordist initials, root file) and time code. These recordings are deposited in the PARADISEC archive.
4   Johnny Namayiwa, 20131107RB01, 00:39:12.675 – 00:39:26.775.
5   Johnny Namayiwa, 20131107RB02, 28:45–28:56.
6   Johnny Namayiwa, 20131107RB01, 55:05–55:20.

were slightly distorted phonetically. The recoverable words, given first in practical orthography and then in IPA[7], were:

1. *ngarta* ([ŋaɖa]): the first singular pronoun in Marrku: 'I, me, my'
2. *ngiro* ([ɲiɻo]): no exact match in Marrku, but a plausible reduction from [ɲiniɻu] *nginiru* 'other, different'
3. *mangurtyi* ([maŋudji]): 'I came, arrived'
4. *kunhi?* ([kuɳi]): no exact match in Marrku, but a plausible reduction from *mukunhi* 'there'
5. *mirakunya martba* ([miɻakuɲa maɖba]): no exact match in Marrku, but looks like it could come from the Marrku word *mira(ng)kuny* ([miɻaŋkuɲ]): 'they went, they had gone', plus the Ilgar/Garig word *yimartba* ([jimaɖba]) 'different, other')
6. Bakarnalinya ([bakaɳaliɲa]): not a known word in either language, but JM stated that it is a place name and that the phrase means 'I'm from Bakarnalinya'.[8]
7. *yakunhi* ([jakuɳi]): exactly matches the Marrku negative 'not'
8. *manbam*: this is the name of another songset associated with the Marrku language, but other Marrku speakers with whom Evans, Barwick and Birch had worked had been unable to supply a meaning. Namayiwa, however, explained that *warramanbam* meant 'little dwarf'; *warra-* is a prefix in Marrku that derives plurals or other animates that can occur in groups. (It occurs as well in the important singular noun *Warramurrungunji* 'founding ancestress'.) Namayiwa also volunteered the further word *warranguridjakud*, which means 'little song-giving dwarves' (these are said to dwell in the mangroves), though it does not occur in this specific song.

Armed with this information, we can piece together a more precise translation for the song, which goes something like: 'I have come from another place, they have gone somewhere else, to Bakarlinya, oh no ... , I have come, I am a *manbam* [ancestor]'. See Musical example 12.1 (next page) for a transcription of the words and music, while listening to Audio example 12.1 (follows Musical example 12.1).

3 Musical features and performance context for Milyarryarr songs

Western Arnhem Land songs have a wide melodic range and strophic or 'sectional' musical form.[9] Songs typically feature a verse, consisting of the song text followed by vocables, (for example 'a yako ni' in bars 14–16, Musical example 12.1). The verse is usually repeated (as in Audio example 12.1 where the verse transcribed in Musical example 12.1 is repeated three times), interspersed with instrumental sections and a coda, in which the singer sings an open vowel and the clapstick beating typically changes, cuing sequences of unified dancing.[10] The song concludes with the vocal part and didjeridu accompaniment finishing first, leaving the

---

7   International Phonetic Alphabet.
8   Though JN offered the translation 'I am from Bakarnalinya', the verb *mirangkuny* would normally mean 'they have gone', suggesting a translation of the phrase as 'they have gone to Bakarnalinya'.
9   In western Arnhem Land *manyardi/kun-borrk*, each verse of the song is sung to the same music, and the melody is coterminous with the text (Barwick 2011:330). This is the case also with other northern Aboriginal song genres, such as *wangga* and *lirrga*, but contrasts with central Australian and north western songs, where the text and melody are independent.
10 Listen to Audio example 12.1 [1:29–1:45]. In this particular instrumental section, the clapstick beating stays the same.

clapsticks to beat a final 'terminating pattern' (Barwick 2002:73).[11] Milyarryarr 'second singer' Jason Mayinaj (who backs up Namayiwa and Guwiyul in ceremonial performance) describes how the different layers of the musical texture are introduced, consistent with western Arnhem Land song conventions:

> Always, with us [in western Arnhem Land], when we start a song, always the didjeridu start it off. We can't just start off ourselves singing, not like eastern [Arnhem Land style] . . . They start with clapsticks, and after, the didjeridu comes in. But us, when we start, it's with didjeridu.[12]

Musical example 12.1: transcription of verse of Milyarryarr song MR07 (0:00–01:28 of Audio example 12.1)[13]

---

11 Listen to Audio example 12.1 [2:32–2:37].
12 Jason Mayinaj, 20110825RB03, 10:30–10:51. See measures 1–5, Musical example 12.1.
13 Recorded by Linda Barwick 20070427MRMP-30-MR07. Musical transcription by Brown and Evans. Transcriptions of didjeridu rhythms in particular are to be taken as indicative; the aim is to show how the clapstick, didjeridu and vocal parts interact and how the music is organised, rather than provide a detailed musical transcription for performance.

Western Arnhem Land *manyardi/kun-borrk* also features a variety of rhythmic modes in slow, moderate and fast tempo, which are performed at particular stages of a ceremony.[14] For example, a singer will usually begin a performance with songs in a slow tempo, building up to a string of songs performed in moderate and fast tempo (which feature men's dancing), before returning at the end of the performance to slow songs (featuring women's dancing) as the ceremonial action draws to a close (Brown 2014:193–194; Brown 2016).

 Audio example 12.1: Verse of Milyarryarr song MR07; Johnny Namayiwa (singer); Solomon Nangamu (didjeridu player)

As discussed in Brown et al. (Chapter 11, this volume), each *manyardi/kun-borrk* songset in western Arnhem Land is associated with a particular language or dialect, which is in turn associated with a particular clan estate (see also Barwick, Birch and Evans 2007:10). The

---

14 Rhythmic modes relate to a combination of the tempo and rhythmic pattern of the clapstick beat that accompanies the singing (i.e. whether the beating is even, uneven, doubled, etc.) with the vocal rhythm and the didjeridu rhythm (Marett 2005:204; Barwick 2002:72).

aesthetics of western Arnhem Land songsets 'follow up'[15] particular living animals (for example, *Mirrijpu/Yalarrkuku* 'seagull'), plants (*Wurrurrumi* 'climbing monsoon forest vine') and spirits (*Mimih* 'stone country spirits' or *Inyjalarrku* 'mermaid spirits').[16] Many of these animals, plants and spirits are associated with the ancestral country of the songs, and feature in creation stories from the region (Berndt 1987). *Milyarryarr*, also referred to as *wukul*, is named after the black heron, whose wings are painted on the body of the singers and dancers (see Figure 12.1). When men and women come together to dance to Milyarryarr songs, they conjure up flocks of black heron. Namayiwa and Guwiyul instruct the male dancers in particular to spread out all over the dance ground and keep moving, calling out in Mawng: *kurrungmarrajbukbu niga*[17] ('walk/roll along there!') Namayiwa explains the context behind this instruction: 'because the birds don't stay in one place – [they're] always moving around hunting, you know? Looking around for their food.'[18]

Together with the body design and the dance, each songset has unique musical features which help to create its 'aural identity' (Barwick 2002; Marett 2013:56). Certain melodic sequences and rhythmic modes are prominent among particular songsets, while individual singers have a precise understanding of the tempo band (often within a range of 1–5 beats per minute) which constitutes 'slow', 'moderate' or 'fast' beating in their songset (Barwick 2002). Table 12.1 summarises some of the unique rhythmic modes which feature in Milyarryarr songs but are not common among other songsets (Brown 2016).

Table 12.1: Distinct rhythmic modes featured in Milyarryarr songs performed by Johnny Namayiwa and Henry Guwiyul

RHYTHMIC MODE DESCRIPTION	CLAPSTICK PATTERN	SONGS FEATURED
Slow tempo uneven clapstick beating pattern	♪♩ ♩ ♪♩ ♩	Verse and Coda of MR01 (*nigi*), where it is reinforced by vocal rhythm: ♪♩ ♪♩ ♫♩ ♩. alart rrajba ngimarrartba a i
Fast even beating, featuring rhythmic pattern punctuated by dance call (*)	♪♩ ♩ ♩ 𝄽 *	Verse of MR04, Instrumental section of MR09
Slow-moderate even beating, followed by clapstick terminating pattern: didjeridu (Dj) cuts out and dancers call (*) on the final beat	♩♩♩♩ ♪♩ ♩♩ Dj – – *	Coda of MR01 (*nigi*), MR02, MR03, MR06, MR07 (Listen to Audio example 12.1 [2:30–2:38]), MR12
Fast uneven clapstick beating pattern, decreasing in tempo	♩♩♩ ♪♩ ♩♩	Coda of MR05, where it is reinforced by vocal rhythm: ♪ ♩ ♩ ♪ ♪ ♩ ♪ ♩. Bardada rramartba rrekodjba rregome

---

15 W. E. H. Stanner (1953:61) suggests that the 'meaning' of the Dreaming is enacted in the present through the performance of songs and dances which 'follow up' the ancestral beings that shaped the country and left their presence at particular sites.
16 The Mirrijpu/Yalarrkuku songset belongs to Solomon Nangamu and is examined in Brown's (2016) dissertation, alongside performances of the Inyjalarrku songset owned by David Manmurulu and family. The Wurrurrumi songset belongs to Kuninjku song man Kevin Djimarr (discussed in Garde 2007). The Mimih/Yawkyawk songset belonged to Kuninjku songman Crusoe Guningbal and was passed on to Guningbal's sons Owen Yalandja, Crusoe Kurddal and Timothy Wulanjbirr (Garde 2006: 81–86).
17 Johnny Namayiwa, 20131107RB02, 24:10–24:23.
18 Johnny Namayiwa, 20131107RB02, 24:52–25:00.

RHYTHMIC MODE DESCRIPTION	CLAPSTICK PATTERN	SONGS FEATURED
Fast doubled beating followed by uneven clapstick (CS) beating pattern, then fast doubled beating (with dance call on first doubled beat)	♩♩♩♩♩ 𝄾 ♩ 𝄾 .♪ ♫♫♫♫ *	Verse of MR04, where it is reinforced by vocal rhythm: ♪♩ ♩♩♩ ♩♩♪ ♪♩ ♩ o rrarrajba rrajba yartba yako ni CS: ♩ ♩♩♩♩ 𝄾 ♩𝄾.♪♫♫♫♫
Didjeridu cuts out, fast doubled beating gets faster in tempo, vocals (Voc) sing sustained open vowel 'i'	♫ (increasing in tempo)	MR04 (below), MR08, MR09 and MR13 Voc i_____ CS ♫♫♫♫♫♫♫♫♫♫♫♫♫♫♫♩♩ Dj – – *
Singing with didjeridu accompaniment but no clapstick accompaniment	N/A	Verse of MR13

The analysis of songs in Table 12.1 draws on a corpus of Milyarryarr songs recorded over a period of seven years by a team of musicologists and linguists documenting *kun-borrk/manyardi* in collaboration with western Arnhem Land singers. In 2006, Isabel O'Keeffe recorded Guwiyul singing Milyarryarr songs at a funeral at Warruwi, and Johnny Namayiwa and Tommy Madjalkaidj singing Milyarryarr songs (accompanied by Johnny 'Blackbook' Namaruda on didjeridu) at an *Inyimany ja najaman* (girls' puberty) ceremony. In 2007 Linda Barwick and O'Keeffe recorded Namayiwa, Henry Guwiyul and other performers singing Milyarryarr songs (accompanied by Solomon Nangamu and others on didjeridu) at a funeral at Warruwi. Reuben Brown also recorded Namayiwa in 2011 as part of a song documentation session led by Nangamu, at local music festivals in Gunbalanya and Jabiru. The most recent recording was made at Warruwi in 2013 during a ceremony staged for the documentary film *Language matters* (Grubin 2014) at which Brown and Evans were also present, as well as Ruth Singer. Based on this corpus, Brown identified 13 individual songs from the songset for playback and elicitation with Namayiwa – some of which appear in Grubin's film. The different performance

Figure 12.1: Johnny Namayiwa and Henry Guwiyul singing Milyarryarr; still from film by David Grubin (Namayiwa has a body design that follows the black heron.)

contexts in which these songs were recorded highlights the primary role of *kun-borrk/manyardi* in western Arnhem Land social life, and the prevalence of ceremonial performance at Warruwi in particular.

Table 12.2: Events involving the performance of Milyarryarr, recorded by musicologists and linguists in western Arnhem Land

YEAR	EVENT	PLACE	REPERTORIES PERFORMED	RECORDIST/S
2006	Funeral ceremony	Warruwi	Gumatj *manikay*, Milyarryarr	O'Keeffe
2006	Igeny Warlk	Warruwi	Milyarryarr	O'Keeffe
2007	Funeral ceremony	Warruwi	Milyarryarr, Galpu *manikay*, Murrungun, Nginji and Inyjalarrku	Barwick, O'Keeffe
2011	Song documentation and elicitation session	Gunbalanya	Milyarryarr, Inyjalarrku, Mirrijpu/Yalarrkuku	Brown
2011	Stone Country Festival	Gunbalanya	Karrbarda, Gurrumba Gurrumba clan *bungurrl*, Milyarryarr	Brown
2011	Mahbilil Festival	Jabiru	Karrbarda, Milyarryarr	Brown
2013	Performance staged for film *Language matters*	Warruwi	Milyarryarr, Mirrijpu, Inyjalarrku	Brown

4 Musical innovation and the dreaming of new songs

Namayiwa continues to dream new songs which are added to the performed repertory of songs he has inherited. Musical creativity and inspiration for new songs comes through an association with the deceased spirit of the songman [in the case of Milyarryarr, Charlie Wardaga] who first composed the songs:

> sometimes when I ... want to sing new song, what I do is get the clapsticks that he [Wardaga] made it for me and gave it to me, and I put it under the pillow, and then the dream comes.[19]

Dream-conceived songs are often the site of musical innovation; while these songs retain the same song text as previously inherited songs, and feature similar melodies and rhythmic modes, the text, melodic or rhythmic mode structure may be subtly re-arranged. One such example for Milyarryarr is the song MR13, which Namayiwa first played on his mobile phone for Brown in 2011 from a recording that his grandson made at a recent funeral at Warruwi. Namayiwa explained: 'this is my latest one here, it's a fast song, which ... I got that in a dream.' Namayiwa often performs the song at funerals when an up-tempo mood is required, or at festivals where such fast tempo songs give dancers an opportunity to display spectacular dancing for an international audience (see Figure 12.2).

The song features the same distinct rhythmic mode also identified in MR04, MR08 and MR09 and described in Table 12.1 (row 6), where the didjeridu cuts out and the singer's clapstick beat gets faster as he sings a sustained open vowel on the tonic (see bars 19–21, Musical example 12.2). Unusually for western Arnhem Land, the song begins with a long passage of singing accompanied by didjeridu without the clapstick beat. Eventually a fast tempo beat is established, first with even beating, and then beating in double (see bars 1–6, Musical example 12.2). Namayiwa explains how this song is 'a bit tricky one for the dancers', who need to be alert to the entry point of the clapstick beat before they can start dancing.[20]

---

19 Johnny Namayiwa, 20131107RB02, 30:48–31:09.
20 Johnny Namayiwa, 20110825RB03, 13:13–13:57.

Musical example 12.2: Transcription of Milyarryarr song MR13[21]

---

21 Recorded by Reuben Brown 20131106MR01-04-MR13_MR05. Musical transcription by Brown and Evans.

Audio example 12.2: Milyarryarr song MR13; Johnny Namayiwa, Jason Mayinaj, Henry Guwiyul (singers); Alfred Gawaradji (didjeridu player)

Figure 12.2: Toby Cooper executes a spectacular leap while dancing to uneven clapstick pattern in MR04, Stone Country Festival, Gunbalanya 2011; photo by David Mackenzie

6 Conclusion

The performance of Namayiwa's Milyarryarr songs illustrates an important path by which languages – or at least parts of them – can go on being transmitted through the medium of song even after regular transmission through speech has ceased. Although virtually no one now speaks Marrku[22], key words from the Marrku language, as discussed in this paper, are heard each time the Milyarryarr songset is performed, and kept alive by Namayiwa through his singing.

Songs are also kept 'alive' through frequent public performance – as in the case of Milyarryarr. This attests to the great value attached to this songset. Its distinctive flavour is supported by musical characteristics that give the set its own unique aural identity – such as rhythmic modes that echo the rhythmic setting of the song text (as in rhythmic modes illustrated for MR01, MR04 and MR05, Table 12.1). Musical innovation is significant here for three reasons. First, it helps to sustain interest and participation in the song tradition by drawing in dancers who are invited to listen to the words and vocal phrase of the song and respond to 'tricky' new clapstick rhythms. Second, it also enables songmen to adapt their music to the social action taking place in a variety of ceremonial contexts (for example, performing a greater number of fast-tempo songs featuring complex dancing for festival audiences). And third, it helps to keep alive the spiritual connections between current and previous songmen and their ancestors, through the process of dreaming and working up new songs.

Clearly, the multilingual environment of western Arnhem Land fosters an appreciation for language diversity (as discussed in Brown et al., this volume). It is also conducive to at least

---

22 At the time of writing, the one living person who knows some Marrku is Khaki Marrala, whose dominant language is Iwaidja. Around 90 and showing some initial signs of dementia, he can nonetheless recall fragments of Marrku, but unfortunately the fact that he is childless and living in aged care in Darwin reduces the opportunities for him to pass on his knowledge.

passive knowledge of many different languages among speakers such as Namayiwa, who may not consider themselves to be conversant in all of them. Transcription of Milyarryarr in this instance relied upon the combination of Namayiwa's ability to identify some song words and provide some context for the song text, and Evans' experience of having worked with Wardaga and others on the Marrku language.

As discussed, in many parts of Arnhem Land, song words are said to be drawn from 'spirit language'. The 'vocables' of these spirit languages often combine specific phonological profiles with a distinct sense of language and place, even when they can't be translated:

> Vocables do not simply draw from the phonology of a language to select ways of making sounds with the vocal apparatus. In exploiting the linguistic form of language, they take on the aesthetic and associative properties of the language. There are certain sounds that we associate with certain languages regardless of whether we can understand those languages, and within any language, quite specific associations between certain sounds and meanings may be developed (Apted 2010:101).

It may remain very much in the ear of the singer, or the audience, as to whether the text of a songset like Milyarryarr gets parsed as words or vocables. And, against a context of language shift, this is clearly a choice that will change through time: Namayiwa's masterful renditions show how the song-words can be transmitted with significant fidelity, without him actually being able to speak the language they were originally composed in. We may see this as a case where parts of a language are preserved through song transmission. But for the singers and listeners of this plangent songset what is more important is the abiding spiritual connection between song, language, country, clan, and the singers who have maintained these links as the clapsticks are passed on.

References

Apted, Meiki Elizabeth, 2010, Songs from the Inyjalarrku: the use of a non-translatable spirit language in a song set from north-west Arnhem Land, Australia. Australian Journal of Linguistics 30:93–103.

Barwick, Linda, 2002, Tempo bands, metre and rhythmic mode in Marri Ngarr 'Church *Lirrga*' songs. Australasian Music Research 7:67–83.

—— 2011, Musical form and style in Murriny Patha *Djanba* songs at Wadeye (Northern Territory, Australia). In Michael Tenzer and John Roeder, eds. Analytical and cross-cultural studies in world music, 317–351. Oxford Scholarship Online: Oxford University Press.

Barwick, Linda, Bruce Birch, and Nicholas Evans, 2007, Iwaidja *Jurtbirrk*: bringing language and music together. Australian Aboriginal Studies 2007 (2):6–34.

Barwick, Linda, Bruce Birch, Nicholas Evans, Murray Garde, Alan Marett, Isabel O'Keeffe, and Ruth Singer, 2011–2015, The west Arnhem Land song project metadata database, 2011–2015 https://elar.soas.ac.uk/Collection/MPI1013566 [accessed 7 September 2017].

Berndt, Ronald, 1987, Other creatures in human guise and vice versa: a dilemma in understanding. In Margret Clunies Ross, Tamsin Donaldson, and Stephen Wild, eds. Songs of Aboriginal Australia, 169–191. Sydney: Oceania Monographs (University of Sydney).

Brown, Reuben, 2014, The role of songs in connecting the living and the dead: a funeral ceremony for Nakodjok in western Arnhem Land. In Amanda Harris, ed. Circulating cultures: exchanges of Australian Indigenous music, dance and media, 169–201. Canberra: ANU Press.

—— 2016, Following footsteps: the *kun-borrk/manyardi* song tradition and its role in western Arnhem Land society. PhD dissertation, University of Sydney, Sydney.

Evans, Nicholas, 2001, The last speaker is dead – long live the last speaker! In Paul Newman and Martha Ratliff, eds. Linguistic field work, 250–281. Cambridge: Cambridge University Press.

—— 2003, Introduction: comparative non-Pama-Nyungan and Australian historical linguistics. In Nicholas Evans, ed. The non-Pama-Nyungan languages of northern Australia: comparative studies of the continent's most linguistically complex region, 3–25. Canberra: Pacific Linguistics.

—— 2006, Warramurrungunji undone: Australian languages into the 51st millennium. In Matthias Brenzinger, ed. Language diversity endangered, 342–373. Berlin: Mouton de Gruyter. Reprinted in Linguistische Berichte, Sonderheft 14, 19–44.

—— 2010, Dying words: endangered languages and what they have to tell us. Maldon & Oxford: Wiley-Blackwell.

—— 2011, A tale of many tongues: documenting polyglot narrative in North Australian oral traditions. In Brett Baker, Ilana Mushin, Mark Harvey and Rod Gardner, eds. Indigenous language and social identity: papers in honour of Michael Walsh, 291–314. Canberra: Pacific Linguistics.

—— 2016, As intimate as it gets: paradigm borrowing in Marrku and its implications for the emergence of mixed languages. In Felicity Meakins and Carmel O'Shannessy, eds. Loss and renewal: Australian languages since colonisation, 29–56. Berlin: Mouton de Gruyter.

Evans, Nicholas, Joy Williams Malwagag and Khaki Marrala, 2006, Majila Inkawart. Jabiru: Iwaidja Inyman.

Garde, Murray, 2006, The language of Kun-borrk in western Arnhem Land. Musicology Australia 28:59–89.

—— 2007, Warrurrumi Kun-Borrk: songs from western Arnhem Land by Kevin Djimarr [booklet accompanying CD]. The Indigenous music of Australia, vol. 1. Sydney: Sydney University Press.

Grubin, David, 2014, Language matters, with Bob Holman [video documentary]. New York: David Grubin Productions.

Koch, Grace and Myfany Turpin, 2008, The language of Central Australian Aboriginal songs. In Claire Bowern, Bethwyn Evans and Luisa Miceli, eds. Morphology and language history: in honour of Harold Koch. Amsterdam: John Benjamins.

Marett, Allan, 2005, Songs, dreamings, and ghosts: the *Wangga* of North Australia. Middletown, CT: Wesleyan University Press.

Marett, Alan, Linda Barwick and Lysbeth Ford, 2013, For the sake of a song: *Wangga* songmen and their repertories. Sydney: Sydney University Press.

Stanner, W. E. H., 1953, The Dreaming. In Stanner, The Dreaming and other essays, 61–62. Collingwood, Victoria: Black Inc. Agenda.

Treloyn, Sally, 2006, Songs that pull: *Jadmi Junba* from the Kimberley region of Northwest Australia. PhD thesis, University of Sydney, Sydney.

13 Singing with the ancestors: musical conversations with archived ethnographic recordings

Genevieve Campbell
University of Sydney, Conservatorium of Music

Abstract

Approximately 1300 song items are preserved among the ethnographic recordings made on the Tiwi Islands (northern Australia) between 1912 and 1981. Housed in the Australian Institute of Aboriginal and Torres Strait Islander Studies, Canberra, they were repatriated to the Tiwi community in 2010. Almost all of the song texts use the first person and present tense. For Tiwi listeners this brings the time, place and – importantly – the original performer of each song into the present at each hearing, creating a personal relationship between the (deceased) performer and the (living) listener and transmitting an experience of the original occasion. Extemporisation within cultural, linguistic and musical frameworks is fundamental to Tiwi song practice, with perhaps its most defining feature being the composition of text specific to a song's performance and audience context.

This chapter discusses a project[1] that brought together Tiwi and non-Tiwi musicians to explore notions of improvisation and performance intuition, as we created a series of 'duets' with the recorded voices of deceased Tiwi singers, selected from the archive by elders. As well as engaging with the rich musical heritage of the recordings, this project invited the ancestors themselves into the recording studio as co-performers, re-establishing the important role of musical and poetic extemporisation and the 'now' of Tiwi song. This has been a way of keeping the ancestors' voices and knowledge active in an ongoing dialogue between the past and the present.

Keywords: Tiwi Islands, endangered song culture, Tiwi language, improvisation, jazz

1 Introduction: Tiwi music

Bathurst and Melville Islands lie just north of Darwin, in northern Australia. Together they are known as the Tiwi Islands and are the home of about 2500 Tiwi people. I have been working

---

[1] This project was funded through the Phonographic Performance Company of Australia, Australia Council for the Arts Recording Artists Initiative.

with a group of Tiwi singers and elders for the last 10 years, focusing on Tiwi songs in both traditional and contemporary composition and performance contexts. I have also worked extensively with the older singers on a collection of ethnographic recordings that are archived in the Australian Institute of Aboriginal and Torres Strait Islander Studies (AIATSIS) in Canberra. These were recorded between 1912 and 1981 and repatriated to the islands in 2010.

Ngarukuruwala ('we sing songs'), founded in 2007, is a collaborative ensemble comprising Tiwi singers and non-Tiwi instrumentalists. Our aim is to create contemporary Australian music of high artistic and intellectual quality that blends the complementary skills of the musicians and engages both performers and audience in meaningful cultural exchange and mutual respect. Being closely informed by Tiwi song practice, which is based on extemporisation, our body of work comprises loosely arranged but fundamentally improvised versions of traditional Tiwi songs, sung in the language by the Tiwi Strong Women's Group.[2] These women, in their 50s, 60s and 70s, are called 'Strong Women' as a mark of respect for their position in the community as knowledge holders and role models. Our early projects centred on the women's 'modern' guitar-accompanied songs, composed by them in the 1980s and 1990s. As our work together moved towards the transcription and analysis of the ethnographic recordings, we began to use more of the old song forms in our performance and recording projects. It was with a growing sense of pride in the complexities of Tiwi song culture and concern at the state of its endangerment that the Tiwi singers with whom I had been working really began to look at how their songs fit into Australia's contemporary landscape – musically, spiritually, politically and in terms of cultural heritage. In this chapter I will discuss the recording project '*Ngiya awungarra* – I am here now' and place it in the context of the present volume's focus on the maintenance of traditional cultures through contemporary forms.

Tiwi song practice is fundamentally based on extemporisation. Each singer brings his or her own vocal idiosyncrasies to 'standards'[3]; that is, to set melodies. Perhaps the tradition's most defining feature is the composition of text specific to the time and place of a song's performance. Almost all of the 1300 unique song items recorded by ethnographers across last century use the first person and present tense. Thus, every time a recording is heard, it has the effect of recreating the original occasion. In the context of the repatriation and audition of the archived recordings, this brings the time and place, the story and the voice of each song into the present, in this way creating a personal connection between the living listener and the original performer.

Tiwi music is primarily vocal,[4] and there are 11 song types, each having a specific function, whether ceremonial, secular, political or social. Learning to create metrically, rhythmically, melodically and stylistically correct song forms across these 11 types was traditionally a heuristic process of engagement with senior songpersons. From about the age of 10, boys and girls would watch, listen and learn from their elders until they were ready to create and perform their own song. This achievement was regarded as the symbolic attainment of adulthood – the point at which a young man or woman was able to contribute to the cultural activities of the community (Goodale 2003:161; see also Stubington 2007).

---

2   28-year-old Francis Orsto is a Tiwi man in the unique position of having learned songs from the old ladies, as well as now being initiated into song by senior songmen. He and Eustace Tipiloura, leading senior culture and song man, have become closely involved with the project and also perform with the group.
3   I use the term 'standard' in the jazz sense: a well-known song that is treated in different ways by different performers, while remaining recognisably similar to the original.
4   There is no aerophone (such as a didjeridu) in Tiwi musical culture.

The complexity of this process, plus the fact that it relies heavily on fluent knowledge of the 'Old' (and now largely obsolete) form[5] of the Tiwi language, means that today there are fewer than 10 singers capable of performing traditional Tiwi songs[6], and perhaps five seniors who can compose in this form. With the survival of the song practices in such peril, elders have been urgently looking for ways to revitalise interest in and maintain essential elements of the song language. This has led them to the use of ethnographic recordings, not only as a rich resource for linguistic, musical, historical and cultural knowledge and learning material, but also as a means of direct contact with the original singers themselves – and with the moments of their performance.

2 Singing now

All Tiwi people, past, present and future, exist concurrently. The *Pitapitui* (the as yet unborn), the *Tiwi* (the living) and the *Mopaditi* (the dead) all inhabit the islands and are referred to in ceremony, in narrative and in social etiquette, behaviours and traditions. (In the latter case, this occurs more, at the present time, among the older, more culturally orthodox Tiwi people.) The *Pitapitui* live on the same Country[7] and within the same kinship networks as the living do, and when they are 'found' or 'dreamed' by their future father, they are born (Goodale, 1971:140).[8]

When someone dies they become *Mopaditi*. For a while they will stay around the places they frequented when alive, until the proper ceremonies are held to convince them to move on and join the world of the dead. In that world all of the kinship ties, interactions and activities that happened in the world of the living continue. Whenever living people move around the islands they call out to both *Pitapitui* and *Mopaditi* family members. The term 'ancestors' is one that has been added to current usage, although there is no equivalent Tiwi word that has the sense of 'people who lived in the past'. Tungutalum, who sang for Spencer in 1912 and Hart in 1928, and so, for me is a person (and a voice) of the past, is referred to by my colleagues as the man who *sings* in a certain way, not a man who *sang* in a certain way.

In almost all the Tiwi songs I have witnessed personally or come across in the recordings the text includes the first person singular pronoun *ngiya*, 'I (am)'. This means that each performance is a dramatic personification, usually of an ancestral being, such as a deceased person or the animal of their Dreaming. The pronoun is used with verbs in the present tense, and this brings a sense of immediacy to the listener's experience. In this way, Tiwi singing reflects the 'self-manifesting and eternally active nature of the Dreaming' (Marett and Barwick, 2003:145).

As the singer performs, s/he becomes the embodiment of the subject of the song and (re) tells the story or describes the imagery as though it is happening *now*. With each performance,

---

5   See Lee (1988) for an explanation of the shift from 'Old', through 'Modern' to 'New' Tiwi. Tiwi language has been described in terms of these three broadly identifiable manifestations in the last 100 years (Lee 1987). 'Old' Tiwi refers to the pre-contact language. 'Modern' Tiwi developed through the introduction of English in the Mission school. It features simplified grammatical structures and some English loan-words, but keeps many features of the Old language. 'New' Tiwi is the term for what is spoken today and is a further mixing of English and Tiwi. It differs sufficiently from Modern Tiwi that people under 20 understand very little of the songs (composed in Modern Tiwi) that the older women sing

6   In the face of the impending loss of songs essential for ceremonies related to death and mourning, a set of songs is being taught by rote to young adults, who do not necessarily understand the words. Nonetheless, the songs are being passed on in this way so that the correct ceremonial procedures can be maintained.

7   Capitalised to indicate that 'in Aboriginal English the word "country" is not only a common noun but also a proper noun. People talk about country in the same way that they would talk about a person: they speak to country, sing to country, visit country, worry about country, grieve for country, and long for country' (Harrison and Rose 2010:257).

8   This symbolic finding of the unborn child by the father is why Tiwi have their father's 'Dreaming' and their affiliation to Country is patrilineal, but they belong to their mother's skin group and blood kinship line (matrineal). See Goodale (2003:158).

therefore, a folding over of time is occurring, with the deep past and the present co-existing.[9] Whether it is a *Kulama*[10] song telling of current news, such as 'I am the falling cotton tree' (Campbell 2014a:159), a bereavement song sung in the voice of the deceased (Campbell 2014a:150), or a Dreaming song such as 'I am the crocodile' (Campbell 2014a:45), Tiwi songs are occasion-specific, tailored to the audience, the place and the time of day in which they are being created and (simultaneously) performed.

A feature of the language spoken by people older than 60 is the grammatical encoding of three general times of the day.[11] The verbal marking of 'time of day' is in addition to tense and aspect (Campbell 2013). To some extent this has been retained in the speech of older Tiwi people and their songs, which suggests that it is a feature of Modern Tiwi but not New Tiwi.

When listening to old recordings, the elder singers who are more familiar with Old Tiwi often commented on the time of day when the song was sung; for example, 'he's singing for the morning, morning words, sounds like morning'. They were hearing the verbal affixes that mark 'temporality'.[12] These encode the time of the performance/utterance rather than the time of the events narrated in the song; for example, (in the *Kulama* song recordings) crocodile running or ship waiting for the tide (Osborne 1989:281).

In the old songs we hear the parts of speech that not only place the story 'now' but also position the *performance* at the particular time of day it was presented.[13] It is interesting, in the context of this project, to note that this caused some confusion amongst my Tiwi colleagues when, for instance, we were listening to song recordings elicited in organised sessions rather than recorded in ceremony. Mountford's recordings contain sequences of songs that would not normally be performed together, and older listeners were confused by the time of day switching from one song to the next. Was the singer repeating a song from a recent *Kulama* ceremony, and therefore using the language as he would have sung it on the third evening of *Kulama*, for the purposes of putting it on record and perhaps following a 'set-list'? Or was he inserting evening words and affixation into what would be a morning song, because he was singing for Mountford in the evening? There is no real way of knowing, but it certainly raised a lot of questions for Tiwi listeners.

The fact that Tiwi singers encode for temporality means that the text of any song (and so its phrase lengths) will change slightly from one rehearsal or recording session to the next, if these are at different times of the day. This kind of variability can be observed in performances of the Ngarukuruwala band, where it demonstrates an aspect of Tiwi extemporisation that follows quite different conventions from Western jazz improvisation.[14]

---

9   For a fuller explanation of concepts of time in Indigenous Australian cultures see Ellis (1984).
10 The annual *Kulama* ceremony is held over four days at the beginning of the dry season. For more detail on the event and the songs within it see Brandl (1970), Goodale (1971), Grau (1983), Hart, Pilling and Goodale (1988), Osborne (1989), Campbell (2013).
11 There is no affix specifically meaning midday, but the absence of any temporal affix implies the general middle of the day (neither morning nor evening).
12 There is no single word, analogous to 'tense' or 'aspect', that is commonly used to refer to the grammatical function of affixes of this type. R. M. W. Dixon (2009:205) uses the phrase 'temporal specification'. Bernard Comrie, more discursively, calls such affixes 'bound morphemes, attachable to the verb, which indicate the time of day at which a situation holds' and notes that they are rare across the languages of the world (Comrie 1985:17–18). In Australia they occur in Yandruwandha as well as Tiwi, but elsewhere the only example Comrie gives is from the West African language Kom. In Tiwi, they have been described in grammars by Osborne (1974:37, 46) and Lee (1987:151, 186).
13 This has added a fascinating level of detail to the metadata associated with the archive recordings because Tiwi listeners are able to pinpoint the time of day the song was sung.
14 This became very clear when we were creating the track 'Brolga' for this project. Eustace Tipiloura recorded his Brolga song twice, the first time at my home one late afternoon. I gave this recording to trombonist Simon Bartlett to work with. Then the song was taken down again in the studio at about 11am, for Simon to record onto. While the main body

3 Why duets? The origins of the 'Ngiya Awungarra' recording project

The idea of creating 'duets'[15] came initially from comments made by my Tiwi colleagues when we were together at AIATSIS and the National Film and Sound Archive (NFSA) in Canberra in 2009. On hearing a particular voice that they recognised among the old recordings, my colleagues invariably said *awana* 'hello' to them and spoke in the present tense when explaining what the person was singing about. There was never the sense that these were people singing in the past, but rather that the recordings brought the person into the room. At the NFSA we watched some archival films[16], one of which showed young Tiwi children at the Bathurst Island Mission during WWII.[17] Leonie Tipiloura, an Elder, was in the room watching, and those around her recognised her among the children pictured. She became very upset and left the room, saying that she could not be in the same place twice. This was a very different reaction to what might be expected from someone brought up in Western society, who is more likely to distinguish consciously between their current self and their past self: 'Look at me there on the screen, back then, look how I've changed'.

Leonie was saying that she was here and *here*. She found it impossible to dissociate her contemporary self from the image on the screen, even though she was a small child in the film and an old lady in the room.[18] Later in that visit Leonie looked at the film again and was able to enjoy seeing her five-year-old self. The group decided that photographs and films were easier than sound recordings to rationalise as being in the past and therefore not *now*, partly because people looked obviously younger in the visual media, but also because group members are familiar with historical photographs in books about the Tiwi islands. Recorded voices, however, were, and still are, quite a different matter. Calista Kantilla explained to me[19] that a person's voice is still there even when they have died. The voice can still be heard in the bush, even though the body has gone into the ground. Hearing these voices loud and clear in recordings therefore renders them very much alive.

It is widely recognised that archived ethnographic recordings can become valuable as historical documents, since they preserve geographical and kinship information that enables ties to Country to be traced, and also provide evidence of ownership and custodial obligations (Lancefield 1998, Toner 2003). We are now starting to think, as well, of the voice itself (with its particular vocal quality, pitch centre and performance idiosyncrasies) as a significant heritage item, since it is both traceable to an individual and able to be passed down through descendants.[20]

The next occasion that brought this home to me was a listening session at Wurrumiyanga in 2010, when I was with senior songwoman Clementine Puruntatameri (now deceased). A group

---

of the text is almost identical in the two versions, Mr Tipiloura used morning words at the studio, rather than the afternoon words he had used previously. This meant that the rhythmic motifs Simon had identified to use in his improvised accompaniment no longer fitted, because Eustace was singing different words. Rather than forcing the issue and making Eustace wait until 5pm, we went ahead and Simon played something else.

15 Not all the pieces are strictly duets, but the project centres on the sense of dialogue between the archive track and the musician/s.

16 Tiwi people do not have the long-term restrictions on the voices/images of deceased persons that some other Indigenous Australian communities do. The period of mourning (during which the voice, name and image of the deceased are closed) lasts approximately one year, or until a particular ceremony is performed. All recorded voices in this project have been chosen by Tiwi singers and their use authorised by elders.

17 Movietone News #A0418: 'Island Mission sends native kiddies south', 1942.

18 I have come across this also with the most senior elders when looking at photographs of themselves as young people.

19 Personal communication, Wurrumiyanga/Nguiu February 2012.

20 Marett (2000:23–24) has made similar observations about the transmission of 'voice' in the Belyuen area of the Northern Territory.

was listening to a recording from 1928. There was some discussion about who the singer might be. Clementine became quite adamant that the voice she was hearing was that of a gentleman I knew could not have been singing in 1928, because he would either have been very young or not yet born. She insisted that she was hearing his voice and recognised it by the vocal quality as well as elements of his singing style. It transpired that we were listening to this man's father, so it makes sense that Clementine would recognise qualities of the voice and performance that could have been passed down orally. The most interesting aspect of this discussion was that Clementine, although conversant with 'modern' concepts of time, watches, calendars etc., had no real understanding of the linear order of years. She would not accept that the man she was sure was the singer was not alive (yet) in 1928. Even after much discussion and input from others, she stuck with her theory that this was the voice of that man, but decided it must have been coming through his father's body.

Figure 13.1: Clementine Puruntatamerit† (right) with Leonie Tipiloura (left) and Stephanie Tipuamantimerit† listening to the old recordings, 2010[21] (photograph by the author)

I also experienced old women singing the line that the wife would traditionally sing to accompany certain song-types, when (presumably for reasons of recording logistics at the time) the man had sung alone. They told me that it was wrong for these men not to have the 'follow up' line with their song and so would always add it on, even if they were simply walking past as I was auditioning with somebody else. Gradually I began to understand that the recordings were not just pieces of history. They actually brought the singers back into the contemporary world as protagonists. This had implications for the way we treated the recordings in our projects. The singers on these recordings in fact became participants.

---

21   † denotes that the person is now deceased.

Figure 13.2: Recording, Bathurst Island 2015 (photograph by Simon Bartlett)

4 Questions of ownership: of songs, of performances and of recordings

Most of the archival recordings have now been successfully repatriated, but it has been an unusually complex process (and one that is still ongoing) to find out what legal rights the elders have to use them in settings that require different permissions. For example, can they be played publicly at (Tiwi) community events, or in the background at the local art centre? Can copies be made to share with family? The use of the recordings in our live performances and in this new recording project has necessitated the negotiation of another round of permissions, payments and copyright restrictions.[22] Learning that copyright of the physical material is owned by the person who made the recording or by the institution in which it is now housed has been confronting for many of my Tiwi colleagues, who then draw the logical conclusion that their ancestor's voice is owned by a (non-Tiwi) third party. This results in the distressing perception that the essence of those people is trapped or held by others, elsewhere. A central and continuing aspiration during our current project has therefore been to engage personally with those voices and to welcome them as people, not merely as recordings.

While there is little doubt or argument that the artistic and moral rights of the songs belong to Tiwi traditional owners, ownership of the recordings themselves is a complex issue. After *requesting* repatriation of the recordings in 2008, the Tiwi traditional owners also had to *give permission* for their repatriation.[23] As the holders of the moral rights and cultural authority they were (in some paperwork, literally) signatories both as the party requesting release of material and as the party granting permission for its release.[24] Their experience with the repatriation

---

22 Disc copies were given to 11 Tiwi ladies and gentlemen on their visit to AIATSIS in 2009, but these were for personal use only, not to be broadcast or played publicly and not to be copied.
23 The complications and implications of the repatriation of indigenous material are beyond the scope of this paper. See Brown (1998), Nakata (2003), Toner (2003), Thomas (2007) and Treloyn (2012) for wider discussion pertinent to this subject.
24 Permission for use, replication and publication was requested for each particular recording prior to its inclusion in the project. Permission for the use of the musical, cultural and linguistic content had already been given, because it was the senior Tiwi song-men and -women (who give such authority) who chose the recordings to be worked with. It has

process has motivated Tiwi community leaders to ensure that these recordings are 'reclaimed' in an artistic and cultural sense as well as by having them physically returned.

5 The recording project

A detailed track-list of the 'Ngiya awungarra' album is provided below, in Table 13.1. It shows track numbers, titles, performers, recordists, and dates of original recording.[25] The sequencing of the songs is intended to give the album a meaningful shape in terms of mood, musical style, tempo and dynamic, with the aim of enabling the whole work to be listened to (and potentially performed) as a thematically-connected piece. Since we knew roughly what time of day each song pertained to, we decided to structure the album with this in mind. So, for example, 'Love song' is cushioned between sounds of the bush in the early morning[26]; 'Goose, moonfish and the footy' takes place in the middle of the day, when we would expect to hear public *Yoi*[27] gatherings as well as the football game; and the women's healing and *Amparruwu* songs come out of the sounds of the outskirts of town at dusk.[28]

Table 13.1: List of ethnographic field recordings used in Ngiya Awungarra CD, showing song-type and subject, performers[29] (living and deceased), AIATSIS catalogue references and dates of recording

SONG ITEM, CD TRACK NUMBER, SINGERS AND INSTRUMENTATION	AIATSIS REFERENCE AND TIMESTAMP	DATE RECORDED
Apajirupwaya **(Love song)** Payaningamayuwu† 1. with band and Tiwi singers 2. with violin, horn 18. with bass clarinet	Mountford C01-002916 -9 @00:26:52	1954
Kuwiyini Mirri Ilityipiti 3. Allie Miller Mungatopi†, and Mary Elizabeth Moreen with viola	Mountford C01-002916-9 @00:11:39	1954

---

been an ongoing, often uncomfortable and largely unresolved circle of questions and discussion amongst the group as we have waited for (and sometimes had rejected) permission to use songs that, by any ethical reasoning, belong to the Tiwi people and voices that are their direct ancestors, and sometimes even themselves. At all stages I have followed the direct advice and responded to the wishes of Tiwi custodians. More details of this process are longer than space permits here, so I direct the reader to Campbell 2014b.

25 For more detailed explanation of the song types, see Osborne (1989) and Campbell (2013:238). Contemporary Tiwi vocalists who made solo contributions are named in the 'song item' column. Tiwi vocalists marked with † are deceased, and, with the exception of Casmira Munkara, their voices are contained in the archive recordings. She was a member of the Strong Women's group and involved in this project until her death in November 2015. Permission has been granted to use her voice in the recording project and to name her in this chapter. Tracks 6, 15 and 19, while directly related to specific Tiwi songs, do not contain archival recordings and so are not included in the list at Table 13.1. The discographic details of the published recording are included in the reference list at the end of the chapter, under 'Ngarukuruwala 2016'.

26 The 'Love song' returns later on the CD (and so is within dusk bush sounds) for purposes of musical balance.

27 *Yoi* is a song/dance form performed at group events.

28 I recorded Eunice Orsto's *Amparruwu* contribution in the evening, outside the Wurrumiyanga women's centre, after a funeral earlier that day. The sounds of insects, distant voices, dogs and a radio in a house nearby were 'background noise' that I was, at first, disappointed to have captured. I realised later though that this is in fact the perfect accompaniment to an informal singing session. Eunice sang as people walked by, as children were called home and as the bush settled into evening. In the studio we overlapped some of the evening's wild sound with each end of Eunice's track, so that it became part of the aural background.

29 Violin: Michelle Kelly; viola: Virginia Comerford; bass clarinet: Jason Noble; horn: Genevieve Campbell; trumpet: Casey Nicholson; trombone: Simon Bartlett; double bass: Dave Ellis (tracks 7, 12, 13, 16), Brendan Clarke (track 1); guitar, blues harp: Dan Dinnen; drums: Jamie Cameron.

SONG ITEM, CD TRACK NUMBER, SINGERS AND INSTRUMENTATION	AIATSIS REFERENCE AND TIMESTAMP	DATE RECORDED
God sitting in the bush Daniel Paujimi† 4. with viola, 5. with bass clarinet	Sims_M03-002480-2 @00:06:15	1972
Yamparriparri: 'Falling star' 7. Pujuta Long Stephen† with band	Osborne C04-003854-132 @00:28:04	1975
Gramophone 8. Tungutalum†	Hart C01-004240B-D33 @00:04:52	1928
Going to Canberra 9. Unidentified men, and Eustace Tipiloura with horn	Short edits of archivists' identifying introductions from each of the collections used. Group call Holmes_S03 – 000184A @01:20:18	various 1966
Nyingawi 10. Enrail Munkara†, Munkara†, and Casmira Munkara† with trumpet, horn, trombone	Mountford C01-002916-1 @00:04:25 Hart C01-004240B-D49 @00:23:28 C. Munkara recorded by G. Campbell	1954 1928 2008
Goose, moonfish and the footy 11. Bartholemew Kerinaiua†, Eustace Tipiloura, unidentified group with bass clarinet, digital sampling	ABC ABC_36-004069-4 @00:05:37 Holmes_S03 – 000184A @02:15:00	1955 1966
Yoi pirrawa: 'Boat' 12. Tungutalum† with double bass, drums, bass clarinet	Spencer C01-00701-11 @00:18:22 Hart C01-004240B D38 @00:12:55	1912 1928
Ampirrimarrikimili: 'Crocodile' 13. Unidentified women† with drums, band	ABC, Simpson Island of Yoi @00:16:25	1948
Mamanunkuni: 'Silent land' 14. Long Stephen† with guitar, blues harp	Osborne C04-003855-201 @00:34:38	1975
Ariwangilinjiya (Lullaby) 16. Payaningamayuwu†, Calista Kantilla with violin, double bass,	Mountford C01-002916 @00:17:00	1954
Amparruwu: 'Snake' 17. Mary Curry†, Eunice Orsto with horn, trombone, trumpet	Osborne C04-003855-197 @00:27:24	1954
Yinjula: 'Old lady' 20. Leonie Tipiloura, Strong Women's group, unidentified Milikapiti children.	Wurm 508A @00:19:32	1967

6 Musical responses and devices

The non-Tiwi musicians were sent the old recording a few months ahead of the time we proposed to meet in the studio. Following their own personal methods, they devised their own response. They were given only limited information about the material. I did not want them to 'over-think' things and create a contrived countermove. They were advised of the song's function and given a transcription and general gloss of the Tiwi text. I did not (unless specifically asked) provide detailed metrical or musical analysis. The brief was for the performer to respond instinctively, emotionally and musically to the sound and the voice, in real time, not to a written transcription. We included a small amount of English transliteration in the liner notes, so that the listener would have a starting point for their own experience with the piece, but we didn't want to speak for the singer by transposing into another language what he or she is saying so eloquently in Tiwi.

I provide here a representative sampling of the different approaches the musicians took to the task at hand, as a way of illuminating the variety of responses.[30]

- Track 12 (*Yoi pirrawa* 'Boat') illustrates a spontaneous combining of instruments in a one-take improvisation, to create a soundscape based on a visual image conjured up by the text. Three players (on double bass, drums and bass clarinet) improvised freely to a 1912 and a 1928 recording of songs alluding to boats on the sea. Their responses to the recordings and to each other were informed by their own images of the sea as well as by the sounds of the recording itself – the melodic, rhythmic and dynamic fluctuations of the voice and of the recording machine.
- In track 16 (*Ariwangilinjiya*) a violin solo and a double bass solo were added to a woman's rendition and a man's rendition (respectively) of a traditional Tiwi lullaby song. Both instrumentalists approached this piece knowing it was a lullaby and, although they worked separately, used the same tonal centre. Each response is similarly mannered, pre-composed and repeatable, but fundamentally based on the musicians' imagined version of the Tiwi melody, using the implied harmonies that it would perhaps be surrounded by if played in a western classical setting.
- In the widow's grieving song of track 17 (*Amparruwu* 'Snake'), the horn and trombone improvised freely over one take, playing in dialogue with the other instrument as well as with the recorded voice, to create a trio in which the two musicians were responding to the same Tiwi source material, but also to each other. The original vocal recording of Eunice Orsto (recorded in 2010) includes spoken words as well as singing, as Eunice translates and explains parts of what she has just sung. The brass players therefore found that they naturally followed the ebb and flow of the conversation as well as the undulations of the melody and the imagery of the text, which describes the entwining of two people in embrace, 'like a snake'. Towards the end of the piece, an archival recording of Mary Curry (deceased) adds her *Amparruwu*, with responses from trumpet, creating a circling and layering of time as well as melody.

 Audio example 13.1: *Amparruwu* 'Snake' (track 17 of *Ngiya Awungarra* CD)

- Tracks 4 and 5 (Daniel Paujimi's song, called 'God sitting in the bush') are a digitally produced composition, using multi-tracking of instrumental lines, and editing and/or altering effects on the song recording and the instrument. It was produced so as to magnify the undulation of pitch caused by warping of the archive tape from the heat. Multi-tracked bass clarinet lines have been added to overlayering of the original vocal track, with production effects enhancing the pitch fluctuations and giving the impression of echoes as the voice fades in and out in volume. In the viola treatment of this recording, these undulations are created physically by the player, with no digital effects used.

---

30 On a personal note: having transcribed and analysed these songs in previous research, I had a strong pre-conception of what I thought I heard in them in terms of melody, rhythmic and textual metre and meaning, allusion and function. I found it fascinating and at times overwhelming to hear the musical treatment that each musician brought to them. In every case the essence of the music and the integrity of the song was honoured beautifully and the care and respect with which each musician had approached the project was clear.

- Track 3 (Mary Elizabeth's song, *Kuwiyini Mirri Ilityipiti*) was the result of a completely unplanned response to a recording on the day. Mary Elizabeth Moreen (Tiwi Elder) and Virginia Comerford (viola) had never met before they sat together in the studio. Virginia had prepared to play to a recording of Mary Elizabeth's father, singing her naming song when she was a baby in 1954. Mary Elizabeth, initially just there to observe, decided to tell her story, then sing in response to her father. She intuitively modified the phrasing, pitch centre and tempo of her speech and singing to blend with Virginia's playing. This incredible first (and only) take was an extremely powerful experience for all present.

A number of other tracks involved loosely prepared but freely improvised instrumental soloing over repeats of the Tiwi song item, set onto a loop by the sound engineer. The players then chose the iteration that they preferred. Tracks 1, 7, and 10 are a combination of written arrangements and improvisation, so musically, there were no set ways that the musicians were asked to respond to the recordings. It was left to each musician to react in their own way to what they heard and felt. The result is therefore multi-stylistic. Moreover, it incorporates not just the daily sounds of the Tiwi bush – where the songs came from – but also those of the archives – where the songs were preserved.

7 The recordings themselves become the protagonist

We regarded our project as a dialogue not just between people but also between soundscapes, so it was important to us that Tiwi musicians recorded in Sydney and Sydney musicians recorded on the islands. The Sydney recording sessions were held at a professional studio, where four Tiwi singers (two elders and two younger people) were present to add their voices, their opinions and their ideas. On Bathurst and Melville Islands the sessions took place in the old church at Wurrumiyanga and on Country. We were not aiming to produce a 'studio' sound, so we could allow the aural atmosphere in each venue to become an important part of the recording process. Most of the old field recordings include background noise, whether the sounds of a townscape or of birds, insects, dogs or the movement of a person sitting nearby. This has all been incorporated into the music as a feature of each track, and indeed as part of the overall narrative of the project.

The sound quality of the actual recordings has also become an audible interlocutor in the project, with the hum, crackle and distortion on the tracks being embraced to add interest, colour and atmosphere. Sometimes these components become the focus of the track itself. Other features of the old recordings that have played their part include the politely formal words of the AIATSIS librarian (recording the identification of material being transferred from reel-to-reel to cassette tape) and the voice of the recordist in the field. These add further dimensions to the polyphonic conversation between the various sonic protagonists. It is perhaps the sound engineer who has had the most fun with these elements, in some cases keeping (and even replicating) the print-through[31] sound for effect, or leaving in the blips and flares of level and the white noise crackle on the older recordings. This has created a distinct feel for each song.[32]

The song entitled 'Going to Canberra' celebrates the recording process as a soundscape in itself. While Eustace Tipiloura sings a *Kulama* song about going to Canberra to reclaim the

---
31 Print-through refers to the accidental imprinting of a segment of the recording from one part of the tape to another after being wound up on a reel for many years.
32 In addition to retaining some 'naturally occurring' extraneous sound on each item, sound engineer Bob Wheatley also copied sections of tape noise to add to some of the pieces and between tracks.

Figure 13.3: Sydney musicians in the recording studio, January 2016 (photograph by the author)

Figure 13.4: Eustace Tipiloura, Nelsina Portaminni and Karen Tipiloura in the recording studio, Sydney, October 2015 (photograph by the author)

material[33], we hear an emblematic array of voices and tapes the Tiwi group heard. These include an overlapping of librarians' and researchers' voices, giving tape identifications and catalogue numbers and snippets of a number of archive recordings. This piece is suggestive of the way that the songs and their performers have been obscured by catalogue numbers, since more often than not they are not named. Eustace sings of how important the material is, describing the long journey to reclaim it.

Audio example 13.2: 'Going to Canberra' (track 9 of *Ngiya Awungarra* CD)

All of the pieces recorded for our project defer in some way to the original recordings (as well as to their songs, texts, melodies etc.). Rather than cleaning them up, we have embraced the beating of wax cylinders on the 1912 recordings, the crackle of poor quality tape on the 1928 material, the print through on reel-to-reels from 1954, as well as pitch and tempo fluctuations, accidental over-dubbings at the time of transfer and the warp of the cassette tape that must have been heat damaged at some stage in the 1970s.

Although the pitch of some of the old recordings created interesting sounds, it proved difficult to work with when playing instruments tuned to A440. A few of us found it impossible to locate a definitive pitch on the tonal scale, and this made it very difficult to create melodic accompaniments. In some cases a combination of retuning the recording and tuning the instrument brought the pitch closer together, but it was not always possible to get 'properly' in tune without affecting the sound quality of either the instrument or the recorded voice, so we chose to live with some discrepancies of intonation. The microtonal nature of many of the Tiwi melodies also posed an interesting challenge to the instrumentalists, as did rhythmic and metric units, phrase-lengths and melodic ornamentations added by the singers.

All the Sydney musicians commented that only after a substantial amount of close listening did they really feel that they were hearing all that there was to hear within the recording. Only then could they attempt to create a musical response by adapting something of their own playing to what they were hearing. The acoustic power of the old recordings had an extra impact on the musicians' responses. They remarked how different the experience was when they were actually performing in the studio, where the old recordings filled the space, or were in headphones, as opposed to when they were doing their preparatory listening to the archive track in preparation at home. In the studio the Tiwi voice, as an ever-present revered ancestor, became very much an equal protagonist.

8 Items of intangible cultural heritage are in fact tangible

There has been much discussion in recent literature around the relationship between intangible and tangible heritage. For example, van Zanten (2004:39) observes as follows:

> The intangible cultural heritage cannot be entirely separated from the tangible heritage. Some human knowledge systems do not even differentiate tangible from intangible forms of heritage, or cultural from natural ... The intangible cultural heritage is manifested in tangible forms. For

---

33 Eustace sang this at *Kulama* in March 2010, putting on public record the visit to AIATSIS by himself and his colleagues. He then sang it again, some time later, for me to record for this project.

instance, knowledge and skills to build musical instruments are manifested in the products: the instruments built. Therefore, the definition of intangible cultural heritage had to mention this close connection: 'The "intangible cultural heritage" means the practices, representations, expressions, knowledge, skills – as well as the instruments, objects, artefacts and cultural spaces associated therewith . . .'.

Others approaching the same issue, from various angles that bear on my theme, include Munjeri (2004), Ahmad (2006), Giaccardi and Palen (2008), Ruggles and Silverman (2009), Harrison and Rose (2010), Falk and Ingram (2011), Howard (2012), Leader-Elliott and Trimboli (2012), Yelmi (2016) and Kearney and Kowalewski (2017).

As a further dimension to this discussion, one might argue that singing itself is in fact tangible. It can be felt physically, not just through its sonic vibrations but also through the emotions it arouses. There is no Tiwi word for 'song'. The closest words are *miraka* (voice), *kuruwala* (to sing), *yimunga* (life/skin group/pulse/soul; also used to refer to breath/lung support when singing) and *ngirramini* (words/news/stories), and all of these can be tangible. Add to this the experience my Tiwi colleagues had in reclaiming the recordings: initially, these were objects sitting on a shelf in Canberra, but they became the 'vehicles' for carrying home the *yimunga* of the ancestors. The production of an artefact (the CD) that is tangible as well as audible will reflect the real physical presence of the ancestral voices it hosts. It will also mean that these voices come to reside in a physically holdable, protectable, cherishable and 'ownable' form. Mainly for this reason, the Tiwi participants – in spite of knowing that these days most products of the recorded music industry exist in digital download form – regarded a compact disc as the preferred outcome of our project.

The CD format has other advantages. It will allow the Tiwi community to access the music without the need for a computer or internet connection. This will give the recording the best chance of contributing to cultural preservation and the 'musical health' (Grant 2010:46) of the islands, through bringing the ancestors back as teachers and co-performers. Also, in the context of a slowly growing tourist market, it will provide an item for the women's group to sell to visitors, with proceeds going towards their activities in the women's centres at Wurrumiyanga, Milikapiti and Pirlangimpi.

For the non-Tiwi who hear this music, it will be a reminder that 'every inch of Australia is a sung country. Its archaeology is deeply inscribed with sound by the longest continuing culture on earth' (Bandt 2014:88). The listener is not just 'hearing places' (Bandt, Duffy & MacKinnon 2007) and 'hearing the past' (Buckley 1998). They are also hearing a multi-layered journey through space-time: the journeys to Sydney and Canberra; the journey of almost 10 years to discover and reclaim the recordings and recover copyright; the even longer journey from the earliest ethnographic recordings to the present.

Through this project, the ancestors we invited into the studio as partners in a musical dialogue have made themselves available for ongoing conversations with others, both Tiwi and non-Tiwi, who journey through this present that we are sharing.

Eunice Mirrukuku Palipuaminni Orsto, revered Tiwi song and culture woman, passed away 1 December 2017. Her family has given permission for her voice and words to be included in this chapter and are proud that she will be remembered and honoured in this way.

References

Ahmad, Yahaya, 2006, The scope and definitions of heritage: from tangible to intangible. International Journal of Heritage Studies 12(3):292–300.

Bandt, Ros, 2014, Sonic archaeologies: towards a methodology for 're-hearing' the past – Lake Mungo, Australia and the Yerebatan Sarnici, Istanbul. In Linda C. Eneix, ed. Archaeoacoustics: the archaeology of sound (publication of proceedings from the 2014 Conference in Malta), 87–98. Myakka City, Florida: The OTS Foundation.

Bandt, Ros, Michelle Duffy and Dolly MacKinnon, eds, 2007, Hearing places: sound, place, time and culture. Newcastle UK: Cambridge Scholars.

Brandl, Maria, 1970, Adaptation or disintegration? changes in the Kulama initiation and increase ritual of Melville and Bathurst Islands, Northern Territory of Australia. Anthropological Forum 2(4):464–479.

Brown, Michael F., 1998, Can culture be copyrighted? [with comments and reply]. Current Anthropology 39(2):193–222.

Buckley, Ann, ed., 1998, Hearing the past: essays in historical ethnomusicology and the archaeology of sound. Liège: Etudes et recherches archéologiques de l'Université de Liège.

Campbell, Genevieve, 2013, Sustaining Tiwi song practice through Kulama. Musicology Australia (special issue: An introduction to sustainability and ethnomusicology in the Australian context) 35(2):237–252.

—— 2014a, Ngarukuruwala: the songs of the Tiwi Islands, northern Australia. PhD thesis, University of Sydney.

—— 2014b, Song as artefact: the reclaiming of song recordings empowering Indigenous stakeholders – and the recordings themselves. In Amanda Harris, ed. Circulating cultures: exchanges of Australian Indigenous music, dance and media, 101–127. Canberra: ANU Press.

Comrie, Bernard, 1985, Tense. Cambridge: Cambridge University Press.

Dixon, Robert M. W., 2009, Basic linguistic theory volume 1: methodology. Oxford: Oxford University Press.

Ellis, Catherine J., 1984, Time consciousness of Aboriginal performers. In J. C. Kassler and J. Stubington, eds. Problems and solutions: occasional essays presented to Alice M. Moyle, 149–185. Sydney: Hale & Iremonger.

Falk, Catherine and Catherine Ingram, 2011, From intangible cultural heritage to collectable artefact: the theory and practice of enacting ethical responsibilities in ethnomusicological research. In R. Cribb, ed. Transmission of academic values in Asian Studies: workshop proceedings. Canberra: Australia–Netherlands Research Collaboration. Online at *http://hdl.handle.net/1885/8329*

Giaccardi, Elisa, and Leysia Palen, 2008, The social production of heritage through cross-media interaction: making place for place-making. International Journal of Heritage Studies 14(3):281–297.

Goodale, Jane C., 1971, Tiwi wives: a study of the women of Melville Island, North Australia. Seattle: University of Washington Press.

—— 2003, Tiwi Island dreams. In Roger Ivar Lohmann, ed. Dream travelers: sleep experiences and culture in the western Pacific, 149–167. New York: Palgrave Macmillan.

Grant, Catherine, 2010, The links between safeguarding language and safeguarding musical heritage. International Journal of Intangible Heritage 5:46–59.

Grau, Andrée, 1983, Dreaming, dancing, kinship: the study of Yoi, the dance of the Tiwi of Melville and Bathurst Islands, North Australia. PhD thesis, the Queen's University of Belfast, Belfast.

Harrison, Rodney, and Deborah Rose, 2010, Intangible heritage. In T. Benton, ed. Understanding heritage and memory, 238–276. Manchester: Manchester University Press in association with the Open University.

Hart, Charles W. M., Arnold R. Pilling and Jane C. Goodale, 1988, The Tiwi of north Australia (3rd ed.). New York: Holt, Rinehart and Winston.

Howard, Keith, 2012, Music as intangible cultural heritage: policy, ideology, and practice in the preservation of East Asian traditions. Farnham UK: Ashgate.

Kearney, Amanda, and Gabrielle Kowalewski, 2017, Refuting timelessness: emerging relationships to intangible cultural heritage for younger Indigenous Australians. In Peter Davis and Michelle L. Stefano, eds. The Routledge companion to intangible cultural heritage, ch. 22. London: Routledge.

Lancefield, Robert C., 1998, Musical traces' retraceable paths: the repatriation of recorded sound. Journal of Folklore Research 35(1):47–68.

Leader-Elliott, Lyn, and Daniella Trimboli, 2012, Government and intangible heritage in Australia. In Michelle L. Stefano, Peter Davis and Gerard Corsane, eds. Safeguarding intangible cultural heritage, 111–124. Woodbridge UK: Boydell Press.

Lee, Jennifer, 1987, Tiwi today: a study of language change in a contact situation. Canberra: Pacific Linguistics.

—— 1988, Tiwi: a language struggling to survive. Darwin: Australian Aborigines and Islanders Branch, Summer Institute of Linguistics.

Marett, Allan, 2000, Ghostly voices: some observations on song-creation, ceremony and being in NW Australia. Oceania 71(1):18–29.

Marett, Allan, and Linda Barwick, 2003, Endangered songs and endangered languages. In Joe Blythe and R. McKenna Brown, eds. Maintaining the links: language, identity and the land. (Proceedings of the Seventh FEL Conference, Broom, Western Australia, 22–24 September 2003.) Bath: Foundation for Endangered Languages.

Munjeri, Dawson, 2004, Tangible and intangible heritage: from difference to convergence. Museum International 56(1–2):12–20.

Nakata, N. Martin, 2003, Indigenous knowledge, new times and tomorrow's archives. The Inaugural Ben Haneman Memorial Lecture, State Library of New South Wales, Sydney, 10 September 2003. Online at *http://anthropology-bd.blogspot.com.au/2008/07/indigenous-knowledge-new-times-and.html*)

Ngarukuruwala, 2016, Ngiya awungarra: I am here, now (audio disc). Sydney: Rouseabout Records (RRR75). See *http://www.undercovermusic.com.au/latestreleaes.htm*

Osborne, Charles R., 1974, The Tiwi language. Canberra: Australian Institute of Aboriginal Studies.

—— 1989, Tiwi chanted verse (3 vols). Ann Arbor: UMI. (Final draft of a book, published by UMI and held by AIATSIS as MS 5032.)

Ruggles, D. Fairchild, and Helaine Silverman, 2009, From tangible to intangible heritage. In H. Silverman and D. F. Ruggles, eds. Intangible heritage embodied. Berlin: Springer.

Stubington, Jill, 2007, Singing the land: the power of performance in Aboriginal life. Strawberry Hills NSW: Currency House.

Thomas, Martin, 2007, Taking them back: archival media in Arnhem Land today. Cultural Studies Review 13(2):20–37.

Toner, Peter G., 2003, History, memory and music: the repatriation of digital audio to Yolngu communities, or, memory as metadata. In Linda Barwick, Allan Marett, Jane Simpson and Amanda Harris, eds. Researchers, communities, institutions, sound recordings. Sydney: University of Sydney. Published online at *https://ses.library.usyd.edu.au/bitstream/2123/1518/1/Toner%20rev1.pdf*

Treloyn, Sally, 2012, Stopping the freeze: finding a place for musical analysis in a repatriation-focused song maintenance project. Paper presented at the Joint Annual Meeting of the American Musicological Society, the Society for Ethnomusicology and the Society for Music Theory, 1–4 November, 2012, New Orleans.

Yelmi, Pinar, 2016, Protecting contemporary cultural soundscapes as intangible cultural heritage: sounds of Istanbul. International Journal of Heritage Studies, 22(4):302–311.

Zanten, Wim van, 2004, Constructing new terminology for intangible cultural heritage. Museum International 56(1–2):36–44.

14 Children, knowledge, Country: child and youth-based approaches to revitalising musical traditions in the Kimberley

Andrea Emberly,[1] Sally Treloyn[2] and Rona Googninda Charles[3]
York University, Toronto,[1] University of Melbourne[2] and Wilinggin Aboriginal Corporation[3]

Abstract

Children and young people are often positioned as future beneficiaries of efforts to revitalise language, song, and culture. While accounts of dance-song traditions in Australia often include evidence of the participation of children, or are explicitly directed at children, rarely, if ever, has the position and role of children in these initiatives been examined. This paper turns attention to the activities, attitudes and roles of children and young people in the practice and revitalisation of the Junba dance-song tradition in the northern Kimberley.

Keywords: revitalisation, singing, song, Junba, Kimberley, digital cultural heritage, repatriation, children and young people

Introduction

The public dance-song genre known as Junba is practised by Ngarinyin, Worrorra and Wunambal peoples in Mowanjum and associated Communities[1] located along the Gibb River Road (Kimberley, Western Australia). Strategies to sustain and revitalise Junba traditions have been the focus of previous research that investigates how collaborative and community-led repatriation supports intergenerational knowledge transmission (Treloyn and Charles 2015). This chapter builds on previous work that outlines how children and young people are beneficiaries (Treloyn and Martin 2014) and key participants in Junba initiatives (Treloyn, Charles and Nulgit 2013, Treloyn and Charles 2015) in order to foreground and understand the key role they play in sustaining Junba.

The data for this chapter is based on research from a current project titled 'Children, knowledge, Country: music-based strategies for teaching and learning in remote Aboriginal

---

1   The word 'community' is capitalised ('Community') when referring to a particular settlement that is called a Community by residents and is declared a Community by the Western Australian Government, under the *Aboriginal Communities Act* 1979. The word 'community' is not capitalised when referring to a group of people defined by common language, cultural practice, or other association.

communities of Western Australia', conducted in partnership with the Kimberley Language Resource Centre (KLRC).[2] The authors of this chapter include two academic researchers (Emberly and Treloyn) and a community investigator who is also a leader in the revitalisation of Junba (Charles). The pictures, photos, words and data from child and youth participants are included here with permission from each participant and their guardians.

Among activists and academics there is an emergent movement to encourage children to 'become active partners and participants in research conducted about them and among them', rather than just to observe or record their views (Montgomery and Kellett 2009:47). This movement challenges researchers to consider children's participation in the research process: how do we shift away from representations of children based on unexamined notions of childhood towards informed, child-directed and child-initiated research participation, while at the same time balancing issues of consent, access, and dissemination (e.g., Alderson and Morrow 2011; Greig, Taylor and McKay 2013)? The 'Children, knowledge, Country' project has attempted to take up this challenge, and our research meshes with a number of local and regional research priorities in relation to the revitalisation of language and Junba.

The important role of children and young people in revitalisation activities is recognised by the KLRC, which was established in 1984 to advocate for Aboriginal languages and language speakers of the Kimberley and to ensure that languages and associated knowledge systems are passed onto children (Hudson and McConvell 1985, Kimberley Land Council and Waringarri Resource Centre 1991, KLRC 2010). The KLRC understood that local song and dance traditions such as Junba play an important role in the transmission of knowledge about language, land and culture to children in their home communities and in 'on Country' contexts, but that these rich and diverse educational experiences were not necessarily reflected in classroom learning. This motivated them to collaborate on the 'Children, knowledge, Country' project. (By 'Country', we mean the places that are intertwined with the identities and knowledge systems of the participants). Moreover, there has been local concern about the health of the Junba tradition, so these disconnections in the educational worlds of children risk reinforcing both poor outcomes not just for children but for the state of Junba as well.

This paper seeks to understand the perspectives of children and young people in relation to the factors that guide revitalisation of Junba. Specifically, our interest is in the role of children and young people in prompting and stimulating intergenerational knowledge transmission and in communicating their knowledge of Junba through workshops and performances, for each other and for diverse audiences. It also aims to expand on the interest in understanding Aboriginal children's roles in the production and use of cultural media (Kral 2011; Kral and Schwab 2012); in cultural practices on Country (Palmer et al 2006; Eickelkamp 2011); and in the practice and revitalisation of ceremony and dance-song (Campbell 2012; Corn and Patrick 2014).

Children, young people and intergenerational knowledge transmission on Country and through performance

Maintenance of Junba is a primary concern for Ngarinyin, Worrorra and Wunambal communities. It is a holistic practice that plays an important role in maintaining the wellbeing of all living things: people, Country, and spirits in Country (Treloyn and Martin 2014). In 2002, elder singer and expert composer Scotty Nyalgodi Martin[†] (see Redmond 2000, Treloyn 2003)

---

2   Australian Research Council Linkage Project 120020721. Investigators: Patsy Bedford, Siobhan Casson, Rona Googninda Charles, Jane Davidson, Andrea Emberly, Robert Faulkner, Kathryn Marsh, Sally Treloyn.

explained that practising Junba is essential for sustaining life, because Junba (which Martin refers to below as 'culture') and the spirits that created life are inseparable:

> [I]f we don't have any any sort of totem [the painted boards and string crosses carried by dancers] or culture [Junba dance-songs], you know, well … we haven't got a Galaru [Rainbow Serpent] … we haven't got Wanjina [localised ancestral spirits] … You've got to have that [Junba] because you belong to Wanjina. See those song and dance? Everything, that Wanjina gave us. And our body is … the power of it. See we got to have that otherwise we will be lost, without the culture (Scotty Nyalgodi Martin speaking to Treloyn, 20 February 2002, Derby).

Junba is a public dance-song genre that has many of the hallmarks of Central Australian song style, including short text strings that are repeated cyclically, performed isorhythmically and set to a cyclical melody. These are accompanied by clapsticks and clapping, and by dance that is performed by adults and children. There are two broad sub-genres: Jadmi, which is only danced by men and boys, and Jerregorl[3], which is danced by all. The decline in the health of the Junba tradition can be, broadly, attributed to the complex historical and contemporary circumstances that limit opportunities to practise. By contrast, when reflecting on childhoods in the 1970s and earlier, elders refer to experiencing, year after year, an extended period of two to three months during which they walked with their elders and families attending Law ceremonies. This happened in the wet season 'holiday time', when mustering on the cattle stations was halted. Elders have described the rich diversity of Junba repertories that were performed during these periods. Charles describes her experience as a child in the 1960s and 70s at Old Mowanjum mission:[4]

> If it was a concert night, singing and Junba, you could take your blanket and go with your parents to listen, or to night worship, if they were having that. They would have singing every night (Charles 2008:116).

> When the old people were singing at night, our parents took us with them. We weren't allowed to stay in the house. We went to the morning prayer place at Old Mowanjum, laying down under the stars and watching and listening until they fell asleep. This was in the 1970s.

> We used to spend all Christmas holidays – two to three months – travelling for Law business, because my dad was a singer. Daisy Jurruwala (dad's sister, my aunty), and Amy Wurrngany Peters, were also there.

> At New Mowanjum the singing ground was near where the office is today, this is where I saw Biyende[5] [a dance-song about two *agula* spirits (one male, referred to as 'Mr Agula', and one female, referred to as 'Mrs Agula') and a *yila* ('baby') composed by Martin] and Wanalirri [a dance-song about the Wanjina spirit named Wanalirri composed by Watty Ngerdu] and Ninbi [a dance-song about Ngarinyin, Worrorra and Wunambal peoples coming together as *ninbi* ('three tribes') composed by Watty Ngerdu], danced by old Laurie Utemorrah and Watty Ngerdu. Mum used to sing in the group with them, Ngerdu and Utemorrah. William Banjak was a dancer. Laurie Gowanalli was the Biyende dancer, Mrs Agula. He used to walk cross legged. We used to laugh all the time (Charles speaking to Treloyn, 12 June 2016, Mowanjum).

These two to three month periods, with family, Law and culture as the focus, repeated year after year throughout a child's life, provided an opportunity for immersion in both ceremonial (Wolungarri) and public (Junba) dance and song. The childhood experience of going to sleep

---

3   Generally, the term 'Jerregorl' is used to refer to Ngarinyin Junba repertories and 'Galinda' to refer to Worrorra Junba repertories of this sub-genre. Most commonly, however, all repertories are referred to as just 'Junba'.
4   Mowanjum was founded in 1956 as a new home for Ngarinyin, Worrorra and Wunambal peoples. The site of the community was moved in 1980, to accommodate the federal government's extensions to the airport near the old site (Jebb 2008:138–9). The first site is referred to as Old Mowanjum and the second as New Mowanjum.
5   Song names are capitalised.

to sounds of family singing is one frequently described by elders. In recent years, by contrast, perhaps due to the modern conditions that limit mobility and new forms of entertainment, this opportunity for immersion has been interrupted.

The annual Mowanjum Festival first took place in 1997. It has continued to the present as the focal performance event of the year, attracting hundreds of performers and visitors to the Mowanjum Community. It provides Ngarinyin, Worrorra, Wunambal, and visiting groups with a feature event to motivate their practice of Junba and Wangga (the two primary public dance-song genres in the region). The one-night festival and its lead-up, however, often bring some concern that there are not more opportunities to practise Junba. There is a particular need for more opportunities to practise on Country – that is, in the homelands to which Mowanjum's diverse communities are indigenous.

When Junba practitioners are asked how Junba can be sustained, they express a desire and need for additional face-to-face teaching and learning opportunities. While opportunity to practise is recognised as an important requirement for music vitality across the world (Grant 2014), in the case of Junba, the preferred location for teaching and learning Junba is on Country.

'Teaching on Country' has similarly emerged as a priority for the KLRC. There was an internal review in 2005 that sought to understand how Aboriginal people view their heritage, languages and knowledge practices in relation to the education that is provided by remote Community schools. In response, and as a result of ongoing consultation with communities, the KLRC developed curriculum programming centred on recognising and supporting Aboriginal teaching and learning methods in and out of school contexts, including 'Teaching on Country' (Bedford and Casson 2010). Thus, the notion of 'Junba camps on Country' became key to the collaborative planning for the 'Children, knowledge, Country' project.

Using the research projects as support, in 2011 elders Rona Charles, Matthew Martin and Pansy Nulgit ran the first Ngarinyin Junba camp, as part of an ARC Linkage Project (LP0990650) and assisted by the Mowanjum Art and Culture Centre, structured around a range of activities aimed at providing opportunities for children, young people and adults to practise Junba. These included dance, song and associated activities, such as: locating and harvesting *ornmal* 'white ochre' for body paint, or paperbark for *ngadarri* 'headcaps' to be worn by dancers; clearing and planning the *bororru* 'dance ground'; 'brightening' totems by repainting their designs; storytelling; and the study of dance practice using video recordings (Treloyn, Charles and Nulgit 2013). With the support of the Mowanjum Art and Culture Centre, children and young people led the documentation of the event using iPads and handheld recorders. Charles led a second camp in 2015.

Conversations about the importance of sustaining Junba and holding Junba camps on Country have identified children as beneficiaries and as motivators of adults' practice. Describing the benefits for children that come from their participation in Junba teaching and learning events, Scotty Martin's son, Matthew Dembal Martin, focuses on children's emotional and physical wellbeing:

> We just do it for the children, showing them... Like last week I was down in Perth. We had that NAIDOC [National Aboriginal and Indigenous Day of Observance Committee] week, but some students from Mowanjum they are schooling there, high school. They're all dancers. So they called me up, so I came down for that NAIDOC week. I had one week there going from school to school singing, dancing, make them dance, showing their teachers. They were very happy. They have the Country and for themselves they feel strong. They are not weak. The spirit, the singing, the dancing – that makes them healthy. It's always with them (Matthew Martin, 24 July 2012, Melbourne).

Junba camp participants of multiple generations express the benefits for children that stem from the location of the campsite, particularly its distance from town. For the 2011 camp, elders decided that the location should be on Ngarinyin land, some 300 kilometres away from the nearest town of Derby where many of the participants were based. The chosen site, known as Anbada (Old Mount Barnett Station), is close to the Community of Kupungarri and situated in the heart of Wilinggin (Ngarinyin Country). The distractions and troubles associated with town life were seen to be lessened in a remote location.[6]

The social, physical and aural environment of 'on Country' locations also supports immersive learning. 'On Country' camps provide opportunities for Junba listening and contemplation. For elder singer and camp leader Matthew Martin, the week-long camps provide an opportunity to remove children from the day to day distractions associated with mobile phone network coverage, television, radio and town-based activities. This allows space in their minds to concentrate and learn:

> When we get them out bush they will learn quicker. They have got nothing to do in the bush. They'll start talking about the old things that we are trying to teach now. They'll be talking about it. … We learn [teach] them so they can get that thing in their mind (Martin speaking to Treloyn, 15 March 2011, Mowanjum).

Children have the opportunity to go to sleep listening to elders singing, as did their grandparents (and some of their parents) when they were children. These 'on Country' activities provide a context not just for intergenerational teaching and learning, but also for intergenerational bonding (Palmer et al. 2006). Significantly, it provides an opportunity for young people and older children to learn, but also to lead the learning of those younger than themselves.

At the centre of the perceived efficacy of Junba camps for children's learning is the local cultural significance of 'Country'. Country – and the ancestors and spirits residing within it – is core to Ngarinyin, Worrorra and Wunambal peoples' cultural identities and wellbeing. Despite waves of displacement and colonisation, connection to Country has driven major social and political movements in the region throughout the twentieth century and up to today. Learning on Country is considered to be not only an effective space for teaching and learning, free of distractions, but also the right way to learn, in the company of the spirits that inhabit place. Junba Camps begin with a welcome to Country, where a traditional owner 'sings out' to the spirits in Country in language, announcing the participants' presence. Through appropriate welcomes to Country, by learning and dancing on Country with spirits, the bones of children and their social and emotional wellbeing are supported (Treloyn and Martin 2014). In response to a question put to him by an audience member at the 2013 Symposium on Aboriginal and Torres Strait Islander Music and Wellbeing, John Divilli, a participant in Junba Camps then aged 16 years, reflected on the longer-term effects of Junba camp for wellbeing. He pointed out that 'it takes away all the young kids to bush, takes them away from drugs and alcohol and all that stuff. So it helps us, it's good' (John Divilli, 28 November 2013, Melbourne).

While it is clear that elders position children and young people as beneficiaries of Junba, and young people such as Divilli articulate their own views on the subject, the younger generations also play an active role in enabling these benefits to be realised. On a practical level, while elders tend to be the singers, Junba performance requires the participation, motivation and action of children and young people in the dances. Counter to an understanding of intergenerational knowledge transmission that regards it as solely or primarily a process of elders

---

6   This approach has also been adopted by the Yiriman Project. This is a program designed to improve the lives of youth by supporting elders to take young people on trips to Country (Palmer et al. 2006).

teaching younger people, it is clear that, in Mowanjum and related Communities, young people in fact create opportunities for this transmission. For example, in the lead-up to the 2012, 2013, 2014, 2015 and 2016 Mowanjum Festivals, young people have been active in research, using archival photographs, video and audio recordings, and the song knowledge of their elders, to prepare for, practise and then perform dances that have fallen from the contemporary canon. By undertaking this revitalisation work, young people are instrumental in motivating elders to recall and perform the songs that accompany their dances. This work is a source of pride for family members, who praise their young people for such efforts. Speaking to an audience of several hundred at the 2012 Mowanjum Festival, following a performance of Scotty Martin's dance-song Biyende, after a hiatus of some 16 years, by teenagers Johnny Divilli and Larry Wungundin Smith, Rona Charles exclaimed over the microphone:

> What a performance … That particular Jadmi wasn't danced for a very long time. Good on you boys! That was really good boys, well done! (Rona Charles, 11 July 2013, Mowanjum).

Matthew Martin also explains how he has developed his methods of teaching children and young people in response to their interest in audio and video recording technologies and media:

> We have to get that thing straight. Get it down in computers and, like in CDs, many Junba [songs and repertories], dancing and singing. That's the special thing for our kids then—our next generation coming up. They got to pick all that [up] like the old people did. They pass it on to generation after generation. Well that's what I'm trying to get now, trying to teach these kids properly you know? Proper way of dancing, proper way of singing, to learn to sing. So if I am not around, well they got a CD there to look at. A picture to see. They can listen to CD, DVD, look at the pictures. That spirit will bring their mind back, and the kids will carry on from there. When they get older, older, older, they'll, sort of, get everything in their mind. Just in case something happens to us. … They can have their Junba but they can [also] have another song, [from] other old people, that [have] all passed away now. They [the old people are] not singing here with us but we have got to keep carrying on how, teaching our children, let them listen. We can show them our dancing, how they dance from old, old songs. … DVDs that's the main thing. They can watch the pictures, see the show (Martin speaking with Treloyn, 15 March 2011, Mowanjum).

Importantly, it is recognised by elders that children and young people play a role in sustaining and revitalising not only Junba, but also – due to the interconnectedness of Junba dance, people, spirits and environment – the health of their communities and Country (Treloyn and Martin 2014).

The contribution that children make more broadly to their communities is evidenced also by their approach to the workshops designed by the research team. These have the purpose of understanding better the children's experience of teaching and learning Junba. This will be the focus of the second section of this paper.

What children and young people say and show about the importance of Junba

Here we highlight the perspectives, ideas, and concerns of children and young people, as articulated through discussion, drawings, song writing, oral presentation and performance. Insofar as they play an important role in stimulating and leading intergenerational knowledge transmission, finding ways to understand their ideas about why and how they integrate song and dance into their communities and youth cultures is significant for revitalisation methodologies.

Integrating children and young people into research processes demands diverse, attentive and creative methodologies that do not dictate outcomes but rather find meaningful pathways for children to collaborate on outcomes that they deem beneficial and important in their lives. As Punch (2002: 325) notes:

> A common concern for qualitative research with adults or children is not to impose the researcher's own views and to enable the research subjects to express their perceptions freely. The difference for research with children is that it is difficult for an adult researcher ever to totally understand the world from a child's point of view ... Children are not used to expressing their views freely or being taken seriously by adults because of their position in adult-dominated society. The challenge is how best to enable children to express their views to an adult researcher.

Traditional research methods of participant observation and interviews do not necessarily provide a space for children to articulate their perspectives on how the Junba traditions can be sustained and what they mean to youth cultures of today. However, methods that position children and young people as collaborative participants rather than subjects help to integrate their perspectives into research processes and findings (Alderson and Morrow 2011; Greig, Taylor and MacKay 2013 Mitchell 2011). In the 'Children, knowledge, Country' project, we have embraced this approach by incorporating various projects led by children and youth. These include documentation of Junba by children and youth, youth-led activities in Junba Camps on Country, and revitalisation practices developed by youth.

As a means of furthering the aims of this project, members of the research team gathered for a week-long workshop at the Sydney Conservatorium of Music, preceding the 2015 conference of the Musicological Society of Australia (MSA). At this workshop, the culture teachers and community researchers (Rona Charles, Sherika Nulgit and Heather Wungundin) worked towards articulating a Junba-congruent curriculum with Sally Treloyn and Kathryn Marsh. At the same time, six young people between the ages of seven and 15, from the Communities of Mowanjum, Kupungarri and Yumurlun (Pandanus Park), shared their ideas about why Junba is important in their lives and communities. They worked with Emberly to frame their ideas for sustaining Junba and for supporting intergenerational knowledge transmission in their communities and beyond. The methods that emerged as important methods to children for expressing their ideas were: collaborative brainstorming, drawing, song writing, and presenting to an audience and performing. This provided insights into how they view their participation in these traditions as meaningful, and gave us a better understanding of the motivations behind their roles in Junba revitalisation. The youth team was not given explicit methods to follow, but their brainstorming sessions led them to choose song-writing, drawing, and performance as the means for explaining their connection to Junba most effectively.

Scholars argue that drawing and visual methodologies can reveal 'experiences and perspectives while at the same time democratically involving children as 'producers of knowledge" (Eldén 2012: 69). Thus visual methodologies shift the focus away from research *on* children and young people to research *with* children and youth (Thomson 2008). During the Sydney Junba workshop, the children and young people produced knowledge about the interconnectedness of Junba, Country, and wellbeing, and their role in supporting family and Country through Junba. This knowledge was produced by the children themselves, through a collage of words and concepts that addressed the issue of what it is about Junba that is important to them.

In the word list and collage, the participants named several of the Communities in which they and their families live (Mowanjum, Pandanus Park/Yumurlun), and Mount Barnett/Kupungarri). They also named one of the language groups with which they identify (Ngarinyin), as well as that of the land on which the workshop was held ('Gadigal'). (They had learnt this name from the Welcome to Country that opened the MSA conference.) They also used this activity to develop and share their knowledge of the Junba dance-songs that they perform.

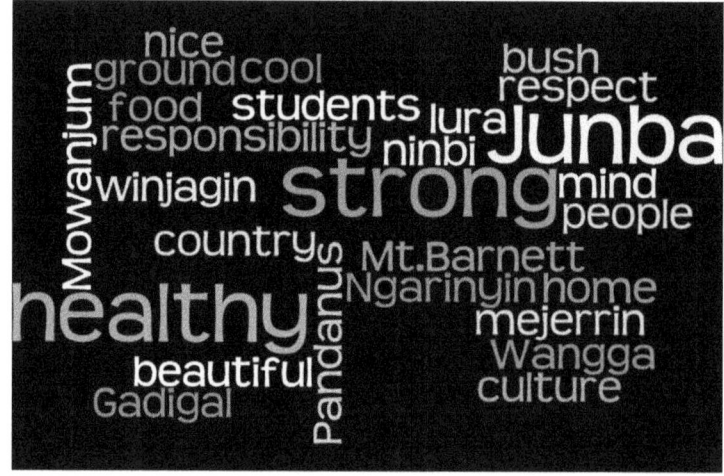

Figure 14.1: The importance of Junba (word collage created by youth participants, 28–30 September 2015)

The word *lura* (upper right) refers to the dance-song Lura Ganinji, in which two *agula* spirits scratch themselves and peer at the audience. Underneath *lura*, *ninbi* refers to the dance-song Ninbi that represents all three Mowanjum groups (the Ngarinyin, Worrorra and Wunambal) coming together. *Mejerrin* (bottom right) and *winjagin* (middle left) refer to two dance-songs that depict ancestral stories for important places in Ngarinyin Country. Linking these references to Country, people and Junba – and adding significantly to our understanding of the importance of Junba and its revitalision for children's lives – are words that attribute affective values, both personal and cultural, to place and people ('home', 'respect', 'responsibility', 'nice', 'cool', 'beautiful').

Building on these themes and assemblages, each participant used drawings to illustrate what the ideas meant to them. Laurenzia Divilli used illustration and key words to show how important it is to stay healthy on the land and to remember the land from which you come.

Clintisha Bangmorra spoke about her enjoyment of witnessing old people playing the clapsticks and teaching Junba to younger generations. Clintisha's drawing (see Figure 14.3) transforms the action and aural effect of the rhythmic striking into an active image, showing paired clapsticks with repeated, multi-coloured parallel lines (top right). Clintisha's drawing also illustrates a comprehensive range of Junba dance-song sub-genres, including two subgenres of Junba. Jadmi is indicated by the conical paperbark headcap (top left) and Jerregorl by the totem (bottom left). The genre Wangga is signalled by the didjeridu (bottom right).

Other drawings illustrate dancing and dances. In the drawing on the left in Figure 14.4, Selwyn Wungundin portrays the *Lura Ganinji* dance that he himself enjoys to perform. He represents the dancer's body with skeletal jagged lines, pointed toes, blank eyes and teeth, to show that the dancer does not dance as a living person but, rather, embodies and enacts one of the *agula* spirits that the song lyrics describe (two *agula* spirits looking for their tribe). In his second drawing, the depiction of a dancer performing a *jerregorl* style *junba* shows the happiness of the dancer as he carries over Country the heavy dance board painted with Wunggurr and Wanjina creative spirits.

In addition to these activities (brainstorming, talking about and drawing Junba, preparing for and practising it), the children and young people also wrote a song in collaboration with the other community participants at the workshop. In this exercise, they connected new

14. CHILDREN, KNOWLEDGE, COUNTRY   313

Figure 14.2: Drawings by Laurenzia Divilli illustrating Junba dancing ground and healthy Country, September 28–30, 2015

Figure 14.3: Drawing by Clintisha Bangmorra, September 29, 2015

Figure 14.4: Drawings of Junba dancing by Selwyn Wungundin, September 29, 2015

lyrics with a traditional melody and song texts (namely, Wanalirri and the warm up song Goobardwardangoo).

Goobardwardangoo (Song by Laurenzia Divilli, Lakeisha and Selwyn Wungundin, Clintisha, Sherayna and Tilenia Bangmora, and Eamarldon Rivers)

This is our land, this is our home
Bush country is where we belong
Junba is the dance for our song

Wanalirri wa yamowul yamowul
yamowul gambani
Wanalirri wa[7]

This is our culture, this is our identity
We are the Ngarinyin People
From Wilinggin Land
This is how we stand
Junba keeps us strong and proud
So *ngalanybabidi*[8] out loud!

Goobardwardangoo
Barlja goomandangi
Woorre gowadnerri[9]

Wanalirri wa yamowul yamowul
yamowul gambani
Wanalirri wa

Following the workshop sessions, the children and young people participated in a panel session at the MSA conference, where they presented their word collage, drawings, and song. After their presentation, they performed Junba for the conference audience, with dance boards they had made during the week. Demonstrating the embodiment of *agula* spirits by dancers in Lura Ganinji (as illustrated in Figure 14.4), the boys approached and lunged towards audience members, soliciting engagement and participation in their performance. The group ended their bracket of Junba performances with Ninbi, which refers to three Mowanjum groups (Worrorra, Wunambal and Ngarinyin) coming together. Finally, they danced Wangga with conference participants.

Conclusion

This paper suggests that children are not only beneficiaries of revitalisation processes, but can also lead them by their participation. Elders describe the physical and emotional benefits for children's wellbeing that emerge from their participation in preparing for and conducting dance. Additionally, however, the forms of intergenerational knowledge transmission that emerge in Junba camps and performances exhibit a fundamental reciprocity and interdependence between

---

7 Gloss: Wanalirri is coming, boggy ground. Explanation provided by elder Matthew Dembal Martin: this is the story of Wanalirri finding the boys and bringing the rain. The ground became soft and boggy, like jelly and quicksand, drowning all the people.
8 Singing group.
9 Gloss (Matthew Dembal Martin): they [all the Wandjinas] were talking, making it big [for Wanalirri]; 'let him come here, and see this for himself', they were saying.

Figure 14.5: Laurenzia Divilli leading the song writing session, September 29, 2015

the actions of learners (children and young people), on the one hand, and teachers (elders) on the other. Children and young people, rather than being the recipients of a unidirectional flow of knowledge from elder to child, motivate elders to sing and teach. They also become teachers to those younger than themselves. Moreover, they lead innovation of the modes by which Junba is taught and learnt, prompting elders to embrace new technologies, and researching dance and song with archival materials. In these ways, children play an active role in the revitalisation of Junba. In addition, by reinforcing connections with family and Country through their performance activities, children and young people contribute to their wider communities and Country by supporting and nurturing the fundamental link between Junba performance, spirits, people and place.

Adopting child-centred methodologies for research focused on child-led production of knowledge, we have drawn attention to the ways in which children and young people articulate their knowledge of Junba as a practice that is an integral part of their identities and communities of childhood. We also see how children affirm their role in communicating the interconnectedness of Junba with people and place. They are advocates for keeping traditions of knowledge strong. They understand that this entails self-reflection as well as presentation and performance to diverse audiences, in both their own communities and elsewhere. They are active in processes of innovation, planning and performance of dance-song activities. The continuation and revitalisation of songs is not just *for* them, but is, in fact, dependent on them. Accordingly, research focused not just on observations of their behaviour and presumption of the benefits, but rather on their views and opinions about revitalisation activities, will enhance our understanding of how endangered dance song practices, such as Junba, are maintained and revitalised.

References

Alderson, Priscilla and Virginia Morrow, 2011, The ethics of research with children and young people: a practical handbook. London: Sage.

Bedford, Patsy Ngalu and Siobhan Casson, 2010, Conflicting knowledges: barriers to language continuation in the Kimberley. Australian Journal of Indigenous Education (Supplement) 39:76–86.

Campbell, Genevieve, 2012, *Ngariwanajirri*, the Tiwi 'Strong Kids Song': using repatriated song recordings in a contemporary music project. Yearbook for Traditional Music 44:1–23.

Charles, Rona, 2008, That's how I really experienced my country. In Maryanne Jebb, ed. Mowanjum: 50 years community history, 116–122. Derby, WA: Mowanjum Aboriginal Community and Mowanjum Artists Spirit of the Wandjina Aboriginal Corporation.

Corn, Aaron (Japangardi) and Wantarri Jampijinpa Patrick, 2014, Singing the winds of change: ethnomusicology and the generation of new collaborative contexts for the teaching of Warlpiri knowledge across generations and cultures. In Katelyn Barney ed. Collaborative ethnomusicology: new approaches to music research between Indigenous and non-Indigenous Australians, 147–168. Melbourne: Lyrebird Press.

Eickelkamp, Ute, ed. 2011, Growing up in Central Australia: New anthropological studies of Aboriginal childhood and adolescence. New York and Oxford: Berghahn Books.

Eldén, Sara, 2012, Inviting the messy: drawing methods and 'children's voices'. Childhood 20(1):66–81.

Grant, Catherine, 2014, Music endangerment: how language maintenance can help. New York: Oxford University Press.

Greig, Anne, Jayne Taylor, and Tommy MacKay, 2013, Doing research with children: a practical guide. London: Sage.

Hudson, Joyce, and Patrick McConvell, 1985, Keeping language strong (long version). Kimberley Language Resource Centre.

Jebb, Maryanne, ed., 2008, Mowanjum: 50 years community history. Derby, WA: Mowanjum Aboriginal Community and Mowanjum Artists Spirit of the Wandjina Aboriginal Corporation.

Kimberley Land Council and Waringarri Resource Centre, 1991. The Crocodile Hole report. Derby: Kimberley Land Council and Waringarri Resource Centre.

Kimberley Language Resource Centre, 2010, Whose language centre is it anyway? In John Hobson, Kevin Lowe, Susan Poetsch and Michael Walsh, eds. Re-awakening languages: theory and practice in the revitalisation of Australia's Indigenous languages, 131–145. Sydney: University of Sydney Press.

Kral, Inge, 2011, Youth media as cultural practice: remote Indigenous youth speaking out loud. Australian Aboriginal Studies 1:4–16.

Kral, Inge, and Robert Schwab, 2012, Learning Spaces: Youth, literacy and new media in remote Indigenous Australia. Canberra, ACT: ANU E Press.

Mitchell, Claudia, 2011, Doing visual research. London: Sage.

Montgomery, Heather and Mary Kellett, 2009, Children and young people's worlds: developing frameworks for integrated practice. Bristol, UK: Policy Press.

Palmer, Dave, John Watson, Anthony Watson, Peter Ljubic, Hugh Wallace-Smith and Mel Johnson, 2006, 'Going back to Country with bosses': The Yiriman Project, youth participation and walking along with elders. Children Youth and Environments 16(2): 317–337.

Punch, Samantha, 2002, Research with children: the same or different from research with adults? Childhood 9(3): 321–341.

Redmond, Anthony, 2000, Nyalgodi Scotty Martin. In Margo Neale and Sylvia Kleinert, eds. The Oxford companion to Aboriginal art and culture, 639–640. South Melbourne: Oxford University Press.

Thomson, Pat, 2008, Doing visual research with children and young people. London: Routledge.

Treloyn, Sally, 2003, Scotty Martin's Jadmi Junba: a song series from the Kimberley region of northwest Australia. Oceania 73:208–220.

Treloyn, Sally and Rona Googninda Charles, 2015, Repatriation and innovation: the impact of archival recordings on endangered dance-song traditions and ethnomusicological research. In Linda Barwick, Nick Thieberger and Amanda Harris, eds. Research, records and responsibility: ten years of PARADISEC, 187–205. Sydney: University of Sydney Press.

Treloyn, Sally, Rona Googninda Charles and Sherika Nulgit, 2013, Repatriation of song materials to support intergenerational transmission of knowledge about language in the Kimberley region of northwest Australia. In Mary Jane Norris, Erik Anonby and Marie-Odile Junker, eds. Endangered languages beyond boundaries: proceedings of the 17th Foundation for Endangered Languages conference, 18–24. Bath, UK: Foundation for Endangered Languages.

Treloyn, Sally and Matthew Dembal Martin, 2014, Perspectives on dancing, singing and wellbeing from the Kimberley region of northwest Australia. Journal for the Anthropological Study of Human Movement 21(1): unpaginated. Online at *http://jashm.press.illinois.edu/21.1/treloyn.html* [accessed 20 June 2016].

15 Revitalising Meriam Mir through sacred song

Helen Fairweather[1] and Philip Matthias[1] with Toby Whaleboat[1]
The University of Newcastle[1]

Abstract

Many Elders and other members of the eastern Torres Strait Islander community are concerned about the future of their language, Meriam Mir, and other intangible expressions of their culture. This heritage includes a repertoire of hymns and choruses that developed following the arrival of Christian missionaries in the late nineteenth century. These sacred songs are still valued within the community as a living tradition, and new songs continue to be added to the repertoire. As a young boy growing up in Townsville, Toby Whaleboat learned Christian songs with texts in Meriam Mir, Torres Strait Creole and English. In collaboration with Meriam Elders and with support of the University of Newcastle, Toby Whaleboat is currently facilitating a number of activities to preserve, revitalise, and disseminate the rich tradition of songs in his ancestral language. This paper focuses on eastern Torres Strait Islanders in mainland Australia, and their ongoing efforts to strengthen language and culture through song. Drawing upon Toby Whaleboat's personal experience, it examines some of the methods by which the Christian song repertoire is maintained and revitalised in mainland Islander communities, particularly in relation to contemporary performance and the dissemination of these songs. The authors identify some of the challenges inherent in revitalising Meriam Mir through sacred song and discuss the Torres Strait Islander Sacred Music Network, a collaborative approach to identifying, recording, notating and performing Christian hymns and choruses with Meriam Mir songtexts.

Keywords: Meriam Mir, Torres Strait Islanders, hymnody, Christianity, songtexts, endangered language

1 Introduction

Situated in Torres Strait – a band of water that both links and separates the Australian mainland from mainland Papua New Guinea – are many islands, reefs, cays and islets. The inhabited eastern islands of this region are Ugar (Stephen Island), Erub (Darnley Island) and Mer (Murray Island). Lying close to the northern tip of the Great Barrier Reef, the island of Mer, together with the neighbouring islands Dauar and Waier, form the Murray Islands group. The volcanic soils of the eastern islands are fertile and the surrounding sea and reefs rich in marine life.

Formerly, the Melanesian Australians who live in eastern Torres Strait spoke Meriam Mir, a Papuan language that had two dialects: one spoken in Ugar and Erub; the other in Mer and Dauar.[1] Meriam Mir is no longer spoken in Erub or Ugar, the last full speaker having died in Erub around 1940 (Shnukal 2004:123, n. 25), and people now communicate using Torres Strait Creole (Yumplatok) – the lingua franca of Torres Strait – or English, or a combination of these two languages.

In the latter half of the twentieth century many eastern Torres Strait Islanders, seeking opportunities in employment and education, moved to mainland Australia, the majority settling in Queensland. The result was that the remaining speakers of Meriam Mir were either in Mer or among small groups of eastern Islanders within the wider Australian community. In the late 1970s, it was thought that approximately 700 Meriam people spoke Meriam Mir as their first language, 'which presumably included eastern Torres Strait Islanders living on other islands of the Torres Strait, and on the mainland of Australia' (Piper 1989:1), in towns and cities such as Cairns, Innisfail, Mackay, Mareeba and Townsville.

According to data in the Catalogue of Endangered Languages (ELCat)[2], in 1996 there were around 320 speakers of Meriam Mir. The *National Indigenous Languages Survey 2005* reported that there were around half this number. The linguist Nick Piper[3] estimates the number of fluent speakers to be currently fewer than 50. This is confirmed by speaker Elimo Tapim (pers. com. 2015), who believes that, at present, perhaps 200 people are passive speakers (that is, they understand Meriam Mir), but only around 40 people are fluent speakers. Piper has observed that 'today the language is at risk of dying out as young people are learning the Torres Strait Creole rather than Meriam. Most of the Meriam speakers are now aged in their 60s or 70s and when they pass away, so will their knowledge'. Thus Meriam Mir could be described as a critically endangered language.

The aim of this chapter is to focus specifically on one Torres Strait Islander language (Meriam Mir) and to examine how it may be revitalised through Christian song in contemporary mainland communities. Although Torres Strait Islanders sing hymns and choruses with texts in English, Yumplatok and some other languages, these are not considered here, since our discussion centres on the particular case of Meriam Mir. The chapter includes an interview with Toby Whaleboat (see section 5 below), recorded by Matthias in 2015. The information contained in the interview exemplifies how, in recent years, knowledgeable Torres Strait Islander musicians have used their specific agency and Christian beliefs to instigate cultural maintenance programs with an emphasis on language and song revitalisation.

This interview is framed within a discussion of examples of the Christian song repertoire ('language hymns' and choruses with Meriam Mir songtexts) of eastern Torres Strait, focusing on Islanders in mainland Australia, and their ongoing efforts to strengthen language and culture through song. This approach allows for an exploration of some of the methods by which

---

1   For some examples of differences in the two dialects, see Haddon (1935:193).
2   *http://www.endangeredlanguages.com* [accessed January 2016].
3   To date, Nick Piper is the only non-Islander in Australia to have studied Meriam Mir in depth. She is currently a doctoral candidate at James Cook University, where she is continuing her linguistic research into Meriam Mir. She is also a member of the Torres Strait Islander Sacred Music Network at the University of Newcastle. For these and other observations by Nick Piper, see Torres Strait Islander Sacred Music page, University of Newcastle website [accessed December 2015]. For further information about the project, and other personnel involved in the Torres Strait Islander Sacred Music Network, see *http://www.newcastle.edu.au*, and follow the pathway: research and innovation / institutes and centres / education and arts research / torres strait islander sacred music / about us.

this repertoire is being maintained and revitalised in mainland Islander communities, particularly through contemporary performance and dissemination of the songs. In the concluding section of the chapter, we identify some of the challenges inherent in revitalising Meriam Mir through sacred song and discuss the Torres Strait Islander Sacred Music Network, a collaborative approach to identifying, recording, notating and performing Christian hymns and choruses with Meriam Mir songtexts.

2 'Language hymns' and songtexts

Many Elders and other members of the Meriam community are concerned about the future of their language and other intangible expressions of their culture. These include 'language hymns'; that is, Christian hymns with songtexts in Meriam Mir that have been performed by eastern Torres Strait Islanders since the arrival of the first Protestant missionaries in the early 1870s.[4] They are usually accompanied by rhythmic beating on a *warup* 'single-headed skin drum'.[5] There are two types of language hymns: polyphonic hymns, in two or three vocal parts, that have their origins in the Polynesian-style *hīmene*; and gospel or Sankey-type hymns[6] with tuneful melodies and triadic harmonies, often featuring a refrain. Some hymns blend musical features of both styles.[7]

For the younger generation of Meriam who were born and raised on the mainland, these sacred songs are generally the main repository of Meriam Mir. As Lawrence (1998:59) has observed, 'hymns with vernacular texts provide an important resource of language knowledge and cultural heritage'. For a number of reasons, however, language knowledge gained mainly through a study of Meriam Mir hymn texts is necessarily incomplete:

- The songtexts function as poetry and, as such, do not exhibit complete sentences that occur in the spoken language.
- Meriam Mir is a complex language having many grammatical and other linguistic features that are not found in English; such features are not fully represented in Meriam Mir songtexts where the grammar has often been simplified.
- The subject matter of the hymns is limited to religious topics and consequently the vocabulary is similarly limited.

Moreover, any study of the language forming the songtexts needs to be based on the actual sung versions, since the published hymnbooks incorporate many alterations and errors (see below).

---

4   Elsewhere, Fairweather (formerly Lawrence) has given accounts of the introduction of Christianity to eastern Torres Strait, the development of Christian hymns and choruses, their musical characteristics and performance practice, and of the outside influences on the sacred song repertoire (see Lawrence 1998 & 2004).
5   The London Missionary Society (LMS) forbad the use of drums in church, but after 1915, when the LMS ceded its churches in Torres Strait to the Church of England (later, the Anglican Church of Australia), the use of drums to accompany hymn-singing was permitted. This practice continues to the present day. On the mainland, the Sankey-type language hymns are occasionally accompanied by both drum and guitar.
6   Ira D Sankey was an American solo gospel singer who composed Christian songs in the gospel-hymn genre. In the late nineteenth century he worked with evangelical preacher Dwight L. Moody, a fellow American, as part of the Protestant revivalist movement in the USA and Great Britain. In the 1870s, Moody and Sankey published a collection of hymns (widely referred to as 'Moody and Sankey'); Sankey later revised and enlarged this work (see Sankey n.d.). Many of the gospel hymns became popular within the Protestant churches and with their missionaries, including the LMS, which introduced them into Torres Strait, translating the songtexts into the vernacular languages of Torres Strait, including Meriam Mir (see, for example, Hunt 1888).
7   Some of the early British missionaries also composed hymns by setting Meriam Mir words to existing Protestant English hymn tunes (see, for example, Hunt 1888); but it was the Pacific Islander missionaries who had a lasting impact on the Christian hymn repertoire of the eastern Islands.

Through both internal and external influences, the spoken and written forms of Meriam language have undergone many changes. Owing to early missionary endeavours in the late nineteenth century, for example, the written form of Meriam Mir gradually became divorced from the spoken language; the grammar was simplified and the pronunciation of existing words was sometimes altered (see Ray 1907:5, 152 & 228; Mullins 1995:175). Additionally, new words referring to Christian concepts and Biblical events were introduced.[8] A further complication is that some of the differences between sung texts and speech evidently existed in the years preceding the introduction of Christianity. For example, the traditional pre-Christian sacred songs – specifically those relating to the Malo-Bomai cult in eastern Torres Strait – were described by the linguist, Sidney Ray (1907:50):

> The language in which these songs were given differed considerably from the common speech of the natives. Sometimes the difference appeared to consist in the use of archaic Miriam [Meriam Mir] forms, sometimes in the use of strange or foreign words. Sometimes the differences seemed to arise from the alteration of words to suit the air to which they were sung.

The alteration of words to suit the melodies of songs is a common practice in the Christian hymnody of eastern Torres Strait. The most common form of alteration is the addition of syllables; these are usually formed by inserting a vowel, for example:

spoken word	sung word
dasmer	*dasemer*
gair	*gaire*
gerger	*gereger*
kupkup	*kupikupi*
laglag	*lagelag*
ople	*opole*
urut	*urute*

Added vowels do not normally occur in initial position. In Meriam Mir hymn texts, however, such added vowels are largely the result of errors in transcription, translation and orthography by the early Pacific Islander pastors and teachers, particularly those who were from Sāmoa and other islands in Polynesia. An added complexity was the difference between the Erub/Ugar and Mer/Dauar dialects of Meriam Mir, which seems to have been either confused or ignored.

A vocable (usually *e* or sometimes *a*) can also be added within a line, or at the beginning or end of a line. These sounds are normally non-lexical; they are added as euphonic or eurhythmic particles (for musical reasons), or for emphasis. As such, they serve to add greater emotional meaning to part of a text (as is common practice in many Pacific music cultures). Two examples of vocable insertion in language hymn songtexts are:

- *(A) ad keriba ad*   (Ah) God, our God; and
- *Wi marau abara mer (e)*   They preached His word (eh).

Hymn texts may also contain combinations of added vowels and vocables.

In addition to the above, the problems inherent in the printed hymnbooks of the late twentieth century have developed largely as a result of earlier errors in translation, transcription and orthography, and the women who are lead singers[9] today still find it necessary to make corrections to printed hymn texts. Thus, texts that are printed in the hymnbook published

---

8   For a list of and information about these words, introduced in the late nineteenth century, see Ray (1907:166 & 167).
9   For a description of the custodial role of individual women who are lead singers in the performance and maintenance of language hymns, see Lawrence (1998:59, 61).

around 1973[10] do not accurately represent the sung texts as they are performed by Erub, Ugar or Mer singers. Furthermore, with the 1995 reprint of the hymnbook, more typographical errors occurred – thereby compounding earlier orthographical problems – and hymns composed since 1973 were not included. Lead singers therefore need to keep their own exercise books in which they write down the texts of language hymns, including newly composed ones, although some texts have obviously been memorised but not written down. Additionally, there are older hymns that were not published in the hymnbooks; they remain in the current repertoire as part of the oral tradition. Even today, there is no standardised orthography for Meriam Mir; nor is there a complete dictionary (but see McConvell et al. 1983; Piper 1989 (and footnote 3, above); Ray 1907:49–87 & 131–165; and Ray 2001). In mainland communities, there are few lead singers with the breadth of musical expertise to be able to pass on their knowledge to the next generation. Confirming Piper's observation about the endangerment of Meriam Mir as a spoken language (see above), these women are ageing and there is a serious risk that, when they pass away, so will their knowledge of sacred song repertoire and performance practice.

All of these factors make learning hymn texts extremely difficult for younger singers. As a result, in many instances, the oral transmission of hymns is of greater relevance than the reading of hymn texts from the printed books, which nowadays seem to serve mainly as a mnemonic device. To redress this situation, a small group of Elders who are fluent in Meriam Mir recently formed a committee in Townsville to review, correct and republish the songtexts of eastern Islands language hymns.[11] A draft document was drawn up in 2009 and an edited version (a second draft) produced in 2010 (Elimo Tapim pers. com. 2015). This revised hymnbook – 'Eastern Island Hymns: Torres Strait' – remains a work in progress. It is uncertain, at this stage, whether it will include language hymns that were composed since the early 1970s and also older existing hymns that, for one reason or another, were omitted from earlier publications.

An example of a language hymn songtext that had many errors in the earlier hymnbooks is the following well-known hymn of thanksgiving. It is here presented in its corrected version.

Audio example 15.1: Language hymn: Eastern Islands hymn no. 199 *Peirdi esoao meriba Ad*, composer unknown, performed by St Stephen's Torres Strait Islands Ministry Choir, Townsville, North Queensland (from Songs of Praise from Torres Strait [CD with booklet], Track 11, produced by Karl Neuenfeldt and Nigel Pegrum, 2007; used with permission)

Eastern Islands language hymn no. 199: ***Peirdi esoao meriba Ad***[12]
Composer: Not known. Text by Lui Bon, c.1942

| *Peirdi esoao meriba Ad* | Now (we) thank our God |
| Now thank our God | |

---

10 An outline of the early LMS publications that included Meriam Mir hymn texts can be found in Ray (1907:226–227). By 1885, the sacred song repertoire, as published in *Euangelia Mareko Detarer* (LMS 1885), had increased to 112 hymns. In 1924, when the Church of England hymnbook was first published, the number of hymns in Meriam Mir had grown to 131 (*Credo* 1924). When Rev. Boggo Pilot (*c*.1973) first published his updated liturgy and hymnbook, 204 Eastern Islands hymns were included. The hymnbook *Island language hymns*, published by the Anglican Church of Australia (1995), was a reprint of Pilot (*c*.1973) in an abridged form, but contained many errors. (For further details, see Lawrence 2004:59, 60.)
11 Its members, supported by staff at the North Queensland Diocesan office (Anglican Church of Australia), are: Gaidan Gisu, Mamam Martin, Elimo Tapim and Gretne Cloudy. The late Anemah Ghee and the late Renah Tapim were also members of this group. All of these people in Townsville are originally from Mer, except Gretne Cloudy who is from Ugar (Elimo Tapim pers. comm. 2015).
12 Corrections to Meriam Mir text (as printed in the hymnbook) and literal translation by Bill Bourne, Erub, January

Nerkep lam a kodomer lam	From our hearts and voices,
Heart from and voice from	
Merbi tadaisa okakis dikoda	You've brought us together
Us brought together gathered	
Debele erkepsam waiskeder.	(It would be) good to raise up our prayers.
Very good prayer will rise up.	

Refrain:
Mi abi tag lam sikak uridili	Because of his actions, we are happy.
We his hand from bad not are	
Abara werkab meribim au degdeg	His blessing for us (is) boundless.
His blessing us for over beyond	
Kaka ko omar	I too love (Him).
I too love.	
Lu bakedida abele gerger	Something happened today
Thing happened this day	
(E) mimi op bapita.	(When) we met together.
We met together.	

Peirdi esoao meriba Ad	Now (we) thank our God
Now thank our God	
Nerkep lam a kodomer lam	From our hearts and voices,
Heart from and voice from	
E debe lu ikeli merbim	He's making good things for us.
He good thing making us for.	
Abele gesep au sererge.	The world rejoices.
This earth very happy.	

Younger generations of eastern Torres Strait Islander musicians raised on the mainland do not have the skills or depth of knowledge required for the composition of new language hymns, for such polyphonic hymns are musically complex. Language hymns also require specialised performance practices (such as those undertaken by the lead singer) that may not be feasible among smaller mainland populations. Also, as the Anglican priest Elimo Tapim[13] (pers. com. 2015) pointed out, younger singers on the mainland often do not understand the purpose or function of specific language hymns; hymns that are appropriate for different occasions – such as burials, the Coming of the Light commemoration, or tombstone openings – or for particular parts of a church service.

Such difficulties are even more pronounced for younger Meriam living in locations like Newcastle, New South Wales, where there are no resident Elders and only a tiny group of Torres Strait Islanders. Consequently, while new language hymns may be composed in the islands of eastern Torres Strait, they are rarely composed on the mainland where the majority of newly composed Christian songs are choruses (Creole, *kores*).

1996. Free translation by Helen Fairweather with assistance from Bill Bourne. Later corrections to Meriam Mir text and English translations by Mabege Tabo and Nick Piper, December 2015.

13 Rev. Elimo Tapim is the priest-in-charge at St Stephen's Anglican church in Townsville (Torres Strait Islander Ministries, North Queensland Diocese). Now in his 70s, he is one of the remaining fluent speakers of Meriam Mir, with an extensive knowledge of the hymnody of eastern Torres Strait. He is a respected Elder and an associate member of the Torres Strait Islander Sacred Music Network at the University of Newcastle.

3 Christian kores[14]

Whereas language hymns are maintained and performed on the mainland within Torres Strait Islander Anglican congregations, *kores* are more popular among members of the Pentecostal churches and other smaller church groups. For non-denominational community events, however, language hymns as well as *kores*, are sung. Anglican congregations also sing *kores* in their church services and at interdenominational fellowship gatherings.

As Lawrence (2000:35) has observed:

> Broadly speaking, the texts of *kores* are usually much simpler in structure than the older style hymns, often consisting of a single brief stanza or verse that is repeated a number of times. Likewise, the melodies and harmonic structures – generally based on the Western triadic chordal system – are less complex than those of language hymns. Because of these features, *kores* are relatively easy to learn and memorise.

With their basic harmonic structures, musically simpler melodies and guitar accompaniment, the performance of *kores* does not require the technical expertise of a lead female singer or a knowledge of intricate vocal parts. Most often it is a man who plays the guitar; he usually selects the appropriate *kores* to be sung and he leads the group. Among younger members of mainland church congregations, the Sankey-type language hymns are sometimes adapted to be sung in a similar style to *kores*, accompanied by guitar, or guitar and *warup*. In the Pentecostal churches, younger singers may also accompany *kores* with electric guitars, drum kit, electronic keyboard or computer-generated music. *Kores* composed by mainland Islanders can have stanzas in various languages (see Lawrence, 2000 & 2004:67). Texts of *kores* are often in English, Yumplatok (Torres Strait Creole), or combinations of these languages. Songtexts may also be in Meriam Mir, especially those that have been composed in Mer but are now performed by Meriam in mainland communities.

In mainland performances, a *kores* with a songtext in English – originally composed by a non-Islander – may have an additional stanza consisting of a translation into Meriam Mir, written by an Islander. Conversely, an English version of a Meriam Mir songtext occasionally forms an extra stanza in some *kores*. The main reason seems to be so that younger Meriam, who have English as their main language, can understand the Meriam Mir words that they sing. In this way, some *kores* serve as a language knowledge resource for younger singers. This is important because, to date, there are no collected works or published books of eastern Torres Strait Islander *kores*. There are, however, various audio recordings commercially available, although few of these have been made in mainland communities.

4 Audiovisual recordings

Will Kepa, Karl Neuenfeldt[15] and Nigel Pegrum have, in recent years, been involved in recording Islander performances, as part of a project in producing Torres Strait Islander community CDs/DVDs. This project is sponsored by the Torres Strait Regional Authority (TSRA) and is ongoing. Two CDs, recorded in Erub (*Erub era kodo mer* 2010) and Mer (*Keriba ged* 2014), contain examples of language hymns and *kores*; community recording in Ugar has yet to be completed.[16]

---

14 For a detailed account of the history and development of Christian choruses in eastern Torres Strait, see Lawrence (2000:35–41).
15 Dr Karl Neuenfeldt, a musician and a cultural studies scholar, has been actively researching and recording Torres Strait Islander music, in all its forms, for many years. He is a Conjoint Fellow, School of Creative Arts, University of Newcastle, and a member of its Torres Strait Islander Sacred Music Network.
16 For details of the practice and process involved in the project, see Neuenfeldt and Kepa (2011). Details of these commercially available recordings are listed in References below.

Recordings, produced by Neuenfeldt and Pegrum, of eastern Torres Strait Islander musicians in a mainland community (Townsville) include: *Songs of Praise from Torres Strait* (St Stephen's Torres Strait Islands Ministry Choir 2007), and language hymn selections from a CD released as part of an exhibition at the National Museum of Australia (n.d.[2002?]).

It is important to note that the printed hymnbooks, and the exercise books kept by lead singers, contain songtexts only; they do not include music notation. Consequently, audio recordings play an essential role in documenting the melodies, vocal parts and instrumental accompaniments of the musical settings of Meriam Mir texts. Apart from the commercial recordings mentioned above, there are various audio recordings that provide examples of sung texts in Meriam Mir, and many of these are from the repertoire of Christian songs. The anthropologist Jeremy Beckett (2001:75–77) has provided an informative overview of earlier field recordings, archival collections and discography, including reference to music notation of Torres Strait Islander songs. In Mer, from 1958 to 1961, Beckett recorded songs, including language hymns, using a reel-to-reel tape recorder. From 1995 to 1997, Helen Lawrence (now Fairweather) made audio recordings in Erub, using a cassette tape recorder. Both of these field collections, held in the sound archive of the Australian Institute of Aboriginal and Torres Strait Islander Studies (AIATSIS), have been digitised and are available to eastern Torres Strait Islanders and, with some restrictions, to other researchers.

In the 1990s, the Torres Strait Islander Media Association (TSIMA) established small recording studios and editorial suites, with basic equipment, in some of the outer islands, including eastern Torres Strait. This enabled trained local personnel to undertake audiovisual recordings in their own communities which, in turn, could be broadcast from Thursday Island. On an informal basis, individual Islanders make their own audiovisual records of special events, especially those that include singing and dancing. Contemporary songwriters in mainland communities occasionally make audio recordings of newly-composed Christian *kores* as learning aids for use by other members of their congregations (Toby Whaleboat pers. com. 2013). Additionally, some Torres Strait Islander churches have recorded congregational singing and, in the past, have released cassette tapes, many of which are no longer readily available. Young Torres Strait Islanders in mainland Australia now make their own recordings of language hymns and *kores*, as well as secular songs and dances, using readily available digital technology and smartphones.

All of these recordings form a significant and valuable resource for language maintenance. Nonetheless, they cannot replace live music performance, for the customary methods of music transmission and performance practice cannot be learned from audio recordings alone. Performance practice, in particular, can only be learned and understood within its cultural and communal setting, and directed by knowledgeable music practitioners.

5 A contemporary singer-songwriter: Toby Whaleboat

One singer-songwriter of the mainland-born younger generation is Toby Whaleboat, whose mother was born in Mer and father in Erub. In this section we present an interview with Toby Whaleboat – a knowledge-holder who is keen to preserve his ancestral language – in which he explains the motivation for his work on revitalising Meriam Mir through song. Toby lives in Newcastle with other members of his family, including his two older brothers, Tat Whaleboat and Dalton Whaleboat. They belong to an extended family of well-respected musicians, dancers, composers and Christian pastors. He composes secular songs, dance songs and Christian *kores*, and teaches these songs and existing language hymns in Meriam Mir to non-Islander musicians in Newcastle, including his New Zealand-born wife, Elise Whaleboat. Much of this cross-cultural work has been done with the support of Philip Matthias at the University of Newcastle and members of its Echology choir. Matthias is currently initiating, with assistance from Benjamin Lambert, the music notation of some of these songs. Bernadette Matthias – a non-Islander who is an accomplished singer – has, under the mentorship of Toby Whaleboat, also publicly performed solo in Meriam Mir *kores*. Whaleboat's original songs – and hymns and *kores* with Meriam Mir songtexts by other composers – have already been performed by Echology at various venues in Newcastle and Townsville, with the collaboration of members of the eastern Torres Strait Islander community. Additionally, Echology has performed Meriam songs at overseas venues, including Sunday Mass at St Peter's Basilica, Vatican City, in 2013 and at workshops in 2012 at the Lincoln Center, New York, as part of the Rhythms of One World Festival.

In the 1960s when the pearling industry came to a close in Torres Strait, many eastern Islanders moved to the mainland in search of employment and educational opportunities for their children. Harry Whaleboat, Toby Whaleboat's father, became a fettler on the railways in the Hughenden district of North Queensland, and it was here that Toby was born. He later lived in Townsville where he received his schooling. Toby Whaleboat's mother, Akazi Whaleboat (née Tapim), was a fluent speaker of Meriam Mir. His father, having been raised in Erub, spoke Torres Strait Creole (Toby Whaleboat pers. com. 2013). Thus, Toby and his siblings grew up hearing both languages spoken, as well as learning English, and listening to their mother sing Meriam songs. Akazi Whaleboat was a lead singer with an extensive knowledge of the Christian song repertoire, and Harry Whaleboat was a talented singer-songwriter (Toby Whaleboat pers. com. 2015).

Figure 15.1: Toby Whaleboat (photo by Helen Fairweather)

Interview with Toby Whaleboat[17]

In 2015, Philip Matthias interviewed Toby Whaleboat about language, identity and cultural transmission. This interview formed part of a video presentation at the workshop entitled 'Revitalising ancestral song traditions in Indigenous Australia', held at the Australian National University on 6 March 2015, as part of the 14th annual Australian Languages Workshop.

> I was brought up in Townsville and that's where I grew up speaking Torres Strait Creole and Meriam Mir. I'd like to see the younger generations today growing up and speaking Meriam Mir as well. My Dad was born on Darnley Island [Erub]. My Mum was born on Murray Island [Mer]. But my heritage comes from Murray Island. My Grandad [Weser Whaleboat] is a Murray Islander. So we come from the village of Umar, and the other village on the Island that we have. My clan is Peibre clan . . .
>
> In the late 1890s Cambridge University undertook an anthropological expedition in the Torres Strait and the purpose of the expedition was to study an Indigenous Australian group of people that still had their language, their culture, [and] their tradition intact.[18] So Murray Island, Mer island, in the eastern Torres Strait, was the island chosen for this expedition. Murray Islanders still had in those times their cultures, their dancing, their singing.
>
> The Meriam language was 100 per cent spoken in the eastern Torres Strait Islands. However, over many decades following colonisation, the majority of Murray Islanders, [and other] eastern Torres Strait Islanders, moved to the [Australian] mainland. Now the majority of eastern Torres Strait Islanders are living on the mainland. A lot of our people today, because of living on the mainland, they had to adjust to the system on the mainland.
>
> It was a necessity for Murray Islanders, for eastern Islanders, to speak English. They were on the mainland because they wanted a better standard of living, because Murray Island wasn't that developed yet with education, with infrastructure. So a lot of Murray Islanders moved down to the south, and eastern Islanders moved down to the south for employment and for education purpose for their families.
>
> However today, living here on the mainland, a lot of Torres Strait eastern Islanders have lost the Meriam Mir language. It's starting to die within the community and die out, because the teaching is not there for the younger generation. That's one of the reasons Philip [Matthias] and I have been working for many years now to try and revitalise the Meriam language again. It's very important to bring our language back, for our kids to learn that language, the Meriam language.
>
> It gives our generation, the younger generation and our people a sense of identity, who they are . . . They can say that they are Meriam people because Meriam people speak Meriam Mir. If they lose that Meriam Mir, they lose their identity. My grandfather [Weser Whaleboat], he was a composer and a writer of eastern Island Torres Strait songs. He wrote many hymns in the early 1900s to the mid 1900s.
>
> He also went to war in World War II. He was stationed in Horn Island [in western

---

17 The transcript of this interview was edited, and explanatory notes added, by Helen Fairweather, January 2016, with permission and suggestions from Toby Whaleboat.
18 The Cambridge Anthropological Expedition to Torres Straits in 1898 was led by Alfred Cort Haddon, who had earlier visited Torres Strait as a marine zoologist in 1888–89. The first Christian missionaries from the LMS had arrived in 1871 but, as the Expedition in 1898 was mainly concerned with salvage anthropology, its members did not take a close interest in Torres Strait Islander Christian music of the late nineteenth century.

Torres Strait] and that's where he wrote one of his pieces. It's called 'Debe lamar e zogo'. It means 'good Holy Spirit'. . . . He wrote that song and he taught it to the Meriam community and still today, in churches up in Far North Queensland or in North Queensland, some churches still sing that language hymn that he wrote in the 1940s.

Audio example 15.2: Kores: *Debe lamar e zogo*, composed by Weser Whaleboat, performed by Toby Whaleboat and Elise Whaleboat (recorded by Philip Matthias, Adamstown Heights, NSW, 27 June 2014)

Kores: **Debe lamar e zogo**[19] 'The Holy Spirit'
Composer: Weser Whaleboat, *c.* early 1940s

Debe lamar (e) zogo   The Holy Spirit
Good spirit   sacred
Keribim (e) watabu   will come down (to earth) for us.
Us for   comes down

Ad   ira mir   natomelu   I'll show you God's word,
God of word I'll show you
Ki lage abele.   which we want.
We want this.

Debe lamar (e) zogo   The Holy Spirit
Good spirit   sacred
Keribim (e) watabu   will come down (to earth) for us,
Us for   comes down
Ko keribim tigarede   To also deliver us
Also us to   take
(E) gaire adud, adudelam.   from all evil.
    every evil, evil from.

Philip [Matthias] and I have actually taught that song as well to the [Echology] choir here in Newcastle, and Philip has written it in a music manuscript. It's the first time we've seen it written down in that format and it's very exciting. When I showed it to the Elders in Townsville, they were very inspired and excited to see it written down.

Philip and I will be undertaking some workshops in Newcastle and also in Townsville, Queensland. These workshops will involve teaching Meriam songs to the Meriam people in the community, in Newcastle and in Townsville, and also teaching the wider community as well [about] the significance of Meriam songs, and to encourage the wider community to be involved, to keep our songs and our language alive. This is a vital part of keeping the Meriam Mir language alive.

These workshops we will do, we hope to involve our Meriam traditional Elders that still have the language, that still speak the language fluently. We'd like them to come along and be involved in the workshops. So they can teach the younger generation and the wider community. Philip and I, we've written many songs down. Philip has written

---

[19] Meriam Mir text transcribed by Toby Whaleboat, 2014. English literal translation and free translation by Helen Fairweather, December 2015. Corrections to orthography and translations by Nick Piper and Mabege Tabo, March 2016.

these songs in music manuscripts. It is the first time I've ever seen Meriam songs written down in music format.

We've taught these songs to the community here [in Newcastle], to Philip's [Echology] choir, and we've sung these songs at the July 1 Festival[20] in Townsville. And one of the Meriam Elders there, Uncle Elimo Tapim, quite a prominent Elder in the community, he's actually said that it was reinvigorating that he saw the Newcastle choir, Philip's choir, sing those songs in Meriam Mir. It was quite an inspiration for him to hear it and for the community to hear it as well. So that's why they've asked us to bring the workshops to Townsville.

Figure 15.2: Toby Whaleboat (centre, front) with members of the Torres Strait Islander community, the University of Newcastle chamber choir 'Echology', and members of the Torres Strait Islander Sacred Music Network, with Canon Rod MacDonald, St James Cathedral, Townsville, 2015 (photograph by Karl Neuenfeldt)

So we are hoping within the workshops to teach younger Meriam people how to write Meriam language songs. This is really important for our younger generations to learn how to write Meriam songs and to speak Meriam songs and to sing; speak the language and sing the language songs, and teach it to other people in their community. I spoke to Philip about my dream, you can call it, about having a large concert in Townsville. Townsville consists of a large majority of eastern Islanders, and around North Queensland and Cairns and Mackay, a lot of eastern Islander communities, they live in those towns.

We just recently had a Christmas concert, only last Christmas [2014], and we sung a few of our songs there at the concert . . . one of the songs was 'Omar, Omar, Omar', which is love, the love of God. This song is a special song. It was taught to me by my Mum when

---

20 The festival referred to here is the Coming of the Light. It is celebrated annually by Torres Strait Islanders on 1 July, the anniversary of the arrival of the first LMS missionaries in Erub, eastern Torres Strait, in 1871. The commemorative service for the Coming of the Light in Townsville was held at St Stephen's Anglican Church. The priest-in-charge was Rev. Elimo Tapim, Toby Whaleboat's maternal uncle (see note 13, above).

I was a very young child and she would sing it to me at night and she would sing it in the house. When I was in her room she would sing the song to us as children.

Audio example 15.3: Kores: *Omar, omar, omar*, composed by Jimmy [?] Wailu; all vocal parts (unaccompanied) performed and recorded by Toby Whaleboat (Shortland, NSW, 18 June 2015)

Kores: **Omar, Omar, Omar**[21]
Composer: Jimmy [?] Wailu c.1970s

Omar, omar, omar ide igardi Love, love, love (doer) took	(It was) love that carried Him;
Bamrerdi sataurogo Hang Himself the cross on	(And left) Him hanging on (the) cross.
Asiasi E digier, Pain He suffer	He suffered and suffered, in great pain.
Watwet mam ide poni desami Dry blood (doer) eye closed	(The) dry blood forced His eyes shut.
Tepaiterdi Tabara mam egomdari Poured His blood pooled	His blood spilled over and pooled below.
Au muimui omar ko meribim Big deep love also us to	He also has a great love for us;
E meriba, meriba Agud. He our, our God.	He (is) our God.

> I taught that to the [Echology] choir here [in Newcastle] and to Bernadette [Matthias], and Bernadette performed the song in the Christmas concert. At the Christmas concert, in the audience were a lot of non-Indigenous people sitting there. There were other songs that we sung as well. *Opole Audlam* ['The Lord rose from the dead'], another great hymn from the eastern Torres Strait Islands; we sung that and we sung many other eastern Torres Strait Islander songs. The response that we got from the audience after the concert, it was overwhelming.
>
> They really loved the performances and just to hear Meriam Mir language, an Indigenous Australian language, sung here . . . we taught that song to the whole audience that was there in the concert and everyone participated and sung this song. It was very special. It was a very special performance to hear the wider community, the non-Indigenous community, sing Meriam Mir language songs. It was very special to me. Very important for us, as Indigenous people, to hear the wider community sing our songs, so we know that our songs will be revived and it won't die. If everyone sings our songs, and keeps it ongoing, and [we] teach it to our younger generation, then this is who we are as Australians: non-Indigenous and Indigenous coming together singing those songs.
>
> So, my Granddad, he was a composer, and he is a well-known composer for his generation and in his time. My Dad wrote a lot of songs as well. He composed a lot of songs,

---

21 Corrections to Meriam Mir text, and English literal translation, by Rev. Elimo Tapim, Townsville, December 2015. English free translation by Elimo Tapim and Helen Fairweather. Later corrections to orthography and translations by Adimabo Noah, Nick Piper, and Mabege Tabo, January 2016. Elimo Tapim (pers. comm. 2015) explained: '*Omar* has two meanings – love and pity. You feel pity for someone that you love'.

language songs and English songs. [This is] a farewell song, farewell to everyone. May God's Holy Spirit go with you, and the angels guide and keep you safe, and God's love will always be with you forever.

Audio example 15.4: Kores: *Debe ki wabim gaire le*, composed by Harry Whaleboat, performed by Gai Bero, Wya Sailor, May Simbolo, Merwez Whaleboat, Toby Whaleboat, Lelay Wailu and Victor Wailu (recorded by Karl Neuenfeldt and Nigel Pegrum, Townsville, North Queensland, 4 July 2015)

Kores: ***Debe ki wabim gaire le***[22] 'Goodnight everybody'
Composer: Harry Whaleboat *c.*1994

Debe ki wabim gaire le	Goodnight everybody,
Good night you for every person	
Wa bakauware wabi uteb ge	You are going home.
You going your place at	
Ad ira lamar zogo mena wadawer	God's Holy Spirit goes with you,
God of spirit sacred continually you with	
Angela giz ko kemem	Angels will guide (you) all.
Angels all will guide	
Ad ira niai eded, a eded asemurkak.	God of eternal life, and life without end
God of forever life, and life finish not.	
Ad ira eded, Ad ira niai, niai karem,	God of life, God of eternity,
God of life, God of always, always ever for,	
Ad ira eded, Ad ira niai, niai karem.	God of life, God of eternity.
God of life, God of always, always ever for.	

🌀 Now, I have been writing songs as well and I love writing songs. I'm beginning to write a lot of Meriam Mir songs now. I've written a lot of English language songs. But I would like to encourage more and more Meriam people to write and sing Meriam Mir songs, with English translation.

Philip and I have been working for many years now to try and revitalise the Meriam language again. It's very important to bring our language back, for our kids to learn that language, the Meriam language, because it gives our generation, the younger generation, and our people a sense of identity of who they are . . . They can say that they are Meriam people, because Meriam people speak Meriam Mir. If they lose that Meriam Mir, they lose their identity. I'd like to encourage a lot of Meriam people and also the wider community, to write and sing Meriam Mir songs. 🌀

6 Challenges

From the information that Toby Whaleboat shared in this interview we can begin to understand the value of, and the limitations inherent in, the cultural transmission of sacred songs among

---

22 Transcribed by Helen Fairweather with assistance from Donald and Dulcie Whaleboat. Meriam Mir text and literal translation by Dulcie Whaleboat. Free translation by Helen Fairweather, December 2015. Minor corrections to the orthography by Nick Piper, March 2016.

eastern Torres Strait Islanders in mainland Australian communities. For passive speakers of Meriam Mir – who are neither fully literate in nor fluent speakers of Meriam Mir – composing new *kores* and other songs can be problematic. In a location such as Newcastle, where there are no musically or linguistically knowledgeable Elders in the immediate community, it is difficult for young songwriters and performers to readily access advice or relevant cultural information. Instructing non-Islander musicians in performing sacred songs, such as language hymns in Meriam Mir, poses another, yet related, set of challenges that need to be met.

Some of these challenges may be broadly identified as:

- difficulties encountered in writing new songtexts using Meriam Mir, as language knowledge (e.g. vocabulary) might be limited
- inexperience in speaking and writing Meriam Mir, sometimes leading to inconsistencies in orthography and grammatical construction of songtexts
- cross-cultural transmission of existing Meriam Mir *kores* and language hymns to non-Islander singers, resulting in changes to musical interpretation and to Islander performance practice.

Through a process of collaboration with Meriam Elders in North Queensland, and with the support of the University of Newcastle, the Torres Strait Islander Sacred Music Network aims to resolve some of these difficulties. One of its goals is to bring the eastern Torres Strait Islander sacred song repertoire to the attention of the wider community in Australia. A variety of strategies is being employed, including notating, teaching, recording and performing the music. A community 'Singing Space' is planned for the Wollotuka Institute at the University of Newcastle, in part to engage this music with Indigenous and non-Indigenous communities alike. Toby Whaleboat further aims to facilitate a number of activities to preserve, revitalise, and disseminate this rich tradition of songs in Meriam Mir and, as he outlined in his interview (above), he plans to lead songwriting workshops for younger eastern Torres Strait Islanders living in North Queensland. These workshops are timed to coincide with the Coming of the Light celebrations each year.

7 Conclusion

These ongoing efforts to strengthen language and culture through song raise complex issues of authenticity, innovation, ownership and appropriation, particularly in relation to contemporary performance and dissemination of songs within the broader Australian community. Moreover, as Matthias has observed during public performances of Meriam Mir songs given by Echology, both singers and audiences alike become engaged with the rhythmic, melodic and polyphonic aspects of the music, especially in the singing of language hymns. He also noticed that performers and audiences seem able to sense that this music has real connection for Torres Strait Islanders and their identity, and that this connection can engage, in a wider sense, with contemporary performers and audiences of all backgrounds. This is in keeping with Anna Shnukal's (2004:111–2) observation that: 'Islander custom and language were apparently always syncretic, receptive to difference and outside influence and eager to accept and transform them' (see also, Lawrence 2004). It may well be that what is being experienced now, among the younger generation of mainlander Meriam, is a continuation and further extension of such syncretism and transformation.

Although this chapter has focused on the texts of contemporary sacred songs, it is important to consider that Meriam Mir also survives in eastern Torres Strait and in mainland Islander communities in the form of texts of secular songs, such as those performed for Island Dance (*segur kab wed*, 'play' dance songs), and in songs and chants for Old Fashioned Dance (*kab kar wed*, 'real' dance songs) (Lawrence 1997). More than 10 years ago Jeremy Beckett (2004:13), who earlier recorded many of these dance songs, expressed the view that Torres Strait Islander music was 'on the threshold of change . . . Also largely unexplored is the mainland-born generation of Islanders.' He posed two important questions:

- What kind of identity have the next generation of mainland-born Islanders made for themselves?
- Who are their models and how do they identify themselves to their own and to others?

Beckett (2004:13) concluded that to 'be an Islander you must have an island, but for the mainland-born this "island" has to be discovered all over again, and imagined'. He further concluded that writing about this will necessitate focusing on individuals 'rather than some homogenised Islander constituency'.

In this paper, we have focused attention on Toby Whaleboat as one such creative individual. The views of Toby Whaleboat provide a basis for non-Islanders to begin to reach a deeper understanding of how mainland-born eastern Torres Strait Islanders rediscover and imagine their ancestral islands – Erub, Ugar and Mer – especially within the context of creating, recreating and interpreting Christian songs. In particular, Toby Whaleboat's willingness to share his knowledge and music experiences expresses a generosity of spirit and a way forward for reconciliation, even if within the boundaries of a Christian music repertoire that previously was unknown to the majority of non-Islander Australians. As Toby Whaleboat stated earlier (see Interview above), 'this is who we are as Australians: non-Indigenous and Indigenous coming together singing those songs'.

We need, however, not only to sing these songs but to record, notate and disseminate them and, by encouraging others to recognise their value and significance, bring them into the mainstream music traditions of Australia. The responsibility, then, in preserving and revitalising Meriam Mir through sacred song, lies not only with eastern Torres Strait Islanders themselves, but with those singers, musicians and linguists in mainland Australia who are concerned that Meriam Mir is among those languages on the critically endangered list. In lending assistance to the revitalisation project, and in providing a respectful learning environment, we shall not only contribute to our diverse Australian heritage but we shall enrich our musical lives, and possibly our spiritual lives as well. The current project proposed by the University of Newcastle's Torres Strait Islander Sacred Song Network encompasses a collaborative approach. It has the potential to serve as a template for similar projects and to lead towards a wider study that includes the secular in addition to the sacred.

Acknowledgements

First and foremost, Fairweather and Matthias express their gratitude to Toby Whaleboat for his generosity in sharing his knowledge and recollections. We also thank all those who assisted with the 2015 conference video presentation or contributed to an understanding of the sacred songs that are discussed in this paper, especially Bill Bourne, Dr Catherine Grant, Dr Karl Neuenfeldt, Adimabo Noah, the late Ruth Pau, Nick Piper, Dr Anna Shnukal, Sedey Stephen, Mabege Tabo, Rev Elimo Tapim, Donald Whaleboat, Dulcie Whaleboat and Tat Whaleboat. We acknowledge, with appreciation, the support of the School of Creative Arts, the University of Newcastle, and members of the eastern Torres Strait Islander communities in Newcastle and

Townsville. We also acknowledge the (anonymous) reviewers and the editors of this volume who provided critical comments and useful suggestions.

Dedication

Dedicated to the memory of Renah Tapim, an esteemed and knowledgeable singer of language hymns, a member of St Stephen's Torres Strait Islands Ministry Choir in Townsville, and a fluent speaker of Meriam Mir, who died during the final stages of the preparation of this chapter.

References

Anglican Church of Australia, 1995, Island language hymns. Thursday Island: The Diocese of Carpentaria, Torres Strait Region.

Beckett, Jeremy, 2001, 'This music crept by me upon the waters': recollections of researching Torres Strait Islander music, 1958–1961. Perfect Beat 5(2):75–99.

—— 2004, Writing about Islanders: recent research and future directions. In Richard Davis, ed. Woven histories, dancing lives: Torres Strait Islander identity, culture and history, 2–14. Canberra: Aboriginal Studies Press.

Catalogue of endangered languages (ELCat). The endangered languages project: a project by the Alliance for Linguistic Diversity: *http://www.endangeredlanguages.com* [accessed January 2016]. (Information from: Ethnologue: languages of the world, 16th edn, 2009, M. Paul Lewis, SIL International.)

Credo, Iesu Keriso ra Erkepasam, agude ra Gelar, a Meriam wed (The Creed, the Lord's Prayer, the Ten Commandments, and hymns in the Murray Island language, Torres Straits.) (Published under the direction of the Bishop of Carpentaria.), 1924. Sydney: D. S. Ford, printer.

Erub era kodo mer: traditional and contemporary music and dance from Erub (Darnley Island) Torres Strait, 2010. [CD with DVD and booklet.] CD produced by Will Kepa, Karl Neuenfeldt and Nigel Pegrum. TSRA 005.

Haddon, Alfred Cort, ed., 1935, Reports of the Cambridge Anthropological Expedition to Torres Straits, vol. 1. Cambridge: Cambridge University Press. (Reprinted 1971, New York: Johnson Reprint Corporation.)

Hunt, (Rev.) Archibald E., 1888, Letter to Rev. R. W. Thompson, 3 August, 1888. LMS Letters, MS94, Australian Joint Copying Project, National Library of Australia.

Keriba ged: traditional and contemporary music and dance from the Murray Islands, Torres Strait, 2014. [CD with DVD and booklet.] CD produced by Will Kepa, Karl Neuenfeldt and Nigel Pegrum. TSRA 012.

Lawrence, Helen Reeves [Helen Fairweather], 1997, Torres Strait Islands. In Warren Bebbington, ed. The Oxford companion to Australian music, 556–558. Melbourne: Oxford University Press.

—— 1998, 'Bethlehem' in Torres Strait: music, dance and Christianity in Erub (Darnley Island). Australian Aboriginal Studies, 1998(2):51–63.

—— 2000, 'Mipla preize nem blo Yu': contemporary Christian songs of eastern Torres Strait. In Tony Mitchell and Peter Doyle with Bruce Johnson, eds. Changing sounds: new directions and configurations in popular music, 35–41. [Proceedings of the 10th International Conference of the International Association for the Study of Popular Music, Sydney, July 1999.] Sydney: Faculty of Humanities and Social Sciences, University of Technology.

—— 2004, 'The great traffic in tunes': agents of religious and musical change in eastern Torres Strait. In Richard Davis, ed. Woven histories, dancing lives: Torres Strait Islander identity, culture and history, 46–72. Canberra: Aboriginal Studies Press.

London Missionary Society, 1885, Gaire ued Miriam mer debele Adim uedakiriar (Songs Miriam speech that may to God be sung). In Euangelia Mareko Detarer (Gospel of Mark, Murray Island language), 147–183. Sydney: s.n.

McConvell, Patrick, Ron Day and Paul Black, 1983, Making a Meriam Mir dictionary. In Peter Austin, ed. Papers in Australian linguistics no. 15: Australian Aboriginal lexicography, 19–30. Pacific linguistics series A no. 66. Canberra: Australian National University.

Mullins, Steve, 1995, Torres Strait: a history of colonial occupation and culture contact 1864–1897. Rockhampton: Central Queensland University Press.

National Indigenous Languages Survey report 2005: report submitted to the Department of Communications, Information Technology and the Arts by the Australian Institute of Aboriginal and Torres Strait Islander Studies in association with the Federation of Aboriginal and Torres Strait Islander Languages, 2005. Canberra: Department of Communications, Information Technology and the Arts (DCITA).

National Museum of Australia, n.d. [2002?], Coming of the Light religious songs [tracks 15–18]. In Music from the National Museum of Australia's Torres Strait Islander paipa exhibition. [CD with booklet.] Produced by Karl Neuenfeldt and Nigel Pegrum in collaboration with Torres Strait Islander communities.

Neuenfeldt, Karl, and Will Kepa, 2011, Indigenising the documentation of musical cultural practices: Torres Strait Islander community CDs/DVDs. In Graham Seal and Jennifer Gall, eds. Antipodean traditions: Australian folklore in the 21st century, 72–90. Studies in Australia, Asia and the Pacific no. 6. Perth: Black Swan Press.

Pilot, (Rev.) Boggo, comp., n.d. [c.1973], Eastern and Western hymn book and liturgy, Torres Strait Island ministry, arranged by Rev. Boggo Pilot. Townsville: The Diocese of North Queensland.

Piper, Nick, 1989, A sketch grammar of Meriam Mir. MA thesis. [Canberra]: Australian National University. [Published in 2013 as A sketch grammar of Meryam Mir. Outstanding Grammars from Australia 14. Series editor, R. M. W. Dixon. Munich: Lincom Europa.]

Ray, Sidney H., 1907, Reports of the Cambridge anthropological expedition to Torres Straits, vol. 3. Cambridge: Cambridge University Press. (Reprinted 1971, New York: Johnson Reprint Corporation.)

Ray, Sydney [Sidney] H., 2001, Dictionary of Torres Strait languages, edited and illustrated by Ron Edwards. ('Drawn from Reports of the Cambridge Anthropological Expedition to Torres Straits, edited by A. C. Haddon, volume 3 Linguistics'.) Kuranda, QLD: Rams Skull Press.

Sankey, Ira D., comp., n.d. [188–?], Sacred songs and solos: revised and enlarged, with standard hymns. London: Morgan and Scott.

Shnukal, Anna, 2004, Language diversity, pan-Islander identity and 'national' identity in Torres Strait. In Richard Davis, ed. Woven histories, dancing lives: Torres Strait Islander identity, culture and history, 107–123. Canberra: Aboriginal Studies Press.

St Stephen's Torres Strait Islands Ministry Choir, 2007, Songs of praise from Torres Strait. [CD with booklet]. Produced by Karl Neuenfeldt and Nigel Pegrum.

16 Recovering musical data from colonial era transcriptions of Indigenous songs: some practical considerations

Graeme Skinner
University of Sydney

Abstract

To date, fewer than 150 surviving musical transcriptions of Indigenous traditional songs have been identified from Australia's colonial era (long nineteenth century). Most of these use standard Western pitch and rhythmic notation, although there are also three invaluable sets of sound recordings made at the end of this period (1898–1903). Many of the earlier notated transcriptions (1793–c.1850) are formatted as harmonised and sometimes varied arrangements of the source melodies, a standard practice in late eighteenth and early nineteenth century British, European, and American editions of the 'national music' of non-European peoples (most notably also Chinese, Hindu, and Native American). After 1850, however, most of the melodic transcriptions are un-harmonised, and more attentive to details of pitch, rhythm, and word underlay.

But although earlier arrangements are often presumed to be unreliable, as unique musical evidence they cannot be simply ignored. The fortuitous preservation of versions of the Tasmanian song *Popela* both in an 1836 musical transcription and three sound recordings made in 1899 and 1903 was first reported by Alice Moyle in 1968, but the unexpected similarities revealed in comparing transcription and recordings have seldom been further explored since then. Digital streaming of some of the late colonial recordings, including one of *Popela*, offers us the means and impetus to again reconsider how a wide range of available evidence can be effectively used in song study and revitalisation. Also drawing on documentation presented in the Skinner and Wafer 'Checklist' in this volume (Chapter 17), this chapter offers some preliminary reflections on how musicologists, singers, and listeners might approach the task of extracting usable musical information from the often problematic, but potentially useful resources available.

Keywords: Indigenous Australian music in the colonial era, documentary history of Australian Indigenous song and dance, revitalisation of Aboriginal and Torres Strait Islander song; European-Australian musical arrangements of Indigenous songs.

16. RECOVERING MUSICAL DATA FROM COLONIAL ERA TRANSCRIPTIONS

FOR ANYONE COLLECTING specific musical data on Indigenous songs in colonial Australia, the surviving documentation is conveniently bounded at the latter end by the neat coincidence of Australian nationhood in 1901 with the local advent of mechanical recording. Between 1898 and 1903, three or four years on either side of Federation, examples from three distinct Australian Indigenous song repertories were recorded in separate projects in Tasmania, the Torres Straits, and Central Australia. These were cylinder recordings made, respectively, in Hobart in 1899 and 1903 by Horace Watson of the singing of Fanny Cochrane Smith; at several sites from a large number of informants by members of Alfred Haddon's Cambridge Expedition to the Torres Strait in 1898, musical transcriptions of which were published by the investigators in 1908 and 1912; and from Arrernte singers in Central Australia by Baldwin Spencer and Frank Gillen in 1901, of which three takes were transcribed by Percy Grainger in Melbourne in 1909, and two published in 1912. One restored recorded example from each of Tasmania and the Torres Straits, and half a dozen from the Arrernte, are now digitally streamed in Australia, and publicly accessible. Accordingly, all three of Grainger's musical transcriptions and one of those by Charles Myers of a song from the island of Yam can be directly compared with the recordings they were made from.[1] Recording technology quickly transformed the practice of musical ethnography, largely rendering notated transcriptions redundant in much academic discourse. At the time, however, both the new recording technology itself, and the increased accuracy of written transcriptions made possible by mechanical reproduction, were ground breaking. Wax cylinder recordings had been first used by an American ethnographer in 1890 to record songs of the Passamaquoddy people of Maine.[2] The Cambridge team was the first British group to make systematic use of the technology, closely followed by Horace Watson in Hobart only a year later.

Yam song (1898)

A physician and psychologist, Charles Myers (1873–1946) is widely known for his 1915 paper on shell-shock. But as a key member of Haddon's expedition who was also musically trained, Myers effectively served as its musicologist, recruiting Murray/Mer Islander singers to perform and record their songs on his Edison phonograph, and later transcribing and analysing these musical artefacts for publication.[3] For his published account of songs from the Western Islands and Saibai, Myers relied on recordings made by his colleague, the linguist Sidney Ray (1858–1939).[4] Ray's recording of this Yam song is (as of 2017) digitally streamed both by the British

---

1 A much larger selection of 30 recordings from the Cambridge Torres Strait expedition is now streamed in Britain (and accessible internationally) by the British Library: see 'Australia' under *http://sounds.bl.uk/World-and-traditional-music/Ethnographic-wax-cylinders*; the featured recordings are mainly traditional songs, also transcribed by Myers (see below), but include as well performances by Islanders of several European songs they had already appropriated and hybridised.
2 Victoria Lindsay Levine, *Writing American Indian music: historic transcriptions, notations, and arrangements* (Music of the United States of America 11) (Middleton: A-R Editions, 2002), 28–29, 54.
3 Charles S. Myers, 'Music', in Alfred Haddon (ed.), *Reports of the Cambridge Anthropological Expedition to Torres Straits (1898), volume 4: arts and crafts* (Cambridge: The University Press, 1912), 238–69: *https://archive.org/stream/reports191204cambuoft#page/238/mode/2up*; on Myers's role in the expedition, see Ben Shepherd, *Headhunters: the pioneers of neuroscience* (London: Vintage Books, 2015), 58–59.
4 Myers, 'Music', 261, 266; on Ray see Roberta Wells, 'Sidney Herbert Ray: linguist and educationalist', *The Cambridge Journal of Anthropology* 21/1 (1999), 79–99; and Helen Reeves Lawrence, '"The great traffic in tunes": agents of religious and musical change in eastern Torres Strait', in Richard Davis (ed.), *Woven histories, dancing lives: Torres Strait Islander identity, culture and history* (Canberra: Aboriginal Studies Press, 2004), 46–72; on the published songs from the expedition, see Skinner and Wafer, *Checklist*, this volume, **30.1–28**.

Library and Australian Screen Online (ASO), and can be compared with Myers's melody-only transcription (Musical example 16.1).[5]

 Audio example 16.1: 'Yamaz Sibarud, sung by Maino of Yam', recorded by Sidney Ray, Torres Strait, 1898 (British Library, Torres Strait Cylinder 77 T.S.)[6]; Canberra, National Film and Sound Archive, ASO, streamed online

🔊 http://videomedia.aso.gov.au/titles/torstsoa/torstsoa1_bb.mp3

Musical example 16.1: Yam II ['Yamaz Sibarud'], musical transcription by Charles Myers (1912, p. 263) https://archive.org/stream/reports191204cambuoft#page/263/mode/2up

Ray's published notes give no information about the singer, or context of the performance, but he did gloss the opening words, *Yamazi barid*, as meaning 'Along Yam Island cuscus'.[7] In the digital restoration the tonality – defined by the upper and lower notes – is higher, closer to F sharp than F, but otherwise Myers's transcription plots the roughly pentatonic contour of Ray's recording reasonably accurately (note his use of the figures to pitch certain notes more closely in cents). For most listeners, however, the streamed sound alone is an eloquent enough account of the anonymous Yam singer and his song.

Tjitjingalla corroboree song (1901)

Grainger's 1909 transcriptions of Arrernte songs are more problematic. Unlike Myers and Ray, Percy Grainger (1882–1961) worked in Melbourne, at a great distance from the recording site, and had no firsthand experience of the singers or the performance context.[8] Vagaries of reproduction, both in Melbourne in 1909 and today, only partly explain why the pitch level of his transcriptions vary so significantly from those of streamed recordings. Further complicating the evidence, simplified versions of his manuscript transcriptions appeared in print in 1912. One song must serve as an example here.[9] In his spoken introduction to the recording streamed by Museum Victoria, Spencer tells us that the song is from the Tjitjingalla Corroboree, recorded at Stevenson's Creek, South Australia, on 22 March 1901:[10]

---

5   Throughout, every care has been taken in providing live links to web addresses of sources, to reference permanent archives and persistent identifiers; the Yam song is **30.26** in Skinner and Wafer, *Checklist*, this volume.
6   Also streamed by the British Library:
    http://sounds.bl.uk/World-and-traditional-music/Ethnographic-wax-cylinders/025M-C0080X1093XX-0100V0.
7   Myers, 'Music', 263, 269.
8   Elinor Wrobel (editor, curator), *Percy Grainger: the passionate folklorist and ethnomusicologist* [exhibition catalogue] (Parkville: Grainger Museum, University of Melbourne, 1999):
    http://grainger.unimelb.edu.au/__data/assets/pdf_file/0004/2036659/PG_and_Folk_Music_catalogue.pdf
9   See Skinner and Wafer, *Checklist*, this volume, **33.3**.
10 Museum Victoria, Spencer & Gillen: a journey through Aboriginal Australia (Reconstructing the Spencer and Gillen Collection Project): *http://spencerandgillen.net*

 Audio example 16.2: Tjitjingalla Corroboree song, recorded by Spencer and Gillen at Stevenson's Creek, 1901 (Adelaide, Royal Geographical Society of South Australia, RGSSA02; online at Museum Victoria)

🔊 http://spencerandgillen.net/objects/4fac699d023fd704f475b641

Musical example 16.2: Tjitjingalla Corroboree song, as transcribed by Percy Grainger, 1909 (Melbourne, Museum Victoria)
http://spencerandgillen.net/objects/50ce72f5023fd7358c8a957d

As can be seen from the online image of his manuscript (Musical example 16.2), Grainger originally transcribed the four 'verses' separately three times ('First time', '2nd and 3rd time', '4th time'), and noted:

> Dadji dadji – Medium speed, flowingly . . . The 2nd, 3rd, & 4th times seem to be more representative of the tune than the first times, the singularities of which are probably owing to the singer's not having got thoroughly into the swing of the tune at once.

Musical example 16.3: Transcription of first of two 'corrobboree songs' (published version) by Percy Grainger; in Spencer and Gillen 1912, vol. 2, Appendix, p. 502

The 1912 printed transcription (Musical example 16.3, above)[11] collapsed these variants into a single version, sacrificing accuracy and detail, but usefully imagining a single melodic model that withstands comparison with all four 'verses' of the streamed recording, allowing that first and last notes of the latter as currently streamed are not now pitched on D, but around B flat. In this respect, it can be appreciated that, for many attempting to learn or perform from transcriptions, those that are forensically more accurate (like Grainger's 'difficult' manuscript version) might not necessarily always be as useful as more schematic generalisations (like the 'easier' printed version).

Of the performers and performance, in his announcement on the recording Spencer merely reported: 'This corroboree was sung on the Stevenson River on March the 22nd, 1901'. But in his diary for the same day, he was more forthcoming:[12]

> At dusk 5 or 6 old natives came in and so we got our phonograph out and got them to sing corrobboree songs into it. They were very much excited and interested especially as we let them hear

---

11 Baldwin Spencer and F. J. Gillen, *Across Australia*. London: Macmillan, 1912 (vol. 2, p. 502).
12 Alice M. Moyle, 'Sir Baldwin Spencer's recordings of Australian Aboriginal singing', *Memoirs of the National Museum of Victoria* 24 (1959), 9:
   http://www.biodiversitylibrary.org/item/120198#page/9/mode/1up; Jason Gibson and Heather Milton (ed., transc.), *Walter Baldwin Spencer's diary from the Spencer and Gillen expedition 1901–1902* ([Melbourne: Museum Victoria, n.d.]): http://spencerandgillen.net/files/Spencers%20Expedition%20Diary.pdf.

> the instrument repeating what they had said. The phonograph is a beauty: it was given to us in Adelaide and we can both take records with it and repeat them as soon as they are taken . . . Gillen & myself felt quite happy to be amongst the blacks again & to hear the old corroboree songs once more and I don't know whether we or the natives were the more excited.

But at this point in his edition of the expedition diaries, Jason Gibson helpfully mentions that Spencer later passed on a quite different recollection of the playbacks that day to his daughter, Alline:[13]

> This nearly ended in disaster . . . my father played the songs back to the natives, who were horrified and ran for their lives. He never let them hear themselves again and I don't know how he calmed the fears of the first batch . . .

From a strictly musical perspective, the 1898 Torres Strait and 1901 Arrernte recordings are invaluable baselines against which later observations of their respective repertories may be objectively measured, compared, and analysed. But they also preserve important evidence of earlier, un-recordable practice both within and outside the host traditions. Compared with what Myers saw as the more 'primitive' cult songs of Murray/Mer Island that were the main focus of his study of the Torres Strait songs, he noted the 'greater (to *our* [British] ears) tunefulness and tonality' in some secular songs originating in the western islands, like Yam, where singers already had some contact with exotic instruments like flutes and jaw-harps.[14] And Spencer, in his recorded introduction to the Tjitjingalla song, noted his belief that it derived from the same source as the Molonga/Mulunga corroborees Walter Roth had witnessed in Queensland in 1894. This song and dance complex is thought to have originated in the 1880s, perhaps as a ritual protest against white aggression and dispossession, and spread widely among peoples in the central, northern, and north eastern parts of the continent into the early years of last century.[15] Questions will always remain as to how much of this unique early recording's musical detail belonged to the shared 'composition', and how much was inherent in the singer's distinctive Arrernte musical identity (how different or similar would the song as sung by different people, hundreds of miles away, actually sound?). Yet, as the only fully provenanced musical documentation of this then still quite recent travelling complex, the four short recorded Tjitjingalla verses are crucial to the understanding of one of the most powerful new productions of Indigenous shared songmaking traditions in the late colonial era. It is ironic, then, that Grainger's minor role as transcriber has so far generated more interest among music historians than the songs themselves.

---

13 Gibson and Milton, *Spencer's diary*, 8 note 21.
14 Myers, 'Music', 239, 266.
15 W. E. Roth, *Ethnological studies among the north-west-central Queensland Aborigines* (Brisbane: E. Gregory, Government Printer, 1898), 120–25:
   https://archive.org/stream/cu31924029890328#page/n143/mode/2up; D. J. Mulvaney, '"The chain of connection": the material evidence', in Nicolas Peterson (ed.), Tribes and boundaries in Australia: ecology, spatial organisation and process in Aboriginal Australia (Canberra: Australian Institute of Aboriginal Studies, 1976), 90–92; Luise A. Hercus, '"How we danced the Mudlunga": memories of 1901 and 1902', *Aboriginal History* 4 (1980), 5–32:
   http://press-files.anu.edu.au/downloads/press/p71161/pdf/article013.pdf; Tony Swain, 'A new sky hero from a conquered land', History of Religions 29/3 (February 1990), 195–232, esp. 219, 229: *http://www.jstor.org/stable/1062852*; Tony Swain, *A place for strangers: towards a history of Australian Aboriginal being* (Cambridge: Cambridge University Press, 1993), 219–33; Jason Gibson, 'Central Australian songs: a history and reinterpretation of their distribution through the earliest recordings', Oceania 85/2 (2015), 165–82: *http://dx.doi.org/10.1002/ocea.5084*.

Popela (1899)

Already at the time they were made, the Tasmanian recordings were recognised as being evidence of a song tradition dating back at least to the 1840s. Subsequent scholarship traced documentation of one of the songs, *Popela* (or *Popeller*), back a further decade. Given the possibilities of transmission available, this Tasmanian song, alone of all colonial era survivals, ticks all the boxes. Beginning in 1831, there is the first of George Augustus Robinson's two transcriptions of the words of the song, along with his observations on its dissemination, use, and meaning; next, there is a notated transcription of the music dating from 1835–36; several further independent text transcriptions and descriptions follow; and the transmission history culminates in three separate versions of the song mechanically recorded in 1899 and 1903 from the singing of Fanny Cochrane Smith (1834–1905).[16] The contents of the first of the original cylinders (Tasmanian Museum 15685/M 3317) as recorded by Horace Watson (1862–1930) in the rooms of the Royal Society of Tasmania on 5 August 1899, are currently freely streamed in their entirety (approx. 2 minutes 23 seconds):[17]

Audio example 16.3: Fanny Cochrane Smith singing 'Popela', recorded by Horace Watson, Hobart, 5 August 1899 (Hobart, Tasmanian Museum 15685/M 3317; Canberra, National Film and Sound Archive)

🔊 *http://aso.gov.au/titles/music/fanny-cochrane-smith-songs/clip1*

The first minute and a half of the clip consists of an introduction in English, declaimed into the recording horn by Mrs Smith:[18]

> I'm Fanny Smith. I was born on Flinders Island. I'm the last of the Tasmanians. I'll (put this morning) a very long story about it. I'll tell you the truth, to let you know a little about us. My mother's name was Tanganitara. I – we are some true born sisters from Flinders Island, where we were for seven years. And I'm here speaking to-day. [in answer to a question] Have we got for mother and my father? My father Noona. Noona (nitara-noota). (Sing a song. Noota, mother and me). My father Noona. My father was a (whaler). Lose-a my mother, all gone. [in answer to another question] My family? I'm married. Goodbye. My father [? family] no more.

At 1 minute 49 seconds, the first of Mrs Smith's three renditions of versions of the song begins; this one, the shortest, only 33 seconds long. A very approximate musical transcription of the melody appears as Musical example 16.4; made specifically from the digital sound-clip, it may be compared with Alice Moyle's transcriptions of this and the other versions, taken from earlier analogue transfers at slightly differing speeds and pitches, that she published in 1960 and 1968.[19]

---

16 For resources and documentation on Mrs Smith, see Trove public tag (curated by Australharmony): *http://trove.nla.gov.au/newspaper/result?l-publictag=Fanny+Cochrane+Smith*; on the various iterations of the song *Popela*, see Skinner and Wafer, *Checklist*, this volume, **9**, and **32.1**.

17 On Watson, see 'OBITUARY', *The Mercury* (12 April 1930), 8: *http://nla.gov.au/nla.news-article29792914*, and Trove public tag (curated by Australharmony): *http://trove.nla.gov.au/newspaper/result?l-publictag=Horace+Watson*.

18 Murray Longman, 'Songs of the Tasmanian aborigines as recorded by Mrs. Fanny Cochrane Smith', *Papers and Proceedings of the Royal Society of Tasmania* 94 (1960), 79–86 (80): *http://eprints.utas.edu.au/14096*.

19 Alice Moyle, 'Two native song-styles recorded in Tasmania', *Papers and Proceedings of the Royal Society of Tasmania* 94 (1960), 73–78: *http://eprints.utas.edu.au/14095*; Alice M. Moyle, 'Tasmanian music, an impasse?', *Records of the Queen Victoria Museum, Launceston* 26 (May 1968), 1–10 (henceforth Moyle 1968), 1–18.

Musical example 16.4: Musical transcription of first recorded version of Fanny Cochrane Smith's song 'Popela', based on the sound clip at the National Film and Sound Archive, Canberra (original held in Hobart, Tasmanian Museum 15685/M 3317); the transcribed section runs from 1:49 to the end (as the rests in the first bar are intended to suggest, the roughly 6/8 song sometimes appears to be sung against a 4-in-a-bar beat).

As Murray Longman and Alice Moyle showed in 1960, all three takes were versions of the same 'master' song, which they traced to multiple mid-nineteenth century transcriptions of the words alone, the earliest by George Washington Walker in 1832. Longman first reported on the existence of an early colonial musical arrangement of the song made by a 'Mrs. Logan', while Moyle believed she had traced Logan's informant to the 'Mifs' mentioned in an added inscription to the manuscript, 'an Aboriginal woman living in the Bothwell district between 1840 and 1850'. By 1968, Moyle had tentatively identified Mrs Logan as a music teacher who had arrived in the colony in February 1835. Brian Plomley shared with Moyle his opinion that, based on his knowledge of the Indigenous visitors to the Hobart area around that time, Logan was most likely to have met her informant (whether or not the putative 'Mifs') before September 1835. The clinching piece of evidence, also discovered by Plomley, was an entry in George Augustus Robinson's journal, made in Hobart on 22 October 1836, which recorded:[20]

> Spent the evening at [Charles] Logan's in Macquarie Street. Mr[s]. Logan set to music a song of the aborigines, POPELLER etc., the first ever attempted.

Moyle first compared her own music-only transcriptions of two of the sound recordings of the song with the melody line of Logan's arrangement in her 1960 paper, and repeated the process more thoroughly in 1968, making new words-and-music transcriptions of all three sound takes, and printing a facsimile of the Logan manuscript. Brian Plomley had, by 1966, also published

---

20 Moyle, Tasmanian music, an impasse?, 9 note 2; N. J. B. Plomley (ed.), *Weep in silence: a history of the Flinders Island Aboriginal settlement with the Flinders Island journal of George Augustus Robinson, 1835–1839* (Hobart: Blubber Head Press, 1987), 391.

two more transcriptions of the words from Robinson's journals, the earlier taken, with partial translation, at Mount Cameron on the north east coast on 13 August 1831.[21]

Moyle's partial identification of Mrs Logan was correct. We now know that she was Maria Logan (1808–86), daughter of Dublin music-seller Andrew Ellard and his first wife Ann, sister of the Sydney music-seller and publisher Francis Ellard, and a first cousin of the composer William Vincent Wallace and of the singer and teacher Eliza Wallace-Bushelle. Maria's husband, Charles, had organised two shiploads of female emigrants from Dublin, and the Logans accompanied the first of these, as superintendents on the *Sarah*, to Hobart, arriving there on 15 February 1835. Having moved to Sydney with her family in 1842, Logan was one of Sydney's leading piano teachers for many decades.[22]

Two colonial era manuscript copies of Logan's lost original arrangement survive—each consisting of a vocal transcription of the melody and words, with a harmonised accompaniment for piano. Both copies contain glaring musical errors, especially in the added accompaniment, and differ from each other at many points; but they largely agree on the essential details of the melody and words. For ease of comparison, Musical example 16.5 is a modern edition of the melody and words only, as given in the two copies, transposed to the same approximate pitch as the streamed 1899 recording and its transcription in Musical example 16.4. In the 1960s, Longman and Moyle knew of, and reported on, only what is clearly the earlier and cleaner of the two copies ('Logan 1' in Musical example 16.5), which Moyle thought was probably the 1835–36 original, albeit 'inexpertly done' (more on this, and the later copy, below).

A very simplified melodic analysis of the basic elements of the song is added above the staves in the two Musical examples 16.4 and 16.5, by means of the large letters **R** (recitation), **M** (mediation), **E** (ending), **LM** (lower mediation), and **LE** (lower ending). Even allowing for the absence of the **LM** and **LE** elements in both copies of the Logan transcription (Musical example 16.5), which merely repeat **M** and **E** at the same pitch, the similarities with the transcription of the 1899 recording (Musical example 16.4) are clear. Pitch and timbre are surprisingly well represented in the streamed recording, though phonemes are not. Nevertheless, in her 1968 paper Moyle hazarded an attempt to fit words from Walker's 1832 text transcription to her music transcriptions of all three recorded versions. Rather than vainly trying to add words to the transcription of the streamed recording (Musical example 16.4 above), Table 16.1 presents Plomley's edition of the two Robinson text transcriptions (neither of which Moyle or Longman collated) in parallel columns with the Logan text. Though only enough material for a temporary and very partial 'revitalisation' are presented here, further important evidence may be found along with their transcriptions in Moyle's and Longman's papers, while solutions of more permanent value may well flow from a systematic use of all the available evidence, if and when all of the Smith recordings are made freely accessible.

---

21 N. J. Brian Plomley (ed.), *Friendly mission: the Tasmanian journals and papers of George Augustus Robinson, 1829–1834* (Hobart: Tasmanian Historical Research Association, 1966), 399, 469–70.
22 On Logan, see Trove public tag: *http://trove.nla.gov.au/result?l-publictag=Maria+Logan*; and Graeme Skinner, Toward a general history of Australian musical composition: first national music, 1788-c.1860 (Ph.D thesis, Sydney Conservatorium of Music, University of Sydney, 2011), 125–28: *http://ses.library.usyd.edu.au/handle/2123/7264*.

Musical example 16.5: Edited transcription of the melody and words only, from the two manuscript copies of 'Song of the Aborigines of Van Diemen's Land arranged by Mrs Logan'

Table 16.1: Textual comparison of three versions of 'Popela'

ROBINSON 1831[22]	ROBINSON 1834[23]	LOGAN 1836
pop.per. rane.nen.er goen.ner.er.	pap.el.er rane.er. gun.nen.er	popela ranea gonne ne popela ranea gone ne na
lur.me. gun.ne.yer	lur.me.gun.ne	lea me gonne a lea me gonne a
toke.her.me. gun.ne.yer	take.er.me.gun.ne	to kea me gun ne a to kea me gun ne a lea me gun ne a lea me gun ne a
neen.ner.tape.er.rane. ner pone.nen.ner	neen.er pape.er.rane.ner rone.nen.er.neen.er	ni na te pea ra nea po ne na ni na te pea ra nea po ne na ni na te pea
nee.nar nee.nar pue.wil.le parn.ner pue.wil.le bal.ler.hoo bal.ler.hoo	nar.er bue.mel.er.par.ner nar.er bue.wel.er bal.er.hoo bal.er.ho	ra ne ni na na re bu wil la pa ne na ra bur wil la bal la hoo! bal la hoo!
		ni na na ra bu wil la pa na pa ra bu wil la bal la hoo! bal la hoo!
	drue.de.cum mine.dim	

None of the above touches on the song's meaning, function, or cultural context, upon which, anyway, colonial reporters vary. They variously described it as a dance song 'in honour of a great chief', as belonging to the 'Ben Lomond tribe' or to the whole of 'north east Tasmania', and even as 'a favourite song chiefly of the men – stated to be learned from the Sydney blacks, but known by most of the aborigines of V.D. Land.'[25] Robinson, in 1831, described its subject as 'indelicate' – according to his gloss, it concerns expelling evil spirits from the feet by defecating; though, in 1899, that evidently did not unduly trouble Mrs Smith, a devout Methodist since her younger days.[26] But even without unmediated access to its context, the survival of the song's words and music in multiple formats is by itself of unparalleled significance.

On Mrs Smith's own say so, she was taught the song by her family, probably as a child at Robinson's station, Wybalenna, on Flinders Island in the years around 1840. Thus, a song that was widely sung by the surviving Tasmanians in the early 1830s and 1840s, and which was then plausibly very much older, survived into the recording age. Having recorded *Popela* and another song in August 1899, Mrs Smith appears not to have had been troubled about treating these

23 Plomley, *Friendly mission*, 469.
24 Plomley, *Friendly mission*, 470.
25 Plomley, *Weep in silence*, 289 (from G. W. Walker's journal).
26 In 1908, Herman Ritz reviewed three other documented early text versions of the song, and proposed 'translations' for each; see 'ABORIGINAL SONGS', *Daily Post* (21 November 1908), 10: http://nla.gov.au/nla.news-article181621319, and Hermann B. Ritz, 'An introduction to the study of the Aboriginal speech of Tasmania (read November 16, 1908)', *Papers and proceedings of the Royal Society of Tasmania* (1908), 73–83: http://eprints.utas.edu.au/16462; Robinson's transcriptions, and probably more accurate translations, were then still unknown and uncollated.

vocal remnants of her cultural heritage as discrete musical artefacts in the European manner. She sang one song at a Wesleyan social a few months before the 1899 recordings (the audience reportedly found it 'very amusing'), and two songs at a public 'entertainment' organised by Watson for her benefit a couple of months later (they were, *The Mercury* said, 'simple and melodious').[27] Many years afterwards in 1949, an 82-year-old friend, Emily Keens, did however recall that Mrs Smith had some initial misgivings when Watson first played the recordings back to her:[28]

> She cried: 'My poor race. What have I done.' We could not pacify her for a long time . . . She thought the voice she had heard was that of her mother.

As complete a documentary profile of *Popela* as we will probably now ever possess was in place by 1968. Writing in that year, of records of Tasmanian Indigenous music generally, Alice Moyle concluded that:[29]

> the chances of adding to these meagre remains are now slight. But even today more than a hundred years after the last full-blood Tasmanians performed their songs and dances, might it still not be possible to find a second or third generation descendent still able to recall tribal song-fragments which have been learned and passed on by older relatives?

Yet Moyle's 'faint hope underlying this question' was in fact partially fulfilled. In 1972, financed by a $720 grant from the Australian Institute of Aboriginal Studies (later AIATSIS), Robert Dixon and Terry Crowley made further investigations, during which Crowley 'tape recorded five words and a short song' from two grand-daughters of Fanny Cochrane Smith.[30] Crowley's recording of Dot Heffernan's singing contained 'a fragment of a lilting corroboree song, the meaning of which is not remembered'.[31] Moyle made an unpublished transcription of it[32], and it proved not to be any of the three songs recorded by Fanny herself at the turn of the century – *Popela*, a 'spring song', and a 'hymn improvisation' – but another one, a 'bird call song', that Fanny had taught her grand-daughter around the same time. The jazz singer Judy Jacques taught herself to perform it from Moyle's transcription[33], and, having done so, was inclined to believe that the 'primary triad structure' of the song, as Heffernan sang it 'in a nursery rhyme

---

27 'LOVETT', *Tasmanian News* (7 April 1899), 3: *http://nla.gov.au/nla.news-article176605899*; 'THE LAST OF THE ABORIGINES', *The Mercury* (31 October 1899), 2: *http://nla.gov.au/nla.news-article12762342*; Andrew Kirk, [Letter to the editor], 'THE LAST OF THE TASMANIANS', *Tasmanian News* (1 November 1899), 3: *http://nla.gov.au/nla.news-article185227458*.
28 'Aboriginal Recordings. VOICE OF EXTINCT PEOPLE LIVES ON IN MEMORY AND WAX', *The Mercury* (23 March 1949), 5: *http://nla.gov.au/nla.news-article26511589*.
29 Moyle, *Tasmanian music, an impasse?*, 1.
30 R. M. W. Dixon, 'Tasmanian language', *The Canberra Times* (1 September 1976), 2:
http://nla.gov.au/nla.news-article110823780; Terry Crowley and R. M. W. Dixon, 'Tasmanian', in R. M. W. Dixon et B. J. Blake (eds), *Handbook of Australian languages* (Canberra: Australian National University Press, 1981), volume 2, 394–421; see 398 for the transcriptions.
31 R. M. W. Dixon, *The languages of Australia* (Cambridge; Cambridge University Press, 1980; facsimile reprint, 2010), 230; for the recording, Canberra, AIATSIS, audio collection, CROWLEY_T02, archive tape no. 002751 (*http://trove.nla.gov.au/version/211580876*).
32 Canberra, AIATSIS, Alice Moyle collection, MS 3501, series 12:
http://aiatsis.gov.au/sites/default/files/catalogue_resources/MS3501.htm; Judy Jacques, 'Passing the torch: commemorating the songs of Fanny Cochrane Smith', in Denis Crowdy (ed.), *Popular music: commemoration, commodification and communication: proceedings of the 2004 IASPM Australia New Zealand Conference, held in conjunction with the Symposium of the International Musicological Society, 11–16 July, 2004* (Melbourne: International Association for the Study of Popular Music, Australia New Zealand Branch, 2004), 11–19.
33 Judy Jacques, 'Passing the torch: commemorating the songs of Fanny Cochrane Smith', in Denis Crowdy (ed.), *Popular music: commemoration, commodification and communication: proceedings of the 2004 IASPM Australia New Zealand Conference, held in conjunction with the Symposium of the International Musicological Society, 11–16 July, 2004* (Melbourne: International Association for the Study of Popular Music, Australia New Zealand Branch, 2004), 11–19.

or sailors' hornpipe style', projected a 'westernised' flavour typical of Fanny's upbringing in the mixed race community at Wybalenna, 'where she arguably absorbed the musical hybridities of settler hymns, folk and whaling songs'. Jacques herself was descended from a convict arrival, some of whose family were, like Mrs Smith's father, Bass Strait whalers, and in a fascinating account of her own practical attempts at creative revitalisation, did conclude that the song's 'western traits . . . do not in themselves discount Tasmanian provenance'. Yet, in the absence of enough independent musical evidence to draw such comparisons, perhaps we should ask again if we can really be so sure of these 'western traits' and 'hybridities' as to identify them reliably.

Looking a little more closely at Logan's *Popela* arrangement, and considering it in isolation from the recordings, even the earlier and slightly more musically 'correct' copy (the opening shown as Musical example 16.6, below) looks and sounds about as unpromising as any colonial transcription could be, were it not for the additional musical evidence of the second copy, dating from late in the century, and apparently made in Victoria.[34] This second copy appears slightly more accurate in some details (for instance, the syllabification of the words), but is worse in some other respects (notably in details of the added accompaniment). Both are, anyway, sufficiently problematic for it to be doubtful that either of them is a reliable record of the first intentions of a reasonably experienced musician like Maria Logan.[35] Nor can we be sure that Logan ever issued only one 'authorised' version of her arrangement. Perhaps she altered and 'improved' details over time, and this accounts for some of the differences in the copies (as for instance in the vocal-line setting of the final 'ballahoos' in Musical example 16.5).

One thing that we might reasonably infer from the existence of two copies made some decades apart, however, is that the Logan arrangement had some continuing currency, probably first among her Hobart music pupils, and later considerably more widely. Yet even after allowing for apparent errors in one or other of them (the obviously corrupt introduction for piano alone in the earlier copy, seems to appear more correctly in the later), the copies agree sufficiently for us to be certain that Logan's arrangement was always going to be considered something of an oddity. Judged by the basic conventions of late eighteenth and early nineteenth century Western musical syntax, the added piano accompaniment must have seemed barely coherent tonally, and the pervasive lilting rhythm (according to the earlier copy, in 3/4 time, but actually in 6/8) implausible. Yet, in dressing up the song melody in Western guise, Logan's arrangement did surprisingly little to make it sound *less* monotonous to colonial ears. Pointedly omitting to take advantage of a fuller range of possible harmonisations, Logan limited her accompaniment to a very occasional alternation of only two repeated and functionally unrelated chords, A major (root position) and F sharp minor (second inversion), in effect using them as harmonic drones, thereby underlining and accentuating, rather than dressing-up and disguising ('colonialising'), the song melody's non-Western traits. Such planned 'primitivism' might today seem almost of a piece with post-Stravinsky minimalism, but in 1836 the arrangement must simply have appeared to many to border on the musically illiterate. Yet it is so *determinedly* 'illiterate' that Logan must surely have known what she was doing. Might not it reflect Logan's desire to

---

34 The second copy (Royal Society of Tasmania, University of Tasmania Library Special and Rare Materials Collection: *http://eprints.utas.edu.au/id/document/2752*) appears to have been made by Henry Lloyd, a violinist, in the late 1890s. Lloyd, who died in 1910 aged 78, had been professionally active in Castlemaine since the late 1860s, before moving to Prahran in 1895, where he also worked as a photographer.

35 A song composed by her, *The vow that's breathed in solitude*, published in Hobart in 1839, does not survive. However, another manuscript piano setting by her, of the song *Those evening bells* (from Thomas Moore's *Irish melodies*), does exist in a copy made Sarah Cross Bingle in Sydney in January 1853. A perfectly respectable, if uninspiring arrangement probably made for her own piano pupils, it is now in a bound music album in the Bingle Family papers, State Library of New South Wales, MLMSS 7115/2–3: *http://archival.sl.nsw.gov.au/Details/archive/110317809*.

document the spirit, if not the letter, of the 'primitive' performance as she heard it? And adding in the corroborative evidence of the 1899 recording, Logan's arrangement does, in fact, appear to be a far more reliable musical account of *Popela* in its essential details than we might otherwise have dared to imagine.

Musical example 16.6: Song of the Aborigines of Van Diemans Land [sic] arranged by Mrs. Logan. (Hobart: Archives Office of Tasmania, photographic copies of original manuscript in the Tasmanian Museum, online at State Library of Tasmania;
page 1: *http://trove.nla.gov.au/work/36693478?q&versionId=47636937*,
page 2: *http://trove.nla.gov.au/work/36693479?q&versionId=47636938*)

Maranoa songs (c.1890, 1937)

Arguing from necessity, music historians wanting to reimagine the actual sound of Aboriginal song in the colonial era have little choice, anyway, but to come to terms with such transcriptions. So too, for Indigenous people and the editors of this book: non-Indigenous documentation, however obviously flawed, needs must be pre-supposed to be of at least some use in revival of broken song traditions or the revitalisation of endangered ones, and in the 'resuscitation' of actual songs long supposed to be dead, but perhaps merely only sleeping. A Gunggari elder, Ethel Munn, gave eloquent testimony to a recent instance of song reclamation on a video for First Language Australia. She recounted how she has treasured for over 40 years a copy of Harold Lethbridge and Arthur Loam's *Australian Aboriginal songs* (1937)[36] as a tangible but mute record of the language and music of her people in the Maranoa area of south-west Queensland. Finally, on camera in 2014, she got the chance to sing the *Maranoa lullaby* with a group of friends:[37]

---

36 *Australian Aboriginal songs: melodies, rhythm and words truly and authentically Aboriginal, collected and translated by H. O. Lethbridge, accompaniments arranged by Arthur S. Loam* (Melbourne: Allan & Co., 1937); exemplar, National Library of Australia, digitised: *http://trove.nla.gov.au/version/44491053*.
37 Lethbridge, Australian Aboriginal songs, 4–5:
   http://nla.gov.au/nla.obj-172234124/view#page/n4/mode/1up.

 Video example 16.1: Ethel Munn and friends from south-east Queensland singing the 'Maranoa lullaby', 2014; streamed by First Languages Australia (Vimeo), and Queensland Indigenous Languages Advisory Committee (QILAC)

https://vimeo.com/99494828 OR
http://www.qilac.org.au/film/maranoa-lullaby

The singer Harold Blair (1924–76) had already publicly 'reappropriated' the Lullaby in the early 1950s, on behalf of southern Queensland Indigenous people (Blair was born at the Cherbourg mission), performing it in Australia and abroad in concerts and recordings.[38] But Ethel Munn's video returned the song much closer still to its origins. Though Harold Lethbridge (1880–1944) did not write them down until the 1930s, his transcriptions were made from his own and his sister's memories of Indigenous songs they'd heard, and been taught to sing themselves, by traditional singers at Forest Vale station on the Maranoa in the 1890s.[39] As he told *The Australian Musical News* in 1937, Lethbridge himself considered that his transcriptions, despite their late date, nevertheless gave a true account of Indigenous music at Maranoa in the late colonial era:[40]

> Station life in Western Queensland in the 80s was very different from present conditions. No wireless – no cars, we lived a life centred round our own home. My father always liked the blacks and they would do anything for him. As boys they were our playmates – we used to hunt with them and eat witchetty grubs with them. We knew their language and sang their songs and even learnt their corroborees. A love of music and a retentive memory have given me the opportunity of knowing these songs still. I can therefore speak truth when I say the words, rhythm, melody and tempo of these songs is as they sang them and absolutely unaltered. Therein lies their value.

Despite this line of authority back to the colonial era, the transcriptions have often been tacitly assumed to be unreliable, and even fatally flawed, probably largely because of a failure to consider the melodies and original words in isolation from Arthur Loam's harmonised accompaniments, and Lethbridge's well-intended, but unfashionably prosy English translations. Among Lethbridge's five transcriptions the most firmly provenanced are the three strophes that make up *The Bingo Corroborees*, which he identified as 'compositions' – words and music – of Boss Davey, or Mundâlo, dating from 'about 1900'.[41] According to Lethbridge:[42]

> The Bingo Series. These I know well. They were the result of a renaissance in music that occurred among the Maranoa Tribe in the 80s. I knew the composer, one Boss Davey. I saw these corroborees night after night and we sang them with the blacks. The translation is quite correct in meaning.

The composer was probably the 'Davey' described in local police records as a 50-year-old 'full-blood' working at 'scalping' at Forest Vale in 1904; and certainly the 'Boss Davey' who, in

---

38 'OVATION FOR HAROLD BLAIR', The Sydney Morning Herald (20 March 1951), 3:
http://nla.gov.au/nla.news-article18204825; Bill Casey, 'Modernity denied: Harold Blair's 1956 EP Australian Aboriginal Songs and its critical reception', in Robert Dixon and Veronica Kelly (eds), *Impact of the modern: vernacular modernities in Australia 1870s–1960s* (Sydney: Sydney University Press, 2008), 52–61; for a 30 second out-take from an unissued 1950 recording, see:
http://aso.gov.au/titles/music/maranoa-lullaby/clip1.
39 On Lethbridge, see Trove public tag: *http://trove.nla.gov.au/result?q=Harold+Octavius+Lethbridge*; on the songs, see Skinner and Wafer, *Checklist*, this volume, **27.1–5**.
40 H. O. Lethbridge, 'ABORIGINAL SONGS. A Valuable Collection, Aboriginal songs explained', *The Australian Musical News* (1 July 1937), 22.
41 Lethbridge, *Australian Aboriginal songs*, 6–9:
http://nla.gov.au/nla.obj-172234124/view#page/n6/mode/1up.
42 Lethbridge, 'ABORIGINAL SONGS. A Valuable Collection', 22.

1914, Lethbridge's father called upon the police to remove to Taroom Aboriginal Settlement. Boss Davey died there on 25 March 1916 of 'senile decay', some months short of witnessing the 'coloured Queensland Pug' [pugilist], Jerry Jerome, lead some of his fellow inmates in the famous 1916 Taroom strike for pay.[43]

Had Lethbridge stopped at naming Davey as the 'composer' of the *Bingo Corroborees*, we might think he meant 'owner', were it not for the added mention of the songs resulting from a 'renaissance in music' among the Maranoa people in the 1880s, itself an interesting, if as yet unverifiable, cultural and historical proposition. Perhaps one other song Lethbridge remembered from the time of this 'renaissance' may yet be found to have some musical connection with the anti-white millennialism of the Tjitjingalla/Mulunga corroborees.[44] War dance-songs execrating 'the whites' are, so far, hard to identify among colonial era word-and-music, or even words-only, transcriptions; but perhaps *The Warrego lament* ('Introduced from the Warrego Tribe. It is the anguished cry of a doomed race – stricken by disease brought by the invading white man') is one of them. And if Lethbridge's designation of it as a 'lament' seems to sit oddly with the indicated *Allegro con brio* tempo, his translation, though hum-drum, leaves very little to the imagination:[45]

> *Happy hunting ours before,*
> *Happy hunts we know no more:*
> *Sick and sad are we*
> *Broken hearts wasting till we die,*
> *Curse the whites! Curse the whites!*

A Cape York song (1876)

Another case of apparently flawed transcriptions whose potential may yet be more fully realised are the four Cape York songs written down in France in 1876 by the composer, critic, and musicologist Edouard Garnier, from the singing of the famous 'castaway', Narcisse Pelletier (1844–94), and published that year.[46] Perforce, Pelletier spent 17 years on Cape York from 1858 to 1875, living as an adopted member of a family of Uutaalnganu speakers (Sandbeach people, Pama Malngkana), going by the name of 'Anco'.[47] Sixty years earlier than Loam, though in remarkably similar style, Garnier added harmonised accompaniments to Pelletier's songs, believing them to be essential to European reception:[48]

---

43 Mitchell Police Letterbook 1889–1921; QS 636/1 (3) and (11), Queensland State Archives:
  http://www.cifhs.com/qldrecords/qldmitchell.html; Chief Protector of Aborigines, Register of Aboriginal Deaths 1910–1928, A/58973, Queensland State Archives:
  http://www.cifhs.com/qldrecords/A58973_Qld_Deaths_1910_1928.html.
44 Swain 1993, and see footnote 15 of the present chapter.
45 Lethbridge, *Australian Aboriginal songs*, 10–11:
  http://nla.gov.au/nla.obj-172234124/view#page/n10/mode/1up.
46 Edouard Garnier, 'Observations musicales sur les chants de Narcisse Pelletier', appendix in Constant Merland, *Dix-sept ans chez les sauvages: aventures de Narcisse Pelletier* (Paris: E. Dentu, 1876), 127–35 (commentary), and four plates (music); on the 4 songs, see Skinner and Wafer, *Checklist*, this volume, **22.1–4**.
47 Stephanie Anderson (trans.), *Pelletier: the forgotten castaway of Cape York*, introductory essay and translation by *Stephanie Anderson; from the original book Dix-sept ans chez les sauvages: les aventure de Narcisse Pelletier by Constant Merland; ethnographic commentary by Athol Chase* (Melbourne: Melbourne Books, 2009).
48 Garnier, 'Observations musicales', 135; translation, Anderson 2009.

Musical example 16.7: Edouard Garnier, 'Observations musicales sur les chants de Narcisse Pelletier (1876), plate 2

Ces airs, avec leur seule ligne vocale, auraient peu de signification. Présentés avec cette partie accompagnante, ils acquièrent, croyons-nous, un certain caractère; ils prennent une sorte de saveur lointaine, et, à ces différents titres, peut-être offriront-ils quelque intérêt aux lecteurs musiciens. *These airs, given with their single vocal line alone, would have little meaning. Presented with the accompaniment, they acquire, we believe, a certain character; they take on a distant flavour; and, as such, perhaps will be of some interest to musical readers.*

There has been no detailed musical historical discussion or analysis of the music Garnier transcribed from Pelletier's multiple performances. Garnier explained that his task was not easy: Pelletier had no Western musical knowledge, would alter his rendition each time, his rhythm was often hard to discern.[49] However, Garnier claimed to have been meticulous in notating what he heard Pelletier singing. He also transcribed the sung text as best he could, inventing the spelling. Perhaps of greatest interest is the second song, which appears to have been composed for, and about, Pelletier himself. Based on Garnier's account and transcription, anthropologist David Thompson reconstructed the likely original words of song, which Pelletier said was 'sung at night' (see Musical example 16.7):[50]

---

49   Garnier, 'Observations musicales', 127: 'Ces airs ou ces chants—est-ce bien là le nom ambitieux qui leur convient—n'ont pas été faciles à recueillir, car Pelletier, ne possédant aucune connaissance musicale, variait à chaque reprise ses formules, à tel point qu'elles devenaient d'un choix fort embarrassant. Sa voix, quoique assez juste, n'avait rien de fixe; par suite, la version s'égarait et se présentait constamment différente. Le rhythme, cet élément pourtant naturel, constitutif, prédominant dans toute musique rudimentaire, était lui-même le plus souvent difficile à démêler par son manque de franchise.'
50   Anderson, *Pelletier: the forgotten castaway*, 357 note 2; music example, Garnier, 'Observations musicales', plate 2.

Yunthu kalinan, kalinan, yunthu kalinan, kalinan,
para kalinan, kalinan, para kalinan, kalinan.

Waterlily root carry-we, carry-we. Waterlily root carry-we, carry-we.
White man carry-we, carry we. White man carry-we, carry we.

Reconsidering the making of transcriptions and arrangements

The diaries of George Augustus Robinson, among others, give some insight into the process of the transcription, transliteration, and translation of song text. But most transcribers of music are silent on precisely how they went about the process. Some, like Lethbridge, merely reported that they had been taught them as children. In Garnier's case, though there was no actual 'field work' involved, he relied totally on what he could glean from the singing of his sole informant, Pelletier. Percy Sheaffe, who settled on the south coast of New South Wales in the mid-nineteenth century, learned the song *Tshemer burra buna* in the field, and found the right pitches to notate using his flute[51], something we can only regret that George Augustus Robinson – who also took his flute with him on his Tasmanian and Victorian expeditions in the 1830s and 1840s – did not also do. Occasionally a report hints at how Indigenous people went about 'teaching' whites their songs in the first place. Numerous colonial reports attest to Indigenous Australians' acuity as mimics generally and copiers of European songs, but, as George Bass observed at Moreton Bay in August 1799, mimicry and copying was, quite naturally, crucial to how Indigenous people *taught*, as well as learned, their own songs[52]:

> Observing that they were attentively listened to, they each selected one of our people, and placed his mouth close to his ear, as if to produce a greater effect, or, it might be, to teach them the song, which their silent attention might seem to express a desire to learn.

The most thorough and systematic colonial account of the transcription process was that given by George Torrance (1835–1907), an Anglican priest and professionally trained musician, in his description of dictation sessions near Melbourne in the mid 1880s with his sole informant, Wurundjeri man and Ngurungaeta headman, William Barak (1824–1903).[53] Before commencing the song-taking proper, Torrance administered a series of ear tests to the singer, from which he observed that Barak's voice was 'a baritone of average compass', and his ear 'quick and accurate'. Barak chose his own starting notes, and Torrance, conscious of the constraints of the semitone scale, was scrupulous in registering slight changes in pitch, sometimes including portamentos ('a curious sliding of one sound into another, not unlike the slow tuning of a violin string'). Notably, he did not force his transcriptions of the three chant-like songs into readymade tonal or metrical schemes. Even one corroboree song, sung to a regular clapping and stamping beat, Torrance transcribed in an irregular mix of duple and triple bars.[54] The sessions probably took place at Barak's home, Coranderrk Station; we know that Barak and Torrance had an audience,

---

51 See Skinner and Wafer, *Checklist*, this volume, **31**.
52 David Collins, *An account of the English colony in New South Wales, from its first settlement in January 1788, to August 1801 ... and an account of a voyage performed by Captain Flinders and Mr. Bass ... abstracted from the journal of Mr. Bass ... volume 2* (London: T. Cadell and W. Davies, 1802), 251:
  https://books.google.com.au/books?id=ghRcAAAAcAAJ&pg=PA251.
53 G. W. Torrance, 'Music of the Australian Aboriginals', *The Journal of the Anthropological Institute of Great Britain and Ireland* 16 (1887), 335–340:
  https://archive.org/stream/journalofroyalan16royauoft#page/334/mode/2up; also
  https://archive.org/details/musicaustralian00howigoog; see also Skinner and Wafer, *Checklist*, this volume **25.1–3**.
54 Anon., 'Ethnological notes', *Science* (8 April 1887), 335: 'Torrance gives three tunes, which he has divided into bars, according to the style of our music. This, however, is not correct, as the irregular accent does not allow their being arranged in this way. Fortunately the study of aboriginal poetry and music is being taken up now by several students.'

and Torrance attests that Barak's 'patience, good temper, and evident pleasure at seeing his song committed to paper, were very remarkable'.[55]

Torrance self-consciously presented his published transcriptions of these very simple, and apparently formulaic chants as a scientific report, with critical apparatus, but without doing anything further to encourage future performances; though when his paper was read, in his absence, to the Royal Anthropological Institute in London late in 1886, it was reportedly 'illustrated vocally by the assistant secretary', George W. Bloxam. Many earlier transcriptions were also largely scientific in intent, starting with Barron Field's 1823 unharmonised transcription of Harry's song[56], and Lesueur and Bernier's 1802 transcriptions, belatedly published in 1824.[57] And after 1850, unharmonised ('scientific') transcriptions seem to have become the norm.

Apart from the Pelletier songs already discussed, George Taplin's *Narrinyeri Corrobbery* was the only new, harmonised arrangement to appear in the second half of the nineteenth century.[58] Taplin claimed that it was 'a specimen of the music of a genuine aboriginal "corrobbery", or song, written down as it was sung by the aborigines about eighteen years ago [c.1861]'; but his arrangement, which he imagined being best performed accompanied by a 'couple of clarionets, with a flute, and, for the bass, a drum', appears to be more like a picturesque sketch than a detailed pitch specific account of a sung melody.[59] By the 1860s and 1870s, if there was any remaining colonial 'market' for Indigenous song arrangements, its demands were increasingly being met by settler-colonist composers, with popular faux-Indigenous imitations. 'Aboriginal songs' were occasionally encountered in the theatre as early as the 1830s, a notable example from the 1840s being *Merry-jig, me sing*, 'written' by the playwright James Ruthven McLauglin in Melbourne.[60] Though only the words survive, it must presumably have been sung to some sort of concocted melody by the 'black-face' professional actors who eventually performed it on stage in McLauglin's play, *Arabin; or, Adventures of a settler*, in 1849.

Another notable example was the 'corroboree chorus' from the lyric masque *The South-sea sisters*, by Charles Edward Horsley (1822–76). So effective was it evoking 'all the grotesque points' of its subject matter that the chorus was 'three times encored' during the masque's premiere at the Melbourne Exhibition of 1866. Horsley's music is lost, and was probably, anyway, little more than an imaginative confection, despite the claim of his librettist, Richard Horne (1802–84), to have borrowed 'the rhythm of the Song-dance ... of the blacks on Goulburn river' (the Taungurung, or Daung wurrung, people) for the words, which do survive:[61]

---

55 Torrance, 1887, 336.
56 B. F. [Barron Field], 'Journal of an excursion across the Blue Mountains of New South Wales (October 1822)', *The London Magazine* (November 1823), 465–66:
    http://books.google.com.au/books?id=o9gYAAAAMAAJ&pg=PA465; see Skinner and Wafer, *Checklist*, this volume, **6**.
57 Charles Alexandre Lesueur and Nicolas-Martin Petit, *Voyage de découvertes aux terres Australes. Historique, atlas par MM. Lesueur et Petit, seconde édition* (Paris: Chez Arthus Bertrand, 1824), plate 32, page 52, no. 3,
    https://books.google.com.au/books?id=aXVdAAAAcAAJ&pg=PT76; Skinner and Wafer, *Checklist*, this volume, **1, 3.1–2**.
58 George Taplin, *The folklore, manners, customs, and languages of the South Australian Aborigines: gathered from inquiries made by authority of South Australian government* (Adelaide: E. Spiller, 1879), 106 (music and text), 107 (commentary): https://archive.org/stream/folkloremannersc00taplrich#page/106/mode/2up; see Skinner and Wafer, *Checklist*, this volume, **20**.
59 For further details of Taplin's transcription, and a synthesised sound-clip of it, see:
    http://sydney.edu.au/paradisec/australharmony/checklist-indigenous-music-1.php#020.
60 Also published separately as 'ABORIGINAL SONG', *Port Philip Gazette* (23 March 1844), 4:
    http://nla.gov.au/nla.news-article224809937.
61 Horne, one of the founders in 1860 of the Chateau Tahbilk vineyards on the Goulburn River near Nagambie, probably witnessed such a 'song-dance' there. On the chorus, see 'THE INTERCOLONIAL EXHIBITION', *The Age* (25 October 1866), 7: http://nla.gov.au/nla.news-article160215604; and word book, *South-sea sisters: a lyric masque written for the opening of the Intercolonial Exhibition of Australasia, 1866, by R. H. Horne; the incidental music composed by Charles Edward Horsley, op. 73* (Melbourne: H. T. Dwight, [1866]), http://nla.gov.au/nla.obj-179572384/view#page/n7/mode/1up.

From creek of Worooboomi – boo!
And sheep-run Woolagoola – goo!
Come Dibble Fellow dancing in fog!
All over Mount Wooloola – yah!
And earth holes of Worondi – wah!
Till he vanish in the yellow Wog-wog!

Old chief of Woolonara – nah!
From the great river banks, far – far!
Hasten here with spear and boomerang –
Then to snowy Woologoomerang –
For white fellow comes to make war.

An atmospheric and exhilarating instrumental example was the orchestral *Danse aboriginale* (1889) by Walter James Turner senior (1857–1900), then organist of old St Paul's Cathedral, Melbourne, and father of the future poet and music critic of the same name.[62]

But what of the rest of those earlier, and presumably more or less authentic songs that were not only shoe-horned into European tonal and metrical schemes, but fitted out with harmonised accompaniments with the obvious intention that they be sung and played by colonists or homeland Europeans, whether for education, edification, or entertainment?[63] In the case of the very earliest, taken down in London in 1793 from the singing of two Wangal men, Bennelong (c.1764–1813) and Yamroweney (c.1775–1794), but not published until 1811, the transcriber, Edward Jones (1752–1824), actually printed two versions, one with the melody un-harmonised and accompanied by a single note bass line representing the singers beating time with sticks.[64] The second version he harmonised in a manner suited to either being played on a piano or, plausibly, on his own first instrument, the Welsh harp. Which leads one to wonder whether, during the process of 'learning' the tune from their no doubt repeated performances of the song, Jones might at some point have joined in with the two Australians by improvising a similar harp accompaniment? Or, if not, whether he at least played his version of the song back to them later? How consultative, in other words, was the process? Was it just a one-direction transaction, whereby Jones took down the song from dictation, or were the singers themselves also somehow further involved in the generation and performance of the arrangement?[65] No colonial transcriber ever says as much, though most of them say little or nothing anyway about the transfer process. But an 1834 account by George Fletcher Moore, of witnessing two men from King George's Sound perform a 'kangaroo dance' in a Perth settler's parlour to a grand piano accompaniment, is suggestive:[66]

> On the 10th I rode to Guildford; walked thence to Perth, which I did not leave until the 12th; at Mr. Leake's, and enjoyed the grand piano which Mrs. Leake, who had recently arrived, had

---

62 *Danse aboriginale [by] W. J. Turner ... performed with great success by the Victorian Orchestra* (Melbourne: W. H. Glen & Co., [1889]); exemplar, National Library of Australia, digitised: *http://trove.nla.gov.au/version/13526570*; see also review, 'Working Men's Choral Society', *Table Talk* (20 December 1889), 16: *http://nla.gov.au/nla.news-article147280749*; for the scores and synthesised sound-clip of Turner's *Danse*, see:
  http://sydney.edu.au/paradisec/australharmony/turner-walter-james-and-family.php.

63 On what is probably the first musical song transcription ever to be published, *A New-South-Wales Song* (c.1805), see Graeme Skinner, 'The invention of Australian music', *Musicology Australia* 37/2 (2015), 289–306: *http://dx.doi.org/10.1080/08145857.2015.1076594*.

64 See Skinner and Wafer, Checklist, this volume, **2**.

65 A synthesised sound-clip of Jones's harp arrangement can be heard at:
  http://sydney.edu.au/paradisec/australharmony/checklist-indigenous-music-1.php#002.

66 Martin Doyle (ed.), *Extracts from the letters and journals of George Fletcher Moore: Esq., now filling a judicial office at the Swan River settlement ...* (London: Orr and Smith, 1834), 224–25:
  https://archive.org/stream/extractsfromlet00doylgoog#page/n252/mode/2up.

brought with her. The two natives of King George's Sound (who are on their return) were greatly delighted with the music; they danced the kangaroo dance ... Afterwards they seated themselves in arm-chairs, with the greatest self-complacency, and drank tea.

Moore's account at least challenges us to think twice before entirely rejecting even such a highly unlikely sounding arrangement as, for instance, bishop Rosendo Salvado's only slightly later transcription of a Western Australian dance song[67], as *ipso facto* inauthentic.[68]

And a final word on Isaac Nathan

The much-discussed arrangements by Isaac Nathan (1792–1864), sometimes called the 'father of Australian music', probably do, on the other hand, remain open to that charge. Nathan, uncharacteristically, stopped short of claiming that any of his arrangements were based on his own transcriptions (albeit he did claim to have been 'an eye-witness [to corroborees] on more than one occasion'). Neither did he leave any evidence that he envisaged, let alone actively enabled, direct Indigenous participation in the performance of his arrangements (though he did once claim that 'one of them ... alternately laughed and wept from excessive joy, at hearing his own native, melody, sung and accompanied by us on our Piano Forte'). For the first of his arrangements, Nathan 'found' both the words-and-melody already in print, John Lhotsky's 1834 publication, *A song of the women of the Menero tribe*.[69] And in 'correcting' and repackaging Lhotsky's earlier transcription as *The Aboriginal father*[70], Nathan merely registered that he had since heard 'the same melody sung in all its genuine purity and simplicity, by one of the Maneroo tribe.' Henry Tingcombe (1810–74), an Anglican priest who had been a station manager in the Monaro area in the late 1830s, provided Nathan with the two other short, but attractive word-and-tune song fragments that he later reconfigured, by a process of repetition and simple variation, into the more elaborate Monaro arrangements, *Koorinda braia* and *Wargoonda minyarrah*.[71] And since Tingcombe is on record as being a skilled musical amateur, he may well have made the original transcriptions himself.

Nathan does not say how he came by the two song fragments ascribed to the Wellington Valley people, *Ah! Wy-a-boo-ka*, and *Dital dital baloonai*, likewise worked into arrangements.[72] Perhaps they were somehow associated with the Wellington Valley Mission, or collected by one of the men or women of the Montefiore family, landholders in the district, and of whom Jacob Montefiore (1819–85) was also the librettist of Nathan's 1847 Sydney opera *Don John of Austria*. Given Nathan's own uncharacteristic silence on their mechanics of transmission, it also seems unlikely that he himself received either of these two songs directly from Indigenous informants.

---

67 Rosendo Salvado, *Memorias históricas sobre la Australia: y particularmente acerca la misión Benedictina de Nueva Nursia y los usos y costumbres de los salvajes* (Barcelona: Impr. de los Herederos de la V. Pla, 1853), page after 314 (music): *https://books.google.com.au/books?id=z_YaZIk1YLQC&pg=PA314*.

68 See Skinner and Wafer, *Checklist*, this volume, **14**; for more on Salvado's transcription, and a synthesised sound-clip of it, see:
    http://sydney.edu.au/paradisec/australharmony/checklist-indigenous-music-1.php#014.

69 *A song of the women of the Menero Tribe arranged with the assistance of several musical gentlemen for the voice and pianoforte, most humbly inscribed as the first specimen of Australian music, to her most gracious majesty Adelaide ... by Dr. J. Lhotsky, colonist N. S. Wales* (Sydney: Sold by John Innes, [1834]): *http://acms.sl.nsw.gov.au/album/albumView.aspx?itemID=846215&acmsid=0*.

70 *The Aboriginal father, a native song of the Maneroo tribe ... the melody, as sung by the Aborigines, put into rhythm & harmonized with appropriate symphonies & accompaniments ... by I. Nathan* (Sydney: T. Bluett, [1843]): *http://trove.nla.gov.au/version/19363034*; Skinner and Wafer, *Checklist*, this volume, **8**.

71 Skinner and Wafer, *Checklist*, this volume, **10.1–2**.

72 Skinner and Wafer, *Checklist*, this volume, **13.1–2**.

For all that, Nathan was quite evidently guided by a belief that his five published Indigenous song arrangements (music for a sixth is lost) were not only intrinsically valuable as musical and ethnographic artefacts, but also potentially of some local interest and practical use to colonists. As such they belong among a larger body of work from the mid 1840s that he called 'Australian melodies'. Also including several entirely original compositions, he clearly hoped they might win him a similar measure of colonial popularity to that which his London theatre songs and *Hebrew melodies* had earned him back in homeland Britain in the 1820s. Nathan notably claimed in 1848 that, in the five and a half years since he first published it, *Koorinda braia* had become 'as popular and as well known to every Australian, as God Save the Queen to every Englishman'.[73]

But this was patently little more than spin, yet another example of Nathan's self-promotional streak that so riled some of his colonial contemporaries. Meanwhile, his collaboration with the radical poet Eliza Hamilton Dunlop (1796–1880) on some original songs on Aboriginal subjects, as well as on his Lhotsky re-arrangement (for which she supplied a versified singing 'translation'), probably also earned him further critics among the squatters' party, smarting from Dunlop's pro-Indigenous public stance on the Myall Creek massacre. In any case, Nathan's practical engagement with Indigenous song appears to have lasted no more than four or five years (1842–47), while his comparatively brief involvement in Mrs Dunlop's Aboriginal causes already took an unexpectedly unfortunate turn with the publication in February 1845 of the last of his self-styled 'Australian melodies', a scurrilous – and scabrous – 'comic' song to words by naval lieutenant J. W. Dent, *A good black gin*.[74] Yet even this outright fall-from-grace need not – does not – call into question the likely authenticity of the original Indigenous song transcriptions Nathan drew upon, the last of which he worked up for publication in his eccentric and idiosyncratic anthology, *The southern Euphrosyne*, released on New Year's day 1848. And in so far as some usable details of melody and rhythm can be recovered, or reconstituted hypothetically, by stripping out their 'improvements', even the most unpromising cases of colonial arrangements – like Nathan's, Salvado's, and Taplin's – potentially retain real value for song revitalisation.[75]

References

(All electronic sources accessed 22 August 2017)

Anderson, Stephanie, trans., 2009, Pelletier: the forgotten castaway of Cape York, introductory essay and translation by Stephanie Anderson; from the original book Dix-sept ans chez les sauvages: les aventures de Narcisse Pelletier by Constant Merland; ethnographic commentary by Athol Chase. Melbourne: Melbourne Books.

Anon., 1844, Aboriginal song. Port Philip Gazette, 23 March, 4. Online at *http://nla.gov.au/nla.news-article224809937*.

Anon., 1866, The intercolonial exhibition. The Age [Melbourne], 25 October, 7. Online at *http://nla.gov.au/nla.news-article160215604*.

---

[73] Isaac Nathan, *The southern Euphrosyne, and Australian miscellany: containing oriental moral tales, original anecdote, poetry and music* (Sydney: I. Nathan, [1848]), 126:
https://books.google.com.au/books?id=ziwieom4lBQC&pg=PA126.

[74] *A good black gin, an Australian melody, an Australian melody, inscribed with great deference and profound respect, to the loyal subjects of his late most gracious, highly accomplished, and revered, antipodal majesty, king Bungaree; poet, Lieut. J. W. Dent, R.N.; composer, I. Nathan* (Sydney: W. Baker, 1845), copy at State Library of New South Wales, DSM/Q784/N.

[75] Further details and synthesised sound-clips of several of Nathan's arrangements can be found at: *http://sydney.edu.au/paradisec/australharmony/checklist-indigenous-music-1.php#008* (*The Aboriginal father*); *http://sydney.edu.au/paradisec/australharmony/checklist-indigenous-music-1.php#010* (*Koorinda braia*); and *http://sydney.edu.au/paradisec/australharmony/checklist-indigenous-music-1.php#013* (*Ah! Wy-a-boo-ka* and *Dital dital baloonai*).

Anon., 1887, Ethnological notes. Science 9(218):335.

Anon., 1889, Working Men's Choral Society [review]. Table Talk [Melbourne], 20 December, 16. Online at *http://nla.gov.au/nla.news-article147280749.*

Anon., 1899, Lovett. Tasmanian News, 7 April, 3. Online at *http://nla.gov.au/nla.news-article176605899.*

Anon., 1899, The last of the aborigines. The Mercury [Hobart], 31 October, 2. Online at *http://nla.gov.au/nla.news-article12762342.*

Anon., 1930, Obituary: Mr. Horace Watson. The Mercury [Hobart], 12 April, 8. Online at *http://nla.gov.au/nla.news-article29792914.*

Anon., 1949, Aboriginal recordings. Voice of extinct people lives on in memory and wax. The Mercury [Hobart], 23 March, 5. Online at *http://nla.gov.au/nla.news-article26511589.*

Anon., 1951, Ovation for Harold Blair. The Sydney Morning Herald, 20 March, 3. Online at *http://nla.gov.au/nla.news-article18204825.*

Casey, Bill, 2008, Modernity denied: Harold Blair's 1956 EP Australian Aboriginal Songs and its critical reception. In Robert Dixon and Veronica Kelly, eds. Impact of the modern: vernacular modernities in Australia 1870s–1960s. Sydney: Sydney University Press.

Collins, David, 1802, An account of the English colony in New South Wales, from its first settlement in January 1788, to August 1801 . . . and an account of a voyage performed by Captain Flinders and Mr. Bass . . . abstracted from the journal of Mr. Bass . . . volume 2. London: T. Cadell and W. Davies. Online at *https://books.google.com.au/books?id=ghRcAAAAcAAJ&pg=PA251* (opens at p. 251).

Crowley, Terry, and R. M. W. Dixon, 1981, Tasmanian. In R. M. W. Dixon and B. J. Blake, eds. Handbook of Australian languages (volume 2), 394–421. Canberra: Australian National University Press.

Dent, J. W., 1845, A good black gin, an Australian melody . . . inscribed with great deference and profound respect, to the loyal subjects of his late most gracious, highly accomplished, and revered, antipodal majesty, king Bungaree; poet, Lieut. J. W. Dent, R.N.; composer, I. Nathan. Sydney: W. Baker. Held by State Library of New South Wales, DSM/Q784/N.

Dixon, R. M. W., 1976, Tasmanian language. The Canberra Times, 1 September, 2. Online at *http://nla.gov.au/nla.news-article110823780.*

Doyle, Martin, ed., 1834, Extracts from the letters and journals of George Fletcher Moore, Esq., now filling a judicial office at the Swan River settlement . . . London: Orr and Smith.

Field, Barron [writing as 'B. F.'], 1823, Journal of an excursion across the Blue Mountains of New South Wales (October 1822). The London Magazine (November 1823), 461–475. Online at *http://books.google.com.au/books?id=o9gYAAAAMAAJ&pg=PA461.*

Garnier, Edouard, 1876, Observations musicales sur les chants de Narcisse Pelletier. Appendix in Constant Merland, Dix-sept ans chez les sauvages: aventures de Narcisse Pelletier, 127–135 (commentary) and four plates (music). Paris: E. Dentu.

Gibson, Jason, 2015, Central Australian songs: a history and reinterpretation of their distribution through the earliest recordings. Oceania 85(2):165–82.

Gibson, Jason, and Heather Milton, eds, transc., n.d. Walter Baldwin Spencer's diary from the Spencer and Gillen expedition 1901–1902. Melbourne: Museum Victoria. Online at *http://spencerandgillen.net/files/Spencers%20Expedition%20Diary.pdf.*

Hercus, Luise A., 1980, 'How we danced the Mudlunga': memories of 1901 and 1902. Aboriginal History 4:5–32. Online at *http://press.anu.edu.au/wp-content/uploads/2016/01/article013.pdf.*

Horne, R. H., 1866, South-sea sisters: a lyric masque written for the opening of the Intercolonial Exhibition of Australasia, 1866, by R. H. Horne; the incidental music composed by Charles Edward Horsley, op. 73. Melbourne: H. T. Dwight. Online at *http://nla.gov.au/nla.obj-179572384/view#page/n7/mode/1up* (opens at exemplar on p. 7).

Jaques, Judy, 2004, Passing the torch: commemorating the songs of Fanny Cochrane Smith. In Denis Crowdy, ed. Popular music: commemoration, commodification and communication: proceedings of the 2004 IASPM Australia New Zealand Conference, held in conjunction with the Symposium of the International Musicological Society, 11–16 July, 2004, 11–19. Melbourne: International Association for the Study of Popular Music, Australia New Zealand Branch.

Kirk, Andrew, 1899, The last of the Tasmanians [letter to the editor]. Tasmanian News, 1 November, 3. Online at *http://nla.gov.au/nla.news-article185227458*.

Lawrence, Helen Reeves, 2004, 'The great traffic in tunes': agents of religious and musical change in eastern Torres Strait. In Richard Davis, ed. Woven histories, dancing lives: Torres Strait Islander identity, culture and history, 46–72. Canberra: Aboriginal Studies Press.

Lesueur, Charles Alexandre, and Nicolas-Martin Petit, 1824, Voyage de découvertes aux terres australes. Historique, atlas par MM. Lesueur et Petit, seconde édition. Paris: Chez Arthus Bertrand. Online at *https://books.google.com.au/books?id=aXVdAAAAcAAJ&pg=PT76*. (opens at exemplars on p. 32).

Lethbridge, Harold Octavius, 1937a, Aboriginal songs. A valuable collection, Aboriginal songs explained. The Australian Musical News, 1 July, 22.

—— ed., 1937b, Australian Aboriginal songs: melodies, rhythm and words truly and authentically Aboriginal: accompaniments arranged by Arthur S. Loam. Melbourne: Allan & Co. Online at *http://nla.gov.au/nla.obj-172234124*.

Levine, Victoria Lindsay, 2002, Writing American Indian music: historic transcriptions, notations, and arrangements. Middleton: A-R Editions (Music of the United States of America 11).

Lhotsky, John, 1834, A song of the women of the Menero Tribe arranged with the assistance of several musical gentlemen for the voice and pianoforte, most humbly inscribed as the first specimen of Australian music, to her most gracious majesty Adelaide . . . by Dr. J. Lhotsky, colonist N. S. Wales. Sydney: Sold by John Innes. Online at *http://acms.sl.nsw.gov.au/album/albumView.aspx?itemID=846215&acmsid=0*.

Longman Murray, 1960, Songs of the Tasmanian aborigines as recorded by Mrs. Fanny Cochrane Smith. Papers and Proceedings of the Royal Society of Tasmania 94:79–86: *http://eprints.utas.edu.au/14096*.

Moyle, Alice M., 1959, Sir Baldwin Spencer's recordings of Australian Aboriginal singing. Memoirs of the National Museum of Victoria 24:7–36. Online at *http://www.biodiversitylibrary.org/item/120198#page/9/mode/1up*.

—— 1960, Two native song-styles recorded in Tasmania. Papers and Proceedings of the Royal Society of Tasmania 94:73–78. Online at *http://eprints.utas.edu.au/14095*.

—— 1968, Tasmanian music, an impasse? Records of the Queen Victoria Museum, Launceston 26:1–18.

Mulvaney, D. J., 1976, 'The chain of connection': the material evidence. In Nicolas Peterson, ed. Tribes and boundaries in Australia: ecology, spatial organisation and process in Aboriginal Australia, 90–92. Canberra: Australian Institute of Aboriginal Studies.

Museum Victoria, n.d., Spencer & Gillen: a journey through Aboriginal Australia (website). Online at *http://spencerandgillen.net*.

Myers, Charles S., 1912, Music. In Alfred Haddon, ed. Reports of the Cambridge Anthropological Expedition to Torres Straits (1898), volume 4: Arts and crafts, 238–269. Cambridge: The University Press. Online at *https://archive.org/stream/reports191204cambuoft#page/238/mode/2up*.

Nathan, Isaac, 1843, The Aboriginal father, a native song of the Maneroo tribe . . . the melody, as sung by the Aborigines, put into rhythm & harmonized with appropriate symphonies & accompaniments . . . by I. Nathan. Sydney: T. Bluett. Online at *http://trove.nla.gov.au/version/19363034*.

—— 1848, The southern Euphrosyne, and Australian miscellany: containing oriental moral tales, original anecdote, poetry and music. Sydney: I. Nathan. Online at *http://nla.gov.au/nla.obj-166023361*.

Plomley, N. J. Brian, ed., 1966, Friendly mission: the Tasmanian journals and papers of George Augustus Robinson, 1829–1834. Hobart: Tasmanian Historical Research Association.

—— 1987, Weep in silence: a history of the Flinders Island Aboriginal settlement with the Flinders Island journal of George Augustus Robinson, 1835–1839. Hobart: Blubber Head Press.

Ritz, Hermann B., 1908a, Aboriginal songs. Daily Post [Hobart], 21 November, 10. Online at *http://nla.gov.au/nla.news-article181621319*.

—— 1908b, An introduction to the study of the Aboriginal speech of Tasmania (read November 16, 1908). Papers and proceedings of the Royal Society of Tasmania (1908), 73–83. Online at *http://eprints.utas.edu.au/16462*.

Roth, W. E., 1898, Ethnological studies among the north-west-central Queensland Aborigines. Brisbane: E. Gregory, Government Printer. Online at *https://archive.org/stream/cu31924029890328#page/n143/mode/2up* (opens at p. 120).

Salvado, Rosendo, 1853, Memorias históricas sobre la Australia: y particularmente acerca la misión Benedictina de Nueva Nursia y los usos y costumbres de los salvajes. Barcelona: Impr. de los Herederos de la V. Pla.

Shepherd, Ben, 2015, Headhunters: the pioneers of neuroscience. London: Vintage Books.

Skinner, Graeme, 2011, Toward a general history of Australian musical composition: first national music, 1788–c.1860. Ph.D thesis, Sydney Conservatorium of Music, University of Sydney. Online at *http://ses.library.usyd.edu.au/handle/2123/7264*.

—— 2015, The invention of Australian music. Musicology Australia 37(2):289–306.

—— 2017, Australharmony (an online resource toward the history of music and musicians in colonial and early Federation Australia). Online at *http://sydney.edu.au/paradisec/australharmony*.

Skinner, Graeme and Jim Wafer, 2017, A checklist of colonial era musical transcriptions of Australian Indigenous songs. In Australharmony (an online resource toward the history of music and musicians in colonial and early Federation Australia). Online at *http://sydney.edu.au/paradisec/australharmony/checklist-indigenous-music-1.php*.

Swain, Tony, 1990, A new sky hero from a conquered land. History of Religions 29(3): 195–232.

—— 1993, A place for strangers: towards a history of Australian Aboriginal being. Cambridge: Cambridge University Press.

Taplin, George, 1879, The folklore, manners, customs, and languages of the South Australian Aborigines: gathered from inquiries made by authority of South Australian government. Adelaide: E. Spiller. Online at *https://archive.org/stream/folkloremannersc00taplrich#page/106/mode/2up* (opens at exemplar on p. 106).

Torrance, G. W., 1887, Music of the Australian Aboriginals. The Journal of the Anthropological Institute of Great Britain and Ireland 16, 335–340. Online at *https://archive.org/stream/journalofroyalan16royauoft#page/334/mode/2up*.

Turner, W. J., 1889, Danse aboriginale . . . performed with great success by the Victorian Orchestra. Melbourne: W. H. Glen & Co.

Wells, Roberta, 1999, Sidney Herbert Ray: linguist and educationalist. The Cambridge Journal of Anthropology 21(1):79–99.

Wrobel, Elinor, ed. & curator, 1999, Percy Grainger: the passionate folklorist and ethnomusicologist [exhibition catalogue]. Parkville: Grainger Museum, University of Melbourne.

17 A checklist of colonial era musical transcriptions of Australian Indigenous songs

Graeme Skinner[1] and Jim Wafer[2]
University of Sydney[1] and University of Newcastle[2]

Abstract

This checklist is intended as a basic resource guide for those who wish to explore the revitalisation of Indigenous song traditions using colonial era documentation of ancestral songs, in the form of written musical transcriptions or mechanical recordings made with early sound-capture technology. It includes a range of pertinent data on 113 songs from the colonial era; that is, notionally from first contact to 1 January 1901, though here actually from c.1789 to 1903. For each song, this checklist provides details of the sources and a link to the musical transcription or sound file. As well, it includes the song text and a gloss (where available), further bibliography, and information on likely regional affiliations, both linguistic and musical.

These resources will be useful to Aboriginal and Torres Strait Islander people undertaking song revitalisation projects and also to researchers interested in reconstructing the musical profiles of those parts of Indigenous Australia where the ancestral performance traditions suffered severe damage in the colonial era. We are not suggesting that the list is complete or exhaustive; indeed, we hope that by printing it here as a work in progress we might encourage others to look for, and in due course, report on yet more relevant musical survivals. This checklist also serves as a bibliographic appendix to the other chapters in the present volume that are concerned specifically with Australian historical ethnomusicology, in particular those by Skinner (chapter 16), McDonald (chapter 7) and Wafer (chapter 9).

Keywords: Indigenous Australian music in the colonial era, documentary history of Australian Indigenous song and dance, revitalisation of Aboriginal and Torres Strait Islander song

Introduction

This checklist is a hard-copy report on the first stage of a long-term project to create an open-access web-log of all surviving colonial era documentation of Australian Indigenous song and dance as a specifically musical resource. The first-stage of the project appears fully in webpage format at:

http://sydney.edu.au/paradisec/australharmony/checklist-indigenous-music-1.php

The documentation of ceremonial and recreational song-making, singing and dancing from the period can be sorted into four categories:

[1] pictorial depictions
[2] written verbal descriptions
[3] written transcriptions of song texts
[4] written musical transcriptions and, at the very end of the colonial era, mechanical recordings.

While category [4] data constitute the principal focus of the above webpage, and of this checklist, many of the actual documents also record song texts [3] and give further details of performance, meaning, and context, described verbally [2] and pictorially [1]. Other complementary pages will be created, in due course, to log systematically colonial documents that lack category [4] data, but are sources for categories [1], [2], and [3].

Simply then, this first checklist provides comprehensive coverage of those Australian Indigenous songs documented during the colonial era for which music survives. Until 1898, all the musical records listed here take the form of manual musical transcriptions into Western notation, from live performances or the observer's memories of live performances. In many cases these are accompanied by transliterated song texts that survive in printed or (occasionally) manuscript forms.

Some of the musical transcriptions listed were published after 1901 (in one instance, as late as 1937); but we can be fairly sure that they were all based on performances that took place before c.1901. Beginning in 1898, we also list three sets of mechanical recordings of songs, the latest of which were taken from live performances in 1901 and 1903, thus extending slightly across the divide (1 January 1901) between the colonial and federated eras.

There are 113 songs in the checklist, and 94 of these include transcriptions of the words. In many cases there is also some kind of gloss.[1] These items are divided, in the inventory that follows below, into 35 entries, or groups of songs, presented in chronological order.

Layout

Each entry is indicated by a number, from 1 to 35, preceded by the estimated likely (best-guess) date of the performance/recording of each group of song transcriptions, or, where there is prior documentation, at the date of the very earliest certain record of the song. The content of the entry is built around the source or sources that provide the relevant data (minimally, a form of musical notation or a sound recording). In almost all cases, a persistent live link is given to take the reader directly to the relevant web-page images of the original transcriptions, or the sound-file of the original recording, where available.

The individual songs within each entry are given a sub-number of the entry number (e.g. 35.3 is the third song in entry 35). Where a single melody has a number of variant texts, these

---

1   All items in the checklist are treated as 'songs', even when they are not accompanied by words, or are referred to in the sources by other names ('dance', 'call', etc.); variants (for example, where the same melody is used with different words) are not treated as separate items. Transcriptions of song words have been included in our calculations even when they are indecipherable. Our use of the term 'gloss' is very broad, and includes any commentary that provides some clue about the meaning of the song text.

are distinguished with a letter that follows the sub-number. So, for example, the three variants of song 27.2 (the 'Bingo corroborees') are numbered 27.2a, 27.2b and 27.2c.

Each song is also identified by a title, either the one provided by the original author or, where none is given, an appropriate word or phrase from the author's text, sometimes with, for disambiguation, the author's surname. So, for example, the song identification line for one of the songs from south-western Western Australia published in 1892 reads thus: '**28.3** Calvert 3 (corroborie)'.

Where text and gloss for a song occur in the source, these are transcribed after the song identification line. So, for example, the first three lines of the entry for the 'Aboriginal native song' made famous by Isaac Nathan in the 1840s read as follows:

10.1 'An Aboriginal Native Song'
text: *Koorinda braia* ... [repeat]
gloss: 'the red and white chalk with which they paint their faces on days of festivity' (Nathan 1848:107)

The 'analytics' line that follows consists of three components: first, the name of the place or district in which the evidence suggests the song was performed; second the 'music region' that the place or district pertains to, based on the Australian Indigenous music regions hypothesised by Alice Moyle (1966:xv–xvii and map 3; see also Moyle 1967:35–43); third, the language sub-family, language group and language, separated by slashes. In the case of the example just given, the analytics line reads thus:

analytics: Monaro area, southern NSW; ECA; South-eastern PN/ Yuin/ Ngarigu

To Moyle's seven music regions (ECA, CA, NWCA, NW, BMI, NE and YCA) we have added two: TAS and TSI (see list of abbreviations, below). Of the nine resulting regions, four (NWCA, NW, NE and BMI), all in the far north of Western Australia and the Northern Territory, are not represented in the data available for this period – at least, not with any certainty. (The song identified as '**7** *Air australien des sauvages de la terre d'Arnheim*' was purportedly collected in Arnhem Land but without any further specification of the locality, so it could conceivably pertain to NW or NE.) For further discussion of Australian music regions, see the Introduction to the present volume.

Our presentation of the linguistic data proceeds from the general to the specific (language sub-family / language group / language) and is hypothetical in most cases, based on the linguistic affiliations of the region in which the recording was made. (We have included these data even when the musical annotation is not accompanied by any text.) Note well that, in some cases, the language of the region is not necessarily the language of the song, which may have originated in a distant location. Where there is an apparent discrepancy, this is noted in the 'commentary' section.

Only one Australian language family, Pama-Nyungan, is represented in the data, since there is no relevant material for the regions in the far north where the non-Pama-Nyungan languages are spoken. (There is, however, one entry, '**30** Torres Strait Island songs', that includes several songsets from the Eastern Torres Strait, where the language is said to belong to the Papuan family.) We have adopted the four-fold division of Pama-Nyungan proposed by Bowern and Atkinson (2012): 'South-eastern', 'Northern', 'Central' and 'Western', so the language sub-family given for most entries is an abbreviated form of one of these ('South-eastern PN' etc.). Our language group names are also based largely on Bowern and Atkinson, and our language names on the most representative current usage. To give an example: the linguistic analytics for the first song read thus: 'South-eastern PN/ Yuin-Kuri [Sydney subgroup]/ Dharug'. The analytics line is followed by a list of sources for the particular song, and this concludes the (indented) basic information for each individual item within the entry.

The indented section(s) may be followed by a listing of '(other) documentation'; that is, sources that furnish other versions of the music or texts of the songs in the entry. This is in turn followed by a 'select bibliography' of relevant secondary sources. Where a particular resource is accessible via the internet, we provide the relevant hyperlink. Sources that are referred to repeatedly in the text are followed on their first occurrence by this alert: (henceforth ***Surname YYYY*** [year of publication]). In cases where the data require explication or elaboration, there is also a 'commentary' section.

Each entry has a brief introduction that begins with the likely language name (in bold italics) associated with the area in which the song was recorded, followed by the name of that area (in italics), then by details of personnel – performer(s) or informant(s) (in bold), recorder(s), transcriber(s), author(s) – and relevant dates (such as likely date of recording and date of first publishing).

Each entry concludes with a 'checklist web link' that provides access to the relevant entry in 'A checklist of colonial era musical transcriptions of Australian Indigenous songs' on the Australharmony website:

http://sydney.edu.au/paradisec/australharmony/checklist-indigenous-music-1.php. These entries provide fuller versions of the data provided in the present condensed print edition of the checklist.

Conventions and abbreviations

The names of Australian states and territories have been abbreviated in the usual way:

NSW	New South Wales
NT	Northern Territory
QLD	Queensland
SA	South Australia
TAS	Tasmania
VIC	Victoria
WA	Western Australia

The abbreviated terms used by Moyle for her music regions (1966) can be interpreted as follows:

ECA	East Central Arid
CA	Central Arid
NWCA	North-west Central Arid
NW	North-west;
BMI	Bathurst and Melville Islands
NE	North-east
YCA	Cape York Central Arid

Note that we have added two:

TAS	Tasmania
TSI	Torres Strait Islands

Other abbreviations

AIATSIS	Australian Institute of Aboriginal and Torres Strait Island Studies
NLA	National Library of Australia
PN	Pama-Nyungan [language family]

References

Bowern, Claire and Quentin Atkinson, 2012, Computational phylogenetics and the internal structure of Pama-Nyungan. Language 88:817–845. Online at *http://elischolar.library.yale.edu/ling_faculty/1*. 'Supplementary materials' online at *http://www.pamanyungan.net/papers/computational-phylogenetics-and-the-internal-structure-of-pama-nyungan/*

Moyle, Alice M., 1966, A handlist of field collections of recorded music in Australia and Torres Strait. Canberra: Australian Institute of Aboriginal Studies.

—— 1967, Songs from the Northern Territory: companion booklet. Canberra: Australian Institute of Aboriginal Studies.

Index of entries in the checklist

		Page
1	1 song call (**Dharug**), c.1789–1802, Sydney area NSW, published Lesueur and Petit 1824	365
2	1 song (**Dharug**), c.1790–93, Sydney area NSW, Jones 1811	367
3	2 songs (**Dharug**), 1802, Sydney area NSW, Lesueur and Petit 1824	368
4	1 song (**Dharug**), c.1800–05, Sydney area NSW, unidentified UK print, c.1802–10	369
5	2 songs (**Dharug**), 1819, Sydney area NSW, Freycinet 1839	369
6	1 song (**Dharug**), c.1820, Sydney area, NSW, Field 1823	370
7	1 song (**Arnhem Land**), by 1830, Arnhem Land NT, Domeny de Rienzi 1836	371
8	1 song (**Ngarigu**), 1834, South-east NSW, Lhotsky 1834	372
9	1 song (**Tasmanian**), 1831–36, Hobart area TAS, MSS 1840s and 1890s	373
10	2 songs (**Ngarigu**), c.1836–38, South east NSW, Nathan 1842 & 1848	374
11	3 songs (**Dharug**), 1839, Sydney area NSW, Wilkes 1845	375
12	1 song (**Yuin**), c.1845, South coast NSW, Townsend 1849	376
13	2 songs (**Wiradjuri**), by 1848, Wellington Valley NSW, Nathan 1848	377
14	1 song (**Nyungar**), c.1846–48, South west WA, Salvado 1853	378
15	1 song (**Wiradjuri**), c.1840s–80s, Upper Murray NSW, MS	379
16	2 songs (**Yagara**), c.1840–50, Brisbane district QLD, Petrie 1904	379
17	1 song (**Nyungar**), c.1850, South west WA, Chauncy 1878	380
18	7 songs (**various language groups of QLD and NSW**), 1858–61, South-east QLD and western NSW, Beckler 1868 & MS	381
19	1 song (**Paakantyi**), 1860, Far west NSW, MS	382
20	1 song (**Narrinyeri**), c.1861, South-east SA, Taplin 1879	383
21	4 songs (**Gureng-Gureng**), c.1863–65, Central QLD, Marett 1910	384
22	4 songs (**Uutaalnganu**), 1858–75, Cape York Peninsula QLD, Merland 1876	386
23	2 songs (**Gabi gabi**), c.1865–84, Central QLD, Mathew 1887	387
24	3 songs (**Queensland language groups**), 1882–83, Northern and western QLD, Lumholtz 1889	387
25	3 songs (**Kulin**), c.1840–c.1885, Southern VIC, Torrance 1887	388
26	1 song (**Western Torres Strait**), 1888, Torres Strait QLD, Haddon 1890	390
27	5 songs (**Maric**), c.1890–c.1900, South east QLD, Lethbridge and Loam 1937	391
28	4 songs (**Nyungar**), c.1893, South west WA, Calvert 1894	392
29	1 song (**Waka-Kabic**), by c.1895, Central QLD, Handley 1897	393
30	28 songs (**Eastern and Western Torres Strait**), 1898, Torres Strait QLD, recordings 1898	394
31	1 song (**Yuin**), 1899, South coast NSW, MS Sheaffe	398
32	3 songs (**Tasmanian**), 1899 & 1903, Hobart area TAS, recordings 1899 & 1903	399
33	7 songs (**various language groups of Central Australia**), 1901, Central Australia SA NT, recordings 1901	400
34	6 songs (**Dhurga**), c.1900, South coast NSW, Mathews 1901 & 1902	403
35	3 songs (**Dhurga**), c.1900–04, South coast NSW, Mathews 1904	404

The checklist

By 1789

1   *1 song-call (Dharug)*

Dharug, Sydney area, NSW; first reported by John Hunter (1737–1821), central coast NSW, 5 July 1789; first musical notation, made by Charles Alexandre Lesueur (1778–1846) and Pierre François Bernier (1779–1803), from unidentified performers, probably in the Sydney area, sometime between late June and November 1802; first published Paris, 1824

---

1   '3. Cri de ralliement' ('rallying cry')
text: *Cou-hé cou-hé cou-hé*
gloss: 'Come here' (and see **Commentary** below)
analytics: Sydney area; ECA; South-eastern PN/ Yuin-Kuri [Sydney subgroup]/ Dharug
source: Charles Alexandre Lesueur and Nicolas-Martin Petit, *Voyage de découvertes aux terres Australes. Historique, atlas par MM. Lesueur et Petit, seconde édition* (Paris: Chez Arthus Bertrand, 1824) (henceforth **Lesueur and Petit 1824**), plate 32, page 52, no. 3,
https://books.google.com.au/books?id=aXVdAAAAcAAJ&pg=PT76
earlier word source: John Hunter, *An historical journal at Port Jackson and Norfolk Island . . .* [abridged] (London: John Stockdale, [1793]), 120:
https://books.google.com.au/books?id=t0tfAAAAcAAJ&pg=PA120

Commentary: The 'cooee' was first documented with musical notation by members of the Baudin expedition in NSW in 1802, and belatedly appeared in print as the third of the three now famous music examples in Lesueur and Petit's 1824 *Atlas*. The other two songs are dealt with below at **3**. There are, however, several prior documentary references to the 'cooee', the earliest that by Hunter on 5 July 1789: 'we called to them in their own manner, by frequently repeating the word Co-wee, which signifies come here.' James Backhouse Walker (1890, 131) surmised that 'a sound like to trumpet or small gong' heard by Abel Tasman's party in Tasmania in 1642 was also 'probably a cooey'. Based on a comparison of various historical records, Troy (1994, 79) reconstructs the phonology as /gawi/ and derives the expression from the verb *gama*, 'to call', suffixed with (a contraction of) the third person marker *-wawi* (1994, 29). Dixon, Ramson and Thomas (1990, 208), on the other hand, reconstruct the phonology as /ˈkui/ or /kuˈi/ and represent it orthographically as *guuu-wi*. Both analyses adopt Hunter's gloss ('come here'), although a number of the sources suggest that the expression was more a generic signal indicating one's presence and location and soliciting the same kind of response from others. Freycinet (1839, 744), for example, says that 'ce signal . . . n'est que d'avertissement' ('this signal . . . is only an alert'; see also e.g. Cunningham 1827 v.2, 23).

Select bibliography before 1901: Peter Cunningham, *Two years in New South Wales: comprising sketches of the actual state of society in that colony . . . second edition, revised and enlarged* (London: Henry Colburn, 1827), volume 2, 23:
https://books.google.com.au/books?id=lfxEAAAAIAAJ&pg=PA23;
Louis de Freycinet, *Voyage autour du monde entrepris par ordre du Roi . . . exécuté sur les corvettes de S. M. l'Uranie et la Physicienne, pendant les années 1817, 1818, 1819 et 1820, historique, tome deuxième – deuxième partie* (Paris: Chez Pillet Ainé, 1839) (henceforth

Freycinet 1839), tome 2, 2 part, 744, 775 (music example no. 5):
http://books.google.com.au/books?id=pWNNAAAAYAAJ&pg=PA744 ('*Cri pour se reconnoître*. – Leur cri particulier pour se reconnoître de loin, est *kouhi*, ou encore *kouh* …; 'Cry for recognising one another – their special cry for recognising one another from a distance is *kouhi* or else *kouh*');

Charles Griffith, *The present state and prospects of the Port Phillip district of New South Wales* (Dublin: William Curry, 1845), 65:
https://archive.org/stream/presentstateand00grifgoog#page/n76/mode/2up;

Isaac Nathan, *The southern Euphrosyne, and Australian miscellany: containing oriental moral tales, original anecdote, poetry and music* (Sydney: I. Nathan, [1848]) (henceforth **Nathan 1848**, 102–104 (commentary and music 'The koo-ee'):
https://books.google.com.au/books?id=ziwieom4lBQC&pg=PA102, 129–132 (second edition of *Koorinda Braia*, with koo-ees newly added):
https://books.google.com.au/books?id=ziwieom4lBQC&pg=PA129;

Cooey! an Australian song, words by an Australian lady, music by Spagnoletti R.A. (Sydney: John Davis, [1860]): http://trove.nla.gov.au/version/16033732;

James Backhouse Walker, 'The discovery of Van Diemen's Land in 1642: notes on the localities mentioned in Tasman's journal of the voyage', *Papers and Proceedings of the Royal Society of Tasmania* (1890); reprint (1902), 131:
https://archive.org/stream/earlytasmaniapap00walk#page/131/mode/2up

Edward E. Morris, *Austral English: a dictionary of Australasian words, phrases and usages* (London: Macmillan and Co., 1898), 95–96:
https://archive.org/stream/australenglishdi00morruoft#page/95/mode/2up

Since 1901: Roger Covell, *Australia's music: themes of a new society* (Melbourne: Sun Books, 1967) (henceforth **Covell 1967**), 69, 325;

R. M. W. Dixon, W. S. Ramson and Mandy Thomas, *Australian Aboriginal words in English: their origin and meaning* (Melbourne: Oxford University Press, 1990), 208–209;

Nicole Saintilan, 'Music – if so it may be called': perception and response in the documentation of Aboriginal music in nineteenth century Australia (M.Mus thesis, University of New South Wales, 1993) (henceforth **Saintilan 1993**), 11–16:
http://handle.unsw.edu.au/1959.4/50383;

Jakelin Troy, *The Sydney language* (Canberra: the author, with assistance from the Australian Dictionaries Project and AIATSIS, 1994):
http://www.williamdawes.org/docs/troy_sydney_language_publication.pdf

Pru Neidorf, 'Coo-ee', in John Whiteoak and Aline Scott-Maxwell (eds), *Currency companion to music and dance in Australia* (Sydney: Currency House, 2003), 188;

Graeme Skinner, Toward a general history of Australian musical composition: first national music, 1788–c.1860 (Ph.D thesis, Sydney Conservatorium of Music, University of Sydney, 2011) (henceforth **Skinner 2011**), 62: http://ses.library.usyd.edu.au/handle/2123/7264;

Keith Vincent Smith, '1793: A song of the natives of New South Wales', *eBLJ* (Electronic British Library Journal) (2011, article 14), 1–7 (henceforth **Smith 2011**):
http://www.bl.uk/eblj/2011articles/pdf/ebljarticle142011.pdf;

Jean Fornasiero and John West-Sooby, 'Cross-cultural inquiry in 1802: musical performance on the Baudin expedition to Australia', in Kate Darian-Smith and Penelope Edmonds (eds), *Conciliation on colonial frontiers: conflict, performance, and commemoration in Australia and the Pacific rim* (New York and Oxford: Routledge, 2015) (henceforth

Fornasiero and West-Sooby 2015), 17–35, esp. 25:
https://books.google.com.au/books?id=VVehBgAAQBAJ&pg=PA25

Checklist web link:
http://sydney.edu.au/paradisec/australharmony/checklist-indigenous-music-1.php#001

c.1790

2   1 song (Dharug)

Dharug, Sydney area, NSW; known to have been sung by Wangal and perhaps also Cadigal people, the words separately recorded by William Dawes (c.1790/1) and David Collins (before 1796); music and words transcribed by Edward Jones (1752-1824), from two Wangal men, **Woollarawarre Bennelong** (c.1764-1813) and **Yemmerrawanne** (c.1775-94), in London, England, mid 1793; musical transcription first published London, 1811

2   'A SONG OF THE NATIVES OF NEW SOUTH WALES; Which was written down from the Singing of BENELONG, and YAM-ROWENY, the two Chiefs, who were brought to England some years ago from Botany Bay, by Governor Phillips [sic].'
text: *Barrabu-la barra ma, manginè wey en-gu-na . . .* [repeats]
gloss: 'The subject of the Song, is in praise of their Lovers'
analytics: Sydney area; ECA; South-eastern PN/ Yuin-Kuri [Sydney subgroup]/ Dharug
source: Edward Jones (ed.), *Musical curiosities: or a selection of the most characteristic national songs and airs . . . consisting of Spanish, Portuguese, Russian, Danish, Lapland, Malabar, New South Wales* (London: Printed for the author, 1811), 15; facsimile in Smith 2011, 1:
http://www.bl.uk/eblj/2011articles/pdf/ebljarticle142011.pdf

Other early sources: William Dawes, Sydney, NSW, 1790-91; University of London, School of Oriental and African Studies, MS 41645, Notebooks of William Dawes (1790-91), Book B, 31: 'A Song of New South Wales', perhaps taken from the singing of the young Cadigal woman, Patyegarang (words only):
http://www.williamdawes.org/ms/msview.php?image-id=book-b-page-31;
David Collins, *An account of the English colony in New South Wales: with remarks on the dispositions, customs, manners, &c. of the native inhabitants of that country . . .* (London: Printed for T. Cadell Jun. and W. Davies, 1798), 616 (words only); from unidentified performer, Sydney area, before August 1796:
https://books.google.com.au/books?id=eRZcAAAAcAAJ&pg=PA616

Commentary: The music and words of this song were taken down by Jones in London in mid 1793 from the singing of Bennelong and Yemmerrawanne, the two Wangal men brought from Sydney to England by retiring governor Arthur Phillip. Keith Vincent Smith reliably fixed the performance at sometime between late May and October 1793, when the singers were lodging in the house of William Waterhouse at 125 Mount Street, Mayfair, near Berkeley Square, London. Smith discovered that Jones, Welsh harpist and bard to the Prince of Wales (later George IV), was then living at 122 Mount Street. Jones (1811:15) noted that, in the 1793 performance he transcribed, 'when they Sang, it seem'd indispensable to them to have two sticks, one in each hand to beat time with the Tune; one end of the left hand stick rested on the ground, while the other in the right hand was used to beat against it, according to the time of the notes.'

Select bibliography: [Review], *The Monthly Magazine* 34 (1 August 1812), 54:
  http://books.google.com.au/books?id=C2eP-ZRhnOwC&pg=PA54;
Carl Engel, *An introduction to the study of national music: comprising researches into popular songs, traditions, and customs* (London: Longmans, Green, Reader, and Dyer, 1866) (henceforth **Engel 1866**), 26–27:
  https://archive.org/stream/introductiontost00enge#page/26/mode/2up;
James Bonwick, *Daily life and origins of the Tasmanians* (London: Samson, Low, Son, and Marston: 1870) (henceforth **Bonwick 1870**), 33:
  https://archive.org/stream/dailylifeandori02bonwgoog#page/n51/mode/2up;
Richard Wallaschek, *Primitive music: an inquiry into the origin and development of music, songs, instruments, dances, and pantomimes of savage races* (London; New York: Longmans, Green, and Co., 1893) (henceforth **Wallaschek 1893**), 41:
  https://archive.org/stream/primitivemusicin00wall#page/41/mode/2up;
Skinner 2011, 62–63;
Smith 2011

Sound: Smith 2011, 7: *http://www.bl.uk/eblj/2011articles/pdf/ebljarticle142011.pdf*. Page 7 of the pdf has an embedded sound file of this song (and also **6**) performed in traditional style by Indigenous performers, Clarence Slockee and Matthew Doyle, at the opening of the Mari Wari exhibition, State Library of New South Wales, Sydney, 24 September 2010.

Checklist web link:
  http://sydney.edu.au/paradisec/australharmony/checklist-indigenous-music-1.php#002

1802

3   2 songs (Dharug)

Dharug, Sydney area, NSW; transcribed by Charles Alexandre Lesueur (1778–1846) and Pierre François Bernier (1779–1803), members of the Baudin expedition, from unidentified singers, probably in the Sydney area, between late June and November 1802; first published Paris, 1824

3.1   '1. Chant' ('song')
text: [music only, no words]
analytics: Sydney area; ECA; South-eastern PN/ Yuin-Kuri [Sydney subgroup]/ Dharug
source: Lesueur and Petit 1824, plate 32, page 52, no. 1:
  https://books.google.com.au/books?id=aXVdAAAAcAAJ&pg=PT76

3.2   '2. Air de danse' ('dance song')
text: [Women] é é Con gô Lœmba Lœmba é é Con gô Lœmba Con gô . . . [repeats]; [Men] pouhé pouhé pouhé pouhé pouhé pouhé pouhé . . . [repeats] [music in 2 parts, rhythms only notated, no melodies]
analytics: As for **3.1**
source: As for **3.1**, no. 2

Select bibliography: Freycinet 1839, volume 2, part 2, 775 (music example no. 3):
  http://books.google.com.au/books?id=pWNNAAAAYAAJ&pg=PA775;

Karl Hagen, **Über die Musik einiger Naturvölker (Australier, Melanesier, Polynesier)**
(Dissertation, University of Jena) (Hamburg: Ferdinand Schlotke, 1892) (henceforth
Hagen 1892): *http://trove.nla.gov.au/version/46275598*;
Wallaschek 1893, 36–37 (commentary), [343] (music, example 5c):
https://archive.org/stream/primitivemusicin00wall#page/n343/mode/2up;
Saintilan 1993, 11–16;
Skinner 2011, 62;
Smith 2011;
Fornasiero and West-Sooby 2015, especially 24–25

Checklist web link:
http://sydney.edu.au/paradisec/australharmony/checklist-indigenous-music-1.php#003

c.1800–05

4   1 song (Dharug)

? Dharug, *? Sydney area, NSW*; transcribed from unidentified performers, probably in the Sydney region, probably c.1800–05, and 'brought over [to UK] by an officer from NSW'; first published Britain, c.1802–10

4   '36. A New-South-Wales song'
text: *Wa ha bin deh bang ha nel ha Wa ha bin deh bang ha nel ha Wa ha bin deh bang ha nel ha Hoh hoh hoh hoh hoh hoh* (D.C. ad lib.)
analytics: ? Sydney area; ECA; South-eastern PN/ ? Yuin-Kuri [Sydney subgroup]/ ? Dharug
source: National Library of Scotland, Inglis Collection of printed music, Ing.72(1–3) [ID: 94733017], a composite music volume in 3 sections; section 3 (unidentified collection of national music of various nations, including airs, glees, catches, etc., titlepage missing, ? published London, Glasgow or Edinburgh, c.1802–1810), no. 36, page [43]:
http://digital.nls.uk/special-collections-of-printed-music/pageturner.cfm?id=94737053

Select bibliography: Graeme Skinner, 'The invention of Australian music', *Musicology Australia* 37/2 (2015), 296–98: *http://dx.doi.org/10.1080/08145857.2015.1076594*

Checklist web link:
http://sydney.edu.au/paradisec/australharmony/checklist-indigenous-music-1.php#004

1819

5   2 songs (Dharug)

Dharug, Sydney area, NSW; transcribed by, or on behalf of, Louis de Freycinet (1779–1842), Sydney area, between 19 November and 25 December 1819; first published Paris, 1839

5.1   'No. 1. *Danse du Kanguroo*' ('Kangaroo dance')
text: [music only, no words]
analytics: Sydney area; ECA; South-eastern PN/ Yuin-Kuri [Sydney subgroup]/ Dharug
source: Freycinet 1839, 774–75 (commentary and music):
http://books.google.com.au/books?id=pWNNAAAAYAAJ&pg=PA774

5.2 'No. 4. *Air de pêche*' ('Fishing song')

text: *E-ya Wan-djé-oua, Tché-en-go Wan-dé-go* ['Je n'ai pu avoir les dernières paroles de cet air' ('I was unable to catch the last words of this song')]
analytics: As for **5.1**
source: Freycinet 1839, 775:
http://books.google.com.au/books?id=pWNNAAAAYAAJ&pg=PA775

Commentary: Of the 5 music examples in Freycinet's 1839 account of his 1819 return visit to Australia (19 November to 26 December), only nos. 1 and 4 (above) appeared for the first time. Freycinet's commentary on Indigenous music making (korroberis) draws partly on sources dating from after his 1819 visit. As evidence of the breadth of his recent reading, Freycinet (830) corrected Lhotsky's claim that his 1834 transcription (entry **8** below) was the 'première spécimen de musique australienne', citing the priority of the 1802 Baudin (Lesueur and Petit 1824, source of his music examples 3 and 5) and Field (Field 1825, source of his example 2). Concerning **5.2**, David Collins had also described a women's fishing song (Collins 1798, 601: *https://books.google.com.au/books?id=eRZcAAAAcAAJ&pg=PA601*). During the 1830s and later, kangaroo songs and dances were widely documented from Tasmania to Western Australia; however, Bonwick's 1870 claim that the Sydney Kangaroo dance melody given by Freycinet was 'a true Tasmanian tune of the oldest date' is self-evidently preposterous.

Select bibliography: Engel 1866, 238:
https://books.google.com.au/books?id=0k4QAAAAYAAJ&pg=PA238;
Bonwick 1870, 31:|
https://archive.org/stream/dailylifeandori02bonwgoog#page/n50/mode/2up;
C. Hubert H. Parry, *The art of music* (London: K. Paul, Trench, Trübner, 1893), 54:
https://archive.org/stream/artofmusic00parrrich#page/54/mode/2up;
(4th edition of same work, under title *The evolution of the art of music*, 1905), 49:
https://archive.org/stream/4thevolutionofar00parruoft#page/48/mode/2up

Checklist web link:
http://sydney.edu.au/paradisec/australharmony/checklist-indigenous-music-1.php#005

c.1820

6   1 song (Dharug)

Dharug, Sydney area, NSW; music and words (no translation) transcribed by Barron Field (1786–1846), from the singing of Harry (c.1787–?), brother-in-law of Bennelong, between c.1820 and early 1823; first published London, November 1823; second edition London, 1825

6 'Australian national melody'

text: *I-ah i-ah i-ah i-ah i-ah i-ah i-ah gumbery jah jingun velah gumbery jah jingun velah i-ah i-ah i-ah i-ah i-ah i-ah i-ah i-ah* &c. [Field 1825 has *a-bang* . . . instead of *i-ah* . . .]
analytics: Sydney area; ECA; South-eastern PN/ Yuin-Kuri [Sydney subgroup]/ Dharug
sources: B. F. [Barron Field], 'Journal of an excursion across the Blue Mountains of New South Wales (October 1822)', *The London Magazine* (November 1823), 465–66:
http://books.google.com.au/books?id=o9gYAAAAMAAJ&pg=PA465 (**Field 1823**);

Barron Field, *Geographical memoirs on New South Wales; by various hands* (London: John Murray, 1825), 433–34:
http://books.google.com.au/books?id=P7kBAAAAYAAJ&pg=PA433 (**Field 1825**)

Select bibliography: Hannover, Stadtbibliothek, Musikabteilung (D-HVs), MS Kestner No. 140 (Nr. 19) [RISM ID no.: 451010544], 'Neuholländisches Lied, Jahiah gumbery jah' [= Field 1823]; copied by Hermann Kestner (1810–90), 1836; see Theodor Georg Wilhelm Werner, 'Die Musikhandschriften des Kestnerschen Nachlasses im Stadtarchiv zu Hannover' (Hannoversche Geschichtsblätter), *Zeitschrift für Musikwissenschaft* 1/8 (1919), 241–372;

Freycinet 1839, tome 2, part 2, 775 (no. 2. Air de danse = Field 1825):
http://books.google.com.au/books?id=pWNNAAAAYAAJ&pg=PA775, see also p. 830 footnote 1: *http://books.google.com.au/books?id=pWNNAAAAYAAJ&pg=PA830*;

Charles Wilkes, *Narrative of the United States Exploring Expedition during the years 1838, 1839, 1840, 1841, 1842* Volume 2 (Philadelphia: Lee and Blanchard, 1845), 200:
https://archive.org/stream/narrativeofunite02wilk#page/200/mode/2up;

Covell 1967, 65–66, 324;

Saintilan 1993, 36–39;

Skinner 2011, 104

Sound: Smith 2011, 7: *http://www.bl.uk/eblj/2011articles/pdf/ebljarticle142011.pdf*. Page 7 of the pdf has an embedded sound file of this song (and also **2**) performed in traditional style by Indigenous performers, Clarence Slockee and Matthew Doyle, at the opening of the Mari Wari exhibition, State Library of New South Wales, Sydney, 24 September 2010.

Checklist web link:
http://sydney.edu.au/paradisec/australharmony/checklist-indigenous-music-1.php#006

By c.1830

7   *1 song (Arnhem Land)*

?, Arnhem Land, NT; music only, transcribed by, or on behalf of, Grégoire Louis Domeny de Rienzi (1789–1843), c. late 1820s (by 1830); first published Paris, 1836

7   **'No. 12. Air australien des sauvages de la terre d'Arnheim'**
text: [music only, no words]
analytics: Arnhem Land; ? NW ? NE ? BMI; ? Australian
source: Grégoire Louis Domeny de Rienzi, *Océanie; ou cinquième partie du monde . . . tome premier* (Paris: Firmin Didot Frères, 1836), 78 (commentary), 81 (music):
https://archive.org/stream/ocanieoucinqui01dome#page/81/mode/2up; also volume 3, 480–81 (commentary): *https://books.google.com.au/books?id=LZlQAAAAYAAJ&pg=PA481*

Commentary: It is unclear when, or indeed whether, Domeny de Rienzi actually set foot in northern Australia; but he had reportedly arrived at Bombay, via the Red Sea, before the end of 1825. Arnhem Land is the most linguistically complex and diverse region in Australia. It is home to numerous non-Pama-Nyungan languages as well as members of the Pama-Nyungan Yolngu group, so it is impossible even to speculate which language or language group the music might be associated with.

Select bibliography: Saintilan 1993, 16–21;
Skinner 2015, 296

Checklist web link:
http://sydney.edu.au/paradisec/australharmony/checklist-indigenous-music-1.php#007

1834

8   1 song (Ngarigu)

Ngarigu, *Monaro area, south east NSW*; words and music (? translation) transcribed by John Lhotsky (1795–1865), 1834; first published Sydney, November 1834

8 'Song of the women of the Menero tribe'
text: *Kon-gi kawel-go yue-re/ con-gi kawel-go yue-re/ Kuma gi ko-ko kawel-go/ kuma-gi ka-ba/ ko-ma gi ko-ko/ koma-gi ko-ko kabel-go/ Koma gi ka-ba/ ko-ma-gi yue-re* (Lhotsky)
gloss: Unprotected race of people, unprotected all we are; and our children shrink so fastly, unprotected why are we? (Lhotsky)
analytics: Monaro area, south east NSW; ECA; South-eastern PN/ Yuin/ Ngarigu
source: *A song of the women of the Menero Tribe arranged with the assistance of several musical gentlemen for the voice and pianoforte, most humbly inscribed as the first specimen of Australian music, to her most gracious majesty Adelaide, queen of Great Britain & Hanover, by Dr. J. Lhotsky, colonist N. S. Wales* (Sydney: Sold by John Innes, [1834]): *http://digital.sl.nsw.gov.au/delivery/DeliveryManagerServlet?embedded=true&toolbar=false&dps_pid=IE3727874*
later edition: *The Aboriginal father, a native song of the Maneroo Tribe . . . the melody, as sung by the Aborigines, put into rhythm & harmonized with appropriate symphonies & accompaniments . . . by I. Nathan* (Sydney: T. Bluett, [1843]): *http://trove.nla.gov.au/version/19363034*

Documentation: 'Domestic Intelligence', *The Australian* (7 November 1834), 2:
  http://nla.gov.au/nla.news-article42007225;
[Advertisement], *The Sydney Gazette* (11 November 1834), 3:
  http://nla.gov.au/nla.news-article2217523;
'NEW MUSIC', *The Sydney Morning Herald* (19 January 1843), 2:
  http://nla.gov.au/nla.news-article12411279;
'NEW PUBLICATION', *Australasian Chronicle* (19 January 1843), 2:
  http://nla.gov.au/nla.news-article31738598;
'THE ABORIGINAL FATHER', *The Australian* (27 January 1843), 3:
  http://nla.gov.au/nla.news-article37116848;
'KOON-GI KAWEL GHO', in Nathan 1848, 104-07:
  https://books.google.com.au/books?id=ziwieom4lBQC&pg=PA104

Select bibliography: Freycinet 1839, 830 footnote:
  http://books.google.com.au/books?id=pWNNAAAAYAAJ&pg=PA830;
W. Arundel Orchard, *Music in Australia: more than 150 years of development* (Melbourne:
  Georgian House, 1952), 7, 212;
Covell 1967, 67, 325;

Harold Hort, 'An aspect of interaction between Aboriginal and western music in the songs of Isaac Nathan', *Miscellanea musicologica: Adelaide studies in musicology* 12 (1987), 205–06;
Saintilan 1993, 53–58;
Skinner 2011, 105–116, 196–202;
Skinner 2017 (this volume)

Checklist web link:
http://sydney.edu.au/paradisec/australharmony/checklist-indigenous-music-1.php#008

1831

9   1 song (Tasmanian)

Tasmanian language, 'Van Diemen's Land' (Tasmania), c. early 1830s; earliest words only transcription by George Augustus Robinson, 13 August 1831, several later words only transcriptions; music and words transcribed by Maria Logan, Hobart, 1836 (2 unpublished MS copies, ? c.1840s and ? c.1850s); 3 sound recordings of at least 2 distinct versions of the song by Fanny Cochrane Smith, Hobart, 1899 and 1903 (see **32.1** below); music (facsimile of MS [1]) published Launceston, 1968

9 'Song of the Aborigines of Van Diemans Land'
text: *Popela ranea gonne ne popela ranea gone ne na lea me gonne a lea me gonne a to kea me gun ne a to kea me gun ne a lea me gun ne a lea me gun ne a ni na te pea ra nea po ne na ni na te pea ra nea po ne na ni na te pea ra ne ni na na re bu wil la pa ne na ra bur wil la bal la hoo! bal la hoo! ni na na ra bu wil la pa na pa ra bu wil la bal la hoo! bal la hoo!*
gloss: G. A. Robinson first transcribed a similar version of the words in 1831 (Plomley 1966, 469 note 250) with a translation 'the evil spirit in the native / the ankle / sole of the foot / to evacuate / to clean the wobbeltenn'. G. W. Walker, who collected another similar version of the text in 1832, noted that it was 'a popular song among all the [Tasmanian] aboriginal tribes, of which I have not obtained the meaning, it being involved by them in some mystery' (Moyle 1968, 2).
analytics: Tasmania; TAS; Tasmanian
sources: [1] *Song of the Aborigines of Van Diemen's Land (arranged by Mrs. Logan)*, MS, copy, ? c.1840s, Archives Office of Tasmania; holographic copies, State Library of Tasmania: *https://stors.tas.gov.au/AB713-1-4961* (page 1), *https://stors.tas.gov.au/AB713-1-4960* (page 2); [2] *Song of the Aborigines (arranged by Mrs. Logan)*, MS, copy, c.1890s, at University of Tasmania Library: *http://eprints.utas.edu.au/1866*; see also later recordings (as specified in **32.1** below).

Other sources and documentation: George Augustus Robinson, journal, 13 August 1831, transcribed in N. J. Brian Plomley, *Friendly mission: the Tasmanian journals and papers of George Augustus Robinson, 1829–1834* (Hobart: Tasmanian Historical Research Association, 1966), 399, 469–70 note 250 (words and gloss only);
Robinson, journal, 22 October 1836, transcribed in N. J. B. Plomley (ed.), *Weep in silence: a history of the Flinders Island Aboriginal settlement with the Flinders Island journal of George Augustus Robinson, 1835–1839* (Hobart: Blubber Head Press, 1987), 391: 'Spent the evening at Logan's in Macquarie Street. Mr[s] Logan set to music a song of the aborigines, POPELLER etc., the first ever attempted.'

Select bibliography: Hermann B. Ritz, 'An introduction to the study of the Aboriginal speech of Tasmania (read November 16, 1908)', *Papers and Proceedings of the Royal Society of Tasmania* (1908), 73–83:

https://archive.org/stream/papersproceeding190809roya#page/n109/mode/2up;

'ABORIGINAL SONGS', *Daily Post* (21 November 1908), 10:

http://nla.gov.au/nla.news-article181621319;

Murray Longman, 'Songs of the Tasmanian aborigines as recorded by Mrs. Fanny Cochrane Smith', *Papers and Proceedings of the Royal Society of Tasmania* 94 (1960), 79–86 (henceforth **Longman 1960**): *http://eprints.utas.edu.au/14096*;

Alice M. Moyle, 'Two native song-styles recorded in Tasmania', *Papers and Proceedings of the Royal Society of Tasmania* 94 (1960), 73–78 (henceforth **Moyle 1960**): *http://eprints.utas.edu.au/14095*;

Alice M. Moyle, 'Tasmanian music, an impasse?', *Records of the Queen Victoria Museum, Launceston* 26 (May 1968), 1–10 (henceforth **Moyle 1968**): *http://www.qvmag.tas.gov.au/qvmag/index.php?c=160*;

Skinner 2011, 127, 442

Skinner 2017 (this volume)

Checklist web link:

http://sydney.edu.au/paradisec/australharmony/checklist-indigenous-music-1.php#009

c.1836–38

10 *2 songs (Ngarigu)*

Ngarigu, Monaro area, southern NSW; collected (? and transcribed) by Henry Tingcombe (1810–74), probably during his residence there, c.1836–38; arranged by Isaac Nathan (1792–1864), **10.1** by May 1842, first published Sydney, July 1842; **10.2** by July 1844; first published Sydney, January 1848

10.1 'Koorinda braia'

text: *Koorinda braia . . .* [repeat]

gloss: 'the red and white chalk with which the paint their faces on days of festivity' (Nathan 1848, 107)

analytics: Monaro area, southern NSW; ECA; South-eastern PN/ Yuin/ Ngarigu

sources: [1] *Koorinda braia, an Aboriginal native song, put into rhythm, harmonised, and inscribed to Mrs. E. Deas Thomson, by I. Nathan. Sydney. 1842*:

http://nla.gov.au/nla.obj-168218284; [2] Nathan 1848, 99–101 and 108 (commentary), 127–32 (music, second 'new' edition, with 'koo-ees' added):

https://books.google.com.au/books?id=ziwieom4lBQC&pg=PA127

other documentation: [Advertisement], *The Sydney Gazette* (24 May 1842), 3:

http://nla.gov.au/nla.news-article2556557; 'MR. NATHAN'S CONCERT', *The Sydney Herald* (30 May 1842), 2: *http://nla.gov.au/nla.news-article12875453*; 'NEW MUSIC', *Australasian Chronicle* (2 July 1842), 3: *http://nla.gov.au/nla.news-article31736395*

10.2 'War-goon-da min-ya-rah'

text: *Wargoonda min-ya-rah / min-ya-kol-ba-wan-de-re?/ Wargoonda min-ya-rah / min-ya kol-ba wan-de-re?/ Wande-re wande-re / min-ya kol-ba wande-re / wande-re wande-re/*

wande-re wande-re/ wande-re wande-re wande-re/ Wan-de-re wan-de-re / min-ya kol-ba wan-de-re/ wan-de-re wan-de-re/ min-ya kol-ba wan-de-re / wan-de-re wan-de-re / wan-de-re wandere wande-re (Nathan 1848, 109–13)
gloss: What is the matter? Where were you? (or:) What did you do? How is this? What have you been doing? On the Rocky Mountains. Did white man give bread? (Nathan 1848, 108)
analytics: As for **10.1**
source: 'War-goon-da min-ya-rah, an aboriginal melody, sung by the Maneroo tribes of Australia, put into modern rhythm, harmonized and arranged, with characteristic additions, by I. Nathan, esq.', in Nathan 1848, 108 (description), 109–13 (music):
https://books.google.com.au/books?id=ziwieom4lBQC&pg=PA108
other documentation: [Advertisement], *The Australian* (9 July 1844), 1:
http://nla.gov.au/nla.news-article37123781;

Select bibliography: 'ORANGE', *Bathurst Free Press and Mining Journal* (1 December 1858), 2: *http://nla.gov.au/nla.news-article64376514*;
Robert Etheridge, *Contributions to a catalogue of works, reports, and papers on the anthropology, ethnology, and geological history of the Australian and Tasmanian Aborigines . . . part 2* (Memoirs of the Geological Survey of New South Wales, palaeontology 8) (Sydney: Government Printer, 1891) (henceforth **Etheridge 1891**), 36: *https://archive.org/stream/contributionsto00ethegoog#page/n83/mode/2up*;
S. M. Mowle, 'Aboriginal songs and words', *Australian Town and Country Journal* (16 May 1896), 24: *http://nla.gov.au/nla.news-article71245725*;
Covell 1967, 68;
Saintilan 1993, 68–72;
Skinner 2011, 189–196, 198–200
Skinner 2017 (this volume)

Checklist web link:
http://sydney.edu.au/paradisec/australharmony/checklist-indigenous-music-1.php#010

1839

11 *3 songs (Dharug)*
? Dharug, *Sydney area*, NSW; transcribed by Joseph Drayton (1798–1877), member of the United States Exploring Expedition (1838–42), from unidentified singer or singers, December 1839; first published Philadelphia, USA, 1845

11.1 [No. 1] [music example no. 1 of 4]
text: [music only, no words]: 'The above [i.e. **11.1**] is thought by Mr. Drayton not to be entirely native music, but the following [i.e. **11.2**] he has no doubt of; the words are given as he heard them'
analytics: Sydney area; ECA; South-eastern PN/ Yuin-Kuri [Sydney subgroup]/ Dharug
source: Charles Wilkes, *Narrative of the United States Exploring Expedition during the years 1838, 1839, 1840, 1841, 1842* (Philadelphia: Lee and Blanchard, 1845) (**Wilkes 1845**), volume 2, 199: *https://archive.org/stream/narrativeofunite02wilk#page/n245/mode/2up*

11.2 [No. 2] [music example no. 2 of 4]
text: *Mer-ry dunbar a-roa Merry dunbar a-roa O man gar merry own dunbar run mun gar*

analytics: As for **11.1**
source: Wilkes 1845, volume 2, 200:
https://archive.org/stream/narrativeofunite02wilk#page/200/mode/2up

11.3 [**No. 3**] [music example no. 3 of 4]
text: [music only, no words]: 'The above [i.e. **11.2**], as well as those which follow [i.e. **11.3** and Drayton's version of **6**], were obtained from a native who was on his way with the new song to his tribe.'
analytics: As for **11.1**
source: As for **11.2**

Commentary: When the United States Exploring Squadron was anchored in Sydney Harbour in December 1839, one of the expedition's artists, Joseph Drayton, made and later published several song transcriptions. He claimed that all 4 of his published examples had been taken from live performances, all by the same 'native', who was taking a 'new song' back to his tribe. Drayton suspected **11.1** 'not to be entirely native music'. Despite the claim also to have sourced it directly from the 'native', a fourth chant, the last given on page 200 [music example no. 4 of 4], to the words '*Abang abang . . .* ', was clearly sourced from Field's 'Australian National Melody' (Field 1825, **6** above).

Select bibliography: Hagen 1892;
Joseph Lauterer, *Australien und Tasmanien: nach eigener Anschauung und Forschung* (Freiburg im Breisgau: Herdersche Verlagshandlung, 1900) (henceforth **Lauterer 1900**), 293:
https://archive.org/stream/australienundta00lautgoog#page/n316/mode/2up;
Saintilan 1993, 22–25, 86, 88;
Skinner 2011, 116, 445

Checklist web link:
http://sydney.edu.au/paradisec/australharmony/checklist-indigenous-music-1.php#011

c.1845

12   *1 song (Yuin)*

Yuin, Ulladulla, South Coast, NSW; transcribed by, or for, Joseph Phipps Townsend (1812–88), mid 1840s, perhaps from the performance of **Jimmy Woodbury**; first published London, 1849

12 'An Aboriginal chant'
text: *Ma-la-yah, Ma-la-yah,/ In-go-bra-yah, Mah-la-yah,/ Ma-la-yah, Ma-la-yah/ In-go-bra-yah, Ma-la-yah, Ma-la*
analytics: Ulladulla, South Coast, NSW; ECA; South-eastern PN/ Yuin/ ? Dhurga ? Dharumba
source: Joseph Phipps Townsend, *Rambles and observations in New South Wales with sketches of men and manners, notices of the Aborigines, glimpses of scenery, and some hints to emigrants* (London: Chapman and Hall, 1849), 88–90, 98–100 (commentary), 91 (music):
https://archive.org/stream/ramblesandobser01towngoog#page/n104/mode/2up

Commentary: Townsend arrived in Australia in 1842, and travelled country New South Wales, from Ulladulla to the Illawarra, before returning to Britain in 1846. He explained that one of his most admired native guides, 'Jimmy Woodbury', was 'a great man at corrobbories . . . and

I know that he has walked fifty miles, in one day, in order to join in a dance at night' (89, also 97). Townsend gave only vague hints as to where, when and how he collected this song ('About Ulladulla . . . '?).

Select bibliography: [Review], *The Athenaeum* (28 April 1849), 433–34:
https://books.google.com.au/books?id=RZRHAQAAIAAJ&pg=PA433;
Etheridge 1891, 45:
https://archive.org/stream/contributionsto00ethegoog#page/n91/mode/2up;
Skinner 2011a, 202, 468

Checklist web link:
http://sydney.edu.au/paradisec/australharmony/checklist-indigenous-music-1.php#012

Before 1848

13 *2 songs (Wiradjuri)*

Wiradjuri, Wellington Valley, NSW; unidentified performers and transcribers, ? between c.1835–45; arranged by Isaac Nathan (1792–1864); published Sydney, 1848

13.1 'Ah! Wy-a-boo-ka, the turtle song'
text: *Ah wyabooka . . .* [repeat]
gloss: 'a species of turtle' (Nathan 1848, 114)
analytics: Wellington Valley, NSW; ECA; South-eastern PN/ Central NSW/ Wiradjuri
source: 'Ah! Wy-a-boo-ka, the turtle song, an Aboriginal melody sung by the Wellington valley Tribe of Australia, put into modern rhythm, harmonized and arranged, with a piano forte accompaniment, by I. Nathan', in Nathan 1848, 114 (commentary), 115–18 (music):
https://books.google.com.au/books?id=ziwieom4lBQC&pg=PA115

13.2 'Dital dital baloonai' ('The battle song')
text: *Dital dital baloonai . . .* [repeat]
gloss: 'Brothers, brothers, on we go, / to meet the foe' (etc. Nathan 1848, 113. We have omitted the following five lines of Nathan's free rendition, since they constitute an unnecessarily fanciful elaboration of the first two lines, as given here.)
analytics: As for **13.1**
source: 'Dital dital baloonai', in Nathan 1848, 113 (commentary), 119–26 (music):
https://books.google.com.au/books?id=ziwieom4lBQC&pg=PA119

Commentary: Nathan (1848, 114) also gave the title only (no music) of another song, 'Ah Warin-ee Ah Warin-e', 'a sweetly flowing melancholy strain, supposed to be a song of lamentation'.

Select bibliography: 'AH WY-A-BOO-KA, THE TURTLE SONG', *Australian Town and Country Journal* (28 January 1888), 33: *http://nla.gov.au/nla.news-article71093723*;
Etheridge 1891, 36: *https://archive.org/stream/contributionsto00ethegoog#page/n83/mode/2up*;
'EUMALGA', *Leader* [Orange, NSW] (2 July 1912), 4:
http://nla.gov.au/nla.news-article117798877;
Skinner 2011, 198, 473
Skinner 2017 (this volume)

c.1846–48

14   1 song (Nyungar)

? *Nyungar*, south-west WA; from unidentified performers, transcribed and 'reduced to the piano forte' by Rosendo Salvado (1814–1900), south-east WA, c.1846–48; first published Barcelona, 1853

14 'Maquielo: cancion de baile de los Australianos occidentales' (Dance song of the Western Australians)
text: [music only, no words]
analytics: south-west WA; CA; Western PN/ Nyungar/ ? Nyungar
source: Rosendo Salvado, *Memorias históricas sobre la Australia: y particularmente acerca la misión Benedictina de Nueva Nursia y los usos y costumbres de los salvajes* (Barcelona: Impr. de los Herederos de la V. Pla, 1853), page after 314 (music):
https://books.google.com.au/books?id=z_YaZIk1YLQC&pg=PA314

Commentary: Salvado's transcription is based on a song he heard during his first Western Australian sojourn, between his arrival at Fremantle in January 1846 and his temporary return to Europe in January 1849. Salvado's brief commentary on Aboriginal song and dance appears in all three original editions of his book, in Italian (1852), Spanish (1853), and French (1854), however the musical transcription appears only in the Spanish (1853) edition.

Select bibliography: Théophile Bérengier, *La Nouvelle-Nursie: histoire d'une colonie bénédictine dans l'Australie occidentale (1846–1878)* (Paris: Lecoffre fils et cie., 1879), 193–194:
https://archive.org/stream/lanouvellenursi00brgoog#page/n226/mode/2up;
Lauterer 1900, 293–94:
https://archive.org/stream/australienundta00lautgoog#page/n316/mode/2up;
E. J. Stormon (ed.), *The Salvado memoirs: historical memoirs of Australia . . .* (Nedlands: University of Western Australia Press, 1977), 132–35, plate facing 125;
Xoan-Manuel Carreira, 'The piano music of Rosendo Salvado', *Studies in Music* 23 (1989);
Xavier Groba González, O legado musical de casto sampedro folgar (1848–1937): o canto galego de tradición oral (doctoral thesis, University of Santiago de Compostella, 2011), 76–79:
http://dspace.usc.es/handle/10347/3621;
Skinner 2011, 347, 475
Skinner 2017 (this volume)

Checklist web link:
http://sydney.edu.au/paradisec/australharmony/checklist-indigenous-music-1.php#014

c.1840s–80s

15   1 song (Wiradjuri)

Wiradjuri, Upper Murray, NSW; ? c.1840, unknown provenance, words only first published Albury, NSW, 1904

15 'Aboriginal chant . . . Woradgery Tribe, upper Murray, 1840'

15 text: *Ah-a-a-a Wein bra-bra wie wie Bun-gam-bin-yah th'longa-la jung-ar mekel boom'ry-ah-a-a wein bra-bra, wein bra-bra ber-gan yel-ar yel-ar yan- lay gunning yea, gunning yea ber-gan yel-ar boon-mar yel-ar boon-mar boon-mar boon-mar-a-a boon-mar-a-a*
gloss: ? 'In peaceful happy days' [2]
analytics: Upper Murray, NSW; ECA; South-eastern PN/ Central NSW/ Wiradjuri
sources: [1] Photocopy at AIATSIS; original manuscript, one folio, 2 pages, provenance and current whereabouts unknown: *http://trove.nla.gov.au/version/41567043*; [2] 'SONG', *Albury Banner and Wodonga Express* (27 May 1904), 34: *http://nla.gov.au/nla.news-article100603667*

Commentary: The manuscript [1] appears to have been copied at the latest in the very early twentieth century. It bears the name 'N. L. Rolfe', perhaps the compiler and composer of the framing song 'Australian song', entitled *Little boy lost*. Apparently about a lost settler child found by the Wiradjuri around 1840s, the framing song, and the 'Aboriginal chant', would seem to connect the song personally with John Francis Huon Mitchell (1831–1923) (*http://nla.gov.au/nla.party-550361*).

Select bibliography: Saintilan 1993, 46–50

Other references: 'A VOCABULARY OF ABORIGINAL TERMS', *Albury Banner and Wodonga Express* (27 May 1904), 34: *http://nla.gov.au/nla.news-article100603675*;
W. M. Sherrie, 'THE WORADGERY TRIBE', *The Argus* (23 June 1906), 5: *http://nla.gov.au/nla.news-article10038425*;
'PERSONAL', *The Argus* (3 March 1923), 30: *http://nla.gov.au/nla.news-article1880156*;
'A PIONEER OF RIVERINA', *Daily Advertiser* (9 March 1923), 2: *http://nla.gov.au/nla.news-article143183376*

Checklist web link:
http://sydney.edu.au/paradisec/australharmony/checklist-indigenous-music-1.php#015

c.1840–1850

16   2 songs (Yagara)

? Yagara, Brisbane district, southern QLD; words and melody transcribed by W. A. Ogg, c.1900, from the singing of Tom Petrie (1831–1910), songs he had learned as a child, c.1840–50, with commentary by Petrie; first published Brisbane, 1904

16.1 'Bobbiwinta's mysterious disappearance'

text: *Tabal-kan wad-li/ tabal-kan wad-li/ tabal-kan wad-li/ 'ngo kun-dul nga-ri wai-yar/ ngat-la in-en-in-go/ tal-lo car-bu / ngat-la ye-ri du-wa*

gloss: 'The words had this meaning: "My oar is bad, my oar is bad; send me my boat, I'm sitting here waiting," and so on, sung slowly. Then quickly, "dulpai-i-la ngari kimmo-man" (jump over for me friends), and so to the finish. The following [musical transcription with words] is the first portion of the song' (Petrie 1904, 25)
analytics: Brisbane district, Southern QLD; ? YCA ? ECA; South-eastern PN/ Durubulic/ ? Yagara
source: Constance Campbell Petrie, *Tom Petrie's reminiscences of early Queensland (dating from 1837) recorded by his daughter* (Brisbane: Watson, Ferguson & Co., 1904) (**Petrie 1904**), 25: https://archive.org/stream/cu31924063745495#page/n49/mode/2up

16.2 'Mina'
16.2 text: *Mi-na lo-ran-da/ mi-na mar-man-do-yar-ni/ mar-man-do-yar-ni/ ko-ko-je-kó-ni/ dam-an-da-dum/ Wa! Wa!*
16.2 gloss: Petrie, who was himself taught it as a child, indicated that this is a lullaby, but could give no gloss of words or phrases.
16.2 analytics: As for **16.1**
16.2 source: Petrie 1904, 27 (commentary), 28 (music): https://archive.org/stream/cu31924063745495#page/n53/mode/2up

Select bibliography: Henry Tate, 'Aboriginal music: its artistic possibilities', *The Argus* (30 June 1923), 7 (henceforth **Tate 1923**): http://nla.gov.au/nla.news-article2002080; Saintilan 1993, 43–46

Checklist web link:
http://sydney.edu.au/paradisec/australharmony/checklist-indigenous-music-1.php#016

c.1850

17 1 song (Nyungar)
? Nyungar, south-west WA; music only, collected by Philip Chauncy (1816–1880) from unidentified performers, Swan River, WA, probably between 1841 and 1853; published Melbourne, 1878

17 'A line of one of their chants'
text: [music only, no words]
analytics: south-west WA; CA; Western PN/ Nyungar/ ? Nyungar
source: Philip Chauncy, 'Notes and anecdotes of the Aborigines of Australia', in R. Brough Smyth (ed.), *The Aborigines of Victoria: with notes relating to the habits of the natives of other parts of Australia and Tasmania* (Melbourne: John Ferres, Government Printer, 1878), volume 2, 266: https://archive.org/stream/aboriginesofvict02smyt#page/266/mode/2up

Commentary: Chauncy served as a government assistant surveyor in the colony of Western Australia from 1841 to 1853. The notes he published in 1878 also reproduced 10 portrait sketches of King George's Sound people that he had made in 1846.

Select bibliography: Hagen 1892;
Lauterer 1900, 297:
   https://archive.org/stream/australienundta00lautgoog#page/n320/mode/2up;
Saintilan 1993, 85–86, 89

Other resources: Philip Chauncy, diaries and survey books, 1840–75; DLMSQ 11, State Library of New South Wales: *http://archival.sl.nsw.gov.au/Details/archive/110347579*

Checklist web link:
http://sydney.edu.au/paradisec/australharmony/checklist-indigenous-music-1.php#017

1858–1867

18   7 songs (various language groups of QLD and NSW)

? Barunggam, Darling Downs, QLD; no. 1 (18.1), music only collected by Hermann Beckler (1828–1914), Darling Downs, 25 March 1858; no. 2 (18.2), music only collected Darling Downs, 9 April 1858; published Germany, 1868

Paakantyi, Menindee ('Meninder'), NSW; no. 3 (18.3), music and words, collected by Beckler 'some years later' (? 1861); published Germany, 1868

? Barunggam, Gayndah, QLD; no. 4 (18.4), 'Corroberri 3', music only collected by 'a German friend [of Beckler's], who was superintendent of a sheep station . . . vicinity of Gayndah'; published Germany, 1868

? Geynyan, Warwick, QLD; manuscript items, 2 further songs (18.5 and 18.6), music and words, collected near Warwick, 28 November 1857, 25 March and 9 April 1858; sent by Beckler in letter(s) to his brother in Germany; first published (facsimile of MS) Germany 1991

18.1 'Corroberri I. Darling Downs'
text: [music only, no words]
analytics: Darling Downs, QLD; YCA; South-eastern PN/ Waka-Kabi/ ? Barunggam
sources: Hermann Beckler, 'Corroberri: Ein Beitrag zur Kenntnis der Musik bei den australischen Ureinwohnern', *Globus: illustrierte Zeitschrift für Länder-und Völkerkunde* 13 (1868) (**Beckler 1868**), 82–84:
https://books.google.com.au/books?id=D6BBAAAAcAAJ&pg=PA82;
J. H. Voigt, 'Die Musik der Aborigines im südlichen Queensland: eine frühe Quelle', in Martin Kintzinger, Wolfgang Sturner, and Johannes Zahlten (eds), *Das andere Wahrnehmen; Beiträge zur europäischen Geschichte; August Nitschke zum 65. Geburtstag gewidmet* (Cologne: Bohlau Verlag, 1991) (**Voigt 1991**), 547–552 (reproduces Beckler's MS transcriptions);
David Parsons, *Waringh waringh: a history of Aboriginal people in the Warwick area and their land* (Maryvale: David Parsons, 2003) (**Parsons 2003**):
http://eprints.usq.edu.au/4687 (pages 77 and 79 reproduce Beckler's MS transcriptions from Voigt 1991) (this song MS = Parsons 2003, 77, top of page)

18.2 'Klage oder Todtenlied [lament or death song], Darling Downs'
text: [music only, no words]
analytics: As for **18.1**
sources: As for **18.1** (MS = Parsons 2003, 77, bottom of page)

18.3 'Corroberri II. Upper Darling River. Meninder' [i.e. Menindee]
text: Bai indi bai indi balema balegna onbai indi bai indi gan on bale
gloss: *Hier möge nur noch der den Anfang machende Gesang, eine Hymne, wenn man will, Musik und Text treu wiedergegeben, Platz finden. Ich ließ mir nachher sagen, es sei ein Gebet, eine Bitte an ihren Gott, um ein großes Uebel, vielleicht eine Krankheit, von ihnen abzuwenden*

(Beckler 1868, 84), 'Here there is only space for the opening song, a hymn, if you like, with music and text faithfully represented. I heard from later enquiries that it was a prayer, a request to their god, to avert a great evil, perhaps an illness.'
analytics: Menindee ('Meninder'), Darling River, NSW; CA; South-eastern PN/ Darling Group/ Paakantyi
sources: As for **18.1**

18.4 'Corrobberri III. Gayndah'
text: [music only, no words]
analytics: Gayndah, QLD; YCA; South-eastern PN/ Waka-Kabi/ ? Waga-Waga
sources: As for **18.1** (MS = Parsons 2003, 79 [example 1 of 4])

18.5 [Beckler MS]
text: [indecipherable]
analytics: ? Warwick, QLD; ECA; South-eastern PN/ Bandjalangic/ Geynyan
source: MS = Voigt 1991, Parsons 2003, 79 [example 1 of 4]

18.6 'I' [Beckler MS]
text: [indecipherable]
analytics: As for **18.5**
source: MS = Voigt 1991, Parsons 2003, 79 [example 2 of 4]

18.7 'IV' [Beckler MS]
text: (music only, no words)
analytics: As for **18.5**
source: MS = Voigt 1991, Parsons 2003, 79 [example 4 of 4]

Select bibliography: Hagen 1892;
Wallaschek 1893, [343]:
> *https://archive.org/stream/primitivemusicin00wall#page/n343/mode/2up* (**18.2** from Beckler 1868);

Stephen Jeffries and Michael Kertesz (eds), *A journey to Cooper's Creek: Hermann Beckler* (Carlton: Melbourne University Press, Miegunyah Press, State Library of Victoria, 1993); Saintilan 1993, 74–76, 86–87;

Ian D. Clark and Fred Cahir (eds), *The Aboriginal story of Burke and Wills: forgotten narratives* (Collingwood: CSIRO Publishing, 2013), 85 (commentary), 111–13 (appendix 5.2: English translation of Beckler 1868 by D. M. Dodd), 114

Checklist web link:
http://sydney.edu.au/paradisec/australharmony/checklist-indigenous-music-1.php#018

1860

19 *1 song (Paakantyi)*

Paakantyi, *far west NSW*; music and words sung and translated by **Walwallim**, transcribed by Ludwig Becker (1808–61), Menindee NSW, November 1860; MS; music first published 1979

---

19 'Anaruka-song (Creek-song)' (Song of Walwallim)
text: *Anaruka wal-li walli madin haa na-ruk car rol-gun na ge all san-u-ri wai ki-wai ki yen dai lom hnai geng na da mi*

gloss: 'Anaruka! you must be quick, come down, I can not wait for you long; No man can wait for you long I am going to sleep (to die)' (Becker 27 Nov. 1860). Becker precedes this gloss with a note: 'Anaruka is the word for creek but often given as a name to girls. There is a truly poetical conception in the double meaning of this word. Wallwallim (name of a Blackfellow) sings: . . . .'.
analytics: Menindee, Darling River, far west NSW; ? CA; South-eastern PN/ Darling Group/ Paakantyi
sources and documentation: Ludwig Becker, despatch to the Royal Society of Victoria, from Menindee NSW, 27 November 1860, State Library of Victoria, MS13071, Box 2082/4: *http://www.burkeandwills.net.au/Despatches/Becker/Beckers_Letter_09.htm*; *http://www.burkeandwills.net.au/Despatches/Becker/Beckers_Letter_11.htm* (omits music); 'ROYAL SOCIETY OF VICTORIA', *The Argus* (11 December 1860), 5: *http://nla.gov.au/nla.news-article5694801* (printed from Becker's MS, omits music); Marjorie Tipping (ed.), *Ludwig Becker: artist & naturalist with the Burke & Wills expedition* (Melbourne: Melbourne University Press, The Library Council of Victoria, 1979), 190 (modern edition 0of Becker's musical transcription)

Select bibliography: Tipping 1979 (as above)

Other resources: Ludwig Becker, [watercolour sketch] Depot Junction: The Bamamoro Cr. with the Darling, 7 miles from Minindie [sic], up the Darling, Nov. 1. 60; State Library of Victoria: *http://handle.slv.vic.gov.au/10381/140047*

Checklist web link:
http://sydney.edu.au/paradisec/australharmony/checklist-indigenous-music-1.php#019

c.1861

20 1 song (Narrinyeri)

***Narrinyeri (Ngarrindjeri)**, south-east SA*; collected by George Taplin (1831–79), 'written down as it sung by the aborigines about eighteen years ago' (so about 1861), probably near Lake Alexandrina (Raukkan); published 1879

20 'Narrinyeri corrobbery'
text: *Puntin Narrinyerar Puntin Narrinyerar O, O, O/ Puntin Narrinyerar O, O, O, O, O/ Yun terpulani ar/ Tuppun an wangamar/ Tyiwewar ngoppun ar O, O, O, O/ Puntin Narrinyerar, &c./* (Taplin 1879b, 39)
gloss: The Narrinyeri are coming, soon they will appear, carrying kangaroos, quickly they are walking (Taplin 1879b, 39)
analytics: Lake Alexandrina, south-east SA; ECA; South-eastern PN/ Lower Murray/ Ngarrindjeri
sources: [1] George Taplin, *The folklore, manners, customs, and languages of the South Australian Aborigines: gathered from inquiries made by authority of South Australian government* (Adelaide: E. Spiller, 1879a), 106 (music and text), 107 (commentary): *https://archive.org/stream/folkloremannersc00taplrich#page/106/mode/2up*;
[2] George Taplin, 'The Narrinyeri', in J. D. Woods (introd.), *The native tribes of South Australia: comprising the Narrinyeri by the Rev. George Taplin* . . . (Adelaide: E. S. Wigg & Son,

1879b), 39 (song text and translation without music):
https://archive.org/stream/nativetribessou00taplgoog#page/n103/mode/2up

Other documentation: George Taplin, diary 1859–79, State Library of South Australia, PRG 186–1/3;

Joe Lane (ed.), *The journals of the reverend George Taplin, missionary to the Ngarrindjeri people of the Lower Murray, Lakes and the Coorong, 1859–1879* (1997):
http://www.firstsources.info/uploads/3/4/5/4/34544232/taplins_diary_1859-79.pdf;

P. A. Clarke, 'Myth as history? The Ngurunderi Dreaming of the Lower Murray, South Australia', *Records of the South Australian Museum* 28/1 (1995), 143–157, esp. 146:
https://archive.org/stream/RecordsSouthAus28Sout#page/146/mode/2up

Commentary: In [2], Taplin also gave words and translation of another song (without music), 'A native song or corrobery, on *The railway train*.' In his journal (30 June 1859), Taplin made reference to similar chants: 'Two of their songs in particular attracted my attention. One was called "The Nurundere", and is about God, and the other is about "Shall I ever see my country again", a sort of native "Ranz des vaches". The former began with a low chant as if they were chanting Latin. However, all through the piece they say the same words over and over again, then the chant rose higher and higher with beat of the Tartengk and native drum, then it sank again and the men's voices broke in shouting in time to the chant and brandishing the weapons with tartengk. Then the shrill treble of the women broke in like an imploring vociferation in answer to the shouts of the men. These ceased, and the whole concluded with a loud chant to the beat of the tartengk and drum. The latter piece was to slower time, and was very plaintive and wild. One of the men asked while I listened if I could write what they sang in a letter.'

Select bibliography: George Taplin, *The Narrinyeri: an account of the tribes of South Australian Aborigines inhabiting the country around the Lakes Alexandrina, Albert, and Coorong, and the lower part of the River Murray: their manners and customs, also, an account of the mission at Port Macleay* (Adelaide: J. T. Shawyer, 1874):
http://catalog.hathitrust.org/Record/008399650;

'THE NARRINYERI', *South Australian Register* (28 May 1874), 5:
http://nla.gov.au/nla.news-article39819493;

James Duff Brown, *Characteristic songs and dances of all nations* (London: Bayley and Ferguson, 1901), 258:
https://archive.org/stream/characteristicso00brow2#page/258/mode/2up;

Tate 1923: *http://nla.gov.au/nla.news-article2002080*;

W. W. T., 'Music, Aboriginal', in Arthur Wilberforce Jose and James Carter (eds), *Australian encyclopaedia, volume 2 (Mab-Z)* (Sydney: Angus & Robertson, 1926), 169 (music and words from [1])

Checklist web link:
http://sydney.edu.au/paradisec/australharmony/checklist-indigenous-music-1.php#020

c.1863–65

21 4 songs (Gureng-Gureng)

Gureng-Gureng, Three Moon Creek, Upper Burnett River, QLD; spelt phonetically in the 'Goorang-Goorang' dialect, obtained by Reginald Byard Buchanan Clayton (1845–1927),

Moon Creek, Upper Burnett River, Queensland, about the years 1863–5; the musical notation is by Isabel S. Clayton (1873–1925); published London, 1910

21.1 'No. I' (Queensland corroboree song 1)
text: *Yar yung-ein mar-ar moon-ie yung-ein mar-ar ce-leen-bar ar ce-leen-bar ar ce-leen-bar ar. Joo vari yung-ein mar-ar ce-leen-bar ar ar. Joo-oo-vari yar yung-ein mar-ar moonie*
analytics (21.1–4): Three Moon Creek, Upper Burnett River, QLD; YCA; South-eastern PN/ Waka-Kabic/ Gureng-Gureng
source: R. R. Marett, 'Queensland corroboree songs', *Folklore* 21/1 (March 1910) (**Marett 1910**), 86–87:
https://en.wikisource.org/wiki/Page:Folk-lore_-_A_Quarterly_Review._Volume_21,_1910. djvu/114; *https://en.wikisource.org/wiki/Page:Folk-lore_-_A_Quarterly_Review._ Volume_21,_1910.djvu/115*

21.2 'No. II' (Queensland corroboree song 2)
text: *A milearah vun-gah tooey bithera beera too varina bithera berra anama-danava ar-ar merah anadadanava ava our our merah anamadanava our anama-danava our iddlety way*
source: As for **21.1**

21.3 'No. III' (Queensland corroboree song 3)
text: *Animularine mong aliong animularine mong aliong amarabula la la clang amarabula la la clang animularine mong aliong amarabula la la clang animularine mong aliong*
source: Marett 1910, 87–88
https://en.wikisource.org/wiki/Page:Folk-lore_-_A_Quarterly_Review._Volume_21,_1910. djvu/115; *https://en.wikisource.org/wiki/Page:Folk-lore_-_A_Quarterly_Review._ Volume_21,_1910.djvu/116*

21.4 'No. IV' (Queensland corroboree song 4)
text: *Cuniem cuniem ia cawar barney vous bundah boomerah lar bundah boomerah lar ar bundah boomerah lar*
source: Marett 1910, 88: *https://en.wikisource.org/wiki/Page:Folk-lore_-_A_Quarterly_ Review._Volume_21,_1910.djvu/116*

Select bibliography: R. C. Riley and M. Curr, 'No. 165 – Upper Burnett River, Mount Debateable, and Gayndah', in Edward Micklethwaite Curr (ed.), *The Australian race: its origin, languages, customs, place of landing in Australia and the routes by which it spread itself over the continent . . . volume 3* (Melbourne: John Ferres, Government Printer, 1887), 150–51:
https://archive.org/stream/cu31924026093835#page/n163/mode/2up;
'TO AUSTRALIA IN 61. PIONEERING IN THE BURNETT. MR. R. B. B. CLAYTON'S REMINISCENCES', *The Queenslander* (31 October 1925), 11:
http://nla.gov.au/nla.news-article25107759;
Lisa Marcussen, Selected bibliography of the Gooreng Gooreng / Gureng Gureng / Gurang Gurang language and people held in the AIATSIS Library (Canberra: AIATSIS, April 2015): *http://aiatsis.gov.au/research/guides-and-resources/ language-and-people-bibliographies*

Checklist web link:
http://sydney.edu.au/paradisec/australharmony/checklist-indigenous-music-1.php#021

c.1858–75

22   4 songs (Uutaalnganu)

Uutaalnganu, *Cape York Peninsula, north QLD*; words and music transcribed by Edouard Garnier, France, 1876, from the singing of adoptive Uutaalnganu man, Narcisse Pelletier (1844–94), or 'Anco', who learned them there between 1858 and 1875; published Paris, 1876

22.1   'No. 1' ('Air de danse' ['dance tune'])
text: *Pakiéro aré pakiéro aré ia méouais kia pour naré ia méouais kia pour naré ia men kaaié ia men kaaié*
analytics (22.1–4): Cape York; YCA; Northern PN/ Northern Paman/ Uutaalnganu
source (22.1–4): Constant Merland, *Dix-sept ans chez les sauvages: Narcisse Pelletier avec portrait, fac-simile, musique et dessin d'armes* (Paris: E. Dentu, 1876), appendice: Édouard Garnier, 'Observations musicales sur les chants de Narcisse Pelletier', 127–35 (music transcriptions, unpaginated, follow p. 135):
http://aiatsis.gov.au/sites/default/files/catalogue_resources/a394874.pdf

22.2   'No. 2' ('Le Hiento – se chante la nuit' ['sung at night'])
text: *Hiento gallinand galliand hienlo gallinand gallinand para gallinand gallinand para gallinand gallinand*
gloss: Waterlily root carry-we, carry-we. Waterlily root carry-we, carry-we. White man carry-we, carry we. White man carry-we, carry we (see **Commentary** below)

22.3   'No. 3' ('Air de danse' ['dance tune'])
text: *Boba ia boba boba ia boba turba turba turba vouloi turba turba turba vouloi boba ia boba*

22.4   'No. 4' ('La ponghé lapon – une invocation à la lune' ['an invocation of the moon'])
text: *La ponghé lapon la ponghé lapon laniméné laniméné cout chiava tcher poulai cout chiava tcher poulai la ponghé lapon*

Commentary: According to Pelletier, the first and third songs were dance tunes, the second sung at night, and the fourth was an invocation of the moon. However, the words of songs 1, 3, and 4 meant nothing to Pelletier, who understood they belonged to 'another tribe'. The second song, however, he was able to explain, and based on Garnier's account and transcription, anthropologist David Thompson (Anderson, 357 note 2) reconstructed the second song as: *Yunthu kalinan kalinan yunthu kalinan kalinan para kalinan kalinan para kalinan kalinan* (Waterlily root carry-we, carry-we. Waterlily root carry-we, carry-we. White man carry-we, carry we. White man carry-we, carry we).

Select bibliography: Stephanie Anderson (trans.), *Pelletier: the forgotten castaway of Cape York, introductory essay and translation by Stephanie Anderson; from the original book Dix-sept ans chez les sauvages: les aventure de Narcisse Pelletier by Constant Merland; ethnographic commentary by Athol Chase* (Melbourne: Melbourne Books, 2009);
Graeme Skinner, 'Narcisse Pelletier', *Australharmony* (an online resource toward the history of music and musicians in colonial and early Federation Australia):
http://sydney.edu.au/paradisec/australharmony/pelletier-narcisse.php

Checklist web link:
http://sydney.edu.au/paradisec/australharmony/checklist-indigenous-music-1.php#022

c.1867–84

23 2 songs (Gabi Gabi)

Gabi Gabi, Mary River, Burnett River district, central QLD; collected and transcribed by John Mathew (1849–1929); published Melbourne, 1887

23.1 'Corroboree I' [Mary River]
text: *Milo longo wombo laililaiya . . . guvai alinge, guvai alingo . . . ye lingo*
analytics: Mary River, Burnett River district, central QLD; ECA; South-eastern PN/ Waka-Kabic/ Gabi Gabi
Source: John Mathew, 'Mary River and the Bunya Bunya country', in Edward Micklethwaite Curr (ed.), *The Australian race: its origin, languages, customs, place of landing in Australia and the routes by which it spread itself over the continent . . . volume 3* (Melbourne: John Ferres, Government Printer, 1887) (***Mathew 1887***), 167–69 (commentary), 170–71 (music):
https://archive.org/stream/cu31924026093835#page/n183/mode/2up

23.2 'Corroboree II' [Mary River]
text: *Weño karinga dha kalana nuyum nuyuma . . . tuanboroma buburindika wone dhomkiya worethe . . .*
analytics: As for **23.1**
source: Mathew 1887, 172–23:
https://archive.org/stream/cu31924026093835#page/n185/mode/2up

Commentary: Of the first song, Mathew (1887, 169) said, 'The words are not Kabi', but 'the second example . . . is written in Kabi'.

Select bibliography: John Mathew, *Eaglehawk and crow; a study of the Australian Aborigines, including an inquiry into their origin and a survey of Australian languages* (London: David Nutt; Melbourne: Mullen and Slade, 1899), 140–41:
https://archive.org/stream/eaglehawkcrowstu00math#page/140/mode/2up;
Tate 1923: *http://nla.gov.au/nla.news-article2002080*;
Saintilan 1993, 83–85;
Malcolm D. Prentis, 'Research and friendship: John Mathew and his Aboriginal informants', *Aboriginal History* 22 (1998), 62–93:
http://press.anu.edu.au/wp-content/uploads/2016/02/article0516.pdf

Checklist web link:
http://sydney.edu.au/paradisec/australharmony/checklist-indigenous-music-1.php#023

1882–83

24 3 songs (Queensland language groups)

? Pirriya, Thomson River, western QLD [1] (**24.1**);
? Wargamay, Herbert River, north QLD [2] and [3] (**24.2** and **24.3**); all three collected by Carl Lumholtz (1851–1922) between August 1882 and July 1883; published London, 1889

24.1 'Korroboree . . . the melody sung to this dance'
text: *La la la la la . . . altogether yarn away . . . Bahl bood'gry borando . . .*

analytics: Thomson River, western QLD; YCA; Northern PN/ Maric/ ? Pirriya
sources: Carl Lumholtz, *Among cannibals: an account of four years' travels in Australia and of camp life with the aborigines of Queensland* (London: J. Murray, 1889) (**Lumholtz 1889**), 41–42:

https://archive.org/stream/amongcannibalsac1889lumh#page/41/mode/2up

24.2 'The song in vogue at this time, and which was sung repeatedly'

text: *Mollemombâ (à) mombâ varinâ katsuburâ indangô gângoril-la* . . .
analytics: Herbert River, north QLD; YCA; Northern PN/ Dyirbalic/ ? Wargamay
source: Lumholtz 1889, 156–57:

https://archive.org/stream/amongcannibalsac1889lumh#page/156/mode/2up

24.3 'War-song'

text: *Wombon maraery! wombon maraery! moridan koby beebon bindalgoh!*
gloss: 'war-song, which celebrates the knob on the throwing stick' (Lumholtz 1889, 158)
analytics: As for **24.2**
source: Lumholtz 1889, 158:

https://archive.org/stream/amongcannibalsac1889lumh#page/158/mode/2up

Commentary: Of the first of these songs, Lumholtz (1889, 41) says, 'melody sung to this dance was genuine Australian, but the text was mixed with English words'; of the second, 'Doubtless it originated in the vicinity of Rockhampton . . . [but] on the Herbert River . . . it was sung without being understood' (Lumholtz 1889, 157).

Select bibliography: Covell 1967, 67, 325;

Terry G. Birtles, 'Carl Lumholtz: a translation of answers to a questionnaire', *Queensland Heritage* 3/4 (1976): 4–22: *http://espace.library.uq.edu.au/view/UQ:246314*;

Grace Koch, 'Dyirbal Gama songs of Cape York', 46–47, in Margaret Clunies Ross et al., *Songs of Aboriginal Australia* (Sydney: University of Sydney, 1987), 43–62;

Saintilan 1993, 39–43

Checklist web link:

http://sydney.edu.au/paradisec/australharmony/checklist-indigenous-music-1.php#024

c.1840–c.1885

25 3 songs (Kulin)

Kulin, Yarra region, VIC; song [1] (**25.1**) (in 'Woiwurrung') composed by or about **Kurburu** (c.1798–1849), c.1840s; song [2] (**25.2**) composed by or about **Wenberi**/Winberri (c.1817–40), c.1840s; song 3 (**25.3**) (in 'Wurunjerri'); all sung by **William Barak** (1824–1903), music and words transcribed by George W. Torrance (1835–1907), Melbourne, VIC, c.1885, published 1887; words transcribed and translated separately by A. W. Howitt (1830–1908), published 1887

25.1 'Kurburu's song'

text: *Enagūréa nŭng ngalourma barein gūrŭkba mŭrnein būrŭnbai nganŭngba lilira mŭringa* [Howitt's transcription]

gloss: 'You cut across my track, you spilled my blood, and broke your tomahawk on me' (translated by Barak; Howitt 1887, 333)

analytics: Yarra River, VIC; ECA; South-eastern PN/ Kulin/ Woiwurung
source: G. W. Torrance, 'Music of the Australian Aboriginals', *The Journal of the Anthropological Institute of Great Britain and Ireland* 16 (1887) (**Torrance 1887**), 337:
https://archive.org/stream/journalofroyalan16royauoft#page/337/mode/2up

25.2 'Wenberi's song'
text: *Nge tuigár ngalá ngibnba ngalūgá diudirŭnding nga Dŭlŭr wīlūit wa weindŭng bŭnjil mameng-ngata yenin thŭlŭrmeik nga wŭrngalŭk-eik* [Howitt's transcription]
gloss: 'We go all (the) bones to all of them/ shining white (in) this Dulur country./ The noise rushing (of) Bunjil father ours singing / (in) breast mine this inside-mine' (Howitt 1887, 331). Howitt notes that the song is 'a good example of the belief held by these "sacred singers" that they were inspired by something more than mortal when composing them. In this case it is "Bunjil" himself who "rushes down" into the heart of the singer.'
analytics: Mount Macedon; ECA; South-eastern PN/ Kulin/ Woiworung (Mount Macedon dialect)
source: Torrance 1887, 338:
https://archive.org/stream/journalofroyalan16royauoft#page/338/mode/2up

25.3 'Corroboree song' (Barak)
text: *ē ngā wăjĕlāi̯ya bŭn-dĕ́a gĕnunwĭ́l/ ngā burdăngală̄ yĕlengĕ́a gŏnowăra/ ngā wăgelāi̯ya bŭn-dĕ́a, &c.* [Torrances's transcription]
gloss: This 'corrobboree song ... is one used by the Wurunjerri, but of which I have no translation' (Howitt 1904, 422).
analytics: Yarra region; ECA; South-eastern PN/ Kulin/ Wurunjeri
source: Torrance 1887, 339:
https://archive.org/stream/journalofroyalan16royauoft#page/339/mode/2up

Additional sources and documentation: A. W. Howitt, 'Notes on songs and songmakers of some Australian tribes', *Journal of the Anthropological Institute of Great Britain and Ireland* 16 (1887), 327–35: *https://archive.org/stream/journalofroyalan16royauoft#page/326/mode/2up* (words and translations of 1 and 2 only);
A. W. Howitt, *The native tribes of south-east Australia* (London: Macmillan and Co., 1904), 418–425: *https://archive.org/stream/nativetribesofso00howiuoft#page/420/mode/2up* (Torrance's 3 music examples reproduced, 420–421)

Commentary: Wurunjeri *ngurungaeta* (elder) William Barak was one of the leading Aboriginal public figures in colonial era Victoria (*http://nla.gov.au/nla.party-1308870*). Torrance's transcription session with Barak probably took place at Coranderrk, and appears to have been arranged not only by Howitt, but also by their mutual friend, anthropologist Lorimer Fison (1832–1907). Kurburu's and Wenberi's songs almost certainly date back to the 1840s. According to William Thomas (1791–1867), 'Kur-bo-roo, a well-known Western Port black, and held in high esteem as a sorcerer, a dreamer, and diviner, was named "The Bear" … [the native bear]' (Brough Smyth 1878, volume 1, 447–448 footnote).

Select bibliography: Etheridge 1891, 45:
https://archive.org/stream/contributionsto00ethegoog#page/n91/mode/2up;
Tate 1923: *http://nla.gov.au/nla.news-article2002080*;
Saintilan 1993, 80–82;

Marie Hansen Fels, *'I succeeded once': the Aboriginal protectorate on the Mornington Peninsula, 1839–1840* (Aboriginal History Monograph 22) (Canberra: ANU Press; Aboriginal History Inc, 2011), 114–15, 241–44: *http://press.anu.edu.au/?p=110711*;

Lisa Marcussen (comp.), Selected bibliography of material on the Woiwurrung / Wurundjeri / Woiwurung language and people held in the AIATSIS Library (2015):
http://aiatsis.gov.au/research/guides-and-resources/language-and-people-bibliographies;

Skinner 2017, this volume

Other references: R. Brough Smyth (ed.), *The Aborigines of Victoria: with notes relating to the habits of the natives of other parts of Australia and Tasmania* (Melbourne: John Ferres, Government Printer, 1878), volume 1, 447–48 footnote:
https://archive.org/stream/aboriginesofvict01smyt#page/447/mode/2up

Checklist web link:
http://sydney.edu.au/paradisec/australharmony/checklist-indigenous-music-1.php#025

1888

26 1 song (Western Torres Strait)

Western Torres Strait dialect ('Mabuiagic'), Western Torres Strait Islands, QLD; music and words transcribed by Alfred Haddon, November 1888, from performance by Mabuiag and Naghir Islanders (**Kudumu** of Nagirm and **Maruděn** and **Zagăra** of Muralug) on Thursday Island, QLD; first published Britain, 1890

26 'Waiitut kap kudu' (Saw-fish dance song)
text: *Ngai natan he! Danabi he! Mari naiděm he! he, he, wa! / Ngita kai he! Ngai keka he! – he – ! Tuwa patan he! He – he! / Yawa bōi he! Wa pōnipan he! Yawa bōi he! he, he, wa! / Wapi sěnu ngapa! Iaubu ulaipa he! Pula sena ngapa. Iabu mulsipa! Sanděral he!*
gloss: Now I can see myself reflected in the pools on the reef as in a mirror / You cut the shoot of the coco palm for me / Farewell dead coco palm leaves. Ho! there's the lightning / Fish now approach the shore, and we must build fish-weirs in their route.
analytics: Western Torres Strait; TSI; Northern PN/ Western Torres Strait/ Kala Lagaw Ya
source: A. C. Haddon, 'Ethnography of the western tribes of Torres Straits', *The Journal of the Anthropological Institute of Great Britain and Ireland* 19 (1890), 376–80:
https://archive.org/stream/journalanthropo08irelgoog#page/n411/mode/2up

Additional documentation: A. C. Haddon, 'The secular and ceremonial dances of Torres Straits', *Internationales Archiv für Ethnographie* 6 (1893), 131–62:
https://archive.org/stream/bub_gb_inBGAAAAMAAJ#page/n137/mode/2up;

A. C. Haddon et al., 'Magic and religion', in Haddon (ed.), *Reports of the Cambridge Anthropological Expedition to Torres Straits* (1898), volume 5: sociology, magic and religion of the western islanders (Cambridge: The University Press, 1904), 343:
https://archive.org/stream/reportsofcambrid05hadd#page/342/mode/2up

Select bibliography: Alice Bertha Gomme, *The traditional games of England, Scotland and Ireland: with tunes, singing rhymes and methods of playing according to the variants extant and recorded in different parts of the kingdom . . . volume 2, Oats and beans – Would you*

know (London: David Nutt, 1898), 519-20:
https://archive.org/stream/traditionalgames02gommuoft#page/519/mode/2up

Checklist web link:
http://sydney.edu.au/paradisec/australharmony/checklist-indigenous-music-1.php#026

c.1890–1900

27 5 songs (Maric)

Maric, Maranoa and Warrego districts, NSW/QLD border; transcribed and translated by Harold Octavius Lethbridge (1880–1944) and his sister Flora Josepha Lethbridge (1873/4–1956; 'Mrs. Murphy' – see **27.5**), from various performers including **Boss Davey (Mundâlo)** (d.1916), Forest Vale Station, near Mitchell, c.1890–1900; published 1937

27.1 'I. Maranoa lullaby'
text: *Mumma warrunno murra wathunno* [repeat]
gloss: 'To this song the mother rocked her baby to sleep in the bark cradle, using her foot to avoid stooping.'
analytics: Maranoa district, NSW/QLD border; YCA; Northern PN/ Maric/ ? Gunggari
source: H. O. Lethbridge and Arthur S. Loam, *Australian aboriginal songs: melodies, rhythm and words truly and authentically aboriginal collected and translated . . . accompaniments arranged . . .* (Melbourne: Allan & Co., 1937) (**Lethbridge and Loam 1937**), 4–5:
http://nla.gov.au/nla.obj-172234124/view#page/n4/mode/1up

27.2a 'II. Bingo corroborees: (a) Bingo bingo'
text: *Bingo bingo carmoo curree . . . cowal cowal cowal cowal . . .*
gloss: 'This is a warning to a youth against bathing in a water-hole at the junction of Bailey's Creek with the Maranoa River. This water-hole was inhabited by a Bunyip.'
analytics: As for **27.1**
source: Lethbridge and Loam 1937, 6–7:
http://nla.gov.au/nla.obj-172234124/view#page/n6/mode/1up

27.2b 'II. Bingo corroborees: (b) The porcupine song'
text: *Wangur dthunnee dthunee dthunee . . . Goolgoo boora goolgoo boora goolgoo boora*
gloss: 'The droll behaviour of the *ECHIDNA never failed to fill these simple-minded and altogether delightful children of nature with uncontrollable laughter. Wai! and Yakai! are words of exclamation.'
analytics: As for **27.1**
source: Lethbridge and Loam 1937, 8–9:
http://nla.gov.au/nla.obj-172234124/view#page/n8/mode/1up

27.2c 'II. Bingo corroborees: (c) The blind blackfellow'
text: *Ngunee ngunee dthara goon doo . . . Ngia ngia ngian ngia . . .*
gloss: 'A blind blackfellow finding his way back to camp' ('The performers in this Corroboree, coming forward to the cleared ground (stage) lit by a semicircle of fires, would imitate the movements of a blind man endeavouring to cross a gully. The orchestra – gins, piccaninnies and non-performers would sing the melody whilst the performers would maintain perfect rhythm and graceful poise.')

analytics: As for **27.1**
source: Lethbridge and Loam 1937, 9:
http://nla.gov.au/nla.obj-172234124/view#page/n9/mode/1up

27.3 'III. A Warrego lament'
text: *Meen gutte meen galina yarin ja ya reen yer mo dtharrbinga buthee marber go thun bin a yun ga ween jin ah! ween jin ah! been a guttee booki yaka!*
gloss: 'It is the anguished cry of a doomed race – stricken by disease brought by the invading white man.' ('Introduced from the Warrego Tribe.')
analytics: Warrego district, south central QLD; YCA; Northern PN/ Maric/ ? Pirriya
source: Lethbridge and Loam 1937, 10–11:
http://nla.gov.au/nla.obj-172234124/view#page/n10/mode/1up

27.4 'IV. Bangee rang ananah'
text: *Bangee rang anan-ah dthiblurrah bangee rang anan-ah dthiblurrah bangee rang anan-ah willy nurry no urmunday wowowo injiaco mookooloo dthoorroo wookoonin*
gloss: 'A Hunting Song'
analytics: As for **27.1**
source: Lethbridge and Loam 1937, 12–13:
http://nla.gov.au/nla.obj-172234124/view#page/n12/mode/1up

27.5 'V. Jabbin jabbin'
text: *Jabbin jabbin kirroo kagla kurra kurra kirroo ka jabbin jabbin kirroo ka*
gloss: 'This is not a corroboree. It is a song sung round the camp fire.'
analytics: As for **27.1**
source: Lethbridge and Loam 1937, 14–15:
http://nla.gov.au/nla.obj-172234124/view#page/n14/mode/1up

Other documentation: Lethbridge and Loam 1937, 2:
 http://nla.gov.au/nla.obj-172234124/view#page/n2/mode/1up [commentary];
'ABORIGINAL SONGS', *The Independent* (9 April 1937), 3:
 http://nla.gov.au/nla.news-article130217175;
'ABORIGINAL SONGS. A Valuable Collection' and 'Aboriginal songs explained (By H. O. Lethbridge)', *The Australian Musical News* (1 July 1937), 22

Other media resources: Harold Blair singing Maranoa Lullaby on an unreleased recording from 1950, opening only (Australian Screen):
 http://aso.gov.au/titles/music/maranoa-lullaby/clip1;
Ethel Munn, Maranoa Lullaby, First Languages Australia, posted 29 June 2014:
 https://vimeo.com/99494828; *http://www.qilac.org.au/film/maranoa-lullaby*

Checklist web link:
 http://sydney.edu.au/paradisec/australharmony/checklist-indigenous-music-1.php#027

c.1893

28 *4 songs (Nyungar)*

***Nyungar**, Gingin and South-west region, WA*; music and words transcribed and sent to A. F. Calvert (1872–1946) by an unidentified reporter, by c.1893; published London, 1894

28.1 'During the ceremony of presentation … song' [Calvert 1]
text: *Wilbeniah yandiwirrie …* [words repeated and alternated]
gloss: 'Some time ago … one of the white colonists, held in high esteem by one of the native tribes near Guigin, was presented by them with what may be best described as "tribal rights" (corresponding to citizenship) over certain lands. During the ceremony of presentation was sung the following song, and it may be explained that "Wilbeniah" was the name of the land, and "Yandiwirrie" the name by which the natives knew their friend. When they sang the first word they pointed to the land, and when they sang the second they pointed to the adopted tribesman, indicating by this probably that the land was his, and that he belonged to the land' (Calvert 1892, 34–35).
analytics (28.1–4): South-west region, WA; CA; Western PN/ Nyungar/ Nyungar
source (28.1–4): Albert F. Calvert, *The Aborigines of Western Australia* (London: W. Milligan and Co., 1894), 34–38: *https://archive.org/stream/aboriginesofwest00calv#page/35/mode/2up*

28.2 'After the marriage … [song]' [Calvert 2]
text: *Harinan oh! harinan oh! … woorinan oh! woorinan oh! …*
gloss: 'Two natives were married … After the marriage, a party of natives, male and female, belonging to their tribe gathered round the fire in front of their hut and sang the following measure, scores of times: "Harinan" was the name of the Benedict, and "Woorinan" that of his Beatrice' (Calvert 1892, 35–36).

28.3 'Corroborie' [Calvert 3]
text: *Ah barrabahnddurrah birrin goorah ah* [repeated six times] *barrabahndidurrah birringoorah ah, barrabahndidurrah! ah barrabahndidurrah! ah, barrabahndidurrah! birringoorah ah!* [Da capo]
gloss: 'sung at a corroborie, or native dance … What the words mean I was never able to learn' (Calvert 1892, 36).

28.4 'Recitative' [Calvert 4]
text: *What for you white fellow wongy you gib'em chickpence and you nothing giberem poor old debbil me poor granny me me nothing nalgo and want'em bread and you big fellow lie tell'em*
gloss: '*Wongy* means *say* or *promise*, and that I had promised her something was one of her pleasant little fictions' (Calvert 1892, 38).

Select bibliography: Calvert 1892: *https://archive.org/details/aboriginesofwest00calvuoft* [earlier version of Calvert 1894, without reference to the songs];
Clint Bracknell, 'Kooral Dwonk-katitjiny (listening to the past): Aboriginal language, songs and history in south-western Australia', *Aboriginal History* 38 (2014), 1–19: *http://press-files.anu.edu.au/downloads/press/p308321/pdf/ch01.pdf*

Checklist web link:
http://sydney.edu.au/paradisec/australharmony/checklist-indigenous-music-1.php#028

c.1895 (possibly much earlier)

29 1 song (Waka-Kabic)

Waka-Kabic, Burnett River, QLD; music transcription only, probably collected and transcribed by Charles Handley, possibly much earlier than the publication date of 1897

29 'Burnett River corroboree'

text: music transcription only
analytics: Burnett River, QLD; YCA; South-eastern PN/ Waka-Kabic/ ? Gureng Gureng
source: [Communication], *The Journal of the Anthropological Institute of Great Britain and Ireland* 26 (1897), 436: *http://www.jstor.org/stable/2842015*

Commentary: 'Burnett River corroboree: MR. JAMES EDGE-PARTINGTON sends the following corroboree music from the Burnett River, Queensland, forwarded to him by Mr. Charles Handley: [music transcription] * Signifies the beat of boomerangs, nullah nullahs, etc., while the gins pad the opossum skins.'

Select bibliography: Saintilan 1993, 78–79

Checklist web link:
http://sydney.edu.au/paradisec/australharmony/checklist-indigenous-music-1.php#029

1898

30 28 songs (Eastern and Western Torres Strait)

Meriam Mir (and possibly Torres Strait Creole), Murray Island (Eastern Torres Strait); sound recordings by Charles Samuel Myers (1873–1946), collected 1898; text transcriptions by Alfred Cort Haddon (1855–1940) and Sidney Herbert Ray (1858–1939); musical transcriptions by Charles Myers; first published Cambridge, 1908 and 1912 (**30.1–18**)

Western Torres Strait dialects ('Mabuiagic'), such as Kala Lagaw Ya, Western Torres Strait Islands (Mabuiag, Yam, and Saibai); sound recordings, text transcriptions and glosses by Sidney Ray, 1898; musical transcriptions by Charles Myers, first published Cambridge, 1912 (**30.19–28**)

A note on the sources: As of 2017, the original 1898 recordings of some 30 of the songs listed are being streamed live by the British Library:
http://sounds.bl.uk/World-and-traditional-music/Ethnographic-wax-cylinders;
see pull-down list by clicking on 'Australia'). The source reference given with each song below is to the musical transcription in Charles M. Myers, 'Music', in Alfred C. Haddon et al., *Reports of the Cambridge Anthropological Expedition to Torres Straits (1898), volume 4, Arts and Crafts* (Cambridge: The University Press, 1912) (**Myers 1912**), 244–47 (Eastern Islands songs):
https://archive.org/stream/reports191204cambuoft#page/244/mode/2up;
and 262–63 (Western Islands songs):
https://archive.org/stream/reports191204cambuoft#page/262/mode/2up;

As reported below in the **gloss** for each song, Myers also gave an appendix 'Words of the songs', transcribed and translated or glossed by Sidney Ray, at pages 266–69:
https://archive.org/stream/reports191204cambuoft#page/266/mode/2up.
Musical transcriptions of 12 of the 13 funeral songs below (**30.1–13**) were previously published in Charles M. Myers and Alfred C. Haddon, 'Funeral ceremonies', in Alfred C. Haddon et al., *Reports of the Cambridge Anthropological Expedition to Torres Straits (1898): volume 6, Sociology, Magic, and Religion of the Eastern Islanders* (Cambridge: The University Press, 1908), 150–53: *https://archive.org/stream/reports190806cambuoft#page/150/mode/2up*

20 Eastern Islands songs

30.1–4A   4 Malu songs

30.1 'Malu songs I' (Funeral song 1)
text: *Wau aka o adeet Maluet e padet emarar*
gloss: Yea why O holy one Malu at the creek sways
analytics (30.1–4A): Murray Island, Eastern Torres Strait; TSI; Papuan/ Miriamic/ Meriam Mir
source (30.1–4A): Myers 1912, 244–45: https://archive.org/stream/reports191204cambuoft#page/244/mode/2up

30.2 'Malu songs II' (Funeral song 2)
text: *Wau o weluba o lewerlewer o meriba tamera*
gloss: Yea O pigeon's feather O food our Malu's club

30.3 'Malu songs III' (Funeral song 3)
text: *Wau Izib eiriam, wau Izibe dirker ewatur*
gloss: Yea Izib ye two drink, Yea Izib he sinks it pulls him down

30.4 'Malu songs IV' (Funeral song 4)
text: *Ib' abara lewer kerim abara lewer* (see source for additional words, not sung)
gloss: Jaw his food head his food

30.4A 'Malu songs IVA' (Funeral song 4A)
text: *Wau aka Maluet au adud leluti adud tereget* (see source for alternative texts to same music)
gloss: Yea why Malu very bad man bad teeth

30.5–13A   9 Keber songs

30.5 'Keber songs V' (Funeral song 5)
text: *Kodiaba kodiaba moiaba dagaba lagiaba sigapa*
gloss: To the ring to the ring to fire to place to there
analytics (30.5–9A): Murray Island, Eastern Torres Strait; TSI; Papuan/ Miriamic/ Meriam Mir and ? Torres Strait Creole
source (30.5–9A): Myers 1912, 245–46: https://archive.org/stream/reports191204cambuoft#page/245/mode/2up

30.6 'Keber songs VI' (Funeral song 6)
text: (music only)

30.7 'Keber songs VII' (Funeral song 7)
text: *Wau kubi uti sa baibai ita...* (see source for additional words sung in monotone)
gloss: Yea dark sleep now eyebrows cover

30.8 'Keber songs VIII' (Funeral song 8)
text: *O meluba Dudiie*
gloss: ? along Daudai

30.9 'Keber songs IX' (Funeral song 9)
text: (music only)

30.10 'Keber songs X' (Funeral song 10)
text: (music only)

30.11 'Keber songs XI' (Funeral song 11)
text: *O obarasa gainau teir dimer*
gloss: recognize pigeon ornament sew/tie on

30.12 'Keber songs XII' (Funeral song 12)
text: *O Dudiaba. . .Gebariaba Mukeriaba tatarmauke Amiaba*
gloss: to Daudai to Gebar to Mukwa comes between to Yam

30.13 'Keber songs XIII' (Funeral song 13)
text: *Pua pua. . .er pua. . .er etc., tokaiba namiedra (? namiadaba) wer a wer*
gloss: (no gloss)

30.13A 'Keber song XIIIA' (Funeral song 13A)
text: *O dia. . .ina wara si kalapudema wa waia tanu abu wali guba gol mina*
gloss: this other there put on back along coconut they ? fishing line club canoe mark

30.14–18 5 secular songs

30.14 'Secular songs XIV'
text: *Isia ba ba walsika O. . .umuru* (see source for other versions)
gloss: name of plant for a basket plait
analytics (30.14–18): Murray Island, Eastern Torres Strait; TSI; Papuan/ Miriamic/ Meriam Mir and ? Torres Strait Creole
source (30.14–18): Myers 1912, 246–47:
https://archive.org/stream/reports191204cambuoft#page/246/mode/2up

30.15 'Secular songs XV'
text: *Kolap nab ulai kolap pogaipa kolap nino wagel (? walgen) pogaipa*
gloss: Spinning top this go along top fails top yours after fails

30.16 'Secular songs XVI'
text: *Babim mena taiseda*
gloss: to father always brought back

30.17 'Secular songs XVII'
text: *Saiba ala mitge we mitge*
gloss: on lip on lip

30.18 'Secular song XVIII'
text: *Iriboa kukia iriboa*
gloss: along N.W.

11 Western Islands songs

30.19–24 6 Mabuiag songs

30.19 'Mabuiag III'
text: *Ngata kaba nau puidaik*

gloss: I dance song sing
analytics (30.19–24): Mabuiag Island, Western Torres Strait; TSI; Northern PN/ Western Torres Strait/ Kala Lagaw Ya
source (30.19–24): Myers 1912, 262–63:
https://archive.org/stream/reports191204cambuoft#page/262/mode/2up

30.20 'Mabuiag IV'
text: *Gana sagulau nau*
gloss: Ga's play's song

30.21 Mabuiag IX
text: *Korara kwiku puidaik*
gloss: ? crocodile head sing

30.22 Mabuiag XI
text: *Waiatana na puidaik*
gloss: Waiat's song

30.23 Mabuiag XIII
text: *Ur kawa*
gloss: Sea [and] island

30.24 Mabuiag XIV
text: *Ngato madubau nau puidaik*
gloss: I madub's (= charm's) song sing

30.25–26 2 Yam songs

30.25 'Yam I'
text: *Awaia gulabwi kabutan*
gloss: pelican in canoe put
analytics (30.25–26): Yam Island, Western Torres Strait; TSI; Northern PN/ Western Torres Strait/ Kulkalgaw Ya
source (30.25–26): Myers 1912, 263:
https://archive.org/stream/reports191204cambuoft#page/263/mode/2up

30.26 'Yam II' (sung by **Maino** of Yam, listen to Audio example 16.1 in Chapter 16)
text: *Yamazi barid*
gloss: along Yam Id. cuscus

30.27–28 2 Saibai songs

30.27A 'Saibai IA'
text: *Mawa na puidam*
gloss: Mawa [ceremony] song sung
analytics (30.27–28): Saibai Island, Western Torres Strait; TSI; Northern PN/ Western Torres Strait/ Kalaw Kawaw Ya
source (30.27–28): Myers 1912, 263:
https://archive.org/stream/reports191204cambuoft#page/263/mode/2up

30.27B 'Saibai IB'
text: Unclear if the text for Saibai I (Haddon 1912:269) applies to the music for Saibai IA or Saibai IB (Haddon 1912:263)

30.28 'Saibai II'
text: *Madub na puidam*
gloss: Charm song sung

Commentary: Haddon's anthropological work was 'confined to Murray Island' (Haddon 1912:261) – that is, to the main island of the Eastern Torres Strait, where the language is Meriam Mir – as so too were Charles Myers's recordings and musical observations. For the western islands (Mabuiag, Yam and Saibai), where there are various dialects of the of the Western Torres Strait language, the song data were collected by Sidney Ray (Haddon 1912:261), the expedition's linguist, who provided phonographic records and glosses of the texts. Haddon says of the language of the Keber songs (30.5–30.13A) of the eastern islands that it is a 'debased form of the language of the western islands of the Torres Strait', so we have tentatively added 'Torres Strait Creole' as a plausible component of the linguistic mix of these songs. As of 2017, links to original recordings of those songs streamed by the British Library can be found on the webpage version of the checklist (see web link below).

Select bibliography: Sidney H. Ray, *Reports of the Cambridge Anthropological Expedition to Torres Straits (1898), volume 3: Linguistics* (Cambridge: Cambridge University Press 1907);
Alice Moyle, 'The Torres Strait phonograph recordings: a preliminary listing of contents', *Australian Aboriginal Studies* (1985, issue 2), 53–57;
Roberta Wells, 'Sidney Herbert Ray: linguist and educationalist', *The Cambridge Journal of Anthropology* 21/1 (1999), 79–99;
Sidney H. Ray, *Dictionary of Torres Strait languages*, edited by Ron Edwards (Kuranda QLD: Rams Skull Press, 2003; 2nd ed.)
Helen Reeves Lawrence, '"The great traffic in tunes": agents of religious and musical change in eastern Torres Strait', in Richard Davis (ed.), *Woven histories, dancing lives: Torres Strait Islander identity, culture and history* (Canberra: Aboriginal Studies Press, 2004), 46–72;
Bennett Zon, *Representing mon-western music in nineteenth-century Britain* (Rochester, NY: University of Rochester Press, 2007), 218–32;
Fairweather, Matthias and Whaleboat 2017 (this volume);
Skinner 2017 (this volume)

Checklist web link:
http://sydney.edu.au/paradisec/australharmony/checklist-indigenous-music-1.php#030

c.1899 (possibly much earlier)

31 *1 song (Yuin)*

Yuin, 'Yatte Yattah', Milton, South Coast, NSW, transcribed by Percy Hale Sheaffe (1832–1913); published 1900, but probably learnt by Sheaffe much earlier

31 'All about whale ship"
text: *Tshemer burra buna ny toonaoo na [repeat ad lib.] parn wate*
gloss: 'all about whale ship'

analytics: Milton, South Coast, NSW; ECA; South-eastern PN/ Yuin/ ? Dharumba
source: [1] Percy Hale Sheaffe, letter to Robert Waddell (District Registrar, Milton, NSW), 30 October 1899; in correspondence attached to Waddell's completed return of a questionnaire sent out by W. Wentworth-Bucknell, on behalf of the Anthropological Society of Australasia, 'Collection of native names of places with their meanings'; Royal Anthropological Society of Australasia – Records, 1885–1914, with additional material, 1921–26, ca. 1991, and papers of Alan Carroll, 1886–92, State Library of New South Wales, MLMSS 7603, box 4, folder 3, 209a (image 10):
http://digital.sl.nsw.gov.au/delivery/DeliveryManagerServlet?dps_pid=FL452840;
[2] Captain Sheafe [Percy Sheaffe], 'Two native songs', *Science of Man and Journal of the Royal Anthropological Society of Australasia* 2/12 (1900), 227 (based on [1])

Commentary: Sheaffe gave only the text for a second song, which was 'all about two gallons'. He explained, 'I began to work on this land, more than 42 years since', and it is likely that he remembered the songs from a much earlier period in his life.

Select bibliography: Saintilan 1993, 78

Checklist web link:
http://sydney.edu.au/paradisec/australharmony/checklist-indigenous-music-1.php#031

1899 & 1903

32 3 songs (Tasmanian)

Tasmanian language, Hobart, TAS; sung by **Fanny Cochrane Smith** (1834–1905) in 1899 and 1903, sound recording by Horace Watson (1862–1930); words of song **31.1** published 1908, musical published 1968; words of songs **32.2-3** published 1960, music 1968 (see entry **9**, above, for further details)

32.1 'Popela' ('popeller') ('Corroboree song')
text: *Poppyla (wala wala pawalawa) / Poppyla (wala wala pawalawa) / Nyna tepe rene pogana / Nyna tepe rene pogana / Nyna tepe re' pogana / Tepe nara pewilly / Para nara pewilly / Pallawoo / a Nyna nara pewilly / Para nara pewilly / Pallawoo pallawoo* (version A, from Moyle 1968, 3)
gloss: As for entry **9** (above).
analytics: Tasmania; TAS; Tasmanian
source: One of 3 original sound recordings of this song, streamed as 'Fanny Cochrane Smith's Tasmanian Aboriginal Songs ('1903') [this recording recte 1899]), National Film and Sound Archive: *http://aso.gov.au/titles/music/fanny-cochrane-smith-songs/clip1*; transcriptions into musical notation from original recordings in Moyle 1960, 76; Moyle 1968, 11, 12.

32.2 'Spring song'
text: *A le di:-- gu:-- la:-- ga a da-ŋa / mi-a pa-la a mi-e- -a mi:-e-a lu:-- pa-du-da ŋa / a mi: mi-e-a ŋu: lu:-- da-ŋa a la mi:-a mi-a ŋu-ma / a da-ŋa a ga:-- mi-a-a lu:-- gu-la-ŋa a-a / a da mi-a du mi: a gu:-la a la mi-e-a ma / a mi: za-li-a-gu-la a ga-li-a ma-na* (transcription from Moyle 1968, 14)
gloss: Spoken by Mrs. Fanny Cochrane Smith (from Moyle 1968:8)
It's Spring time, / The birds is whistling, / The spring is come, / The flowers are all budding, / The (red) fuschia is on the top, / Birds are whistling, / Everything is pretty / 'cause it's spring, (The birds are still dancing) For the springtime

analytics: As for **32.1**
source: Recordings (see **32.1**); transcriptions into musical notation in Moyle 1960, 78; Moyle 1968, 14

32.3 'Hymn *Praise the Lord*'
text: *Praise the Lord, / Hail the Lord, / Abide in Heaven above.*
analytics: Tasmania; TAS; Tasmanian and English
source: Recording (see **32.1**); transcription into musical notation in Moyle 1968, 14

Commentary: Mrs Smith recorded song **32.1** at least three times, in different versions (**9** above is another version of the same song). Only the first of the original cylinders (Tasmanian Museum 15685/M 3317), recorded by Horace Watson in the rooms of the Royal Society of Tasmania on 5 August 1899, is currently (2017) freely streamed in its entirety (approx. 2 minutes 23 seconds) in a sound clip on the National Film and Sound Archive's website (see **source** above). The first minute and a half is an introduction in English, declaimed into the recording horn by Mrs Smith:

> I'm Fanny Smith. I was born on Flinders Island. I'm the last of the Tasmanians. I'll (put this morning) a very long story about it. I'll tell you the truth, to let you know a little about us. My mother's name was Tanganitara. I – we are some true born sisters from Flinders Island, where we were for seven years. And I'm here speaking to-day. [? in answer to a question] have we got for mother and my father? My father [? family] Noona. Noona (nitara-noota). (Sing a song. Noota, mother and me). My father Noona. My father was a (whaler). Lose-a my mother, all gone. [? in answer to a question] . . . My family? I'm married. Goodbye. My father [? family] no more.

At 1 minute 49 seconds, Mrs Smith begins the first and shortest of her three recorded renditions of 'Popela' (**32.1**), 33 seconds in length.

Select bibliography: Longman 1960: *http://eprints.utas.edu.au/14096*;
Moyle 1960: *http://eprints.utas.edu.au/14095*;
Moyle 1968 [includes transcriptions of all 3 songs];
Martin Thomas, 'The rush to record: transmitting the sound of Aboriginal culture', *Journal of Australian Studies* 90 (2007), 107–21 (**Thomas 2007**):
   http://trove.nla.gov.au/version/52218549;
Skinner 2017, this volume

Checklist web link:
   http://sydney.edu.au/paradisec/australharmony/checklist-indigenous-music-1.php#032

1901

33 *7 songs (various language groups of Central Australia)*

Lower Arrernte ('Arunta') country, Stevenson's Creek, SA, and Charlotte Waters, NT; sound recording by Baldwin Spencer, 1901; 3 music transcriptions by Percy Grainger (1909), versions of 2 of these published by Spencer and F. J. Gillen (1912)

33.1 'Song of the Erkita corroboree'
text: *Tangaramba/ Ibitalbita* (T. G. H. Strehlow transcription, published in Gibson 2015, 171)
gloss: 'Bob Rubuntja confidently explained to Strehlow that the verse was part of the *altharte*

Aremaye, a type of large sand goanna song series from a place in Warlpiri territory known as Puturlu (Mt. Theo) and although not being able to provide a meaning, claimed the verse was: *angaramba/Ibitalbita*' (Gibson 2015, 171).
analytics: Stevenson River, northern SA; CA; Central PN/ Arandic/ Anmatyerr
commentary: There is a manuscript (1909) musical transcription of this song by Percy Grainger, the first of two under the title 'Native Australian tunes'. Spencer and Gillen (1912 v.2, 502) subsequently published a version of Grainger's transcription (the second of two in their appendix to volume 2). Gibson (2015, 171) has traced the language of this song (and the next one) to Anmatyerr (an Arandic language that lies to the north-west of Central Arrernte).
sources: Recording by Baldwin Spencer, from an Arunta singer, Stevenson's Creek, SA, 22 March 1901, Royal Geographical Society of South Australia; streamed by Museum Victoria: *http://spencerandgillen.net/objects/4fac6982023fd704f475b5dc* [sound file]; music only transcription, MS, Percy Grainger, Melbourne 1909, Museum Victoria: *http://spencerandgillen.net/objects/50ce72f5023fd7358c8a957d* [image 2].

33.2 'Song of the Ilyarnpa corroboree'
analytics: As for **33.1**
gloss: 'Upon first hearing the recording Bob Rubuntja confidently attributed the verse to an *Altharte Atnyemayte* (witchetty grub dance) from the Anmatyerr estate of Arlekwarr ("Lukara" in Strehlow's spelling)' (Gibson 2015, 171).
commentary: There is a manuscript (1909) musical transcription of this song by Percy Grainger, the second of two under the title 'Native Australian tunes'. Gibson (2015, 171) has traced the language of this song (and the previous one) to Anmatyerr.
sources: As for **33.1**

33.3 'Song of the Chitchingalla corroboree' ('Tjitjingalla')
text: *Tjantjirtjantjirla/ walamburbmarei* (T. G. H. Strehlow transcription, published in Gibson 2015, 170–171)
gloss: 'The text of the recorded verse was, according to Strehlow *antjirtjantjirla/ walamburbmarei*; however, none of his informants knew the meaning of the verse words as it originated from far to the north and was sung in a foreign language ... All three of his main informants did however know this song and dance as the *altharte* "molunga"' (Gibson 2015, 171) – that is, the 'Molonga Set of Corrobborees', so named by Roth (1897, 120), who notes: 'The meaning of the word *Molonga* (*cf*. Pitta-Pitta *mo-ma*) is difficult to interpret in European fashion. It hardly corresponds with our conception of the 'devil,' and yet at the same time it does signify an evil-doer from whom mischief may be expected' (Roth 1897, 121). (See also Hercus 1980.)
analytics: Stevenson River, northern SA; CA; Central PN/ Wakayic or Wambayan/ Wakaya or Wambaya
commentary: Percy Grainger gave his 1909 manuscript musical transcription of this song the title 'Dadji dadji' (possibly his version of the opening words). Spencer and Gillen (1912 v.2, 502) published a version of Grainger's transcription as the first of their music examples. Gibson (2015, 170) has traced the language of this song to Wakaya or Wambaya.
sources: Recording by Baldwin Spencer, Arunta singer, Stevenson's Creek, SA, 22 March 1901. Royal Geographical Society of South Australia; streamed by Museum Victoria: *http://spencerandgillen.net/objects/4fac699d023fd704f475b641* [sound file]; music only transcription (MS) by Percy Grainger, Melbourne 1909 (Museum Victoria): *http://spencerandgillen.net/objects/50ce72f5023fd7358c8a957d* [image 1]

33.4 '2 songs sung by women [1]'
text: *Maljatatjeire/ tambirrkula* (T. G. H. Strehlow transcription, published in Gibson 2015, 174; unclear which of the two women's songs this text relates to)
analytics: Charlotte Waters, southern NT; CA; Central PN/ Warumungic/ Warumungu
commentary: Gibson (2015, 174) has traced the language of this song (and the following) to Warumungu.
source: Recording by Baldwin Spencer, Charlotte Waters, NT, 29 March 1901, Royal Geographical Society of South Australia, RGSSA07; streamed by Museum Victoria: *http://spencerandgillen.net/objects/4fac699f023fd704f475b64d*

33.5 '2 songs sung by women [2]'
analytics: As for **33.4**
commentary: Gibson (2015, 174) has traced the language of this song (and the previous) to Warumungu.
source: As for **33.4**

33.6 'Another song sung by the same women on the same occasion'
analytics: As for **33.4**
source: Recording by Baldwin Spencer, Charlotte Waters, NT, 29 March 1901, Royal Geographical Society of South Australia, RGSSA28; streamed by Museum Victoria: *http://spencerandgillen.net/objects/4fac6984023fd704f475b5ec*

33.7 'Corroboree song'
analytics: Charlotte Waters, southern NT; CA; Central PN/ ? Arandic / ? Lower Arrernte
commentary: Unclear which corroboree this song comes from. If it is one of the two 'totemic' verses (Gibson 2015, 174) recorded at Charlotte Waters on this date (3 April 1901), then the identities of the singers are available from Spencer's journal (Gibson 2015, 175–176).
source: Recording by Baldwin Spencer, Charlotte Waters, 3 April 1901, Royal Geographical Society of South Australia, RGSSA46; streamed by Museum Victoria: *http://spencerandgillen.net/objects/4fac69a6023fd704f475b655*

Select bibliography: Baldwin Spencer and F. J. Gillen, Tape copies of recordings of the 1901 expedition to Central Australia and accompanying correspondence, notes, etc. 1901–80; University of Adelaide, Rare books and special collections, MSS 305.89915 S745A: *https://www.adelaide.edu.au/library/special/mss/spencer_b/?m=tms* [finding guide];

Spencer and Gillen, *Across Australia* (London: Macmillan and Co., 1912), volume 2, 502: *https://archive.org/stream/cu31924088412923#page/n545/mode/2up*;

Alice M. Moyle, 'Sir Baldwin Spencer's recordings of Australian Aboriginal singing', *Memoirs of the National Museum of Victoria* 24 (1959), 7–36:
http://www.biodiversitylibrary.org/item/120198#page/9/mode/1up;

Walter E. Roth, *Ethnological studies among the north-west-central Queensland Aborigines* (Brisbane: Edmund Gregory, Govt Printer):
https://archive.org/stream/ethnologicalstu00rothgoog#page/n139/mode/2up;

Luise A. Hercus, '"How we danced the Mudlunga": memories of 1901 and 1902', *Aboriginal History* 4 (1980), 5–32:
http://press.anu.edu.au/wp-content/uploads/2016/01/article013.pdf;

Thomas 2007: *http://trove.nla.gov.au/version/52218549*;

Jason Gibson, 'Central Australian songs: a history and reinterpretation of their distribution through the earliest recordings', *Oceania* 85/2 (2015), 165–82:
http://dx.doi.org/10.1002/ocea.5084

Checklist web link:
http://sydney.edu.au/paradisec/australharmony/checklist-indigenous-music-1.php#033

c.1900–02

34 6 songs (Dhurga)

Dhurga ('Thoorga'), Ulladulla area, south coast NSW; music and words transcribed by R. H. Mathews c.1900–02, first published 1902 (republished 1907)

34.1 'Dhurramooloon' ('Dharramooloon') [Bunân 1]
text: *Dhurramooloon dhurramooloon binggilbee moondanuna gummerawarawa*
gloss: 'one of the songs chanted by the old men in the presence of the boys' at 'the *Bunân* initiation ceremony' (Mathews 1902, 61)
analytics (34.1–6): Ulladulla area, south coast NSW; ECA; South-eastern PN/ Yuin/ Dhurga
sources (34.1–6): R. H. Mathews, 'The Thoorga language', *Queensland Geographical Journal* 17 (1902), 61–63: *https://archive.org/stream/queenslandgeogra15roya#page/n389/mode/2up*; R. H. Mathews, *Notes on the Aborigines of New South Wales* (Sydney: Government Printer, 1907), 33–35: *https://archive.org/stream/notesonaborigine00math#page/33/mode/2up*

34.2 'Dhurramooloonga' ('Dharramooloonga') [Bunân 2]
text: *Dharramooloonga gale wirrabroo ganga ngoorungga wirraleema*
gloss: As for **34.1**

34.3 'Ngalalbā' [Bunân 3]
text: *Ngalalbā walloolbā jilleejilleen*
gloss: As for **34.1**

34.4 'Jilbarara' [Bunân 4]
text: *Jil´barara mur´ragadyah´ yam´ungad´yeenah´*
gloss: 'One of the songs used by the women in the morning during the time their sons are away with the chief men undergoing initiation' (Mathews 1902, 62)

34.5 'Ngulleejee' [Bunân 5]
text: *Ngul´leejee gawinjee mullinda gunalyee niong´gajee*
gloss: 'During the same period the mothers of the boys chant songs in the evening, of which the following is a specimen' (Mathews 1902, 62)

34.6 'Millingalee' [Bunân 6]
text: *Millingalee kuberinya millingalee kuberinya bingandabee pambeeloonya mirreewala pambeeloonya*
gloss: 'Another song sung by the boys' mothers' (Mathews 1902, 62)

Other documentation: R. H. Mathews and Mary M. Everitt, 'The organisation, language and initiation ceremonies of the Aborigines of the south-east coast of N. S. Wales', *Journal and Proceedings of the Royal Society of New South Wales* 34 (1900), 279–280: *https://archive.org/stream/journalproceedi341900roya#page/279/mode/2up* [words only **34.2, 34.1** (? variant), **34.3**; also words only of two customary songs sung by the old women]

Commentary: Mathews had previously described 'the *Bunân* ceremony of initiation in force among the native tribes occupying the south-east coast of New South Wales from the Victorian boundary to Bulli, and extending inland from eighty to a hundred miles.' Mathews describes nos. 1–3 as 'Dharamoolan's songs' (Mathews 1900, 279). His 'Thurga and Jirringany notebook' (Canberra, NLA, MS 8006/3/5) lists the names of his Dhurga informants as **Harry Walker**, **Annie Wood** (**Benson**), **Bill Chapman**, **James Walker**, and **Huggany** (a Wandandian man); on page 153 Mathews also transcribed three short lyrics headed 'Annie's Songs' (Besold 2013, 19, 20).

Select bibliography: Martin Thomas, *The many worlds of R. H. Mathews: in search of an Australian anthropologist* (Sydney: Allen & Unwin, 2011) (henceforth ***Thomas 2011***); Jutta Besold, Language recovery of the New South Wales south coast Aboriginal languages (Ph.D thesis, Australian National University, 2013) (henceforth ***Besold 2013***): *http://hdl.handle.net/1885/10133*

Checklist web link:
http://sydney.edu.au/paradisec/australharmony/checklist-indigenous-music-1.php#034

c.1900–04

35 *3 songs (Dhurga)*

Dhurga ('Thoorga'), Ulladulla area, south coast NSW, music and words transcribed by R. H. Mathews c. 1900–04, published 1904

35.1 'Chant No. 1' ('dirge') [Pirrimbir 1]
text: *Agh kunumbu kunumbu dyirri wanangunna Manganyingal wallagin ginahiya*
gloss: The first of three songs that Mathews gave as examples in his discussion of the 'Pirrimbir, or avenging expedition' in 'Thoorga territory' (Mathews 1904, 240); this one is a 'tribal dirge' sung by 'two of the eldest men' (Mathews 1904, 239)
Analytics (35.1–3): Ulladulla area, south coast NSW; ECA; South-eastern PN/ Yuin/ Dhurga
source (35.1–3): R. H. Mathews, 'Ethnological notes on the Aboriginal Tribes of New South Wales and Victoria', *Journal and Proceedings of the Royal Society of New South Wales* 38 (1904), 239–241: *https://archive.org/stream/journalproceedi381904roya#page/240/mode/2up*

35.2 'Chant No. 2' ('weeping song') [Pirrimbir 2]
text: *Yanawa berriga malah . . .*
gloss: The second 'Pirrimbir' song (see **35.1**); 'At the same time the women are also mustered in the camp . . . singing a 'nyūnggoan' or weeping song, of which 'Chant No. 2' . . . is an example' (Mathews 1904, 240)

35.3 'Chant No. 3' ('departure of the warriors') [Pirrimbir 3]
text: *Kunumbu kunumbu ngodyiramba urarumba ngurgambawi*
gloss: The third 'Pirrimbir' song (see **35.1**); this one sung during the 'departure of the warriors,' who, while singing, 'gesticulate with their weapons as if assaulting an enemy' (Mathews 1904, 241)

Commentary: On Mathews and his south coast informants, see **34** commentary.

Select bibliography: Thomas 2007;
Besold 2013

Checklist web link:
http://sydney.edu.au/paradisec/australharmony/checklist-indigenous-music-1.php#035

Index

Aboriginal/Islander Dance Theatre (AIDT), 250
acoustemology, 34
acoustic ecology, 9, 34, 37, 205, 231
active imagination, 229, 235
adaptation, 18, 22–3, 40, 42, 66, 193, 197, 199, 214–15, 244, 246, 303
Adelaide, 10, 20, 86, 96–7, 117, 206, 249, 339–40, 402
aesthetics, 7, 18, 31, 33, 35, 38–9, 141, 159, 228, 272, 281
age-groups, 17, 58, 175
Ah! Wy-a-boo-ka (Nathan), 355–6, 377
AIATSIS, *see Australian Institute of Aboriginal and Torres Strait Islander Studies*
Alice Springs NT, 13, 88–9, 93–4, 96, 98–9
alignment, 60, 125, 176, 224
Allen, Archie, 107, 115
Alyawarr, Alyawarra, 87, 89, 102, 118, 186, 238
a-Marndiwa, ceremony, Yanyuwa (*see also* ceremonies), 71–2
Ammaroo Station NT, 102
Amparruwu (Tiwi snake song), 296–8
ancestors, 5, 23, 28, 50, 90, 99, 149–50, 159, 181, 187–8, 190, 208, 219, 232, 248, 278, 286, 289, 296, 301–2, 309
Anmatyerr, Anmatyerre, 15, 89, 401
Anthropological Society of Australasia, 226, 231–2, 399
applied ethnomusicology, 2, 9, 36, 39–40
Arabana, 107, 109
Ara Irititja (digital archive program), 252
Arandic, 13, 15, 123, 126, 139, 142, 401–2
archaeoacoustics, 6, 31, 34, 40, 205, 227, 231, 241, 303
Archibald, Frank, 148–9, 169–70, 174, 334
archives (*see also* museums), 25, 28, 40, 47–8, 53, 55–8, 62, 64, 66–7, 96–7, 117–18, 157, 172–3, 185, 245, 251–2, 259, 263–4, 272, 277, 289, 292–3, 296, 298–9, 301, 304, 325, 337–8, 340, 342, 346–7, 352, 354, 358–9, 366, 368, 371, 374, 378, 380, 385, 387, 391, 393, 397, 399, 402, 404
Armidale NSW, 13, 86, 147, 166, 168–75, 241
Arnhem Land NT, 3, 9, 11–12, 17, 20–1, 25, 33, 38, 42, 53, 72, 86, 100, 141, 185, 189, 192, 206, 219, 227–9, 231–2, 234–5, 237, 257–62, 267, 269–70, 272–6, 278–83, 286–8, 304, 362, 364, 371
Arrarrkpi (Arnhem Land term meaning 'Indigenous'), 260, 270–1
Arrernte, 13, 23, 88–94, 96–100, 107, 111, 204, 219, 221, 234, 337–8, 340, 400–2
arts of memory, mnemotechnical practices, 45, 187, 201–2, 204, 210, 229, 241, 244, 322
atyelpe 'native cat', Arrernte (*see also* Urumpula), 107
audience, 22, 24, 64, 66–7, 72, 85, 162, 184, 189, 215, 219, 249–51, 254, 283, 286–7, 289–90, 292, 306, 309, 312, 314–15, 330, 332, 346, 352
Australia Council for the Arts, 39, 289

Australian Institute of Aboriginal and Torres Strait Islander Studies, 44, 57, 59–60, 62, 89, 100, 97, 102, 117–18, 120, 131, 138, 170–3, 251, 259, 264, 270, 289–90, 293, 295–7, 299, 301, 325, 346, 379, 385, 390
authenticity, 184, 245, 332, 356
Awabakal poem (Haslam), 195, 234
Baayami (Baiame), 194–5, 220–4
Bakarnalinya NT, 278
Banyjima, 57
Barak, William, 109, 156, 352, 388–9
barinma (spirit messengers), 191
Barkly Tablelands NT, 71–2
Barlgabi, genre, Ngardi-ngarli (*see also* song genres), 588
Barraba (mountain, NSW), 226
Baudin expedition (1802), 365–6, 368, 370
Becker, Ludwig, 97, 100, 212, 228, 382–3
Beckler, Hermann, 364, 381–2
Bellbrook NSW, 22, 173
Belyuen NT, 205, 293
Benesh dance terms, 77, 84, 87
Bennelong (Woollarawarre), 160, 354, 367, 370
  Harry (brother-in-law), 370
Berak, *see Barak, William*
Bernier, Pierre François, 365, 368
Bidyadanga WA, 59
Bidyara, 122, 128, 138
bilingual education, 3, 20–1, 33, 44, 173, 185
Bingo Corroborees (Lethbridge), 349–50, 362, 391
Bininj Gunwok, 258, 261, 265, 273, 275–6
Biraban, 194, 234
bird calls, 52, 155, 346
bird call song (Fanny Cochrane Smith), 346
Birdsville SA, 104, 111, 118
Blair, Harold, 349, 357, 392
body percussion (*see also* musical instruments, hand-clapping, knee clapping, thigh slapping), 144, 160
Bon, Lui, 322
boomerangs, clapped or struck (*see also* musical instruments), 58, 72, 143, 146, 159, 253–4, 354
Bora, ceremony, south-eastern (*see also* ceremonies), 152, 191, 221–2
Borroloola NT, 13, 24, 68–72, 86–7, 247
Boss Davey (Mundâlo), 349–50, 391
buljurr, drum, Gumbaynggirr (*see also* musical instruments), 145
Bunan, ceremony, Yuin (*see also* ceremonies), 403
Bungarun (Derby leprosarium, WA), 59
Burbung (*burbang*), ceremony, Wiradjuri (*see also* ceremonies), 191, 222
burdal, genre, Lardil (*see also* song genres), 245, 247–8, 250–6
Burnett River Qld, 129, 384–5, 387, 393–4
Burns, Michael, 57, 61
Burragurra NSW, *see Devil's Rock*

CAAMA, 93
Cadigal, 367
Calvert, Albert F., 46, 53, 362, 364, 392–3
Cambridge Anthropological Expedition to Torres Straits (1898), 327, 334–5, 337, 358, 390, 394, 398
Cape Arid National Park WA, 43
Cape York, 11, 15, 125, 141–2, 145, 158, 206, 350, 356, 363–4, 386
CASM, *see Centre for Aboriginal Studies in Music*
Cavenagh, Maria Bird, 96
Central Australia, 4, 7, 15, 20, 24, 39–40, 46, 55, 69, 86–8, 90, 92, 98, 101–4, 119, 123–4, 142–3, 146, 149, 153, 158, 160, 162, 204, 231–2, 234, 240, 242, 316, 337, 364, 400, 402
Central Australian Aboriginal Media Association, *see CAAMA*
Central Queensland, 138, 335
Centre for Aboriginal Studies in Music, 10, 20
ceremonies, 146, 257, 259–60, 264, 269–70, 286, 307, 361, 393;

  ceremonies by region/language:
  Arrernte, 88–93, 99; Gippsland, 105; Gumbaynggirr, 161; Hunter Valley, 200, 223; Kimberley, 306–7; Kuyani, 106; Lardil, 246–7, 250, 255; Ngarluma, 62, 66; Nyungar, 393; south-eastern, 102, 105, 109–11, 144, 146, 149–54, 157, 159, 160, 161, 163, 178–81, 191–2, 211, 221–2, 403; Tiwi, 290–1, 293; Torres Strait Islands, 390, 394, 397; western Arnhem Land, 261, 267, 269, 272, 275–7, 279, 283; Wiradjuri, 191, 222; Yanyuwa, 1, 24, 71–2, 85; Yuin, 403;

  ceremonies by name, *see*: *a Marndiwa*, Bora, Bunan, Burbung (*burbang*), Inyimany ja najaman, Junba, *Kalwangarra*, *kujika*, Kulama, Kunapipi (*a-Kunapipi*), Malkara, Malo-Bomai, Mamurrng, *manyardi*, *marndar*, *mura*, *Ngadiji*, *Ngakaráwarra*, *Warrthampa*, Wolungarri, *Yalkawarru*, *Yoi*
ceremony holders (*see also* songman), 259, 262
Chapman, Bill (Dhurga), 404
Chauncy, Philip, 45, 53, 364, 380–1
Cherbourg Qld, 349
children, 9, 17, 20, 25, 37, 49, 77, 92, 94–5, 174–5, 184, 217–18, 247, 249, 257–8, 261, 267, 293, 296–7, 305–12, 314–16, 326, 330, 352, 372, 391
Chong, Stanley, 249
chorus, 145, 166, 353
Christianity, 21, 230, 235, 318, 320–1, 334
Christian
  music, 237, 327, 333
  choruses, *see kores*
Churnside, Patrick, 57, 66
Churnside, Robert, 59, 62–3, 65
clapsticks (*see also* musical instruments), 143, 153, 192, 254, 277, 279, 283, 287, 307, 312
Clayton, Reginald Byard Buchanan, 384–5

INDEX

'clever' person, doctor, 150, 152, 191–2, 211, 226, 228
Coast Murring, 151, 162, 192
code-switching, 172, 176
composition, 3, 18, 20, 22, 36, 51, 60, 76, 140, 143, 146, 151, 155, 158, 187–9, 195, 206, 243, 289–90, 298, 323, 343, 359, 366
Conway, Eddie, 120, 131
Coogoon Station via Roma Qld, 119–20
Coombra, Sadie, 121–2, 132
Cooper, Toby, 286
Coranderrk Station VIC, 117, 352, 389
corroborees (*see also ceremonies, Erkita, Ilyarnpa, Tjitjingalla, Molonga*), 71, 123, 127, 129, 143–50, 152–3, 155–6, 159–60, 162, 191, 200, 211, 246, 248, 346, 349–50, 352–3, 387, 389, 391, 394, 399, 400–2
cosmology, 5
counter-mapping, 28–9, 39
Country
  meaning, 26–7, 205, 291
  idiomatic Aboriginal usage, 1, 21, 25–8, 32, 42–3, 59, 61–2, 66, 72, 81–2, 84, 86, 90–2, 99–101, 105, 111, 121, 148, 150–1, 153–4, 157, 160, 173, 180, 182, 204–10, 220–1, 223, 233–5, 238, 241, 248–51, 257–8, 260, 267, 270, 272, 281, 283, 286–7, 291, 293, 299, 302, 305–6, 308–16, 384, 387, 389, 400
Countrylines archive, 28
Creole (Mornington Island), 246, (Torres Strait, Yumplatok), 23, 318–19, 323–4, 394–6, 398
Croker Island NT, 13, 260, 262, 270, 276–7
daladala board, 76
Daly River region, 12, 14, 32, 243, 275
dance, 3, 6, 8, 11, 16, 21, 23–5, 30, 33, 35, 38–9, 42, 48–9, 51, 56, 58, 68–9, 71–2, 74, 76, 80, 82, 85, 87–8, 90–2, 94, 100, 105, 111, 140, 143, 145, 147–9, 151–2, 155, 159, 162–3, 167–8, 170, 182, 189, 191, 193, 197, 199, 201, 204, 208, 229–30, 236, 238, 243, 246–7, 250–3, 255, 257–8, 261–2, 264, 270, 273–4, 281–2, 287, 296, 303, 306, 308–10, 312, 314–15, 325, 333–4, 336, 340, 345–6, 355, 360–1, 366, 368, 370, 377–8, 384, 386, 388, 390, 393, 397, 401
dance genres (*see also song genres, ceremonies, corroborees*), 76; see also Malkirri, yumparrparr
Dareton NSW, 108, 116, 118
Darkinyung, 196, 215–17, 226, 235
Darnley Island TSI, *see* Erub
Dauar TSI, 319, 321
Dawes, William, 367
Day, Stan, 71, 109, 117, 308, 335
Densmore, Frances, 189, 213, 230, 234
Derby WA (*see also Bungarun*), 59, 307, 309, 316
De Salis, Margaret, 193, 218–19, 230
designs (ceremonial), 91, 146, 159, 162–3, 182, 189, 261, 271, 281–2, 308
Devil's Rock NSW, 220, 224, 226, 239, 241
Dhanggati~Thangatti (*see also Thangatti~Dhanggati*), 13, 22, 172–4, 176–83, 186

didjeridu (*see also musical instruments*), 21, 76, 261, 265, 271, 278–83, 285, 290, 312
digging stick, 79, 203
digital archive (*see also Ara Irititja and PARADISEC*), 252
diplomacy ceremony (*see also Mamurrng*), 264, 286, 361, 258, 261–2, 270, 275
Dital dital baloonai (Nathan), 355–6, 377
diversity, 2, 7, 18, 25, 35, 37, 48, 91, 142, 257–60, 269–70, 272, 276, 286, 288, 307, 335
Diyari, 104–5, 138
Djanba, genre, Murriny Patha, 57, 67, 240, 272, 287
Djiagween, Paddy, 59
Domeny de Rienzi, Grégoire Louis, 364, 371
Drayton, Joseph, 375–6
dream (*see also re-dreaming*), 4–5, 16, 18, 27, 35, 68, 71, 151, 186–9, 191–2, 194–5, 205–9, 211–13, 227–8, 231–2, 234–42, 247–8, 255, 261, 283, 329
Dreaming, 28, 38, 68, 71, 80, 84, 86, 90, 99, 121–2, 161, 182, 205, 234–5, 237, 239, 243, 245, 248, 253, 277, 281, 288, 291–2, 303, 384
drum (*see also buljurr, tartengk, warup, musical instruments*), 145, 244, 296–8, 320, 324, 384
duets, 293
Dunlop, Eliza Hamilton, 152, 161, 167, 187, 193, 195–7, 199, 201–2, 208, 212, 214–16, 218–19, 227, 230, 233, 239, 356
Eastern Arnhem Land, 11, 20, 259
Eastern Gulf, 13
Echuca, 103, 109, 117–18
ecomusicology, 8, 40
Edgar, Tommy, 59
Edwards, Henry, 59
ellipsis, 177, 179, 181–2
Ellis, Catherine, 1, 4–6, 9–10, 20, 27, 31, 33–4, 41, 69, 86, 92, 100, 103, 106, 108, 117, 124, 139, 145–6, 148–51, 153–63, 167, 185, 201, 212–13, 231, 233, 235, 237, 292, 303
emu, 123, 221–2, 224
endangerment (of music, language), 20, 23–5, 36, 38, 43, 45–8, 52–3, 56–7, 62–3, 67, 100–1, 186–7, 237, 245, 263, 273–4, 276, 288–9, 304, 315–16, 318–19, 333–4, 348
entertainment songs, 150
environment, 7, 8, 29, 39, 41, 57, 61, 66, 86, 175, 179, 202, 205, 241, 271, 286, 309–10, 333
environmental crisis, environmental activism, 26, 39
Erkita corroboree, Arandic (*see also corroborees*), 400
Erub TSI, 318–19, 321–2, 324–7, 329, 333–4
ethnomusicology (*see also applied ethnomusicology*), 1–2, 6–9, 18, 31–2, 36–40, 69, 163, 170, 185, 229, 231, 303, 316, 360
Euroka Creek NSW, 180
festival, 10, 20, 23–6, 36, 71, 85, 89, 91, 99, 101, 246, 249, 253–5, 258, 274–5, 282–3, 286, 308, 310, 326, 329
Field, Barron, 353, 357, 364, 370–1, 376
Finke NT, 103, 107, 115, 118

Flint, Elwyn, 21, 119–20, 122–3, 125, 127, 129, 131–2, 139
folk music, 2, 39, 61, 92, 164, 347
folklore, folklorist, 2, 7, 33, 35, 39, 229, 235, 244, 335, 353, 359, 383
Freycinet, Louis de, 364–6, 368–72
funerary rites (*see also ceremonies*), 85, 258, 283, 394
fur (vs scales or feathers), 203–4
Gamilaraay (*see also Kamilaroi*), 191, 196, 199, 201–2, 215–17, 219–23, 232
Garnier, Edouard, 350–1, 357, 386
Gathang, 173, 199, 226, 236
genre, *see* song genres, songsets, ceremonies, corroborees, dance genres
gesture, gesture language in song and dance (*see also sign language*), 77–8, 141, 154, 162–3
ghosts, 33, 34, 38, 205, 208–9, 211, 220, 228–31, 237–8, 288
Gillen, Frank, 110, 212, 232, 242, 337–40, 357–8, 400–2
Gippsland Vic, 102–3, 105, 145
girls' ceremony, *see* Inyimany ja najaman
Githabul, 221, 238
Goddard, Roy Hamilton, 148, 150–2, 161, 168, 193, 196, 218–21, 224, 226, 233
Goodman, Cecil, 248, 253–4
Goulburn Island NT, 13, 258–9, 266, 273, 276
Gowanalli, Laurie, 307
Grainger, Percy, 337–9, 359, 400–1
Grannie Moisey, 111
group composition, interauthorial composition, 18, 146
Gulamuwu, James, 260
Gulf festival, 255
Gulf of Carpentaria, 11–12, 28, 32, 42, 68–9, 86–7, 229, 245, 255
Gumbaynggirr, 19, 144–5, 152, 157, 160–1, 168–70, 184–5
gum-leaf, bush leaf (*see also musical instruments*), 105, 145
Gunangu, genre, Ngardi-ngarli (*see also song genres*), 58
Gunbalanya NT, 258, 260–1, 282–3, 286
Gunggari, 13, 119–24, 131, 138, 348, 391
Gunwinyguan, 258, 276
Gunya, 123, 125, 129, 138
Gunyaŋara, 3
Gurrumul (Geoffrey Yunupingu), 8
Guwiyul, Henry, 260, 277, 279, 281–2, 285
Haddon, Alfred Cort, 319, 327, 334–5, 337, 358, 364, 390, 394, 398
hand-clapping (*see also body percussion, musical instruments*), 76–7, 144
Handley, Charles, 364, 393–4
Harry (brother-in-law of Bennelong), 370
Haslam, Percy, 195, 230, 234
Henderson, Lana, 93,
heritage, 1, 9, 31–2, 34–6, 44–5, 56, 58, 66, 88, 90–1, 111, 184, 238, 241, 244, 273, 289–90, 293, 301–5, 308, 318, 327, 333, 346
heritage, intangible, 34–6, 301–5, 318, 320

heterophony, 103
Howe, John, 225, 234, 237
Howitt, A. W., 121, 145-7, 149-51, 154-5, 158, 162, 168, 188, 192, 202-3, 212, 220, 222-3, 234, 236, 388-9
HRLM, *see Hunter River-Lake Macquarie language*
Huckitta Station NT, 98
Huggany (Wandandian man), 404
Hunter River-Lake Macquarie language, 13, 193-4, 196, 198-9, 201-3, 215-16, 220, 226
Hunter Valley NSW, 13, 20, 152, 161, 187-8, 193, 195, 203, 209, 223, 227-30, 239
hunting songs (*see also song genres*), 148, 151, 246, 392
hymns (*see also song genres*), 23, 195, 318, 320, 322, 325, 327-8, 330, 332, 334-5, 346-7, 382
identity, 16, 26, 33, 36, 38-40, 43-4, 63, 67, 88, 90-1, 96-7, 99, 101, 141, 150, 163, 184-5, 188, 192, 195, 219, 227, 232, 236-7, 239-40, 253, 261-2, 271, 275, 286, 288, 304, 306, 309, 314-15, 327, 331, 335, 337, 340, 358, 398, 402
idiom, 195, 209, 257, 263-4, 271-2
Ilgar, 260, 275-8
Ilyarnpa corroboree, Arandic (*see also corroborees*), 401
improvisation, 22, 227, 289, 292, 298-9
increase songs (*see also song genres*), 148, 151, 246, 392
incubation, 187, 191-4, 205-7, 221, 234, 238-40
initiation ceremonies (*see also ceremonies*), 71-2, 106, 152, 191, 221-2, 246-7, 403
innovation, 5, 9, 21, 23, 35, 39, 42, 61, 66, 140, 142, 224, 232, 243-4, 252, 283, 286, 315-16, 319, 332
instrumental music, 1, 16-17, 20, 143-4, 164, 182, 278, 281, 290, 298-9, 301, 325, 354
internet, 25, 29, 62, 90, 302, 363
intonation, 180, 246, 301
Inyimany ja najaman, girls' puberty ceremony, western Arnhem Land (*see also ceremonies*), 261, 282
Inyjalarrku 'mermaid' songset, Mawng (Ngurtikin) (*see also song genres*), 53, 227, 257, 259-62, 265-72, 281, 283, 287
irrerntarenye (spirits of place), 204-5
Iwaidjan, 13, 258, 275-6
Jabiru NT, 282-3, 288
Jacob, Kenneth, 206, 247, 249, 253
Jadmi (song genre), 243, 288, 307, 310, 312, 316
jarada (Lardil 'love magic' song genre), 246
Jenolan Caves NSW, 206, 249
Jigalong WA, 192, 205, 243
Johnson, Edward, 89
Jones, Edward, 354, 364, 367
Julian Rocks NSW, 221
Junba, genre, ceremony, north-western (*see also song genres, ceremonies*), 25, 243, 288, 305-16
Jung, C. G., 191, 229, 235
Kalwangarra, replace with:
Kalwangarra, song-dance sequence, Yanyuwa

(*see also ceremonies*), 71
Kamilaroi (see also Gamilaraay), 169, 191, 232-3, 236, 238
Kantilla, Calista, 293, 297
Kariyarra, 56-7, 59-60, 65
Kaurna, 206, 249
Kaytetye, 97, 101, 103
Keens, Emily, 346
Keeping Culture, *see Ara Irititja*
Kepa, Will, 2, 39, 324, 334-5
Kimberley WA, 4, 11, 13, 25, 50, 55, 57, 59, 139, 141, 190, 192, 204-5, 231-2, 235, 239, 243, 275, 288, 305-6, 316-17
Kimberley Downs Station WA, 59
King George's Sound WA, 231, 354-5, 380
kinship, kin classification, 4, 15, 17, 34, 38, 62, 71, 81-2, 84, 150, 175, 182, 187, 192, 194, 201-3, 219, 223-4, 228, 230, 262, 291, 293, 303
knee clapping (*see also body percussion, musical instruments*), 77, 86
Koorinda braia (Nathan), 355-6, 362, 374
kores 'chorus', genre, Torres Strait Creole (*see also song genres*), 323-6, 332
Kransky, George, 251
kujika, genre, ceremony, Lardil (*see also song genres, ceremonies*), 346-7, 251
Kulama, ceremony, Tiwi (*see also ceremonies*), 291
Kunapipi (*a-Kunapipi*), ceremony, Top End (*see also ceremonies*), 71
Kun-barlang, 258-60, 265, 267, 274, 276
kun-borrk, genre, Bininj Gunwok (*see also song genres*), 185, 258-9
Kungkari, 121
Kunwinjku, 259, 262, 273, 276
Kupungarri Community WA, 309, 311
Kurburu (Woiwurrung singer), 388
Kurrama, 56
Kutthung, *see Gathang*
Kuyani, 106, 113
La Grange mission WA, *see Bidyadanga*
laka, dance movements, Lardil (*see also dance*), 245, 247-8, 254
Lake Alexandrina SA, 205, 383
Lake Eyre SA, 13, 24, 104, 107, 112
Lake Gregory WA, 111
Lake Macquarie NSW, 30, 187-8, 195, 202-3, 210, 214-16, 223, 232, 236, 243
Lake Mungo NSW, 31, 205, 227, 303
Lake Tyers Vic, 105, 112, 118
Lambert, Benjamin, 326
land management, 27-8
Lardil, 13, 206, 245-51, 253-6
Laughton, Ada Sylvia, 94-9
lead singer, 272, 323, 326, 265, 321-2, 325
Lesueur, Charles Alexandre, 353, 358, 364-5, 368, 370
Lethbridge, Harold Octavius, 132, 139, 348-50, 352, 358, 364, 391-2
Lhotsky, John, 355-6, 358, 364, 372
literacy, 20-1, 37, 92-3, 316
Loam, Arthur Steadman, 139, 348, 350, 358, 364, 391-2

Lockyer, Gordon, 61
Logan, Maria (Ellard), 235, 342-3, 345, 347-8, 373
Lommel, Andreas, 190, 192, 211-12, 236
Longman, Murray, 169, 341-3, 358, 374, 400
love magic songs (*see also song genres*), 17, 97-8, 246, 151
Ltyentye Apurte NT, 98
Lumholtz, Carl, 364, 387-8
Lyelthe NT, 98
lyrics, 4, 7, 43, 45, 47-9, 51, 92, 122-3, 166, 312, 314, 404
Madjalkaidj, Tommy, 282
Maino of Yam, 397
Mala (Wollombi Brook) NSW, 193, 219
Malkara, ceremony, Kuyani (*see also ceremonies*), 106, 113
Malkirri, fun dances, Yanyuwa (from Mornington Island area) (*see also dance genres*), 68
Malo-Bomai, ceremony, eastern Torres Strait (*see also ceremonies*), 321
Mamurrng, diplomacy ceremony, western Arnhem Land (*see also ceremonies*), 258, 261-2, 270, 275
management, 23-4, 27-8, 32, 41-2, 88, 150, 205
Manangkardi, 259-60, 275-7
Manbam, songset, Marrku (*see also songsets*), 276
manikay, genre, Yolngu (*see also song genres*), 259
manyardi, genre, ceremony, Mawng (*see also song genres, ceremonies*), 257, 259-61, 265, 269-74, 276, 278, 280, 282-3, 287
Maranoa Lullaby, 392
Maranoa River SW Qld, 120, 391
Mararabarna (Dreaming women), 80
Margany, 123, 131, 138
Maric, 13, 15, 119, 121, 123-5, 127, 129-30, 138-9, 364, 388, 391-2
marndar, genre, Lardil (*see also song genres, ceremonies*), 246-7
Marree SA, 107
Marsh, Kathryn, 306, 311
Martin, Matthew Dembal, 59, 308-10, 314, 317
Martin, Scotty Nyalgodi, 243, 306-8, 310, 316
Martuthunira, 56
Mathew, John, 203, 237, 364, 387
Mathews, R. H., 146-7, 149-50, 152, 154, 169, 191-2, 220-3, 227, 237, 364, 403-4
Mawng, 13, 257-5, 267, 271-2, 274, 276, 281
Mayinaj, Jason, 279, 285
McCardell, Anthony, 60-1, 67
McDermott, George, 104, 111
McDinny, Eileen, 1, 27
McLauglin, James Ruthven, 353
melody, 16, 21, 45, 48, 51, 60-1, 92, 102-3, 106, 108, 119, 123-6, 128-32, 139, 155-6, 158, 161, 163-6, 180, 182-3, 200-1, 271, 278, 283, 290, 298, 301, 307, 314, 320-1, 324-5, 336, 341, 344, 347, 349, 353, 356, 358, 361, 368, 370, 372, 375, 377, 379, 387-8, 391

men's ceremonies (see also ceremonies), 64, 76, 89, 146, 246-7
Mer (Murray Islands) TSI, 318-19, 321-2, 324-5, 327, 333, 337, 340
Meriam Mir, 13-14, 23, 318-35, 394-6, 398
'mermaid' songset, see *Inyjalarrku*
metre, 61, 92, 105, 123, 125, 128, 139, 164-6, 176, 183, 199-200, 287, 298
Mid North Coast NSW, 172-3, 175
Milikapiti NT, 297, 302
Millar, King Frank, 108
Milson, Rachel, 150, 169, 196, 199, 201, 216, 218-20, 238
Milyarryarr 'black heron', songset, Marrku *(see also songsets)*, 259-61, 275-87
Mimih/Yawkyawk (Kuninjku songset), 281
miriru (mystical ability, Wunambal), 190
Mirndiyan Gununa (formerly Woomera Aboriginal Corporation), 249, 252, 255
Mirrijpu/Yalarrkuku, songset, Manangkardi (see also songsets), 259
mirrimba or *walbarra*, rasp idiophone, Ngarluma (see also musical instruments), 60
missions, 56, 57, 59, 120, 151, 162, 222, 234, 240, 246, 249, 291, 293, 307, 343, 345, 349, 355, 358, 373, 384
Mitchell, John Francis Huon, 379
mnemonic (see also arts of memory), 45, 201, 322
mobile phone, 25, 61, 90, 283, 309
Molonga/Molunga corroboree, Qld (see also corroborees), 340, 350
Monaro NSW, 355, 362, 372, 374
Moon Island NSW, 195, 232
Moore, George Fletcher, 354-5, 357
Mopaditi (the dead, Tiwi), 291
Morialta Falls SA, 206, 249
Mornington Island Qld, 13, 23, 68, 245-51, 253-6
Mountford, Charles, 292, 296-7
Mount Lindesay Qld, 221
Mount Playfair Station via Tambo Qld, 120
Mount Yango NSW, 195, 202-3, 219-21, 223-7, 241
Mowanjum WA, 13, 25, 305, 307-12, 314, 316
Moyle, Alice, 4, 6, 10-11, 13-16, 22, 34, 38, 54, 57, 59-61, 67, 71, 87, 123, 125, 139, 141, 150, 155-8, 169-70, 183, 185-6, 213, 231, 237-9, 251-2, 303, 336, 339, 341-3, 346, 358, 362-4, 373-4, 398-400, 402
Mulla Villa NSW, 219
Mulladad, Louis, 96-7
Mulladad, Tilly Nelson, 96-7
Munn, Ethel, 348-9, 392
mura, ceremony type, SA (see also ceremonies), 104-5
Murray Island TSI, 13, 22, 318, 327, 334, 394-6
museums, 26, 35, 40, 86, 118, 122, 167, 219, 228, 234, 236, 242, 244, 273, 304, 325, 335, 338-9, 341-2, 348, 357-9, 374, 384, 400-2
musical instruments (see also *buljurr, mirrimba, tartengk, warup*; body percussion,

boomerangs, clapsticks, didjeridu, drum, gum-leaf, hand-clapping, knee-clapping, percussion, possum skin bundle, rasp idiophone, rattle, thigh-slapping), 1, 16-17, 20, 143-4, 164, 182, 278, 281, 290, 298-9, 301, 325, 354
musical regions, 10-12, 14, 141
Myall Creek (massacre site NSW), 356
Myers, Charles, 337-8, 340, 358, 394-7
NAIDOC Week (National Aboriginal and Islanders Day Observance Committee), 24, 66, 68, 71, 308
Nakamarra or Nimala people (characters in Ngadiji story, Yanyuwa), 84-5
Namayiwa, Johnny, 260, 275-83, 285-7
Nangamu, Solomon, 260, 280-2
Narrinyeri, 161, 242, 353, 364, 383-4
Nathan, Isaac, 230, 238, 355-8, 362, 364, 366, 372, 374-5, 377
National Film and Sound Archive, 293, 338, 341-2, 399
National Indigenous Languages Policy (2009), 3
National Policy on Languages (1987), 3
National Recording Project for Indigenous Performance in Australia (see also Symposium on Indigenous Music and Dance), 3, 33
Native Americans, American Indians, 18, 36, 188-9, 227-8, 230, 232, 234-6, 238, 240, 242, 244, 336-7, 358
Neale, Jessie, 96
Newcastle NSW, 1, 31, 36, 40, 172, 186-7, 195, 200, 227-8, 230, 232, 234, 303, 318-19, 323-6, 328-30, 332-3, 360
Ngadiji, genre, ceremony, Yanyuwa (see also song genres, ceremonies), 24, 68-73, 76-80, 84-5, 87
Ngakaparáwarra, duck increase ceremony, Wangkumara (see also ceremonies), 104
Ngarda-ngarli (west Pilbara cultural heritage community), 56-9
Ngarinyin, 13, 59, 305-9, 311-12, 314
Ngarla, 56-7, 67
Ngarluma, 13, 56, 59-67
Ngarukuruwala (Tiwi Islands musical ensemble), 290, 292, 296, 303-4
Ngerdu, Watty, 307
Ngiya awungarra ('I am here, now', music CD), 290, 304
Ngurungaeta ('headman', Wurundjeri), 352
Nguyulnguyul (women's compositions, Yanyuwa), 76
nigi ('mother song', Mawng), 265, 267, 281
non-Pama-Nyungan languages (NPN), 11-12, 15, 34, 287, 362, 371
Norman, Donald (Piniingu), 61
North Queensland, 190, 241, 255, 322-3, 326, 328-9, 331-2, 335
Nulgit, Pansy, 308
Nung-Ngnun (Dunlop, 'Native poetry'), 167, 187, 193, 196-8, 214, 216-17, 227, 230
Nyamal, 56-7, 60, 67, 186

Nyingawi (mangrove-dwelling hairy beings, Tiwi), 189, 297
Nyirrbu, genre, Nyiyaparli (see also song genres), 56
Nyiyaparli, 56, 60
Nyungar, Noongar, 13, 24-5, 43-55, 364, 378, 380, 392-3
Oceania, 214
O'Grady, Geoffrey, 57, 59, 61
onomatopoeia, 51-2, 155
oral tradition, oral transmission, oral texts, oral literature, 2, 7, 26, 33, 37, 40, 42, 44, 47, 52, 54-5, 90, 92, 139, 153, 167, 174, 181, 185-6, 228, 244, 288, 294, 322
owlet nightjar song, *Yerrateth-kurrk*, Wemba-wemba, 103, 109, 117
ownership, intellectual property, 17, 23-4, 29, 31-3, 35-6, 38, 40, 48, 90, 93, 245, 250-1, 275, 293, 295, 332
Pacific and Regional Archive for Digital Sources in Endangered Cultures, 96, 259, 272, 277, 316
Pacific Islanders, 320-1
Palyku, 56
Pama-Nyungan language family (PN), 11-12, 15, 30, 32, 48, 362-4, 371
Papuan, 13-14, 319, 362, 395-6
PARADISEC, see Pacific and Regional Archive for Digital Sources in Endangered Cultures
Parker, K. Langloh, 190, 194-5, 212, 220-3, 239
Parr, William, 224, 237-8
Patterson, Percy, 105-6, 113
Patterson, Stuart, 105-6, 113
Patyegarang, 367
Peake Creek SA, 107, 118
Pegrum, Nigel, 322, 324-5, 331, 334-5
Pelletier, Narcisse ('Anco'), 350-3, 356-7, 386
percussion (see also body percussion, musical instruments), 103, 106, 108, 144, 146, 155, 159, 161, 182
Perkins, Rachel, 89, 93-4, 96, 98-9, 101
Perkins, Tony, 19, 40, 144-5, 150-1, 160-1, 171
Perth, 43, 308, 354
Peters, Amy, 307
Petri, Helmut, 57, 59, 212-13, 239
Petrie, Tom, 364, 379-80
Phonographic Performance Company of Australia, 289
phylogenetic analysis, 12, 15-16, 37
Pidgin, NSW Pidgin, 22, 172-3, 176-7, 179, 183-4, 215
Pilbara WA, 13, 15, 25, 49, 56-9, 61-3, 66-7, 276
Pilot, Boggo (Rev.), 322, 335
Pilot, Sam, 251, 255
Pintupi, 17, 38, 102, 118, 205, 238
Pirlangimpi NT, 302
Pitapitui ('the as yet unborn', Tiwi), 291
pitch, 73-4, 76, 102, 106, 108-9, 126, 131, 154-6, 160, 162-6, 264-5, 293, 298-9, 301, 336, 338, 341, 343, 352-3
policy, 3, 9, 33, 36-7, 91, 186, 303, 316
Polynesia, 190, 321
polyphony, 103, 239

Popela (song, Fanny Cochrane Smith), 336, 341, 345–8, 373
popular music, 4–5, 7, 31–3, 35–7, 39–40, 101, 168, 237, 241, 334, 346, 357, 368
possum skin bundle (*see also musical instruments*), 144–5, 394
public ceremonies (*see also ceremonies, corroborees*), 16, 146, 247, 257, 259–60, 269–70, 307
Puruntatameri, Clementine, 293–4
Queensland, 13–15, 20–1, 71, 103, 111, 119–21, 131–2, 173, 190, 226, 319, 322–3, 326, 328–9, 331–2, 340, 348–50, 364, 380–1, 385, 387–8, 394, 402–3
Queensland Speech Survey, 120, 139
Rainbow Serpent, 249, 307
rain-making ceremonies (*see also ceremonies*), 90, 105, 110, 148, 150, 314
range (pitch), 73–4, 105, 109, 160, 164, 278
rasp idiophone (*see also mirrimba, musical instruments*), 58, 60–1
rattle (*see also musical instruments*), 63, 144, 160
Ray, Sidney, 321–2, 335, 337–8, 359, 394, 398
reconciliation, 9, 27, 31, 333
recording, 3, 22, 33, 37, 51, 53–5, 57, 59, 64–5, 70, 72, 80, 88, 90, 93–4, 96–7, 106–8, 111, 120, 123–4, 128–9, 138, 141–2, 148, 160–1, 173–4, 181–2, 245, 251, 254–5, 259, 265, 267–8, 270, 274, 276, 282–3, 289–90, 292–302, 310, 318, 320, 324–5, 332, 337–9, 341, 343, 345–6, 348–9, 361–3, 392, 399–401
recordings, 19, 23–5, 43–7, 52–4, 56–60, 62–7, 76, 88–94, 96–100, 102–3, 105, 111, 120, 122, 131–2, 139, 157, 173–4, 178, 182–3, 200, 249, 251–3, 259, 270, 277, 289–96, 298–9, 301–4, 308, 310, 316, 324–5, 336–43, 346–7, 349, 357–8, 360–1, 364, 373, 394, 398–9, 402
re-dreaming, 4, 17, 187, 206
regionality, 141
repatriation, 41, 56–7, 245, 290, 295, 303–5
repertoire, 17, 22–3, 25, 33, 43, 59, 68, 105, 157, 188, 250, 261, 275, 318–20, 322, 325–6, 332–3
repetition, 51–2, 60, 73–4, 76, 92, 105, 108–9, 124, 126, 128, 131, 154, 158, 179, 200–1, 355
representation, 147, 167, 175, 238, 248, 302, 306
rhyme, 154, 176, 179, 199, 201, 346, 390
rhythm, 21, 48, 51, 55, 60–1, 68, 70, 72, 80, 106, 108, 119, 123, 126, 128, 132, 139, 153, 155–6, 158, 161, 163–6, 176, 182–3, 253–4, 261, 271, 279–80, 282, 286, 336, 347, 349, 351, 353, 355–6, 358, 368, 372, 374–5, 377, 391
Ridley, William, 191, 220–3, 240
Robinson, George Augustus, 342–3, 345, 352, 358, 373
Robinvale Vic, 206, 249
Roe, Paddy, 59
Roebourne WA, 20, 25, 57, 60–3
Rookwood, Willie, 21, 119–25, 127, 129, 131–2
Rookwood Station Qld, 120
Roughsey, Kenny, 248
Roughsey, Lindsay, 248

Royal Society of Tasmania, 169–70, 341, 345, 347, 358, 366, 374, 400
Rubuntja, Bob, 400–1
sacred sites, 28, 32, 40, 42, 205, 219
sacrifice zone, 209, 229, 234
Saibai Island TSI, 337, 394, 397–8
Salvado, Rosendo, 355, 359, 364, 378
Sankey, Ira D., 320, 335
Santa Teresa NT, *see* Ltyentye Apurte
Scandinavia, 211
Schafer, Murray, 8, 26–7, 40, 205, 231, 241
school, 20, 23, 33, 174, 247, 249–51, 253–4, 269, 291, 308
Scott, Doug, 174, 181–2
sea, 27–8, 49–50, 71–2, 86, 152, 192, 195, 260, 298, 319
secular songs and dances, 16, 103, 290, 325, 333, 340, 390, 396
Seven Sisters song line, Arabana (*see also songsets*), 103, 106–7, 109, 111, 114
Sheaffe, Percy, 352, 364, 398–9
sign language (*see also gesture*), 162
skin names, *see* kinship
Smith, Fanny Cochrane, 101, 156, 169, 337, 341–3, 345–7, 373–4, 399–400
Smyth, R. Brough, 53, 212, 242, 380, 389–90
solos, 24–5, 58, 78, 102–3, 105, 109, 143, 150, 182, 191, 261, 296, 298, 320, 326, 335
song genres (*see also: songsets, ceremonies, corroborees, dance genres*), 2, 4, 7, 16–17, 22, 45, 65, 76, 90, 92, 148–150, 156, 158, 185, 195, 209; **song genres by region/language:** Arrernte/Arandic, 97–8, 123, 125, 401–2; Bardi, 17; Bininj Gunwok, 185, 258–9; Kimberley, 312; Lardil, 245–8, 250–6; Marri Ngarr, 278; Mawng, 257, 259–61, 265, 269–74, 276, 278, 280, 282–3, 287; Murriny Patha, 57, 67, 240, 272, 287; Ngardi-ngarli, 58; Ngarinyin, 312; Ngarla, 56, 59; north-western, 25, 243, 278, 288, 305–16; Nyiyaparli, 56; Pilbara, 25, 56–60, 62, 66; south-eastern, 148–50, 156, 158, 185, 195; Top End NT, 4, 22, 260; Torres Strait Creole, 23, 318–19, 323–4, 394–6, 398; Worrorra, 307; Yanyuwa, 69, 77; Yolngu, 259; **song genres by name:** *see anggwuy, Barlgabi, burdal, Djanba, Galinda, Gunangu, gurungara, ilma , ilpentye, Jadmi, jarada, Jerregorl, Junba, kores, kujika, kun-borrk, lirrga, ludiny, manikay, manyardi, marndar, Ngadiji, Nyirrbu, Thabi, ululung , Wangga, wujuj, Yirraru*
songman, songperson, 194–5, 206, 208, 227, 237, 245, 247–9, 253, 255, 257, 259, 261, 268, 275–6, 281, 283, 286, 288, 290
songsets of *manyardi/kun-borrk* and *manikay* genres, Arnhem Land (table), 259–60
songsets, song series, *see: Inyjalarrku, Manbam , Milyarryarr, Mirrijpu, Urumbula, Seven Sisters, Wurrurrumi, Yanajanak*
songtext, 159, 183, 318–22, 324–6, 332
soundscape, 8, 9, 19, 26, 37, 39–40, 237, 240–1, 298–9, 304

sound studies, 9, 39–40, 209
Spencer, Baldwin, 105, 110, 118, 212, 232, 242, 291, 297, 337–40, 357–8, 400–2
Spencer and Gillen, 110, 212, 242, 337–9, 357–8, 401–2
spirit familiar, 190
spirit language, 53, 227, 275, 287
spiritscapes, 25, 28, 30, 38, 40
spirits of place, *see irrerntarenye*
stanza, 124, 166, 200, 324
Stevenson River Vic, 339, 401
Strangways, Tim, 106–7, 109, 114
Strehlow, Theodor G. H., 1, 40, 89, 101, 201, 203, 212–13, 219, 221, 242, 400–2
strophic form, 156, 166
St Stephen's Anglican Church (Townsville Qld), 329
Stubbs, Dacre, 15, 40
succession, 165–6, 194, 224
Sumba (island, Indonesia), 28
Sunday Island WA, 205
Swansea NSW, 195
Sydney, 5, 7, 61, 77, 139, 144–5, 157, 162, 193, 196, 199, 214–17, 226, 246, 248–9, 256, 299–302, 311, 343, 345, 347, 349, 362, 364–72, 374–7, 384, 388, 403–4
Sydney Island Qld, 248
Sydney language, 199, 215, 243, 366
Symposium on Indigenous Music and Dance, 3, 8
Tanganitara (mother of Fanny Cochrane Smith), 341, 400
Tapim, Elimo (Rev.), 319, 322–3, 326, 329–30, 333–4
Taplin, George, 161, 205, 242, 353, 359, 364, 383–4
Taroom Qld, 120–1, 350
tartengk, drum, Narrinyerri (*see also musical instruments*), 145, 384
Tasmania, 11, 23, 90, 141, 156–7, 217, 336–7, 341–3, 345–8, 352, 364–6, 370, 373–4, 380, 390, 399–400
Tasmanian language, 357, 373, 399
Taungurung (Daung wurrung), 353
tempo, 21, 61, 72–3, 125, 128, 267, 280–3, 296, 299, 301, 349–50
Thabi, genre, Pilbara (*see also song genres*), 25, 56–60, 62, 66
Thangatti~Dhanggati (see also Dhanggati~Thangatti), 13, 22, 172–4, 176–83, 186
thigh-slapping (*see also body percussion, musical instruments*), 144
Threlkeld, Lancelot Edward, 168, 170, 172, 186, 193–5, 197, 200–1, 203, 208, 212, 223, 226, 232–3, 235, 243
time of day (temporal specification), 292
Tingcombe, Henry, 355, 374
Tiny, Webb, 96
Tipiloura, Eustace, 290, 292–3, 297, 299–300
Tiwi, 13, 22, 35, 189, 229, 233, 289–93, 295–9, 301–4, 316
ceremony, *see* Kulama

Tjitjingalla corroboree, Arandic? (*see also corroborees*), 338-40, 350, 401
Tomlinson, Gary, 1, 6, 19, 22, 24, 41, 47, 54, 202, 243
tonic, 73-4, 78, 124, 126, 128-31, 156-8, 164-6, 265, 283
Top End NT, 4, 22, 258, 260
Torrance, George W. (Rev.), 109, 118, 155-7, 170, 352-3, 359, 364, 388-9
Torres Strait, 3, 9, 11, 14, 22-6, 30, 32, 34, 36-9, 57, 62, 86, 89, 91, 100-2, 120, 139, 168-71, 173, 229, 255, 272-3, 289-90, 309, 318-30, 332-8, 340, 358, 360, 362-4, 390, 394-8
totemism, 149-50, 170, 203
Townsend, Joseph Phipps, 364, 376-7
Townsville Qld, 255, 318-19, 322-3, 325-31, 334-5
tradition (*see also oral tradition*), 2-4, 6-7, 9, 23, 25, 28, 30, 32-7, 39, 41, 43, 47-8, 52, 55-7, 62, 66-9, 72, 74, 86-7, 89, 90, 92, 101-2, 109-10, 119, 123-4, 131, 141, 143, 147, 167, 169, 173-4, 181, 186, 188-9, 191, 194, 200, 203, 205-6, 219, 223, 229, 232-5, 237, 239-40, 245, 247, 255, 257, 269-70, 272-4, 276, 286-8, 291, 303, 305-7, 311, 315-16, 318, 322, 327, 332-3, 335, 340-1, 348, 360, 368
trance, 87, 100, 190, 212, 228, 241
Tropic of Capricorn, 15
Tungutalum (Tiwi singer), 291, 297
Turner, M. K. (Margaret Kemarre), 4, 10, 23, 41, 89-90, 93, 96-8, 101, 204, 209, 213, 243
Turner, Walter James, 354, 359
Ugar (Stephen Island) TSI, 318-19, 321-2, 324, 333
Umbara (Coast Murring singer), 151, 192
Unemarre NT, 98
UNESCO, 28, 33, 255
Ungkari~Ungorri, 121
unison singing, 103
United States Exploring Expedition (1839), 195, 371, 375
University of Newcastle, 318-19, 323-4, 326, 329, 332-3
Urumbula (*urrempele*), song series, Arrernte (*see also songsets*), 103, 107, 115
Utemorrah, Laurie, 307
Uutaalnganu, 350, 364, 386
Vale, Lachlan ('Locky'), 173-5, 177
variation, 22, 46, 54, 60, 73-5, 77, 98, 103, 106-7, 124, 127, 148, 151, 154, 158, 167, 180, 185, 200, 355
verse, 24, 68-70, 72-4, 76-7, 80, 84-5, 92-4, 97-8, 100, 102-3, 106, 111, 114, 119, 123, 126, 128, 131, 153-4, 157, 166, 172, 185, 193, 197, 200-1, 204, 211, 278-9, 304, 324, 340, 400-2
Victoria, 102-3, 105, 112, 145-7, 156, 224, 338-9, 347, 352, 354, 380, 382-3, 389-90, 401-2
Victoria River District NT, 205
vocable, 123-4, 127-9, 321
voice, 1, 22, 27, 35, 38, 41, 62, 65, 76, 106, 110, 155, 160, 162, 165, 167, 170, 174-5, 179, 193-4, 207-30, 233, 237, 239, 244, 254-5, 273, 277, 289-90, 293, 295-6, 299, 301-2, 304, 323, 346, 352, 355, 358, 372, 384

voice quality, 76
Wadeye (Port Keats) NT, 7, 38, 57-8, 67, 272, 275, 287
Wahwee (song-giving monster), 191, 194
Waier TSI, 319
Wailu, Jimmy, 330-1
Wailwan, 191
Wakawaka, 129
Wakaya, 71
Wakka-Kabic, 129-30, 139
walbarra, see *mirrimba*
Walker, George Washington, 342-3, 345, 373, 404
Walker, Harry (Dhurga), 404
Walker, James (Dhurga), 404
Walker, James Backhouse, 365-6
Walwallim (Paakantyi singer), 382
Wangaaypuwan, 203, 224
Wangal, 354, 367
Wangga, genre, north-western (*see also song genres*), 278, 308, 312
Wangkamadla, 111
Wangkangurru, 13, 104-5, 109, 111-12
Wangkumara, 104, 108, 121
Wardaga, Charlie, 275-7, 283, 287
Wargoonda minyarrah (Nathan), 355
Warlpiri, 15, 17, 20, 41-2, 55, 69, 76, 86-7, 97, 100, 123, 126, 139, 170, 177, 185, 192, 221, 229, 242, 244, 316, 401
Warramurrungurrunji (founding ancestress, Marrku), 278
warranguridjakud (song-giving dwarves, Marrku), 189, 278
Warrthampa, ceremony, Wangkangurru (*see also ceremonies*), 104
Warruwi Community NT, 13, 25, 257-63, 269-71, 274, 276, 282-3
warup, drum, Torres Strait Islands (*see also musical instruments*), 320, 324
Watson, Horace, 337, 341, 346, 357, 399-400
Watt, Gordon, 249, 253
wax cylinder recordings, 23, 173, 301, 337, 346, 357,
Wellington Valley mission NSW, 151, 162, 222, 355, 364, 377
Wenberi (Woiwurrung singer), 388-9
western Arnhem Land NT, 21, 25, 100, 185, 189, 192, 206, 228-9, 232, 257-62, 267, 269-70, 272-6, 278-83, 286-8
Western Australia, 15, 24, 43-4, 48, 50, 52, 156, 194, 221, 226, 305-6, 355, 362, 370, 378, 380, 393
Western Desert, 60, 108, 192, 205, 238, 240, 243
west Pilbara, 56-8, 66
Williams, Joy, 277, 288
Wilson, Nancy, 247, 252
Wilson, Renee, 252
Wiradjuri, 152, 191, 194, 199, 201-2, 220-2, 233, 364, 377, 379
Wirlomin (Nyungar clan), 44, 49-50, 52-4
Woiwurung, 109, 389-90
Wollombi NSW, 161, 187, 193, 195-6, 202, 215, 217-20, 227, 230-1, 233, 239

Wollombi Brook, *see Mala*
Wollotuka Institute (University of Newcastle), 332
Wolungarri, ceremony, Kimberley (*see also ceremonies*), 307
women's ceremonies (*see also ceremonies*), 24, 71, 86, 88, 146, 267
Wonnarua, 209
Wood, Annie (Benson) (Dhurga), 404
Woodbury, Jimmy, 376
Woomera Aboriginal Corporation (*see also Mirndiyan Gununa*), 249, 255
Woorabinda Qld, 13, 119-20, 122, 138
wordplay, 51
world music, 7, 34, 41, 67, 87, 272, 287
Worrorra, 305-9, 312, 314
wukul 'black heron', Marrku (*see also Milyarryarr songset*), 281
Wulatji (Wallatu, songman, Hunter Valley), 187, 193-6, 200, 202-3, 207-8, 210
Wunambal, 59, 190, 226, 236,
wurnan (trade paths, north-western Australia), 276
Wurrumiyanga NT, 293, 296, 299, 302, 305-9, 312, 314
Wurrurrumi, songset, Kuninjku (*see also songsets*), 281
Wurundjeri, 352, 390
Wybalenna (Flinders Island) Tas, 345, 347
Yalkawarru, song-dance type, Yanyuwa (*see also ceremonies*), 85
Yaluyandi, 111
Yam Island TSI, 337-8, 340, 394, 396-8
Yamroweney (Yemmerrawanne, singer, Wangal), 354
Yanajanak, songset, Amurdak (*see also songsets*), 260-2
Yanyuwa, 1, 12-13, 15, 27-8, 32, 42, 68-72, 75-7, 83, 85-7, 229, 247-8, 255
Yarmirr, Mick, 277
Yawulhu, song-dance type, Yanyuwa (from Mount Isa area) (*see also ceremonies*), 68
Yindjibarndi, 56, 59-61
Yinhawangka, 57
Yirraru, genre, Pilbara (*see also song genres*), 56, 59
Yirrinju~Yurrunju (male spirit of Ngadiji ceremony, Yanyuwa), 68, 71-2, 76, 80, 84
Yoi, public song-dance type, Tiwi (*see also ceremonies*), 296-8
Yolngu, 8-9, 12, 15, 17, 20, 33, 38, 189, 219, 237, 264, 304, 371
Yuendumu NT, 192
yumparrparr 'giant dance', Mawng (*see also dance genres*), 267
Yumpi Jack, 107, 115
Yumplatok (*see also Creole, Torres Strait*), 319, 324
Yunupingu, Galarrwuy, 19
Yunupingu, Geoffrey, see *Gurrumul*
Yuwaalaraay, 196, 199, 201, 216, 222, 227, 232